W9-AUI-004

How Students Learn

Reforming Schools Through Learner-Centered Education

Edited by Nadine M. Lambert &
Barbara L. McCombs

American Psychological Association • Washington, DC

Published by
American Psychological Association
750 First Street, NE
Washington, DC 20002

Copies may be ordered from
APA Order Department
P.O. Box 92984
Washington, DC 20090-2984

In the UK and Europe, copies may be ordered from
American Psychological Association
3 Henrietta Street
Covent Garden, London
WC2E 8LU England

Typeset in Futura and New Baskerville by EPS Group Inc., Easton, MD

Printer: Braceland, Philadelphia, PA
Jacket Designer: Kachergis Book Design, Pittsboro, NC
Technical/Production Editor: Tanya Y. Alexander

Library of Congress Cataloging-in-Publication Data
How students learn : reforming schools through learner-centered education / edited
  by Nadine M. Lambert and Barbara L. McCombs.
      p.   cm.
   Includes bibliographical references and index.
   ISBN1-55798-464-6 (pbk.)
   1. Learning, Psychology of.   2. Cognition.   3. Teaching—United
States.   4. Educational tests and measurements—United States.   5. Teachers—
Training of—United States.   6. Educational change—United States.   I. Lambert,
Nadine M.   II. McCombs, Barbara L.
LB1060.H674   1997
371.102'0973—dc21   97-37185
                                                                            CIP

British Library Cataloguing-in-Publication Data
A CIP record is available from the British Library

Printed in the United States of America
First edition

Contents

Contributors

Patricia A. Alexander, University of Maryland, College Park
Paul Ammon, University of California, Berkeley
Joan Boykoff Baron, Connecticut State Department of Education, Hartford
Allen Black, University of California, Berkeley
Ann L. Brown, University of California, Berkeley
Joseph C. Campione, University of California, Berkeley
Joseph P. DuCette, Temple University, Philadelphia, PA
Craig L. Frisby, University of Florida, Gainesville
Linda R. Kroll, Mills College, Oakland, CA
Nadine M. Lambert, University of California, Berkeley
Hermine H. Marshall, University of California, Berkeley
Robert J. Marzano, Mid-Continent Regional Educational Laboratory, Aurora, CO
Richard E. Mayer, University of California, Santa Barbara
Barbara L. McCombs, Mid-Continent Regional Educational Laboratory, Aurora, CO
Marcia Mentkowski, Alverno College, Milwaukee, WI
P. Karen Murphy, University of Maryland, College Park
Scott G. Paris, Ann Arbor, MI
Andrew C. Porter, University of Wisconsin, Madison
Trevor E. Sewell, Temple University, Philadelphia, PA
Joan Poliner Shapiro, Temple University, Philadelphia, PA
Rhona S. Weinstein, University of California, Berkeley
Merlin C. Wittrock, University of California, Los Angeles

Foreword

Declining levels of academic performance in science and mathematics, disciplinary and drug abuse problems, and increasing violence in America's schools have generated extensive national debate over the past two decades. These concerns are viewed not only as a crisis in education that requires imperative reform but also as reflecting significant deficiencies in American society. Early concerns were voiced in *A Nation at Risk*, the report of the National Commission on Excellence in Education, published in 1983 by the U.S. Department of Education. A summit meeting of the nation's governors in 1989, along with active leadership by former President George Bush, further highlighted the national concerns about education and what was needed to improve it.

The last 20 years have witnessed tremendous advances in theory and research in developmental and cognitive psychology, and on the emotional, motivational, personality, and social processes of individual learners that contribute to the dynamics of the learning process. Such findings obviously have considerable significance for education, but transfer of the accumulated psychological knowledge to education has been limited at best, especially in terms of applications in classroom and school settings.

Although learning has been a major area of research in American psychology since the beginning of the 20th century, and this interest has been strongly expressed in the research literature and at regional meetings and the Annual Convention of the American Psychological Association (APA), the APA Education and Training Board has been concerned almost exclusively with the education of psychologists, rather than the contributions of psychology to education. In keeping with the prevailing concerns about American education and the potentially important, but heretofore limited, contributions of psychology to solving these problems, shortly after my election as president of APA in 1989, I prevailed on the APA Board of Directors to establish a presidential task force on "psychology in education."

The first meeting of the Psychology in Education Task Force was convened in Denver in March 1990, hosted by the Mid-Continent Regional Educational Laboratory (McREL). The editors of this volume, Nadine Lambert and Barbara McCombs, served as co-chairs of the task force, along with Frank Farley, who was subsequently elected president of APA and continued to support the association's programs pertaining to the contributions of psychology to education. Barbara McCombs established the collaborative relation between APA and McREL, which gave the task force a direct link to cutting-edge theory and research on applications of psychology to learning and educational programs in public school settings.

In addition to serving as co-chair of the Psychology in Education Task Force, Nadine Lambert, professor of educational psychology and former director of the School Psychology Training Program at the University of California in Berkeley, was a member of the APA Board of Directors when the Education Directorate was established and also served as chair of the APA Education and Training Board. With the establishment of the APA Board of Educational Affairs (BEA), which replaced the Education and Training Board in 1990, Professor Lambert served for two terms as chair of the BEA. The establishment of the BEA and the APA Education Directorate provide further evidence of the association's growing commitment to enhancing the contributions of psychology to education.

Dr. McCombs was primarily responsible for developing the initial draft of the *Learner-Centered Psychological Principles: Guidelines for School Redesign and Reform* (APA Presidential Task Force on Psychology in Education, 1993) and for revising and editing subsequent drafts. She has also pioneered applications of the learner-centered psychological principles in school settings, working closely with teachers in communities located in diverse areas of the United States. She recently completed a program for teachers based on the principles, and has extended her work on community involvement and developed empowerment programs for students at risk for school failure.

This volume presents theoretical perspectives and research findings of leading contributors to educational psychology relating to the needs of learners and the context of the learning process. The individual chapters reflect the work of these distinguished educators and psychologists in developing and articulating the psychological knowledge base that is most relevant to education. Most of them are also actively involved in disseminating this information to teachers, educational administrators, and policy makers.

Collaboratively developed by McREL and APA, the learner-centered psychological principles are described in detail by the editors in their introductory chapter. The principles provide a coherent theoretical framework for examining critical problems in education and psychology. Recommendations that will contribute to successful solutions to these problems are noted by the chapter authors and by the editors in the final chapter. The learner-centered reform agenda, which is articulated in the final chapter, gives equal emphasis to the learner, what is learned, and the learning process, and sounds the clarion call for future contributions of psychology to education.

Charles D. Spielberger, past president, 1991–1992
American Psychological Association

Preface

As psychologists, parents, and educators, we share a deep concern about signs that our nation's children are not learning and valuing learning sufficiently to succeed in our complex and rapidly changing world. The burden placed on our nation's schools and the educators who are committed to making a difference to reach increasingly diverse student needs, while also meeting increasingly more demanding knowledge and performance standards, warrants our additional concern. How can some of these pressures be eased and schools rise to the challenge of better preparing our nation's youth?

We believe a big part of the answer lies in taking seriously the accumulated knowledge base on the psychology of learning and individual differences. Part of our belief stems from our obvious bias as educational psychologists that the knowledge base we have amassed offers valuable guidelines and insights into what is needed in today's schools and classrooms. Another reason for this belief is directly attributable to the nature of the learning process. That is, learning is by definition a psychological process. It occurs inside the heads and hearts of individual learners. Teachers and others can influence learning, but it is the individual learner who must decide to learn and must engage attentional, intellectual, and emotional processes in learning. The social context can also influence learning, but again, it is the individual learner who decides what and how much to learn.

Because of our belief about the significant role the psychological knowledge base can play in helping to inform the educational reform agenda, we have been actively involved in both defining the knowledge base and disseminating it to teachers, educators, researchers, and policy makers. This book represents a part of that effort and also offers the best thinking and recommendations for learner-centered practice from a world-class group of psychologists concerned with learning, education, and the systemic change of our educational system to better meet the learning and development needs of every learner.

In the chapters ahead, we have assembled the writings of noted leaders in the psychological and educational community to share the research base on learning and learners. These leaders also share their recommendations on the topics of learner-centered classroom teaching, assessment systems, teacher education, and policy implications. They provide evidence from a variety of psychological perspectives of the need for a learner-centered model to guide the current educational reform agenda. We invite you to read and reflect on these perspectives.

Introduction: Learner-Centered Schools and Classrooms as a Direction for School Reform

Nadine M. Lambert and Barbara L. McCombs

Schools must be "learner-centered," concerned not about "whether the child is ready for school" but "whether the school is ready for the child."
—Edwin J. Delattre

From what we know from the research about learners and learning, students need to be active participants in the learning process.
—Barbara L. McCombs

As the debate about the quality of the American educational system continues in this country as well as internationally, concerned citizens, parents, educators, researchers, policymakers, and even the students themselves question whether problems facing schools represent educational or social issues. That is, many are questioning whether there is a crisis in education or a crisis in society. The answer to this question is an important one because it dictates the kinds of solutions and approaches taken to educational reform. If the crisis is centered in education and the system that supports this function, solutions center on the ingredients of education: the content standards, the curricula and frameworks for organizing content, the teaching and learning processes, the way what is learned is assessed, and how schools are managed. On the other hand, if the crisis extends beyond the educational system and includes the social system, solutions center on meeting both the academic and nonacademic needs of students; on removing boundaries between and among the school, family, and community; and on addressing both educational and social policies that impact student learning and achievement.

Our view is that what has been called a crisis in education must also be viewed as a crisis in society. A national commitment to excellence in education is necessary because the more each individual is able to contribute, the better society will be. The more society improves, the more capable it will be to educate its citizens, bringing even greater rewards. Fundamental shifts in education will occur only when there are shifts in how people *think* about education, including their fundamental assumptions, their attitudes, and their beliefs. This volume is our attempt to help create a new vision of what is possible in schools of the future—schools that help every learner maximize his or her unique talents.

We believe that the focus of education needs to be on clear expectations and high standards for each student while also respecting each student's diversity and unique talents. For us, current emphasis on standards-based education is a necessary but not sufficient condition. Also necessary is an emphasis on meeting the needs and developing the capabilities of each learner. To accomplish learner-centered, standards-based education, a holistic consideration of the learner, learning, and learning context are required as well as the broader social, economic, and political realities that form the backgrounds and perspectives of each learner.

In creating a new vision of schools, some tough questions must be asked and answered. What do schools do? What do we want them to do? Are schools reflections of what we value in our society? If our society is *not* what we want, are schools the places where our children can become what they want to be and what society values? How do we raise children to live in a world that we cannot anticipate? These are just a few of the questions that we and our colleagues in psychology and education are attempting to answer. They are not simple questions; there are no simple, easy answers. To find answers to these and other related questions will take a widespread effort to find solutions that will fit the diverse cultures that currently exist in this country and in our schools. It is no longer good enough for education to succeed for some children. It must be successful for every child, every person. Those failed by our educational system will not just "go away." They will become persons that our society has to care for, in one way or another. The rising number of homeless, criminals, and welfare recipients give testimony to what happens to many of those who "fall through the cracks." For a nation to grow and prosper, it is vital that its citizens work together to make the educational system succeed with *all* children, not just some children.

The Learner in the Context of Educational Reform

Proposals for education reform over the past several years, beginning with the publication of *A Nation At Risk: The Imperative for Educational Reform* (National Commission on Excellence in Education, 1983) and culminating with the 1994 publication of *Striving for Excellence: The National Education Goals* (U.S. Department of Education, 1991), have focused attention on new designs for our nation's schools. The impetus for this volume came from several sources. Foremost among them during this period of heightened attention on needed reforms in education was the establishment in 1990 of the American Psychological Association's (APA) Presidential Task Force on Psychology in Education. The goals of the task force were to focus attention on the contributions of American psychology to understanding the learner in educational contexts, and to examine ways that such a focus would highlight psychology's century-long contributions to understanding learners and the learning process.

A focus on the learner, rather than on teaching and pedagogy, curriculum and instruction, or the administrative structure of the school enables psychology to make its contributions to educational processes and programs explicit and focused. The topics presented in this volume are a derivative of the work of the many psychologists involved in schooling over almost a century and direct attention to the contribution of psychological principles and scientific discoveries to a better understanding of what learners require if schools are to fulfill their primary objectives of educating the nation's youth.

National and state educational reform agendas are having a significant impact on neighborhood schools in most communities. Although some psychologists at national, state, and local levels have been active in promoting psychology and psychological services in educational reform initiatives, knowledge about their efforts is fragmented. APA has undertaken the task of promoting psychology and psychologists in educational reform. As the rhetoric on education reform has cycled through policy-driven, outcomes-based, and teacher-accountability perspectives, the learner has seemed to have gotten lost in the process. It is reasonable to argue that whatever the perspective of educational reform, goals for education that assure an optimum education for *all* children require the achievement of learning goals for *every* child.

School Reform Proposals: From Policy to Learner Perspectives

The first wave of educational reform (1983–1986) was a top-down approach in reaction to the 1983 report, *A Nation at Risk* (National Commission on Excellence in Education, 1983). The report argues that educational problems in the United States were attributed to low academic standards and poor quality of instruction. Solutions were to be driven by state government actions that would require improvement in achievement by raising state achievement standards. It followed that the classroom teacher was to be held accountable for improving educational outcomes. These reform efforts targeted an increase in the number of math and science classes, stiffer high school graduation requirements, increased teacher salaries, tougher qualifications and requirements for teaching credentials, and increased frequency of testing and assessment of students. The proposed strategies for improving schooling ignored local boards of education, administrators, and teachers.

During the mid-1980s, many argued that increasing state-mandated educational standards and prescribed content and form of schooling were too rigid, passive, and rote-oriented to produce the thinkers needed to be workers in the 21st century. To be truly effective, change initiatives must take into account specific local needs and must begin at the local level (Conley, 1991). This approach emphasized the need to empower teachers, not manage them. The empowerment effort called for enhancing the professional status of teachers by providing them more autonomy, training, trust, and a collegial environment in which to carry out their job. At this point discussions centered on decentralization of decision making, particularly site-based management, flexibility in how local districts meet state standards, and teacher ownership and involvement in change—all considered to be prerequisite for accountability and outcomes.

In the 1990s educational reform focuses on systemic restructuring of education in a comprehensive systems approach to change. Systemic reform is based on and incorporates the change approach called *restructuring,* a term borrowed from the private business sector, adopted and adapted by educators. *Educational restructuring* has been defined in a variety of ways, but there are common themes throughout. One theme is the emphasis on challenging fundamental assumptions about student learning, where *learning* is defined as the ability to retain, synthesize, and apply conceptually complex information in meaningful ways. Another theme is that restructuring involves changes in roles, rules, and relationships between and among students and teachers, teachers and administrators, and administrators at various levels from the school building to the district office to the state level, all with the aim of improving student outcomes.

Ultimately restructuring involves decentralizing authority; changing accountability standards; redesigning curriculum, including meaningful standards of achievement and performance in every curriculum area; modifying instruction, with an emphasis on mastery or outcome-based learning; working toward developmentally based learning and the personalization of learning; and finding new ways of assessing performance and progress, particularly more authentic ways to find out what students know and can do, that are consistent with changes in curriculum and instruction and increased professionalism of teaching. Learners are central to restructuring efforts and systemic change.

When we shift attention to what the national reform agenda has identified as the overwhelming need facing American education, it is consistent with the need to facilitate learning and achievement for *every* student. Since the publication of *A Nation at Risk* (National Commission on Excellence in Education, 1983), national attention has been focused on declining student achievement in critical subject areas (e.g., mathematics, science, reading, and writing) and the disparity in achievement between more advantaged and less advantaged students. More recently, first with the publication of *America 2000* under President Bush and our nation's governors (ERIC, 1991) and currently with President Clinton's Goals 2000 and subsequent legislation, the nation's awareness of the wide set of interrelated and system goals needed to address the problem of improved achievement for all students has been heightened. Parents and the public are openly sharing their concerns about the quality of public schools, and parents of disadvantaged children, in particular, are becoming increasingly vocal about conditions they perceive to be responsible for their children's failure in the traditional educational system. Issues of equity, parent involvement, standards that speak to an uneven playing field, and reform solutions that go beyond the school walls to family, community, and business responsibilities are all part of the national discussion about factors that need to be addressed in raising student achievement.

In a recent *Phi Delta Kappa* and Gallup poll of adults in the United States that surveyed the public's attitudes toward public schools (Elam, Rose, & Gallup, 1994), respondents found the five biggest problems facing public schools to be fighting/violence/gangs, lack of discipline, lack of proper financial support, drug abuse, and standards/quality of education. A national survey of the nation's educational leaders reported by the Council of Great City Schools (1993) found a similar list of issues: The need for new models of and strategies for implementing student performance assessment and alternative assessment, eliminating violence and gang-related activity, creating national standards and assessment, restructuring the management of schools, creating bilingual education, and expanding early childhood education. Clearly, then, these polls and surveys show concerns that span educational and social issues, calling for a systemic response.

In the context of restructuring or transforming the nation's schools, we are proposing that education again look at the learner—much as Aristotle did as he taught young boys in Greece, working with each one to develop that child's strengths and provide the education that child would need as an adult. By building on the knowledge base from research and theory on how learning occurs and the individual differences that influence learning, we can see how best to work with each person's strengths and provide the education that all people will need to maximize their development and learning. We can no longer assume that all learners bring similar experiences and needs to the learning context. We need to find those successful schools, programs, and practices that have worked in helping every student succeed to the highest levels of achievement on content standards valued at local and national levels. We need to learn how successful schools have transformed themselves through collaborations and shared responsibility with families and communities to maintain a learner-centered focus in the context of high academic and personal expectations and standards for all students.

A first step in accomplishing these goals is to provide an array of learner-centered theoretical and empirically based psychological perspectives that provide frames of reference for rethinking and transforming classroom teaching, classroom assessment systems, and teacher education. We have selected these topics to provide a sample of the possibilities for designing schooling from a learner-centered perspective. By no means does this volume represent all of the relevant psychological literature with potential applications for learner-centered schools. It does, however, represent the views of contemporary educational and school psychologists on those issues of importance to the success of each learner on valued standards (cf. McCombs & Whisler, 1997).

Taking What Research Shows About Learners and Learning Seriously

As the reform agenda proceeds multidirectionally and at an accelerated rate in addressing the national education goals, the need for a defensible framework to guide complex decisions regarding standards, curricula, assessment, instruction, and the very structure and organization of schools becomes critical. What have we learned about effective interventions that contribute to high achievement levels on desired educational outcomes for *every* student? What are the major considerations in choosing among alternative approaches—considerations that include principles of learning and effective practice that are derived from the knowledge base both on the psychology of learning and individual differences and on "what works" from educational research?

The Learner-Centered Psychological Principles

We believe a foundation for guiding educational reform decisions is the knowledge base on learners and learning that has been derived from research in education and psychology. That knowledge base specifies factors that influence learning and academic achievement from the perspective of the individual learner. It provides a holistic conception of what research shows about individual learner needs and capacities for learning that can ensure that educational decisions will be responsive to the student, thereby avoiding issues of alienation, boredom, perceptions of irrelevancy, and other current issues students express with the traditional educational system and reform efforts that do not consider the individual student.

A summary of key principles defining major factors that influence learning and achievement, the learner-centered psychological principles, was jointly developed by APA and the Mid-Continent Regional Educational Laboratory (McREL; APA Presidential Task Force on Psychology in Education, 1993). Prior to its initial publication, drafts of the *Learner-Centered Psychological Principles: Guidelines for School Redesign and Reform* document were reviewed by major scientific societies, psychology organizations, and professional educational associations. The original document lists 12 principles that are divided into 5 major categories or factors that describe aspects of learners and the learning process that must be attended to in making educational decisions at all levels of the system and for all learners. The 5 categories of factors are metacognitive and cognitive, affective, developmental, personal and social, and individual differences. In the original document, the goal was that educators understand the validity of a learner-centered perspective—a perspective substantiated by research and one that provides a foundation for systemic educational decision making. For this reason, the original document laid out implications of the principles for effective instruction, curriculum, assessment, instructional management, teacher education, parent and community involvement, and policy practices.

A revision of the original document, recently undertaken by another APA task force in 1995–1996, slightly modified the original 12 principles and defined a total of 14 principles (*Learner-Centered Principles: A Framework for School Redesign and Reform* (APA, 1995), reorganized into 4 major categories, or factors. These factors include (a) cognitive and metacognitive factors that summarize what is known about the constructive nature of the learning process and the value of helping learners become more aware of their thinking and learning processes; (b) motivational and affective factors that summarize what is known about the influence of emotions and motivation on learning; (c) developmental and social factors that summarize the importance of positive learning climates and relationships in establishing the social context that facilitates meaningful learning as well as important differences in not only intellectual but also emotional, social, and physical development within and among learners; and (d) individual differences factors that summarize the commonality of principles describing all learners and the learning process and remind us of unique individual differences that shape the underpinnings of effective standards and assessment for *every* learner. An abbreviated version of the 14 principles is presented in the Appendix at the end of this chapter. The original 12 principles and discussion of their implications for the systemic redesign of education (instruction, curriculum, etc.) are presented in the Appendix to this volume.

Defining *Learner-Centered*

We believe a lot of confusion has existed about what is meant by *learner-centered*—what it is and what it isn't. Some people equate the term with child or student-centered. We think it goes well beyond a concern with preschool and other school-aged students. When one examines the 14 learner-centered principles, it is clear that the concept suggests more than that. The principles apply to all of us, cradle to grave, from students in the classroom to teachers, administrators, parents, and others influenced by the process of schooling. Other people equate *learner-centered* with the affective side of education—quality interpersonal relationships, climates of caring, and focus on fostering students' competence and sense of well-being. Again, we think that's only part of the picture. When one looks across the domains covered in the principles —the metacognitive and cognitive, affective, personal and social, developmental, and other individual differences factors—it is clear that there is an emphasis on both the learner and learning. The central understanding that emerges from an integrated and holistic look at the principles, however, is that for educational systems to serve the needs of every learner, it is essential that every instructional decision focus on the individual learner—with an understanding of the learning process (see Figure 1).

McCombs and Whisler (1997) defined learner-centered as

> the perspective that couples a focus on individual learners (their heredity, experiences, perspectives, backgrounds, talents, interests, capacities, and needs) with a focus on learning (the best available knowledge about learning and how it occurs and about teaching practices that are most effective in promoting the highest levels of motivation, learning, and achievement for all learners). This dual focus, then, informs and drives educational decision making. (p. 9)

Learner-centered is an application of the learner-centered psychological principles in practice—in the programs, policies, and people that support learning for all. Furthermore, this definition and the principles, themselves, lead to some fundamental conclusions about learners and learning. The following are the premises of a learner-centered model:

1. Learners have distinctive perspectives or frames of reference, contributed to by their history, the environment, their interests and goals, their beliefs, their ways of thinking, and the like. These must be attended to and respected if learners are to engage in and take responsibility for their own learning.

Figure 1

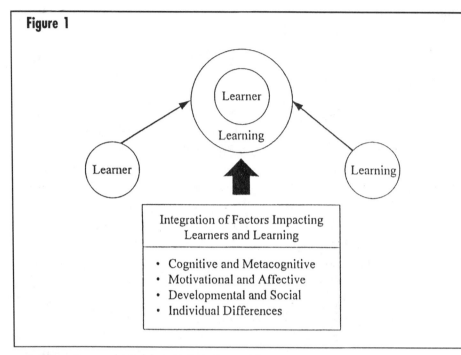

Learner-Centered Model: A Holistic Perspective

2. Learners have unique differences, including emotional states of mind, learning rates, learning styles, stages of development, abilities, talents, feelings of efficacy, and other needs. These must be taken into account if all learners are going to be provided with the challenges and opportunities for learning and self-development they need.

3. Learning is a constructive process that occurs best when what is being learned is relevant and meaningful to the learner and when the learner is actively engaged in creating his or her own knowledge and understanding by connecting what is being learned with prior knowledge and experience.

4. Learning occurs best in an environment that contains positive interpersonal relationships and interactions, comfort and order, and in which the learner feels appreciated, acknowledged, respected, and validated.

5. Learning is seen as a fundamentally natural process; learners are viewed as naturally curious and basically interested in learning about and mastering their world. Although negative thoughts and feelings sometimes interfere with this natural in-

clination and must be dealt with, the learner is neither regarded nor related to as deficient or needing to be "fixed."

None of the above premises need take a particular form or look a particular way. However, each must be reflected in the beliefs and actions of teachers, in the nature of their interactions with learners, and in the programs and structures they adopt. Generally, this means that (a) learners are included in educational decision-making processes, whether it be what they focus on in their learning or the rules that are established in the classroom; (b) the diverse perspectives of learners are encouraged and regarded during learning experiences; (c) the differences of learners' cultures, abilities, styles, developmental stages, and needs are accounted for and respected; and (d) teachers treat learners as co-creators in the teaching and learning process, as individuals with ideas and issues that deserve attention and consideration.

What Characterizes a Learner-Centered Model?

Many educators, including teachers and administrators, implicitly sense a conflict between learner- and learning-centered approaches. In sorting this out, Goldenberg (1991) contrasted these two views of how students learn and the conditions under which learning is optimized. The first view focuses on the *learner* and emphasizes that learning is a natural process guided by individual learners' goals, arising from the activity itself and interactions with others stemming from the activity, in which students try to make sense of their experience by constructing knowledge, meaning, and understanding. Current constructivist, social constructivist, and intrinsic motivation theories support this view (e.g., Brooks & Brooks, 1993; Deci & Ryan, 1991; Gardner, 1991; Gardner & Boix-Mansilla, 1994; McCombs, 1993, 1995; Oldfather, 1991, 1993; Ryan, 1995).

In the second view, focusing on *learning*, the emphasis is on the role of well-done explicit teaching in enhancing learning. This includes teaching procedures such as stating goals to students, summarizing prior learning, clearly presenting information, checking for understanding, modeling successful performance, guiding student practice toward fostering independent learners, and providing correctives and feedback on student performance. Cognitive theories of learning and instruction support this view, such as those of Marzano (1995), Marzano and Pickering (1991), Resnick (1987), and Shuell (1986, 1993).

Because research can be found to support both views, Goldenberg (1991) argued that the two views should be reconciled. The learner-centered psychological principles provide a knowledge and research base for the integration of what research shows about factors impacting learners and learning in concert with Goldenberg's perspective. Because the principles constitute an integration of research from a variety of perspectives and disciplines, they are concerned with both the learner and learning. That is, the current knowledge base suggests that focusing on learner needs and capacities in the context of understanding how learning occurs uniquely for each learner requires such an integration for maximum learning and motivation. As shown in Figure 1, the learner-centered model and the principles that underlie this model logically lead to the integration of learner and learning perspectives as well as promote a view that puts the learner focus in the forefront.

The model brings together what is important in what is referred to as a learner-centered versus learning-centered approach. In essence, the learner-centered model provides a perspective that rests on whether an educator's practice is based on an understanding of the nature of the individual learner (his or her characteristics, cultural and family background, experiences, and needs) and what research shows about learning. Focusing on the learner should not be interpreted as meaning there is no concern with learning achievement. Rather, the learner-centered model—by focusing on the individual learner and research on how best to support that learner's learning—provides a foundation for every learner to perform better on whatever outcomes or achievement measures might be chosen at the classroom, school, or district level.

We believe that to fully engage students in learning and meet basic needs, such as those of choice, competency, and connectedness, educational programs must be concerned with all of the unique individual differences of each learner. That means the focus is not just on intellectual gains. It means that what we know about learning and how it can best be facilitated is considered after first focusing on the needs, experiences, capacities, and perspectives of individual learners. It also means getting to know and respecting the uniqueness of each learner as a prerequisite to effective teaching and learning.

Psychological Perspectives on Learning and Teaching Practices, Assessment Systems, Assessment Policies, and Teacher Education Reform

The national debate on reforming America's schools requires significant restructuring efforts that are designed with a learner-centered perspective, and the learner-centered psychological principles provide a useful framework for guiding the restructuring efforts. We have noted that considerable national attention has been focused on basing educational reform decisions on a foundational knowledge base about learners and learning. There is a growing recognition that to the degree that instructional processes are consistent with this knowledge base, the educational system is more responsive to learner needs and potential for learning and that a learner-centered system, in turn, can ensure the promise of enhanced learning outcomes for every learner. These enhanced outcomes include not only higher achievement on educational standards but also enhanced motivation to learn.

To provide a complete account of psychology's contributions to learner-centered perspectives would be an impossible task. We have, however, selected some examples of promising thinking and research in four domains: learner-centered perspectives on (a) learning and teaching practices, (b) assessment systems, (c) assessment policy and reform strategies, and (d) teacher education. We offer this volume in the hope that it will initiate widespread and continued discussion about ways to make schooling more accessible to every one of the nation's learners, and promote the development of learner-centered schooling.

Organization of the Book

The first section of the book presents chapters on learning and teaching practices that reflect a rich array of thinking about the research base for the learner-centered principles, contextual factors that influence their application at the classroom level, the role of teacher expectations when informed by a learner-centered perspective, the importance of the cognitive principles for the development of literacy, how the principles contribute to subject matter learning, and what the principles mean for designing a community of young learners. In the second section, the criticality of a learner-centered perspective for the design of effective assessment systems at the classroom, school, and district or state levels is discussed, and strategies for looking comprehensively at assessment practices such that they address multiple domains of learner characteristics (cognitive, metacognitive, and conative) are provided.

The third section specifically addresses what has become central in our educational reform agenda—assessment policy and its role in reform. The authors look at the relationship of assessment policy to the national goals and what is done in higher education, how policy can address diversity, and various dilemmas when assessing academic achievement. The fourth section focuses on teacher education and what the knowledge base represented by the learner-centered psychological principles contributes to defining what teachers need to know, how their professional development experiences are designed and implemented, developmental issues that must be addressed as beginning teachers progress toward becoming expert teachers, and what the principles imply for how the knowledge base of educational psychology is conveyed to teachers and other educators. Finally, the book concludes with our summary remarks about what our research indicates and what the learner-centered perspective contributes to school reform.

References

American Psychological Association Board of Educational Affairs. (1995, Dec.). *Learner-centered psychological principles: A framework for school redesign and reform* [On-line]. Available: http://www.apa.org/ed/lcp.html.

American Psychological Association Presidential Task Force on Psychology in Education. (1993, January). *Learner-centered psychological principles: Guidelines for school redesign and reform.* Washington, DC: American Psychological Association/Mid-Continent Regional Educational Laboratory.

Brooks, J. G., & Brooks, M. G. (1993). *The case for constructivist classrooms.* Alexandria, VA: Association for Supervision and Curriculum Development.

Conley, D. T (1991). *Restructuring schools: Educators adapt to a changing world.* Eugene, OR: University of Oregon ERIC Clearinghouse on Educational Management.

Council of Great City Schools. (1993). *Diversifying our great city school teachers: Twenty-year trends.* Washington, DC: Author.

Deci, E. L., & Ryan, R. M. (1991). A motivational approach to self: Integration in personality. In R. Dienstbier (Ed.), *Nebraska symposium on motivation. Vol. 38: Perspectives on motivation.* Lincoln: University of Nebraska Press.

Elam, S. M., Rose, L. C., & Gallup, A. M. (1994). The 26th Annual Phi Delta Kappa/Gallup Poll of the public's attitudes toward the public schools. *Phi Delta Kappan, 76*(1), 41–56.

ERIC. (1991, October). *Striving for excellence: The national education goals.* Washington, DC: U.S. Department of Education.

Gardner, H. (1991). *The unschooled mind.* New York: Basic Books.

Gardner, H., & Boix-Mansilla, V. (1994). Teaching for understanding: Within and across the disciplines. *Educational Leadership, 51,* 14–18.

Goldenberg, C. (1991, June). *Two views of learning and their implications for literacy education.* Paper presented at the Language Minority Literacy Roundtable, University of California, Santa Barbara.

Marzano, R. J. (1995). Elements of a comprehensive approach to critical thinking. In J. Block, T. R. Guskey, & S. T. Everson (Eds.), *Choosing research-based school improvement innovations.* New York: Scholastic.

Marzano, R. J., & Pickering, D. (1991). Dimensions of learning: An integrative instructional framework. In A. Costa (Ed.), *Developing minds: A resource book for teaching thinking* (Vol., pp. 94–99). Alexandria, VA: Association for Supervision and Curriculum Development.

McCombs, B. L. (1993). Learner-centered psychological principles for enhancing education: Applications in school settings. In L. A. Penner, G. M. Batsche, H. M. Knoff, and D. L. Nelson (Eds.), *The challenge in mathematics and science education: Psychology's response.* Washington, DC: American Psychological Association.

McCombs, B. L. (1995). Putting the learner and learning in learner-centered classrooms: The learner-centered model as a framework. *Michigan ASCD Focus, 17,* 7–12.

McCombs, B. L., & Whisler, J. S. (1997). *The learner centered classroom and school: Strategies for enhancing student motivation and achievement.* San Francisco, CA: Jossey-Bass.

National Commission on Excellence in Education. (1983, April). *A nation at risk: The imperative for educational reform.* Washington, DC: U.S. Department of Education.

Oldfather, P. (1991, April). *When the bird and the book disagree, always believe the bird: Children's perceptions of their impulse to learn.* Paper presented at the annual meeting of the American Educational Research Association, Chicago.

Oldfather, P. (1993, Summer). *Students' perspectives on motivating experiences in literacy learning.* Athens, GA: National Reading Research Center.

Resnick, L. B. (1987). Learning in school and out. *Educational Researcher, 16*(9), 13–20.

Ryan, R. M. (1995). Psychological needs and the facilitation of integrative processes. *Journal of Personality, 63,* 397–427.

Shuell, T. J. (1986). Cognitive conceptions of learning. *Review of Educational Research, 56,* 411–436.

Shuell, T. J. (1993). Toward an integrated theory of teaching and learning. *Educational Psychologist, 27,* 291–311.

U.S. Department of Education. (1991, October). Striving for excellence: The national education goals. Washington, DC: Author.

Appendix

The Learner-Centered Psychological Principles

The following 14 psychological principles pertain to the learner and the learning process. They focus on psychological factors that are primarily internal to and under the control of the learner rather than conditioned habits or physiological factors. However, the principles also

Note. In developing and revising the principles, the original task force and the subsequent work group have endeavored to substantiate the research base for each principle. The multidisciplinary research expertise of the task force and work group members facilitated an examination of each principle from a number of different research perspectives. The development of each principle also involved thorough discussions of the research supporting that principle. From "Learner-Centered Psychological Principles: A Framework for School Redesign and Reform," American Psychological Association Board of Educational Affairs, December 1995 [on-line]. Available: http://www.apa.org/ed/lcp.html. Copyright 1995 by the American Psychological Association.

attempt to acknowledge external environment or contextual factors that interact with these internal factors.

The principles are intended to deal holistically with learners in the context of real-world learning situations. Thus, they are best understood as an organized set; no principle should be viewed in isolation. The 14 principles are divided into groups referring to cognitive and metacognitive, motivational and affective, developmental and social, and individual difference factors influencing learners and learning. Finally, the principles are intended to apply to *all* learners from children, to teachers, to administrators, to parents, and to community members involved in our educational system.

Cognitive and Metacognitive Factors

1. Nature of the learning process. The learning of complex subject matter is most effective when it is an intentional process of constructing meaning from information and experience.

There are different types of learning processes (e.g., habit formation in motor learning and learning that involves the generation of knowledge, or cognitive skills and strategies, by constructing or integrating some form of mental representation). Learning in schools emphasizes the use of intentional processes that students can use to construct meaning from information, experiences, and their own thoughts and beliefs. Successful learners are active, goal-directed, self-regulating, and assume personal responsibility for contributing to their own learning. The principles set forth in this document focus on this type of learning.

2. Goals of the learning process. The successful learner, over time and with support and instructional guidance, can create meaningful, coherent representations of knowledge.

The strategic nature of learning requires students to be goal directed. To construct useful representations of knowledge and to acquire the thinking and learning strategies necessary for continued learning success across the life span, students must generate and pursue personally relevant goals. Initially, students' short-term goals and learning may be sketchy in an area, but over time their understanding can be refined by filling gaps, resolving inconsistencies, and deepening their understanding of the subject matter so that they can reach longer term goals.

Educators can assist learners in creating meaningful learning goals that are consistent with both personal and educational aspirations and interests.

3. Construction of knowledge. The successful learner can link new information with existing knowledge in meaningful ways.

Knowledge widens and deepens as students continue to build links between new information and experiences and their existing knowledge base. The nature of these links can take a variety of forms, such as adding to, modifying, or reorganizing existing knowledge or skills. How these links are made or develop may vary in different subject areas, and among students with varying talents, interests, and abilities. However, unless new knowledge becomes integrated with the learner's prior knowledge and understanding, this new knowledge remains isolated, cannot be used most effectively in new tasks, and does not transfer readily to new situations. Educators can assist learners in acquiring and integrating knowledge by a number of strategies that have been shown to be effective with learners of varying abilities, such as concept mapping and thematic organization or categorizing.

4. Strategic thinking. The successful learner can create and use a repertoire of thinking and reasoning strategies to achieve complex learning goals.

Successful learners use strategic thinking in their approach to learning, reasoning, problem solving, and concept learning. They understand and can use a variety of strategies to help them reach learning and performance goals, and to apply their knowledge in novel situations. They also continue to expand their repertoire of strategies by reflecting on the methods they use to see which approach works best for them, by receiving guided instruction and feedback, and by observing or interacting with appropriate models. Learning outcomes can be enhanced if educators assist learners in developing, applying, and assessing their strategic learning skills.

5. Thinking about thinking. Higher order strategies for selecting and monitoring mental operations facilitate creative and critical thinking.

Successful learners can reflect on how they think and learn, set reasonable learning or performance goals, select potentially appropriate learning strategies or methods, and monitor their progress toward these goals. In addition, successful learners know what to do if a problem occurs or if they are not making sufficient or timely progress toward a goal. They can generate alternative methods to reach their goal (or reassess the appropriateness and utility of the goal). Instructional methods that focus on helping learners develop these higher order (metacognitive) strategies can enhance student learning and personal responsibility for learning.

6. Context of learning. Learning is influenced by environmental factors, including culture, technology, and instructional practices.

Learning does not occur in a vacuum. Environmental factors can have strong positive or negative influences on learning. Cultural or group influences on students can impact many educationally relevant variables, such as motivation, orientation toward learning, and ways of thinking. Technologies and instructional practices must be appropriate for learners' level of prior knowledge, cognitive abilities, and their learning and thinking strategies. The nature of the classroom environment, particularly the degree to which it is nurturing or not, can also have significant impacts on student learning.

Motivational and Affective Factors

7. Motivational and emotional influences on learning. What and how much is learned is influenced by the learner's motivation. Motivation to learn, in turn, is influenced by the individual's emotional states, beliefs, interests and goals, and habits of thinking.

The rich internal world of thoughts, beliefs, goals, and expectations for success or failure can enhance or interfere with the learner's quality of thinking and information processing. Motivational and emotional factors have a marked influence on the cognitive component of learning. Moods and feelings influence both the quality of thinking and information processing as well as an individual's motivation to learn. Positive emotions, such as curiosity, generally enhance motivation and facilitate learning and performance. Mild anxiety can also enhance learning and performance by focusing the learner's attention on a particular task. Similarly, mild frustration and anger can increase the learner's determination to demonstrate knowledge and competence. However, intense negative emotions (e.g., anxiety, panic, rage, insecurity) and related thoughts (e.g., worrying about competence, ruminating about failure, fearing punishment, ridicule, or stigmatizing labels) generally detract from motivation, interfere with learning, and contribute to low performance. Educators need to be aware of learners' emotional states and the influence of their practices on these states.

8. Intrinsic motivation to learn. The learner's creativity, higher order thinking, and natural curiosity all contribute to motivation to learn. Intrinsic motivation is stimulated by tasks the learner perceives to be of optimal novelty and difficulty, relevant to personal interests, and providing for personal choice and control.

Curiosity, flexible and insightful thinking, and creativity are major indicators of the learners' intrinsic motivation to learn. Intrinsic motivation to learn is in large part a function of meeting basic needs to be competent and to exercise personal control. Intrinsic motivation is facilitated on tasks that learners perceive as personally relevant and meaningful, appropriate in complexity and difficulty to the learners' abilities, and on which they believe they can succeed. Intrinsic motivation is also facilitated on tasks that are comparable to real-world situations and meet needs for choice and control. Educators can encourage and support learners' natural curiosity and motivation to learn by attending to individual differences in learners' perceptions of optimal novelty and difficulty, relevance, and personal choice and control.

9. Effects of motivation on effort. Acquisition of complex knowledge and skills requires extended learner effort and guided practice. Without learners' motivation to learn, the willingness to exert this effort is unlikely without coercion.

Effort is another major indicator of motivation to learn. The acquisition of complex knowledge and skills demands the investment of considerable learner energy and strategic effort, along with persistence over time. Educators need to be concerned with facilitating motivation by strategies that enhance learner effort and commitment to learning and to achieving high standards of comprehension and understanding. Effective strategies include purposeful learning activities, guided by practices that enhance positive emotions and intrinsic motivation to learn, and methods that increase learners' perceptions that a task is interesting and personally relevant.

Developmental and Social Factors

10. Developmental influences on learning. As individuals develop, there are different opportunities and constraints for learning. Learning is most effective when differential development within and across physical, intellectual, emotional, and social domains is taken into account.

Individuals learn best when material is appropriate to their developmental level and is presented in an enjoyable and interesting way. Because individual development varies across intellectual, social, emotional, and physical domains, achievement in different instructional domains may also vary. Overemphasis on one type of developmental readiness—such as reading readiness, for example—may preclude learners from demonstrating that they are more capable in other areas of performance. The cognitive, emotional, and social development of individual learners and how they interpret life experiences are affected by prior schooling, home, culture, and community factors. Early and continuing parental involvement in schooling and the quality of language interactions between parents and their children can influence these developmental areas. Awareness and understanding of developmental differences among children with and without emotional, physical, or intellectual disabilities can facilitate the creation of optimal learning contexts.

11. Social influences on learning. Learning is influenced by social interactions, interpersonal relations, and communication with others.

Learning can be enhanced when the learner has an opportunity to interact and to collaborate with others on instructional tasks. Learning settings that allow for social interactions and that respect diversity encourage flexible thinking and social competence. In interactive and collaborative instructional contexts, individuals have an opportunity for perspective taking and reflective thinking that may lead to higher levels of social and moral development and self-esteem. Quality personal relationships that provide stability, trust, and caring can increase learners' sense of belonging, self-respect, and self-acceptance, and provide a positive climate for learning. Positive interpersonal support and instruction in self-motivation strategies can offset factors that interfere with optimal learning such as negative beliefs about competence in a particular subject, high levels of test anxiety, negative sex role expectations, and undue pressure to perform well. Positive learning climates can also help establish the context for healthier levels of thinking, feeling, and behaving. Such contexts help learners feel safe to share ideas, actively participate in the learning process, and create a learning community.

Individual Differences

12. Individual differences in learning. Learners have different strategies, approaches, and capabilities for learning that are a function of prior experience and heredity.

Individuals are born with and develop their own capabilities and talents. In addition, through learning and social acculturation, they have acquired their own preferences for how they like to learn and the pace at which they learn. However, these preferences are not always useful in helping learners reach their learning goals. Educators need to help students examine their learning preferences and expand or modify them, if necessary. The interaction between learner differences and curricular and environmental conditions is another key factor affecting learning outcomes. Educators need to be sensitive to individual differences, in general. They also need to attend to learner perceptions of the degree to which these differences are accepted and adapted to by varying instructional methods and materials.

13. Learning and diversity. Learning is most effective when differences in learners' linguistic, cultural, and social backgrounds are taken into account.

The same basic principles of learning, motivation, and effective instruction apply to all learners. However, language, ethnicity, race, beliefs, and socioeconomic status all can influence learning. Careful attention to these factors in the instructional setting enhances the possibilities for designing and implementing appropriate learning environments. When learners perceive that their individual differences in abilities, backgrounds, cultures, and experiences are valued, respected, and accommodated in learning tasks and contexts, levels of motivation and achievement are enhanced.

14. Standards and assessment. Setting appropriately high and challenging standards and assessing the learner as well as learning progress—including diagnostic, process, and outcome assessment—are integral parts of the learning process.

Assessment provides important information to both the learner and the teacher at all stages of the learning process. Effective learning takes place when learners feel challenged to work toward appropriately high goals; therefore, appraisal of the learner's cognitive strengths and weaknesses, as well as current knowledge and skills, is important for the selection of instructional materials of an optimal degree of difficulty. Ongoing assessment of the learner's understanding of the curricular material can provide valuable feedback to both learners and teachers about progress toward the learning goals. Standardized assessment of learner progress and outcomes assessment provides one type of information about achievement levels both within and across individuals that can inform various types of programmatic decisions. Performance assessments can provide other sources of information about the attainment of learning outcomes. Self-assessments of learning progress can also enhance motivation and self-directed learning.

Part I

Learner-Centered Perspectives for Classroom Teaching

The Research Base for APA's Learner-Centered Psychological Principles

Patricia A. Alexander and P. Karen Murphy

Between 1990 and 1996, an impressive collection of educational researchers contributed their wisdom and years of well-honed insights to a set of 14 psychological principles that they hoped would guide the redesign and reform of American schools (e.g., American Psychological Association [APA] Presidential Task Force on Psychology in Education and Mid-Continent Regional Educational Laboratory [McREL], 1993). These psychological principles and the philosophical statement framing them have subsequently been revised and are currently under review (APA Board of Educational Affairs, 1995). In our view, these resulting principles can be invaluable tools for practicing professionals as they seek to understand and facilitate the learning of others.

Our role in this critical enterprise began several years ago. At that time, we were asked to offer an analysis of the literatures in learning and instruction, motivation, and development that might underlie the initial set of 12 principles forwarded in the original APA–McREL document (Alexander & Murphy, 1994). Thankfully, during the past decade, Alexander and colleagues (Alexander & Judy, 1988; Alexander & Kulikowich, 1994; Alexander, Kulikowich, & Jetton, 1994; Alexander, Parsons, & Nash, 1996; Alexander, Schallert, & Hare, 1991) engaged in multidimensional reviews of the literature that have synthesized research in these same areas (i.e., learning and instruction, motivation, and development). As we illustrate in this chapter, the general premises

A version of this chapter was presented at the annual meeting of the American Educational Research Association, New Orleans, April 1994.

or postulates that were formulated in these reviews provide strong support for many of the ideas represented in both the original and revised learner-centered principles, described by Lambert and McCombs in the opening chapter of this volume (see chap. 1).

To perform our review of these literatures, we took an initial step of distilling the original 12 statements offered by the task force into 5 more general statements (see Exhibit 1), which we felt could meaningfully serve educators at all instructional levels. We then proceeded to identify bodies of research that we felt were relevant to these general premises. Further, we specified emerging psychological issues that we found missing or only weakly addressed in the original 12 principles outlined by the task force. The resulting research review, which we present in this chapter, served as one of the sources of information that APA's Board of Educational Affairs used in its preparation of the revised learner-centered psychological principles (APA, 1995). For this reason, several of the missing or weakly addressed areas of concern we describe in this chapter are now evident or more strongly articulated in the revised 14 principles. For the reader's convenience, our discussion of the 5 guiding premises makes reference to the pertinent principles as stated

---

Exhibit 1

Five General Statements Related to the Learner-Centered Principles

The knowledge base
   One's existing knowledge serves as the foundation of all future learning by guiding organization and representations, by serving as a basis of association with new information, and by coloring and filtering all new experiences.
Strategic processing or executive control
   The ability to reflect on and regulate one's thoughts and behaviors is essential to learning and development.
Motivation and affect
   Motivational or affective factors, such as intrinsic motivation, attributions for learning, and personal goals, along with the motivational characteristics of learning tasks, play a significant role in the learning process.
Development and individual differences
   Learning, although ultimately a unique adventure for all, progresses through various common stages of development influenced by both inherited and experiential/environmental factors.
Situation or context
   Learning is as much a socially shared undertaking as it is an individually constructed enterprise.

in the lastest revision. In addition, we have noted any significant deviation between our initial concern (e.g., lack of a specific principle related to assessment) and the modifications that are reflected in the document prepared by the Board of Educational Affairs.

We conclude our literature survey in this chapter by considering the potential impact of these psychological premises on future educational practices—the explicit goal of the APA task force. Before we proceed, however, it is important to place the subsequent analysis within an appropriate theoretical and philosophical context. First, we heartily concur with the mission of the task force to infuse knowledge of human learning, motivation, and development into ongoing efforts to improve the educational experience of all people. Educational reform has too long overlooked or undervalued the beneficial knowledge that can be contributed by research in psychology and related fields. In the judgment of Alexander and Knight (1993), this devaluing of psychological processes has been a contributing factor to the failure of reform movements in education to bring about meaningful progress. Instead, basic issues are updated and recycled, often without regard to their philosophical and psychological roots (Alexander, Murphy, & Woods, 1996).

Second, as with any collaborative effort, even one as effective as the work of the aforementioned task force and the Board of Educational Affairs, the resulting set of principles must be recognized as a compromise among members who came to the task with their own research interests and constructions. This is not to question, in any way, the outcome of these renowned researchers' efforts, but only to recognize that no committee report results without negotiation, collaboration, and ultimately compromise. This observation is one reason why we have chosen to focus our analysis on the underlying tenets espoused in the principles rather than concentrate on their specific language or phrasing.

Third, the guidelines offered by the task force are, indeed, principles that are still undergoing review and revision. As with any "living" document grounded in research that is continually developing, such ongoing review and revision are to be welcomed and encouraged. Consequently, these espoused principles should not be viewed as prescriptions that ensure or even promise effective educational redesign or reformation. Nothing short of long-term, concerted, and cooperative effort on the part of all partners in the educational enterprise can achieve such a laudable goal.

A Reframing of the Learner-Centered Principles

To frame the contents of the original 12 psychological principles proposed by the task force, within the existing literature, we found it helpful to distill them into 5 more general statements that pertain to broad dimensions of learning. By formulating fewer and more general statements, we were better able to specify a body of recent works that substantiates the gist of the original principles. In essence, our goal, as mentioned earlier, was to evaluate the general intention of the learner-centered principles rather than focus our energies on assessing their exact wording or phrasing.

Parsed down to their fundamental roots, we hold that the learner-centered principles relate to five essential dimensions of meaningful learning that have been systematically investigated in psychology and related disciplines for decades. Those dimensions are

1. the knowledge base,
2. strategic processing or executive control,
3. motivation and affect,
4. development and individual differences, and
5. situation or context.

Specifically, it is our judgment that the original 12 statements, as well as the revised 14 principles, can be combined and simplified into these 5 premises, presented in Exhibit 1.

The Knowledge Base

One's existing knowledge serves as the foundation of all future learning by guiding organization and representations, by serving as a basis of association with new information, and by coloring and filtering all new experiences.

Several of the principles formulated by the task force (e.g., Principles 1, 2, and 3) speak to one of the most powerful and consistent findings to emerge from the research in cognition over the past several decades. Simply stated, the knowledge that learners possess becomes an extremely powerful force, not only in what information they attend to (e.g., Anderson, Pichert, & Shirey, 1983; Hidi, 1990; Reynolds & Shirey, 1988) or how that information is perceived (e.g., Gibson, 1966) but also in what is judged by learners as relevant or important (e.g., Alexander, Jetton, Kulikowich, & Woehler, 1994; Pichert & Anderson, 1977; Schraw

& Dennison, 1994) and what is comprehended and remembered (e.g., Alvermann, Smith, & Readence, 1985; Anderson, Reynolds, Schallert, & Goetz, 1977; Pritchard, 1990). In essence, the knowledge base is the total of all an individual knows or believes (Alexander et al., 1991). Truly one's knowledge base is the scaffold that supports the construction of all future learning (Principle 3). Further, because each individual's knowledge base is unique, so too are his or her constructions within that scaffold (Principle 12).

Through the 1970s and into the 1980s, a great flood of research appeared concomitantly with the rise of cognitive psychology that demonstrated how prior knowledge was predictive of learning outcomes (e.g., Alexander, 1996; Anderson, 1977; Bransford & Franks, 1972). Classic studies during this period further demonstrated how the organization and structure of that knowledge often differentiated novice learners from those with greater expertise (e.g., Chi, Feltovich, & Glaser, 1981; Larkin, McDermott, Simon, & Simon, 1980). However, as research on the knowledge base matured, several changes in understanding about the nature and role of that knowledge occurred.

First, since the early information-processing studies, knowledge has come to be viewed as a multifaceted construct that encompasses many interactive dimensions (Alexander et al., 1991), including sociocultural knowledge (Principles 11 and 13), strategic abilities (Principle 4), personal beliefs (Principle 13), and goals (Principle 2). For example, Lipson (1983) examined how students' religious orientation influenced the way they comprehended and recalled passages about religious practices, whereas Chambliss and Garner (1996) investigated how adults' views on logging practices in the western United States altered their reading of persuasive texts. In addition, Alexander and Kulikowich (1991) found that readers' knowledge about human biology was a significant factor in their strategic processing of analogies embedded in exposition. Thus, although researchers have continued to study the knowledge base and substantiate its powerful role in subsequent learning, they conceive of it in an increasingly more complex, multidimensional way (Alexander, Murphy, Woods, Duhon, & Parker, 1997).

Sometimes the dimensions of one's knowledge base, just described, work in concert. At other times, however, these dimensions operate in conflict with one another, as when one's informal knowledge or spontaneous concepts are in opposition to the formal or scientific concepts that are the mainstay of the instructional enterprise (e.g., Alexander, 1992; Gardner, 1991; Vygotsky, 1934/1986). Further, the knowledge base is not constructed solely of factual or schooled content stored and organized in memory, knowledge that can be retrieved and reflected on (Prawat, 1989), or knowledge that can be externally validated (Alexander & Dochy, 1994, 1995; Mayer, this volume, chap. 14). Instead, it is accepted that the knowledge learners possess is often acquired from nonacademic life experiences (Gardner, 1991) and is, thus, a unique reflection of their sociocultural heritage (Principle 13).

Also, this knowledge can remain buried in memory, as in the case of implicit theories (e.g., Alexander, 1992; Gardner, 1991; Prawat, 1989; Sternberg, Conway, Ketron, & Bernstein, 1981), or can be seriously flawed or misleading (e.g., Alvermann et al., 1985; Champagne, Kloper, & Anderson, 1980; Marshall, in press). Therefore, although knowledge is generally held to be a positive force in the learning process, it is no longer judged to always be so (Principle 3). Because learners operate on the incomplete and inaccurate knowledge they possess, their existing knowledge and the misconceptions that are part of it can actually deter or interfere with future growth (e.g., Chinn & Brewer, 1993; Perkins & Simmons, 1988). Consequently, educators must be aware of the misconceptions that students may commonly hold in an area of study and must work to challenge those misconceptions within the context of meaningful instruction (Roth, 1985).

Finally, another change that has occurred in the study of the knowledge base over the past 30 years is the recognition that knowledge, particularly as it relates to academic learning, is associated with specific fields of studies (i.e., domains) and is applied differentially on the basis of the characteristics of the learning task or the context in which it is situated (Principle 6). In our own work, for example, we have begun to systematically investigate students' learning across different topics in the same field (e.g., bacteriophages vs. viral nucleic acids; Alexander, Pate, Kulikowich, Farrell, & Wright, 1989), across different fields of study (e.g., human immunology vs. physics; Alexander, Jetton, & Kulikowich, 1995), and under varying task conditions (e.g., linear vs. nonlinear text processing; Alexander, Kulikowich, & Jetton, 1994).

The outcomes of the studies just referenced and others (e.g., Cognition and Technology Group at Vanderbilt, 1990; Hidi & Baird, 1986, 1988; Schiefele, 1991; Wittrock, this volume) corroborate that a learner's knowledge can vary dramatically from topic to topic, from domain to domain, and from situation to situation (Murphy & Woods, 1996). For example, the child who demonstrates competence in one area (e.g., dinosaurs) or with one task (e.g., multiplication tables) may perform like a novice in another area or with an alternate learning task (Alexander, in press-b). Likewise, the adult who is considered an expert in one domain (e.g., educational psychology) may best be described as a competent learner in some other domain (e.g., statistics) or even naive or acclimated in another (e.g., physics). This finding suggests that the knowledge base is not only complex but also fluid and dynamic in terms of its application. Thus, global and unconditional judgments of student capabilities and competencies on the basis of the assessment of the knowledge base may be unfounded and potentially detrimental to subsequent learning.

Strategic Processing or Executive Control

The ability to reflect on and regulate one's thoughts and behaviors is essential to learning and development.

Since the ground-breaking work of Flavell (1977) and Brown (1975), and with support of research in creative or critical thinking (e.g., Ennis, 1985, 1987, 1989; Nickerson, 1989), it is widely accepted that effective learners not only possess a body of organized and relevant knowledge, but they also have the ability, and at times the willingness, to reflect on and to oversee their own mental functioning and to assess their own performance (Principles 4 and 5). Studies have demonstrated that learning is enhanced when individuals have knowledge of and apply appropriate monitoring or executive strategies during the learning process (e.g., Elliott-Faust & Pressley, 1986; Garner & Alexander, 1989; Weinstein & Mayer, 1986). Whether these mental actions and self-regulations are specifically identified as general cognitive strategies (Pressley, Goodchild, Fleet, Zajchowski, & Evans, 1989), metacognitive strategies (Flavell, 1976; Garner, 1987), executive control or monitoring (Brown, 1975), executive components (Sternberg, 1980), or creative or critical thinking (Ennis, 1989), the findings are much the same. Those who reflect on their own thinking and learning performance and use that self-knowledge to alter their processing are more likely to show significant academic growth than those who do not (e.g., Garner, 1987).

Yet, the research in strategic processing or executive control has also undergone change over the past decades. Initially, there was lively debate in the literature over whether general or domain-specific strategies were more essential to learning (e.g., Glaser, 1984; Sternberg, 1985). The flurry of discussion around this debate has since quieted. It is no longer a question of which is better. It is strongly held that both general cognitive and metacognitive strategies and domain-specific strategies are critical for learning (Alexander & Judy, 1988). The leading question has now become one of when, where, and for whom certain types of strategies are more effective for learning (Alexander, in press-b; Schoenfeld, 1988). In addition, there have been attempts to clarify the meaning of such fundamental terms as *strategies* (Alexander et al., 1991; Pressley et al., 1989). Even the notion of metacognition and creativity has undergone reexamination in recent years (e.g., Alexander, Parsons, & Nash, 1996; Gardner, 1993; Garner & Alexander, 1989; Paris & Winograd, 1990; Sternberg & Lubart, 1991).

Just as the research in knowledge has matured, so too have the investigations of strategic processing. For instance, during the height of research on metacognitive and cognitive strategies during the 1970s and 1980s, there was great hope that training in strategic processing or executive control would give rise to significant and long-term changes in students' learning. Yet, so many of those dreams were never realized. It became clearer and clearer to those engaged in this research and those who attempted to implement relevant findings in schools that strategic processing or executive control alone is necessary, but not sufficient, to ensure greater learning (Alexander & Judy, 1988; Garner, 1990). If training was limited in scope, not extended over time, or did not adequately address transfer to new tasks or situations; if the attributions and goals in the classroom did not support or reward strategic thinking; if students failed to see the relevance or value of the trained strategies; or if their self-judgments did not justify the effortfulness required of strategic behavior, then little if any real impact on learning could be expected from the teaching of cognitive or metacognitive strategies (e.g., Borkowski, Carr, Rellinger, & Pressley, 1990; Garner, 1990; McCombs, 1988; Palmer & Goetz, 1988; Paris & Winograd, 1990).

As with the dimensions discussed in the other principles, it is better understood that strategic processing or executive control must be coordinated with other factors, such as the learner's emotional state or the instructional climate, if optimal learning is to be achieved (Alexander, in press-a, in press-b). There is also greater understanding that learners' strategic processing should vary as their knowledge in a field grows and develops (Alexander & Judy, 1988; Hasselhorn & Körkel, 1986; McCutchen, 1986). For example, McCutchen (1986) found that students' writing performance varied as their knowledge of content, discourse, and strategies changed. Likewise, Hasselhorn and Körkel

(1986) investigated how instruction in a general knowledge activation strategy benefited children with differing amounts of content knowledge. Specifically, Hasselhorn and Körkel demonstrated that metacognitive training was most useful with novices, whereas a more traditional knowledge-activation study worked best with experts. On the basis of these results, the researchers concluded that there were "greater benefits of metacognitive instruction in selected settings" (p. 88).

Further, the reflection and strategic efforts must, almost by definition, vary as the demands of the task or the nature of the context changes (e.g., Lave, 1988, 1991; Pressley et al., 1992; Resnick, 1991). To assume that one can simply have students memorize and routinely execute a set of strategies is to misconceive the nature of strategic processing or executive control. Such rote applications of these procedures represents, in essence, a true oxymoron—nonstrategic strategic processing. It has become increasingly clear, as well, that strategic processing or executive control is not only a purposeful undertaking but an effortful one as well (Borkowski, Carr, & Pressley, 1987). This means that it is difficult to bring about changes in students' strategic processing without addressing issues of motivation, interest, and self-regulation (Palmer & Goetz, 1988). This interplay among dimensions is a theme we return to later in this chapter.

Motivation and Affect

Motivational or affective factors, such as intrinsic motivation, attributions for learning, and personal goals, along with the motivational characteristics of learning tasks, play a significant role in the learning process.

Edison is credited with saying that "Genius is 1% inspiration and 99% perspiration." Much the same can be said for learning in general, because learning is strongly influenced by the degree to which individuals are invested in the learning process. In other words, learning is altered by motivational and affective factors within the learner and in the learning environment. Indeed, many of the learner-centered principles from the APA task force (1993) relate to this dimension (i.e., Principles 2, 6, 7, 8, and 9). Whereas semantic issues about the construct of motivation persist (Pintrich, 1991), it is useful to view motivation as the general process by which the individuals' needs and desires are activated and, thus, directs their thoughts and their behaviors (e.g., Pintrich, Marx, &

Boyle, 1993). Affect, as a related construct, can be understood as the feelings or emotions that individuals typically have and that, likewise, influence their thoughts and behaviors (e.g., Ames & Ames, 1985).

The research in motivation and affect has documented well over the decades that personal involvement, intrinsic motivation, and commitment contribute to greater learning (Principle 8; e.g., Ames & Ames, 1985, 1989; Corno & Rohrkemper, 1985; Dweck & Leggett, 1988; Gottfried, 1985, 1990). Those learners who have positive self-concepts (e.g., Wigfield & Karpathian, 1991; Wylie, 1974, 1979, 1989), believe themselves to be in control of their learning (e.g., deCharms, 1968; Deci & Ryan, 1985, 1991; Deci, Valleran, Pelletier, & Ryan, 1991), and have goals of understanding rather than performing (e.g., Dweck, 1986; Nicholls, 1984; Principle 2) are more apt to be those who achieve in schools. In addition, the students who are capable of setting appropriately high goals for themselves (e.g., Bandura, 1977, 1993; Schunk, 1991; Tolman, 1932) and those who find their academic work to be personally relevant (Principle 8) are more likely to succeed in schools (e.g., Lepper, 1988; Maehr & Braskamp, 1986; Meece, Blumenfeld, & Hoyle, 1988). The classroom environment in which students operate also plays a significant role in learning (Principle 6). When the teacher acknowledges students' personal goals and interests, or when learners perceive the academic climate as supportive and encouraging, they are more likely to perform well within the academic environment (e.g., Ames, 1992; Newman & Schwager, 1992; Pintrich et al., 1993).

Yet, motivational or affective influences are not restricted to general personality or emotional factors or to global orientations toward school or learning. These dimensions, as with the strategic factors we described earlier, have a domain-specific or task-specific character, as well as some general nature that is not clearly conveyed in the original principles. That is, although we can say that the research has supported the notion that the more motivated student performs better than the unmotivated student, we should also consider that no individual is equally motivated in all situations or contexts (e.g., Csikszentmihalyi, 1990; Schiefele & Csikszentmihalyi, 1994, 1995). To the contrary, learners are apt to show higher levels of motivation (e.g., interest or involvement) for some fields of study than others and for certain tasks but not for others (e.g., Alexander, Kulikowich, & Schulze, 1994a; Phillips & Zimmerman, 1990; Renninger, 1992).

These variations in motivation or affect may be attributed to a number of factors, including students' knowledge of the content (e.g., Alexander, Kulikowich, & Schulze, 1994b; Schiefele, Krapp, & Winteler, 1992), their perception of instructional priorities or teacher expectations (e.g., Alexander, Jetton, Kulikowich, & Woehler, 1994; Jetton & Alexander, 1997; Wigfield & Harold, 1992), or the perceived climate in the classroom (e.g., Ames, 1992; Schunk & Meece, 1992). In a recent study, for example, Schiefele and Csikszentmihalyi (1994) found that high school students' interest was significantly associated with the perceived quality of their experiences in their classes. In addition, the researchers reported that regression results suggested that performance in students' more difficult subjects (e.g., mathematics and physics) was more affected by ability, whereas performance in the easier to learn subjects (e.g., biology and social studies) was more influenced by motivational factors.

For the reasons just stated, there is an increasing trend in the literature on motivation and affect to investigate more specific dimensions of human learning and performance (e.g., Monroe, 1991). Thus, although the research on motivation and affect continues to flourish, there is a growing body of work in interest (e.g., Renninger, Hidi, & Krapp, 1992; Tobias, 1994), which, by definition, conveys the domain or task specificity that we have been addressing. That is, as with the Schiefele and Csikszentmihalyi (1994) study, we do not typically describe learners as globally interested, but rather as possessing interest in some subject, topic, task, or even text segment (e.g., Asher, Hymel, & Wigfield, 1978; Baldwin, Peleg-Bruckner, & McClintock, 1985; Hidi, Baird, & Hildyard, 1982; Pintrich et al., 1993; Schank, 1979).

One outcome of this changed focus in research on motivation and affect is the recognition that individuals' investment or involvement, even when positive, does not always result in a rise in learning. Indeed, under certain conditions, individuals' arousal or attention to information or factors that are not important or even tangential to academic goals can prove detrimental to the learning process (e.g., Garner, Alexander, Gillingham, Kulikowich, & Brown, 1991; Garner, Gillingham, & White, 1989; Wade, Schraw, Buxton, & Hayes, 1993). Garner et al. (1991) discovered, for example, that the presence of highly interesting, but relatively unimportant, information about a wager made by Stephen Hawking appeared to negatively impact students' ability to recall highly important but less interesting scientific content.

This recognition has important implications for educators, because it suggests that it is not sufficient for teachers to merely pique the attention or interest of their students without consideration of potential ramifications. Rather, teachers' attempts to motivate must consider the personal goals and interests of the student (Dewey, 1913) and the relative value of the content (Wade et al., 1993), along with the desired outcomes of the instructional process (Alexander, in press-b). Further, the teacher must create an instructional climate in which the students have opportunities to engage their personal interests in meaningful ways and in a manner that acknowledges their personal control or regulation of their own learning (e.g., Pintrich & Schrauben, 1992; Zimmerman & Martinez-Pons, 1992). In sum, it would seem that the application of the literatures in motivation and affect to the reshaping and reformation of the educational system will need to consider not only learners' general needs, desires, self-perceptions, and emotional states or orientations but also their specific interests, goals, and desires.

Development and Individual Differences

Learning, although ultimately a unique adventure for all, progresses through various common stages of development influenced by both inherited and experiential/environmental factors.

Of the various dimensions of learning that we have analyzed, none has a longer or richer history than that of development. Indeed, the philosophical roots of traditional developmental theory reach well back to Plato, Rousseau, and Locke and are marked by attempts to understand the nature and growth of the human species. Although the philosophical foundations of individual differences may be relatively more recent (e.g., Luther, J. S. Mill), the resulting body of research is no less rich and impressive. The focus of this research is the variability that differentiates one person from another. As John Stuart Mill (1859/1947) so aptly stated, "The free development of individuality is one of the leading essentials of well-being" (p. 58).

In their articulation of learner-centered principles, the members of the APA task force (1993) saw fit to devote a specific guideline to development (Principle 10) and another to individual differences (Principle 12). This approach is quite understandable in light of the tendency among psychologists to think either in terms of global trends in human development (e.g., Case, 1985, 1993) or in terms of unique, individualistic patterns of change (e.g., Dillon & Schmeck, 1983; Reynolds & Willson, 1985). According to Scarr (1992), this separateness between development and individual differences is attributable, in large measure, to the distinct philosophical traditions that underlie each, and to which we have alluded. Certainly, there is a rich and extensive literature that attests to progressive and predictable patterns in human development (e.g., Farrar & Goodman, 1992; Flavell, Mumme, Green, & Flavell, 1992; Zelazo & Reznick, 1991). Likewise, there is a plethora of research that speaks to variations in development at the level of the individual learner (e.g., Galton, 1908; Jensen, 1989; Plomin & Daniels, 1987; Plomin & DeFries, 1985).

Yet, there is no reason to assume that development must be conceptualized as either typical or individualistic in nature. Our goal here, therefore, is to reframe the original principles dealing with development and individual differences into one statement that conveys human growth as a process that entails not only commonalties across individuals but also unique variations within individuals. For instance, we can discuss the rather stable nature of IQ scores substantiated in populations over time, or we can describe the large variation in such scores that can be evidenced within individuals (e.g., Bayley, 1943; McCall, Applebaum, & Hogarty, 1973). According to Cole and Cole (1993), there are three questions that have marked the history of developmental studies. First, there are issues that concern the continuity or continuous development of the human species. Second, there are studies that focus on individual differences or the patterns that distinguish one person from all others, whereas, third, there are questions regarding the sources of development. For our purposes, we intentionally juxtapose discussions of typical population development against the theme of individual variability, thus, reducing our guiding foci to two: development (both group and individual) and sources of that development.

Of course, by choosing to combine these two original principles, we have undoubtedly made our task of analysis more demanding. However, we felt that this step was important so as to establish the perspective that learning is characterized by the continual interplay between the nomothetic and idiographic components of human development, that is, between the generalizable patterns that give human thoughts and actions more predictability and the individualistic constructions that are inevitable. Indeed, whether the focus is on cognitive (e.g., Case, 1985; Flavell, Miller, & Miller, 1993; Piaget, 1952; Vygotsky, 1934/1986), socioemotional (e.g., Barrett & Campos, 1987; Dabrowski, 1964; Dodge, 1980, 1986; Erickson, 1963; Hoffman, 1975; Skinner, 1953), or moral dimensions (e.g., Gilligan, 1977, 1982; Kohlberg, 1981; Wainryb & Turiel, 1993) of human development, educators must be knowledgeable of the typical stages that mark the pathways through which individuals of shared characteristics (e.g., age, gender, or experiential background) appear to travel. Simultaneously, educators must not be blind to the fact that no two pathways of development are identical. Because every individual enters the world with a different genetic or biological history (e.g., Jenkins, 1979; Piaget, 1952; Plomin, 1986), particular psychological makeups, and idiosyncratic preferences (e.g., Csikszentmihalyi, 1990; Gardner, 1983), and because individuals develop within varied sociocultural environments (e.g., Ogbu, 1974), their ultimate constructions are unique and nonreplicable (e.g., Nicholls, Chueng, Lauer, & Patashnick, 1989; Schmeck & Geisler-Brenstein, 1989).

This interplay between nomothetic and idiographic perspectives on human development was the basis for Scarr's 1991 Presidential Address to the Society for Research in Child Development. As Scarr noted, traditional developmental theories historically centered their attention on typical patterns of behavior and viewed deviations from those typical patterns as distractions (see, e.g., Chomsky, 1975; Luria, 1976). Reciprocally, other perspectives on human development, particularly some recent views, have seemingly discounted the commonalities that are basic to populations of learners and have chosen, instead, to focus solely on the unique constructions or personal realities that characterize individual thought and action (e.g., Tobin, 1991; von Glaserfeld, 1991). Still, there is no reason to assume that these dimensions of human development must remain separate, and there is good reason to expect them to become more integrated in emerging theories of development. Educational research and instructional practice can be well informed by both philosophical traditions and related literatures. This was exactly Scarr's (1992) intention when she proposed that

> it is possible now to incorporate both typical development and individual variations on typical patterns in new theory that describe and explain human development as both human and uniquely so. I argue that most developmental theories today are unnecessarily limited in the observations they subsume and that they seldom address the issues of causality in development and individual variations with the same concepts. (p. 2)

If educators are to bring about the restructuring of schools that is the espoused goal of the APA task force, and of many other researchers and practitioners, then understanding and valuing of both the typical and unique dimensions of human growth and development must occur. These are indeed complementary, not contradictory or even separate, dimensions of human growth. Thus, as with other dimensions we have reviewed here, it is not a matter of one perspective or another. Rather, optimal learning results when one accepts and appreciates the fluid and complex nature of human change. Perhaps our decision to combine the information on development and individual differences arises from occasions in our own teaching and research endeavors that have pointed out the potential ramifications of strict adherence to either of these two complementary perspectives. For instance, we have seen educators who make instructional and research decisions on the basis of notions about cognitive capabilities that resulted in the disregard of evidence to the contrary (e.g., Alexander, White, Haensly, & Crimmins-Jeanes, 1987; Alexander, Willson, White, & Fuqua, 1987; Gelman, 1969). In contrast, we have been witness to the instructional difficulties that emerge when novice teachers enter the classroom without an understanding of the general patterns that learners of particular attributes (e.g., age) are likely to exhibit (Alexander & Knight, 1993).

But what of the sources of development? Is growth and change in learners the consequence of inheritance or of experience? As the task force recognized in its learner-centered principles, human growth is influenced by both inherited and experiential factors. It remains debatable and empirically testable as to which of these powerful forces exerts the most influence on learners' growth. Depending on the specific aspects being examined, it may at times appear that changes in human thinking, feeling, or actions are more a reflection of one's inherent abilities, capabilities, conditions, or predispositions (e.g., Chomsky, 1986; Newport, 1991; Piatelli-Palamarini, 1980; Scarr, 1992). At other times, however, the research would seem to support the position that development is more than the outcome of one's life experiences and the context in which one learns and grows (e.g., Bronfrenbrenner, 1986; Howes, Matheson, & Hamilton, 1994; Ogbu, 1974). By strategically acknowledging the potency of both heredity and environment, we and the task force avoid entering this debate and intentionally give both contributing powers their due.

Situation or Context

Learning is as much a socially shared undertaking as it is an individually constructed enterprise.

One of the most powerful observations that has emerged in the psychological literature in the past several years, and a premise that has been woven throughout our discussion of the preceding dimensions, is the recognition that learning is continuously and markedly shaped by the social context in which it occurs (e.g., Alexander, in press-a; Cognition and Technology Group at Vanderbilt, 1990; Lave, 1988; Resnick, Levine, & Teasley, 1991; Rogoff, 1990). It is difficult to pick up a volume of research written in the past several years without encountering some reference to *socially shared cognition* (Resnick et al., 1991), *distributed intelligence* (Pea, 1988, 1989), *shared expertise* (Brown & Palincsar, 1989), *guided participation* (Rogoff, 1990), or some related terminology such as *situated action* (Greeno & Moore, 1993; Vera & Simon, 1993) or *anchored instruction* (Cognition and Technology Group at Vanderbilt, 1990). Principle 11 of the learner-centered psychological principles specifically acknowledges the social nature of learning and the value that shared thinking can have on learner performance. Indirectly, Principle 13, with its discussion of cognitive filters also attends to the external circumstances that are reflected in individual understandings and awareness.

Overall, what the literature underlying the work of the task force stresses foremost is the within-individual processes and conditions that are central to learning. This orientation is readily apparent in the task force's choice of title for its document—*Learner-Centered Psychological Principles: Guidelines for School Redesign and Reform*. Concurrently, the dimensions dealing with the knowledge base, strategic processing or executive control, motivation and affect, and development and individual differences discussed here are more concerned with the internal state of human learning than with social or contextual considerations. Yet, this internal state of the learner is in constant interface with external conditions and influences. With its inclusion of Principle 11, the task force encourages deeper examination of the impact of external forces on individual learning.

In many ways, the biological structure that separates the individual mind from the sociocultural context in which that mind functions can be thought of as a highly permeable fabric through which thoughts, feelings, and impressions move freely. Further, with each passage through this permeable fabric, those thoughts, feelings, and impressions are filtered and transformed, often without a conscious awareness on the part of the learner or those within the situation or context. Thus, educational change or reformation of the kind advocated by APA, the American Educational Research Association, as well as many other national associations and organizations (e.g., the National Council of Teachers of Mathematics and the National Research Council) cannot be realized unless the power of the social or contextual factors involved in learning is also given credence (Yinger & Hendricks-Lee, 1993). Otherwise, the picture of learning remains largely incomplete.

As we see it, there are two general issues to be considered in this discussion of the socially shared nature of learning. The first relates to the potential effect of social interactions within the classroom, and the second pertains to the potential discrepancies in learning that can arise between in-school and out-of-school contexts. To understand the effect that social interactions and the learning contexts have on students' learning, one must first understand that schools are, after all, social institutions in which groups of individuals are brought together to share the educational experience. Students are in constant contact with peers and with other adults during the course of instruction. Rather than overlook this fact, various researchers have systematically investigated how these classroom interactions can be perceived or orchestrated to contribute to greater learning (e.g., Brown & Palincsar, 1989; Collins, Brown, & Newman, 1989; Johnson & Johnson, 1985; Palincsar & Brown, 1984; Slavin, 1978, 1987). As Resnick (1991) put it,

> Recent theories of *situated cognition* are challenging views that the social and the cognitive can be studied independently, arguing that the social context in which cognitive activity takes place is an integral part of that activity, not just the surrounding context for it . . . every cognitive act must be viewed as a specific response to a specific set of circumstances. Only by understanding the circumstances and the participants' construal of the situation can a valid interpretation of the cognitive activity be made. (p. 4)

Although some socially interactive approaches, such as cooperative learning (Johnson & Johnson, 1985; Slavin, 1987), have been around for some time, a plethora of new orientations or instructional approaches have begun to appear in the literature that also advocate social interaction. Among these approaches are reciprocal teaching (Palincsar & Brown, 1984), cognitive apprenticeship (Collins et al., 1989), anchored instruction (Cognition and Technology Group at Vanderbilt, 1990), and Jigsaw (Aronson, 1978; Brown & Campione, 1990). Overall, the data on these various approaches have generally been favorable (e.g., Palincsar & Brown, 1984; Slavin, 1987). However, the empirical base for a number of these popular and theoretically appealing movements is still in an emergent phase. Educational researchers and practitioners, therefore, should continue their cooperative efforts to test the effectiveness of these and other approaches within the most appropriate laboratory for such research—the classroom.

Yet, learning, as we discussed earlier, does not occur only within the confines of the school or the classroom (Murphy & Woods, 1996). Learning takes place wherever the individual interacts with his or her world. Indeed, much of the influential works of Rogoff (e.g., Radziszewska & Rogoff, 1988; Rogoff & Gauvain, 1986) and Lave (1988) have documented the outcomes of socially shared learning among children and adults functioning in nonschool situations. Radziszewska and Rogoff (1988), for example, observed errand planning in 9-year-olds working with both same-age peers and adults. One of the most interesting results of this particular study was the researchers' determination that the 9-year-olds gained more skills in errand planning when they collaborated with a parent than with a same-age partner. It would appear that the knowledge and skills of those with whom a child collaborates or cooperates may be a significant component in the learning equation, both in and out of school.

Because the school, itself, is a unique and socially contrived context, there are instances when knowledge and skills acquired within that context do not transfer to other potentially relevant situations (e.g., Perret-Claremont, Perret, & Bell, 1980). Likewise, there is evidence that the knowledge and skills that individuals manifest in their daily lives fail to find their way into the school classroom (e.g., Lave, 1991; Rogoff & Lave, 1984). Lave (1991) argued that this lack of transfer is attributable to the absence of interconnectedness among communities of practice. It would appear that the artificial barrier between schooled and nonschooled contexts contributes to the inapplicability of valuable knowledge (e.g., Lave, 1988). Thus, the student who seemingly demonstrates competency in physics fails to apply that knowledge in out-of-school situations where it can be useful (e.g., diSessa, 1982). Reciprocally, the young man who can buy and sell baseball cards in expert fashion after school can actually appear rather mathematically incompetent when faced with school-like mathematics problems (e.g., Schoenfeld, 1985; Stewart, 1987).

One outcome of this growing body of research is the understanding that the context in which learning occurs is certainly nontrivial (Bereiter & Scardamalia, 1989; Cognition and Technology Group at Vanderbilt, 1990; Greeno, 1989; Greeno & Moore, 1993). It is also apparent that the role of the teacher as the facilitator and guide of these social exchanges is vital (Ellis & Rogoff, 1986; Radziszewska & Rogoff, 1988; Rogoff & Gauvain, 1986). In essence, when learners were able to benefit from the guidance of a knowledgeable adult (e.g., teacher) who promoted their exploration and interchange, performance was found to be better. It has also been suggested, in line with Vygotsky's (1934/1986) concept of a zone of proximal development, that the guidance provided by the more knowledgeable and skilled adult be commensurate with the knowledge and skill of the learner. Thus, as the learner develops in an area or in relation to a given task, the direct or indirect assistance provided by the teacher should decrease proportionately (e.g., Alexander, in press-b; Brown & Palincsar, 1989). This lessening of external direction and support from teacher or adult should theoretically contribute to more independent functioning on the part of the student and, likewise, enhance the possibility of transfer of the acquired knowledge or skill both in class and out (e.g., Rogoff, 1990).

Issues for Further Consideration

As we stated at the outset of this chapter, the original set of 12 psychological principles (APA, 1993) we reviewed in 1994 have already undergone revision (APA, 1995). This revision was intended, in part, to address several important issues that we and others believed were only indirectly addressed in the original learner-centered principles, or not specifically addressed at all. Those issues, some of which we alluded to previously, include an attention to the multidimensional, interactive character of learning and a recognition of the domain-specific or context-specific nature of learning. Further, we wanted to consider the issue of assessment, not in terms of its role in measuring student outcomes or progress, but in terms of its contributions to planning more effective curricula and to building optimal learning environments for students. Finally, we caution educational researchers and practitioners against falling victim to premature and overly optimistic support of emerging and largely untested ideas or approaches, regardless of their political power or their intuitive appeal.

Interactive Dimensions of Learning

In its preface to the original learner-centered principles, the APA task force stated that the principles they championed "must be understood as an organized set of principles and not be treated in isolation" (APA, 1993, p. 6). We concur with that statement, but we wish to extend it somewhat. Although the task force may say to educators that the learner-centered principles should not be dealt with in isolation, the specific format and wording of the report may unintentionally reinforce that perception. That is, among the original principles, there are several that speak to metacognitive and cognitive factors, affect, personal and social factors, and individual differences, and another that overviews development. Of course, the pragmatic and theoretical rationales for quartering off learning into foundational areas are certainly justifiable—particularly in light of the massive literatures on which each is grounded. For those awarded the honor of substantiating these principles from the research base, that rationale is evident indeed. However, even as we consciously dissect learning into its essential dimensions, we must strongly acclaim the serious limitations of this organizational strategy.

Specifically, if meaningful change is to occur within the educational system, then it must be better understood by educators and educational researchers that these dimensions of learning are not really separable entities in "real-world learning situations" (APA, 1993, p. 6). Although, as researchers, we can theoretically and empirically extract cognition from affect, knowledge from strategic processing, or sociocultural background from development, these dimensions, as with the others addressed in the principles, remain inextricably intertwined in the real world. For example, the knowledge base is both an aspect of development (e.g., Chi, 1985; Chi et al., 1981) and a part of motivation (e.g., Renninger, 1992; Schiefele, 1991), just as development is integrated with individual differences and sociocultural background (e.g., Ogbu, 1974; Scarr, 1992) and strategic processing is correlated with one's motivational or affective state (e.g., Garner, Brown, Sanders, & Menke, 1992; Hidi & Anderson, 1992; Weinert & Kluwe, 1987).

By approaching learning in a systemic fashion, attending simultaneously to the interplay of its various dimensions, educators perhaps have a greater chance to make significant and long-term changes in students' learning and in the institutions created especially to promote such learning (Salomon, 1991). In his analysis of human behavior and the experiences from which it arises, Dewey (1930) expressed this precept: "No act can be understood apart from the series to which it belongs" (p. 412). We could not agree more.

The Domain-Specific Nature of Learning

As we have noted at various points in our analysis of the research literature, the subject matter with which a student deals, as well as the learning tasks and the contexts in which that individual operates, must be given its rightful due, not only in the learner-centered principles but also in the educational practice that these principles seek to impact. This domain and context specificity is addressed to some extent in the task force's presentation of the implications of the learner-centered principles for school redesign and reform. However, this orientation is less apparent in the principles themselves, which are likely to be discussed and highlighted separately from any implications the task force has chosen to advance. Therefore, we would prefer to see this issue of domain and context specificity more directly considered in each of the relevant principles.

For instance, individuals' knowledge base and their motivation to achieve or to learn have a significant impact in the process of schooling. However, we cannot overlook the fact that knowledge, motivation, and the other dimensions that we have described here are highly complex and varied phenomena. Whether students are asked to function in a subject matter area for which they feel competent or for which they have an abiding interest versus one for which they possess only fragmented knowledge, or little if any interest, is critical (Alexander, in press-b). Teachers should not expect students to be consistently and invariantly knowledgeable or motivated in classrooms. In addition, teachers should have a realization that the motivational character and the meaningfulness of tasks and learning environments are not solely inherent in the tasks or environments, themselves. Rather, these positive attributes are as much a consequence of the knowledge and interest that the learner brings to that task or that environment. Further, as Spiro argued (Spiro, Feltovich, Jacobson, & Coulson, 1992; Spiro & Jehng, 1990), domains of knowledge are different, and those differences should be attended to as educators attempt to enhance student understanding in classrooms. For example, learning physics is unique from learning literature or social studies (Alexander & Kulikowich, 1994; diSessa, 1989; Larkin, 1985; Larkin et al., 1980). By identifying the specific attributes and concomitant challenges that each domain may present to students, and students' knowledge and interests relative to each domain, teachers will be better equipped to organize the instructional tasks and the learning environment more effectively.

After our previous discussion about the interactive and multidimensional nature of learning, we think it necessary to explain further our call for more consideration of the domain-specific nature of learning. Specifically, the acknowledgment of domain-specific influences in the learning process has importance for two reasons. First, it is our contention that an individual's progression from a naive or acclimated learner to one who is competent and, potentially, even expert seems reliant in large measure on his or her ability to function with a "principled" understanding in a given domain (Alexander, in press-b; Gelman & Greeno, 1989).

Principles can be thought of simply as the guiding concepts or understandings that give a domain its particular configuration or structure. In mathematics, for example, one such principle deals with the "conservation of number," whereas in reading, one guiding principle relates to the "meaningfulness of text." Until learners grasp these fundamental understandings, their acquisition of relevant information in the domain is apt to be fragmented and incoherent. Therefore, domain-specific principles become organizing concepts for students' knowledge base. According to Gelman and Greeno (1989), the presence of domain-specific principles serves another role in the learning process. These principles provide learners with a mechanism for ascertaining the relevance of new information. In addition, Gelman and Greeno hold that principles offer clues to the interpretation of ambiguous information within the environment—information that has the potential to either foster or frustrate learning.

Our second purpose for stressing the domain-specific characteristics in learning is related to the first. Specifically, as educators pursue the laudable goal of integrating bodies of knowledge within the learning environment (as in the case of the dimensions of learning we analyze here), they should appreciate that this integration is aided by students' ability to build meaningful connections across those bodies of knowledge (e.g., Holyoak, 1991). Yet, to build connections across two or more areas of knowledge, learners must possess some clear conceptualization of each contributing factor. For example, to see the relationships that exist between early American literature and the historical events of that time, students must have or be given both relevant literary and historical information around which these relationships can be forged. In essence, the ability to see relationships across seemingly diverse areas of learning requires awareness of what makes each area unique in and of itself. Otherwise, efforts to create a beneficial confluence of bodies of knowledge can, regrettably, result in little more than a hodgepodge of unusable and disjointed content.

The Instructional Value of Assessment

Although multiple chapters of this volume (e.g., Paris, this volume, chap. 8) are dedicated to the various aspects of assessment, learner assessment is not treated as a statement of principle in the original publication of the learner-centered psychological principles. We found this particularly interesting in light of the fact that more space was devoted to the discussion of assessment than to any other issue. Perhaps it was the judgment of the task force that assessment did not qualify as a within-individual psychological factor appropriate for consideration as a principle of teaching and learning. However, the attention to "relevant, authentic learning tasks" (APA, 1993, p. 7) would seem to open the door to discussions of assessment, especially as it pertains to creating effective learning tasks and optimal learning environments. Nonetheless, in light of the weight given to assessment in American classrooms and to the political and philosophical debates that this topic engenders, some specific statement of principle about assessment seems warranted. If we were to incorporate a principle relative to assessment, it might read as follows:

> The development of relevant learning tasks and the orchestration of optimal learning environments is predicated on access to accurate and useful information about such dimensions of learning as students' knowledge base (e.g., sociocultural background and beliefs), their strategic processing, as well as motivational and affective factors (e.g., interests and preferences).

We are pleased to note that the revised version of the document (APA, 1995) now contains a specific principle addressing the topic of assessment (Principle 14). Moreover, this principle incorporates and extends our proffered statement.

Our goal from a psychological perspective in this discussion is to alert the educational community to the fundamental point that assessment does not simply equate to the evaluation of student achievement nor to standardized measures. Instead, assessment should be viewed simply as the gathering of pertinent information in a systematic and useful fashion. Sometimes that information concerns the outcomes of the instructional process or includes formal tests or standardized measures of achievement, aptitude, personality, or other dimensions of learning. However, this is not the only intent or nature of assessment.

When teachers gather information on student interests, analyze responses to oral or written questions, gauge strategic processing, or monitor student reactions to particular learning conditions or tasks, they are engaged in assessment. What separates relevant from nonrelevant assessment then becomes a matter of the appropriate interpretation and application of the assembled information. Thus, *assessment*, defined in this admittedly liberal manner, should be seen as integral to effective teaching and learning and should not be held as something apart from them (e.g., Alexander, Kulikowich, & Jetton, 1994; Kulikowich & Alexander, 1994; Weinstein & Meyer, 1991; Wittrock, 1991).

We realize that some of these same concerns and perspectives were contained within the 1993 task force presentation of the implications and applications of the learner-centered principles. In addition, to our knowledge this topic has received much deserved attention during the revision of these principles, as evidenced by the addition of the specific assessment principle (14). Our issue is that the distinction between assessment, as broadly conceived, and evaluation, as narrowly portrayed in certain educational or political circles, needs to be made more emphatically.

Cautionary Note

Perhaps in a far too idealistic fashion, we would hope that research of whatever paradigm or perspective would serve as a voice for reasoned and informed practice, rather than as an inciter of untested or potentially risky actions. It is critical that the educational research community not become part of the very problems or conditions it purports to study (Alexander, Murphy, & Woods, 1996, 1997). If practitioners are to take researchers and their findings seriously, then it is mandatory that the educational research community establish and maintain credibility with the community of practitioners that must bring our ideas to light in the instructional setting. If the judgments and stances of the research community are perceived to shift too easily or too willingly with the winds of political pressure or in the direction of external funding, then it is likely that this credibility will suffer. Although it is not necessary that they always lead the way in instructional practice, educational researchers should at least share their knowledge with that leadership.

Therefore, as partners in school reform and redesign, educational researchers must be careful not to fuel the fires of debate or ignite passions when such emotionalism is unjustified or unsupported. This is not to say that educational researchers should not be proactive and vocal when issues are clearly warranted, as in the case of the extended discussion of assessment found in the task force report. Where we wish to take issue is with the choice of wording in several of the principles— words that project a particular bias or orientation that is, in our opinion, unsubstantiated or unclarified from the perspective of the research. We focus on just one principle to illustrate our argument.

In the original principle dealing with learning tasks, the task force stated that "curiosity, creativity, and higher order thinking are stimulated by relevant, authentic learning tasks of optimal difficulty and novelty for each student" (APA, 1993, p. 7). The gist of this statement would seem to be that better instructional tasks produce better learning. However, the presence of such terms as *authentic* give this principle a character that becomes more difficult to substantiate. Is the literature clear on what constitutes an "authentic" task? As the term is sometimes used in the literature, is there an evident causal relationship between authenticity and student curiosity, creativity, and higher level thinking? Are all tasks that fall outside the rubric "authentic" assumed to be nonauthentic or fraudulent? Are there, as the task force suggests in its introductory remarks, decades, if not "more than a century" (APA, 1993, p. 5) of research to uphold this claim? As our position in this discussion suggests, we contend otherwise.

Indeed, as we stated at the outset of this chapter, we recognize that any report of a committee, such as the task force document, represents a compromise among many individuals from many perspectives. It is likely, therefore, that the inclusion of such emotionally laden terms as *authentic* is an outcome of this compromise. We feel that the goal of educational reform and redesign would have been better served by offering a more bottom-line analysis of learning that indeed has a long history of rather consistent outcomes to substantiate it. (The current version of the learner-centered psychological principles prepared by the APA Board of Educational Affairs, 1995, does not include this reference to authentic tasks.)

Conclusion

Again, we support the APA Presidential Task Force on Psychology in Education (APA, 1993), as well as the APA Board of Educational Affairs (APA, 1995), in their attempts to interject psychological principles into current efforts to reform and redesign schools. Educational practice certainly can benefit from the valuable and essential knowledge that has been contributed by generations of educational researchers. As our analysis demonstrates, there are indeed massive bodies of research that uphold the role that the knowledge base, strategic processing or executive control, motivation and affect, development and individual differences, and situation or context play in student learning. Sadly, too little of that research has made its way into the public and political mainstream and, likewise, into American classrooms. Perhaps the efforts of the task force will help alter this regrettable situation. Yet, some equally powerful statements authored by the research community in the past have fallen short of their promise to bring about relevant change in instructional practice (e.g., Anderson, Hiebert, Scott, & Wilkinson, 1985). This observation leaves us cautiously optimistic about the prospects for the future with respect to the goals of the task force. Of course, the future is not yet written, and the concerted efforts of the educational research community, in partnership with others who are invested in the learners of today and tomorrow, can possibly make the hopes expressed in the learner-centered principles a reality. As individuals who share these hopes, we anxiously await the outcome.

References

Alexander, P. A. (1992). Domain knowledge: Evolving themes and emerging concerns. *Educational Psychologist, 27*, 33–51.

Alexander, P. A. (Ed.). (1996). The role of knowledge in learning and instruction [Special issue]. *Educational Psychologist, 31*(2).

Alexander, P. A. (in press-a). The interplay between domain and general strategy knowledge: Exploring the influence of motivation and situation. In A. Pace (Ed.), *Beyond prior knowledge: Issues in text processing and conceptual change.* Norwood, NJ: Ablex.

Alexander, P. A. (in press-b). Stages and phases of domain learning: The dynamics of subject-matter knowledge, strategy knowledge, and motivation. In C. E. Weinstein & B. L. McCombs (Eds.), *Skill, will, and self-regulation.* Hillsdale, NJ: Erlbaum.

Alexander, P. A., & Dochy, F. J. R. C. (1994). Adults' views about knowing and believing. In R. Garner & P. A. Alexander (Eds.), *Beliefs about text and about instruction with text* (pp. 223–244). Hillsdale, NJ: Erlbaum.

Alexander, P. A., & Dochy, F. J. R. C. (1995). Conceptions of knowledge and beliefs: A comparison across varying cultural and educational communities. *American Educational Research Journal, 32*, 413–442.

Alexander, P. A., Jetton, T. L., & Kulikowich, J. M. (1995). Interrelationship of knowledge, interest, and recall: Assessing a model of domain learning. *Journal of Educational Psychology, 87*, 559–575.

Alexander, P. A., Jetton, T. L., Kulikowich, J. M., & Woehler, C. (1994). Contrasting instructional and structural importance: The seductive effect of teacher questions. *Journal of Reading Behavior, 26,* 19–45.

Alexander, P. A., & Judy, J. E. (1988). The interaction of domain-specific and strategic knowledge in academic performance. *Review of Educational Research, 58,* 375–404.

Alexander, P. A., & Knight, S. L. (1993). Dimensions of the interplay between learning and teaching. *Educational Forum, 57,* 232–245.

Alexander, P. A., & Kulikowich, J. M. (1991). Domain knowledge and analogic reasoning ability as predictors of expository text comprehension. *Journal of Reading Behavior, 23,* 165–190.

Alexander, P. A., & Kulikowich, J. M. (1994). Learning from physics text: A synthesis of recent research. *Journal of Research in Science Teaching, 31,* 895–911.

Alexander, P. A., Kulikowich, J. M., & Jetton, T. L. (1994). The role of subject-matter knowledge and interest in the processing of linear and nonlinear texts. *Review of Educational Research, 64,* 201–252.

Alexander, P. A., Kulikowich, J. M., & Schulze, S. K. (1994a). How subject-matter knowledge affects recall and interest on the comprehension of scientific exposition. *American Educational Research Journal, 31,* 313–337.

Alexander, P. A., Kulikowich, J. M., & Schulze, S. K. (1994b). The influence of topic knowledge, domain knowledge, and interest on the comprehension of scientific exposition. *Learning and Individual Differences, 6,* 379–397.

Alexander, P. A., & Murphy, P. K. (1994, April). *The research base for APA's learner-centered principles.* Invited symposium presented at the annual meeting of the American Educational Research Association, New Orleans.

Alexander, P. A., Murphy, P. K., & Woods, B. S. (1996). Of squalls and fathoms: Navigating the seas of educational innovation. *Educational Researcher, 25*(3), 31–36, 39.

Alexander, P. A., Murphy, P. K., & Woods, B. S. (1997). Unearthing academic roots: Educators' perceptions of the interrelationship of philosophy, psychology, and education. *Educational Forum, 61,* 172–186.

Alexander, P. A., Murphy, P. K., Woods, B. S., Duhon, K. E., & Parker, D. (1997). College instruction and concomitant changes in students' knowledge, interest, and strategy use: A study of domain learning. *Contemporary Educational Psychology, 22,* 125–146.

Alexander, P. A., Parsons, J. L., & Nash, W. R. (1996). *Toward a theory of creativity.* Washington, DC: National Association for Gifted Children.

Alexander, P. A., Pate, P. E., Kulikowich, J. M., Farrell, D. M., & Wright, N. L. (1989). Domain-specific and strategic knowledge: Effects of training on students of differing ages or competence levels. *Learning and Individual Differences, 1,* 283–325.

Alexander, P. A., Schallert, D. L., & Hare, V. C. (1991). Coming to terms: How researchers in learning and literacy talk about knowledge. *Review of Educational Research, 61,* 315–343.

Alexander, P. A., White, C. S., Haensly, P. A., & Crimmins-Jeanes, M. (1987). Training in analogical reasoning. *American Educational Research Journal, 24,* 387–404.

Alexander, P. A., Willson, V. L., White, C. S., & Fuqua, J. D. (1987). Analogical reasoning in young children. *Journal of Educational Psychology, 79,* 401–408.

Alvermann, D. E., Smith, L. C., & Readence, J. E. (1985). Prior knowledge activation and the comprehension of compatible and incompatible text. *Reading Research Quarterly, 20,* 420–436.

American Psychological Association Board of Educational Affairs. (1995, Dec.). *Learner-centered psychological principles: A framework for school redesign and reform* [On-line]. Available: http://www.apa.org/ed/lcp.html.

American Psychological Association Presidential Task Force on Psychology in Education. (1993, January). *Learner-centered psychological principles: Guidelines for school redesign and reform.* Washington, DC: American Psychological Association and Mid-Continent Regional Educational Laboratory.

Ames, C. (1992). Achievement goals and the classroom motivational climate. In D. H. Schunk & J. L. Meece (Eds.), *Student perceptions in the classroom* (pp. 327–348). Hillsdale, NJ: Erlbaum.

Ames, C., & Ames, R. (Eds.). (1985). *Research on motivation in education: The classroom milieu* (Vol. 2). San Diego, CA: Academic Press.

Ames, C., & Ames, R. (Eds.). (1989). *Research on motivation in education: The classroom milieu* (Vol. 3). San Diego, CA: Academic Press.

Anderson, R. C. (1977). The notion of schemata and the educational enterprise. In R. C. Anderson, R. J. Spiro, & W. E. Montague (Eds.), *Schooling and the acquisition of knowledge* (pp. 415–431). Hillsdale, NJ: Erlbaum.

Anderson, R. C., Hiebert, E. H., Scott, J. A., & Wilkinson, I. A. G. (1985). *Becoming a nation of readers: The report of the commission on reading.* Washington, DC: National Institute of Education.

Anderson, R. C., Pichert, J. W., & Shirey, L. L. (1983). Effects of reader's schema at different points in time. *Journal of Educational Psychology, 75,* 271–279.

Anderson, R. C., Reynolds, R. E., Schallert, D. L., & Goetz, E. T. (1977). Frameworks for comprehending discourse. *American Educational Research Journal, 14,* 367–381.

Aronson, E. (1978). *The jigsaw classroom.* Beverly Hills, CA: Sage.

Asher, S. R., Hymel, S., & Wigfield, A. (1978). Influence of topic interest on children's reading comprehension. *Journal of Reading Behavior, 10,* 35–47.

Baldwin, R. S., Peleg-Bruckner, Z., & McClintock, A. H. (1985). Effects of topic interest and prior knowledge on reading comprehension. *Reading Research Quarterly, 20,* 497–508.

Bandura, A. (1977). Self-efficacy: Toward a unifying theory of behavioral change. *Psychological Review, 84,* 191–215.

Bandura, A. (1993). Perceived self-efficacy in cognitive development and functioning. *Educational Psychologist, 28,* 117–148.

Barrett, K. C., & Campos, J. J. (1987). Perspectives on emotional development: II. A functionalist approach to emotions. In J. D. Osofsky (Ed.), *Handbook of infant development* (2nd ed., pp. 555–575). New York: Wiley.

Bayley, N. (1943). Mental growth during the first three years. In R. G. Barker, J. S. Kounin, & H. F. Wright (Eds.), *Child behavior and development* (pp. 85–107). New York: McGraw-Hill.

Bereiter, C., & Scardamalia, M. (1989). Intentional learning as a goal of instruction. In L. B. Resnick (Ed.), *Knowing, learning, and instruction: Essays in honor of Robert Glaser* (pp. 361–392). Hillsdale, NJ: Erlbaum.

Borkowski, J. G., Carr, M., & Pressley, M. (1987). "Spontaneous" strategy use: Perspectives from metacognitive theory. *Intelligence, 11,* 61–75.

Borkowski, J. G., Carr, M., Rellinger, E., & Pressley, M. (1990). Self-regulated cognition: Interdependence of metacognition, attributions, and self-esteem. In B. F. Jones & L. Idol (Eds.), *Dimensions of thinking and cognitive instruction* (pp. 53–92). Hillsdale, NJ: Erlbaum.

Bransford, J. D., & Franks, J. J. (1972). The abstraction of linguistic ideas. *Cognitive Psychology, 2,* 331–350.

Bronfrenbrenner, U. (1986). Ecology of the family as a context for human development: Research perspectives. *Developmental Psychology, 22,* 723–742.

Brown, A. L. (1975). The development of memory: Knowing, knowing about knowing, and knowing how to know. In H. W. Reese (Ed.), *Advances in child development and behavior* (Vol. 10, pp. 103–152). San Diego, CA: Academic Press.

Brown, A. L., & Campione, J. S. (1990). Communities of learning and thinking, or a context by any other name. *Contributions to Human Development, 21,* 108–126.

Brown, A. L., & Palincsar, A. S. (1989). Guided, cooperative learning and individual knowledge acquisition. In L. B. Resnick (Ed.), *Knowing, learning, and instruction: Essays in honor of Robert Glaser* (pp. 393–451). Hillsdale, NJ: Erlbaum.

Case, R. (1985). *Intellectual development: Birth to adulthood.* San Diego, CA: Academic Press.

Case, R. (1993). Theories of learning and theories of development. *Educational Psychologist, 28,* 219–233.

Chambliss, M. J., & Garner, R. (1996). Do adults change their minds after reading persuasive text? *Written Communication, 13,* 291–313.

Champagne, A. B., Kloper, L. E., & Anderson, J. H. (1980). Factors influencing the learning of classical mechanics. *American Journal of Physics, 48,* 1074–1079.

Chi, M. T. H. (1985). Interactive roles of knowledge and strategies in the development of organized sorting and recall. In S. F. Chipman, J. W. Segal, & R. Glaser (Eds.), *Thinking and learning skills: Research and open questions* (Vol. 2, pp. 457–483). Hillsdale, NJ: Erlbaum.

Chi, M. T. H., Feltovich, P., & Glaser, R. (1981). Categorization and representation of physics problems by experts and novices. *Cognitive Science, 5,* 121–152.

Chinn, C. A., & Brewer, W. F. (1993). The role of anomalous data in knowledge acquisition: A theoretical framework and implications for science instruction. *Review of Educational Research, 63,* 1–49.

Chomsky, N. (1975). *Reflections on language.* New York: Pantheon Books.

Chomsky, N. (1986). *Knowledge of language: Its nature, origin, and use.* New York: Praeger.

Cognition and Technology Group at Vanderbilt. (1990). Anchored instruction and its relationship to situated cognition. *Educational Researcher, 19*(6), 2–10.

Cole, M., & Cole, S. R. (1993). *The development of children* (2nd ed.). New York: Scientific American Books.

Collins, A., Brown, J. S., & Newman, S. E. (1989). Cognitive apprenticeships: Teaching the crafts of reading, writing, and mathematics. In L. B. Resnick (Ed.), *Knowing, learning, and instruction: Essays in honor of Robert Glaser* (pp. 453–494). Hillsdale, NJ: Erlbaum.

Corno, L., & Rohrkemper, M. (1985). The intrinsic motivation to learn in classrooms. In C. Ames & R. Ames (Eds.), *Research on motivation in education: The classroom milieu* (Vol. 2, pp. 53–84). San Diego, CA: Academic Press.

Csikszentmihalyi, M. (1990). *Flow: The psychology of optimal experience.* Cambridge, England: Cambridge University Press.

Dabrowski, K. (1964). *Positive disintegration.* Boston: Little, Brown.

deCharms, R. (1968). *Personal causation: The internal affective determinants of behavior.* San Diego, CA: Academic Press.

Deci, E. L., & Ryan, R. M. (1985). Intrinsic motivation and self-determination in human behavior. San Diego, CA: Academic Press.

Deci, E. L., & Ryan, R. M. (1991). A motivational approach to self: Integration in personality. In R. Dienstbier (Ed.), *Nebraska Symposium on Motivation: Perspectives on Motivation* (Vol. 38, pp. 237–288). Lincoln: University of Nebraska Press.

Deci, E. L., Valleran, R. J., Pelletier, L. G., & Ryan, R. M. (1991). Motivation and education: The self-determination perspective. *Educational Psychologist, 26,* 325–346.

Dewey, J. (1913). *Interest and effort in education.* Boston: Riverside.

Dewey, J. (1930). Conduct and experience. In C. Murchism (Ed.), *Psychologies of 1930* (pp. 410–429). Worchester, MA: Clark University Press.

Dillon, R. F., & Schmeck, R. R. (1983). *Individual differences in cognition* (Vol. 1). San Diego, CA: Academic Press.

diSessa, A. A. (1982). Unlearning Aristotelian physics: A study of knowledge-based learning. *Cognitive Science, 6,* 37–75.

diSessa, A. A. (1989). Toward an epistemology of physics. *Cognitive Science, 13,* 145–182.

Dodge, K. A. (1980). Social cognition and children's aggressive behavior. *Child Development, 51,* 162–170.

Dodge, K. A. (1986). A social information processing model of social competence in children. In M. Perlmutter (Ed.), *Minnesota Symposium on Child Psychology* (Vol. 18, pp. 77–126). Hillsdale, NJ: Erlbaum.

Dweck, C. S. (1986). Motivational processes affecting learning. *American Psychologist, 10,* 1040–1048.

Dweck, C. S., & Leggett, E. L. (1988). A social–cognitive approach to motivation and personality. *Psychological Review, 95,* 256–273.

Elliott-Faust, D. J., & Pressley, M. (1986). Self-controlled training of comparison strategies increases children's comprehension monitoring. *Journal of Educational Psychology, 78,* 27–33.

Ellis, S., & Rogoff, B. (1986). Problem solving in children's management of instruction. In E. Mueller & C. Cooper (Eds.), *Process and outcome in peer relationships* (pp. 301–325). San Diego, CA: Academic Press.

Ennis, R. H. (1985). Critical thinking and the curriculum. *National Forum, 65,* 28–31.

Ennis, R. H. (1987). A taxonomy of critical thinking dispositions and abilities. In J. B. Baron & R. J. Sternberg (Eds.), *Teaching for thinking* (pp. 9–26). New York: Freeman.

Ennis, R. H. (1989). Critical thinking and subject specificity: Clarification and needed research. *Educational Researcher, 18*(3), 4–10.

Erickson, E. H. (1963). *Childhood and society* (2nd ed.). New York: W. W. Norton.

Farrar, M. J., & Goodman, G. S. (1992). Developmental changes in event memory. *Child Development, 63,* 173–187.

Flavell, J. H. (1976). Metacognitive aspects of problem solving. In L. B. Resnick (Ed.), *The nature of intelligence* (pp. 231–235). Hillsdale, NJ: Erlbaum.

Flavell, J. H. (1977). *Cognitive development* (1st ed.). Englewood Cliffs, NJ: Prentice-Hall.

Flavell, J. H., Miller, P. H., & Miller, S. A. (1993). *Cognitive development* (3rd ed.). Englewood Cliffs, NJ: Prentice-Hall.

Flavell, J. H., Mumme, D. L., Green, F. L., & Flavell, E. R. (1992). Young children's understanding of different types of beliefs. *Child Development, 63,* 960–977.

Galton, F. (1908). *Memories of my life.* London: Methuen.

Gardner, H. (1983). *Frames of mind.* New York: Basic Books.

Gardner, H. (1991). *The unschooled mind.* New York: Basic Books.

Gardner, H. (1993). *Creating minds.* New York: Basic Books.

Garner, R. (1987). *Metacognition and reading comprehension.* Norwood, NJ: Ablex.

Garner, R. (1990). When children and adults do not use learning strategies: Toward a theory of settings. *Review of Educational Research, 60,* 517–529.

Garner, R., & Alexander, P. A. (1989). Metacognition: Answered and unanswered questions. *Educational Psychologist, 24,* 143–148.

Garner, R., Alexander, P. A., Gillingham, M. G., Kulikowich, J. M., & Brown, R. (1991). Interest and learning from text. *American Educational Research Journal, 28,* 643–659.

Garner, R., Brown, R., Sanders, S., & Menke, D. J. (1992). "Seductive details" and learning from text. In K. A. Renninger, S. Hidi, & A. Krapp (Eds.), *The role of interest in learning and development* (pp. 239–254). Hillsdale, NJ: Erlbaum.

Garner, R., Gillingham, M. G., & White, C. S. (1989). Effects of "seductive details" on macroprocessing and microprocessing in adults and children. *Cognition and Instruction, 6,* 41–57.

Gelman, R. (1969). Conservation acquisition: A problem of learning to attend to relevant attributes. *Journal of Experimental Child Psychology, 7,* 67–87.

Gelman, R., & Greeno, J. G. (1989). On the nature of competence: Principles for understanding in a domain. In L. B. Resnick (Ed.), *Knowing, learning, and instruction: Essays in honor of Robert Glaser* (pp. 125–186). Hillsdale, NJ: Erlbaum.

Gibson, J. J. (1966). *The senses considered as perceptual systems.* Boston: Houghton-Mifflin.

Gilligan, C. (1977). In a different voice: Women's conceptions of the self and of morality. *Harvard Educational Review, 47,* 481–517.

Gilligan, C. (1982). *In a different voice: Psychological theory and women's development.* Cambridge, MA: Harvard University Press.

Glaser, R. (1984). Education and thinking: The role of knowledge. *American Psychologist, 39,* 93–104.

Gottfried, A. E. (1985). Academic intrinsic motivation in elementary and junior high school students. *Journal of Educational Psychology, 20,* 205–215.

Gottfried, A. E. (1990). Academic intrinsic motivation in young elementary school children. *Journal of Educational Psychology, 82,* 525–538.

Greeno, J. G. (1989). A perspective on thinking. *American Psychologist, 44,* 134–141.

Greeno, J. G., & Moore, J. L. (1993). Situativity and symbols: Response to Vera and Simon. *Cognitive Science, 17,* 49–59.

Hasselhorn, M., & Körkel, J. (1986). Metacognitive versus traditional reading instruction: The mediating role of domain specific knowledge on children's text processing. *Human Learning, 5,* 79–90.

Hidi, S. (1990). Interest and its contribution as a mental resource for learning. *Review of Educational Research, 60,* 549–571.

Hidi, S., & Anderson, V. (1992). Situational interest and its impact on reading and expository writing. In K. A. Renninger, S. Hidi, & A. Krapp (Eds.), *The role of interest in learning and development* (pp. 215–238). Hillsdale, NJ: Erlbaum.

Hidi, S., & Baird, W. (1986). Interestingness—A neglected variable in discourse processing. *Cognitive Science, 10,* 179–194.

Hidi, S., & Baird, W. (1988). Strategies for increasing text-based interest and students' recall of expository texts. *Reading Research Quarterly, 23,* 465–482.

Hidi, S., Baird, W., & Hildyard, A. (1982). That's important, but is it interesting? Two factors in text processing. In A. Flammer & W. Kintsch (Eds.), *Discourse processing* (pp. 63–75). Amsterdam: North-Holland.

Hoffman, M. L. (1975). Altruistic behavior and the parent–child relationship. *Journal of Personality and Social Psychology, 31,* 937–943.

Holyoak, K. L. (1991). Symbolic connectionism: Toward third-generation theories of expertise. In K. A. Erickson & J. Smith (Eds.), *Toward a general theory of expertise: Prospects and limits* (pp. 301–335). Cambridge, England: Cambridge University Press.

Howes, C., Matheson, C. C., & Hamilton, C. E. (1994). Maternal, teacher, and child care history correlates of children's relationships with peers. *Child Development, 65,* 264–273.

Jenkins, J. B. (1979). *Genetics* (2nd ed.). Boston: Houghton-Mifflin.

Jensen, A. R. (1989). The relationship between learning and intelligence. *Learning and Individual Differences, 1,* 37–62.

Jetton, T. L., & Alexander, P. A. (1997). Instructional importance: What teachers value and what students learn. *Reading Research Quarterly, 32*(3), 290–308.

Johnson, D. W., & Johnson, R. T. (1985). Motivational processes in cooperative, competitive, and individualistic learning situations. In C. Ames & R. Ames (Eds.), *Research on motivation in education* (Vol. 2, pp. 249–286). San Diego, CA: Academic Press.

Kohlberg, L. (1981). *The philosophy of moral development.* New York: Harper & Row.

Kulikowich, J. M., & Alexander, P. A. (1994). Evaluating students' errors on cognitive tasks: Applications of polytomous item response theory and log-linear modeling. In C. R. Reynolds (Ed.), *Cognitive assessment: A multidisciplinary perspective* (pp. 137–173). New York: Plenum.

Larkin, J. H. (1985). Understanding, problem representations, and skill in physics. In S. F. Chipman, J. W. Segal, & R. Glaser (Eds.), *Thinking and learning skills* (Vol. 2, pp. 141–159). Hillsdale, NJ: Erlbaum.

Larkin, J., McDermott, J., Simon, D. P., & Simon, H. (1980). Expert and novice performance in solving physics problems. *Science, 208,* 1335–1342.

Lave, J. (1988). *Cognition in practice.* Cambridge, England: Cambridge University Press.

Lave, J. (1991). Situating learning in communities of practice. In L. B. Resnick, J. M. Levine, & S. D. Teasley (Eds.), *Perspectives on socially shared cognition* (pp. 63–84). Washington, DC: American Psychological Association.

Lepper, M. R. (1988). Motivational considerations in the study of instruction. *Cognition and Instruction, 5,* 289–309.

Lipson, M. Y. (1983). The influence of religious affiliation on children's memory for text information. *Reading Research Quarterly, 18,* 448–457.

Luria, A. R. (1976). *Cognitive development.* Cambridge, MA: Harvard University Press.

Maehr, M. L., & Braskamp, L. A. (1986). *The motivation factor: A theory of personal investment.* Lexington, MA: Heath.

Marshall, N. (in press). A search for the source of scientific misconceptions. In A. Pace (Ed.), *Beyond prior knowledge: Issues in text processing and conceptual change.* Norwood, NJ: Ablex.

McCall, R. B., Applebaum, M. I., & Hogarty, P. S. (1973). Developmental changes in mental performance. *Monographs of the Society for Research in Child Development, 38* (Serial No. 150).

McCombs, B. L. (1988). Motivational skills training: Combining metacognitive, cognitive, and affective learning strategies. In C. E. Weinstein, E. T. Goetz, & P. A. Alexander (Eds.), *Learning and study strategies: Issues in assessment, instruction, and evaluation* (pp. 141–169). San Diego, CA: Academic Press.

McCutchen, D. (1986). Domain knowledge and linguistic knowledge in the development of writing ability. *Journal of Memory and Language, 25,* 431–444.

Meece, J. L., Blumenfeld, D. C., & Hoyle, R. H. (1988). Students' goal orientation and cognitive engagement in classroom activities. *Journal of Educational Psychology, 80,* 514–523.

Mill, J. S. (1947). *On liberty.* New York: Appleton-Century-Crofts. (Original published in 1859)

Monroe, M. C. (1991). *The effect of interesting environmental stories on knowledge and action-taking attitudes.* Unpublished doctoral dissertation, University of Michigan.

Murphy, P. K., & Woods, B. S. (1996). Situating knowledge in learning and instruction. *Educational Psychologist, 31*(2), 141–145.

Newman, R. S., & Schwager, M. T. (1992). Student perceptions and academic help-seeking. In D. H. Schunk & J. L. Meece (Eds.), *Student perceptions in the classroom* (pp. 123–148). Hillsdale, NJ: Erlbaum.

Newport, E. (1991). Contrasting concepts of the critical period for language. In S. Carey & R. Gelman (Eds.), *The epigenesis of mind: Essays on biology and cognition* (pp. 111–130). Hillsdale, NJ: Erlbaum.

Nicholls, J. G. (1984). Achievement motivation: Conceptions of ability, subjective experience, task choice, and performance. *Psychological Review, 91,* 328–346.

Nicholls, J. G., Chueng, P. C., Lauer, J., & Patashnick, M. (1989). Individual differences in academic motivation: Perceived ability, goals, beliefs, and values. *Learning and Individual Differences, 1,* 63–84.

Nickerson, R. S. (1989). New directions in educational assessment. *Educational Researcher, 18*(9), 3–7.

Ogbu, J. U. (1974). *The next generation: An ethnography of education in an urban neighborhood.* San Diego, CA: Academic Press.

Palincsar, A. S., & Brown, A. L. (1984). Reciprocal teaching of comprehension-fostering and monitoring activities. *Cognition and Instruction, 1,* 117–175.

Palmer, D. J., & Goetz, E. T. (1988). Selection and use of study strategies: The role of the studier's beliefs about self and strategies. In C. Weinstein, E. T. Goetz, & P. A. Alexander (Eds.), *Learning and study strategies: Issues in assessment, instruction, and evaluation* (pp. 77–100). San Diego, CA: Academic Press.

Paris, S. G., & Winograd, P. (1990). Dimension of thinking and cognitive instruction. In B. F. Jones & L. Idol (Eds.), *How metacognition can promote academic learning and instruction* (pp. 15–51). Hillsdale, NJ: Erlbaum.

Pea, R. D. (1988). Putting knowledge to use. In R. S. Nickerson & P. P. Zodhiates (Eds.), *Technology in education: Looking toward 2020* (pp. 169–212). Hillsdale, NJ: Erlbaum.

Pea, R. D. (1989). Socializing the knowledge transfer problem. *International Journal of Educational Research, 2,* 639–663.

Perkins, D. N., & Simmons, R. (1988). Patterns of misconceptions: An integrative model for science, math, and programming. *Review of Educational Research, 63,* 167–199.

Perret-Claremont, A., Perret, J., & Bell, N. (1980). The social construction of meaning and cognitive activity in elementary school children. In L. B. Resnick, J. M. Levine, & S. D. Teasley (Eds.), *Perspectives on socially shared cognition* (pp. 41–62). Washington, DC: American Psychological Association.

Phillips, D. A., & Zimmerman, M. (1990). The developmental course of perceived competence and incompetence among competent children. In R. J. Sternberg & J. Kolligian (Eds.), *Competence considered* (pp. 41–66). New Haven, CT: Yale University Press.

Piaget, J. (1952). *The origins of intelligence in children.* New York: International Universities Press.

Piatelli-Palamarini, M. (1980). *Language and learning.* Cambridge, MA: Harvard University Press.

Pichert, J. W., & Anderson, R. C. (1977). Taking different perspectives on a story. *Journal of Educational Psychology, 69,* 309–315.

Pintrich, P. R. (1991). Editor's comment. *Educational Psychologist, 26,* 199–205.

Pintrich, P. R., Marx, R. W., & Boyle, R. A. (1993). Beyond cold conceptual change: The role of motivational beliefs and classroom contextual factors in the process of conceptual change. *Review of Educational Research, 63,* 167–199.

Pintrich, P. R., & Schrauben, B. (1992). Students' motivational beliefs and their cognitive engagement in classroom academic tasks. In D. Schunk & J. Meese (Eds.), *Student perceptions in the classroom* (pp. 149–183). Hillsdale, NJ: Erlbaum.

Plomin, R. (1986). *Developmental genetics and psychology.* Hillsdale, NJ: Erlbaum.

Plomin, R., & Daniels, D. (1987). Why are children in the same family so different from each other? *The Behavioral and Brain Sciences, 10,* 1–16.

Plomin, R., & DeFries, J. C. (1985). *Origins of individual differences in infancy.* San Diego, CA: Academic Press.

Prawat, R. S. (1989). Promoting access to knowledge, strategy, and disposition in students: A research synthesis. *Review of Educational Research, 59,* 1–41.

Pressley, M., Goodchild, F., Fleet, J., Zajchowski, R., & Evans, E. D. (1989). The challenges of classroom strategy instruction. *Elementary School Journal, 89,* 301–342.

Pressley, M., Wood, E., Woloshyn, V. E., Martin, V., King, A., & Menke, D. (1992). Encouraging mindful use of prior knowledge: Attempting to construct explanatory answers facilitates learning. *Educational Psychologist, 27,* 91–109.

Pritchard, R. (1990). The effects of cultural schemata on reading processing strategies. *Reading Research Quarterly, 25,* 273–295.

Radziszewska, B., & Rogoff, B. (1988). Influence of adult and peer collaboration on children's planning skills. *Developmental Psychology, 24,* 840–848.

Renninger, K. A. (1992). Individual interest and development: Implications for theory and practice. In K. A. Renninger, S. Hidi, & A. Krapp (Eds.), *The role of interest in learning and development* (pp. 361–395). Hillsdale, NJ: Erlbaum.

Renninger, K. A., Hidi, S., & Krapp, A. (1992). *The role of interest in learning and development.* Hillsdale, NJ: Erlbaum.

Resnick, L. B. (1991). Shared cognition. In L. B. Resnick, J. M., Levine, & S. D. Teasley (Eds.), *Perspectives on socially shared cognition* (pp. 1–20). Washington, DC: American Psychological Association.

Resnick, L. B., Levine, J. M., & Teasley, S. D. (1991). *Perspectives on socially shared cognition.* Washington, DC: American Psychological Association.

Reynolds, C. R., & Willson, V. L. (Eds.). (1985). *Methodological and statistical advances in the study of individual differences.* New York: Plenum.

Reynolds, R. E., & Shirey, L. L. (1988). The role of attention in studying and learning. In C. E. Weinstein, E. T. Goetz, & P. A. Alexander (Eds.), *Learning and study strategies: Issues in assessment, instruction, and evaluation* (pp. 77–100). San Diego, CA: Academic Press.

Rogoff, B. (1990). *Apprenticeship in thinking: Cognitive development in social context.* New York: Oxford University Press.

Rogoff, B., & Gauvain, M. (1986). A method for the analysis of patterns illustrated with data on mother–child instructional interaction. In J. Valsiner (Ed.), *The role of the individual subject on scientific psychology* (pp. 261–290). New York: Plenum.

Rogoff, B., & Lave, J. (1984). *Everyday cognition.* Cambridge, MA: Harvard University Press.

Roth, K. J. (1985). Developing meaningful conceptual understanding in science. In B. F. Jones & L. Idol (Eds.), *Dimensions of thinking and cognitive instruction* (pp. 139–175). Hillsdale, NJ: Erlbaum.

Salomon, G. (1991). Transcending the qualitative-quantitative debate: The analytic and systemic approach to educational research. *Educational Psychologist, 20*(6), 10–18.

Scarr, S. (1992). Developmental theories for the 1990's: Development and individual differences. *Child Development, 63,* 1–19.

Schank, R. C. (1979). Interestingness: Controlling variables. *Artificial Intelligence, 12,* 273–297.

Schiefele, U. (1991). Interest, learning, and motivation. *Educational Psychologist, 26,* 229–323.

Schiefele, U., & Csikszentmihalyi, M. (1994). Interest and the quality of experience in classrooms. *European Journal of Psychology of Education, 9,* 251–270.

Schiefele, U., & Csikszentmihalyi, M. (1995). Motivation and ability in mathematics experience and achievement. *Journal for Research in Mathematics Education, 26,* 163–181.

Schiefele, U., Krapp, A., & Winteler, A. (1992). Interest as a predictor of academic achievement: A meta-analysis of research. In K. A. Renninger, S. Hidi, & A. Krapp (Eds.), *The role of interest in learning and development* (pp. 183–211). Hillsdale, NJ: Erlbaum.

Schmeck, R. R., & Geisler-Brenstein, E. (1989). Individual differences that affect the way students approach learning. *Learning and Individual Differences, 1,* 85–124.

Schoenfeld, A. H. (1985). *Mathematical problem solving.* San Diego, CA: Academic Press.

Schoenfeld, A. H. (1988). When good teaching leads to bad results: The disasters of "well-taught" mathematics courses. *Educational Psychologist, 23,* 145–166.

Schraw, G., & Dennison, R. S. (1994). The effect of reader purpose on interest and recall. *Journal of Reading Behavior, 26,* 1–18.

Schunk, D. (1991). Self-efficacy and academic motivation. *Educational Psychologist, 26,* 207–231.

Schunk, D. H., & Meece, J. L. (Eds.). (1992). *Student perceptions in the classroom.* Hillsdale, NJ: Erlbaum.

Skinner, B. F. (1953). *Science and human behavior.* New York: Appleton-Century-Crofts.

Slavin, R. E. (1978). *Effects of student teams and peer tutoring on academic achievement and time on-task* (Tech. Rep. No. 240). Baltimore, MD: Johns Hopkins University, Center for Social Organization of Schools.

Slavin, R. E. (1987). Development and motivational perspectives on cooperative learning: A reconciliation. *Child Development, 58,* 1161–1167.

Spiro, R. J., Feltovich, P. J., Jacobson, M. J., & Coulson, R. L. (1992). Cognitive flexibility, constructivism, and hypertext: Random access instruction for advanced knowledge acquisition in ill-structured domains. In T. M. Duffy & D. H. Jonassen (Eds.), *Constructivism and the technology of instruction: A conversation* (pp. 57–75). Cambridge, England: Cambridge University Press.

Spiro, R. J., & Jehng, J. C. (1990). Cognitive flexibility and hypertext: Theory and technology for the nonlinear and multidimensional traversal of complex subject matter. In D. Nix & R. J. Spiro (Eds.), *Cognition, education, and multimedia* (pp. 163–205). Hillsdale, NJ: Erlbaum.

Sternberg, R. J. (1980). Factor theories of intelligence are all right almost. *Educational Researcher, 9*(8), 6–13, 18.

Sternberg, R. J. (1985). But it's a sad tale that begins at the end: A reply to Glaser. *American Psychologist, 40,* 571–573.

Sternberg, R. J., Conway, B. E., Ketron, J. L., & Bernstein, M. (1981). People's conceptions of intelligence. *Journal of Personality and Social Psychology, 41,* 37–55.

Sternberg, R. J., & Lubart, T. I. (1991). An investment theory of creativity and its development. *Human Development, 34,* 1–31.

Stewart, I. (1987). *The problem of mathematics.* Oxford, England: Oxford University Press.

Tobias, S. (1994). Interest, prior knowledge, and learning. *Review of Educational Research, 64,* 37–54.

Tobin, K. G. (1991). Learning from interpretive research in science classrooms. In J.

J. Gallagher (Ed.), *Interpretive research in science education* (pp. 199–216). Manhattan, KS: National Association for Research in Science Teaching.

Tolman, E. C. (1932). *Purposive behavior in animals and men.* New York: Appleton-Century-Crofts.

Vera, A. H., & Simon, H. A. (1993). Situated action: A symbolic interpretation. *Cognitive Science, 17,* 7–48.

von Glaserfeld, E. (1991). *Radical constructivism in mathematics education.* Dordrecht, Netherlands: Kluwer Academic Publishers.

Vygotsky, L. (1986). *Thought and language.* A. Kozulin (Trans.). Cambridge, MA: MIT Press. (Original work published in 1934)

Wade, S. E., Schraw, G., Buxton, W. M., & Hayes, M. T. (1993). Seduction of the strategic reader: Effects of interest on strategies and recall. *Reading Research Quarterly, 28,* 93–114.

Wainryb, E., & Turiel, E. (1993). Conceptual and informational features in moral decision-making. *Educational Psychologist, 28,* 205–218.

Weinert, F. E., & Kluwe, R. H. (1987). *Metacognition, motivation, and understanding.* Hillsdale, NJ: Erlbaum.

Weinstein, C. E., & Mayer, R. E. (1986). The teaching of learning strategies. In M. C. Wittrock (Ed.), *Handbook of research on teaching* (3rd ed., pp. 315–327). New York: Macmillan.

Weinstein, C. E., & Meyer, D. K. (1991). Implications of cognitive psychology for testing: Contributions from work in learning strategies. In M. C. Wittrock & E. L. Baker (Eds.), *Testing and cognition* (pp. 40–61). Englewood Cliffs, NJ: Prentice-Hall.

Wigfield, C., & Harold, R. D. (1992). Teacher beliefs and children's achievement self-perceptions: A developmental perspective. In D. H. Schunk & J. L. Meece (Eds.), *Student perceptions in the classroom* (pp. 95–121). Hillsdale, NJ: Erlbaum.

Wigfield, A., & Karpathian, M. (1991). Who am I and what can I do? Children's self-concepts and motivation in achievement situations. *Educational Psychologist, 26*(3 & 4), 233–261.

Wittrock, M. C. (1991). Cognition and testing. In M. C. Wittrock & E. L. Baker (Eds.), *Testing and cognition* (pp. 1–16). Englewood Cliffs, NJ: Prentice-Hall.

Wylie, R. C. (1974). *The self-concept* (Vol. 1). Lincoln: University of Nebraska Press.

Wylie, R. C. (1979). *The self-concept* (Vol. 2). Lincoln: University of Nebraska Press.

Wylie, R. C. (1989). *Measures of the self-concept.* Lincoln: University of Nebraska Press.

Yinger, R. J., & Hendricks-Lee, M. S. (1993). An ecological conception of teaching. *Learning and Individual Differences, 4,* 269–281.

Zelazo, P. D., & Reznick, J. S. (1991). Age-related asynchrony of knowledge and action. *Child Development, 62,* 719–735.

Zimmerman, B. J., & Martinez-Pons, M. (1992). Perceptions of efficacy and strategy use in the self-regulation of learning. In D. H. Schunk & J. L. Meece (Eds.), *Student perceptions in the classroom* (pp. 185–207). Hillsdale, NJ: Erlbaum.

Contextual Factors Influencing the Classroom Application of Learner-Centered Principles

Craig L. Frisby

Learning does not occur in a vacuum. This brief but profound idea is one of the most important educational principles that is implicit in a learner-centered psychological perspective for facilitating educational reform (Principle 6; American Psychological Association [APA] Board of Educational Affairs, 1995). Human beings learn (intentionally or unintentionally) in a variety of contexts, and from a variety of situations experienced within those contexts. The most immediate context for formal learning is, of course, a classroom managed by one or more teachers. However, classrooms exist within the context of schools, which are characterized by a school climate or school culture that often permeates classrooms (i.e., "This is the way we do things at *this* school"). A teacher's interest and enthusiasm for teaching, as well as his or her effectiveness in meeting children's learning needs, is often related to the quality of his or her professional and social relationships with principals, colleagues, and staff.

Schools, in turn, operate within the context of local communities. Characteristics of local communities can exert either direct or indirect effects on individual learners. Communities influence learners in schools indirectly through social class and its correlates; its geographical location and population density; its racial divisions, ethnic characteristics, and cultural traditions; and the extent to which parents are politically astute in their relationships with school boards. Communities consist of family units, which directly influence the learning process in classrooms. It is common knowledge among teachers that some families offer home environments that support their efforts in the classroom, whereas other home environments undermine these same efforts. Finally, the nature of formal schooling occurs within a national context that is uniquely American. American education is shaped by the accumulation of historical and political factors that have not been duplicated in any other country in the world. Historically, American educational trends reflect cycles of proactive versus reactive thinking in response to critical marker events (Pulliam & Van Patten, 1995). During the mid- to late 1950s, for example, a new period of federal activity in education started with the cold war and the launching of the first space satellite (Sputnik) by the Soviets. In the wake of this event, many influential policy makers reacted with the suggestion that American educators should intensify their efforts to produce technological and scientific experts for world competitiveness. As a result, the National Defense Act of 1958 provided monies designed to strengthen the teaching of science, technology, mathematics, and foreign languages in the nation's schools. In 1983, the National Commission on Excellence in Education published *A Nation at Risk: The Imperative for Education Reform*, which had an impact similar to the Soviet's launching of Sputnik. The report began with a scathing discussion of the dismal condition of America's system of public education, particularly its high schools. Its recommendations were to intensify the existing high school curriculum by requiring 4 years of English, 3 years of math, 3 years of science, 3 years of social studies, 6 months of computer science, and up to 6 years of foreign language. In addition, the report recommended more homework, longer school days and a longer school year, increased incentives for good teachers, and the firing of bad teachers.

Following *A Nation at Risk*, over 300 commissions and task forces were created to develop educational reform proposals (O'Brien, 1994). By 1987, virtually every state in America had taken steps to reform its public schools (Kirst, 1988). Trained educational historians have observed that many educational trends, with the exception of those set into motion by technological advances, often reflect repeats of history. Certainly, the promulgation of learner-centered psychological principles is no exception to this rule. Therefore, a knowledge of history has the potential to inform educators of what innovations are most and least likely to be successful.

The general purpose of this chapter is to elaborate on Principle 6 (context of learning) of the *Learner-Centered Psychological Principles: A Framework for School Redesign and Reform* (APA, 1995).

To this end I describe more fully some national, community, and school contextual factors that influence applications of learner-centered principles in classrooms. I end the chapter with a description of four general principles that flow from this discussion.

National Trends

A number of significant events have occurred in education during the last half of the 20th century that are taken for granted today. The first was a move away from an educational philosophy focused on the mastery of subject matter to a broader educational philosophy that stresses social goals and individual objectives (Pulliam & Van Patten, 1995). The writings of John Dewey during the late 19th and early 20th century were influential in education and helped accelerate this trend, particularly during the 1930s. The sole purpose of the Progressive Education Association, an organization that existed from 1919–1955, was to apply the theories of John Dewey in advancing the cause of educational reform. Its influence on American education was profound, and in many ways it was a precursor to the learner-centered psychological principles for educational reform. At its first organizational meeting, the members of the Progressive Education Association adopted the following principles (adapted from Pulliam & Van Patten, 1995):

> (a) The child should be provided freedom to learn according to the social needs of his/her community, and should be provided with a learning environment rich in opportunities for self-expression and initiative; (b) the development of the child's interest through contact with the world, the application of the knowledge gained, and the self-consciousness of achievement; (c) the teacher's role as a learning guide, rather than a taskmaster; (d) scientific data collection as an aid to the facilitation of child development; (e) greater attention to how the educational environment can maximize the health and physical well-being of children; (f) co-operation between school and home to meet children's educational needs; and (g) an openness to the supplanting of tradition with new discoveries and knowledge. (pp. 138–139)

Although the progressive education movement had its critics (which later included Dewey himself), its child-centered philosophy continues to influence modern educational philosophy within teacher education (Pulliam & Van Patten, 1995).

Second, teacher training and instructional methods used in the classroom began to be influenced significantly by the growing field of educational psychology, particularly the work of David Ausubel, Benjamin Bloom, Jerome Bruner, Robert Gagne, Robert Glaser, Jerome Kagan, Jean Piaget, B. F. Skinner, and L. S. Vygotsky.

Third, the last half of the 20th century saw the enactment of federal initiatives designed to protect rights and provide funding for the education of educationally and economically disadvantaged children (e.g., Title 1 of the reauthorized Elementary and Secondary Education Act), disabled children (e.g., Individuals with Disabilities Education Act; Section 504 of the Rehabilitation Act of 1973), children facing numerous language barriers (e.g., reauthorized Bilingual Education Act), children of homeless parents (e.g., McKinney Act of 1987), and to a lesser extent gifted children (e.g., Gifted and Talented Students Education Act of 1988). Although the spirit of these initiatives is to promote equity in the education of vulnerable or previously underserved populations, the practical effect of these initiatives is to hold teachers in federally funded schools accountable for meeting the unique learning needs of a wider variety of students.

Fourth, the impact of developing educational technologies has created conditions that have altered the manner in which instruction and learning occur. For example, teachers are socialized to be responsive to individual differences in the classroom. Unfortunately, good intentions are often thwarted by the demands of assessing, prescribing, and monitoring student progress (Thomas & Knezek, 1991). Computer-based management and delivery of instruction has the potential for permitting teachers to address specific needs and maximize individual learning. Kulik (1994) reviewed findings from several meta-analytic studies of the effects of computer-based instruction on student outcomes. Although Kulik did not find consistent results across all types of computer instruction in all types of settings, several definite patterns did emerge from his review: (a) Students usually learn more in classes in which they receive computer-based instruction; (b) students learn their lessons in less time with computer-based instruction; (c) students also like their classes more when they receive computer help in them; and (d) students develop more positive attitudes toward computers when they receive help from them in school.

With the growth of instructional technology, students have access to efficient information retrieval through electronic bulletin boards and networks. Educational technology also gives learners exposure to expertise outside of the traditional classroom setting. Students are able to complement their studies with videotapes, CD-ROM programming, cable television, telephone conference calls, and satellite broadcasts. These and other innovations in the "distance education" movement allow for learning experiences that are unhindered by the physical separation between the learner and instructor (Hajdu & Schreckengost, 1994). Networking, electronic bulletins boards, and electronic mail systems have the potential to remove feelings of isolation and allow teachers to communicate and work as a team with other teachers (Thomas & Knezek, 1991).

Communities

Communities have various qualitative characteristics that indirectly affect student learning. To appreciate the full effects of community contexts on school learning, communities must be understood wholistically (rather than as an interaction of separate factors). A description of a child's schooling experience in two radically different communities illustrates this principle.

The first example is derived from Hillman's (1994) description of the advantages associated with educational systems in rural Pennsylvania. A school district is considered rural when the number of inhabitants is fewer than 150 per square mile, or when located in counties with 60% or more of the population living in communities no larger than 5,000 inhabitants (Helge, 1992). In these communities, rural schools are characterized by a safe environment, a lack of bureaucratic red tape, an emphasis on "the basics," and a sense of purpose and community morality. School events play a more important role in the day-to-day cultural and social life of rural communities. Rural residents display a sense of ownership of their schools that goes beyond the "mere coagulation of taxpayer groups" (Hillman, 1994, p. 316). In rural communities, two generations of family members may have learned under the same teacher. Students will see their teachers more frequently, and will come to know their teachers and receive help from them on a more personal level. In a family with such a history, the teacher is considered to be almost a family member. In addition, all support staff (e.g., administrators, bus drivers, cafeteria workers, secretaries, and maintenance staff) generally reside in the community. Problems that individual students may have are often identified and dealt with long before they come to the attention of school authorities (Hillman, 1994).

It is instructive to contrast this picture with a very different picture that is all too common in many inner city neighborhoods (Roth, 1994). In these urban communities, students grow up in a chaotic environment where female-headed households are the norm and two-parent families are rarely seen. This, coupled with the density of the population and the anonymity it provides, makes the task of keeping young people in line much more difficult. As a result, the sense of safety in the community is undermined by a delinquent adolescent subculture that preys on law-abiding citizens with little fear of arrest, let alone conviction. The social climate of schools within poor inner city communities has deteriorated to the point where little is expected of students academically, and constant disruption is the norm rather than the exception. Teacher morale is low, and metal detectors and bars on windows are part of the daily school routine. For many students, the lack of social order allows criminal acitivity to be so rewarding as to discourage serious engagement with the drudgery and routine of school work. Since many youth do not take school seriously, their prospects for employment beyond dead-end jobs are slim. Work habits of reliability and punctuality, and ability to delay gratification, are never internalized in many youth in these communities, due to a lack of consistent job experience. With no community norms prohibiting sexual activity before marriage, alarming numbers of young teenage girls allow themselves to become pregnant as a means of accomplishing personal fulfillment and status among peers in the community. Thus, the cycle of social pathology claims another generation of children.

Of course, not all communities fit the description of these two extremes, as there can be significant overlap in characteristics within any one community. The typical approach in social science research is to highlight the effects of specific community variables on student outcomes. Communities are made up of families, and families are the most proximal influence on students outside of schools. The majority of families want their children to do well in school. However, the specific manner in which social class, family structure, and home environment affect school learning is not precisely known. Our current understanding of this complex relationship appears to be a mixture of common sense and fragmented findings from empirical research on both demographic and process variables.

Social Class

Social class is positively correlated with a variety of measures of scholastic ability and achievement (e.g., White, 1982). Social class has been found to be related to the widening achievement gap as children progress through school (Fogelman & Goldstein, 1976) and the highest level a child reaches in the educational system (Sewell & Hauser, 1976). In addition, socioeconomic status is a powerful variable in mediating home-school relationships that in turn may influence learning. Lareau (1989) found that upper-middle-class parents spent time in their children's classroom, talked frequently to teachers, spent money hiring tutors for their children, used their status and influence to argue with teachers and administrators on policies beneficial to their children, and worked with their children on school tasks at home. Teachers, in turn, were impressed by parental involvement of upper-middle-class parents and tended to take their criticisms more seriously (Connell, Ashenden, Kessler, & Dowsett, 1982; Lareau, 1989). In contrast, working class parents tended to be intimidated by the educational system, lacked confidence and competence to criticize teachers and administrators, and generally felt a lack of capability in helping their children at home with school work. Willis (1977) found some evidence that working class boys' resistance to individual competition in school had roots in a family ethos that valued manual work and class solidarity.

Family Configuration

Dawson (1991) studied the effects of different family configurations on children's school problems (e.g., repeated grades, suspensions, and expulsions) in a sample of over 17,000 parent interviews. Dawson found that among school-age children, only 12% of those living with both biological parents had repeated a grade. However, this figure was 22% for children living with formerly married mothers or with mothers and stepfathers, and 30% for those living with never-married mothers. Similarly, only 4% of children living with both biological parents had ever been expelled or suspended, whereas the figure was 15% for those living with never-married mothers (Dawson, 1991). Although there are many factors that covary with family configuration that no doubt contribute to these outcomes, the evidence is strong that children of single mothers are more at-risk for school problems.

Home Environment

Although demographic factors continue to be of strong interest to researchers, a major concern is no longer the description of correlates of school learning but the analysis of the processes whereby demographic and other variables exert their effects. For example, the home environment influences learning differentially according to the child's age. Parent–child interaction declines as children grow older. Limitations in parental education may have little or no influence on the ability of parents to assist with homework when children are young but may present a substantial limitation when children are older. As children grow older, peers often replace parents as the primary source for values and academic goals.

Baurmind (1973) described two important dimensions of the home child-rearing climate. The first is the degree of parental guidance and control, and the second is the amount of emotional support and encouragement parents give to their children. There is evidence that households high in both parental guidance/control and support/encouragement lead to greater academic performance during high school (Dornbusch, Ritter, Leiderman, Roberts, & Fraleigh, 1987; Steinberg, Mounts, Lamborn, & Dornbusch, 1991). However, there is also evidence that these effects vary according to the racial/ethnic group of the household (Dornbusch et al., 1987).

Kellaghan (1994) identified several family processes associated with high student achievement: (a) high parental expectations and aspirations for their children; (b) opportunities for language development and the use of complex levels of language; (c) the availability and quality of help provided by the family on matters relating to school work (academic guidance); (d) parental involvement with their children in a variety of scholastic and nonscholastic activities; (e) amount of opportunities provided to children for thinking and imagination in daily activities; and (f) degree of routine and structure in home management.

School Effects

Teachers impact classroom learning as it is directly experienced by students. The culture of a school impacts student outcomes to the extent that it impacts the culture of teaching (Leithwood & Jantzi, 1994). In some schools, teachers are isolated from professional exchanges with other teachers, whereas in other schools teachers share an ongoing, collaborative professional relationship. In some schools, administrators are expected to refrain from interfering with teachers' routines and instructional decisions, but are expected to shield teachers from outside pressures (e.g., angry parents). In these schools, parents are valued by teachers to the extent that they support the teachers' plans. In other schools, administrators are expected to provide instructional leadership, and parents are considered partners in the education of students (Little, 1982). Smaller schools have an advantage over larger schools in fostering greater student participation in extracurricular activities, lower levels of student alienation, and greater collegiality among administrators and staff (Haller & Monk, 1988; Hamilton, 1983).

The number of instructional days per year and the time actually spent on learning tasks have a significant effect on student achievement. Schools influence the time available for instruction to the extent that they enforce student attendance policies. Individual teachers and students control the actual amount of time spent on tasks, which has been shown to vary from a low of 40% to a high of 85% across a sample of junior high classrooms (Everston, 1980). Increased time on tasks is assisted by the extent to which schools support teachers in neutralizing the effects of disruptive students.

Schools have policies with respect to grouping students by ability within classes, across classes, and across schools (Braddock, 1990). There is substantial evidence of the effects of grouping practices on a variety of student outcomes. For example, the best evidence to date suggests that the effects of homogeneous ability grouping (both between and within classes) is strongest for students of high academic ability (Gamoran & Berends, 1987; Slavin, 1990). Unfortunately, the research evidence reflects neutral or negative effects for low-ability students in lower tracks (Murphy & Hallinger, 1989). The instructional process experienced by students in lower tracks tends to be slower paced, interrupted more frequently by classroom management problems, and characterized by a greater emphasis on noninteractive seat work. Instruction for these students tends to be less varied and less likely to include assigned homework and constructive academic feedback. In short, rigorous encounters with academic content are "traded off" for compliance with classroom routines and nondisruptive behavior for lower track students (Leithwood & Jantzi, 1994).

There is some evidence that the background and personal characteristics of principals influence student learning outcomes. Evidence suggests that principals with longer classroom experience prior to their role, greater formal education, specific curriculum or policy-related knowledge, adequate on-the-job training as vice principal, and personal characteristics of openmindedness and a nurturing attitude toward students are associated with effective instructional leaders. Effective instructional leaders adopt practices that influence students' acquisition of basic skills, attitudes toward school, absenteeism, vandalism, and grade retention. These variables, in turn, are associated with positive learning outcomes for students (Leithwood & Jantzi, 1994).

Alternative schools are designed to provide a special instructional environment and educational philosophy for families seeking experiences for their children that are different from those offered by public or state-controlled schools (Cooper, 1994). Relevant subcategories within alternative schools are private, independent, religious, and model schools (within the existing state-supported public school system). Private schools are not necessarily "alternative" schools in the sense of always providing a radically different educational experience. However, the privatization of education creates the conditions favorable for alternatives not available in public schools. Independent schools are free from the sponsorship of established educational, religious, or governmental institutions. These schools often pride themselves on being "in opposition" to some undesirable aspect of the traditional public school system. Religious schools are run by religious groups that may or may not operate within the guidelines of a parent church. These schools tend to be highly traditional in their emphasis on stricter rules of conduct and an adherence to a curriculum rooted in fundamental religious teachings. A number of public school systems run "model" schools that operate within the system, usually by converting traditional schools to nontraditional ones. In some cases, for example, school districts may create magnet schools that provide more elaborate and creative instruction in a particular subject area. Other school districts may create alternative schools for students who are ineligible for special education, but whose behavioral problems warrant a different educational experience.

Alternative schools are characterized by their freedom to link pedagogy and curriculum with an explicit or implicit educational philosophy. For example, methods used by some alternative schools are based on the assumption that children have a natural love of learning, are intensely curious, and are essentially good natured. As a result, these schools encourage children to explore knowledge outside the walls of the school, take pride in creating a democratic and caring classroom community, and emphasize shared governance among teachers and administrators. Other alternative schools operate under the assumption that children are naturally lazy, unmotivated, and undisciplined. As a result, these schools may stress a more authoritarian classroom atmosphere, a greater emphasis on external methods of enforcing discipline, and a greater emphasis on drill and practice in instruction. Some alternative schools operate under the assumption that the outside world (i.e., those of a different racial, ethnic, or religious group membership) is hostile or "contaminated" in some moral or cultural sense. As a result, these schools may place a heavy emphasis on the inculcation of knowledge about one's own group and its traditions, and may use programmed materials that undermine individualization (Cooper, 1994).

Extensive empirical evaluations of the merits of public versus alternative schools are rare. However, there are some major projects that have addressed this need. For example, Marks and Lee (1994) summarized comparative research in the 1980s on the effectiveness of public versus private schools, which was based on the High School and Beyond (HS&B) database. The HS&B database reflects a nationally representative longitudinal study, sponsored by the National Center for Educational Statistics, of 58,000 students across 1,015 secondary schools. Catholic schools and schools with high proportions of minority children were deliberately oversampled. The Educational Testing Service developed achievement tests in reading, vocabulary, mathematics, writing, civics, and science that served as outcome measures. Although this database was subject to numerous analyses, critiques, and reanalyses (see review by Marks & Lee, 1994), some consistent findings emerged. Catholic schools demonstrated consistent and statistically significant advantages in reading, vocabulary, and mathematics tests. Minorities and students from lower socioeconomic backgrounds did particularly well in Catholic schools compared with public schools. Although critics have charged that private schools usually serve a more selective clientele, there are other qualities that private schools share to which researchers attribute greater academic performance (Marks & Lee, 1994): (a) A generally smaller student population and decision-making autonomy, (b) a consensus that unites the school and community on a common core of values and educational purpose, (c) a safe and orderly environment, (d) clear standards for student behavior and achievement that minimize the role of prior socioeconomic background, (e) traditions and rituals that define a school culture and impart a shared identity, and (f) close monitoring among staff on how school conditions affect student learning and development.

RAND Corporation Study

Hill (1990) described a RAND Corporation study that illustrates the integration of school organizational variables and their effects on student outcomes. Hill and his associates studied 13 inner city high schools in New York and Washington, DC. Eight of these schools were studied intensively. In these intensively studied schools, researchers spent 10 days interviewing school personnel (including students) and observing classes. Researchers also examined student records and administered questionnaires for 50 students in each school. Of these 8 schools, 3 were New York City Catholic high schools; 2 were *zoned* (regular neighborhood) New York City schools; 2 were public schools that provided specially focused vocational or academic programs for a cross-section of New York City students; and 1 was a special school designed for students who had failed in regular high schools and were assigned there for a "last chance" at education (Hill, 1990). Less intensive 3- to 5-day observations were conducted in 3 Washington, DC, and 2 New York City schools. All schools drew from a population of economically disadvantaged youth. While the zoned schools enrolled the largest proportion of poor minority students, 40% of the Catholic school enrollment came from families receiving welfare or families living below official poverty levels (Hill, 1990).

Hill (1990) compared education outcomes in zoned schools versus the Catholic and special purpose schools, which were termed *focus* schools. Hill found that students in focus schools graduated at a much higher rate than students in zoned schools. In addition, the majority of graduating seniors in the focus schools took the Scholastic Aptitude Test (SAT), which is required for entry into selective colleges or universities. Test scores for focus school students approached or exceeded national averages. In contrast, less than one third of the graduating students in zoned schools took the SAT. Among this group, the scores of zoned school students fell far below national and focus school averages.

Hill found important similarities among the focus schools. Contrary to conventional wisdom, focus schools did not uniformly share features associated with private school advantages (e.g., the luxury of admitting the best students, highly motivated parents, freedom to expel disruptive students, freedom to teach moral absolutes, single sex composition of the student body, the wearing of school uniforms, or regimentation and harsh discipline). Although these features may contribute to an individual school's effectiveness, Hill and his research team found that these features were not the most important ones that differentiated focus schools from zoned schools.

Focus schools differed dramatically from zoned public schools in less obvious areas. For example, focus schools were found to have clear, uncomplicated missions centered on the experiences the school intends to provide its students and on the ways it intends to influence its students' performance, attitudes, and behavior (Hill, 1990). They tended to be strong organizations with a capacity to initiate action in pursuit of their missions, to sustain themselves over time, to solve their own problems, and to manage their external relationships. Interestingly, focus schools were not characterized by innovative education. Rather, the key characteristic seems to be a feeling among students and staff that their school is a special creation that reflects their efforts and meets their needs.

In contrast, zoned schools were found to have diffuse missions defined by the demands of external funders and regulators. They were also found to be profoundly compromised organizations, with little capacity to initiate their own solutions to problems, define their internal character, or manage their relationships with external audiences. Because zoned schools are essentially franchises reflecting a standard model established by central authorities, staff and students have less reason to consider the schools uniquely their own (Hill, 1990). The key differences between focus and zoned schools are listed in Exhibit 1.

Ultimately, the most important outcome of focus schools is the effect that they have on students. Hill (1990) found statistically significant differences in students' attitudes toward the different school types. In general, focus school students believed that their schools were safer, cleaner, and more pleasant than did zoned school students. Focus school students were far more likely than their zoned school counterparts to take pride in their school and consider themselves fortunate to attend it. Interestingly, students in zoned schools expressed a desire to learn and to accept behavioral and academic standards consistently applied. However, they cited peer pressure as the key factor that prevented them from appearing to be one of a few students who study hard or appreciate the teacher's efforts. As a result, Hill and his team found that students adopted defiant and oppositional attitudes toward learning simply as a defense against ridicule from other students. Most significant is the change in attitudes of low-achieving students who transferred from a zoned to a focus school. The researchers found that the

Exhibit 1

Key Differences in School Mission and Organizational Strength of Focus and Zoned Schools as Identified by Hill (1990)

Focus schools	Zoned schools
School mission	
1. Concentrate on student outcomes before all other matters	Focus primarily on delivering programs and following procedures
2. Have strong social contracts that communicate the reciprocal responsibilities of students and teachers, establishing the benefits that each derives from fulfilling the contract faithfully	Try whenever possible to let staff and students define their own roles in the school
3. Have a strong commitment to parenting and aggressively mold student attitudes and values; they emphasize the secular ethics of honesty, reliability, fairness, and respect for others	Teachers see themselves primarily as transmitters of information and imparters of skills
4. Have a centripetal curricula that draw all students toward learning certain core skills and perspectives	Distinguish among students in terms of ability and preference and offer profoundly different curricula to different groups
Organizational strength	
1. Operate as problem-solving organizations, taking the initiative to change their programs in response to emerging needs	Problem-solving capability is constrained by external mandates and rigid internal divisions of labor
2. Protect and sustain their distinctive character, both by attracting staff members who accept the school's premises and by socializing new staff members	Have little capacity to select staff or influence the attitudes or behavior of new staff members
3. Consider themselves accountable to the people who depend on their performance, such as parents, students, neighborhood and parish groups, and financial supporters	Answer primarily to bureaucratic superiors—outside rule-making, auditing, and assessment organizations

vast majority of these transfer students portrayed themselves as initially having the same rebellious attitudes that lead to poor attendance and low academic effort in zoned schools. However, the focus school environment made it more acceptable for them to make an effort to attend class and follow rules.

The researchers are careful to make the point that focus schools may not be for everyone. However, if troubled public schools wish to make focus school characteristics a reality in their schools, it requires a committment to initiating those processes that alter the organizational context in which students learn.

Conclusion

In school reform efforts, a commitment to a learner-centered perspective is a worthy goal that cannot exist independently of a consideration of context effects. This chapter has discussed how national, community, and school contexts can influence the content and quality of classroom learning. There are four principles that appear to flow directly from the previous discussion. First and fundamentally, life is unfair. All learners (like all people) are not born under the same set of life circumstances. Learners are born with different genetic constitutions and are raised by caregivers that vary markedly in their own personal stability, skill for and commitment to child rearing, and attitudes toward their children's schooling. Learners have no control over the communities that they grow up in or the historical time period in which they are born. Obvious differences in the extent to which these factors impinge on children's learning experiences constitute a reality that no amount of well-intentioned social engineering will control completely.

However, this axiom is tempered by two additional principles. A second principle is that individual differences in factors influencing learning will continue to exist within commonalities in life circumstances. Consider, for example, contentious debates over the role of genetics and environment in individual and group differences in intelligence. Many staunch environmentalists are convinced that a large part of IQ variation is environmentally determined, which in their view argues for increased efforts to improve environmental conditions for certain segments of the American population. Most Americans favor efforts to enhance environmental conditions for disadvantaged groups on moral grounds, regardless of whether such efforts are motivated by perceived effects on cognitive functioning. Ironically, the more equalized the educational environments become, the greater the role that heredity plays in explaining individual differences in intellectual outcomes (Herrnstein & Murray, 1994). Even if economically disadvantaged environments are not altered for learners, there will continue to be differential influences that are attributable to other environmental processes. Some families are poor, but they sacrifice their limited resources on books, tuition, and school uniforms to provide the best education experiences for their children. In contrast, other families living in the same neighborhood may consist of parents who are largely unavailable or who are so disrupted by marital and personal problems that creating conditions for a sound educational environment at home is a low priority. This has led many researchers to the conviction that the importance of children's learning lies not in who parents are (with respect to SES) but in what they do (Kellaghan, Sloan, Alvarez, & Bloom, 1993).

Third, life circumstances are rarely static but are susceptible to change. This principle is illustrated by families that are able to move to better neighborhoods, or students who are able to transfer to better schools. However, this should not be taken to mean that all contextual change requires a physical move. Contexts can also change in the absence of physical moves. Children who were previously unmotivated to learn can suddenly become motivated as a result of personal changes or after exposure to new learning opportunities. Parents are capable of learning new skills that will benefit their children's education. Hill (1990) made the point that state departments of education, school superintendents, boards of education, and teacher's unions must agree to share a common vision if failing schools are to become successful schools. Specifically, these parties must agree to waive any bureaucratic rules, policies, ineffective incentive schemes, or cumbersome reporting requirements that hinder the creation of decentralized site-managed schools that adhere to the various principles outlined by Hill.

The fourth and most important outcome of a learner-centered psychological perspective is that it challenges educators to think psychologically rather than ideologically. Although educators can strive to make their practices more psychologically sensitive, policy and practice decisions in education cannot escape being shaped to some extent by ideological or philosophical viewpoints. Consider, for example, the following questions: Should schooling be based on the immediate needs and interests of the learner, or should schooling emphasize the development of intellectual skills needed for the realization of human potential? Should schools require a universal core curriculum, or should teachers and students be given autonomy in deciding what is taught? Should the goal of schooling be to promote the economic interests (business and industry) of a nation, or should the goal of schooling be to develop general citizenship skills for solving social problems? Some argue that educational needs are determined not by viewing the child as an isolated unit but rather as a person inevitably linked to broader society. Hence, a community must first make a moral commitment to the type of society it wants before content and authority in education can be established. These and other issues reflect fundamental ideological debates in education that will be argued (in various forms) as long as education continues to exist (Noll, 1991).

Other debates in education reflect narrower (but no less acrimonious) issues that are framed in language shaped by shifting trends. These movements crystallize around various catch phrases, slogans, and buzzwords designed to function as social litmus tests. Here, one's stated position in favor of or in opposition to a particular movement places people into hostile camps of the "good guys" versus the "bad guys." For example, should schools teach multiculturalism or the notion of a common culture? Should parents be provided subsidized free choice among public and private schools? Is inclusion good for children with disabilities? How should sex education be taught in schools? Will yearlong schools increase achievement? Which is better for children: whole language or direct instruction? Is bilingual education effective? These questions are likely to generate strong feelings in those persons for whom education is their life's work, because they tap deep convictions about what is "best" for children. Although empirical research may provide some guidance as to what works or does not work in a specific study, there continues to be much debate over the proper interpretation of various findings, and differences of agreement as to the implications of findings. Because different groups have different opinions as to what is best, resolutions of these debates are often a function of which political parties, superintendents, school boards, teacher's unions, or parent and community groups happen to be in power. Whoever is in power at the moment influences national and state education laws, how teachers are socialized and trained, and what they are allowed (or not allowed) to do in the classroom. The purpose of this book is to sensitize educators to not let the needs of the individual learner become lost in the process.

References

American Psychological Association Board of Educational Affairs. (1995, Dec.). *Learner-centered psychological principles: A framework for school redesign and reform* [On-line]. Available: http://www.apa.org/ed/lcp.html.

Baurmind, D. (1973). The development of instrumental competence through socialization. In A. D. Pick (Ed.), *Minnesota Symposium on Child Psychology* (Vol. 7). Minneapolis: University of Minnesota Press.

Braddock, J. H. (1990). Tracking the middle grades: National patterns of grouping for instruction. *Phi Delta Kappan, 71,* 445–449.

Connell, R. W., Ashenden, D. J., Kessler, S., & Dowsett, G. W. (1982). *Making the difference: Schools, families, and social division.* Sydney, Australia: Allen & Unwin.

Cooper, B. S. (1994). Alternative schools and programs. In T. Husen & T. N. Postlewaite (Eds.), *The international encyclopedia of education* (2nd ed., pp. 260–266). Tarrytown, NY: Elsevier Science.

Dawson, D. (1991). *Family structure and children's health. Series 10: Data from the National Health Survey, No. 178* (DHHS Publication No. PHS 91–1506). Hyattsville, MD: National Center for Health Statistics.

Dornbusch, S., Ritter, P., Leiderman, P., Roberts, D., & Fraleigh, M. (1987). The relation of parenting style to adolescent school performance. *Child Development, 58,* 1244–1257.

Everston, C. M. (1980). Relationships between classroom behaviors and student outcomes in junior high mathematics and English classes. *American Educational Research Journal, 17,* 43–60.

Fogelman, K. R., & Goldstein, H. (1976). Social factors associated with changes in educational attainment between 7 and 11 years of age. *Educational Studies, 2,* 95–109.

Gamoran, A., & Berends, M. (1987). The effects of stratification in secondary schools: Synthesis of survey and ethnographic research. *Review of Educational Research, 57,* 415–436.

Hajdu, D. L., & Schreckengost, D. L. (1994). Distance learning. In C. E. Greenawalt (Ed.), *Educational innovation: An agenda to frame the future* (pp. 285–308). Lanham, MD: University Press of America.

Haller, E. J., & Monk, D. H. (1988). New reforms, old reforms and the consolidation of small rural schools. *Educational Administration Quarterly, 24,* 470–483.

Hamilton, S. F. (1983). The social side of schooling: Ecological studies of classrooms and schools. *Elementary School Journal, 83,* 313–334.

Helge, D. I. (1992). Rural education. In M. C. Aiken (Ed.), *Encyclopedia of educational research* (6th ed., pp. 1118–1123). New York: Macmillan.

Herrnstein, R. J., & Murray, C. (1994). *The bell curve: Intelligence and class structure in American life.* New York: The Free Press.

Hill, P. T. (1990). *High schools with character.* Santa Monica, CA: RAND Corporation. (ERIC Document Reproduction Service No. 327597)

Hillman, A. (1994). The problems of rural education. In C. E. Greenawalt (Ed.), *Educational innovation: An agenda to frame the future* (pp. 309–330). Lanham, MD: University Press of America.

Kellaghan, T. (1994). Family and schooling. In T. Husen & T. N. Postlewaite (Eds.), *The international encyclopedia of education* (2nd ed., pp. 2250–2258). Tarrytown, NY: Elsevier Science.

Kellaghan, T., Sloan, K., Alvarez, B., & Bloom, B. S. (1993). *The home environment and school learning.* San Francisco, CA: Jossey Bass.

Kirst, M.W. (1988). Recent state education reform in the United States, looking backward and forward. *Educational Administration Quarterly, 24,* 319–328.

Kulik, J. A. (1994). Meta-analytic studies of findings on computer-based instruction. In E. L. Baker & H. F. O'Neil (Eds.), *Technology assessment in education and training* (pp. 9–33). Hillsdale, NJ: Erlbaum.

Lareau, A. (1989). *Home advantage: Social class and parental intervention in elementary education.* London: Falmer Press.

Leithwood, K., & Jantzi, D. (1994). School organizational effects on student outcomes. In T. Husen & T. N. Postlewaite (Eds.), *The international encyclopedia of education* (2nd ed., pp. 5259–5264). Tarrytown, NY: Elsevier Science.

Little, J. W. (1982). Norms of collegiality and experimentation: Workplace conditions of school success. *American Educational Research Journal, 19,* 325–340.

Marks, H. M., & Lee, V. E. (1994). Public versus private schools: Research controversies. In T. Husen & T. N. Postlewaite (Eds.), *The international encyclopedia of education* (2nd ed., pp. 4839–4845). Tarrytown, NY: Elsevier Science.

Murphy, J., & Hallinger, P. (1989). Equity as access to learning: Curricular and instructional treatment differences. *Journal of Curriculum Studies, 21,* 129–149.

National Commission on Excellence in Education. (1983). *A nation at risk: The imperative for educational reform.* Washington, DC: U.S. Government Printing Office.

Noll, J. W. (1991). *Taking sides: Clashing views on controversial educational issues.* Guilford, CT: Dushkin Publishing Group.

O'Brien, T. V. (1994). Educational reform movements among the states in the last ten years. In C. E. Greenawalt (Ed.), *Educational innovation: An agenda to frame the future* (pp. 31–58). Lanham, MD: University Press of America.

Pulliam, J. D., & Van Patten, J. (1995). *History of education in America* (6th ed.). Englewood Cliffs, NJ: Prentice-Hall.

Roth, B. (1994). *Prescription for failure: Race relations in the age of social science.* New Brunswick: Transaction.

Sewell, W. H., & Hauser, R. M. (1976). Causes and consequences of higher education: Models of the status attainment process. In W. H. Sewell, R. M. Hauser, & D. L. Featherman (Eds.), *Schooling and achievement in American society* (pp. 9–27). San Diego, CA: Academic Press.

Slavin, R. E. (1990). Achievement effects of ability grouping in secondary schools: A best-evidence synthesis. *Review of Educational Research, 60,* 471–500.

Steinberg, L., Mounts, N., Lamborn, S., & Dornbusch, S. (1991). Authoritative parenting and adolescent adjustment across varied ecological niches. *Journal of Research on Adolescence, 1,* 19–36.

Thomas, L. G., & Knezek, D. (1991). Providing technology leadership for restructured schools. *Journal of Research on Computing in Education, 24,* 265–279.

White, K. R. (1982). The relationship between socioeconomic status and academic achievement. *Psychological Bulletin, 91,* 461–481.

Willis, P. (1977). *Learning to labor: How working class kids get working class jobs.* Farnborough: Saxon House.

4

Promoting Positive Expectations in Schooling

Rhona S. Weinstein

Conceptualizing the Problem

The Motivation to Learn

Children's motivation to learn lies at the very core of achieving success in schooling. Given rapid technological advances, an ever-changing knowledge base, and shifting workforce needs, a continuing motivation to learn may well be the hallmark of individual accomplishment across the life span. In fact, as Sarason (1995) argued, instilling or supporting a continuing motivation to learn may be the most important underlying purpose for schooling. However, despite the importance of motivation as a mediating process that underlies academic accomplishment, current reform efforts focus on the end point of achievement. The nation's report card on education fails to ask—first, how well its educators do in enhancing children's interest in and sustained commitment to learning, and second, wherein lies the source of the problem?

Applying Learner-Centered Psychological Principles

One exception to this limiting end-point perspective can be seen in the work of the American Psychological Association (APA) Presidential Task Force on Psychology in Education (1993). Their report outlined 14 empirically derived learner-centered psychological principles (APA Board

---

The author gratefully acknowledges the support of the Spencer Foundation during the preparation of this chapter.

of Educational Affairs, 1995) that chart a path-breaking direction for school reform efforts. In framing this knowledge base around the learner in educational context rather than around the more common topics of curriculum, instruction, and administration, the task force underscored psychology's unique and critical role in reform efforts. Importantly, these principles place a highly differentiated view of learner psychological processes at the heart of educational reform—a perspective that has been largely missing in the history of school change.

Currently three principles (7–9) speak to the important role of motivational and affective aspects of learning and to their interdependent relationship to cognitive, developmental, social, and individual-difference factors. These principles, which reflect a constructivist perspective, target learner processes that mediate learning (such as emotional states and expectations for success and failure) and teaching practices and policies that impact on these learner processes (such as stigmatizing labels). These principles apply equally to all learners who participate in the educational system, including teachers and administrators. Thus any attempt at school reform must engage teachers and principals in the learning process, just as school reforms seek to engage students.

The underlying message of the APA principles is that learning is maximized when learners are *intellectually challenged* "in linking new information with existing knowledge in meaningful ways" (APA, 1993, p. 5); *intrinsically motivated* to exert effort through positive emotions, personal interest, and control; and *respectfully and appropriately supported* in learning despite differences among learners. The expectations we hold for learners about their capability for learning are key to actualizing this vision of the learning process.

Research evidence points to substantial erosion of student motivation in schooling and to the underlying role of teacher expectations for children in creating negative self-fulfilling prophecies. But relatively little empirical work has addressed the application of this knowledge toward effective preventive intervention—that is, the promotion of positive expectancy climates and enhanced motivational outcomes (Babad, 1993; Weinstein et al., 1991). This chapter addresses the knowledge base for such interventions through an examination of an expectancy-enhancement intervention in an inner-city high school.

Teacher Expectations About Student Capability for Learning

Although most children begin their schooling with great excitement about learning, daily life in schools often erodes children's interest, self-concept as learners, and educational aspirations. Research suggests that this erosion of motivation can arise from learning opportunities, interactions with teachers and peers, and school-wide policies that convey to children low expectations about their capacity to learn (Babad, 1993; Weinstein, 1993). Such low expectations can serve as self-fulfilling prophecies. That is, the expression of low expectations by differential treatment can inadvertently lead children to confirm predictions about their abilities by exerting less effort and ultimately performing more poorly.

Certain groups of children have been found to be at particular risk for low expectations or "underestimated" ability. These include the poor, certain ethnic-minority groups, immigrants, girls in math and science, children with handicaps, and generally students in the bottom half of the achievement hierarchy (Barr & Dreeben, 1983; Franklin, 1994; Meier, Stewart, & England, 1989; Porter, 1990; Sadker, Sadker, & Klein, 1991; Stewart, 1993). Enormous disparities in expectations (beyond those predicted by actual performance differences) and documented gaps in achievement are troubling in and of themselves. They also pose critical societal problems given the high economic, social, and emotional costs of school failure (Schorr, 1988). Early school problems have been found to predict later school failure and school dropout as well as under- and unemployment, and problems with health, mental health, and criminal behavior (Oakland, 1992). Further, these disparities in expectations and performance are forecast to increase with the growing diversity of the children who come to schooling—a diversity reflective of rising rates of poverty and immigration in this country (Stewart, 1993). There is much at risk here in terms of wasted opportunities to develop talent.

Toward Promotion of Positive Expectancy Climates

In order to enhance the motivation of learners amid an increasing diversity of learners, the pivotal role of expectancy processes must be addressed in educational reform efforts. With this goal in mind, I briefly review key aspects of our knowledge about self-fulfilling prophecies in schooling that are essential for framing the direction of application. Given the paucity of applied intervention research and its relative failure to make substantial changes in expectancy climate, I next present an integrative model of expectancy enhancement. Here, I draw both from children's knowledge of expectancy communication in schooling and from the social psychological literature on stereotype change and institutional reform. The model targets eight features of teaching practices for change and creates sustained collaborative conditions for teachers and administrators to work together in bringing about these reforms.

Finally, I report on an evaluation of a 2-year expectancy-enhancement intervention, which, although implemented in high school, is equally appropriate for the elementary school level. I highlight aspects of the process of raising expectations in schooling and selected outcomes that accompany such a venture in an effort to illustrate learner-centered psychological principles in action. Empirically validated expectancy theory thus provides an important opportunity to envision, implement, and test alternatives, more motivationally "nurturing" educational contexts for both teachers and students.

Self-Fulfilling Prophecies in Schooling

Expectancy Effects Exist

It is now 30 years since the classic *Pygmalion in the Classroom* experiment (Rosenthal & Jacobson, 1968) was published. This study is remembered for its dramatic demonstration that giving false information to teachers about a randomly selected group of "intellectual bloomers" resulted in greater IQ gains for the targeted children (in the early grades only) as compared to control students. Despite enormous controversy over the methodological problems in the study and similar studies that followed it, there exists substantial evidence that self-fulfilling prophecies do occur in schooling and in many other interpersonal contexts (Babad, 1993; Blanck, 1993; Jussim, 1986; Jussim, Madon, & Chatman, 1994).

Controversy persists, however, over the magnitude of such effects. Some investigators argue that these effects are small, in light of some failures to replicate findings and substantial evidence that teacher expectations are often accurate, that is, simply reflective of or responsive to student incoming achievement differences (Brophy, 1983; Jussim, 1989). But others underscore that the important task lies in the identification of the conditions under which expectancy effects are magnified or diminished—for example, the qualities of teachers, schools, and students that predict susceptibility to such prophecy effects (Babad, 1993; Weinstein, 1993).

In both experimental and naturalistic contexts, meta-analytic reviews of the available research evidence underscore clear effects of teacher expectations on student achievement and in some cases on IQ (Raudenbush, 1984; Smith, 1980). Raudenbush (1984) pointed out that IQ effects are more likely when expectations are induced early in the school year (prior to the formation of teachers' own expectations) and in the early grades and during the transition to junior high (when teachers have the least prior information about their students). Further, expectancy effects on achievement have been found to be larger for biased teachers (Babad, Inbar, & Rosenthal, 1982) and in classrooms in which children report a great deal of differential teacher treatment (Brattesani, Weinstein, & Marshall, 1984).

Mediating Steps of Communication in Teacher Behavior

Research has also addressed the mediating steps through which expectations can shape children's achievement. Brophy and Good (1970, 1974) provided a model conceptualizing self-fulfilling prophecies as outcomes of observable sequences of behavior. They documented that teachers do indeed differentiate their treatment of students in accord with their naturally occurring expectations; that is, teachers systematically favored *highs* (high-expectancy students) over *lows* (lower expectancy students) in "demanding and reinforcing quality performance" (Brophy & Good, 1970, p. 373). They also hypothesized both a direct route of influence through differential exposure to curriculum or practice and an indirect route where such differential treatment may impact student motivation and self-view.

Reviews of this research describe from 17 to 31 distinct mediation behaviors (Brophy, 1983; Harris & Rosenthal, 1985). The Harris and Rosenthal (1985) meta-analysis concluded with widespread support for three of the four factors of Rosenthal's (1973) theory, with regard to their predictive relationship to an array of outcomes. These factors include climate (teachers' warmth toward highs), input (the teaching of more and more difficult material to highs), and output (greater opportunities for highs to respond). Far less conclusive support was found for teacher feedback (more differentiated and positive information to highs). Ironically, much of the current intervention work has been based around teacher feedback, that is, attempts to equalize praise and criticism to highs and lows.

This focus on single, discrete teacher behaviors has been limited in its explanatory power. Research on student perceptions has high-lighted the subtle and sometimes conflicting nature of expectancy clues such as children's differentiation between types of teacher "call on" behaviors (Babad, 1990a, 1990b; Weinstein, 1989) or nonverbal behavior and potential leakage of teacher expectations across channels of communication. For example, Babad and colleagues (Babad, Bernieri, & Rosenthal, 1989, 1991) have demonstrated such leakage in the presence of negative affect in facial expression but not in speech content. Finally, studies have documented that expectations are also expressed not only to individual students, but also at a group level within the classroom (ability-based grouping), at a classroom level (tracking), and at school and district levels. Such expressions of expectations have implications for differential access to curricular opportunities and to teacher messages about student capacity to succeed (Barr & Dreeben, 1983; Oakes, 1987; Rist, 1970).

Thus, these findings alert us not only to specific teacher behaviors in the teacher–student dyad, but also to the institutional policies and culture of the classroom and the school as sources of expectancy effects. They focus attention on participants' interpretive meaning of such communications. The need is clear for a broader, unifying framework for the expression of low and differential expectations in schooling.

Into the Minds of Teachers

Moving beyond the specification of behaviors, more complex models of expectancy effects evolved to highlight the thinking of both teacher and student as participants in the process (e.g., Darley & Fazio, 1980). The research task focused on the illumination of step-by-step causal processes from the formation of expectancies, to their communication, and to their interpretation and internalization by students. Research studies also identified critical differences in teachers and students that might explain where and when expectancy effects occur.

With regard to teachers, the Dusek and Joseph (1983) meta-analysis of research studies on the formation of expectations underscored the role of student attractiveness, classroom conduct, cumulative folder material, race, and social class as critical factors in shaping teacher expectations. Other studies offered evidence for distinguishing among expectation-prone teachers such as, for example, those who show bias in judgment (Babad, Inbar, & Rosenthal, 1982) and display a need for control over student performance (Cooper, 1979). Others such as Jussim (1991) pressed for distinguishing between evidence for teacher perceptual bias (perceived confirmation) and teacher self-fulfilling prophecy (actual confirmation).

Into the Minds of Students

With regard to students, a growing body of research has documented that children are aware of differential teacher treatment and thus gain knowledge from these patterns about teachers' expectations regarding their relative ability (Babad, 1993; Cooper & Good, 1983; Mitman & Lash, 1988; Weinstein, 1993). Elementary school children as young as first graders report differences in teacher treatment of high and low achievers across a number of studies (Marshall & Weinstein, 1984; Weinstein, Marshall, Botkin, & Sharp, 1987; Weinstein, Marshall, Brattesani, & Middlestadt, 1982; Weinstein & Middlestadt, 1979). Children report observing differential treatment from even brief glimpses of teacher behavior (Babad et al., 1991; Babad & Taylor, 1992). In the Weinstein studies, low achievers were described by students as the recipients of more negative feedback ("the teacher scolds him/her for not listening") and more teacher direction ("the teacher watches him/her closely when he/she is working") than high achievers. In contrast, high achievers were perceived as receiving higher expectations ("the teacher trusts him/her") and more opportunity and choice ("the teacher asks him/her to lead activities") than low achievers.

Consistent with observational studies, these children in the Weinstein studies described marked differential treatment in some classrooms ("the teacher expects more out of 'em than us") and more equitable treatment in other classrooms ("in this class, people who used to not be so smart, they're smart now"). Taking account of these perceived classroom differences provides a window on where expectancy effects are maximized. For example, children are more likely to perceive differences in their own treatment (not only teachers' behavior toward others) consistent with their expectancy status in those classrooms where expectancy cues are more salient (Brattesani et al., 1984; Mitman & Lash, 1988).

Differential Teacher Treatment and Student Motivational Outcomes

That children can identify differential treatment by teachers has enormous predictive consequences. For example, in classrooms where children perceive high differential treatment, children's own academic expectations (and ultimately their achievement) more closely matched teachers' expectations than was the case in equitable-treatment class-rooms (Brattesani et al., 1984; Weinstein et al., 1987). This means that in such higher cue classrooms, the gap among children in their beliefs about their future performance is wider. These findings hold true for younger children, but by fifth grade, children for whom teachers held low expectations report more negative ability perceptions in both high and low differential treatment classrooms. Other studies, using observer-derived rather than student-derived measures of differential treatment, confirm these relationships between higher cue classrooms and greater stratification of ability perceptions by children about them-selves and their peers (Filby & Barnett, 1982; MacIver, 1988; Mitman & Lash, 1988; Rosenholtz & Rosenholtz, 1981; Rosenholtz & Wilson, 1980; Stipek & Daniels, 1988).

These findings underscore that certain teaching practices (of which children are aware) widen the circle of perceived low achievers. Importantly, substantial evidence links the perception of "being capa-ble" with a variety of motivational outcomes, such as intrinsic motiva-tion, task orientation, effort expenditure, preference for challenge, and the valuing of achievement (e.g., Ames, 1992; Covington, 1992; Cum-mins, 1986). A fourth grader described this linkage most poignantly:

> Like if the teacher always yells at you whenever you do something wrong—if you don't understand something and she yells at you and says "You should already know"—then you might not do as well. You might say, "Well, I don't like that part." (Weinstein, 1989)

Thus, the effects of expectations about ability come not only from dif-ferential access to learning (which directly impacts achievement), but also from children's awareness of differential treatment and the subse-quent impact on motivation to learn.

Paucity of Preventive Interventions

Despite substantial evidence of expectancy effects and national atten-tion focused on higher and more equitable expectations, empirically derived and evaluated preventive interventions have been relatively few in number. Virtually every textbook in educational psychology alerts prospective teachers to the potentially harmful effects of low expecta-tions. The setting of high expectations has been identified as a critical quality of effective schools (Good & Weinstein, 1986). Current policy reform in many districts targets the untracking of high school classes so as to equalize expectations for all learners (Oakes, 1992). Further, the recent national and statewide standards movement highlights the setting of curriculum standards (high expectations about what children should learn) and built-in accountability (Cohen, 1995).

But despite this call to raise expectations, evidence is scarce about whether these discrete efforts are effective and whether they address the underpinnings of expectancy effects rather than their surface symptoms. Relatively little is known about the "how" of change, that is, the processes critical to the implementation of higher and more equitable expectations. As Babad (1993) suggested, application of expectancy findings must keep pace with the progress made in theoretical and empirical research.

In reviewing intervention efforts to date, Babad (1993) described three types of application: first, the provision of research-derived recommendations to equalize teacher treatment (Brophy, 1983; Cooper & Tom, 1984; Smith & Luginbuhl, 1976); second, controlled studies in which empirically based feedback is given to teachers about observed patterns of differential treatment (Good & Brophy, 1974) or gaps between student and teacher perceptions of differential treatment (Babad, 1990b); and third, school-wide inservice programs that reflect research findings and address teacher awareness of expectancy practices (Gottfredson, Marciniak, Birdseye, & Gottfredson, 1995; Kerman, 1979; Penman, 1982; Proctor, 1984; Weinstein et al., 1991).

Evaluative data are quite rare and, where available, provide limited support for positive change. For example, empirically based feedback given to teachers about their own practice did not always translate into changed behavior or perceptions. Half of Babad's (1990b) treatment teachers resisted the feedback and, following the intervention, student perceptions did not match changes in teachers' reports of treatment. Good and Brophy (1974) documented teacher-treatment changes on participation and interaction behaviors but not on negative behaviors. There was behavioral change among some students, but not perceptual change in the teachers' expectations. Beyond these two controlled studies, the two evaluations of the school-wide Teacher Expectations and Student Achievement (TESA) program, have had equivocal results (Gottfredson et al., 1995; Penman, 1982).

It is important to underscore the underlying features of these applications, which may help explain the equivocal results. The interventions have been largely prescriptive in nature, insight-focused, and behaviorally targeted. Given evidence for the institutional embeddedness of expectancy processes and for the important role of teacher learning, a more comprehensive and participative model for change may be needed.

An Expectancy-Enhancement Model

The model described in this section and depicted in Tables 1 and 2 was drawn from children's empirically derived descriptions of the communication of teacher expectations as well as from the social psychological literature on the optimal conditions for stereotype change and on institutional reform. It reflects the vision of the learner-centered principles in its attention to issues of substantive change (more challenge, intrinsic motivation, and positive relationships) and of processes of change (motivating teachers in order to motivate students).

Eight Features of Expectancy Communication: As Described by Students

There is much to be discovered from what children describe as the *clues* to their relative position in the classroom achievement hierarchy. Some researchers in this area use trained observers rather than children's reports, believing that "what students perceive and experience in the classroom is identical to the reports of these judges" (Babad, 1993, p. 138). Research has documented both agreement and disagreement between student and observed perceptions in perceptions of teacher treatment (Cooper & Good, 1983; Mitman & Lash, 1988). Children's awareness of teacher expectations rests on subtle interactions, often single critical incidents, and on the interaction of events that mitigate or accentuate the ability differences in the emerging classroom culture (Weinstein, 1993). Insights into children's thinking have led to a very different model of expectancy communication in the classroom shaped by student perceptions (Marshall & Weinstein, 1984; Weinstein, 1986, 1993).

According to research based on children's descriptions (Weinstein et al., 1991), at least eight aspects of classroom and school practice impact student experience and provide information to children about expected ability (see Table 1). These features further elaborate the dimensions of Rosenthal's (1973) original four-factor model (input, output, feedback, and climate). Inputs to the instructional environment include (a) the ways in which students are grouped for instruction, (b)

Table 1

Elements of the Expectancy Communication Model

Elements	Differential Practices
Grouping	Grouping by ability (reading groups, tracks) heightens ability comparisons, framing perceived competence.
Curriculum	Certain tasks/curricular tracks heighten ability comparisons.
	Differential task allocation: highs are enriched and lows are remediated; differential curriculum lessens opportunity to learn for lows.
Motivation	Competitive, ego-evaluative reward systems heighten ability comparisons, limit peer interaction, decrease intrinsic motivation.
	Different motivators are used for high (intrinsic) and low (extrinsic) achievers.
Responsibility for Learning	Limited student agency restricts the uncovering of talent and competence, diminishes motivation.
	Differential opportunities for responsibility and choice for high and low achievers
Evaluation	Certain ability beliefs (that intelligence is stable, global, and distributed along a normal curve) limit the provision of varied types of performance opportunities for evaluation, creating single sets of winners and losers.
	Differential allocation of performance opportunities and feedback to highs and lows
Class Relations	Narrow academic agenda frames relationships, creating a bimodal distribution of stars and isolates, devaluing diversity and community.
	Differential allocation of warmth, trust, humor, and concern to high and low achievers
Parent–Class Relations	Limited and narrow communication opportunities (left to problems or parent initiation) create winner–loser families.
	Differential parent–class relationship for high and low achievers

continued

Table 1, continued

Elements	Differential Practices
School–Class Relations	Limited opportunities for participation and recognition at a school-wide level leave chances for success to just the classroom.
	Differential opportunities for school involvement, leadership, and reward for highs and lows

Table from "Expectations and High School Change: Teacher–Researcher Collaboration to Prevent School Failure," by R. S. Weinstein, C. C. Soule, F. Collins, J. Cone, M. Mehlhorn, and K. Simontacchi, 1991, *American Journal of Community Psychology, 19,* p. 337. Copyright 1991 by Plenum Press. Reprinted with permission.

Table 2

Components of Expectancy-Enhancement Strategy

Substantive Target	Learner-generated model of expectancy communication
Process Target	School–university collaborative partnership
	Diversity of membership (teachers, administrators, researchers)
	Regularized, school-based weekly meetings
	Long time perspective
	Shared responsibility for students
	Translate research findings into practice and policy

	Read
	    Observe
	    Design
	    Implement
	    Evaluate
	    Disseminate/Train

	Monitor multilevel outcomes
	    Working environment of teachers and administrators
	    School policies and opportunities
	    Classroom practices
	    Student outcomes

the tasks through which the curriculum is enacted, (c) the motivational strategies that teachers use to engage learning, and (d) the role that students are asked to play in directing their own learning. By integrating outputs and feedback, (e) the evaluation system shapes the beliefs about ability that undergird the evaluation of student work, the nature of the performance opportunities provided to assess capability, and the feedback given. Finally, interactions around tasks and their evaluation take place in the context of relationships at multiple levels (f) within the class, (g) with parents, and (h) within the school, thus creating the climate of schooling.

These features frame the instructional environment for students in at least three important and distinct ways: first, by expanding or constraining learning opportunities for all children; second, by accentuating or minimizing information about student ability; and third, by equally or differentially allocating educational experiences to different groups of children. Children report that membership (i.e., in reading groups, tracks, and pull-out programs) informs them of their relative smartness (Weinstein, 1993). Students note that higher groups are assigned more difficult work, that classroom competition makes some children feel good about themselves and others feel badly, and that high achievers are given more choice and responsibility for their learning. Children are also sensitive to teachers' beliefs about ability, subtle nuances in teacher feedback, the different qualities of relationships teachers have with students and with parents, and the different opportunities students have for whole-school involvement and leadership.

These components of the empirically derived expectancy communication model are clearly interactive and synergistic. Each component has implications for the others; for example, beliefs about ability also guide the construction of curricula and the grouping choices made. Also, instructional choices made in one arena can accentuate or soften the effects of other features of instruction. For example, the effects of flexible and short-term ability grouping in a classroom can be mitigated by the use of heterogeneous families in seating arrangements and other activities (Marshall & Weinstein, 1984).

Instructional and policy choices that widen motivational and learning opportunities for all children serve to create a more positive expectancy climate. Heterogeneous grouping practices with challenging curricula invite more students to meet the challenge (Gamoran, 1987). Motivational climates that stress intrinsic motivation, learning rather than performance goals, and cooperative rather than competitive rewards focus student attention on "what I am doing" and the challenges of the task rather than "how I am doing" (Ames, 1992; Aronson, 1978; Covington, 1992; Slavin, 1983). Increasing student choice and responsibility for learning serves to uncover new talent and to increase intrinsic motivation (Corno, 1993). Beliefs that intelligence is malleable (Dweck & Leggett, 1988), that there are multiple abilities (Gardner, 1983), and that all students can meet a specified standard (Goodlad, 1990) shift the responsibility for failure from students to teachers, broaden the performance opportunities available, and offer absolute rather than relative criteria for accomplishment. Finally, classrooms and schools with more diverse and differentiated opportunities for participation (with the demand for involvement in excess of the person-power to meet it) create the contexts for warmer, more concerned relationships between teachers, students, and parents (Barker & Gump, 1964; Butterworth & Weinstein, 1996).

Thus, the task of creating a positive expectancy climate includes making changes in the following areas: (a) the curriculum (higher order, more meaningful, more participative tasks); (b) in grouping for instruction (heterogeneous, interest-based, flexible groupings); (c) in the opportunities afforded by the evaluation, motivation, and student responsibility structures (varied performance opportunities, recognizing multiple abilities, intrinsic and cooperative learning strategies, student-directed learning opportunities); and (d) in relationships in the classroom, with parents, and within the school (valuing diversity, creating community, sharing expectations, and providing access to schoolwide activities and rewards). These changes, when coordinated and synchronized, serve to focus attention on the development rather than the selection of talent in schooling.

Collaborative Conditions for Expectancy Change

In this model of expectancy change, the scope of identified practices and policies is broader, moving beyond dyadic interaction patterns between teachers and students to the entrenched culture of schooling. Further, the target for intervention includes the enduring system as well as psychological change (Weinstein, Madison, & Kuklinski, 1995).

The research evidence regarding the necessary conditions for psychological change (in the disconfirmation of stereotypes) and social system change (in the creation of a culture of positive expectations) underscores the importance of active and ongoing participation in the change effort. Research on stereotype change points to the context under which negative perceptions are successfully challenged. These include conditions where disconfirming information is systematically made available, analyzed, and generalized (Bar-Tal, 1989; Olsen & Zanna, 1993; Rothbart & John, 1985); motivational goals stress accuracy and accountability (Neuberg, 1989); and interactions are cooperative, co-equal, successful, and lacking in conflict (Desforges, Lord, Ramsey, Mason, & Van Leeuwen, 1991).

Research on organizational reform highlights the important role of involved participants (as reshapers of the innovation in the context of local conditions and as key players in its ultimate institutionalization) and of collaborative workplace conditions that sustain the hard work of system change (Beer & Walton, 1987; Berman & McLaughlin, 1978; McLaughlin, 1990). School reform researchers also point to the need to systematically address the critical interrelationships among levels of the school culture that might thwart the change effort. For example, Maehr and Midgley (1991) underscored the interdependence between teacher attitudes and practices and school-wide policies in delivering consistent motivational messages to students. Epstein (1985) noted the re-segregation of students in the classrooms of desegregated schools, which appeared as a function of teachers' negative attitudes about integration.

Together, these findings suggest the need for moving beyond prescriptive and behavioral approaches targeted at teachers alone toward collaborative approaches that include administrators also. The task at hand is to provide an ongoing context in which negative beliefs can be disconfirmed, positive beliefs developed, and changes made in practices and policies. Thus, the critical components of the expectancy change process included (a) collaborative methods; (b) diverse membership across teachers, administrators, and university researchers; (c) a regularized, weekly, school-based meeting, with additional planning time; (d) a long time perspective; (e) shared responsibility for students; (f) an opportunity to translate research findings into practice and policy; and (g) the monitoring of multilevel outcomes (Weinstein et al., 1995). Table 2 summarizes the components of this expectancy-enhancement strategy.

This hands-on access to research findings, the built-in monitoring and evaluation of school practices, and the diversity of input to the process both expands and challenges sources of information and analysis critical to promoting expectancy disconfirmation. It is also important to note that the ways in which teachers, administrators, and researchers are asked to work together are analogous to the classroom and school climate they plan to create for their students. Enhancing the expectations for students rests on enhancing the expectations (and motivational climate) for teachers and administrators.

Expectancy Enhancement in Action

This model of expectancy enhancement was implemented and evaluated over a 2-year period in an inner-city high school. Full details of this intervention project are reported in two papers (Weinstein et al., 1991; Weinstein, Madison, & Kuklinski, 1995). Highlights of project methodology, intervention processes, and selected results at multiple levels are reported in this section. The purpose is to illustrate how the dynamics of expectancy change reflect the learner-centered psychological principles in action, as applied to teachers and students. Both teachers (the agents of change) and students (the consumers of these reforms) are engaged in a learning process and both experience important motivational outcomes.

Methodology

School Site and Sample
The intervention study took place during 2 academic years (1986–1988) in a mid-sized urban and ethnically diverse high school (minority enrollment of 68%). The student population numbered 1,500, with a certificated staff of 80. All incoming ninth graders assigned to the lowest track of English classes were targeted for the intervention, yielding a sample of 158 students over the 2-year project as contrasted with 154 comparable students from the 2 previous years' of classes. Overall, the student sample was slightly more male than female (54.2% versus 45.8%) and overrepresentative of African Americans and underrepresentative of Asian Americans and European Americans, relative to the school as a whole (68.3% African American, 7.4% Hispanic, 4.2% Asian American, 10.6% European American, and 9.5% unknown).

All participating faculty had volunteered for the project and had 10 or more years of teaching experience. During the first year, collaborators regularly included 12 staff: eight teachers (English, history, science, computer, and special education) and four administrators (counselor, dean, principal, and vice principal). In the second year, there were staff changes (one maternity leave and three administrative reassignments) and withdrawals (three teachers, citing the heavy demands of the project). Thus, by the second year, membership regularly included 10 staff: four of the original teachers (English), two newly joining teachers (history and math), the returning principal, and three new administrators. In both years, meetings were open, drawing visits from other teachers in the school.

The Expectancy-Enhancement Intervention

Entry began in a university seminar opened to the community, with local teachers and administrators invited to join graduate students in applying the literature on expectancy effects toward school reform efforts. Participants read original research, systematically observed expectancy components in a school or classroom, and demonstrated innovative lessons and policies. This design provided a model for subsequent inservice workshops and for the weekly meeting that served as a key component of the intervention. An invitation from a high school teacher in the seminar began the collaborative process. At her initiation, plans were made to offer a three-session inservice (a miniseminar) to her entire school staff as the first step in creating a collaborative group committed to the expectancy-enhancement intervention. The researcher provided the empirically based model of expectancy change, and the school staff framed other aspects of project design unique to the needs of their site.

As negotiated, targeted low-achieving ninth-grade students (at a critical transition period in risk for high school dropout) were programmed into one or more of the classes of participating teachers, thus creating a smaller school within a school. This enabled teachers to share a common pool of students and a common preparation period each day scheduled around the lunch hour, which facilitated daily collaboration. Teachers, administrators, and researchers met in a weekly 2-hour meeting where they read the research literature, monitored the impact of existing programs, and designed, implemented, and evaluated innovations in practices and policies targeting the eight features of expectancy communication in schooling. From these meetings came the materials, programs, lesson plans, and policies that were then implemented in the classrooms and at a school level.

Sources of Data for Evaluation

The evaluation design was collaboratively and creatively negotiated in the face of existing constraints. Lower enrollments of low-track students by the third week of classes led to cancellation of the control group and the adoption of an archival cohort design. Clashes between the autonomous needs of teacher collaborators and the protective rights (for signed informed consent) of the university Human Subjects Committee stalled collection of classroom data.

The ultimate design reflected a mixed quantitative and qualitative quasi-experimental approach, charting both the course of the intervention over time and evidence for change at the multiple levels of student, teacher, and school policy. Researchers collected pre- and postintervention teacher ratings of practices as an intervention check and kept detailed narrative records of the 2 years of weekly meetings involving teachers, administrators, and researchers. Sample meetings from this sequential record were analyzed by two trained coders to chart the course of changes in expectations over time. Researchers also obtained performance, attendance, and disciplinary information from student records at four time periods: preintervention (second semester 8th grade), early intervention (first semester 9th grade), postintervention (second semester 9th grade), and at one-year follow-up (second semester 10th grade) for project students and for a comparable cohort.

Implementation Highlights

Perceived Constraints in Raising Expectations

The locus of the expectancy change effort occurred in the context of the weekly collaborative meeting between participating teachers, administrators, and researchers. At the start, although members met around a common goal and negotiated the specific features of the intervention (adapting the expectancy model to local conditions), they perceived themselves "as individuals in isolation, not as colleagues in collaboration" (Weinstein et al., 1995).

Enormous skepticism emerged regarding members' potential efficacy with regard to the project. This skepticism concerned perceived obstacles in students, teachers, the system, and the project that would thwart any efforts made. Frequently, the problems identified were substantively similar across the levels and reflected dimensions identical to those identified in the expectancy-communication model. As one example drawn from the narrative records, the perceived limitations of teachers mirrored negative views about students:

> It was noted that, even if the group committed to the work being asked for, some teachers would not be willing to make the time

commitment and some teachers would not be able to profit from it. The researcher noted that these comments had been made before and were similar to negative expectations teachers entertain about students. Some teachers responded that, in their defense, some negative attitudes were justified, about both teachers and students. (Weinstein et al., 1995, p. 137)

Beyond beliefs about limited capabilities, other examples reflected constraints inherent in the teacher tracking system ("they were taking on the most difficult groups in school, ones that other teachers wouldn't work with") and in the competitive and noncollaborative climate of the school ("the inference is I've done that, well, you mean you haven't done that!"). Still other constraints suggested resistance to teacher agency ("I understand that you set up a program to help me discover things for myself, but I guess I wanted to be fed information"), and the uneasy relationships between teachers and administrators ("filled with misunderstandings and differing perspectives").

A Collaborative Reframing of Limiting Perceptions

Despite the initial and recurring skepticism, the engagement in regular meetings, the diversity of group membership, and the infusion of new and challenging information proved critical in creating a context for the exchange of ideas. In contrast to the earlier expressed isolation (e.g., "one teacher said that she could not use other people's ideas directly but needed to develop her own materials"; Weinstein et al., 1995, p. 137), group members were now jumping in to offer alternative interpretations of the problems and to share innovative strategies. One example of this collaborative exchange is as follows:

> One teacher complained of resistance to groups, e.g., kids (despite prior statements about cooperation and rule-setting) who still banter about not liking that person, not working with that person . . . this was followed by the constant need for her to patrol groups to keep them on task. Another teacher suggested that "perhaps we ask too much at first," i.e., time frame too short (e.g., 1–3 days). The first teacher noted that she hadn't run any ice-breaking activities but had plunged into academic work. (Weinstein et al., 1995, p. 141)

This teacher's intervention suggested that it was the teacher's actions, rather than limitations in the students, that may have thwarted student performance in cooperative groups. The first teacher was able to use this interpretation to analyze her lesson sequence and to make appropriate changes. This reattribution from student deficit to teaching practice was pivotal in setting conditions whereby negative perceptions of students could be disconfirmed.

This ongoing collaboration offered enormous support to the school staff in reframing obstacles and planning alternative actions. As one teacher described this support, "It was easier to take risks in the classroom with project backup. You don't throw things out if they don't succeed immediately" (Weinstein et al., 1995, p. 142).

Expanding Teachers' Roles

The changes that occurred across the 2 years of the project included a broadening of teachers' professional roles (as colleague, grant writer, teacher mentor, and researcher). Project members expressed more positive and open attitudes toward colleagues ("the collaborative nature of the project equals support"; "I've become open and vulnerable to support and criticism from my colleagues in the project"). Teachers worked actively to enlarge and secure the participation of a greater number of colleagues, departments, and administrative staff. Teachers became more persistent in negotiating administrative involvement and policy changes. Project members competed for and won both district and national grants for their work. They also began to communicate their findings through mentorship and inservice programs both within and outside of the school district as well as through writing (see, e.g., Cone, 1989).

A highlight of the shared writing came in the presentation of a symposium to a national conference. One of the teachers wrote about the excitement of the writing itself:

> Little did we expect how much the writing would mean to us. As we wrote, we reflected on the growth that we had experienced as teachers, the effect we had had on our school, and the success our students had shown ... I can clearly remember the first day we got together to read our individual papers to each other. All of us fought back tears as we realized how much we had grown and how much we owed that growth to each other. (Cone, 1989)

This particular teacher became an active teacher–researcher contributing extensively to the literature on untracking high school classes. The parallel between the teachers' experiences (of meaningful work and of growth-producing collaboration) and their capacity to create these same conditions for students is evident here.

The Challenge of Engaging the School as a Whole

There were enormous obstacles, however, that were never overcome in the relatively short time frame of 2 years. As described, the model evolved in stages and thus was never fully implemented as designed.

Some teachers withdrew their involvement, given the heavy workload of the project and disillusionment over the administrative hurdles. Gaining administrative participation co-equal to that of the teachers proved daunting. Obstacles to administrative participation included frequent administrative reassignments; a reactive, crisis style of administration leading to frequent absences from meetings; and the differing agenda of the district that clashed with a teacher-directed project. Although the project did attract more teachers and did achieve highly visible policy changes in detracking English classes, without consistent administrative support, the project could not gain a strong foothold across the entire school and hence remained a project within the school.

Change in Expectancy Climate and Student Outcomes

A More Positive Expectancy Environment for Students

Had expectations changed for these low-achieving students and were they the recipients of more positive and challenging teaching practices and policies? Over time, as captured in the narrative records of meetings, teachers began to communicate more complex, differentiated, and positive views of student abilities. Early on, talk focused on the deficits that these students brought to the classroom in terms of the low motivation, negative self-image, lack of skills, and poor behavior. But as the collaboration progressed (as rated by coders), discussion of student obstacles to learning declined and teachers talked more about student capabilities. The shift toward a capability focus is clear in the following excerpt from a discussion about one teacher's remedial English students:

> I don't know if you collect student papers as evidence that below grade level students can think but if you do, these are to me startling examples—both boys are reading at the fifth to sixth grade level. Their papers bowled me over. I don't think that my honors kids will do better. (Weinstein et al., 1991, p. 350)

Talk turned toward the actions teachers could take to solve the problems they experienced with students (Weinstein et al., 1995). For example, one teacher shared that "she was dissatisfied with the effort and productivity in her editing groups and decided that future groups needed more structure" (Weinstein et al., 1995, p. 141).

This change in beliefs about students was further supported by the results from a 44-item teacher-practices survey. This survey, completed early and late in the first intervention year, documented a trend for the predicted increase over time in positive expectancy behaviors (e.g., "each student has varied performance opportunities, which call for different abilities") across the eight domains of the model. Table 3 documents examples of the innovations introduced. The narrative records also underscored evolving but systematic attempts by each teacher to implement each component of the model. By their own characterization, some teachers felt more successful than others and some components proved trickier to implement (e.g., changes in parent–classroom relationships).

Finally, over time, the project pioneered new school policies regarding the tracking of students. Beginning within the context of a highly tracked system—where the English classes for project students did not count for college preparatory credit (a fact not known to these students)—the project members negotiated a series of policy changes, successively broadening the curricular challenge for these low-achieving students. These changes included retroactive college-prep credit on transcripts for successfully completing the project classes, assignment in the second year to college-bound classes, integration of low-stanine students into average-achievement classes, and finally, an open enrollment policy for college placement English classes based on interest and a work contract rather than on test scores.

Student Outcomes

To what extent were students aware of higher, more favorable expectations? Anecdotal information from an outside evaluation of the program provides some provocative evidence. Students described project teachers as "making sure you do your work," and felt "our teachers care, they make you feel comfortable" and "they expect you to finish whole books, discuss them, write about them" (Weinstein et al., 1991). In another example, one student wrote,

> In Mrs. ____'s class—one of my favorite teachers—she make me feel good about myself and she doesn't say well you ought to just stick with something simple. She just let's you think about it and if you would like to take the challenge and if you think that you could actually do it, then she would encourage you to do so (Freedman, 1989, cited in Weinstein et al., 1991, p. 346)

With regard to evidence for increased student motivation and involvement in schooling, the narrative records revealed a variety of examples (Weinstein et al., 1991). In one class, students were described as arriving at school early to use the computers for their writing assign-

Table 3

Innovative Positive Expectancy Practices Implemented

Elements	Innovative Practices
Curriculum	Enriched curriculum materials—adapting readings from honors classes Enriched methods of instruction—editing groups for writing, teams to create history materials
Grouping	Regrouping strategies to help all students work with everyone Heterogeneous grouping—moving selected students to honors classes, encouraging student involvement in school activities Keeping opportunities open—retroactive college prep credit policy if earned
Evaluation	Broadening performance opportunities to increase success—role plays, drama, class newsletter, peer teaching Shared positive feedback across teachers
Motivation	Cooperative rather than competitive teaching strategies—team learning Focus on intrinsic motivation—encouraging student interest (community service project, choice in reading, writing)
Reponsibility for learning	More active student participation—making choices, taking leadership in peer work groups, providing feedback to peers Training in work study skills, conflict management strategies
Class relations	Developing individual relationships with each student—individual conferences, writing assignments about being a ninth grader and school success Encouraging diversity of talent and views
Parent–class relations	Reaching out to parents and bringing parents in—calls to parents with positive news, joint teacher–parent–student conferences, special evening meetings, class newsletter focused on parent writing and questions
School–class relations	Encouraging student participation in school activities—special speakers (coaches, minority student models), creation of community service program

Table from "Expectations and High School Change: Teacher–Researcher Collaboration to Prevent School Failure," by R. S. Weinstein, C. C. Soule, F. Collins, J. Cone, M. Mehlhorn, and K. Simontacchi, 1991, *American Journal of Community Psychology, 19*, p. 345. Copyright 1991 by Plenum Press. Reprinted with permission.

ments. Based on their deep engagement in collaborative writing, one passing teacher mistook the project class for an honors program. Other examples included reports of students applauding each others' work, sharing their accomplishments across project teachers, and expressing excitement about the honors-level materials. Project teachers perceived higher student attendance at school athletic events, and deans perceived fewer referrals for disciplinary actions from project students. Also, for the first time in the school's history, two of the freshman class officers elected to the student council came from project classes.

With regard to achievement and related behaviors, analyses revealed that, after controlling for entering achievement differences, project students obtained higher grades in English and history, higher overall GPAs, and a greater decrease in disciplinary referrals, but not a lower absence rate, in contrast with comparable cohort of students from previous years. These effects (except for absences) can be understood as mediated by changes in teacher perceptions. While not unimportant (as an impact on the school environment, evidenced in deans' perceptions of reduced disciplinary infractions), they reflect only the first step of expectancy confirmation (perceptual confirmation).

Behavioral evidence can be seen in the one-year follow-up data where by the end of tenth grade, only half as many project students (18.6%) had transferred out of the school (to other schools, alternative settings, or dropped out) as compared to 37.7% of the contrast students. This reflects perhaps the greater holding or motivational power of the school for the project students, postintervention. For the continuing students, however, the significant lead they had established in English grades and GPA (although in the predicted direction) was not maintained with nonproject teachers in the next year, nor did their absence rate differ from comparison students. The unevenness of these follow-up findings (greater holding power, but not significantly higher performance) can be explained by two possible confounding factors. The lower attrition rate of project students might have led to a wider band of low achievers among the continuing project students, as contrasted with the continuing comparison students. In addition, these continuing project students (but not comparison students) were also placed in college-bound classes for the first time, and thereby were provided with more challenge and graded in contrast to higher performing students. Both these factors could potentially mask the higher achievement of the project students postintervention.

On What Was Learned

This collaborative expectancy-enhancement intervention resulted in a negotiated and evolving implementation that posed creative challenges to evaluation. Without a control school, one can only suggest that the changes qualitatively documented in teacher thinking, classroom practices, and school policies derived from the intervention itself. However, in the measurement of student change, given an archival cohort sample for comparison, the ground is stronger—both perceived by project teachers (perceptual confirmation) and observed, with regard to the holding power of the school, one full year postintervention (behavioral confirmation).

It is also possible that, given the evolving implementation, the model was not evaluated at a point of fullest strength. Or it can be argued that, given the high-risk group of students targeted and a high absence rate that team members could not affect, one year of a positive expectancy climate at this late date in these students' school careers was an insufficiently strong intervention, in and of itself. Nonetheless, because of the consistencies of changes both across levels of the school and as predicted by expectancy theory, the evidence available does hold considerable promise about the potential of this approach for expectancy change.

Expectancy Change as Exemplifying Learner-Centered Principles

This chapter underscores the important and largely ignored role of student perceptions in illuminating both the dynamics of self-fulfilling prophecy effects in schooling and the often missed institutional nature of expressed expectations about ability. Substantial evidence also links an integrative set of differentiated teaching practices and school policies to greater stratification in children's self-perceptions as capable learners and children's motivation to learn. It is precisely around the enhancement of these critical child-mediating processes of positive emotion, self-view, excitement, and interest that learner-centered school reform is framed. And it is these learner processes that are at enormous risk in environments of low or sharply differentiated expectations for learning.

This chapter also highlights the reciprocal relationship between the working and learning conditions for teachers and the learning context for students in classrooms. Consistent, stimulating, and supportive conditions for school staff to question their expectations for students —not only in addressing beliefs about ability but also in examining teaching practices and policies—were critical to promoting a positive expectancy climate. Perceived obstacles were translated into opportunities, as teachers collaboratively reframed their work with students, other teachers, and the administration. Narrative records reported that school staff addressed intellectually challenging tasks in collaborative ways, with ultimately positive emotions about how much they had learned. Their experience as learners helped them stimulate these same experiences for students.

As others have noted about collaborative workplace conditions for teachers, such conditions enhance teachers' sense of efficacy (Little, 1993; Rosenholtz, 1989). Teachers' beliefs about their capacity to influence student learning have also been found to be critical to promoting student achievement (Ashton & Webb, 1986). Also, as Sarason (1990) has so forcefully argued, "it is virtually impossible to create and sustain over time conditions for productive learning for students when they do not exist for teachers" (p. 145).

In charting the direction for school reform, the APA Presidential Task Force on Psychology in Education (APA, 1993) concluded that

> the learner-centered principles cannot be treated in isolation when deriving policy implications. Taken together, these principles describe a new view of the learner, the learning process, and implications for instruction. (p. 13)

Thus, the challenge, for example, "of providing high standards and optimistic expectations for all students while respecting cultural diversity, developmental variations, and other individual differences" (APA, 1993, p. 12) requires a learner-centered systems approach to instruction, curriculum, assessment, management, teacher education, parent and community involvement, and policy.

The awareness of differential expectations and differential treatment in schooling is only the first step. And the targeting of specific and discrete teaching behaviors for change does not reach quite far enough. Reform efforts will have to address this issue systemically and consistently across multiple features of schooling in order to create positive expectations for all children. Multiple challenges remain such as the need to enlist teachers and administrators as co-equal participants in school reform. Without joint responsibility, efforts to realign school policy and classroom practice in mutually supportive and consistent ways will likely fail. Nonetheless, more positive expectations for students rest on more positive, motivating conditions for teachers and administrators. Their opportunities for meaningful work in sustained and supportive collaborative relationships are critical to the reframing of low and negative expectations in schooling and to the development of a positive climate for motivated learning.

References

American Psychological Association Board of Educational Affairs. (1995, Dec.). *Learner-centered psychological principles: A framework for school redesign and reform* [On-line]. Available: http://www.apa.org/ed/lcp.html.

American Psychological Association Presidential Task Force on Psychology in Education. (1993, January). *Learner-centered psychological principles: Guidelines for school redesign and reform.* Washington, DC: American Psychological Association and Mid-Continent Regional Educational Laboratory.

Ames, C. (1992). Classrooms: Goals, structures, and student motivation. *Journal of Educational Psychology, 84,* 261–271.

Aronson, E. (1978). *The jigsaw classroom.* Beverly Hills, CA: Sage.

Ashton, P. T., & Webb, R. B. (1986). *Making a difference: Teachers' sense of efficacy and student achievement.* White Plains, NY: Longman.

Babad, E. Y. (1990a). Calling on students: How a teachers' behavior can acquire disparate meanings in students' minds. *Journal of Classroom Interaction, 25,* 1–4.

Babad, E. Y. (1990b). Measuring and changing teachers' differential behavior as perceived by students and teachers. *Journal of Educational Psychology, 82,* 683–690.

Babad, E. Y. (1993). Pygmalion—25 years after interpersonal expectations in the classroom. In P. D. Blanck (Ed.), *Interpersonal expectations: Theory, research, and application* (pp. 125–153). London: Cambridge University Press.

Babad, E. Y., Bernieri, F., & Rosenthal, R. (1989). Nonverbal communication and leakage in the behavior of biased and unbiased teachers. *Journal of Personality and Social Psychology, 56,* 89–84.

Babad, E. Y., Bernieri, F., & Rosenthal, R. (1991). Students as judges of teachers' verbal and nonverbal behavior. *American Educational Research Journal, 28,* 211–234.

Babad, E. Y., Inbar, J., & Rosenthal, R. (1982). Pygmalion, Galatea, and the Golem: Investigations of biased and unbiased teachers. *Journal of Educational Psychology, 74,* 459–474.

Babad, E. Y., & Taylor, P. J. (1992). Transparency of teacher expectancies across language, cultural boundaries. *Journal of Educational Research, 86,* 120–125.

Barker, R. G., & Gump, P. V. (1964). *Big school, small school: High school size and student behavior.* Stanford, CA: Stanford University Press.

Barr, R., & Dreeben (1983). *How schools work.* Chicago: The University of Chicago Press.

Bar-Tal, Y. (1989). Can leaders change followers' stereotypes? In D. Bar-Tal, C. F. Graumann, A. W. Kruglanski, and W. Stroebe (Eds.), *Stereotyping and prejudice: Changing conceptions* (pp. 225–242). New York: Springer-Verlag.

Beer, M., & Walton, A. E. (1987). Organizational change and development. *Annual Review of Psychology, 38,* 339–367.

Berman, P., & McLaughlin, M. (1978). *Rethinking the federal role in education.* Santa Monica, CA: Rand Corporation.

Blanck, P. D. (Ed.). (1993). *Interpersonal expectations: Theory, research, and applications.* Cambridge, England: Cambridge University Press.

Brattesani, K. A., Weinstein, R. S., & Marshall, H. H. (1984). Student perceptions of differential teacher treatment as moderators of teacher expectation effects. *Journal of Educational Psychology, 76,* 236–247.

Brophy, J. E. (1983). Research on the self-fulfilling prophecy and teacher expectations. *Journal of Educational Psychology, 75,* 631–661.

Brophy, J. E., & Good, T. L. (1970). Teachers' communication of differential expectations for children's classroom performance: Some behavioral data. *Journal of Educational Psychology, 61,* 365–374.

Brophy, J. E., & Good, T. L. (1974). *Teacher–student relationships: Causes and consequences.* New York: Holt, Rinehart & Winston.

Butterworth, B., & Weinstein, R. S. (1996). Enhancing motivational opportunity in elementary schooling: A case study of the ecology of principal leadership. *The Elementary School Journal, 97,* 57–80.

Cohen, D. K. (1995). What is the system in systemic reform? *Educational Researcher, 24,* 11–17.

Cone, J. (1989, March). *The teacher and motivation researcher relationship: Bridging the gap.* Paper presented at the Annual Meeting of the American Educational Research Association, San Francisco, CA.

Cooper, H. M. (1979). Pygmalion grows up: A model for teacher expectation communication and performance influence. *Review of Educational Research, 49,* 389–410.

Cooper, H. M., & Good, T. L. (1983). *Pygmalion grows up: Studies in the expectation communication process.* New York: Longman.

Cooper, H. M., & Tom, D. Y. H. (1984). Teacher expectation research: A review with implications for classroom instruction. *The Elementary School Journal, 85,* 77–89.

Corno, L. (1993). The best-laid plans: Modern conceptions of volition and educational research. *Educational Researcher, 22,* 14–22.

Covington, M. V. (1992). *Making the grade: A self-worth perspective on motivation and school reform.* Cambridge, England: Cambridge University Press.

Cummins, J. (1986). Empowering minority students: A framework for intervention. *Harvard Educational Review, 56,* 18–36.

Darley, J. M., & Fazio, R. H. (1980). Expectancy confirmation processes arising in the social interaction sequence. *American Psychologist, 35,* 867–881.

Desforges, D. M., Lord, C. G., Ramsey, S. L., Mason, J. A., & Van Leeuwen, M. D. (1991). Effects of structured cooperative contact on changing negative attitudes toward stigmatized social groups. *Journal of Personality and Social Psychology, 60,* 531–544.

Dusek, J. B., & Joseph, G. (1983). The bases of teacher expectancies: A meta-analysis. *Journal of Educational Psychology, 75,* 327–346.

Dweck, C., & Leggett, E. (1988). A social-cognitive approach to motivation and personality. *Psychological Review, 95,* 256–273.

Eden, D. (1992). Leadership and expectations: Pygmalion effects and other self-fulfilling prophecies in organizations. *Leadership Quarterly, 3,* 271–305.

Epstein, J. L. (1985). After the bus arrives: Resegregation in desegregated schools. *Journal of Social Issues, 41,* 23–43.

Filby, N. N., & Barnett, B. G. (1982). Student perceptions of "better readers" in elementary classrooms. *The Elementary School Journal, 82,* 435–449.

Franklin, B. M. (1994). *From "backwardness" to "at-risk": Childhood learning difficulties and the contradictions of school reform.* Albany: The State University of New York Press.

Gamoran, A. (1987). The stratification of high school learning opportunities. *Sociology of Education, 60,* 135–155.

Gardner, H. (1983). *Frames of mind: The theory of multiple intelligences*. New York: Basic.

Good, T. L., & Brophy, J. E. (1974). Changing teacher and student behavior: An empirical examination. *Journal of Educational Psychology, 66*, 390–405.

Good, T. L., & Weinstein, R. S. (1986). Schools make a difference: Evidence, criticisms, and new directions. *American Psychologist, 41*, 1090–1097.

Goodlad, J. I. (1990). *Teachers for our nation's schools*. San Francisco: Jossey-Bass.

Gottfredson, D. C., Marciniak, E. M., Birdseye, A. T., & Gottfredson, G. D. (1995). Increasing teacher expectations for student achievement. *The Journal of Educational Research, 88*, 155–163.

Harris, M. J., & Rosenthal, R. (1985). Mediation of interpersonal expectancy effects: 31 meta-analyses. *Psychological Bulletin, 97*, 363–386.

Jussim, L. (1986). Self-fulfilling prophecies: A theoretical and integrative review. *Psychological Review, 93*, 429–445.

Jussim, L. (1989). Teacher expectations: Self-fulfilling prophecies, perceptual biases, and accuracy. *Journal of Personality and Social Psychology, 57*, 469–480.

Jussim, L. (1991). Social perception and social reality: A reflection–construction model. *Psychological Review, 98*, 54–73.

Jussim, L., Madon, S., & Chatman, C. (1994). Teacher expectations and student achievement: Self-fulfilling prophecies, biases, and accuracy. In L. Heath, R. S. Tindale, J. Edwards, E. J. Posavac, F. B. Bryant, E. Henderson-King, Y. Suarez-Balcazar, & J. Myers (Eds.), *Applications of heuristics and biases to social issues* (pp. 303–334). New York: Plenum.

Kerman, S. (1979). Teacher expectations and student achievement. *Phi Delta Kappan, 60*, 716–718.

Little, J. W. (1993). Teachers' professional development in a climate of educational reform. *Educational Evaluation and Policy Analysis, 15*, 129–151.

MacIver, D. (1988). Classroom environments and the stratification of pupils' ability perceptions. *Journal of Educational Psychology, 80*, 495–505.

Maehr, M. L., & Midgley, C. (1991). Enhancing student motivation: A school-wide approach. *Educational Psychologist, 26*, 399–427.

Marshall, H. H., & Weinstein, R. S. (1984). Classroom factors affecting students' self-evaluations: An interactional model. *Review of Educational Research, 54*, 301–325.

McLaughlin, M. W. (1990). The Rand Change Agent Study revisited: Macro perspectives and micro perspectives. *Educational Researcher, 19*, 11–16.

Meier, K. J., Stewart, J., Jr., & England, R. E. (1989). *Race, class, and education: The politics of second-generation discrimination*. Madison: The University of Wisconsin Press.

Mitman, A. L., & Lash, A. A. (1988). Students' perceptions of their academic standing and classroom behavior. *The Elementary School Journal, 89*, 55–68.

Neuberg, S. L. (1989). The goal of forming accurate impressions during social interactions: Attenuating the impact of negative expectancies. *Journal of Personality and Social Psychology, 56*, 374–386.

Oakes, J. (1987). Tracking in the secondary schools: A contextual perspective. *Educational Psychologist, 22*, 129–153.

Oakes, J. (1992). Can tracking research inform practice?: Technical, normative, and political considerations. *Educational Researcher, 21*, 12–21.

Oakland, T. (1992). School dropouts: Characteristics and prevention. *Applied and Preventive Psychology, 1*, 201–208.

Olsen, J. M., & Zanna, M. P. (1993). Attitudes and attitude change. *Annual Review of Psychology, 44*, 117–154.

Penman, P. R. (1982). *The efficacy of TESA training in changing teacher behaviors and attitudes toward low achievers.* Unpublished doctoral dissertation, Arizona State University, Phoenix.

Porter, R. P. (1990). *Forked tongue: The politics of bilingual education.* New York: Basic.

Proctor, C. P. (1984). Teacher expectations: A model for school improvement. *The Elementary School Journal, 84,* 469–481.

Raudenbush, S. W. (1984). Magnitude of teacher expectancy effects on pupil IQ as a function of the credibility of expectancy induction: A synthesis of findings from 18 experiments. *Journal of Educational Psychology, 76,* 85–97.

Rist, R. (1970). Student social class and teacher expectations: The self-fulfilling prophecy in ghetto education. *Harvard Educational Review, 40,* 411–451.

Rosenholtz, S. J. (1989). *Teachers' workplace: The social organization of schools.* White Plains, NY: Longman.

Rosenholtz, S. J., & Rosenholtz, S. H. (1981). Classroom organization and the perception of ability. *Sociology of Education, 54,* 132–140.

Rosenholtz, S. J., & Wilson, B. (1980). The effect of classroom structure on shared perceptions of ability. *American Educational Research Journal, 17,* 75–82.

Rosenthal, R. (1973). *On the social psychology of the self-fulfilling prophecy: Further evidence for Pygmalion effects and their mediating mechanisms.* New York: MSS Modular Publications.

Rosenthal, R., & Jacobson, L. (1968). *Pygmalion in the classroom.* New York: Holt, Rinehart and Winston.

Rothbart, M., & John, O. P. (1985). Social categorization and behavioral episodes: A cognitive analysis of the effects of intergroup contact. *Journal of Social Issues, 41,* 81–104.

Sadker, M., Sadker, D., & Klein, S. (1991). The issue of gender in elementary school education. *Review of Research in Education, 17,* 269–334.

Sarason, S. B. (1990). *The predictable failure of educational reform.* San Francisco: Jossey-Bass.

Sarason, S. B. (1995). *Parental involvement and the political principle.* San Francisco: Jossey-Bass.

Schorr, L. B. (1988). *Within our reach: Breaking the cycle of disadvantage.* New York: Doubleday.

Slavin, R. E. (1983). *Cooperative learning.* White Plains, NY: Longman.

Smith, F. J., & Luginbuhl, J. E. R. (1976). Inspecting expectancy: Some laboratory results of relevance for teacher training. *Journal of Educational Psychology, 68,* 265–272.

Smith, M. L. (1980). Teacher expectations. *Evaluation in Education, 4,* 53–55.

Snyder, M. (1984). When belief creates reality. In L. Berkowitz (Ed.), *Advances in experimental social psychology* (Vol. 16, pp. 248–305). New York: Academic Press.

Stewart, D. W. (1993). *Immigration and education.* New York: Lexington Books.

Stipek, D. J., & Daniels, D. (1988). Declining perceptions of competence: A consequence of changes in the child or the educational environment? *Journal of Educational Psychology, 80,* 352–356.

Weinstein, R. S. (1986). The teaching of reading and children's awareness of teacher expectations. In Taffy E. Raphael (Ed.), *The contexts of school-based literacy* (pp. 233–252). New York: Random House.

Weinstein, R. S. (1989). Perceptions of classroom processes and student motivation: Children's views of self-fulfilling prophecies. In R. Ames and C. Ames (Eds.), *Research on Motivation in Education* (Vol. 3, pp. 187–221). New York: Academic Press.

Weinstein, R. S. (1993). Children's knowledge of differential treatment in school: Implications for motivation. In T. Tomlinson (Ed.), *Motivating student to learn* (pp. 197–224). Berkeley, CA: McCutchan.

Weinstein, R. S., Madison, S., & Kuklinski, M. (1995). Raising expectations in schooling: Obstacles and opportunities for change. *American Educational Research Journal, 32,* 121–159.

Weinstein, R. S., Marshall, H. H., Botkin, M., & Sharp, L. (1987). Pygmalion and the student: Age and classroom differences in children's awareness of teacher expectations. *Child Development, 58,* 1079–1093.

Weinstein, R. S., Marshall, H. H., Brattesani, K., & Middlestadt, S. E. (1982). Student perceptions of differential teacher treatment in open and traditional classrooms. *Journal of Educational Psychology, 74,* 678–692.

Weinstein, R. S., & Middlestadt, S. E. (1979). Student perceptions of teacher interactions with high and low achievers. *Journal of Educational Psychology, 71,* 421–431.

Weinstein, R. S., Soule, C. C., Collins, F., Cone, J., Mehlhorn, M., & Simontacchi, K. (1991). Expectations and high school change: Teacher–researcher collaboration to prevent school failure. *American Journal of Community Psychology, 19,* 333–363.

5

Cognitive Principles Applied to the Development of Literacy

Linda R. Kroll

This chapter looks primarily at how developmental psychology can help researchers and educators understand learning within the domain of literacy, looking in particular at one aspect of learning to write. Using examples from children's writing samples, I show first how developmental psychology can be pertinent to and serve the needs of effective teaching, and second how the learner-centered psychological principles, which form the framework for this book, are related to the use of developmental psychology to understand both learning and teaching. My research is focused on how children become writers and has been formed and guided by principles of developmental psychology, particularly the work of Jean Piaget (1965). There are several ways in which his theory has shaped my own research in the development of writing. This chapter describes three of them, with particular focus on how developmental psychology can inform educational research.

One basic premise of Piaget's (e.g., see Piaget, 1969) theory is that knowledge is constructed by the individual as a result of interactions between the individual and the environment. For those of us who call ourselves constructivists this premise may seem so obvious that it need not be mentioned. However, if one assumes that all knowledge is constructed in this way, then the ramifications for instruction are legion and require careful consideration. Most school instruction is not based on such an assumption, but rather assumes that knowledge can be transmitted by telling.

Learning to write is a developmental process resulting from the interaction between the child's knowledge and the literary environment to which the child is exposed. This construction process begins long before children enter school, with their first exposure to books, signs, ads, labels, and the trappings of an urban literary environment (Ferreiro, 1978; Harste, Woodward, & Burke, 1984; Heath, 1983). Thus, children enter school with a great deal of knowledge about literacy; yet, in most teaching situations, this knowledge is ignored or discounted. Teachers make assumptions about children's lack of knowledge because it is clear that most children do not come to school with conventional knowledge about reading and writing.

How to find out what knowledge children do have is one of Piaget's contributions. Although his research did not cover literacy development, his method of examining children's knowledge and understanding, the method of critical exploration, has been invaluable in investigating this development. Researchers have observed, collected, and analyzed young children's early writing attempts in an effort to document and understand the process of learning to write. The developmental aspects of this process are represented in the research of, among others, Ferreiro (1978, 1984, 1986; Ferreiro & Teberosky, 1982), Sulzby (1987; Sulzby, Barnhart, & Hieshima, 1989; Teale & Sulzby, 1987), and Dyson (1985, 1989a, 1989b, 1989c). Ferreiro, on the basis of the Piagetian model of research, conducted an extensive study of the development of children's understanding of the alphabetic principle (that the sounds of speech, rather than the meaning of speech, are represented in writing) using the method of critical exploration.

The main focus of this chapter is on how this method of critical exploration can be used in a longitudinal study to trace the development of certain aspects of learning to write over a 5-year period.

I have said that teachers traditionally assume that children have no knowledge when they lack conventional knowledge of literacy issues. (It is important to note that this idea is changing, and the whole language movement in education is helping to promote a more constructivist and developmental viewpoint in the teaching of reading and writing. However, this movement is by no means the norm in literacy instruction.) The result of this assumption is that teachers teach reading and writing in a piecemeal fashion, separating out the mechanical and technical aspects of literacy from the meaningful, social aspects, putting the whole together 2 or 3 years after instruction has begun. The consequences are most serious in the teaching of writing in which early instruction is often seen as primarily training in handwriting and spelling. In contrast, if one takes the developmental point of view that children think and understand things not quantitatively less than adults but qualitatively differently from adults, then instruction must be more holistic, constantly addressing the whole as well as the parts. Ferreiro (1984) made a crucial observation when she pointed out that when children are learning to read, they are trying to understand not just the parts of the system, but that they are constantly trying to reconstruct the system. "They try to understand not only the elements or the results but also, and above all, the very nature of the system " (p. 172).

If one believes that indeed children are constantly trying to understand the nature of the system of literacy, then the nature of their understanding of this system as they reconstruct it for themselves is the crucial aspect to understand. The method of critical exploration can be used for just this purpose. The examples discussed here show how that can be done.

The final contribution of developmental theory to understanding writing development that I discuss herein is the relationship between the development of logical thinking and writing development. Basic logical functions that have been studied in detail by Piaget such as part–whole coordination (e.g., Inhelder & Piaget, 1964), one-to-one correspondence (e.g., Piaget, 1965), seriation (both temporal and spatial; e.g., Inhelder & Piaget, 1964; Piaget & Inhelder, 1967), and classification (e.g., Inhelder & Piaget, 1964) contribute to the development of knowledge within specific domains of knowledge, including the development of literacy. One area of interest in this study is how such logical functions are related to and used in the development of writing.

These three points—the use of the method of critical exploration for research in a specific domain of knowledge, the assumption that children's knowledge is qualitatively rather than quantitatively different from adults' knowledge, and the relationship between logical thinking development and development in a specific domain of knowledge— indicate how influential developmental psychology can be in understanding development in basic school subjects. My purpose in this chapter is first to demonstrate how the method of critical exploration can be used to research and understand how children's concepts of writing change, and second to show how logical thinking is connected to this development.

It should be evident, even from this preliminary discussion, that the revised learner-centered psychological principles (American Psychological Association [APA] Board of Educational Affairs, 1995) that constitute the framework of this volume are consonant with the points drawn from

---

Exhibit 1

Strands of Development in Writing

Strand type	Description
Physical	Representation of text on the page; letter orientation; organization of space; small motor coordination; use of capitals and lowercase letters
Symbolic	Writing represents the sound rather than the meaning of language; invented spelling; invented punctuation
Semantic	Understanding and constructing the meaning of text in writing; relationship between what is written down and what the writer means; physical and symbolic structures the child constructs to make his or her meaning clear; the use of literary models and genres; the different functions of writing and written text
Social	Construction of the communicative aspects of written language; the development of the notion of audience; the context in which writing occurs

---

developmental psychological theory. The assumptions underlying the research perspective, that learners construct knowledge for meaningful purposes and that they attempt to make sense of a whole system, are consonant with cognitive and metacognitive factors, in particular with the nature of the learning process, the goals of the learning process, and the construction of knowledge. Later, I show that constructivist teaching that is based on an understanding of children's literacy development is supported by other aspects of the learner-centered principles.

In my research I have identified four strands of development in writing: physical, symbolic, semantic, and social (Black, Ammon, & Kroll, 1987; Black & Kroll, 1989; see Exhibit 1). The *physical* strand refers to how the child physically represents text on the page and includes consideration of such issues as letter orientation, organization of space, small motor coordination, and use of capitals and lower case letters. The *symbolic* strand refers to how the child uses the symbolic aspects of written language, particularly the development of the idea that writing represents the sound rather than the meaning of language. Issues involving the use of invented spelling and invented punctuation are included in this strand. The *semantic* strand refers to how children understand and construct the meaning of text in writing. Included in this strand is the child's understanding of the relationship between what is written down and what the writer means, the kinds of physical and symbolic structures the child constructs to make his or her meaning clear, how the writer makes use of literary models and genres, and the different functions of writing and written text that the young writer invents. The *social* strand refers to how the young writer constructs the communicative aspects of written language (i.e., how he or she develops a notion of an audience) and the context in which writing itself occurs.

In this chapter I present the semantic strand, how children use physical and symbolic representation systems they have constructed to express meaning, how the meaning they intend is related to the social context and function of written language, and how this constructive process of literacy development is related to more general cognitive development. I discuss an examination of this particular strand of writing development to exemplify how researchers and educators can apply the method of critical exploration to understanding children's writing development and to show the qualitative changes in understanding as children construct their own understandings of how to make meaning in writing.

Using Critical Exploration to Understand Children's Writing Development

To make explicit these issues, I present examples of the writing development of four children: Cathy, Matthew, Scott, and Sally. I followed their writing development, along with that of their classmates, for 5 years. I began when the children entered kindergarten in a small, urban, nonsectarian, private school. The school population was largely white, middle-class, with about 25% ethnic minority. When the children began school, they were between the ages of 4.5 and 5.5 years. I completed the study in their fifth year of school when they were in the fourth grade. During this time, they all remained at the same school, although they were in different classrooms after the first year.

During the first 4 years I spent an hour a week in their classrooms, during a writing period, observing, assisting, and interviewing them about their writing. In the fourth year I also did some teaching of writing in one classroom (with Matthew). The writing for the first 3 years was primarily in journals—bound notebooks where different writing genres were acceptable. In Scott's class, in the third year, children also began to keep writing folders. In the fourth and fifth years both journals and folders were used for writing in all classes. Writing done in the folders tended to be offered for revision more often; however, the distinction between the two physical places for writing was unclear until the final year. In the final year, the journal was clearly for personal writing; there were no topic assignments. Writing in the folders tended to have constraints on topic, genre, or style. I collected all of the journal writing over the entire 5 years and most of the folder writing for the last 2 to 3 years.

During the 5 years the children had a total of six teachers, although not all children had all teachers. Each teacher had an individual writing program, which ran the spectrum from a whole language approach to the teaching of writing to a much more directive approach, with assigned topics and genres. However, all of the teachers encouraged invented spelling in the first 3 years, provided frequent opportunities for writing (two to three times a week), and often allowed topic choice. In most of the classrooms, the sharing of writing was a regular occurrence, although the use of writing conferences was limited, as was discussion of writing processes, styles, and problems. The teachers at the school saw themselves as learning to be good writing teachers. They were committed to trying to implement writers' workshops in their classrooms on a regular basis but were still at different levels of implementing this approach. They were very involved with me in discussing their writing programs and their ideas about writing.

Preliminary results indicate that there are identifiable levels of development within each of the four strands described: physical, symbolic, semantic, and social. Categories or classification of general characteristics and level within each strand are being developed but are not reviewed in this chapter. Herein, I focus on development within the semantic strand, keeping in mind evidence of concurrent development within the other three strands, both from my own work and from the work of other researchers (physical and symbolic: Ferreiro, 1978, 1984, 1986; Ferreiro & Teberosky, 1982; Sulzby, 1987; Teale & Sulzby, 1987; Sulzby et al., 1989; semantic: Kroll, 1990; social: Dyson, 1985, 1989a, 1989b, 1989c; Harste et al., 1984). I use the tracing of this development to exemplify how examining children's writing in detail can be used to interpret their understanding of writing as it develops. I review in detail the writing development of four children, Cathy, Matthew, Scott, and

Sally, to show how they confronted certain fundamental semantic issues as they constructed and reconstructed making meaning in writing.

Issues Within the Semantic Strand

The major issues I observed that undergo a developmental construction and reconstruction process within the semantic strand are (a) the relationship between drawing and writing; (b) differentiation of literary genres such as narrative, exposition, and poetry; (c) coherence within the text; (d) the influence of heard and read literature on structure, style, and content; and (e) the manifestation of part–whole coordination within the writing domain. I have examined development year by year for each of the semantic issues for the four children, but for our purposes here I focus on Condition b (the differentiation of literary genres) and Condition e (the manifestation of part–whole coordination within the writing domain).

The Development and Differentiation of Literary Genres

The development and differentiation of literary genres is at the core of the semantic strand of development in writing. By constructing and reconstructing their own ideas of the different possible structures written language can take, children come to understand the wide variety of ways that one can make meaning. Britton's (1970) view of this process gives a general overview: writing begins as an expressive form of communication and is gradually differentiated into two general categories, poetic and transactional. *Poetic writing* is fiction, narrative prose and poetry; it is written language that integrates poetic style with meaning, focusing more on the personal aspects of writing. *Transactional writing* is informational writing, focusing more on the communication purpose of writing. This view is a useful beginning for examining this strand, but not very helpful in understanding the details of the change in children's writing. More specific categories of literary behavior and attributes are necessary. In examining the development and differentiation of genres I looked at genre category (e.g., narrative, exposition, poetry, etc.), topic, structure (the relation of the organization of the text to conventions of text organization in each genre), genre markers (e.g., *once upon a time*), and voice (personal style).

Year 1

Even in the first year, the roots of different writing genres were apparent. The writing was a personal statement of opinion or fact, a description of a picture, or an elaboration on the action in the pictures (e.g., Cathy's piece, "THSZNTNATTHHLZ" [This is night time at the hills], which is accompanied by a drawing of hills and a triangular moon; see Figure 1). Other pieces involved either wishes or expressions of feelings (e.g., "I wish," "I like," "I hate," etc.). These pieces are good examples of early expressive writing that contain the seeds of both narrative and expository text.

Frequently, children wrote on one topic several times. When this occurred, it was easier to identify genre precursors. Thus, Matthew wrote a number of pieces (all no longer than one sentence) first on "the rabbit" and later on G.I. Joe. The G.I. Joe pieces are story precursors; each one represents a battle between G.I. Joe and his arch enemy Cobra, with G.I. Joe triumphing in the end. Although these pieces lack most narrative characteristics (plot, character development, setting, etc.), they do have the rudiments of narrative structure. There is a hero, G.I. Joe, triumphing repeatedly over the enemy, Cobra (e.g., "G.I. JO IS /FITEN/COBRA" [G.I. Joe is fighting Cobra]). The rabbit pieces, on the other hand, show a mixture of narrative and expository style. The reader can interpret the series of pieces (which occurred over a period of 4 months) as an ongoing story about a rabbit and all his activities or as a series on "what I know about rabbits." In fact, the series seems to be something of both. Some entries have a more narrative flavor (e.g., "HE*STOPPT*4 LNCH"). The text is about an action; it is written in the past tense, it is about a moment in time. Others seem more expository (e.g., "THE RABET iS PREDE"). Part of the series described the rabbit, which can be considered as character description, because Matthew used the definite article to identify the rabbit. However, the collection of entries that is more descriptive in nature seems like a general description of a rabbit, rather than the description of a story character.

Year 2

At the beginning of the second year, personal narrative was the most common form of writing. Scott's soccer team narrative was typical. The entries were short and summarized personal information ("I am ona soocR/ tem stenG Ras/ senR foRRo" [I am on a soccer team. Sting rays. Center forward]). During the year these personal pieces became longer and more elaborated. Many initially had the characteristics of diary entries but eventually developed into full-fledged narratives. Scott's garter snake narrative and Matthew's narratives on his trip to

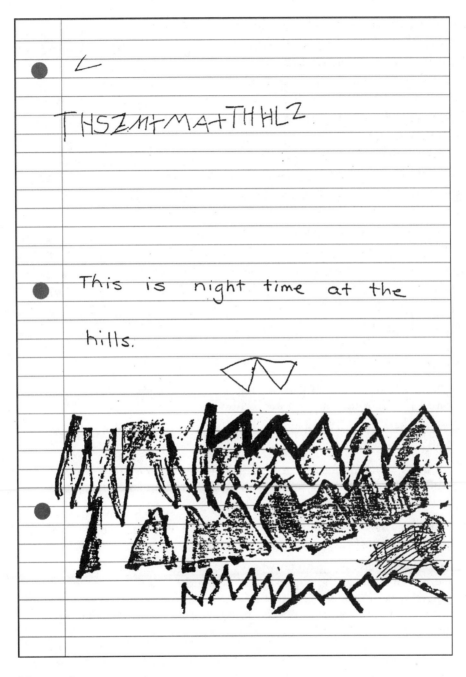

Figure 1

Cathy's writing at Year 1 titled This is night time at the hills and accompanied by hills and a moon.

Alaska and to Los Angeles demonstrate this development (see Figures 2, 3, and 4). These later works have many characteristics of narrative structure: sequence—a beginning, middle, and end—voice, and past tense. Although they include these elements of narratives, they tend to lack all development (as in the garter snake story where Scott's teacher's prompt helps him elaborate his story; see Figure 2), or to trail off at the end (as in Matthew's Los Angeles story; see Figure 4). Graves (1983) and Calkins (1994) called these *bed-to-bed stories*, because often the stories only end when the characters go to bed. As soon as Matthew, Scott, Cathy, and Sally started to write longer works, the bed-to-bed structure appeared.

Not all the narratives were derived solely from personal experiences. The children began to attempt to write fiction, imitating stories and structures they had heard in literature. Sally's Mouse House story is a fantasy that takes off from a possible personal experience. (Original spelling and punctuation are maintained. Each paragraph represents a new page of text.)

> Own day I was eating lunch wen I herd sum litll noysis they were coming from the cuderd. sloly and coshly I opind it.
>
> There wer littele mies in the coder. They wer steeling all the food. Soe I pot then into my red moueshoues.
>
> They wer very bisy little creechers. One of them was even playing ball.
>
> One day I tock them out for a wolk. It was suny. So we tock a loung wolk and wen we came home we wer all tiered and we all went to bed after diner
>
> One day I wocke up and my mise wer gon. There wer plae mise in the mousehouse.
>
> [One day I was eating lunch when I heard some little noises. They were coming from the cupboard. Slowly and cautiously I opened it. There were little mice in the cupboard. They were stealing all the food. So I put them into my red mousehouse. They were very busy little creatures. One of them was even playing ball. One day I took them out for a walk. It was sunny. So we took a long walk and when we came home we were all tired and we all went to bed after dinner. One day I woke up and my mice were gone. There were play mice in the mousehouse.]

In this story one sees the true beginning of a narrative. The story begins with a typical genre marker: *one day*. It consists of a sequence of events with a beginning, middle, and end that show some rudimentary devel-

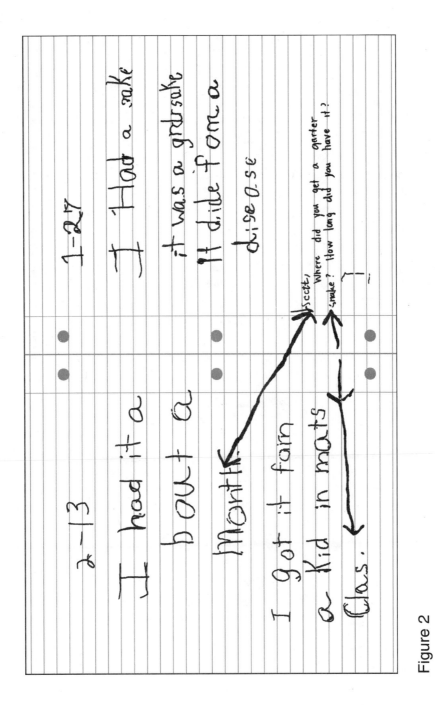

Figure 2

Scott's garter snake story at Year 2 demonstrating his developing use of narrative.

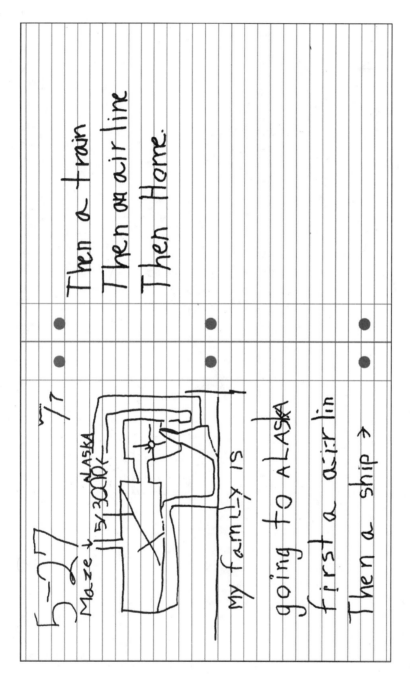

Figure 3

Matthew's narrative on his trip to Alaska at Year 2 demonstrating the development of sequence in narrative.

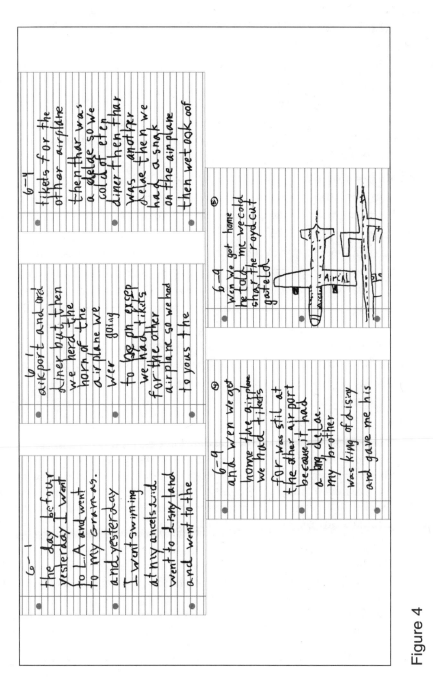

Figure 4

Matthew's story on his trip to Los Angeles at Year 2 demonstrating the development of narrative with trailing off at the end.

opment. Sally began mysteriously, established the mice and herself as characters in the story, and then ended by having the mice disappear just as mysteriously. She used a sequence of events within the sequence wherein she described the long walk. In this section she had difficulty ending, so she ended by putting everyone to bed. Her story is written in the past tense, another genre marker.

Toward the end of the second year the children began writing never-ending stories. From the end of March until the end of the school year Scott periodically added to a story about a boy who meets a dinosaur and the adventures they have together. This development seems an offshoot of the bed-to-bed sequence, but differs because the adventures go on and on, never ending. These stories were more common in the third year, thus I discuss them further in the Year 3 section of this chapter.

Not all personal experience pieces developed into narratives. Protoexpository pieces appeared in several guises. Matthew and Scott, as well as many of the other boys, drew and described numerous mazes, explaining the goals and the point systems in some detail. As their teacher responded to their writing in their journals, the children began to carry on written conversations with her about what they were writing. Sally, and a number of the other girls, wrote interview pieces about each other. These pieces are clearly derived from personal pieces in that they describe the person's likes and dislikes, but they are written in the third person about someone else.

> Helen's favrte food is Macrony and chees. Helen's favrte ise cereme is cooky ise cereme. Helen's favrte hiding plase is under the sters . helen's faverite toy is mister ptadoe hed. helen's faverite is holday is cerismis helen's faverite ferot is woter melllin helen's faverite canb is choclit. Helen's faverit game is spud. Helen's best friend is Sally. Helen's favorite thing in school is girls.

> [Helen's favorite food is macaroni and cheese. Helen's favorite ice cream is cookies and cream. Helen's favorite hiding place is under the stairs. Helen's favorite toy is Mr. Potato Head. Helen's favorite holiday is Christmas. Helen's favorite fruit is watermelon. Helen's favorite candy is chocolate. Helen's favorite game is spud. Helen's best friend is Sally. Helen's favorite thing in school is girls.]

> From the teacher: This is a fun list to read. I am waiting to read more about Helen's favorite things.

Matthew wrote a piece about the solar system, which he also illustrated. This variety of expository writing styles shows that the children were beginning to understand and construct different structures for communicating different kinds of meaning in their writing.

Year 3

In the third year the children's writing consisted mostly of personal narrative and narrative fiction. The children had differentiated narrative from other genres, although there are still samples that show some mixing of genres. Stories consistently began and ended with traditional story markers such as *once upon a time, one day, once there was, happily ever after, the end,* and so forth. Matthew, Scott, and Sally wrote ongoing stories that continued over several entries. The structure of these stories is quite predictable. The story begins with the introduction of a main character and with the introduction of that character's problem. This beginning is followed by a number of incidents that, although coherent within themselves, are connected only minimally. Borrowing a phrase from Applebee (1978), I call these James Bond stories, because the structure reminds me of the typical James Bond thriller in which one exciting event follows another, with almost no connection between events. The ends of these stories, if in fact they are completed, are contracted to a few sentences in which the final problem is resolved without any elaboration and the people all end up happy (e.g., "And so he folled the map and he killed the dragen and reskyoued the princass and got back home. and lived happly ever after"; Sally, King Clumsy IV). The children experimented with different kinds of narratives: fairy tales, sports stories, scary stories, fictional stories of themselves and their friends, and so forth. In spite of the variety of subjects, the stories maintained the same James Bond or bed-to-bed structure.

Although narrative was the dominant genre form used during this year, children did experiment with different expository forms as well. Scott wrote commercials and recipes, which he interspersed into his ongoing story. Sally wrote more friend interview stories, similar to the ones she had written the year before. Cathy was working to make sense of new ideas with a piece, "I wish I was historee and my muthr was historee" (see Figure 5). The children used their journals as diaries, recording reflections about their experiences and their feelings. Sally marked some entries "privit, do not reed!!!" In addition, she experimented with poetry, writing several poems during the year.

The third year was dominated by a construction and reconstruction of several different genres. Narratives, while dominated by two basic structures (James Bond and bed to bed), were constructed with a variety

Figure 5

Cathy's piece at Year 3 showing her attempt to make sense of new ideas.

of content. In expository writing, the children investigated a variety of forms. In personal writing, the children began to use writing as a means for clarifying their own feelings about themselves and their experiences. Writing, in this year, began to take on the epistemic function described by Bereiter (1979) in which the writer writes to learn. In this case, the children are writing to learn more about their own feelings and ideas. Making meaning with writing is starting to become a reciprocal process; the writer makes meaning for both himself or herself and for the audience.

Year 4

In the fourth year the children began to write well-formed narratives. Some of the children used a more anticipatory story structure, setting up events for the reader and then following up on those events. Whereas sequential, linear constructs, rather than true anticipatory constructs, continued to be used within these stories, the overall impression is of a well-formed story. Scott and Sally wrote fish stories in chapters with character descriptions, settings, problems, resolutions, and conclusions. The following is one excerpt that illustrates this advance in story planning and structure:

Chapter 1

How it began

"Hi my name is Skippy. I'm a skipjack tuna. And I have a story to tell you." One day I was swimming along. I was going to the super sewead store and I was carrying my purse. When a shark came up to me and took my purse and swam off!!! I shoted at him but he didn't her me. I had 100 clam shells in my purse. 1 clam shell is werth 1 doller so I was prity mad. To top that off my purse had some very prety perals on it from the most valubal oysters in the sea. I was angry as a wave crashing on the rocks. . . .

The story goes on for two chapters in which Skippy calls the police (swordfish who sharpen their swords on the coral) and describes the thief. They go off to catch him. The story ends in the following manner:

.Finly we saw him he was bieing a tikit to the nexst train out of toun. Gest as he was about to by his tikit Sam [the police chief] snuk up behind him and grabed him he clampd handcufs on him and took him to jail. jail is a big room made out of coral. Well thats the end of my story. I have to go by."
THE END

Sally began the story by speaking directly to the audience. She set the stage, provided the audience with necessary world knowledge (about the value of the stolen objects), and used imagery to express her feelings. All of these are new literary devices, commonly used by adult fiction writers and poets, with which she experimented in order to understand how to use them to make her meaning clear. The ending is not the compacted ending of the year before. She was able to describe the action and the setting at the end of the story, as well as end where she began, with a message to the audience.

Scott's fish story was not nearly so well planned and executed; it still contained James Bond elements. However, the beginning of the story was well developed, setting the scene and the characters:

> One day there was a school of fish. The techer of the school was named Mr. Hammerfish. The biggist fish is named Fred. He can swim the fastest. The secont biggeist was named Jon. Jon went the secont fastest. The third was named Tom. Tom went the third fastestest. The fourth bigist was named Han. He could swim the fourth fastest. now the smallest could not swim fast at all (he could not even swim an inch in a minit) His name was Ty.

Of course, Ty is the hero of the story. He gets lost from the school and has a James Bond series of adventures. He does not end up back with the school, which is what our own sense of good story structure would lead us to expect. In fact, the story ends in an unsatisfying way structurally; Scott tried a new tactic, ending with a joke. Ty gets into a battle with a sea serpent, and Ty is winning:

> ...Ty said "down for the cont 1 2 3 that sure was a knock out.
> The serpent said "that was not a knock out. I could bely even feal it.
> "Than why dident I hear yoaer hart betting?" said Ty.
> "Because you just got an ear efekshin!" yeald the serpent.

> [Ty said, "Down for the count. 1, 2, 3. That sure was a knockout."
> The serpent said, "That was not a knockout. I could barely even feel it."
> "Then why didn't I hear your heart beating?" said Ty.
> "Because you just got an ear infection!" yelled the serpent.]

For Scott, the punch line of the joke sufficed to end the story.

Matthew and Cathy also showed progress in writing more well-formed narratives that included some anticipation, while maintaining the vestiges of the James Bond style. All four children used chapter headings to indicate the different parts of their stories. Most of the stories had real problems that were maintained to a final resolution, if the child finished the story. Finishing a story was an issue, and many stories were begun, set up well but remained unresolved. The lack of an ending indicates that, at this point in their development as story writers, ending a story was the most difficult part of story structure to construct, although when stories did end, the ending was more elaborated, as was seen with Sally's fish story.

The children experimented with more types of narrative, mixing personal experience with narrative structure. Matthew wrote a baseball story that was ongoing, written in the present tense, as if it was the commentary accompanying an actual game. He included interruptions of songs to indicate similar interruptions that occur in real baseball games and told the reader, "Now, back to the game." He also combined book structure with personal narrative when he wrote the book of "My Most Painful Experiences." During this year the children began to write several drafts of stories. They began to recognize the process of making one's meaning clearer through the act of revision.

As well as experimenting with narrative form and structure, the children clarified and constructed a stronger notion of expository text. They experimented with journalism, lists, reporting school events, writing assigned topic reports, and so forth, and with philosophical essays. In his essay on the importance of education, Matthew combined narrative and expository genres to make his point:

> Education means alot to me! It gives me a chance to have fun with math, reading, ext. I can right storys with my friends. If I was not educated I could not do things like read and I would not know about anybody else. I love to be educated. Me and my friends can have lots and lots of fun. Story.

> I am in school. It is nine a.m. school has just started. It is my first day at school. I was not educated yet. I was scared. Quiet my teacher said. I was starteld. My skin allmost flew of my body, but I held it on. After a long time she said "reses" I din't know what in the world she was saying. Everybody else put there stuf ayway and walked outside. I stayed behine my best friend, Joey. Half a year later when Mrs. Rufrok said "reses" I was the first one outside. Then I asked Joey "What does reses mean?" Joey said "time to go to lunch." Two years later I new math. I was almost educated! I was happy. But now I *am* educated! I am happy. The end.

> Education is wonderful espeshaly when you ned it like in school are jest math class.

> Proof that I am educated, I rote this.

In this piece Matthew used everything he knew about writing to make his meaning clear. He mixed and combined narrative and expository elements inappropriately, but he demonstrated a strong personal voice and sense of what an expository essay is supposed to do: convince the reader of a point of view.

The fourth year was a coming together of many of the different constructions in genre with which the children experimented. Narratives began to be well formed, using planning and anticipation to enhance the meaning of the text. Expository prose was still in the beginning stages, with children continuing to experiment with lists, reporting, and so forth, but some of the children began to construct a more advanced view of the purpose of expository text, thus differentiating between the purpose of narrative and exposition. This differentiation represents an advance in understanding different ways of making meaning through writing.

Year 5

The most striking characteristic of the fifth year is the progress the children made in differentiating writing genres. Narratives, descriptions, personal narratives, and exposition all have definite characteristics of which the children made use. For example, the elements of narrative include main characters, setting, plot, problems, and resolutions, often with a number of episodes all leading toward a final, more inclusive conclusion. Three of the children (Scott, Sally, and Matthew) kept journals that were truly personal diaries, reporting daily events and their reactions to those events. All the children wrote reports during this year, which gave them a structure for expository writing. What is significant about these reports is that none of them included a narrative in writing about factual topics. Until now, narrative and exposition were mixed to support each other. At this point, the expository writing seems to have been defined for itself, and not as a variation on the narrative. The reports are too long to quote in their entireties, but Matthew's introduction to his report on snakes gives a sense of his changing understanding of expository writing.

> Most people think they understand snakes very well. Snakes seem to be very simple animals. All they appear to have is a head and a long tail. But snakes are not as simple as they appear. There are many amazing and surprising facts about snakes. This report will reveal some of them.
>
> The snake is a member of the family of animals called reptiles which includes: Turtles, Crocodiles, Lizards and Tuataras. All reptiles are cold blooded. Cold blooded means their blood tempature changes to the air tempature. All reptiles have scales. A snake is

different from other reptiles because it has no eyelids, ears or lims. It can tell if an enemy is coming because it can rest it head on the ground and feel the vibrations.

This report will be about the different kinds of rattle snakes, some facts about king snakes and facts on the cobras.

Matthew's introduction draws the reader into the report, summarizes some basic facts about snakes, and ends by explaining just what he will do in the rest of the report. When one compares this piece with his essay on what education means to him from the previous year it is clear that his understanding of the purpose of expository text has been both refined and changed.

During this year, the children often wrote in response to assigned writing exercises, such as making descriptions, taking a different point of view, continuing a story started by the teacher, and so forth. These assignments seemed to heighten their awareness of genre differences and uses. Sally turned a description into "The Life of a Lemon," complete with narrative and exposition of the development of a lemon—a very sophisticated piece of writing. Scott experimented with playwriting in fulfilling another descriptive, point of view assignment; he also experimented with the shock value of bathroom humor and bad language on his audience. Development during this fifth year seemed to be focused on differentiating and refining the concept and use of different writing genres.

Part–Whole Coordination

Before I conclude, let me share the third point in which developmental theory can inform interpretation and understanding of writing development. One aspect of cognitive development that is reflected in many domains of knowledge is part–whole coordination, an aspect of the development of classification and seriation where children construct hierarchical relations between classes. Issues of part–whole coordination arise in mathematics in many strands (Black & Kroll, 1989; Piaget, 1965), in the development of scientific thinking (Inhelder & Piaget, 1958), and also in the development of literacy (Ferreiro & Teberosky, 1982). Ferreiro and Teberosky discussed the relationship between the development of part–whole coordination and the development of sound–symbol correspondences, in which children have to understand that (in English) one symbol can stand for many different sounds and also that one sound can be represented by more than one symbol. In the semantic strand the influence of the development of part–whole coordination is evident in how children coordinate the different parts of a text, how they are able to add and delete information as they write, and how they account for their audience as they take a more objective stance in their writing. The following is a brief explanation of how this is so.

Development of Part–Whole Coordination in Writing From Year 1 to Year 5

To begin with the part is the whole. In the first year, when writing was mostly drawing and very brief, the picture or concept was the whole and the writing labeled that whole. There was no sequence, and no parts of the picture were discussed or represented separately. By the second year, a sequence of events appeared in some narratives, indicating the beginning of the construction of parts. In fact, the appearance of sequence marks one beginning of a sense of narrative form. Other parts of narrative form began to be used, such as the advent of markers like *once upon a time* and *happily ever after* or *the end*. The parts began to be distinguished but were related sequentially rather than hierarchically. The bed-to-bed structure and the James Bond structure represented a sequential stringing together of events or episodes.

By the third year, as the James Bond–type organization became transitional to a more anticipatory form of story structure (i.e., the episodes became more related to each other), a sense of the relationship between the parts and the whole became more apparent. However, the children were unable to insert revisions or changes and tended to tack them on to the end of a story, indicating a lack of a simultaneous sense of the whole and its parts. During the fourth year, children inserted information as they thought of it, with phrases such as, "I forgot to tell you," indicating a sense of necessity about revision, but an inability to insert new material into an already formed piece.

The mixing of narrative and expository form in the fourth year, although in some ways seeming to show a less definitive attitude toward the separation of parts, in fact, represented an attempt to differentiate the whole from its parts. In other words, the sense of a theme or message became one purpose of the text, and that message had to be coordinated with the parts of the text, which could be relayed by expository or narrative forms, or both. Story structure was anticipatory in nature, using different literary styles to support this coordination of parts. Expository form, which is not sequentially organized in the first place, and is, hence, more difficult to construct, was still at a more rudimentary stage. With narrative the children began with the parts and constructed the whole from the parts. This is less true for expository text, wherein analysis of text must begin with the whole and then be reduced to the parts and their relation to the whole to be understood. It is not surprising, therefore, that the coordination of parts and whole occurred later in exposition than in narration.

By the fifth year the children had more clearly differentiated among genres of writing. This categorization of genres was represented by a better coordination of the parts and the whole. For example, the children wrote research reports that included introductions, chapters that represented the information in the report, and conclusions. The parts of the text had undoubtedly been taught and described by their teachers. What is interesting, however, is not that they included labeled parts in their reports, but that what was in those sections actually coincided with the title; the introduction was truly an introduction, and so forth. In the fifth year, then, the children had developed not only a strong concept of narrative, but also the concept of exposition, at least for simple research reports, was seen as different from narrative, with different parts.

This is just a brief example of how logical thinking processes can and do apply to the learning of specific school subjects. By understanding how part–whole coordination is reflected in literacy development, one gets a larger view of the underlying cognitive processes that support and interact with the development of literacy.

The Development of Meaning Making in Writing and the Learner-Centered Psychological Principles

I have not discussed the development of the physical, symbolic, or social strands of writing, although that information can also be derived from this body of data. I have discussed the children's development in one issue of semantic development year by year to make clear the progression of development that occurred. I now summarize briefly the levels of development within the issue of the differentiation of literary genres and the levels of part–whole coordination that occur (see Exhibit 2), and then show how these levels of development are related to the psychological principles, which can form the basis of appropriate instruction.

Exhibit 2		
Levels of Development in the Semantic Strand		
Level	Characteristics of development	
1a	Differentiation of literary genres Genres undifferentiated; writing is a label	Part–whole coordination Parts and whole undifferentiated
1b	Personal narrative or personal descriptions	
2a	Personal narrative with sequence Bed to bed Different expository genres tried	Parts used to produce sequence; new information added only at the end
2b	Narrative parts are linear; James Bond structure, fairy tales; Exposition = convince reader of point of view	Add new information as they think of it, but recognize it should go elsewhere
3a	Narratives with anticipation; chapters, poetry, new content sources	Revise; insert new information
3b	Well-formed expository styles; narrative show use of text-level planning	Coordinate parts of narrative and expository texts sequentially

The Differentiation of Literary Genres

There are three basic levels in this category, each having sublevels indicating development within:

Level 1a. Genres are undifferentiated. Writing is a label.

Level 1b. Personal narratives or descriptions appear.

Level 2a. Personal narratives with sequence are written. Bed-to-bed constructions are used to create stories. Many genres of expository writing are attempted.

Level 2b. Narratives are better differentiated; parts of narratives are used effectively. The structure of stories is linear or sequential. James Bond structure is used to create more complex stories. Different kinds of stories, such as fairy tales, scary stories, stories about friends, and so forth, are written. Personal writing takes on an epistemic function. Categories of expository writing begin to be differentiated, including using writing to convince the reader of a philosophical point of view.

Level 3a.   Well-formed narratives, true problems, and strong structure as represented by the use of chapters to divide the
text appear. Stories show some planning and anticipatory
organization. Children are experimenting with different
poetic and expository genres, combining and differentiating among styles and types. New content sources are
used.

Level 3b.   Some expository styles are well formed. Simple research
reports that include introductions, subject chapters, and
brief conclusions that essentially restate the conclusion
are written. Children continue to experiment with other
expository genres. Narratives are anticipatory in form,
showing the use of text-level planning. Stories include
several episodes before a resolution is reached.

In the development and differentiation of literary genres, Cathy is
at Level 2b, Scott is at Level 3a, and Matthew and Sally are at Level 3b.
Level 3b seems to represent a concrete level of differentiating literary
genres. Although the forms these children use are not as complex or
flexible as the conventional adult models of these genres, nevertheless
they have achieved some clear definition by this point. It is evident that
development from one level to the next is a reconstruction process of
genre, approximating adult literature more and more at each level. In
the process, children create some of their own genre types, some of
which they find effective and continue to use and some of which they
abandon as failures in their search for making sense in writing.

Part–Whole Coordination

The integration and differentiation of parts of a text from the whole
text is an ongoing process that reflects generic logical development in
this domain. At the first level, the parts and whole are basically undifferentiated, although toward the end of this level some transitional differentiation of parts is evident, for example, through the use of numerous illustrations. At the second level the appearance of sequence
recalls the development of seriation. The children are able to write a
sequence of events or ideas in logical order. However, if they forget
something they add it on to the text, wherever they happen to be,

ignoring its appropriate place in the sequence. In seriation development, the same difficulties with insertion appear (Inhelder & Piaget, 1964). By the end of the second level the children show that they recognize that the added information should have gone earlier by writing "I forgot to tell you" before entering the new information. At the third level children are able to revise and insert new information. At the beginning of this stage they indicate a struggle to differentiate the parts from the whole while simultaneously considering the whole. By the end of this level they have identified rudimentary parts of both narrative and expository texts and are able to coordinate those parts, although usually in a sequential rather than coordinated way.

I have shown the role developmental theory can play in helping researchers and educators understand the learning of writing. Using a combination of the method of critical exploration and literary analysis, we can get a detailed view of each child's development within the larger context of writing development in general. The children in this study came to school with different levels of understanding writing vis-à-vis adult conventional wisdom. They developed in similar ways, along a similar path, despite different methods of teaching. One significant aspect of their education in writing, I believe, is that, even in the most structured writing environments, the children were encouraged to experiment with their own way of completing assignments. (One final example. Sally wrote at the end of one assignment, "Sorry, M—[her teacher], I didn't exactly do the assignment," indicating her own awareness of the difference between her teacher's expectations and her performance, but confident that it would be acceptable, which in fact it was.) This freedom to experiment gave all of them the chance to construct for themselves different literary genres and figure out how to make their own meaning clear to their readers. In such circumstances, it is more likely that one can find children struggling with issues that produce a disequilibrium that leads to progress in understanding, rather than a disequilibrium that leads to children searching for immediate right answers. These children are trying, as Ferreiro (1984) said, to understand not just the pieces but the whole nature of the system.

Using the method of critical exploration to research writing development gives teachers and researchers the opportunity to see what children do know about writing, what hypotheses they are making about what is good writing, and how to use this information. If educators can start with what and how children know, they have a better chance of designing developmentally appropriate instruction.

It is important to note that the developmental levels I have proposed do not correlate exactly with the years the children have been in school. Developmental pace is individual; children do not all develop at the same speed. Cathy's development during this period had been behind that of the other children in some ways, whereas Sally seemed in some ways to be more advanced. All children, given the opportunity, can learn to become good writers. The value of seeing the dissonance between levels and years of experience is that one can identify appropriate activities that will challenge a child to continue in his or her writing development if one understands at what level she or he is confronting a particular issue. Instruction can be designed that is developmentally appropriate for each child.

Learner-Centered Psychological Principles

The psychological factors identified in the learner-centered psychological principles (APA, 1995) can provide guidance for thinking about instruction in literacy, particularly in writing instruction. Whole language instruction as described, for example, by Graves (1994), Goodman and Wilde (1992), and Calkins (1994) builds on the central premise that learning is most effective when it is an intentional process of constructing meaning, that successful learners construct meaningful, coherent representations of knowledge. The writing development exemplified by the four children discussed in this chapter shows children grappling over the 5-year period with making sense of the whole system of literacy. Looking specifically at the development of literary genre enables one not only to identify writing development, per se, but also to see the children's interpretation of their reading experiences as well as their writing experiences. The writing of narrative and expository text was strongly influenced by what the children had the opportunity to read and discuss. For example, Sally's King Clumsy IV has all the trappings of a fairy tale, both in content (a mysterious old man, mysterious map, and magical directions) and in language ("And so he folled [followed] the map and he killed the dragen and reskycued the princass and got back home. and lived happly ever after").

Conclusion

The examination of the development of these children's writing over the 5-year period reveals the importance of providing a context in which students can set meaningful goals for their learning. The story of Cathy, Matthew, Scott, and Sally shows how a writers' workshop format for teaching writing, as practiced in a variety of ways, allows children to develop and refine their own goals for learning, thereby supporting the development of meaningful, coherent representations of knowledge. The four children developed changing concepts of both narrative and expository discourse. Their personal goals for learning to write were encouraged to flourish by an instructional context that allowed them to choose their own topics and genres most of the time. Through the use of journals and writing folders their teachers provided a context in which children felt encouraged to play with and experiment with genre. By the fifth year their concepts of narrative and expository texts were sufficiently differentiated to allow them to benefit greatly from direct instruction regarding the use of genre. Their earlier, less-directed experience had allowed them to develop a voice that subsequently enabled them to integrate their own personal writing goals with the educational writing goals of the curriculum. We can see this integration in the reports they wrote, where their assigned expository text retained the individual voice of each author, and the passion of their interest in the subject matter.

By encouraging and allowing the children to select and explore their own writing content, the teachers made use of motivational and affective factors, as well as the cognitive and metacognitive factors. The children welcomed the writing periods when I came in to either help out or teach. Writers' workshop, which was our model for writing instruction (and which differed in each classroom, depending on the teacher's perspective as well), was always greeted with great enthusiasm. The children delighted in the opportunity not only to write about their own chosen topics but also to work with one another, sharing and supporting each other's writing. The writing conferences, common in many of the classrooms, supported learning that was influenced by social interactions, interpersonal relations, and communication with others. Sharing their writing with one another allowed each novice writer some insight into the writing processes of others, as well as some immediate feedback on his or her own writing. The sharing of styles, strategies, and content encouraged the children to continually confront their own concepts of narrative and exposition and to regularly refine those concepts. Thus, working together was both enjoyable (it is fun to write with a friend) and challenging (your friend may question what you do and force you to think about why you wrote what you did).

Perhaps most significantly, the story of Cathy's, Matthew's, Scott's, and Sally's development makes a strong contribution to diagnosis and assessment within literacy development, with the goal of determining appropriate instruction on the basis of what a child already brings to the writing situation. The use of the method of critical exploration and a careful analysis of children's texts can allow teachers to understand what problems children are attempting to solve in the stories they write. Teachers can then determine appropriate instruction, on the basis of the children's current understanding.

Learning to make meaning in writing is a developmental issue that children begin to construct as soon as they begin to write. The principles and methods of developmental psychology can be used to help researchers and educators understand that development. In this study, issues that children face in striving to construct meaning in their writing can be seen to develop in a consistent way that can be identified within individual children's writing and across their individual experiences. Looking closely at children's writing over a period of years provides insight into the development of writing. Such a fine-grained examination, coupled with knowledge of writing development, can inform elementary teachers of what issues children are currently constructing and reconstructing, thus informing instruction in a developmentally appropriate way. Individual differences can be understood within the whole continuum of writing development, allowing for more effective instruction for individual children.

References

American Psychological Association Board of Educational Affairs. (1995, Dec.). *Learner-centered psychological principles: A framework for school redesign and reform* [On-line]. Available: http://www.apa.org/ed/lcp.html.

Applebee, A. N. (1978). *The child's concept of story: Ages two to seventeen.* Chicago, IL: University of Chicago Press.

Bereiter, C. (1979). Development in writing. In L. W. Gregg & E. R. Steinberg (Eds.), *Cognitive processes in writing* (pp. 73–93). Hillsdale, NJ: Erlbaum.

Black, A., Ammon, P., & Kroll, L. (1987). Development, literacy and the social construction of knowledge. *The Genetic Epistemologist, 15*(3–4), 13–20.

Black, A., & Kroll, L. (1989, April). *Teaching based assessment from a cognitive developmental (Piagetian) perspective.* Invited address at the 23rd Annual University of California—Berkeley School Psychology Conference, Berkeley, CA.

Britton, J. (1970). *Language and learning*. Middlesex, England: Penguin.

Calkins, L. (1994). *The art of teaching writing* (2nd ed.). Portsmouth, NH: Heinemann.

Dyson, A. (1985). Individual differences in emerging writing. In M. Farr (Ed.), *Advances in writing research: Vol. 1. Children's early writing development*. Norwood, NJ: Ablex.

Dyson, A. (1989a). *Multiple worlds of child writers: Friends learning to write*. New York: Teachers College Press.

Dyson, A. (1989b). Negotiating among multiple worlds: The space/time dimensions of young children's composing. *Research in the Teaching of English, 22,* 355–390.

Dyson, A. (1989c, March). *Play, pictures and pencils in the primary school: The development of dialectic between function and form*. Paper presented at the annual meeting of the American Educational Research Association, San Francisco, CA.

Ferreiro, E. (1978). What is written in a written sentence? A developmental answer. *Journal of Education, 160,* 25–39.

Ferreiro, E. (1984). The underlying logic of literacy development. In H. Goelman, A. Oberg, & F. Smith (Eds.), *Awakening to literacy* (pp. 154–173). Exeter, NH: Heinemann.

Ferreiro, E. (1986). The interplay between information and assimilation in beginning literacy. In W. H. Teale & E. Sulzby (Eds.), *Emergent literacy: Writing and reading* (pp. 15–49). Norwood, NJ: Ablex.

Ferreiro, E., & Teberosky, A. (1982). *Literacy before schooling*. Exeter, NH: Heinemann.

Goodman, Y. M., & Wilde, S. (1992). *Literacy events in a community of young writers*. New York: Teachers College Press.

Graves, D. (1983). *Writing: Teachers and children at work*. Portsmouth, NH: Heinemann.

Graves, D. (1994). *A fresh look at writing*. Portsmouth, NH: Heinemann.

Harste, J. C., Woodward, V. A., & Burke, C. L. (1984). *Language stories and literacy lessons*. Portsmouth, NH: Heinemann.

Heath, S. B. (1983). *Ways with words: Language, life, and work in communities and classrooms*. Cambridge, England: Cambridge University Press.

Inhelder, B., & Piaget, J. (1958). *The growth of logical thinking: From childhood to adolescence*. New York: Basic Books.

Inhelder, B., & Piaget, J. (1964). *The early growth of logic in the child*. New York: W. W. Norton & Company.

Kroll, L. (1990, April). *Making meaning in writing: A longitudinal study of young children's writing development*. Paper presented at the annual convention of the American Educational Research Association, Boston.

Piaget, J. (1965). The child's conception of number. New York: W. W. Norton & Company.

Piaget, J. (1969). *Science of education and the psychology of the child*. Dallas, TX: Penguin Books.

Piaget, J., & Inhelder, B. (1967). *The child's conception of space*. New York: W. W. Norton & Company.

Sulzby, E. (1987). Writing and reading: Signs of oral and written language organization in the young child. In W. H. Teale & E. Sulzby (Eds.), *Emergent literacy: Writing and reading* (pp. 50–90). Norwood, NJ: Ablex.

Sulzby, E., Barnhart, J., & Hieshima, J. A. (1989). Forms of writing and rereading from writing: A preliminary report. In J. M. Mason (Ed.), *Reading and writing connections*. Boston: Allyn & Bacon.

Teale, W. H., & Sulzby, E. (Eds.). (1987). *Emergent literacy: Writing and reading*. Norwood, NJ: Ablex.

Cognition and Subject Matter Learning

Merlin C. Wittrock

he learning of subject matter and the training of intelligence present fundamental problems for educational psychologists to study. These apparently different problems relate to each other in important ways that have been written about since antiquity and researched since educational psychology studied faculty psychology. Plato (1924) taught a slave boy the Pythagorean theorem as a way to train thinking, or virtue, not as a way to teach mathematics. Over 2,000 years later, Charles Judd (1908) taught boys a principle about the refraction of light as it leaves water and enters air as a way to train intelligence through increasing transfer of learning, not as a way to teach physics.

Edward L. Thorndike presented a different approach to these problems of learning and the training of intelligence. He (Thorndike & Woodworth, 1901) studied the effects of having learners estimate the areas and magnitudes of certain shapes. Thorndike found that no increase in general ability to observe or to estimate areas and magnitudes occurred as a result of this training. From these and related later studies he developed his theory of identical elements in transfer of training. Later, Thorndike (1922, pp. 70–74) argued for a "psychology of arithmetic," based on the importance of concrete knowledge and of practice at specific skills, hobbies, and associations, rather than on the understanding of general principles.

Research on the "psychologies of subject matters" or more appropriately, I think, the "psychology of learning of a subject matter," began to flourish after the recent reemergence of interest among educational psychologists in human cognition, including cognitive learning, background knowledge, knowledge acquisition, learning strategies, and metacognition. Before this advent of interest in cognition, educational psychologists and experimental psychologists often studied nonsense materials in well-controlled laboratory settings. They chose the laboratory study of these materials to eliminate the confounding effects of past learning on their research. Their goals included the discovery of the fundamental psychological processes important to the development of a theory of learning. Unfortunately, it was often believed in those days that learning theory could be developed and tested in the laboratory, but not in the practical world of the classroom. The unfortunate results of that belief included (a) the elimination of background knowledge—one of the most significant factors in cognitive learning—from research on teaching and instruction and (b) a serious reduction in the content validity and the utility of studies of learning, which focused on artificial situations and tasks not typical of subject matter learned in school classrooms.

With the recently renewed interest in cognition, different approaches to the study of human learning and knowledge acquisition have emerged. Today, educational psychologists have shown that metacognition, learning strategies, prior learning, background knowledge, subject matter areas, and practical teaching contexts and instructional settings are most appropriate parts of the research and theory building of educational psychology. Educational psychologists have also shown that the methods and theories of cognition can be applied to the scientific study of everyday learning in practical contexts, including subject matter learning in schools. They believe that researchers can productively study and theorize about important educational problems by studying how students learn subject matter in realistic, everyday instructional settings.

These commonly held beliefs have led to studies in a variety of subject matters, including reading, mathematics, and physical science. These studies involve methods of research that include classroom observation, student interviews, and protocol analyses, as well as tests and measures that focus on comprehension and students' preconceptions, beliefs, and attitudes (Wittrock, 1987; Wittrock & Baker, 1991).

The thinking that unites and adds coherence to recent studies of subject matter learning is expressed in cognitive theories of learning from teaching that unite several learner-centered psychological principles (e.g., generative teaching theory; Wittrock, 1994). The first of these principles is that learning with understanding is a generative process, in which the learner or student actively builds meaning (Wittrock, 1974, 1990, 1991). The second of these principles is that learning with understanding involves the student construction of relations between experience and knowledge on the one hand and new events, problems, and data on the other hand (see principles 1, 2, and 3 of the APA learner-centered psychological principles [APA Presidential Task Force on Psychology in Education, 1993]).

From these two fundamental principles of cognitive learning, teaching and instruction derive distinct characteristics as well. First, teaching and instruction involve knowing the learners' preconceptions, models of subject matter principles, learning strategies, and metacognitive processes, as well as their attitudes, beliefs, anxieties, and self-concepts. Second, instruction and teaching involve leading the learners to generate meaning and understanding by using their learning strategies and metacognitive processes to construct relations between their background knowledge and the problems and events of the subject matter. In this model of generating teaching and learning, it is the learner who mentally and actively constructs explanations and understanding through generating relations between subject matter and knowledge and experience, and across difficult concepts presented in the subject matter (Wittrock, 1990, 1991).

Some of these principles of cognitive learning and teaching are as ancient as Socrates's attempts to teach logic, virtue, and the Pythagorean theorem by dialogue and questioning, which led the learner to construct understanding. Nonetheless, these principles, some of which are still not well accepted, have important implications for changing current teaching and instructional procedures. For example, these principles imply that teachers do not directly impart meaning to learners. That is, teachers do not teach in the everyday sense of the term. Nor is there only one meaning of instruction that is acquired by the students. Instead, even with direct teaching, that is teaching by telling, learners still construct meanings by use of their background knowledge, learning strategies, and metacognitive processes.

This implication means that direct teaching can still be effective. However, cognitive theory suggests a different way to understand how it or any other type of teaching influences learning. The influence is on the constructive thinking and affective processes of the learner. Effective teaching stimulates these thoughts and affective processes (Kourilsky & Wittrock, 1987, 1992; Mackenzie & White, 1982).

The recent research on the psychology of learning subject matters focuses on some important topics in the study of teaching that enhance our understanding of learning, transfer, and the training of intelligence and aptitude. These topics include (a) the learners' background knowledge and experience, (b) the learners' strategies for knowledge acquisition, (c) the learners' metacognitive processes, (d) the types of text relations (e.g., cause, effect, and sequence), (e) the types of text structure (e.g., enumeration, classification, and generalization), (f) the types of discourse structure (e.g., narration and exposition), (g) the types of constructive teaching procedures, (h) the learners' affective processes, (i) the types of measures of learners' thought processes and affective processes, and (j) the ways to teach comprehension and understanding. The recent research on reading comprehension, science, and mathematics represents the directions of the research on cognition and the teaching of subject matter.

Reading Comprehension

Reading research now focuses on reading comprehension, semantics, and pragmatics (Wittrock, 1981). Within this focus, the research has often demonstrated the critical role of the learners' background knowledge and experience in the construction of meaning. Schema theory builds on this principle. Research on reading comprehension has identified learning strategies used by good readers to actively construct meaning. These learning strategies include summarization, purpose in reading, attention direction, imagery, and inferencing (Wittrock, 1990, 1991). Research on reading comprehension has also studied metacognitive processes that readers can, but often do not, use to increase their comprehension. These metacognitive processes include planning, monitoring, and evaluation. The teaching of these learning strategies and metacognitive processes sometimes greatly (i.e., by a factor of two or more) enhances comprehension with no increase in time to read (Wittrock, 1990).

Somewhat less well-known but still impressive are the advances recently being made in identifying the different types of relations and different types of discourse or text structure involved in reading. The comprehension of narrative text often involves different grammars or organizations than does the comprehension of expository text that typifies many subject matters. McNeil (1987), for example, showed that children's stories often involve a simple four-part story grammar: (a) original setting, (b) problem, (c) solution, and (d) restoration of original setting. On the other hand, expository text often involves, as in biology, a hierarchical organization of specific to general categories and concepts. The types of relations to be constructed across the text concepts and between the text and the learners' experience and knowledge vary according to the type of text.

The teaching of reading comprehension according to these principles involves (a) the differentiation of the learning strategies learners can use best to their advantage with each type of text and with each subject matter, (b) the teaching of learners to identify each type of text, and (c) the teaching of metacognitive procedures that will organize for the learners a sequence of reading strategies appropriate for the text and the subject matter (Wittrock, in press). In this manner, reading comprehension is facilitated, transfer of successful reading processes is enhanced, and, perhaps, intelligence is trained as well. Some of these cognitive procedures are domain specific, such as a four-part story grammar, while other cognitive procedures are relatively domain free, such as summarization and inferencing and metacognitive procedures. These principles have fundamentally important implications for revising teacher education programs. Teachers should be taught how to teach students to generate meaning as they read by constructing summaries, analogies, and images, and by relating text to their experience. Teachers should be taught how to teach learning strategies and metacognitive processes to enable their students to guide their own generative processes as they read.

Science and Mathematics

Cognitive research in physical science and mathematics shows findings related to those of the research on reading comprehension (West & Pines, 1985; Wheatley, 1991). Again, the critical role of the learner's background knowledge, or preconceptions, has been repeatedly demonstrated. In science learning, children consistently show a finite, small number of conceptions of the flow of electrical current (Osborne, 1981; Osborne & Wittrock, 1983, 1985), of matter (Benson, Wittrock, & Baur, 1993), and of gravity and the shape of the earth (Nussbaum & Sharon-Dagan, 1983; Sneider & Pelos, 1983). These preconceptions are highly resistant to change and influence students' ability to learn scientific conceptions of these phenomena.

In mathematics, children's addition and subtraction strategies (Carpenter, Moser, & Romberg, 1982) and childrens' "bugs" or faulty addition and subtraction strategies (Brown & Burton, 1978) markedly influence their ability to learn to add and to subtract. Instruction in addition and subtraction needs to identify and to build on, or to correct, these previously learned strategies.

These, and related research findings, imply that the teaching of science or mathematics involves more than presenting the scientist's view of naturalistic phenomena, such as current flow, or more than presenting the mathematician's conception of addition and subtraction. Teaching involves leading learners to revise their previous conceptions, to modify or to reject procedures that they often feel are adequate and correct (Wittrock, 1994).

The types of expository text involved in word problems in mathematics and in physical science texts also involve learning the reading strategies I discussed earlier under the topic of reading comprehension. In addition, the reading of a scientific text involves structures not all of which are commonly found in narration. Cook and Mayer (1988) listed five types of structures of scientific text: (a) generalization, (b) enumeration, (c) sequence, (d) classification, and (e) comparison and contrast. Again, the structure of the text and the type of reading strategies appropriate for it should be combined into useful metacognitive procedures that will lead the learners to construct the semantic and pragmatic relations and the structure involved in comprehension.

In addition, the affective processes and self-concept involved in learning mathematics and physical science are critical for achievement in these subject matters. Ironically, competent and successful mathematics students sometimes feel that they are unable to learn mathematics as well as other students, who are no more successful, or actually less successful, than the competent students (Kimball, 1989).

In the research on mathematics and science learning there are interesting parallels to the research on reading comprehension in the processes of learning and teaching, such as some of the learning strategies and metacognitive processes. However, there are also important distinctions in the types of problems and text structures, and in the attitudes and beliefs about one's competence and ability to succeed.

The research on mathematics learning and science teaching shows, for example, that the more competent or more advanced learners, compared with the less competent learners, generate better representations of problems (Peled & Wittrock, 1990). The better problem solvers construct pragmatic or individualized contexts for problems that accurately reflect the stated problem. The more advanced learners or experts tend to classify and to represent problems according to their deep structure and according to their underlying mathematical or scientific principles (Alexander & Judy, 1988). These learners also are better at selecting strategies for solving problems than are the less competent learners. They seem to see a different problem than the one seen in the beginning student.

Less competent learners seldom effectively use metacognitive procedures. However, advanced learners in science have well-developed regulatory and self-monitoring metacognitive skills (Glaser, 1990). The more advanced learners frequently engage in conscious planning and frequently move from declarative knowledge to procedural skills.

Advanced learners also transfer their learning to new and related settings better than do the less well-prepared learners. Lehman, Lempert, and Nisbett (1988) explicated the nature of this transfer in relation to content learning. They studied transfer effects of graduate training in psychology, law, medicine, and chemistry. They found that graduate training in psychology and in medicine increased learners' ability to apply statistical and methodological reasoning to everyday problems. Graduate training in law increased learners' abilities to reason logically about complicated everyday problems. Apparently, these types of transfer occurred because training in psychology and medicine involve learning to apply statistics and methodological principles to complex applied problems. Training in law involves learning to apply logic and the law to the analysis and solution of complex practical problems.

Graduate training in chemistry, however, did not increase students' ability to do research on everyday problems. The study of practical problems is not often part of graduate training in chemistry, at least not to the extent that these problems occur in training in psychology, medicine, and law (see Ericcson & Charness, 1994, for related research).

These findings regarding mathematics learning, science teaching, and transfer through metacognition also have fundamental implications for revising teacher education. First, the research on preconceptions in science and mathematics clearly shows that teachers need to know student preconceptions and to understand that their students generate meaning in their classes by use of the models of mathematics and science that they bring to the classroom. Second, teachers need to know how to engage students in experiments, demonstrations, and discussions that involve familiar objects, events, and equipment the results of which they trust as representative of their real-world, everyday experience. Third, the enhancement of transfer by student use of learning strategies and metacognition implies a new focus in teacher education on the learning of ways to lead students to control their own learning processes (Wittrock, in press).

Conclusion

These studies of learning in different content areas show considerable coherence that advances understanding of the fundamental problems of learning, teaching, and transfer that Thorndike and Judd wrote about 90 years ago. The APA learner-centered psychological principles (APA, 1993) reflect many of these findings. These recent studies indicate that there are general metacognitive and executive skills (Belmont, Butterfield, & Ferretti, 1982; Wittrock, in press) that are relatively context free or domain free. These studies also show that there are learning strategies and principles of science and mathematics that are domain specific or content field specific. In addition, these studies indicate that there are procedures and strategies that are specific to principles or topics within a content field or discipline, such as addition and subtraction strategies. Less well understood, but of much significance, are the transfer skills and procedural knowledge involved in applying content areas to complex everyday problems.

In sum, the recent research on cognition and subject matter learning shows that the training of intelligence involves several levels: (a) metacognitive learning; (b) learning strategies; (c) executive skills; (d) subject matter learning; and (e) knowledge of principles and rules and specific situated knowledge. These data show that the training of intelligence involves subject matter learning, but it also involves student learning of metacognitive strategies, learning strategies, and transfer strategies. There is still a psychology of learning, and it has grown to include the psychologies of the learning of subject matters.

Teacher training programs can profit from these findings about the training of intelligence and the learning of subject matter. In teacher education programs, the students should learn the importance of the learners' metacognition, learning strategies, executive skills, and preconceptions in their learning, understanding, and transfer of subject-matter-based principles, rules, and situated knowledge. Learner-based cognitive psychological models of teaching offer a coherent and innovative research-based approach toward the reform and improvement of teacher education that can lead to major improvements in the learning and achievement of elementary and secondary school students.

References

Alexander, P. A., & Judy, J. E. (1988). The interaction of domain-specific and strategic knowledge in academic performance. *Review of Educational Research, 58,* 375–404.

American Psychological Association Presidential Task Force on Psychology in Education. (1993, January). *Learner-centered psychological principles: Guidelines for school redesign and reform.* Washington, DC: American Psychological Association and Mid-Continent Regional Educational Laboratory.

Belmont, J. M., Butterfield, E. C., & Ferretti, R. P. (1982). To secure transfer of training, instruct self-management skills. In D. K. Detterman & R. J. Sternberg (Eds.), *How and how much can intelligence be increased* (pp. 147–154)? Norwood, NJ: Ablex.

Benson, D. L., Wittrock, M. C., & Baur, M. E. (1993). Students' preconceptions of the nature of gases. *Journal of Research in Science Teaching, 30,* 587–597.

Brown, J. S., & Burton, R. R. (1978). Diagnostic models for procedural bugs in basic mathematical skills. *Cognitive Science, 2,* 155–192.

Carpenter, T. P., Moser, J. M., & Romberg, T. A. (1982). *Addition and subtraction: A cognitive perspective.* Hillsdale, NJ: Erlbaum.

Cook, L. K., & Mayer, R. E. (1988). Teaching readers about the structure of scientific text. *Journal of Educational Psychology, 80,* 448–456.

Ericsson, K. A., & Charness, N. (1994). Expert performance, its structure and acquisition. *American Psychologist, 49,* 725–747.

Glaser, R. (1990). The reemergence of learning theory within instructional research. *American Psychologist, 45,* 29–39.

Judd, C. H. (1908). The relation of special training to general intelligence. *Educational Review, 36,* 28–43.

Kimball, M. M. (1989). A new perspective on women's math achievement. *Psychological Bulletin, 105,* 198–214.

Kourilsky, M., & Wittrock, M. C. (1987). Verbal and graphical strategies in the teaching of economics. *Teaching and Teacher Education, 3,* 1–12.

Kourilsky, M., & Wittrock, M. C. (1992). Generative teaching: An enhancement strategy for the learning of economics in cooperative groups. *American Educational Research Journal, 29*(4), 861–876.

Lehman, D. R., Lempert, R. O., & Nisbett, R. E. (1988). The effects of graduate training on reasoning. *American Psychologist, 43,* 431–442.

MacKenzie, A. W., & White, R. T. (1982). Fieldwork in geography and long-term memory structures. *American Educational Research Journal, 19,* 623–632.

McNeil, J. (1987). *Reading comprehension.* Glenview, IL: Scott Foresman.

Nussbaum, J., & Sharon-Dagan, N. (1983). Changes in second grade children's preconceptions about the earth as a cosmic body resulting from a short series of audio-tutorial lessons. *Science Education, 67,* 99–114.

Osborne, R. J. (1981). Children's ideas about electric current. *New Zealand Science Teacher, 29,* 12–19.

Osborne, R. J., & Wittrock, M. C. (1983). Learning science: A generative process. *Science Education, 67*(4), 489–504.

Osborne, R. J., & Wittrock, M. C. (1985). The generative learning model and its implications for science education. *Studies in Science Education, 12,* 59–87.

Peled, Z., & Wittrock, M. C. (1990). Generated meanings in the comprehension of word problems in mathematics. *Instructional Science, 19,* 171–205.

Plato. (1924). Meno. In W. R. M. Lamb (Ed.), *Plato* (pp. 265–377). Cambridge, MA: Harvard University Press, Loeb Classical Library.

Sneider, C., & Pelos, S. (1983). Children's cosmographies: Understanding the earth's shape and gravity. *Science Education, 67,* 205–221.

Thorndike, E. L. (1922). *The psychology of arithmetic.* New York: Macmillan.

Thorndike, E. L., & Woodworth, R. S. (1901). The influence of improvement in one mental function upon the efficiency of other functions. *Psychological Review, 8,* 247–261, 384–395, 553–564.

West, L. H. T., & Pines, A. L. (1985). Cognitive structure and conceptual change. San Diego, CA: Academic Press.

Wheatley, G. H. (1991). Constructivist perspectives on science and mathematics learning. *Science Education, 75,* 9–21.

Wittrock, M. C. (1974). Learning as a generative process. *Educational Psychologist, 11,* 87–95.

Wittrock, M. C. (1981). Reading comprehension. In F. J. Pirozzolo & M. C. Wittrock (Eds.), *Neuropsychological and cognitive processes in reading.* San Diego, CA: Academic Press.

Wittrock, M. C. (1987). Process oriented measures of comprehension. *The Reading Teacher, 40,* 734–737.

Wittrock, M. C. (1990). Generative processes of comprehension. *Educational Psychologist, 24,* 345–376.

Wittrock, M. C. (1991). Generative learning processes of the brain. *Educational Psychologist, 27,* 531–541.

Wittrock, M. C. (1994). Generative science teaching. In P. J. Fensham, R. F. Gunstone, & R. T. White (Eds.), *The content of science: A constructivist approach to its teaching and learning* (pp. 29–38). London: Falmer Press.

Wittrock, M. C. (in press). *Metacognition.* In C. E. Weinstein & B. L. McCombs (Eds.), *Issues in school reform.* Washington, DC: American Psychological Association.

Wittrock, M. C., & Baker, E. (1991). *Testing and cognition.* Englewood Cliffs, NJ: Prentice-Hall.

Designing a Community of Young Learners: Theoretical and Practical Lessons

Ann L. Brown and Joseph C. Campione

A community of learners reflects a classroom ethos different from that found in traditional classrooms. In the traditional classroom, students are perceived as relatively passive learners who receive wisdom from teachers, textbooks, or other media. In the community of learners classroom, students are encouraged to engage in self-reflective learning and critical inquiry. They act as researchers who are responsible, to some extent, for defining their own knowledge and expertise. In the community of learners classroom, teachers are expected to serve as active role models of learning and as responsive guides to students' discovery processes. Teachers learn to provide instruction on a need-to-know basis, which allows them to respond to students' needs, rather than to a fixed scope and sequence schedule or an inflexible lesson plan (Brown & Campione, 1990, 1996). Instead of emphasizing breadth of coverage, the content of the curriculum features a few recurring themes that students come to understand at increasingly sophisticated levels of explanatory coherence and theoretical generality. In addition, the technological environment is designed to foster an intentional learning environment, not to drill and practice or program (Scardamalia & Bereiter, 1991), thereby encouraging student reflection and discussion. Finally, in the community of learners classroom, methods of assessment focus on the students' ability to discover and use knowledge,

The research reported in this chapter was supported by grants from the James S. McDonnell Foundation, the Andrew W. Mellon Foundation, and the Evelyn Lois Carey Research Fund. Preparation of this chapter was supported by grants from the Andrew W. Mellon and James S. McDonnell Foundations.

rather than focusing on basic retention, and on-line dynamic measures of performance are as important as static measures of product.

The History of Learning Theory

The community of learners classroom and the theories that support it are best understood in light of the history and development of learning theory in this century. Neither psychological research nor curriculum reform take place in a vacuum. Psychologists are creatures of their time, and the methods they use to attack such durable problems as learning must be considered in the light of the period in which their research took place. Learning theory has undergone major change in this century, although it is often represented as static and established when in fact it is not. By the same token, methods of studying learning in children have also undergone radical change.

Under the auspices of the so-called cognitive revolution, there has been nothing short of a sea change in theories of learning, with a corresponding revolution in how learning is conceived, observed, and fostered. A dramatic change occurred in what students were required to learn, even in laboratory settings, and an awakening to the fact that real-life learning is intrinsically entangled with situations, one cluster of such situations being the classroom.

This transformation of psychological learning theory had several major facets. First, learners came to be viewed as active constructors of knowledge, rather than passive recipients of static knowledge (Brown, 1975, 1978). Second, learners became imbued with powers of introspection, once verboten: One of the most interesting things about human learning is that the learner has knowledge and feelings about it, sometimes even control of it—an area of research now known as *metacognition* (Brown, Bransford, Ferrara, & Campione, 1983). Third, humans, although excellent all-purpose learning machines, like all biologically evolved creatures, are predisposed to learn certain things more readily than others (Carey & Gelman, 1991).

The field of developmental psychology expanded rapidly during this period, providing research with valuable information concerning children's learning. On the basis of earlier behaviorist theories of learning, a model of the child emerged that severely underestimated young children's capabilities. It was received wisdom that young children had limited attention spans. They were deemed incapable of inferential reasoning, of certain forms of classification, and of insightful learning and transfer. We now know this is not true, but because of these assumed problems of immaturity, it was believed that in school, children should work to mastery on decontextualized skills for short periods of time under conditions of positive and negative reinforcement.

Research now shows that small children understand and can do a great deal more than previously thought. By age 5, children understand basic principles of biological and physical causality. They learn rapidly about number, narrative, and personal intent. They entertain theories of mind. And we now know a great deal about older students' acquisition of disciplined bodies of knowledge characteristic of academic subject areas (e.g., mathematics, science, computer programming, and social studies and history). Higher order thinking has returned as a subject of inquiry (Brown, 1994).

During the latter part of the century, psychologists also began considering input from other branches of cognitive science—anthropology, sociology, and linguistics—and they began to consider learning settings outside the laboratory, or even the classroom walls. It is clear that a strictly laboratory-based psychological theory of learning is, and always was, a chimera.

Transforming Classrooms

Laboratory Learning: Reciprocal Teaching

These changes in learning theory led us to consider forms of learning derived from these new theories of education. Together with our colleagues, we began a series of classroom-based studies concentrating on guided instruction and assessment in social contexts (Brown et al., 1983; Brown, Campione, Reeve, Ferrara, & Palincsar, 1991). In this chapter we focus on the most extensive of these programs, reciprocal teaching —a procedure designed to foster comprehension and cognitive monitoring while reading (Palincsar & Brown, 1984), solving mathematics problems (Campione, Brown, & Connell, 1988; Reeve, Gordon, Campione, & Brown, 1990), and learning science (Brown & Campione, 1990).

Our primary work on reciprocal teaching centered on strategic reading. Although the focus was theoretical—the role of strategies, metacognition, content, and context on learning and understanding—

the applied value of the work is apparent. Students learn to read and understand.

In a typical reciprocal teaching session the participants in a group of about six members take turns leading a discussion about a text. The participants divide themselves into groups consisting of a learning leader (adult or child) and learning listeners/critics for each segment of text. The learning leader begins the discussion by asking a question and ends by summarizing the gist of what has been read. The group rereads and discusses possible problems of interpretation when necessary. Questioning provides the impetus to get the discussion going. Summarizing at the end of a period of discussion helps students establish where they are in preparation for tackling a new segment of text. Attempts to clarify any comprehension problems that might occur arise opportunistically, and the leaders ask for predictions about future content. The four activities—questioning, clarifying, summarizing, and predicting—are selected to bolster the discussion because they are excellent comprehension monitoring devices. For example, if one cannot summarize what one has read, this is an indication that understanding is not proceeding smoothly and that remedial action is needed. The strategies also provide the repeatable structure necessary to begin a discussion, a structure that can be phased out when students are experienced in the discourse mode.

When it is the adult teacher's turn to be the leader, she models mature versions of the strategies. When it is a child's turn, the adult teacher and the rest of the groups are there to provide support. Students exposed to regular practice of this kind improve their reading scores dramatically and transfer their new competence broadly. Reading becomes a tool of wide applicability.

Over time our studies of reciprocal teaching of reading comprehension became more complex as the method became increasingly incorporated into the dynamics of classroom life. We began working one-on-one with children who were reading unconnected passages in laboratory settings (Brown & Palincsar, 1982) and progressed to studying children in groups in resource rooms outside the classroom (Palincsar & Brown, 1984), then to considering naturally occurring reading groups in the classroom (Brown & Palincsar, 1989), and finally to studying reading comprehension groups that were fully integrated into science classrooms (Brown & Campione, 1990). We began by concentrating on a few constrained strategies and proceeded to study complex explanation, argument, and discussion forms. Initially, we looked at students reading unconnected passages and proceeded to look at students reading coherent content (Brown & Campione, 1996; Palincsar, Brown, & Campione, 1990). Now, the procedure is incorporated within the daily life of classroom activity. We observe reading comprehension as it takes place in groups of students who are reading, discussing, and arguing about cohesive material they have prepared themselves, thus acquiring ownership of that knowledge.

Classroom Observations and Experimentation: Communities of Learners

In our current work, reciprocal teaching is only one component of the design experiment intended to encourage distributed expertise (Brown, 1990) in a community of learners (Brown, Ash, Rutherford, Nakagawa, Gordon, & Campione, 1993). Although we have worked with students from 7 to 14 years old, we concentrate in this chapter primarily on sixth graders (11- to 12-year-olds). The setting is a science classroom where sixth-grade students are responsible for doing collaborative research and sharing their expertise with their colleagues.

To foster a community of learners that features students as designers of their own learning, we encourage students to be partially responsible for creating their own curriculum. The two major forms of cooperative learning used to accomplish this are the jigsaw method (Aronson, 1978) and the reciprocal teaching method. Students are assigned curriculum themes (e.g., changing populations) divided into five subtopics (changing populations = extinct, endangered, artificial, assisted, and urbanized populations). Students form five research groups, each assigned responsibility for one of the five subtopics. These research groups prepare teaching materials using computer technology (Campione, Brown, & Jay, 1992). Then, using the jigsaw method, the students separate into learning groups in which each student is expert in one subtopic, responsible for one fifth of the information. Each fifth needs to be combined with the remaining fifths to make a whole unit, hence jigsaw. The choice of a discussion leader is now based on expertise rather than random selection, as was the case in the original reciprocal teaching work. All children in a learning group are expert on one part of the material, teach it to others, and prepare questions for the test that all will take on the complete unit. During this cyclical process, students both acquire content expertise and learn how to learn from texts and other media (Brown & Campione, 1990).

Thus, the students are involved in the following learning behaviors:

(a) extensive reading to research their topic; (b) writing and revision to produce books from which to teach; and (c) computer use to publish, illustrate, and edit their books. In addition, a great deal of cognitive monitoring must take place in order for the students to set priorities concerning what to include in their books, what to teach, what to test, how to explain mechanisms, and so forth. They read, write, discuss, revise, set priorities, and use computers all in the service of learning.

Essential Characteristics of a Community of Learners

The two main activities, reciprocal teaching and jigsaw, form an essential core of the community of learners, where students undertake research and share their knowledge with each other. Adult teachers provide guidance and direction through the design of units and the selection of material to support sustained inquiry on a topic. They also bring the whole class into conference occasionally to track progress and set learning goals.

With a group of teachers and with inner-city students, we have evolved a view of the essential features that characterize our ideal classroom environment. As each new teacher is involved from the outset in the organic growth of his or her version of the program, one compatible with our underlying learning principles and his or her own practices, there is considerable variability in different classes. With the teachers, we have settled on several characteristics of successful classrooms that must be operating for the program to be judged in place. These essential characteristics are discussed in turn.

Individual Responsibility Coupled With Communal Sharing

Students and teachers each have "ownership" of certain forms of expertise, but no one has expertise in all areas. Responsible members of the community share the expertise they have or take responsibility for finding out about needed knowledge. Expertise is distributed deliberately through the jigsaw and reciprocal teaching collaborative learning activities that ensure that students learn complementary material and can thus teach from strength.

Expertise is also distributed by happenstance; variability in expertise arises naturally within these classrooms (Brown & Campione, 1996). We refer to this as *majoring*. Children are free to major in a variety of ways, free to learn and teach whatever they like within the confines of the selected topic. Children select topics as their special areas of interest (e.g., some children become resident experts on DDT and pesticides; some specialize in disease and contagion; younger children often adopt a particular endangered species). Within the community of the classroom, these varieties of expertise are implicitly recognized, although not the subject of much talk.

Subcultures of expertise develop: Varieties of expertise are recognized by the pattern of help-seeking and the role students assume in small group and class discussions. In these discussions, the class defers to expert children in both verbal and nonverbal ways. Status in discussions does not reside "in" the individual child, however, as in the case of established leaders and followers, but is a transient phenomenon that depends on a child's perceived expertise within the domain of discourse. As the domain of discourse changes, so too do the students receiving deferential treatment.

Ritual and Familiar Participant Structures

Principal participation frameworks are few and are practiced repeatedly. One common classroom routine is for the students to be divided into three groups, one composing on the computers, one conducting research using a variety of media, with the remaining children interacting with the teacher in some way: editing manuscripts, discussing progress, or working with the teacher in some other way. Another repetitive frame is that the class is engaged in reciprocal teaching research seminars or jigsaw teaching activities, with approximately five research/teaching groups in simultaneous sessions. Another feature, "crosstalk," a whole class activity, was introduced by the students. In crosstalk students from the various research groups periodically report on their progress to date, and students from other working groups ask questions for clarification or extension. The various working groups thereby talk "across groups" and provide comprehension checks to each other. The final activity features the classroom teacher, or an outside expert, conducting a class lesson, modeling thinking skills and self-reflection, introducing new information, stressing higher order relationships, or encouraging the class to pool their expertise in a novel conceptualization of the topic. The repetitive, indeed, ritualistic nature of these activities is an essential aspect of the classroom, for it enables children to make the transition from one participant structure to another quickly and effortlessly. As soon as students recognize a participant structure, they understand the role expected of them. Thus, although there is room for individual agendas and discovery in these classrooms, they are highly structured to permit students and teachers to navigate between repetitive activities as effortlessly as possible.

A Community of Discourse

It is essential that a community of discourse, an interpretive community (Fish, 1980), be established in which constructive discussion, questioning, and criticism are the mode rather than the exception. Speech activities involving increasingly scientific modes of thinking, such as conjecture, speculation, evidence, and proof become part of the common voice of the community. Successful acculturation into the community leads participants to recognize the difference between, and appropriate place of, both everyday versions of speech activities having to do with the physical and natural world and the discipline-embedded special versions of the same activities (O'Connor, 1991).

Multiple Zones of Proximal Development

Theoretically, we conceive of the classroom as composed of multiple zones of proximal development (Vygotsky, 1978) through which participants can navigate using different routes and at different rates (Brown & Reeve, 1987). A zone of proximal development defines the distance between current levels of comprehension and levels that can be accomplished in collaboration with other people or using powerful artifacts. It can include adults and children with varying expertise, but it can also include artifacts such as books, videos, wall displays, scientific equipment, and a computer environment intended to support intentional learning (Scardamalia & Bereiter, 1991). The zone of proximal development embodies a concept of readiness to learn that emphasizes upper, rather than lower, levels of competence. These boundaries are not immutable but rather constantly changing as the learner becomes increasingly independent at successively more advanced levels.

Seeding, Migration, and Appropriation of Ideas

In our classroom, teachers and students create zones of proximal development by *seeding* the environment with ideas and concepts that they value and by harvesting those that "take" in the community. Ideas seeded by community members *migrate* to other participants and persist over time. Participants in the classroom are free to *appropriate* vocabulary, ideas, methods, and so forth that appear initially as part of the shared discourse, and by appropriation, transform these ideas through personal interpretation. Ideas that are part of the common discourse are not necessarily appropriated by all, or in the same manner by everyone. Because the appropriation of ideas and activities is multidirectional, we use the term *mutual appropriation* (Newman, Griffin, & Cole, 1989).

The Nature of the Curriculum

Although there is considerable room for discovery and individual majoring in these classrooms, we intentionally engineer the curriculum in certain ways. The teacher's role here is complex; he or she must see that curriculum content is "discovered," understood, and transmitted efficiently and at the same time recognize and encourage students' independent majoring attempts. But what is the place of a set curriculum in discovery classrooms? True, it would be possible to allow the students to discover on their own, charting their own course of studies, exploring at will; but, to be responsive to the course requirements of normal schools, we believe it necessary to set boundaries on the curriculum to be covered. In general our approach is to select enduring themes for discussion and to revisit them often, each time at an increasingly more mature level of understanding. This idea of a spiraling curriculum was adapted from Bruner (1963).

Under the general umbrella of the themes and subunits, students are introduced to some critical underlying notions. For example, in biology we concentrate on interdependence and adaptation. Grade school children become increasingly interested in cross-cutting themes that would form the basis of an understanding of such principles as metabolic rate, reproduction strategies, and structural and behavioral adaptations, although at a very elementary level. For example, a member of a group studying elephants became fixated on the amount of food consumed by elephants and, subsequently, by other animals, notably the panda and the sea otter. Although relatively small, the sea otter consumes vast quantities of food because, "It doesn't have blubber, and living in a cold sea, it needs food for energy to keep warm." When an adult observer mentioned the similar case of the hummingbird's need for a great deal of food, this student caught on to the notion of metabolic rate, a concept that he introduced in all subsequent discussions. The notion of metabolic rate, seeded by one student, quickly migrated throughout the classroom, was appropriated by many, came to form part of the common discourse, and eventually made its way into the class book on endangered species.

As a further example, a group of students studying whales became interested in fertility rates and the fate of low birth weight babies. They discovered that one reason that certain species of whales are endangered is that their reproduction rate has slowed dramatically. The same was found to be true of sea otters. These students introduced the concept of declining fertility rates into the discussion, and it was taken up in the common discourse in two forms: simply as the notion of the number of babies a species has and more complexly as the notion of reproductive strategies in general. The skilled teacher appropriates students' spontaneous interest in the common problems of endangered animals—amount of food eaten, amount of land required, number of young, and so forth—and encourages them to consider the deeper general principles of metabolic rate and survival and reproductive strategies.

Evaluating the Success of the Program

Content Knowledge

We concentrated first on the acquisition of biological knowledge. In short, did the students learn anything about the curriculum? We used an extensive battery of static and dynamic pretest and posttest measures as well as on-line indexes of conceptual change. We augmented pretest and posttest scores by the use of portfolios and student products. The database is extremely rich, and we concentrate here on the more traditional pretest-posttest tasks and extension activities of knowledge utilization.

All students receive short-answer tests on the entire theme before and after each unit. Half of the items are generated by the student research teams and half by our staff. The results of short-answer tests over a period of a year with sixth graders are shown in Figure 1. Students in the research classes were compared with a partial control group (PCont) that was treated exactly the same as the research classroom for the first semester (Unit 1) and then taught environmental science by their regular science teacher. The partial control group had exactly the same access to books, videos, computers, and so forth as did the re-

Figure 1

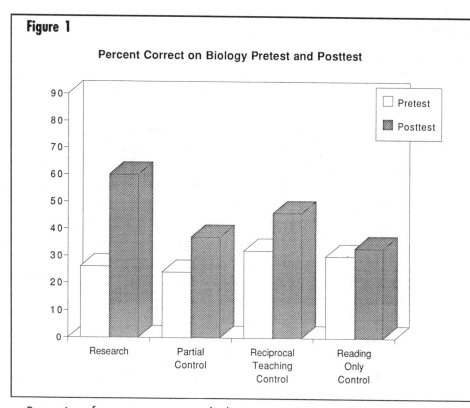

Proportion of correct responses on biology pretest and posttest as a function of experimental condition.

search classrooms. As can be seen, the two groups did not differ from each other on Unit 1, where they were, in effect, treated exactly the same; but the children in the research classrooms outperformed the partial control group on both Units 2 and 3 (second and third semesters). A read only control (ROC) group, that read the key materials but did no research, did poorly throughout. These "quick assessments" given to all students assure us that domain-specific content is retained better by students in the research classrooms.

Using Organized Knowledge Flexibly

The next question is, Can the students use the information flexibly? Students differ in their level of understanding and in the confidence with which they hold opinions. To test this we developed a clinical interview (Ash & Brown, 1993) consisting of a series of questions designed to be sensitive to the bandwidth of competence within which each individual student can navigate (Brown & Reeve, 1987). To map the window of opportunity for learning, the interviewer raises a series of key questions. First, he or she elicits basic expository information (e.g., what does the student know about the herbivore-carnivore distinction?). If the student cannot answer, the interviewer provides hints and examples as necessary to test the student's readiness to learn that concept. If, however, the student seems initially knowledgeable, the interviewer questions the stability of that understanding by introducing counterexamples to the student's beliefs and, again if appropriate, the interviewer might ask the student to engage in thought experiments that demand novel uses of the information. For example, a student who has sorted pictures into herbivores and carnivores, and justified the choices, may be asked, "What would happen on the African plain if there were no gazelles or other meat for cheetahs to eat? Could they eat grain?" Some students are surprisingly uncertain about this, suggesting that cheetahs could eat grain under certain circumstances, although they would not live happily. Some even entertain a critical period hypothesis—that the cheetah could change if it were forced to eat grain from infancy, but once it reached adolescence, it would be too set in its ways to change. Only a few invoked notions of form and function, such as properties of the digestive tract or dentition, to support the assertion that cheetahs could not change. These extension activities of thought experiments and counterexamples are far more revealing of the current state of students' knowledge than their first unchallenged answers.

We see the same benefit of being in the research classroom on novel application tasks, such as when students are asked to design an animal to fit a particular habitat (desert, tundra, or rain forest) or to design an animal of the future. The students in the research classroom outperformed control students in the number of biologically appropriate mechanisms they included in their designs (e.g., mechanisms of defense, reproductive strategies). Over time the research students introduced significantly more novel variations of taught principles along with more truly novel ideas. For example, the class had discussed the notion of mimicry as a defense mechanism. One student's design included the fact that the eggs of his animal were placed in a line and the markings made the eggs look like a "full grown cobra," a novel use of the mimicry principle. Another student incorporated the notion of behavioral mimicry that had not been taught, still another introduced the concept of a predator's injecting a poison to which it was itself immune, so that the predator could safely devour the stunned prey.

Responses to clinical interviews, "what if" thought experiments, and analogy and transfer tests tell us a great deal about the status of a child's accumulating knowledge and ability to reason on the basis of incomplete knowledge. We regard them as fruitful avenues for promoting and evaluating students' ability to think critically about knowledge, an antidote to the stockpiling of passive, inert knowledge (Whitehead, 1916).

Reading Ability

Although regarded as a science curriculum, the program of research is very much an extension of the original reading comprehension work that began with reciprocal teaching (Palincsar & Brown, 1984). Our main "transfer" data, therefore, take the form of (a) improvement in students' reading comprehension scores on materials outside the domain of study; and (b) gradual acquisition of increasingly complex forms of argumentation and explanation strategies. We limit ourselves here to a few representative samples.

We begin with an example of sixth graders' performance on criterion-referenced tests of reading comprehension. At the beginning and end of the year, students read age-appropriate expository passages unrelated to the curriculum and answered a set of questions from memory. These data are shown in Figure 2a. Students in the research classroom outperformed a comparison group reading the same passages using reciprocal teaching, even though the reciprocal teaching groups were given at least twice as much practice in collaborative reading procedures and in taking tests of this nature. A read-only control group failed to show improvement. We also included a partial control group consisting of sixth graders who were treated the same as the experimental group for the first semester but taught by their regular classroom teacher after that. They also failed to achieve the same gains.

On each passage students were asked four fact and four inferential questions, together with a gist question requiring them to summarize the main theme of the entire passage and an analogy question in which they were asked to solve a problem that was analogous to the problem solved in the target passage. In Figure 2b, we show the differential improvement according to question type for the research students. By design, students scored well on simple fact-based questions (to ensure that they achieved some success); as a result, there was no improvement on

Figure 2

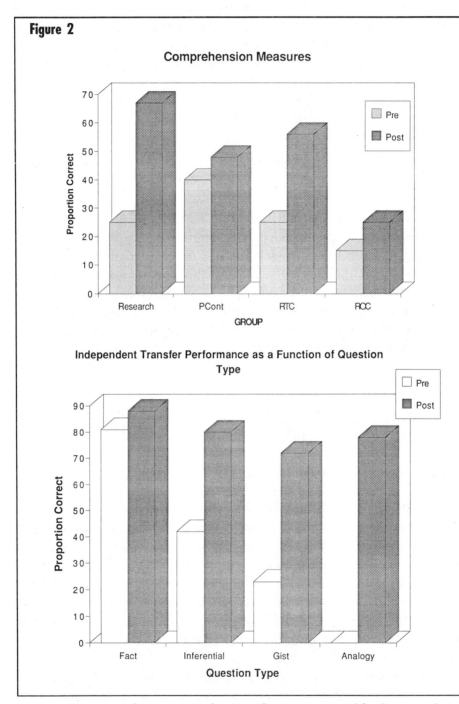

Comprehension performance as a function of groups (top), and for the research group, as a function of question type (bottom).

this measure. On inferential, gist, and analogy questions, however, there was significant improvement. In particular, regular practice greatly improved the students' ability to use analogous information to solve problems; that is, practice created a mind-set to reason by analogy (Brown & Kane, 1988).

Argumentation Skills

Increasingly powerful comprehension-extending activities occurred in the student dialogues. The use of deep analogies and causal explanations increased over time. Explanations were more often supported by warrants and backings (Toulmin, 1958). The nature of what constitutes evidence was discussed, including a consideration of negative evidence. A variety of plausible reasoning strategies (Collins & Stevens, 1982) began to emerge. Argumentation formats developed, in which different points of view and defensible interpretations were compared. The nature and importance of prediction evolved, with students going beyond predictions of simple outcomes to considering possible worlds and engaging in thought experiments about them.

Teaching Techniques

Inside the School

For the Fostering Communities of Learners program to run optimally, adults are needed to lead jigsaw and reciprocal teaching seminars, but of course having a large number of adults available to serve this function is not feasible. We try to design the classroom activities in such a way that they can be sustained in average classrooms conducted by average teachers. As a rule of thumb, we have no more than two adults, the equivalent of a teacher and an aide, interacting with the students. Other adults in the classroom serve purely observational or data collection roles.

For these reasons we rely heavily on the expertise of the students themselves. We use peer- and cross-age tutoring, both face-to-face and by electronic mail, and we also use older students as discussion leaders guiding the reciprocal teaching groups of younger students.

Cross-Age Tutoring

Our cross-age tutoring program involves 10- to 12-year-old students working with 7- and 8-year-olds. The tutors receive 4 weeks of training. The class discusses questioning, listening, relating personal experiences to text, and so forth. In addition, the experienced older students are reminded of (a) reciprocal teaching procedures; (b) guided writing using computers; (c) pair editing in which students work in pairs to compose and edit texts; and (d) the content area of interest to both age groups (note that both older and younger students focus on endangered species in their environmental science units). Finally, the older students are introduced to the rudiments of ethnographic methods—what to look for, field notes, interviewing tutees, and so forth (Heath & Mangiola, 1991).

Students as Discussion Leaders

We also prepare our older students to act as discussion leaders. Although we experience some of the same difficulties with students as with adult teachers, notably the tendency to be too directive, 11-year-olds are remarkably facile at leading discussions. They mimic activities modeled by their own adult teachers and enact them with their young charges. Student teachers introduced examples of both thinking activities and content area knowledge into the wider community. An example of this can be seen in Exhibit 1, which presents an 11-year-old's discussion as she attempts to dispel the common belief of younger children that plants eat soil as food.

Guest Teachers

Because we work primarily with grade school teachers who are not subject area specialists, we provide additional support in the form of outside subject area experts who interact with the teachers and students, either in person or electronically. Exhibit 2 presents the script of an outside expert, a biologist, beginning her second class lesson with this group by modeling thinking and research skills, and introducing biological ideas and terminology. In response to a student's question, the teacher not only introduces the term *sexual dimorphism* but also points out that she has been thinking about the problem all week. The exact answer is not in the books she has, and she invites the students to join her in a thought experiment about how a biologist might reason this

Exhibit 1

Cross-Age Tutoring

First session together (extracted from a 31 page transcript)

Cast:

Fl	Eleven-year-old teacher
Cr, Ke, Je, Da	Eight-year-old returning students
Ri Ne, Tr	Eight-year-olds new to program

Tr Presents (p. 22 of transcript)

[Tells group of her urban wildlife: monkey flower and wild carrot Questioning begins]

Je: When the monkey flower dies, does it turn all brown and all the feathers come off? I mean, you know, the leaves.

Tr: It limps. It goes like that [body movement of limp plant].

Ri: What does it eat?

Tr: Water. It eats water and, this is how you make its food. With air, sunlight and water.

Ri: What does the wild carrot eat?

Tr: It eats the same thing, and it can eat dirt too. That's what it eats—

Ke: Does you animal, I mean plant, need soil? Does it need soil?

Ne: Water.

Tr: [Calls on student teacher, who has her hand up] Fl.

Fl: Plants don't eat soil. They don't eat soil at all. There was this experiment that was—

Je: Soil is dirt. That's where they growing.

Fl: They just grow in it, but they don't eat it. They make their own food. You know how, like how the carbon dioxide and everything, they mix that in, and that act is called photosynthesis. So they don't—

Tr: How do you spell that?

[Fl writes the word on paper, gives to Tr who copies it into her field notes]

Fl: For one thing, there was an experiment—a gallon, I think about five gallons of soil was put under a redwood tree that started growing, and as soon as it was real, real tall, the scientist took the barrel of soil away, and found that only about two ounces were taken away. Only about two ounces were all.

Tr: It doesn't need the earth for food? It makes its own?

through. She then explicitly poses a thinking challenge and introduces the notion of advantages and disadvantages of a particular adaptation. Later, she entertains a student's erroneous suggestion that the larger

---

Exhibit 2

Whole Class Discussion led by Visiting Expert (VE)

R:	There's this one topic that I really want to find out about, is why female peregrine falcons are larger than males.

VE:	I know that question has been on your mind; you've mentioned it three different times. It's been on my mind since Tuesday. Do you know the first thing I did when I got home? I got all my biology books out, and the topic I looked up is sexual dimorphism. I have my biology hat on. Right now I'm talking as a biologist. And I'm going to use some biological terms. Sexual has to do with male and female, right? "Di" means two. "Morph" has to do with how you look. It really means form.

VE:	What's the question? The question was, R?

R:	Why are the female peregrine falcons larger than the males?

VE:	I said OK, the male and female, having two looks, male and female. In my books do you know what they said? They said usually the male bird is more gorgeous and has better feathers and is red and blue. And the female is kind of drab. Drab means kind of dull looking. I said, "Huhh?" That's true right, but that's not the peregrine falcon. In your RT texts, it specifically said they look pretty much the same. Right? And the female is bigger. So we're not talking about pretty males and drab females are we? But the books said this: when you have pretty males and drab females, usually the male does not help take care of the babies. Hint. And I said that probably tells me that the male peregrine helps take care of the baby because he looks like the female. So then I said, "T, you're a biologist. How would a biologist think this problem through? Let's think like a biologist."

[Students make suggestions, mimic putting on biologist hats]

VE:	Now here's a new thinking challenge for you. We need to think what is the advantage, the pros, of being bigger, and what are the disadvantages, the cons. The pros and cons. And in the biological world you add those pros and cons up, and usually you weigh them. Let's think about some advantages and disadvantages. And here is where we are all on the same ground. I couldn't find it in a book, and I'm asking [student teachers] to help me because none of my books said anything about it. Really think, think, think. What might be an advantage of being bigger if you were a female peregrine falcon? Forget the male for now.

El:	She can scare people away because she's bigger.

N:	She can keep the babies warmer?

R:	Protect her babies.

VE:	What's a disadvantage? El?

continued

Exhibit 2, continued

La: This is an advantage because if she is bigger therefore she can produce more babies because she has enough womb to make a lot more babies than if she was smaller than the male.

Ma: She's not going to have more babies because look, humans are bigger than peregrines, and they only have one baby, sometimes twins. And what about elephants? They only have one baby every three years. N?

Two Weeks Later

El: . . . like because all birds of prey are called raptors, and a lot of the raptors are bigger than the . . . have females that are bigger than the males.

Ta: Since the female is larger she's able to feed on a larger prey than the male is.

VE: All right now, we are talking about survival, having babies and not dying, and getting food, right? We talked about advantages and disadvantages. That's a big idea.

VE: All right, let's direct our eyes back to our food chain. [Peregrine falcon food chain designed by students and displayed on board.] Now here's my thought process yesterday. Biologist's hat. Now catch this. What if, because the female is a third larger, in their territory— the place that they live—what if she can take advantage of eating things like ducks and pigeons, which are relatively *large* birds, and the male, because he's a little smaller, he can take advantage of eating relatively *small* birds, how might that give an advantage? Now think this through please. I want some thoughtful processes here. How might this help?

Lee: Well, it would help them because they could, they could use a smaller place to live, like a territory. Because if the male, if it eats different food from the female, it would be less likely to run short on food. Uhm. . .

Ned: It would make it better for them because they would like have, both of them go out and hunt at different times. It's like the female could bring back bigger prey, the male could bring back smaller prey. And they could put it together and have more food.

size of the female might allow her to have more eggs, a suggestion that is rejected by a student by recourse to negative evidence. Still later, while accepting a student's correct solution, the teacher talks about her own thought process and directs them to a crucial part of their readings illustrating the notion of competitive advantage that the students understand.

Beyond the School

We turn next to the use of electronic mail to extend the research community beyond the classroom walls, thereby creating richer zones of proximal development for community members. For example, consider the following exchange between a biologist (MJ) and a group of students. The interaction was initiated by the students, who queried the status of hibernation for bears that live in zoos:

> Our major question is what happens to the bears that live in the zoo if they can't hibernate? DA [the science teacher] said that they don't need to hibernate because they are fed every day. But she said that was only a thought so I am asking you to please help us by giving us all you know and all you can find.

MJ responded with some information; admitting that he didn't really know the answer, he suggested a hypothesis and provided a phone number for the group to find out more information on their own volition. Throughout the interchange, MJ systematically seeded three pieces of information critical for an understanding of hibernation—the availability of resources, longevity, and warm- versus cold-bloodedness:

> You probably think about hibernating in the same way as you think about sleeping, but they aren't the same. Bears hibernate in response to the weather conditions and the availability of food. If the conditions are reasonably fair (not too cold) and food is available, the bear probably won't hibernate. I don't know, but I hypothesize that during the times when bears would usually hibernate, bears in captivity are probably a bit slower, still showing signs of their tendency to hibernate at that time of the year. How could you find out if my hypothesis is true? (Hint: phone number of local zoo)

The topic is then dropped by the group but taken up by one group member (AM) who is majoring in hibernation and wishes to know about hibernation patterns in insects. She inquires to the network in general:

> I was wondering if you can find out an answer to this question. The question is does insects hibernate? The reason why we ask that is because MR [classroom teacher] read a book named *Once There Was a Tree*. And in it, it said something about the insects slept in the bark of the tree when winter came. Then when spring came they got up and did what they usually do till winter comes, then they start all over again.

Receiving no response, the student then addresses MJ directly about the topic. As a gesture of good faith, she begins by offering some facts of her own before asking for information:

> Bears hibernate because whatever they eat is gone during the winter (like berries) and they can't eat so that's what hibernation is for. It is for them to get away from starvation. So what does tarantula's eat? Can they always get their food? If they can't get their food would they have to hibernate or die? Could we ask somebody that knows about insects?

MJ responds with another prompt to encourage the student to take the initiative and approach experts, pointing out that the contact person at another local zoo is ready and willing to help. The persistent AM sends yet another request, and MJ reenters the fray. Following a lengthy discussion on the reproduction and survival strategies of insects, he continues with a series of questions intended to push the student to further and further depths of inquiry, a typical strategy of guides in a zone of proximal development. In this communication, MJ introduces the notion of *longevity*, prompting AM to consider the fact that if an insect lives only one season, hibernation would not have much survival value for the species:

> So you ask, What does this have to do with your questions about hibernation? Consider the difference between the life style of your typical mammal and that of the typical insect. Why is hibernation important to some mammals? Why might hibernation not be a successful strategy for most insects? Some insects, such as tarantula, live for 10 or more years. Do you think that they might hibernate? How might their life style be different from that of other insects.

Resisting this lead, AM again adopts the easier path of asking for direct information, asking "I'm not really sure if a tarantula hibernates. What do you think?" to which MJ again responds with some critical information about warm-bloodedness:

> I'm really not sure either. I do know that insects are cold-blooded, which means that they don't have a constant body temperature. This means that they depend on warmth from the sun or other objects in order to become active (move around and hunt). This happens pretty much every day. As the sun sets and it gets cold, cold-blooded animals slow down. But hibernation is something that happens over a greater period of time (over a year rather than a day). Where do you think we could find out more about this question?

The interaction continued for several days. MJ gradually seeds the zone of proximal development with three critical pieces of information during this exchange. AM picks up on two of these features (availability of resources and longevity), although she never understands warm-bloodedness. Electronic mail as a medium for sustaining and expanding zones of proximal development has exciting possibilities and is an essential feature of our learning environment, freeing teachers from the sole burden of knowledge guardian and allowing the community to extend beyond the classroom walls.

Strengths and Weaknesses of a Guided Discovery Classroom

Strengths

Distributed Expertise

Reliance on the two modes of cooperative learning, reciprocal teaching coupled with jigsaw, ensures that expertise is deliberately distributed across the members of the classroom (Brown & Campione, 1996). In addition, variability in expertise arises opportunistically. The ploy of increasing rather than decreasing diversity and allowing many ways to full or legitimate peripheral participation (Lave & Wenger, 1991) increases the richness of the knowledge base on which the community can draw. Everyone in the community is an expert responsible for sharing his or her expertise with others. Both inside and outside school students and teachers have access to circles of ever-deepening domain expertise.

Teachers Capitalize on Student Expertise

Teachers have at their disposal a variety of experts capable of peer and cross-age tutoring. Adult teachers are not the only source of knowledge. Many members of the community are knowledgeable. This knowledge can be harnessed to provide varieties of expertise, thus enriching the learning environment and at the same time providing opportunities for its members to take responsible leadership roles.

Multiple roles are modeled and appropriated by both students and adult teachers. Because majoring is encouraged, even teachers are free to reveal ignorance of certain topics and to model ways of overcoming that ignorance by consulting outside sources and continuing to develop expertise over sustained periods of time. Children are free to be domain experts, be that in the subject area under study, in the use of technology, or in the role of social facilitator.

Actors and Audience

Everyone in the community is a teacher as well as a learner; everyone is at some stage an actor and an audience. The sense of audience for one's research efforts is an important aspect of the community. Audiences, of both adults and children, demand coherence; they push for higher levels of understanding; they require satisfactory explanations; and they request clarification of obscure points. Students do not have to deal with a single audience, the teacher, as they usually do in school; the sense of audience is not imaginary, but palpable and real. Students are forced to teach what they know, and this is often the impetus for learners to recognize gaps in their knowledge that need attention before they take center stage again.

Weaknesses

Limited Knowledge Capital

Any learning community is limited by the combined knowledge of its members. Classrooms are constrained by four walls. Attempts to expand the knowledge capital of the community by recourse to libraries, field trips, and so forth are as old as school itself. But even so, within traditional schools, members draw on a limited knowledge capital if the faculty and students are relatively static, or face jarring discontinuity if there is rapid turnover of personnel. Furthermore, both teachers' and students' expectations concerning excellence, or even what it means to learn and understand, may be limited if the only standards are local ones. Methods of extending the community beyond the classroom walls are needed to enrich and challenge the knowledge capital of a learning community.

Teacher Competence

A major problem with guided discovery is the load placed on the guide, the official teacher. Invoking comfortable metaphors such as the teacher as coach does not tell us how and when the teacher should coach. How can the teacher foster discovery and at the same time provide guidance?

The role of guide in the discovery process is difficult to maintain. Consider the position of a teacher who knows something that the students do not. Here, he or she must decide whether to intervene. He or she must decide whether the problem centers on an important principle or involves only a trivial error that he or she can let pass for now. Consider the case of the teacher who does not know the answer, or one who may share the students' puzzlement or misconception. In this case the teacher is first required to recognize this fact and, after admitting puzzlement or confusion, find ways to remedy it, for example by seeking help. This is not an easy role for many teachers; it requires them to admit that they do not know and seek help, thereby modeling this important learning strategy for their students.

Teacher as Critical Thinking Model

In addition to guiding a class through the curriculum content, the teacher should also be a role model for certain forms of inquiry activities. If students are apprentice learners, then the teacher is the master craftsman of learning that they must emulate. In this role, the teacher models scientific inquiry through thought and real experiments. Ideally, children should witness teachers learning, discovering, doing research, reading, writing, and using computers as tools for learning, rather than lecturing, managing, assigning work, and controlling the classroom exclusively.

The teacher's job also includes efforts to model habits of mind by which children are encouraged to adopt, extrapolate, and refine the deep underlying themes to which they are exposed. As Bruner (1969) argued,

> [education] should be an invitation to generalize, to extrapolate, to make a tentative intuitive leap, even to build a tentative theory. The leap from mere learning to using what one has learned in thinking is an essential step in the use of the mind. Indeed, plausible guessing, the use of the heuristic hunch, the best employment of necessarily insufficient evidence—these are the activities in which the child needs practice and guidance. They are among the great antidotes to passivity. (p. 124)

But again, note that this requires the expert guidance of a gifted teacher. It requires competence, confidence, and a great deal of sheer energy.

Remedying Misconceptions

Children "discovering" in our biology classrooms are quite adept at inventing scientific misconceptions. For example, they readily become Lamarkians, believing that acquired characteristics of individuals are passed on and that all things exist for a purpose. They overdetermine cause, the teleological stance, thus blinding themselves to essential notions of randomness and spontaneity (Mayr, 1988). We encourage teachers to see these common problems as fruitful errors, waystages on the route to mature understanding that they can manipulate and direct in useful ways. Our teachers are also made aware of common misconceptions that students may harbor concerning, for example, the nature of plants or natural selection (Brumby, 1979). Armed with this information, teachers are better able to recognize the occurrence of misconceptions and fallacious reasoning so that they may then introduce students to counterexamples or other challenges to their inchoate knowledge, for example by having students who believe that plants suck up food through the soil conduct experiments on hydroponic gardening.

The Need for a New Theory of Learning

We argue that a major part of a research agenda such as the one described in this chapter is to contribute to a new theory of learning that would capture the richness of the environment and the flexible learning activities it engenders. The development of theory is critical for two reasons—conceptual understanding and practical dissemination. The development of theory has always been necessary as a guide to research, a lens through which one interprets, that sets things apart and pulls things together. But theory development is essential for practical implementation as well.

As a cautionary tale, consider the fate of the original reciprocal teaching program. The program has enjoyed widespread dissemination. It has been picked up by researchers, teachers, and textbook publishers, and has become part of the discourse of the educational community. But too often something called reciprocal teaching is practiced in such a way that the principles of learning it was meant to foster are lost, or at best relegated to a minor position. The surface rituals of questioning, summarizing, and so forth are engaged in, divorced from the goal of reading for understanding that they were designed to serve. These "strategies" are sometimes practiced out of the context of reading authentic texts. Quite simply, if one wants to disseminate a program on the basis of principles of learning rather than surface procedures, one must be able to specify what those principles are in such a way that they can inform practice.

We try to encourage teachers to reinvent the program in their own fashion. Adaptation and modification are an organic part of any implementation process. We view implementation as evolution constrained by first principles (Brown, 1994; Majone & Wildavsky, 1978); so let us turn to the principles.

Principles of the Community of Learners Program

1. *Learning is an active process.* A great deal of academic learning, though not everyday learning, is active, strategic, self-conscious, self-motivated, and purposeful. Effective learners operate best when they have insight into their own strengths and weaknesses and access to their own repertoires of strategies for learning. In recent years this type of knowledge and control over thinking has been termed *metacognition* (Brown, 1975).

Of course this position is not new, it is just that a concentrated period of research has reaffirmed what was already suspected. A little recognized progenitor was actually Binet. Binet (1909) was interested in the education of the childlike mind, childlike because the learner was biologically or intellectually young. True to the new-found confidence in testing, Binet designed tests of what he called *autocriticism.* For example, what is wrong with this sentence?

> Yesterday we found a woman's body sliced in 18 pieces; we believe she killed herself.

Binet (1909) developed a remedial curriculum called *mental orthopedics* that was intended to strengthen the child's "unreflective mind" by training "habits of work, effort, attention, reasoning and self-criticism" (p. 346). Unfortunately for us, Binet was more than a little vague about how one might do this. Actual descriptions of the program or its outcomes do not survive, a problem in general for "innovative programs" of the past.

One might also argue that all this talk of strategies and metacognition is silly. Who would want passive, unmotivated, purposeless—indeed mindless—learning? Who could possibly argue against active, mindful learning? The point is not that people argued against mindful learning, rather that they did not campaign actively for it. Remember, the belief that rote learning trains the mind has been held for a long time. Advocates of fact acquisition—in and of itself and by whatever means—still stalk the land. One legacy of behaviorism was a concern with capturing the mind in spite of itself. Understanding and reflection were not prominent features of the psychological learning theories of the mid-century. The need for a resurgence of interest in mind and its uses was overdue.

2. *Classrooms create multiple zones of proximal development.* We take it as given that learners develop at different rates. At any time they are ripe for new learning more readily in some arenas than others. They do not

come "ready for school" in some cookie-cutter fashion. This is why we find it fruitful to think of a classroom as fostering multiple zones of proximal development through which its many actors pass in and out by different paths and at different rates.

The central Vygotskian notion is one of tracing the zone between lower and upper bounds of potential, and pushing as much as possible toward the upper bounds. This is also a position that needed to be reinvented (Vygotsky, 1978). The set of influential contrasting theories includes errorless learning, mastery learning, and so on: All attempt to aim instruction at the child's existing level of competence—often interpreted as lower levels of performance. Many misinterpreted Dewey (1929, 1990) as suggesting emphasis on lower bounds when he argued in favor of teaching to the child's level. We argue that an essential role for teachers is to guide the discovery process into forms of disciplined inquiry that would not be reached without expert guidance, to push for the upper bounds.

3. *Legitimization of differences.* A closely related principle is that the community should, to the extent possible, aim for the legitimization of differences. We borrowed this term from studies of out of school learning, specifically Shirley Brice Heath's (1991) work on little league baseball. But we also see reflections in the work of Howard Gardner (1983) and others who stress multiple intelligences, for example, Jean Lave's (Lave & Wenger, 1991) concerns with multiple ways into communities of practice.

It is very much our intention to increase diversity in these classrooms. Traditional school practices have aimed at just the opposite, decreasing diversity, a traditional practice based on several assumptions: that there exist prototypical, normal students who, at a certain age, can do a certain amount of work, or grasp a certain amount of material, in the same amount of time. There is little that we know about learning and development that would support these assumptions. Therefore, although we must aim at conformity on the basics, everyone must read eventually, we also aim at increasing diversity of expertise and interests so that members of the community can benefit from the increasing richness of knowledge available. The essence of teamwork is pooling varieties of expertise. Teams composed of members with homogeneous ideas and skills are denied access to such diversity.

Heath and McLaughlin (1994) described several features of successful youth activities that inner city youth volunteered to join. We try to mimic some aspects of these successful organizations in our restructuring of schools. In addition to the respect and legitimization of diversity, experience, and talent, we believe that the sense of imagined family, where older and more experienced participants guide new members, is important. Seasonal cycles of planning, preparing, practicing, and performing to outside audiences, with real deadlines that provide points for self-reflection and taking stock, also provide the backbone of these organizations. An atmosphere of mutual monitoring and support, with assigned responsibility for group progress, makes these organizations safe havens for youth.

To the extent we are able, we aim to mimic this philosophy within classrooms. We try to create a community of scholastic practice within which expertise is distributed (Brown & Campione, 1996): Everyone is a researcher, everyone is a teacher, everyone is a writer, everyone is an expert at something. Everyone is involved in a plan-prepare-practice-perform cycle with tangible results. Identities are created, and a sense of community with shared values emerges. Students say that they feel ownership, and although it can't be absolute, there is a sense of volunteerism and choice in these classrooms. There are multiple ways to full participation, and peripheral participation in some aspects of the work is legitimized (Campione, Rutherford, Gordon, Walker, & Brown, 1994; Lave & Wenger, 1991).

Coupled with responsibility and the acceptance of legitimate differences comes respect among students, between students and school staff, and among all members of the extended community, including experts outside the school walls. Students' questions are taken seriously. Experts, be they children or adults, do not always know the answers: known answer question and answering games (Heath, 1983; Mehan, 1979) have no home in this environment. Respect is earned by responsible participation in a genuine knowledge-building community (Scardamalia & Bereiter, 1991).

4. *Dialogic base.* These classrooms are intentionally designed to support multiple voices in Bakhtin's (1986; see also Holquist & Emerson, 1981) sense of *voice* as the speaking personality and the speaking consciousness. A major tenet of Bakhtin's (1986) creed was that any true understanding is dialogic in nature.

In these classrooms there is the assumption of shared discourse and common knowledge (Edwards & Mercer, 1987) as well as individual expertise. The core participant structures of our classrooms are essentially dialogic. Sometimes these activities are face to face in small or large group interactions; sometimes they are mediated through print or electronic mail; and at other times they go underground and become part of the thought processes of members of the community (Vygotsky, 1978). Dialogues provide the format for novices to adopt the discourse structure, goals, values, and belief systems of scientific practice. Over time, the community of learners adopts a common voice and common knowledge base, a shared system of meaning, beliefs, and activity that is as often implicit as it is explicit.

5. *Community of practice.* Learning and teaching depend heavily on creating, sustaining, and expanding community because of the key notion of distributed expertise. Members of the community, both inside the classroom and beyond, are critically dependent on each other. No one is an island; no one knows it all; cooperative learning is necessary for survival. This interdependence promotes an atmosphere of joint responsibility, mutual respect, and a sense of personal and group identity.

6. *Developmentally sensitive contexts for learning.* The five principles described above are closely intertwined and form a system. Multiple zones of proximal development presuppose distributed expertise, distributed expertise presupposes legitimization of differences, and so on. The next pair of principles also form a systemic cluster: the need for deep conceptual content that is sensitive to the developmental level of the students.

We are reminded of a story told by Jerome Bruner (1986). After a presentation, a student asked a question about Bruner's claim that any subject could be taught to a child at any age in some intellectually honest way. Bruner was expecting the usual question about teaching calculus in the first grade. But, no, the question was, "How do you know what's honest?" Now that really is the pivotal question.

It is not an easy question to answer. Most contemporary school reform projects finesse the problem by adopting a "one size fits all" philosophy. The principles and structure of the program are the same, independent of the age or background of the students. The developmental model is missing.

However, some implicit developmental assumptions must govern school practices. In America we teach the 6-year-old student social studies in reference to his or her own neighborhood. Why? Because someone decided this was developmentally appropriate. Six-year-olds in the

Dewey Lab School studied "occupations serving the household" (May-hew & Edwards, 1936). Why?

There is a disturbing tradition in educational circles to make up developmental theory. Our favorite example is that of G. Stanley Hall, sometimes called the father of developmental psychology. Brushing aside the need for empirical validation, Hall (1881) championed a developmental theory made up of cultural epochs. The proper curriculum should mimic the history of mental evolution. Young children at the "savage" stage should study material from the corresponding historical epoch, that is, ancient myths and fables. High school boys should study the knights of the feudal period because, developmentally, the boys were in the period of chivalry and honor. Young women were not accorded a corresponding period! There existed no scientific justification for these developmental stages whatsoever.

This story is not just one of historical interest. In contemporary curriculum design, a simplistic interpretation of Piagetian theory has led to the consistent underestimation of students' capabilities. This Piagetian slant encourages sensitivity to what children of a certain age cannot do because they have not yet reached a certain stage of cognitive operations. The "theory" still prevails in the face of 30 years of ingenious work by developmental psychologists emphasizing the impressive cognitive abilities that children do possess. Especially relevant to the design of grade school science curricula is the painstaking documentation of children's evolving knowledge about biological and physical phenomena (Carey & Gelman, 1991). Similarly, we know a great deal about children's impressive reasoning processes within contexts that they do understand (Brown & Campione, 1990).

Conclusion

After 6 years of intensive work on an environmental science curriculum, we have only just begun to take a stab at a spiraling curriculum (Bruner, 1963), where each layer builds on preceding ones in a systematic way. We know that overarching themes of interdependence and adaptation can be visited fruitfully by children from kindergarten to eighth grade. Six-year-olds consider the concept of living thing, a topic of great interest that they refine over a period of years, gradually assimilating plants into this category (Carey, 1985; Hatano & Inagaki, 1987). Second graders concentrate on survival mechanisms and design criteria for animal-

habitat mutuality. Sixth graders delve into concepts such as delayed im-
plantation, biological magnification, and the effect of broad versus
narrow niches. By eighth grade they can cope with complexities such
as variation in the gene pool and its effects on adaptation and survival.
But the development of such a curriculum takes time and intuition.
Straightforward trial and error is needed, even with the information
provided by developmental psychology.

And let us not forget developments in reasoning within domains!
Do children understand the difference between evidence and hypothesis? What is their understanding of the scientific method? What should
it be? Is it Francis Bacon's or is it Karl Popper's? When can we share
with them the insights of Peter Medawar that scientists as human beings
do what everyday people do. They are not omniscient. They tell good
stories, they create imaginary worlds. Indeed the scientific method itself
like any other explanatory process is a dialogue between fact and fancy,
between the actual and the possible, between what could be true and
what is in fact the case—it is a story of justifiable beliefs about a possible
world (Medawar, 1982). And then there is the age old problem for a
developmental psychologist, transition mechanisms—what triggers conceptual change? In short, the amount of work involved in mapping a
spiraling curriculum that is truly developmentally sensitive is quite overwhelming.

A Final Comment

In this chapter, we have described our current attempts to engage in
design experiments intended to transform classrooms from work fac-
tories to learning environments that encourage reflective practice
among students, teachers, and researchers. We traced briefly the history
of our own progression from the study of laboratory learning to classroom observations and experimentation. The need for new and complex theories to capture the systemic nature of learning and teaching
was described. We concluded by describing steps toward a set of first
principles of learning that would guide both theoretical development
and practical dissemination of the program.

References

Aronson, E. (1978). *The jigsaw classroom.* Beverly Hills, CA: Sage.
Ash, D., & Brown, A. L. (1993). *After the jigsaw is over: Children's learning in socially and*

informationally rich environments. Paper presented at the meetings of the American Educational Research Association, Atlanta.

Bakhtin, M. M. (1986). *Speech genres and other late essays.* (C. Emerson & M. Holquist, Eds.). (V. W. McGee, Trans.). Austin, TX: University of Texas Press.

Binet, A. (1909). *Les idees modernes sur les infants.* Paris: Ernest Flatiron.

Brown, A. L. (1975). The development of memory: Knowing, knowing about knowing, and knowing how to know. In H. W. Reese (Ed.), *Advances in child development and behavior* (Vol. 10, pp. 103–152). San Diego, CA: Academic Press.

Brown, A. L. (1978). Knowing when, where, and how to remember: A problem of metacognition. In R. Glaser (Ed.), *Advances in instructional psychology* (Vol. 1, pp. 77–165). Hillsdale, NJ: Erlbaum.

Brown, A. L. (1990). Domain-specific principles affect learning and transfer in children. *Cognitive Science, 14,* 107–133.

Brown, A. L. (1994). *The advancement of learning.* Presidential Address presented at the annual meeting of the American Educational Research Association, New Orleans.

Brown, A. L., Ash, D., Rutherford, M., Nakagawa, K., Gordon, A., & Campione, J. C. (1993). Distributed expertise in the classroom. In G. Salomon (Ed.), *Distributed cognitions: Psychological and educational considerations* (pp. 188–228). Cambridge, England: Cambridge University Press.

Brown, A. L., Bransford, J. D., Ferrara, R. A., & Campione, J. C. (1983). Learning, remembering, and understanding. In J. H. Flavell & E. M. Markman (Eds.), *Handbook of child psychology: Cognitive development* (Vol. 3, pp. 77–166). New York: Wiley.

Brown, A. L., & Campione, J. C. (1990). Communities of learning and thinking, or A context by any other name. *Human Development, 21,* 108–125.

Brown, A. L., & Campione, J. C. (1996). Psychological theory and the design of innovative learning environments: On procedures, principles, and systems. In L. Schauble & R. Glaser (Eds.), *Innovations in learning: New environments for education* (pp. 289–325). Mahwah, NJ: Erlbaum.

Brown, A. L., Campione, J. C., Reeve, R. A., Ferrara, R. A., & Palincsar, A. S. (1991). Interactive learning, individual understanding: The case of reading and mathematics. In L. T. Landsmann (Ed.), *Culture, schooling and psychological development* (pp. 136–170). Hillsdale, NJ: Erlbaum.

Brown, A. L., & Kane, M. J. (1988). Preschool children can learn to transfer: Learning to learn and learning from example. *Cognitive Psychology, 20,* 493–523.

Brown, A. L., & Palincsar, A. S. (1982). Inducing strategic learning from texts by means of informed, self-control training. *Topics in Learning and Learning Disabilities, 2*(1), 1–17.

Brown, A. L., & Palincsar, A. S. (1989). Guided, cooperative learning and individual knowledge acquisition. In L. B. Resnick (Ed.), *Knowing, learning, and instruction: Essays in honor of Robert Glaser* (pp. 393–451). Hillsdale, NJ: Erlbaum.

Brown, A. L., & Reeve, R. A. (1987). Bandwidths of competence: The role of supportive contexts in learning and development. In L. S. Liben (Ed.), *Development and learning: Conflict or congruence?* (pp. 173–223). Hillsdale, NJ: Erlbaum.

Brumby, M. (1979). Problems in learning the concept of natural selection. *Journal of Biological Education, 13,* 119–122.

Bruner, J. S. (1963). *The process of education.* Cambridge, MA: Harvard University Press.

Bruner, J. S. (1969). *On knowing: Essays for the left hand.* Cambridge, MA: Harvard University Press.

Bruner, J. S. (1986). *Actual minds, possible worlds.* Cambridge, MA: Harvard University Press.

Campione, J. C., Brown, A. L., & Connell, M. L. (1988). Metacognition: On the importance of understanding what you are doing. In R. I. Charles & E. A. Silver (Eds.), *Research agenda for mathematics education: The teaching and assessing of mathematical problem solving* (pp. 93–114). Hillsdale, NJ: Erlbaum.

Campione, J. C., Brown, A. L., & Jay, M. (1992). Computers in a community of learners. In E. DeCorte, M. Linn, H. Mandl, & L. Verschaffel (Eds.), Computer-based learning environments and problem solving (pp. 163–192). Berlin: Springer-Verlag.

Campione, J. C., Rutherford, M., Gordon, A., Walker, J., & Brown, A. L. (1994). Now I'm a REAL boy: Zones of proximal development for those at risk. In N. C. Jordan & J. Goldsmith-Phillips (Eds.), *Learning disabilities: New directions for assessment and intervention.* Needham Heights, MA: Allyn & Bacon.

Carey, S. (1985). *Conceptual change in childhood.* Cambridge, MA: Bradford Books, MIT Press.

Carey, S., & Gelman, R. (1991). *The epigenesis of mind.* Hillsdale, NJ: Erlbaum.

Collins, A., & Stevens, A. L. (1982). Goals and strategies of inquiry teachers. In R. Glaser (Ed.), *Advances in instructional psychology* (Vol. 2, pp. 65–119). Hillsdale, NJ: Erlbaum.

Dewey, J. (1929). *My pedagogical creed.* Washington, DC: Progressive Education Association.

Dewey, J. (1990). *The school and society.* Chicago, IL: University of Chicago Press.

Edwards, P., & Mercer, N. (1987). *Common knowledge.* London: Open University Press.

Fish, S. (1980). *Is there a text in this class? The authority of interpretive communities.* Cambridge, MA: Harvard University Press.

Gardner, H. (1983). *Frames of mind: The theory of multiple intelligences.* New York: Basic Books.

Hall, G. S. (1881). The contents of children's minds. *Princeton Review, 11,* 249–272.

Hatano, G., & Inagaki, K. (1987). Everyday biology and school biology: How do they interact? *The Newsletter of the Laboratory of Comparative Human Cognition, 9,* 120–128.

Heath, S. B. (1983). *Ways with words.* Cambridge, England: Cambridge University Press.

Heath, S. B. (1991). "It's about winning!" The language of knowledge in baseball. In L. B. Resnick, J. M. Levine, & S. D. Teasley (Eds.), *Perspectives on socially shared cognition* (pp. 101–126). Washington, DC: American Psychological Association.

Heath, S. B., & Mangiola, L. (1991). *Children of promise: Literate activity in linguistically and culturally diverse classrooms.* Washington, DC: National Education Association.

Heath, S. B., & McLaughlin, M. W. (1994). Learning for anything every day. *Journal of Curriculum Studies, 26,* 471–489.

Lave, J., & Wenger, E. (1991). *Situated learning: Legitimate peripheral participation.* Cambridge, England: Cambridge University Press.

Majone, G., & Wildavsky, A. (1978). Implementation as evolution. In H. E. Freeman (Ed.), *Policy studies review annual* (Vol. 2, pp. 103–117). Beverly Hills, CA: Sage.

Mayhew, K. C., & Edwards, A. C. (1936). *The Dewey School: The laboratory school of the University of Chicago, 1896–1903.* New York: Appleton-Century.

Mayr, E. (1988). *Toward a new philosophy of biology.* Cambridge, England: Belknap Press.

Medawar, P. (1982). *Pluto's republic.* Oxford, England: Oxford University Press.

Mehan, H. (1979). *Learning lessons: Social organization in the classroom.* Cambridge, MA: Harvard University Press.

Newman, D., Griffin, P., & Cole, M. (1989). *The construction zone.* Cambridge, England: Cambridge University Press.

Palincsar, A. S., & Brown, A. L. (1984). Reciprocal teaching of comprehension-fostering and monitoring activities. *Cognition and Instruction, 1*(2), 117–175.

Palincsar, A. L., Brown, A. L., & Campione, J. C. (1990, April). *Discourse as a mechanism for acquiring process and knowledge.* Paper presented at the American Educational Research Association Conference, Boston, MA.

Reeve, R. A., Gordon, A., Campione, J. C., & Brown, A. L. (1990, April). *Enhancing and predicting the math performance of elementary school children using reciprocal teaching and dynamic assessment.* Paper presented at the American Educational Research Association Conference, Boston, MA.

Scardamalia, M., & Bereiter, C. (1991). Higher levels of agency for children in knowledge building: A challenge for the design of new knowledge media. *The Journal of the Learning Sciences, 1,* 37–68.

Toulmin, S. (1958). *The uses of argument.* Cambridge, England: Cambridge University Press.

Vygotsky, L. S. (1978). *Mind in society: The development of higher psychological processes* (M. Cole, V. John-Steiner, S. Scribner, & E. Souberman, Eds. and Trans.). Cambridge, MA: Harvard University Press.

Whitehead, A. N. (1916). *The aims of education.* Address to the British Mathematical Society, Manchester, England.

Part II

Learner-Centered Perspectives in the Design of Assessment Systems

Why Learner-Centered Assessment Is Better Than High-Stakes Testing

Scott G. Paris

A ssessment of students' achievement is fundamental to all school reform efforts because effective instruction depends on effective assessment and because the merits of any reform are usually judged by relative gains in assessment data. Assessment serves as an educational tool with at least these two distinct functions: (a) improving learning and teaching and (b) providing measures of performance for accountability, which are referred to as the *formative* and *summative purposes of assessment.* Formative assessment provides diagnostic information about the products and processes of students' learning so that educators and parents can adjust the curriculum and instruction to foster learning. Ongoing assessments such as teachers' observations, conferences, and performance feedback are intended to motivate students to improve their learning. Formative assessments are usually continuous, connected to the curriculum of daily classroom tasks, teacher controlled, and nonthreatening. In contrast, summative assessment is perceived as "high-stakes" testing, is externally imposed, and may not be directly related to the classroom curriculum content, or instructional methods. Summative assessments are usually reported as test scores that can be used to compare students, classrooms, teachers, and schools. Policy makers and parents make the comparisons to judge the relative accomplishments of students but also the implied effectiveness of teachers, schools, and reforms. Indeed, any school reform plan is likely to be abandoned if it does not raise test scores and visible signs of students' achievements.

In this chapter, I suggest that the emphasis on assessment for accountability purposes has overshadowed and undermined the use of

assessment to improve students' learning and motivation. Both formative and summative assessment are evident in every classroom, but the
increasing public emphasis on accountability of school effectiveness as
measured by test scores has influenced the ways that teachers and students incorporate assessment into their views of education. Although a
purpose of high-stakes testing is to motivate teachers and students to
high levels of performance, this good intention has had many adverse
side effects that require examination. In the first half of this chapter, I
examine some of the reasons for the increased use of standardized
achievement testing in America and consider how high-stakes testing
distorts teachers' instructional practices, students' goals and learning
strategies, and parents' understanding of education. In the second half
of the chapter I describe principles of learner-centered assessment and
how portfolios and performance assessment can help students become
motivated, thoughtful, and reflective and involve teachers and parents
in more fruitful assessment practices with children.

The Rise of High-Stakes Testing

Standardized achievement testing as a means of ensuring educational
accountability was barely evident before 1970, yet it is now mandated
by virtually every state and school district in the United States. The
number of tests, the academic time devoted to test preparation, the
importance of publicly reported scores, and the amount of money spent
on standardized achievement testing continue to increase every year
(Madaus & Tan, 1993). The main explanations for increased testing
include the need for more information about what students have
learned, the public demand for more accountability of schools and
teachers, and the need to establish higher educational standards
through more rigorous testing. These are familiar themes, which are
usually expressed to garner political and financial support for a broad
array of educational reforms. However, it is important to examine some
of the underlying reasons for increased educational testing and to examine the impact of various educational assessments on students.

Some of the factors responsible for increased testing in schools are
related more to political agenda than connected directly to classroom
learning. First, cross-national comparisons of educational achievement
have shown that American students lag far behind students in other
countries (Stevenson & Stigler, 1992). Teachers and schools have be-

come the scapegoats for allegations about the poor quality of education, and many advocates of educational reform support higher standards and increased testing as means to promote higher quality. Indictments through alarmist journalism about inadequate test scores sell newspapers but also increase the public mistrust of teachers and schools. A second reason that standardized testing is increasing is economic gain. Test makers join the chorus of demands for higher test scores and more accountability (and they often equate the two) because they earn money on every test that students take. Many statewide assessment reforms are conducted jointly with test publishers who often make a profit from the sales of test-preparation materials and tests. A third reason is that the people empowered to monitor assessment are the ones who benefit directly from increased testing. Testing specialists at the national, state, and district levels expand their staffs, budgets, and power with more testing and new kinds of assessment. Fourth, test specialists and administrators have forged alliances with politicians and businesses that are mutually beneficial. Businesses will save money if schools provide more relevant job training and provide employers with more specific information about the comparative qualifications of potential workers so they are eager to have better test score data. Politicians enhance their public popularity when they demand greater accountability through testing from teachers and students, partly because the public does not understand educational standards, assessments, and research. "More jobs," "more prisons," "more testing" are familiar political slogans that shift attention to the problems and victims rather than the solutions and causes. Misinformed secretaries of education, presidents, governors, and others display wall charts and other public comparisons of test scores as they bemoan the state of education and call for higher standards and more testing.

This interpretation may be challenged by those who fight to preserve their privilege, power, and profit. Some parents may also disagree because they have been led to expect comparative assessments of achievement test scores as the basis of educational quality. It is a prevailing belief that competitive, demanding, quantitative tests provide quality control in America. Testing proponents argue, "The public needs to know how teachers and students measure up. It is a free-market mentality. Testing helps students prepare for the 'real world' and the rigors of the workplace." Alternatively, some might say that competition weeds out the weak and unsuccessful; it is the "law of the jungle" where only the fittest survive. However, neither analogy works for American education because of the presumption of an acceptable failure rate. A free-market economy must tolerate many businesses that try hard but cannot succeed and an evolutionary analogy accepts that the endangered and fragile members simply die out.

Are American parents willing to accept the same risks and losses in education? Should the weak or unsuccessful or fragile students be dropped by the wayside as victims of healthy competition? Should we focus only on the survivors, the best, the brightest? Most parents would say "no," yet they are tacitly saying "yes" when they accept standardized achievement testing as the fundamental measures of teachers' instructional effectiveness, students' learning, and educational quality. Why? Because norm-referenced standardized tests are designed to compare students, schools, districts, and states and to identify the winners and losers. In a fair test with a normal distribution, half of all students will be below average. Even if everyone improves, the bottom half will always be below average. Tests that sort and compare students lead to negative consequences for those who score poorly and to allocation of selective rewards to those who score well. Thus, normative comparisons based on standardized tests foster a meritocratic orientation to education rather than an approach that is centered on enhancing the development of each individual (Nicholls, 1989). The time is long overdue for the public to debate the dangers of standardized achievement testing and to consider alternative assessment practices that benefit students directly.

How Standardized Testing Undermines Effective Education

Historically, the design and implementation of achievement tests have been guided by concerns for test validity and reliability, which means, "Does the test measure what it purports to assess and are the scores reliable over time?" However, the focus on the psychometric properties of achievement tests fails to consider the impact of the test on teachers and students. Linn, Baker, and Dunbar (1991) have suggested that the concept of validity in educational assessment should be expanded to include the consequences of assessment such as fairness of the test to various groups, use of the data, transfer and generalization of the performance indicators, cognitive complexity of the test, meaningfulness to the test takers, and cost and efficiency. These features of consequential validity call attention to the impact of the test on the primary stakeholders, especially students. In order to focus on the consequences of standardized testing, assume that most popular standardized achievement tests (e.g., the Stanford Achievement Test, the California Achievement Test, and the Iowa Test of Basic Skills) are reliable and valid instruments in the traditional senses so that we can examine their consequential validity and their impact on students, teachers, and parents. My main points in the following sections are that all standardized achievement tests have unintended consequences that can seriously undermine effective teaching and learning and that the potential harm may outweigh the potential benefits of standardized test scores (McGill-Franzen & Allington, 1993).

Misdirected Motivation and Learning

Perhaps the most fundamental problem with standardized achievement tests is that they distort students' motivation and learning by overemphasizing the importance of the scores as outcomes and measures of students' abilities. Tests can redefine students' goals for learning in counterproductive ways that make the outcome more important than learning as inquiry, reflection, and process. Research on academic motivation indicates that a focus on extrinsic goals (such as test scores) and task completion (such as getting through the test) undermines intrinsic motivation, interest, and persistence (Ames & Archer, 1988). In contrast, when students have mastery goals and take pride in their efforts and accomplishments, they use better strategies and display more self-regulated learning (Pintrich & DeGroot, 1990). When high test scores become the goal rather than self-regulated learning, students invest disproportionate value and effort in high-stakes tests. For many students, the consequences of testing are neutral or negative, ranging from the innocuous lack of feedback to negative feedback about one's competence. The ones who suffer most from repeated testing are the students who score poorly each year and are told annually that they do not measure up. Low achievers are left with few choices. If they believe that the tests are good measures of ability, then they may only try half-heartedly so that they can claim their poor test scores reflect low effort rather than low ability (Stipek, 1993). Other choices include discounting the importance of the test entirely, cheating, or sabotaging the test. All these options make the scores meaningless indicators of the students' ability and thus invalidate the test data for those most at risk. With age and practice, these counterproductive strategies become more prevalent and more creative (Paris, Lawton, Turner, & Roth, 1991).

Achievement testing also subverts students' learning strategies because test-taking strategies are usually inconsistent with learning strategies taught everyday in the classroom. For example, young children are frustrated (as are their teachers) when they cannot ask for help and hints on tests. Most students are taught to use people and materials as resources for learning in class, but are disallowed from using them during testing. Children learn, or are sometimes actually taught, that it is useful to read the test questions first and then look for the answers in the text rather than trying to read and comprehend the text. This contradicts good instructional practices. Narrowing options down to two choices and guessing is also a poor strategy to generalize. Likewise, math tests usually do not allow students to use calculators, and writing tests usually do not allow multiple drafts and peer conferences. Why should test-taking strategies contradict the daily academic strategies that are taught by teachers? What do children learn while taking tests? Too often, they learn that high-stakes tests are different from the daily curriculum and assessments, that one needs special tricks to pass achievement tests, that low scores mean a person is dumb, and that teachers cannot help students. The inability of teachers and students to control testing policies and to demonstrate their knowledge increases their frustration. Under these circumstances, they are justified in wanting to abolish standardized achievement testing, but the public often misinterprets their anger as an unwillingness to be evaluated.

Distorted Curricula and Instruction

Teachers across the United States typically give students one or two achievement tests each year and often spend many days preparing students for standardized achievement testing (Urdan & Paris, 1994). The pressure on teachers to improve test scores has a profound impact on teaching practices. One direct consequence is a narrowed curriculum because teachers focus on information covered by the test. Moore (1994) investigated how teachers in one district responded to a new testing program and found that 97% of the teachers had increased their instructional emphasis on the material in the program, 75% eliminated topics from the local curriculum to make time for test-related instruction, and 88% had aligned their instruction with the test skills and objectives. Charlesworth, Fleege, and Weitman (1994) concluded that the effects of standardized testing included "narrowing and fragmenting of the curriculum, limiting the nature of thinking, or forcing teachers to rush too much for students to learn well" (p. 198). Thus, teachers respond to pressure from administrators and parents to raise test scores at the expense of the curriculum. But one may ask, who is the better teacher—the one who provides frequent and rigorous test preparation activities or one who provides minimal test preparation but provides a rich, integrated curriculum? Some may argue that the latter practice should help increase test scores too, but the important point to keep in mind is that teachers change their practices to fit the demands of testing and accountability imposed on them. Many teachers feel confused and angry about the dual and sometimes competing standards that they are expected to meet.

A second consequence of the pressure to improve test scores is that standardized tests cannot match the local curriculum in a district well because the tests are designed for diverse districts across the country. Charlesworth et al. (1994) estimated that standardized tests match only 20–50% of local curricula. They also make the point that items answered correctly by all students are dropped from tests so that the content of the tests is determined by item difficulty, not importance of information for the curriculum, and thus, the tests may underestimate what students learn from their curriculum. Why are districts and teachers encouraged to design innovative curricula and then assess the success of the curricula with standardized tests that do not cover the same material? The public reports of test data never report the degree of overlap between the test and the curriculum nor the variability across schools in the amount of overlap. If test scores are used as the basis to evaluate and compare teachers, then the teacher who provides the most thorough test preparation (or who has the curriculum that most overlaps with the test) will be judged as the most effective teacher (assuming random assignment of students). Yet most parents and educators would worry that students in such a class are being taught "test-wiseness" rather than the regular curriculum.

Consider the investment of teachers' time in achievement testing. If teachers spend 18 of 180 school days each year preparing students for standardized tests, administering the tests, recording, discussing, and interpreting the tests, they are spending 10% of their time away from their usual teaching practices (Haladyna, Nolen, & Haas, 1991). That 10% is not subtracted from time at music, art, gym, recess, and nonacademic activities; it comes directly from the heart of instructional time devoted to reading, writing, math, and core subjects. In fact, the 10% may be a low estimate based on teachers' reports (Madaus & Tan, 1993).

It is ironic that teachers are spending so much time preparing students for tests that they do not believe are worthwhile. The overwhelming conclusion of surveys with teachers is that they view standardized testing negatively. Urdan and Paris (1994) found that fewer than 10% of K–8 teachers thought that standardized tests reflect what students learn in school. Moore (1994) found that 65% of teachers did not find the tests useful to them and 75% thought the tests did not benefit students. Between 77% and 90% of teachers, the professionals who are most affected by testing, reported that standardized tests are not worth the time and money spent on them (Haladyna, Nolen, & Haas, 1991; Moore, 1994; Urdan & Paris, 1994).

Test Pollution

The problems of standardized testing go beyond the amount of time lost in test preparation because it is the large variability in teachers' test preparation and administration that makes all test scores, even scores on a so-called psychometrically perfect test, invalid. Haladyna, Nolen, and Haas (1991) conducted a survey of 2,500 Arizona teachers and administrators and found that there was tremendous variability in the ways that teachers help children prepare for standardized achievement testing. For example, some teachers spent several hours a week for several months helping children learn how to take multiple-choice, timed tests, whereas other teachers spent only an hour or two, usually the week before the test. Some teachers taught test-taking skills and provided repeated practice with test facsimiles, whereas other teachers simply taught their regular curriculum. About 40% of teachers used commercial test-preparation materials (notice the hidden costs); 60% provided practice with sample questions; 13% gave students tests used in previous years as practice; 26% taught vocabulary on the current test; and 10% actually instructed students on items from the current test. The researchers labeled this variability *test pollution* because these highly variable practices contaminate the external validity of the test scores. If two schools or districts vary widely in curricula, time spent teaching test-taking skills, and help given to students during the tests, then all comparisons of the test scores are hopelessly contaminated and uninterpretable. For example, if School A devotes 30 minutes for test preparation and practices test taking twice each week for several months preceding the achievement test and then scores higher than School B who did not do any advance preparation, how can the scores be used as an index of relative educational quality?

Cheating

These test preparation activities may seem like cheating, but it should be noted that teachers have little guidance and no supervision to determine what are appropriate and ethical assessment practices. Is the teacher cheating if she stops students during a test to define an important word or concept? Probably, but what if she teaches it the day before because she knows that her students will have trouble when they encounter it on the test? What should a teacher do if she notices that a child has filled in two bubbles for one answer and then become lost on the answer sheet? Should she erase and re-mark all the answers? What about the students who need more time, who feel dizzy, who are frustrated, and who lose their concentration? What help should be provided? Teachers' test preparation and administration practices can have a large impact on the test scores, but there are no safeguards to limit this "pollution" nor to account for the variability when interpreting the data.

Cheating by teachers and principals is also invited in more subtle ways by manipulating whose scores are reported at which grade levels. Some students are retained in grades and some placed into special education programs in order to improve test scores (McGill-Franzen & Allington, 1993). School boundaries or busing routes that affect test scores may be redrawn. Some principals excuse selected students from testing, some low-scoring students may be absent on test days, and some test booklets are mysteriously lost before being shipped to the district headquarters. Retaining students may raise test scores because the students who are held back will score higher the next year in a lower grade and not pull down the scores in their regular grades. Depending on whether a school district allocates more money to schools that score high or low on the test (a peculiar decision that also deserves discussion), there are many practices that teachers and principals can use to artificially raise or lower their scores. These practices, and many more that educators conceal deliberately, undermine the validity of the reported scores, but enhance class and school averages. When merit pay, public support, and financial allocations depend on test scores, teachers and administrators often "bend the rules" on achievement testing. If the objective is simply to have good numbers reported in the media, these are effective strategies, but if the objective is to improve children's education, they are an unethical waste of time and energy.

Useless Data

Most states administer standardized achievement tests at the end of the
school year, and the results are not available until after school has
ended. This means that the test results arrive too late in the year to be
used by the students' current teacher and they are often ignored by the
students' future teacher who may not even know the child. Furthermore, knowing the test scores before meeting the child may establish
erroneous expectations. The delays in reporting test results are necessitated by the large volume of tests when all students are tested and the
view that testing is most appropriate at the end of the year as a measure
of accountability for what has been learned. Thus, the timing and procedures surrounding traditional standardized achievement tests mitigate the usefulness of the tests and virtually assures that teachers are
unable to use the test results to help individual students. Furthermore,
the data are usually reported incompletely in newspapers and district
flyers so that parents cannot understand or use the data to help their
children.

A Misinformed and Misguided Public

The public consumption of test scores is fueled by the need for accountability and the appearance of scientific rigor in the quantitative
data provided. Yet most parents understand so little about the tests and
the scores that they misinterpret them (Barber, Paris, Evans, & Gadsden,
1992). Not only does the public often misinterpret test data, many people believe scores provide a measure of the quality of education provided in their schools. Indeed, it is virtually the only measure of quality
that is provided, and thus people may rely exclusively on these data.
Many school boards, in their attempt to improve the quality of education, adopt simplistic goals such as raising test scores without understanding how this narrows education in the classroom. They also fail to
understand that it is psychometrically impossible for all students to increase their test scores on an annual basis. Some schools adopt policies
that are doomed to fail when they try to increase standardized test
scores each year. The consequence is that school boards and the public
gauge education by test scores and adopt goals based on the test scores
that inevitably cannot be met. Both students and teachers will be
blamed for failing to increase achievement levels, and the search will
continue for the "cause" of this problem, when, indeed, the fundamental problem is that the public believes that standardized test scores

provide appropriate measures of educational accountability. Standardized achievement test scores assess student characteristics that may or may not be affected by specific curricula and reforms. The misuse of normative test scores to evaluate diverse educational programs and reforms may be part of the reason that educators swing the pendulum of change from one extreme to another.

Runaway Costs

Almost all states and districts administer standardized achievement tests to every student at every grade (at least above second grade) on an annual basis. Although this procedure provides an accountability measure for every student, every class, and every school, *census testing* (testing every student in the population) requires a large investment of time and money for preparation, administration, and feedback. The visible cost of census testing is the $5–7 per pupil spent on test forms and scoring. However, the invisible cost is the time spent in a district to manage and interpret the testing. It is not just testing personnel who are involved with tests. Teachers administer the tests for several days and may spend more time working with principals and parents to interpret the scores. When the administrative and clerical staff are added to the teachers' time and then added to the cost of the tests alone, the expenses become sizable. In a district of 20,000 students, the cost of the test booklets and scoring may be less than $100,000, but the actual costs with staff time figured in may exceed a million dollars. In those districts that yearly administer two or more standardized tests that each occur over 3 to 5 days, the costs can be much higher. Even conservative estimates of the cost of achievement testing in the United States exceed a billion dollars each year (Madaus & Tan, 1993). The time and money devoted to testing are not usually subject to regulation by teachers, school boards, or parents who are often unaware of the escalating costs.

Traditional achievement testing destabilizes many students' feelings of self-efficacy and has potential debilitating effects on students' motivational goals and learning strategies, particularly those of low achievers. Regardless of the psychometric properties of the tests, the ways they are used can suppress motivation and learning in schools. The negative consequences of standardized testing have been ignored because of public and political pressures for educational accountability and comparative, quantifiable measures of students' achievement. Greater accountability, though, has stimulated searches for "new and better'' tests, which, unfortunately, has resulted in more testing with more dire consequences (e.g., diploma certification) imposed on schools with little attention given to the impact of more frequent high-stakes testing on students' learning and motivation.

It is time for a more balanced view of assessment policies in schools in which the liabilities and benefits of assessment are discussed openly. The impact of assessment on the quality of teaching and learning must be evaluated. The attitudes of teachers and students must be considered so that the next generation of assessments elicits their genuine endorsement. This means that teachers and students alike should perceive the assessments as valid, informative, and useful. The strengths of standardized achievement testing, such as efficiency, economy, and comparisons on the same quantitative scales, are already well known. There are many advocates for the use of such tests and a large number of educators who believe that those traditional tests can be revised and used in a satisfactory manner. There are other educators who believe strongly that entirely new forms of assessment are required in schools in order to promote thoughtfulness (Wiggins, 1989; Wolf, Bixby, Glenn, & Gardner, 1991). There is a renewed energy in the debates about test validity and the consequences of assessment for students that will, in the long run, improve educational assessment. In the next section, learner-centered principles of assessment that may help map new directions for classroom assessment that can serve students and teachers effectively are presented.

Designing Assessment to Enhance Learning and Teaching

The pattern of growing disillusionment, decreased motivation, and detachment from a commitment to academic learning because of the primacy of accountability through standardized testing threatens children's orientations to learning and education. New forms of assessment that are sensitive to students' backgrounds, motivation, affect, and attitudes must be created so that students are positively motivated to do their best. New forms of assessment must establish intrinsic goals of mastery, improvement, and success rather than extrinsic comparative goals based on test scores. New forms of assessment should involve students so that they respect the test purposes, content, and format. Assessment should elicit productive strategies and positive motivation so that students can maximize their performance. These positive features of assessment might be attained through performance testing or portfolios of work samples where assessment is linked to the classroom curriculum and is part of an ongoing process in which students monitor their personal progress.

Students may learn to assess and regulate their own performance when they have the responsibility and motivation to improve their own learning and when all students understand that they can progress and succeed in the classroom (Corno, 1992). Students' perspectives on learning and assessment can have long-lasting consequences for education, and it is imperative that policy makers who are revising assessment practices consider the psychological impact on students as well as the political and psychometric features of assessment. In order for assessment practices to support the development of self-regulated learning, educators need to become aware of learner-centered principles of assessment. The following list of learner-centered principles of assessment from Paris and Ayres (1994, p. 50) provides guidelines for assessment reforms that support students' learning:

1. The fundamental purpose of any educational assessment of students should be to promote meaningful learning.
2. Assessment should elicit students' genuine effort, motivation, and commitment to the assessment activity and situation.
3. Assessment should provide credibility and legitimacy to a broad range of talents and accomplishments of students across the curriculum.
4. Assessment should occur continuously in classrooms in order to provide longitudinal evidence of individual progress.
5. The strategies, skills,and knowledge required to excel on academic assessments should be the same as those required to master the curriculum on a daily basis.
6. Assessments should be based on authentic and meaningful tasks that are consistent with the regular curriculum and instruction provided in the classroom.
7. Assessments should be fair and equitable to all students regardless of prior achievement, gender, race, language, or cultural background.
8. Assessments should measure students' motivation, attitudes, and affective reactions about the curriculum as well as their cognitive skills, strategies, and knowledge.
9. Assessments should include exhibits, portfolios, and performances to demonstrate a wide range of behavior and accomplishments.

10. The design of standards of excellence and assessment systems should be negotiated by the participants—including parents, teachers, administrators, and students—in districts and states in order to ensure consensus, commitment, and ownership among the primary stakeholders.

11. The results of assessment should provide clear, comprehensible, and immediate feedback to the participants.

12. All assessments should provide for periodic review and revision among the participants and consumers of assessment information.

These 12 principles are meaningful corollaries to the American Psychological Association (APA) Presidential Task Force's learner-centered psychological principles (APA, 1993) and can be applied directly to assessment situations and tasks. There are numerous classroom activities that are aligned with these principles. In fact, many organizations, such as the National Council for Teachers of Mathematics (NCTM) and the International Reading Association (IRA), have proposed assessment frameworks that are compatible with these principles. During the past 5 years, there have been many demonstrations of the value of performance-based and portfolio assessments (e.g., Herman, Aschbacher, & Winters, 1992; Tierney, Carter, & Desai, 1991). These exciting alternatives have been received enthusiastically by parents, teachers, and students who use them. Although new assessment techniques may not replace standardized testing, they provide valuable supplementary information that redirects the focus of teaching on instructional decision making, redirects students' motivation to self-improvement, and redirects parental concern to supporting the educational progress of their children. In the following pages of this chapter, it is clear how portfolios that include children's work samples, projects, and reflections can promote deeper engagement with learning, higher motivation for assessment, and feelings of pride and efficacy that promote lifelong learning.

Benefits of Portfolios

Portfolios are not a panacea for all the problems with achievement testing. However, they help redress the imbalance of current assessment procedures by placing more emphasis on students' work samples from the regular curriculum. These ongoing assessments complement the more focused assessments that are typically provided by periodic tests. Ongoing assessments such as samples of children's writing, attitudes, reflections, reports, and other work produced during the week may or may not be included in a portfolio system, but they do provide authentic evidence of children's performance in the classroom. Ongoing assessments provide continuous information to teachers, parents, and students about what and how students are learning (Winograd, Paris, & Bridge, 1991).

The most positive feature of portfolios for teachers is that they provide a system for collecting and monitoring students' work. Paris and Ayres (1994) defined *portfolios* as principled and selective collections of students' work that reflect the authentic activities of daily classroom curriculum and instruction. Portfolios usually include a variety of evidence that demonstrate and explain students' classroom performance. The collection should be guided by principles of what is important to assess in children's progress. The judgements about important values or dimensions of learning might be stipulated by the district outcomes, by the schools' objectives, or by the categories included on the periodic report card or pupil progress report. Each of these sources reflects the school district values about what is important to assess and each provides guidance for teachers about what to include in students' portfolios. Thus, it is not necessary to include multiple copies of the same kinds of worksheets or weekly spelling tests, just representative examples that are consistent with the outcomes or objectives being measured.

Another key characteristic of this portfolio system (Paris & Ayres, 1994) is that the system is designed to support existing assessment procedures in a district and does not require additional work on the teacher's part for no apparent purpose. When designing portfolios in a large metropolitan school district, Paris and Ayres linked them closely to parent–teacher conferences and student report cards so that parents and teachers understood clearly the purpose and value of portfolios. Alternative assessment systems must fit clearly with other assessments in the school and provide procedures that are efficient and effective for teachers. New assessment procedures must help teachers do their jobs better with minimal costs in time and resources. Portfolios offer both of these advantages and indeed are the most efficient, low-cost form of assessment that teachers can implement.

The main advantage of portfolios to parents is the increased communication about daily classroom activities and their children's performance. Too often, parents know little about the curriculum and instruction in the class. They rely on periodic letters, work samples, projects, and report cards to tell them about events at school. Because teachers vary considerably in what they send home and how often they send it, parents are often left to guess about the curriculum and their children's progress. That is partly why they have come to rely so much on test scores. Portfolios build a different relationship among the participants. Instead of parent–teacher distrust or confrontation about a student's performance, portfolios and work samples allow shared information and common goals for students, teachers, and parents as they review children's learning and motivation. In schools that use portfolios, parents are enthusiastic about the kinds of work samples they see and the regular communication with teachers that are afforded by portfolios. When they have teacher–parent conferences, they understand what to look for as they examine their own children's work. Frequently, teachers invite students to lead the parent–teacher conferences as they review and display evidence of their accomplishments.

The main advantage of portfolios for students is that students learn to take responsibility for collecting evidence about their own work and assessing their own progress. They become more actively involved in applying criteria of learning and motivation and understanding the standards of performance that are expected from them. They become engaged in self-assessment, which is the critical internalization of both parents' and teachers' standards and expectations. For example, as students review work to include in their portfolios, they must decide whether it reflects the effort and skills that they want to share with teachers and parents. In other words, their work is not just a sample of what is being completed, but a sample of a high standard of performance according to specific criteria. Self-assessment enhances students' motivation and ownership in their own learning in ways that are not provided in traditional achievement testing (Au, Scheu, Kawakami, & Herman, 1990).

Teachers vary tremendously in the ways that they collect work samples, and there is no standard format. Some teachers use hanging file folders in bins to collect samples of work throughout the week; other teachers use file cabinets, boxes, folders, or journals to collect various pieces of evidence. In fact, teachers often use several different systems such as writing folders, journals, math portfolios, and reading logs to organize work samples in different areas of the curriculum. *Portfolios* is a generic term for collections rather than a particular physical system for organizing those collections of work samples. Although the systems may vary, teachers and students should consider three kinds of evidence across the curriculum. First, children should include samples of their performance on daily tasks. This includes what they read, write, compute, and create every day. These are the concrete artifacts and work samples of the curriculum. Second, portfolios should include evidence about the processes of learning used by students so that others can "see their thinking" in the work. Periodically, teachers might include comments from the student or the teacher about children's abilities to revise written material, to use appropriate reading strategies, or to demonstrate their thinking as they solve mathematical problems. The focus on the metacognitive aspects of "learning how to learn" in a portfolio gives this aspect of education an explicit priority that is often missing in classrooms. Third, teachers and students should reflect on their perceptions of their own abilities and achievements. Teachers may periodically ask students to fill out attitude or opinion surveys. Students may include periodic self-reflections in their journals, or they may provide evaluations of their own portfolios before a teacher conference or a report card. These three aspects of daily work—performance, process, and perception—may be labeled knowledge, skill, and attitude (or something else), but they reflect distinct kinds of evidence about children's learning and development. In the Paris and Ayres (1994) project, teachers were encouraged to collect samples of students' performance, process, and perceptions for each of the graded report card categories. This matrix provides a systematic way for teachers and parents to understand how the portfolios include different kinds of evidence for the different criteria on the report card. Thus, it provides a selective and principled system for choosing evidence for the portfolio as well as interpreting the work samples that they review.

Promoting Learning and Motivation With Authentic Assessment

There is no simple way to describe the multiple benefits of using portfolios in classrooms. Portfolios create a totally different atmosphere of collaboration and mutual analysis of students' accomplishments. They shift the emphasis from doing 15-minute, close-ended activities to more open-ended analyses of learning itself, which reflect an integrated curriculum. In other words, better assessment techniques encourage a better curriculum on a daily basis. Better assessment techniques also encourage more active student engagement in learning and in self-assessment, and thus both teachers and students are more enthusiastic and satisfied with the kinds of learning that go on in the classroom. Paris and Turner (1994) discussed these advantages of a motivating classroom in terms of six critical characteristics. These are described briefly in the following paragraphs so that teachers can examine how their current assessment practices support each of these characteristics in their own classrooms.

First, authentic tasks allow students to construct meaning in what they read, write, and create, rather than simply copy sentences off the board or fill in the blanks on worksheets. One of the problems with traditional testing is that students do not construct meaning in a way that is similar to the rich activities they do on a daily basis. Portfolios and authentic assessment allow richer examples of work that reflect children's abilities to construct meaning from authentic problems.

Second, a good curriculum, like good assessment practices, allows children to have choices about what they learn, the pace of their learning, and how they express their understanding. For example, children may all choose to read different passages or books, but they are accountable for their comprehension of them. Choice allows students to tailor a curriculum as well as an assessment portfolio based on their own interests, backgrounds, and knowledge. Third, successful classrooms provide challenges to each and every student. This means that some tasks are made more difficult whereas others are made easier for students according to their level of ability, not that all the classroom activities are raised to the same uniform high or low standard. The trouble with conventional curricula aimed at the middle of the class is that they are frustrating for the "slow" students and boring for the "fast" students. Authentic assessment that allows each child to display their best work or performance allows children to be challenged at a level at which they can succeed.

Fourth, teachers encourage collaboration, but traditional testing is isolated and independent. Authentic assessment allows for group projects, peer conferences, and cooperative learning to be included in evaluations of children's progress. Fifth, students often lose interest in classroom activities, both curricular and assessment, when they have no *control* over the task. They become more involved when they see that they can choose different goals, apply different strategies, and control the pace and direction of their own learning. These feelings of control lead directly to feelings of self-efficacy which promote subsequent motivation.

Sixth, the consequences of self-assessment, such as reviewing and evaluating portfolios, are immediate, gratifying, and beneficial for future learning and motivation. Students do not get feedback about standardized tests for several months, if at all, and the results rarely have any direct impact on their learning or instruction. Students cannot feel good or bad after the test; most are simply relieved that it's over and move on to the next task. Likewise, teachers do not benefit directly from the consequences of achievement tests because the results are usually not timely or diagnostic for individuals, and thus the tests promote benign neglect or cynicism from teachers and students. In contrast, authentic assessments provide immediate diagnostic information for teachers and sources of pride and satisfaction.

In combination, these six characteristics describe vibrant classrooms where teachers and students are engaged in exciting projects that are designed for individual interests and knowledge of students. Assessment and curriculum are intertwined through the use of portfolios because teachers and students are constantly trying to improve what they know and what they produce. These six characteristics are also hallmarks of intrinsic motivation and reflect students who take charge of their own learning in a strategic, independent, and confident manner. The fact that these six characteristics are missing from traditional achievement tests is a stinging criticism of the sterility and uselessness of these tests for teachers and students. The power of portfolios and alternative assessments is that they provide direct and immediate benefits to students, parents, and teachers that promote, rather than undermine, education.

Conclusion

The central message of this chapter is that education professionals can do a better job assessing students' learning than using periodic standardized achievement tests with every student. Standardized testing includes many hidden dangers for parents, teachers, and students that can be removed by more judicious use of these tests and better use of alternative assessment procedures to document the ongoing progress of students. If the goal is to encourage students' learning and motivation in schools year after year, standardized achievement testing must be minimized and alternative assessments must be created that support teachers, inform parents, and motivate students.

References

American Psychological Association Presidential Task Force on Psychology in Education. (1993). *Learner-centered psychological principles: Guidelines for school redesign and reform.* Washington, DC: American Psychological Association and the Mid-Continent Regional Educational Laboratory.

Ames, C., & Archer, J. (1988). Achievement goals in the classroom: Students' learning strategies and motivation processes. *Journal of Educational Psychology, 80,* 260–267.

Au, K. H., Scheu, J. A., Kawakami, A. J., & Herman, P. A. (1990). Assessment and accountability in a whole language curriculum. *The Reading Teacher, 43,* 574–578.

Barber, B. L., Paris, S. G., Evans, M., & Gadsden, V. (1992). Policies for reporting test results to parents. *Educational Measurement: Issues and Practices, 11,* 15–20.

Charlesworth, R., Fleege, P. O., & Weitman, C. J. (1994). Research on the effects of group standardized testing on instruction, pupils, and teachers: New directions for policy. *Early Education and Development, 5,* 195–212.

Corno, L. (1992). Encouraging students to take responsibility for learning and performance. *Elementary School Journal, 93,* 69–83.

Haladyna, T., Nolen, S. B., & Haas, N. S. (1991). Raising standardized achievement test scores and the origins of test score pollution. *Educational Researcher, 20,* 2–7.

Herman, J. L., Aschbacher, P. R., & Winters, L. (1992). *A practical guide to alternative assessment.* Alexandria, VA: Association for Supervision and Curriculum Development.

Linn, R. L., Baker, E. L., & Dunbar, S. B. (1991). Complex, performance-based assessment: Expectations and validation criteria. *Educational Researcher, 20,* 15–21.

Madaus, G. F., & Tan, A. G. A. (1993). The growth of assessment. In G. Cawelti (Ed.), *Challenges and achievements of American education* (pp. 53–79). Alexandria, VA: Association for Supervision and Curriculum Development.

McGill-Franzen, A., & Allington, R. L. (1993). Flunk 'em or get them classified: The contamination of primary grade accountability data. *Educational Researcher, 22,* 19–22.

Moore, W. P. (1994). The devaluation of standardized testing: One district's response to a mandated assessment. *Applied Measurement in Education, 7,* 343–367.

Nicholls, J. G. (1989). *The competitive ethos and democratic education.* Cambridge, MA: Harvard University Press.

Paris, S. G., & Ayres, L. R. (1994). *Becoming reflective students and teachers with authentic assessment.* Washington, DC: American Psychological Association.

Paris, S. G., Lawton, T. A., Turner, J. C., & Roth, J. L. (1991). A developmental perspective on standardized achievement testing. *Educational Researcher, 20,* 12–20.

Paris, S. G., & Turner, J. T. (1994). Situated motivation. In P. Pintrich, C. Weinstein, & D. Brown (Eds.), *Student motivation, cognition, and learning: Essays in honor of Wilbert J. McKeachie* (pp. 213–237). Hillsdale, NJ: Lawrence Erlbaum Associates.

Pintrich, P. R., & DeGroot, E. V. (1990). Motivational and self-regulated learning components of classroom academic performance. *Journal of Educational Psychology, 82,* 33–40.

Stevenson, H. W., & Stigler, J. (1992). *The learning gap.* New York: Summit Books.

Stipek, D. J. (1993). *Motivation to learn: From theory to practice.* Boston: Allyn & Bacon.

Tierney, R. J., Carter, M. A., & Desai, L. E. (1991). *Portfolio assessment in the reading-writing classroom.* Norwood, MA: Christopher-Gordon.

Urdan, T. C., & Paris, S. G. (1994). Teachers' perceptions of standardized achievement tests. *Educational Policy, 8*(2), 137–156.

Wiggins, G. (1989). A true test: Towards more authentic and equitable assessment. *Phi Delta Kappan, 70,* 703–714.

Winograd, P., Paris, S., & Bridge, C. (1991). Improving the assessment of reading. *The Reading Teacher, 45,* 108–116.

Wolf, D., Bixby, J., Glenn, J., & Gardner, H. (1991). To use their minds well: Investigating new forms of student assessment. In G. Grant (Ed.), *Review of research in education* (Vol. 17, pp. 31–74). Washington, DC: American Educational Research Association.

Using Learner-Centered Assessment on a Large Scale

Joan Boykoff Baron

The question addressed in this chapter is whether learner-centered assessment and large-scale state assessment are compatible. After surveying the more common forms of state assessment, one might be tempted to think that the answer is negative. However, the premise of this chapter is that they can be. This chapter begins by defining learner-centered assessment and describing its characteristics. Next, I describe how learner-centered tasks are structured within the Connecticut Common Core of Learning Assessment program and present an extended example. The concluding sections look at the nature of the stakes, incentives, and timelines that should accompany a successful learner-centered state assessment program and explore how such assessments can supplement or potentially replace the assessments that are currently being used for accountability and instructional improvements.

The work reported in this chapter is the result of the efforts of many individuals and I wish to gratefully acknowledge their help. Through a grant from the National Science Foundation (SPA-8954692-Principal Investigator, Joan Boykoff Baron), the Common Core of Learning Assessment Project was able to involve directly close to 200 science and mathematics teachers from Connecticut, Michigan, Minnesota, New York, Texas, Vermont, and Wisconsin; the Coalition of Essential Schools; Project RE:Learning; and the Urban Districts' Leadership Consortium of the American Federation of Teachers. Without the cooperation of these teachers and their students, we could not have developed and revised our assessment tasks. We are also grateful to the nearly 100 project advisors—scientists, science educators, mathematicians, mathematics educators, state education specialists, psychologists, and psychometricians who provided helpful suggestions at key points in the project. The Common Core of Learning Assessment Staff at the Connecticut State Department of Education consisted of Jeffrey Greig, Michal Lomask, and Sigmund Abeles in science, and Bonnie Laird Hole, Steven Leinwand, Susan Dixon, and Judith Collison in mathematics. Pascal D. Forgione and Douglas A. Rindone directed the project with the assistance of Steven Martin, Amy Shively, and Hannah Kruglanski. Claire J. Harrison and Bruce Davey provided psychometric expertise, and Arlene Morrissey and Martha Szykula furnished clerical assistance. The Soda Task grew out of an idea suggested by Dale Wolfgram, a chemistry teacher in Michigan. Following revisions suggested by more than a dozen teachers and the project's science team, the current version of the task emerged. I am especially grateful to Michal Lomask for creatively strengthening the content of the science tasks and suggesting many of the formats and scoring procedures that were finally used. Any opinions expressed in this chapter are my own and are not meant to represent the views of the funding agencies or my colleagues.

Characteristics of Learner-Centered Assessments

Learner-centered assessments are those that are intended to enhance student learning. As such, they have three characteristics. First, they begin with a commitment to helping the learner function successfully in society by representing the content, skills, and dispositions that society currently values and is likely to value over the coming decade. For example, they might include the ability to solve loosely structured problems, work together in groups, and present information orally.

Second, learner-centered assessment tasks themselves function as learning events. The tasks are seen as opportunities for students to learn from one another and deepen their understanding of content. In Gibson's terminology, the assessment tasks provide multiple affordances for learning (cited in MacArthur & Baron, 1983). There are several categories of tasks that provide indexes of students' deepened understanding—integration, application, and transfer. A task requiring integration and synthesis is one in which students are called on to pull together and make sense of previously fragmented bits of prior knowledge. For example, one item developed for our Common Core of Learning Assessment program used an essay format in which students responded to questions such as, "If you were to receive a blood transfusion, for what would you want your blood tested?" (Lomask, Baron, & Greig, 1993). Since all of the information about blood type and disease transmission had already been learned by the students, the assessment task provided an opportunity for students to select what was relevant and put it all together. Application occurs when students are asked to use their previously acquired knowledge and skills in a new situation in which they know, at least generally speaking, what kinds of information are required. Like application, transfer requires that students are able to use their previously acquired knowledge in novel situations. But unlike application, the problem formulation in transfer tasks has no scaffolding; it does not specify the elements of the subject matter that are required to solve the problem. Through tasks like these, the students learn how their school-based knowledge can be used in more real-world settings. The Soda Task, which is described in depth later in this chapter, contains an example of both application and transfer.

A third characteristic of learner-centered assessment is that students are continuously encouraged to self-assess their progress by using publicly stated performance criteria to monitor their own work. In learner-centered classrooms, time is spent making students familiar with the performance standards (i.e., what they mean and what level of performance is required to distinguish an outstanding performance from a satisfactory or unsatisfactory one). Ownership of the standards empowers students to set meaningful goals as well as to make adjustments in their thinking and their performance as they learn how to produce high-quality work and assume the responsibility for doing so.

An Analogy Worth Exploring

Assessment skeptics are fond of warning us that "weighing cattle doesn't make them fatter" (Shanker, 1995). They argue, by analogy, that more testing or even different kinds of testing does not ensure greater student achievement. But, what would happen if cows could read the scales? And what if the cows knew what to eat and how much to eat when (and if) they wanted to gain weight? Let us change the context from fattening cattle to one of the currently popular weight-loss programs. They always begin with an assessment, by having the dieters get on a scale. The scale provides the dieter with the critical data to self-monitor the progress made since the last weigh in. This feedback enables the dieter to make adjustments if two conditions are met. First, the dieter must be motivated to alter his or her behavior and second, the dieter must know what changes to make. Thus, when the assessment data are supplemented by motivation and know-how, the dieter can lose weight and the proverbial cow can be fattened (or slenderized in this particular case).

The client-centered characteristics of successful weight-loss programs can be applied directly to learner-centered assessment. In such a model, the first role of the assessment is to engage and challenge. The learner should perceive the assessment tasks as direct assessments of society's most valued outcomes and as sources of ongoing and meaningful feedback. This will enable the student to use these data for self-assessment, reflecting on the possible next steps and the best strategies for taking those steps. In summary, when assessments have these characteristics they are learner centered.

Why the Need for Learner-Centered Assessment?

There are several reasons why learner-centered assessment is being promoted by educators in Connecticut as well as by several other groups and in many other states in this country, for example, the American Psychological Association (1993), ARTS PROPEL (Wolf, Bixby, Glenn,

& Gardner, 1991), California (Honig, Alexander, & Wolf, 1996), Kentucky (Gong & Reidy, 1996), New York (Darling-Hammond & Snyder, 1992), and Vermont (Mills, 1996). One has to do with the widespread support for the governors' and president's national education goals and the 1992 recommendations for a set of national curriculum and assessment standards deemed to be feasible and desirable by the National Council for Educational Standards and Testing (NCEST). The NCEST report responded to the mounting national concern over the poor showing of United States students in both national and international tests of mathematics and science. It also captured the nation's frustration over the national educational dropout rate of close to 25% and the Black and Latino dropout rates of close to 50%. In sum, it reflected a decade of national embarrassment over being a nation at risk.

The American public continues to grow impatient. It no longer wants to just weigh its cattle; it wants to fatten them. Increasing numbers of educators are beginning to realize that we do not need more traditional assessments. There is a growing realization that merely increasing our present accountability and instructional improvement efforts cannot be counted on to improve achievement. Many reformers recognize that to reduce our educational risk, we need to foster the development of empowered and efficacious learners. Toward this end, many educators believe that we need a learner-centered assessment system in which we motivate students with engaging and challenging performance-based tasks and the criteria to self-assess their own progress.

One might legitimately ask whether this emphasis on better assessment will also result in a better curriculum. If done well and with forethought, it should. New assessments should be designed to both reflect the most challenging curricula and point the way toward them. Reasonable timelines and the commitment to bring both the assessments and the curriculum in line with society's needs and values are necessary. If we are dedicated to preparing more effectively tomorrow's parents, voters, professionals, service workers and elected officials, we will want to develop learning events that enhance students' abilities to solve complex, multidimensional, loosely structured problems (see Baron & Sternberg, 1987; Resnick, 1987a).

Assessing What Our Nation Values

In developing the content categories for our most recent high school assessments in science and mathematics, it has been necessary to decide precisely what aspects of science and mathematics are important. Many professional groups have attempted this task, and it is useful to look at their reports to analyze their commonalities. Notable among these in mathematics is the National Council of Teachers of Mathematics (1988), and in science, the American Association for the Advancement of Science (1989), the National Center for the Improvement of Science Education (Raizen et al., 1989, 1990), the National Research Council (1994), and the National Science Teachers' Association (1992). All of these groups subscribed to the belief that less is more—that it is more important for students to understand fully a few important concepts than to grasp superficially a great many less important concepts. In addition, they all called for students who can solve problems both individually and collaboratively and clearly communicate their ideas orally and in writing. These views were supported by business and labor groups, school boards, and educators across the academic disciplines (Marzano et al., 1988). The Common Core of Learning, adopted by the Connecticut State Board of Education (1987) after extensive public review reflected these important ideas. Following its adoption state department personnel set out to create assessment tasks to illustrate more concretely those beliefs (Baron, 1996; Baron, Forgione, Rindone, Kruglanski, & Davey, 1989).

If one were to develop science and mathematics problems that incorporate the common thinking skills and dispositions that have been identified in the documents cited above, they would include students' abilities to do such things as the following:

1. Frame problems and troubleshoot solutions
2. Tolerate ambiguity
3. Make and specify one's assumptions
4. Consider alternatives and be open to new ideas
5. See issues from different perspectives
6. Develop a line of argument and marshall support for it
7. Value evidence
8. Collect, aggregate, analyze, and portray data
9. Produce and generate solutions
10. Synthesize knowledge from a variety of sources
11. Take responsibility to complete sustained problems
12. Persist in the face of failure
13. Be reflective
14. Self-assess one's own progress and make corrections
15. Recognize that knowledge is tentative

Two recent future-oriented books can be used to add some new and less conventional aspects. Reich's (1991) *The Work of Nations: Preparing Ourselves for 21st Century Capitalism* describes three groups of people needed in today's organizations: "problem-identifiers, problem solvers, and the strategic brokers who link the first two." Sinetar's (1991) *Developing a 21st Century Mind* adds the following attributes:

1. Creatively adaptive
2. Playfully solves problems
3. Incubates solutions
4. Is logically intuitive
5. Is "unfreakable" and challenged by problems
6. Enjoys ordering chaos
7. Is visionary
8. Transcends or resolves paradoxes
9. Is whole-seeing

As we proceed to develop performance-based assessment and curriculum, we may want to consider ways to foster many of these attributes.

Establishing a Synchrony Between Society's Values and Educational Assessment

The learner-centered view subscribed to by the Common Core of Learning Assessment program (Connecticut State Board of Education, 1987) was framed to determine how well students had developed the kinds of skills and attributes listed above. This is quite different from a view of assessment that begins with what schools are currently teaching. Many educators believe that as new assessments are built to reflect society's changing values and as teachers begin to teach to these new assessments, the resultant (or delivered) curriculum and instruction will be more closely aligned to society's values than to the more outdated curriculum that has been falling short. This view harnesses the power of assessment in today's schools. Therefore, one might reasonably argue that attending to the changing needs of contemporary society is more learner centered in the deep sense, because we will be preparing learners to adapt to the world in which they will live and work. This represents a shift from the current emphasis on curricular and instructional validity to something we might call *learner-centered* or *societally valued validity*. Several individual states (U.S. Congress, Office of Technology Assessment, 1992), consortia of states like the New Standards Project (Daro, 1996), and national assessment groups like the National Assessment of Educational Progress (Haertel & Mullis, 1996) and the College Board (Stewart & Johanek, 1996) are beginning to change their course and veer away from assessing what "*is*" toward assessing what "*should be.*"

Learner-Centered Assessment: What We Know From Psychology

Another equally powerful way in which assessments can be learner centered is by attending to what we know about how students learn. Cognitive, motivational, and educational psychology over the past two decades have made dramatic strides in understanding how students can learn more effectively. By incorporating these findings into the design of assessment tasks, we can create powerful learner-centered models for teachers to emulate. Simply stated, these assessment tasks are intended to serve as models of good instructional tasks. They can provide opportunities for students to both foster and demonstrate what they know and can do. In this section, we examine some of these principles.

Contributions of Cognitive Psychology

Students Learn Best When They Actively Construct Their Own Meaning

During the last decade, cognitive psychology has embraced a constructivist philosophy. In this view, students learn best when they are actively engaged. Students are not seen as passive receptacles of knowledge. They are not blank slates, but rather are thinking beings bringing to each new situation prior knowledge, beliefs, and dispositions. For real learning to occur, students must activate their prior knowledge structures (see Driver, 1990) or schemas (see Bransford & Stein, 1984) and examine new information in the light of their past beliefs. Where new information is discrepant, students need to reconcile these discrepancies. Toward this end, students are encouraged to formulate questions, hypotheses, and predictions and then collect evidence by designing and carrying out experiments, doing investigation, and conducting library research. Throughout this process, students will either confirm or reformulate their beliefs.

When tasks are structured in this way, students will be able to tell "a whole story" with many interconnected parts rather than being able to express just a few unconnected fragmentary ideas. This places a heavy burden on curriculum and assessment designers to determine in advance what the most important aspects of the curriculum are, to focus on the "big ideas" in the discipline, and where possible to design tasks that will enable students to frame their stories on the basis of connections among many different aspects of the curriculum.

Students Learn Best When They Use Metacognition and Self-Assessment

Students learn best when expectations are clearly stated and they know what quality works looks like. In this way, they can examine their own work and assess their own progress. Aspects of this process have been referred to as metacognition (Flavell, 1976), executive processing (Sternberg, 1987), reflective practice (Schön, 1982), self-regulation (McCombs & Marzano, 1990), and self-assessment (Wolf, 1988). What these processes entail is a publicly acknowledged set of criteria (dimensions of quality) and standards (i.e., how much is good enough?) along with an understanding of what it looks like to meet those criteria and reach those standards (i.e., exemplars). Effective classroom experiences will include discussions of the meaning of quality along with many concrete examples of effective work. Once students internalize these criteria they are empowered as self-critical and generative learners (Perkins, 1992). Therefore, any worthwhile student assessment program must include this self-assessment or reflective component. Anything short of this is not fully learner centered.

Students Learn Best When They Have Experience in Applying and Transferring Their Knowledge

Many have called the transfer problem the single most important problem in education (ASCD, 1992). Most teachers experience frustration from observing their students' inability to see the connections between something they learned last week and its utility for today. Equally frustrating is the inability of their students to see the relevance of what they do in school to what they do outside of school or the relevance for what they do outside of school to what they do in school (reviews of transfer may be found in Cormier & Hagman, 1987; Covington, 1992; Pea, 1988). Also of interest are recent studies in situated cognition in which students are often able to solve complex problems in the world of work that they cannot solve in school (see Brown, Collins, & Duguid, 1989; Newman, Griffen, & Cole, 1989; Rogoff & Lave, 1984; Scribner & Cole, 1981).

Research shows that students better transfer their knowledge to new situations if they have experience in learning how and under what conditions it is appropriate to do so. Learner-centered assessment should incorporate these principles by giving students multiple opportunities to apply their knowledge in situations that are highly scaffolded and then gradually diminish the scaffolding until they can transfer their knowledge and skills in situations where little or no scaffolding is provided (Collins, Brown, & Newman, 1989).

Contributions of Motivational and Educational Psychology

A summary of the research from motivational and educational psychology (Ames & Ames, 1985; APA, 1993; Covington, 1992; McCombs & Marzano, 1990) provides a set of additional findings that can be incorporated into the design of effective assessments.

Students Learn Best When Problems Are Interesting, Meaningful, Challenging, and Engaging

Related to the transfer issue discussed above is the idea of using interesting and engaging problems. Generally, students will engage more easily with problems that are embedded in challenging real-world contexts that have apparent relevance to their lives (Resnick, 1987b). These problems tend to be intrinsically motivating for students. However, some recent evidence emerging from science assessment in Great Britain (Song & Black, 1991, 1992) indicates that students may need help in recognizing that school-based scientific knowledge is useful in real-world contexts.

Students Learn Best When They Exercise Choice, Control, and Personal Responsibility

Students will perform best when they have some choice and control over their learning. This is enhanced when students can choose their own strategies, design their own experiments, and control their own pace and their use of resources. This underscores the importance of research findings in self-regulation and responsibility. When students feel in control of their decisions, they are more motivated to persist, take responsibility for their own learning, and strive for quality results (DeCharms, 1976; McCombs, 1984).

Students Learn Best When They Have a Sense of Efficacy

Students perform best when they believe they have the requisite knowledge and skills to carry out the task. This will be more likely to occur when teachers have provided opportunities for students to engage in learning experiences that enable them to acquire and apply the knowledge and enabling skills that students require for the assessment tasks. If students confront a problem that they have no hope of solving, many students will not even attempt to solve it (Bandura, 1982).

Students Learn Best When They Work in Groups

There are at least three separate lines of social policy, theory, and research that have encouraged us to ask students to work collaboratively on assessment tasks. An important policy impetus comes from society at large, which has been clamoring for students who can work productively in group settings. This call is heard in both professional and service-oriented work settings. In fast-food restaurants, industrial settings, and research laboratories, people do not work in isolation. They depend on each other for ideas, implementation, follow-through, and general well-being. A second line of support emanates from the writings of Vygotsky (1978), which emphasize the role of social factors in both instigating learning and in facilitating the accelerated development of metacognitive processes through social prompting the zone of proximal development (ZPD). The final line of theory and research has evolved under the title of "cooperative learning," beginning with Deutsch (1949) and continuing with the jigsaw approach to cooperative problem solving of Aronson, Blaney, Stephan, Sikes, and Snapp (1978) and many other lines of related work that illustrate many advantages of working in a group (Hertz-Lazarowitz & Miller, 1992; Hibbard & Baron, 1990; Johnson & Johnson, 1985, 1990; Johnson, Maruyama, Johnson, Nelson, & Skon, 1981; Sharan & Sharan, 1976; Sharan & Shaulov, 1990; Slavin, 1983).

What Should Learner-Centered Performance-Based Assessment Tasks Include?

If one were to incorporate the findings from cognitive and motivational psychology with the goals expressed by current society for what effective learners should display, one would have a very different type of assessment. Learner-centered assessment tasks would be

1. contextualized, real-world, and authentic;
2. engaging;
3. nontrivial; and
4. challenging.

Furthermore, they would involve (a) connecting a big chunk of curriculum, including the most important content, skills, and dispositions, and (b) allowing for multiple solutions and/or solution paths. In learner-centered assessment tasks, students are often expected to

1. formulate the problem;
2. make and specify their assumptions;
3. consider different points of view;
4. make choices and decisions;
5. activate prior knowledge of content and process;
6. design and carry out an investigation;
7. collect, analyze, and interpret data;
8. communicate results in writing and orally;
9. collaborate;
10. tell a whole story;
11. self-assess the quality of their work using a set of pre-specified criteria; and
12. reflect on their own work and the work of other groups.

What Is the Role of Teachers During These Assessment Tasks?

The teacher plays several roles during a performance-based assessment task. The first of these is to ensure that the students have the necessary background of knowledge, skills, and dispositions required to successfully complete the task. Somewhat new for many teachers is the job of ensuring that students understand the criteria for successful work. This means that teachers and students will define, talk about, and find examples of student work that represent high-quality accomplishments. It is expected that as students grow to understand what these qualities are, they will internalize them and be able to apply them to their own work and that of others. The teacher also must continuously support a physically and psychologically safe environment in which the students can feel free to express themselves and take intellectual risks.

Up to this point, I have focused on the student as learner. It is at this juncture that one recognizes that performance-based student assessment places teachers in the role of learners. This is well beyond the learning that teachers generally report from assessments—that of learning about one's own students. Whereas that will indeed occur, there is another type of learning that occurs when teachers use performance-based assessment tasks, analogous to how an expert deepens his or her understanding in the context of the scaffolding role of the ZPD. This has to do with changing basic beliefs about the way students learn and the instructional practices best suited to students' learning. It also has to do with using the scoring guides and students' examples to help structure their own understanding of subject matter.

It is generally acknowledged that teachers teach the way they were taught. This is not unlike Harlow's experiments with the mothering habits of laboratory monkeys. Those monkeys that had not been "mothered" did not know how to mother. Very few teachers have ever been exposed to the kinds of assessment tasks described in this chapter. They have had almost no exposure to classroom-based problems that have more than one right answer or solution path, or require students to design their own experiments, plan together, and make oral reports about their procedures. Therefore, everything I said earlier about how students learn most effectively also applies to their teachers. They too must work in a supportive environment—one that enables them to experience the same psychological safety net that is critical for their students. Teachers must be motivated to engage in these new practices and acquire the skills necessary to do so. This requires a substantial change in the nature and amount of preservice and inservice professional development experiences that are established for teachers. As Cohen (1992) noted, "Any effective new curriculum or assessment must also be an occasion for teachers to learn."

Policy Makers and Parents as Learners

Just as students and teachers are learners in this process, so are policy makers and parents. These groups are accustomed to simple summary statistics to describe the status of a student's or school's achievement. These have taken the form of national and state norms or numbers of items correct on a multiple-choice test. Performance-based assessment requires human judgment. To be maximally useful, it will require multiple judgments on several dimensions of quality. An effective written essay may be judged on the depth of its support and elaboration, its clarity, and its style to name a few possibilities. A mathematics solution might be scored on its problem-solving, reasoning, communication, and accuracy. Just as students and teachers will need to become accustomed to using these descriptive and diagnostic dimensions of quality, policy makers and parents must learn to interpret these dimensions. They will learn that scoring criteria can be subjective without being capricious or arbitrary in nature (Glass, 1978). Scoring criteria should also be sensitive to the particular contexts and populations with whom they are used.

As parents become familiar with the scoring criteria, they will feel more comfortable engaging with their children about their work.

In this sense, performance-based student assessment creates opportunities for many groups to learn. Students can deepen their understanding of the content domain while engaging in a performance-based assessment task. Teachers can sharpen their own understandings of what the qualities of good work are in ways that are tangible enough to enable them to assist their students to internalize theirs. And policy makers and parents can increase their own understandings about the complex nature of what it means for students to really understand something wherein understanding is not some vague abstraction but a multifaceted set of transformations (e.g., integrations, applications, and transfers) students are able to make when they have indeed mastered material (Baron, 1993).

The Structure of Connecticut's Common Core of Learning Performance Tasks

The Connecticut Common Core of Learning performance assessment tasks (Connecticut State Board of Education, 1987) developed for high school science and mathematics have three parts that require a blend of individual work at the beginning and end, and group work in the middle. As originally conceived, when operational, teachers would be able to choose which tasks to administer to their students and when to administer them. In selecting the tasks, teachers would consider what the enabling skills and knowledge are and introduce the tasks once they believe their students have acquired the requisite skills.

Part 1

At the beginning of the task, each student individually generates information about his or her prior knowledge and understandings about the science concepts and processes relevant to the task. Each student is asked for an initial hunch, an estimate of the solution, a preliminary design for a study, some important content-related or procedural understandings, and/or a list of questions the student would like to ask about the concepts being assessed. There are at least four important reasons for beginning by accessing each student's prior knowledge. First, it provides an opportunity for each student to do some preliminary thinking and be better able to make a contribution to the group discussion. Second, it increases the likelihood that each group can begin its deliberations with different perspectives represented. Third, it will make salient what each student brings to the task. The students' conceptions (naive or sophisticated) can be used by the group as a springboard for discussion and as an indication to them of where better clarity or relearning is needed. Teachers can use them to assess where students are beginning (Pecheone, Baron, Forgione, & Abeles, 1988), which provides informal baseline data against which to look at changes in students' thinking that may occur later during the group work. Finally, it provides the students with recorded traces of their early thinking that can be revisited reflectively from time to time. In Part 1 of The Soda Task, students are told as follows:

The Soda Task: Part 1: Starting by Yourself

You will be given two samples of soda, one regular soda containing sugar and the other one diet soda containing an artificial sweetener. Your task is to identify each sample as diet or regular based on your knowledge of physics, chemistry, and/or biology. As in any experiment, you are not allowed to taste any of the samples.

Information about Regular and Diet Soda

Regular soda generally contains fructose and/or sucrose (types of sugar) as sweeteners. Diet soda generally contains aspartame as a sweetener. The chemical formulas for these ingredients are shown below:

Fructose $C_6H_{12}O_6$
Sucrose $C_{12}H_{22}O_{11}$
Aspartame $C_{14}H_{18}N_2O_5$

Aspartame is roughly one hundred times sweeter than sugar. Therefore, significantly less aspartame is needed to make a given amount of diet soda equally sweet as regular soda.

Begin by making a list of the properties of the two sodas which might help to distinguish between the samples. Write down as many as you can think of.

This is a transfer task, offering virtually no scaffolding. It requires the students to draw on their knowledge of the properties of sugared and artificially sweetened substances. The task is loosely structured and there are many possible solutions and solution paths. This Getting Started by Yourself Task is designed to access students' prior knowledge, to give them something to talk about when they begin their group work, and to provide the teacher with a sense of how students approach an ambiguous task.

Part 2

In the middle section of the task, by far the longest phase, students work as a *group* to produce a group product. Students plan together and work together. In the group section of The Soda Task, the students are asked to do the following:

The Soda Task: Part 2: Group Work

1. Make a group list of the properties of the two sodas which will best help you to distinguish between the two samples.
2. Based on your list of properties, design two tests to distinguish between the two types of soda. They should be the ones which your group believes would be the most effective in distinguishing between the two samples. Explain why you chose each of them. Show that you understand the science involved in each test.
3. Write out a complete experimental plan for each of these two tests. Include a list of all the materials and equipment that you will need. Show your plan to your teacher before proceeding.

After getting approval from your teacher carry out your experiments.

4. Summarize your group's findings in a final report which includes:
    a. What your group tried to investigate (dependent and independent variables);
    b. How your group performed your experiments (method);
    c. What your group found (raw data, organized in charts or graphs, as necessary);
    d. What your group concluded (based on experimental findings) and how valid your group thinks these conclusions are.
5. Prepare an oral presentation of your group's experiments, findings, and conclusions. Each member of your group should be ready to participate in any part of the presentation.

In some more complex tasks, work is divided among the group members for part of the time. Throughout the task, interdependence is fostered by having each student feel responsible for telling the whole story, from the development of the group's initial design to its final conclusions. (This is most obvious in Number 5 where students are told that each member of the group should be ready to participate in any part of the presentation.) Also, at various intervals, students are asked to monitor their success both as a total group and as separate individuals working as part of a group. The criteria that will be used to assess the quality of the group project are shared with the students (see Number 4). These should be very familiar to students because they should have used them in their laboratory work during the semester. They should know what a controlled experiment entails as well as how to portray data.

The criteria for the oral presentations should also be familiar to the students. They include a combination of content and stylistic elements. In the first set, related to the content of the message, are the following:

The speaker:
1. Organizes the presentation effectively
2. Reports and explains clearly
3. Fits his/her presentation into the presentations of the other group members
4. Provides thorough and clear answers to questions
5. Uses scientific terminology accurately and appropriately

The second set, related to the medium or style of the presentation, includes the following:

The speaker:
6. Uses a voice clear and loud enough for all to hear
7. Maintains eye contact with the audience
8. Uses a conversational tone rather than reading to the audience
9. Uses visual aids that are easily seen and understood
10. Avoids distracting behaviors

The class should also have worked together in groups before the assessment and become familiar with the dimensions of the Group Performance Rating Form found in Exhibit 1. Students are asked to complete the ratings individually and then circulate their ratings to each member of their group for his or her review and signature. If any member of the group disagrees with the self-ratings, the students are asked to discuss with that person the reasons for the disagreement and then decide whether they want to change their original ratings.

Before students complete the third and last part of the task, Finishing by Yourself, they do an application task as part of their group work. Here they are asked to do the following:

Now that you have heard all of the group oral reports, please discuss the following questions, "If you were diabetic and had to know whether a sample of soda has sugar in it, which test (of all of the ones described by any group) would you trust the most? Which test would you trust the least? Explain fully why you chose each of these?

This gives the students an opportunity to synthesize and evaluate critically the information that they have heard from the different groups.

Exhibit 1

Group Performance Rating Form

Student Name or Code: _____   Date _____

Check One

	Almost Always	Often	Some-times	Rarely
Group Participation				
1. Participated in group discussion without prompting.				
2. Did his or her fair share of the work.				
3. Tried to dominate the group—interrupted others, spoke too much.				
4. *Participated in the Group's Activities.*				
Staying on the Topic				
5. Paid attention, listened to what was being said and done.				
6. Made comments aimed at getting the group back to the topic.				
7. Got off the topic or changed the subject.				
8. *Stayed on the topic.*				
Offering Useful Ideas				
9. Gave ideas and suggestions that helped the group.				
10. Offered helpful criticism and comments.				
11. Influenced the group's decisions and plans.				
12. *Offered Useful Ideas.*				
Consideration				
13. Made positive, encouraging remarks about group members and their ideas.				
14. Gave recognition and credit to others for their ideas.				
15. Made inconsiderate or hostile comments about a group member.				

continued

Exhibit 1, continued

Check One

	Almost Always	Often	Some-times	Rarely
16. *Was Considerate of Others.*				
Involving Others				
17. Got others involved by asking questions, requesting input or challenging others.				
18. Tried to get the group working to reach group agreements.				
19. Seriously considered the ideas of others.				
20. *Involved Others.*				
Communicating				
21. Spoke clearly. Was easy to hear and understand.				
22. Expressed ideas clearly and effectively.				
23. *Communicated Clearly.*				

It also gives teachers, students, and parents a greater feeling of comfort and fairness knowing that students will have the benefit of hearing the solutions of all of the groups before completing the final part of the task individually.

Not every assessment task warrants several hours of group time. To be a successful group task, it must meet one of two criteria: (a) the task provides a forum for students to work and talk together in ways that deepen students' understanding of essential scientific (or mathematical) concepts and processes, or (b) the structure of the task allows students to divide a large amount of work among the group members and share their findings with the group (Aronson et al., 1978). This task provides both—a chance for students to deepen their understanding of the scientific principles involved and the opportunity to divide the work among the group members.

Part 3

In the Finishing by Yourself section of The Soda Task, each student individually responds to three questions. These responses provide teachers, parents, and policy makers with a summative view of what each student knows and can do at the end of a rich set of learning and assessment opportunities. The first question requires students to apply their conceptual understanding of the chemistry involved in the task in a new context.

The Soda Task: Part 3: Finishing By Yourself

1. If you were given two samples of water, one of which is salt water and the other fresh water, which tests that your class tried out for the sodas would be useful in differentiating between the two? Which tests would not be useful? Which other tests might be appropriate for this problem? Explain all of your answers fully.

The second and third questions require students to analyze the experimental procedures and explanations displayed in a report generated by another group of students.

Group Report

Our group tested the following two properties of the sodas:

Test #1: Boiling

The boiling point of soda A was 96 and soda B was 97. The higher sugar content of B must have increased its boiling point.

Test #2: Density

Procedure: Weigh graduated cylinder. Measure 100 ml of soda A and weigh the cylinder and soda together.

Data: Mass of graduated cylinder = 43.26 g
      Mass of cylinder and soda A = 141.45 g
      Mass of cylinder and soda B = 144.02 g

Analysis: Density = mass/volume

Density of soda A = $(141.45 - 43.26)$ g/100 ml = .9819 g/ml
Density of soda B = $(144.01 - 43.26)$ g/100 ml = 1.0075 g/ml

Soda A was less dense than soda B.

Final conclusion: Due to the observations from the boiling test and the calculated density, Soda A was diet soda and soda B was regular soda.

---

2. A scientific report is written to share information and to enable others to replicate (repeat) the same experiment. Does this report give you enough information to replicate the experiment? If not, what is missing or not completely described in the report? Please be specific in your critique.
3. Write a critique of the students' final conclusion.

The data from tasks like these can ultimately be combined and aggregated for use by policy makers. Psychometricians in several states (e.g., California, Connecticut, Maryland, Kentucky, and Vermont) are currently working out the details of such a reporting system. Furthermore, researchers in these states and others are examining the extent to which different tasks provide similar patterns of performance. Although there are some generic aspects to these tasks (e.g., designing and carrying out experiments, collecting and portraying data, analyzing sources of error, delivering oral reports), the content knowledge differs on each task. Therefore, we would not expect two tasks based on different aspects of the curriculum to be equally difficult. This means that to obtain a stable estimate of an individual student or even a group of students, several tasks should be used (Dunbar, Koretz, & Hoover, 1991; Linn & Baker, 1996).

Assessments as Learning Events

It should be obvious by now that well-constructed assessment tasks can function as both assessments and learning events. Students can assess their own work and teachers can assess what their students know and can do. Throughout the task, students are constructing new conceptual models and deepening their understanding as they work together with other students to design and carry out their experiments. When the students listen to the other group reports and reflect on the best experiments, they are sharpening their understanding of quality work. When they reflect on which might be the most reliable test to use if they were diabetic and had to know which soda contained sugar, they are reflecting on the validity, reliability, and sources of error in the work of their own and other groups. This intentionally precedes the individual application task in order to give students additional opportunities to process and assimilate new knowledge. So, in an important sense, learner-centered assessment is also learner-centered curriculum. This is a notion that currently exists in Great Britain, which views its assessment tasks as *bits of curriculum* (Burstall, 1989). It is also consonant with the philosophy of the ARTS PROPEL program, which views its assessments as *episodes of learning* (Wolf, 1988).

During the pilot phase of our project, at the end of each task, we asked students for their reaction to the task. In examining close to 100 responses of students to The Soda Task, we found that students' reactions tended to be related to their academic backgrounds. In general, students in the more advanced classes were more positive about the task, although students from the lowest level class reported that they found it interesting. About a quarter of the students liked creating their own experiments and mentioned things they had learned while doing the task. Many students reported that they liked working in a group— getting new ideas, sharing different perspectives, seeing how others worked. Some students enjoyed working on The Soda Task because "it was a change from the step-by-step labs that we always do and I got to use my imagination," whereas others "didn't like having to make up an experiment because I had never done anything like it before, (but) now I think that making up an experiment is fun." What was particularly illuminating were responses like, "Taking a test can prove you remembered something, (but) this doesn't mean that you understand it. In order to do a performance task, you must remember the information and understand it."

Although it will not happen overnight, based on our experiences to date with a sample of highly motivated volunteer teachers, we believe that it is not unreasonable to predict that after students have tried several tasks like The Soda Task,

1. Students will feel comfortable when confronting loosely structured problems with considerable ambiguity.
2. Students will be able to make and specify their assumptions.
3. Students will consider different points of view and resolve them.
4. Students will make appropriate choices and decisions about how to allocate their time and resources.
5. Students will be able to design and carry out experiments.
6. Students will be able to collect, analyze, portray, and interpret data.
7. Students will be able to communicate their results in writing and orally.
8. Students will feel comfortable working in a group.
9. Students will take responsibility for completing a task, persisting even when unsure.
10. Students will feel comfortable telling a whole story.
11. Students will be able to assess the quality of their work using a set of public criteria.
12. Students will be able to reflect on and critique the work of other groups.
13. Students will know that there will always be sources of error and will be able to identify them and minimize their impact.

14. Students will come to expect to use their knowledge of science and math to solve real-world problems.
15. Students will develop a sense of efficacy.

Embedding Learner-Centered Tasks in the Classroom

What enables tasks like The Soda Task to be learner centered is that they take place in the students' own classroom over several days. Ideally, there should be relatively little anxiety associated with such tasks. From the students' point of view, this task is just like others in the curriculum. The students are not competing with each other. If everyone does well, everyone can get excellent ratings. What is important is that through a series of classroom conversations and with considerable practice students come to recognize and eventually internalize what quality work looks like.

When my colleagues and I applied to the National Science Foundation for a grant to develop learner-centered science and mathematics assessments, we knew that activities like The Soda Task were in short supply in Connecticut classrooms and those around the nation. We hoped to develop assessments that were consistent with the expanded vision of learning portrayed in the NCTM Standards, the AAAS Science for All Americans, and the Connecticut Common Core of Learning. The road has not been an easy one because personal and professional changes do not come about easily. Teachers who are accustomed to lecturing to their students and having them do step-by-step cookbook-type laboratory experiments do not make this transition readily. Teachers who have not used group work are generally uneasy about trying it. Furthermore, students who are not accustomed to thinking hard about loosely structured problems are uncomfortable at first. Unsure teachers need substantial bolstering and confidence before they are able to face unsure students. Changes like those required by this type of assessment will not happen over night. They will require large-scale professional development efforts with teachers having access to models of effective, engaging tasks to try out. Teachers will need time to work together to decide what they value and then develop both appropriate tasks and the accompanying criteria for quality work. Such changes will call for teachers who are more experienced with performance-based assessment to work closely with their less experienced colleagues who are uneasy about getting started with performance tasks. Although I recognize that this is a monumental task, I also know from working with the teachers in our CCL program that every phase of performance assessment—developing, implementing, and scoring—is itself professional development. Professional development should no longer be viewed as something additional to be tacked on.

Is It Worth the Trouble?

When one considers that large numbers of students in the United States know less science and mathematics than their counterparts in other parts of the world and that they report finding school boring and of little value, it can be argued that there is little to lose and much to gain in taking steps toward developing learner-centered assessments and curriculum. We do not know whether such efforts will produce more efficacious students who are better able to think, solve problems, communicate, and collaborate, but a growing number of states and large districts are betting that it will and are developing performance-based assessment systems accordingly.

Toward a Vision of a Learner-Centered Large-Scale Assessment System

While the National Council on Educational Standards and Testing was deliberating on the merits of national examinations, Wolf and Baron (1991) submitted an options paper titled "A Realization of a National Performance-Based Assessment System." This was not written to endorse a single national assessment but rather to provide a very different vision of what a sensible national system might look like. We suggested that such a system might combine a series of approximately seven embedded assessment tasks along with two on-demand tasks, one at the beginning and one at the end of the year. The on-demand tasks would be administered by someone other than the child's own teacher and be scored at a central scoring location. Early in the year, the embedded tasks would be selected by teachers from a bank of tasks. As teachers became comfortable with the implementation and the scoring, they would begin to design three or four of their own tasks. The teacher-designed aspect of the program is central to such an assessment system for several reasons. For one, it will substantially increase the number of viable tasks that will eventually go into the task bank. Second, it will enable teachers to design tasks that are congruent with their curriculum and in so doing, be able to pay more attention to those aspects of the curriculum that they value most highly. But most important, it acknowledges the fact that without teachers' involvement and commitment, nothing in education can change. When teachers design their own assessment tasks, they are increasing their own capacity—both as assessors and as instructors. Through this process they will come face-to-face with their own values, their own knowledge of subject matter and pedagogy, and their understanding of what it means for students to do high-quality work. Before long, teachers in our project found themselves asking, "What do I have to do in order for my students to be successful on these tasks?" When teachers deepen their own understanding and think about ways to enable their students to do the same, we will have taken some major steps toward meaningful educational reform.

Sharing Standards Through Teacher Moderation

Wolf and Baron (1991) felt that it was important for two tasks during the year to be scored by both teachers and other outside raters. This process has been used successfully in Great Britain and the Netherlands as well as in Vermont as part of its portfolio assessment. As teachers score the work of students in other schools and discuss their ratings with the students' teachers, a new level of evaluative sophistication is achieved. A moderation system has the added advantage of building greater credibility and trust for teachers' judgments in the minds of policy makers and parents. For example, Pittsburgh has also been experimenting quite successfully with using panels of raters, including parents and members of the community (Howard & LeMahieu, 1995; LeMahieu & Eresh, 1996).

Wolf and Baron (1991) also suggested that students design one task of their own during the school year, thereby capitalizing on the students' motivation and interests. Finally, each student's collection of embedded tasks would be supplemented with a set of written reflections by both the student and the teacher that describe the student's growth during the school year.[1] Results from both the on-demand and embedded tasks would be aggregated and used for both accountability and instructional improvement.

The Right Mix of Stakes and Incentives

This sort of assessment system is not likely to be incorporated into all of our nation's schools tomorrow. Nor should it be. Substantial resources—both human and material—need to be provided first. In addition, the policy context must be supportive. For teachers and students to be able to take intellectual risks, the psychological climate must

---

[1] In the best of all possible worlds, we also encourage parents and other family members to serve as responders to their children's work (see Darling-Hammond, Ancess, & Falk, 1995; Howard & LeMahieu, 1995) and where possible as mentors to their children.

be conducive. That means that the stakes must be low for superintendents, principals, teachers, and students. For the stakes to be low, the timelines must be sensible. That means that for several years, teachers can try their hand at new practices before anything "counts." In today's educational climate, what is valued is what is tested and test scores capture people's attention (National Commission on Testing and Public Policy, 1990; Shepard, 1989; Smith, 1981). Therefore, it is pragmatic to harness the magnetic power of assessments by phasing in such a learner-centered assessment program over a period of about 5 years, with schools being aware that after the initial grace period, they will be held accountable for the results.

Using Learner-Centered Assessment for Accountability and Program Improvement

After this lengthy phase-in, these learner-centered assessments could be used for both accountability and program improvement. However, unlike many of the curriculum-centered tests of today, they will not spring from a lock-step curriculum. Rather, they will emanate from a flexible set of skills, knowledge, and dispositions that society values—with the expectation that the tasks and emphases will shift as values shift.[2]

A learner-centered assessment program provides a very different model of assessment from the ones to which many teachers and students are accustomed. If these complex and multifaceted embedded assessments are designed and implemented appropriately, using research from cognitive and motivational psychology and attending carefully to the early reactions and needs of students, teachers, administrators, parents, and policy makers, then we may be able to see the dawning of a new age of assessment and curriculum, one that is at its core learner centered.

References

American Association for the Advancement of Science. (1989). *Science for all Americans, A Project 2061 report on literacy goals in science, mathematics, and technology.* Washington, DC: Author.

American Psychological Association Presidential Task Force on Psychology in Education. (1993). *Learner-centered psychological principles: Guidelines for school redesign and*

---

[2]For a detailed description of how the classroom-embedded performance tasks described in this chapter were adapted for use annually in Connecticut on a large-scale, *on-demand* statewide assessment in science for approximately 30,000 students, see Lomask, Baron, and Greig (in press).

reform. Washington, DC: American Psychological Association and Mid-Continent Regional Educational Laboratory.

Ames, C., & Ames, R. (Eds.). (1985). *Research on motivation in education: Vol. 2, Classroom milieu* (pp. 93–140). Orlando, FL: Academic Press.

Aronson, E., Blaney, M., Stephen, C., Sikes, J., & Snapp, M. (1978). *The jigsaw classroom.* Beverly Hills, CA: Sage Publications.

Association for Supervision and Curriculum Development. (1992, June). The transfer question. *Curriculum Update.* Alexandria, VA: Author.

Bandura, A. (1982). Self-efficacy mechanism in human agency. *American Psychologist, 37,* 122–147.

Baron, J. B. (Ed.). (1993). *Assessment as an opportunity to learn: The Connecticut Common Core of Learning alternative assessment of secondary school science and mathematics.* Hartford: Connecticut State Department of Education.

Baron, J. B. (1996). Developing performance-based assessments: The Connecticut experience. In J. B. Baron & D. P. Wolf (Eds.), *Performance-based student assessment: Challenges and possibilities, Ninety-fifth yearbook of the National Society for the Study of Education, Part I* (pp. 166–191). Chicago: University of Chicago Press.

Baron, J. B., Forgione, P. D., Rindone, D. A., Kruglanski, H., & Davey, B. (1989, April). *Toward a new generation of student outcome measures: Connecticut's common core of learning assessment.* Paper presented at the annual meeting of the American Educational Research Association, San Francisco.

Baron, J. B., & Sternberg, R. J. (1987). *Teaching thinking skills: Theory and practice.* New York: W. H. Freeman.

Bransford, J. D., & Stein, B. S. (1984). *The ideal problem solver: A guide for improving thinking, learner, and creativity.* New York: W. H. Freeman.

Brown, J. S., Collins, A., & Duguid, S. (1989). Situated cognition and the culture of learning. *Educational Researcher, 18*(1), 32–42.

Burstall, C. (1989, June). *Update on the new national assessment in Great Britain.* Paper presented at the Large-Scale Assessment Conference sponsored by the Education Commission of the States and the Colorado State Department of Education, Boulder, CO.

Cohen, D. (1992, April). *Opening address.* Paper presented at the American Educational Research Association annual conference.

Collins, A., Brown, J. S., & Newman, S. (1989). Cognitive apprenticeship: Teaching the craft of reading, writing, and mathematics. In L. B. Resnick (Ed.), *Knowing, learning and instruction: Essays in honor of Robert Glaser* (pp. 453–494). Hillsdale, NJ: Erlbaum.

Connecticut State Board of Education. (1987). *Common core of learning.* Hartford, CT: Author.

Cormier, S., & Hagman, J. (Eds.). (1987). *Transfer of learning: Contemporary research and applications.* Orlando, FL: Academic Press.

Covington, M. V. (1992). *Making the grade: A self-worth perspective on motivation and school reform.* Cambridge, England: Cambridge University Press.

Darling-Hammond, L., Ancess, J., & Falk, B. (1995). *Authentic assessment in action: Studies of schools and students at work.* New York: Teachers College Press.

Darling-Hammond, L., & Snyder, J. (1992). Reframing accountability: Creating learner-centered schools. In A. Lieberman (Ed.), *The changing contexts of teaching, Ninety-first yearbook of the National Society for the Study of Education* (pp. 11–36). Chicago: University of Chicago Press.

Daro, P. (1996). Standards and portfolio assessment. In J. B. Baron & D. P. Wolf (Eds.), *Performance-based student assessment: Challenges and possibilities, Ninety-fifth yearbook of the National Society for the Study of Education, Part I* (pp. 239–260). Chicago: University of Chicago Press.

DeCharms, R. (1976). *Enhancing motivation: Change in the classroom.* New York: Irvington (Halsted-Wiley).

Deutsch, M. (1949). A theory of cooperation and competition. *Human Relations, 2,* 129–152.

Driver, R. (1990). Assessing the progress of children's understanding in science: A developmental perspective. In G. Hein (Ed.), *The assessment of trends on elementary school programs* (pp. 204–216). Grand Forks: The North Dakota Study Group.

Dunbar, S. B., Koretz, D. M., & Hoover, H. D. (1991). Quality control in the development and use of performance assessments. *Applied Measurement in Education, 4,* 289–303.

Flavell, J. H. (1976). Metacognitive aspects of problem solving. In L. B. Resnick (Ed.), *The nature of intelligence* (pp. 231–235). Hillsdale, NJ: Erlbaum.

Glass, G. V. (1978). Standards and criteria. *Journal of Educational Measurement, 15,* 237–261.

Gong, B., & Reidy, E. F. (1996). Assessment and accountability in Kentucky's school reform. In J. B. Baron & D. P. Wolf (Eds.), *Performance-based student assessment: Challenges and possibilities, Ninety-fifth yearbook of the National Society for the Study of Education, Part I* (pp. 214–233). Chicago: University of Chicago Press.

Haertel, E., & Mullis, I. V. (1996). The evolution of the National Assessment of Educational Progress: Coherence with best practice. In J. B. Baron & D. P. Wolf (Eds.), *Performance-based student assessments: Challenges and possibilities, Ninety-fifth yearbook of the National Society for the Study of Education, Part I* (pp. 287–304). Chicago: University of Chicago Press.

Hertz-Lazarowitz, R., & Miller, N. (Eds.). (1992). *Interaction in cooperative groups: The theoretical anatomy of group learning.* Cambridge, England: Cambridge University Press.

Hibbard, K. M., & Baron, J. B. (1990, April). *Assessing students working in groups: Lessons from cooperative and collaborative learning.* Paper presented at the annual meeting of the American Educational Research Association, Boston.

Honig, B., Alexander, F., & Wolf, D. P. (1996). Rewriting the tests: Lessons from the California state assessment system. In J. B. Baron & D. P. Wolf (Eds.), *Performance-based student assessments: Challenges and possibilities, Ninety-fifth yearbook of the National Society for the Study of Education, Part I* (pp. 143–165). Chicago: University of Chicago Press.

Howard, K., & LeMahieu, P. G. (1995). Parents as assessors of student writing: Enlarging the community of learners. *Teaching and Change, 2*(4), 392–414.

Johnson, D. W., & Johnson, R. T. (1985). Motivational processes in cooperative, competitive, and individualistic learning situations. In C. Ames & R. Ames (Eds.), *Research on motivation in education: Vol. 2. The classroom milieu* (pp. 249–286). Orlando, FL: Academic Press.

Johnson, D. W., & Johnson, R. T. (1990). Cooperative learning in achievement. In S. Sharan (Ed.), *Cooperative learning: Theory and research* (pp. 249–286). New York: Praeger.

Johnson, D. W., Maruyama, G., Johnson, R., Nelson, D., & Skon, L. (1981). Effects of cooperative, competitive, and individualistic goal structures on achievement: A meta-analysis. *Psychological Bulletin, 89,* 47–69.

LeMahieu, P. L., & Eresh, J. (1996). Coherence, comprehensiveness, and capacity in assessment systems: The Pittsburgh experience. In J. B. Baron & D. P. Wolf (Eds.), *Performance-based student assessments: Challenges and possibilities, Ninety-fifth yearbook of the National Society for the Study of Education, Part I* (pp. 125–142). Chicago: University of Chicago Press.

Linn, R. L., & Baker, E. L. (1996). Can performance-based student assessments be psychometrically sound? In J. B. Baron & D. P. Wolf (Eds.), *Performance-based student assessments: Challenges and possibilities, Ninety-fifth yearbook of the National Society for the Study of Education, Part I* (pp. 84–103). Chicago: University of Chicago Press.

Lomask, M., Baron, J. B., & Greig, J. (1993). Assessing conceptual understanding in science through the use of two- and three-dimensional concept maps. In J. D. Novak (Ed.), *Proceedings of the Third International Seminar on Misconceptions and Educational Strategies in Science and Mathematics.* Ithaca, NY: Cornell University.

Lomask, M. S., Baron, J. B., & Greig, J. (in press). Large-scale science performance assessment in Connecticut: Challenges and resolutions. In B. J. Fraser & K. G. Tobin (Eds.), *The international handbook of science education.* Lancaster, England: Kluwer Academic Publishers.

MacArthur, L. Z., & Baron, R. M. (1983). Toward an ecological theory of social perception. *Psychological Review, 90,* 215–238.

Marzano, R. J., Brandt, R. S., Hughes, C. S., Jones, B. F., Presseisen, B. Z., Rankin, S. C., & Suhor, C. (1988). *Dimensions of thinking: A framework for curriculum and instruction.* Alexandria, VA: Association for Supervision and Curriculum Development.

McCombs, B. L. (1984). Process and skills underlying continuing intrinsic motivation to learn: Toward a definition of motivational skills training interventions. *Educational Psychologist, 19,* 199–218.

McCombs, B. L., & Marzano, R. J. (1990). Putting the self in self-regulated learning: The self as agent in integrating will and skill. *Educational Psychologist, 25,* 51–69.

Mills, R. (1996). Statewide portfolio assessment: The Vermont Experience. In J. B. Baron & D. P. Wolf (Eds.), *Performance-based student assessments: Challenges and possibilities, Ninety-fifth yearbook of the National Society for the Study of Education, Part I* (pp. 192–214). Chicago: University of Chicago Press.

National Commission on Testing and Public Policy. (1990). *Reforming assessment: From gatekeepers to gateway to education.* Chestnut Hill, MA: Boston College.

National Council on Educational Standards and Testing. (1992). *Raising standards for American education. A Report to Congress, the Secretary of Education, the National Education Goals Panel, and the American People.* Washington, DC: Author.

National Council of Teachers of Mathematics. (1988). *Curriculum and evaluation of standards for school mathematics.* Reston, VA: Author.

National Research Council. (1994). *National science education standards.* Washington, DC: National Academy Press.

National Science Teachers' Association. (1992). *Scope, sequence, and coordination. The content core: A guide for curriculum designers.* Washington, DC: NSTA.

Newman, D., Griffen, P., & Cole, M. (1989). *The construction zone: Working for cognitive change in school.* Cambridge, England: Cambridge University Press.

Pea, R. D. (1988). Putting knowledge to use. In R. S. Nickerson & P. P. Zodhaites (Eds.), *Technology in education: Looking toward 2020* (pp. 169–212). Hillsdale, NJ: Erlbaum.

Pecheone, R. L., Baron, J. B., Forgione, P. D., Jr., & Abeles, S. (1988). A comprehensive approach to teacher assessment: Examples from math and science. In A. B. Champagne (Ed.), *This year in school science 1988: Science teaching: Making the system work* (pp. 191–214). Washington, DC: American Association for the Advancement of Science.

Perkins, D. (1992). *Smart schools: From training memories to educating minds.* New York: Free Press.

Raizen, S. A., Baron, J. B., Champagne, A. B., Haertel, E., Mullis, I. V. S., & Oakes, J. (1989). *Assessment in elementary science education.* Washington, DC: National Center for Improving Science Education.

Raizen, S. A., Baron, J. B., Champagne, A. B., Haertel, E., Mullis, I. V. S., & Oakes, J. (1990). *Assessment in science education: The middle years.* Washington, DC: National Center for Improving Science Education.

Reich, R. (1991). *The work of nations: Preparing ourselves for 21st century capitalism.* New York: Vintage (Random House).

Resnick, L. B. (1987a). *Education and learning to think.* Washington, DC: National Academy Press.

Resnick, L. B. (1987b). Learning in school and out. *Educational Researcher, 16,* 13–20.

Rogoff, B., & Lave, J. (Eds.). (1984). *Everyday cognition: Its development in social context.* Cambridge, MA: Harvard University Press.

Schön, D. A. (1982). *The reflective practitioner: How professionals teach in action.* New York: Basic Books.

Scribner, S., & Cole, M. (1981). *The psychology of literacy.* Cambridge, MA: Harvard University Press.

Shanker, A. (1995, April 9). Where we stand: Feeding and weighing. *New York Times, Section 4,* p. 7.

Sharan, S., & Sharan, Y. (1976). *Small group teaching.* Englewood Cliffs, NJ: Educational Technology Publications.

Sharan, S., & Shaulov, A. (1990). Cooperative learning, motivation to learn, and academic achievement. In S. Sharan (Ed.), *Cooperative learning: Theory and research* (pp. 173–202). New York: Praeger.

Shepard, L. (1989). Why we need better assessment. Educational Leadership, 46, 4–9.

Sinetar, M. (1991). *Developing a 21st century mind.* New York: Villard.

Slavin, R. (1983). *Cooperative learning.* New York: Longman.

Smith, M. L. (1981). Put to the test: The effects of external testing on teachers. *Educational Researcher, 20,* 10.

Song, J., & Black, P. (1991). The effects of task contexts on pupils' performance in science process skills. *International Journal of Science Education, 13,* 49–53.

Song, J., & Black, P. (1992). The effects of concept requirements and task contexts on pupils' performance in control of variables. *International Journal of Science Education, 14,* 83–93.

Sternberg, R. J. (1987). Teaching intelligence: The application of cognitive psychology to the improvement of intellectual skills. In J. B. Baron & R. J. Sternberg (Eds.), *Teaching thinking skills: Theory and practice* (pp. 182–218). New York: W. H. Freeman.

Stewart, D. M., & Johanek, M. (1996). The evolution of college entrance examinations. In J. B. Baron & D. P. Wolf (Eds.), *Performance-based student assessments: Challenges and possibilities, Ninety-fifth yearbook of the National Society for the Study of Education, Part I* (pp. 261–286). Chicago: University of Chicago Press.

U.S. Congress, Office of Technology Assessment. (1992). *Testing in American schools: Asking the right questions* (OTA-SET-519). Washington, DC: U.S. Government Printing Office.

Vygotsky, L. S. (1978). *Mind in society: The development of higher psychological processes* (M. Cole, V. John-Steiner, S. Scribner, & E. Souberman, Trans. and Eds.). Cambridge, MA: Harvard University Press. (Original work published 1935)

Wolf, D. P. (1988). Opening up assessment. *Educational Leadership, 45,* 224–229.

Wolf, D. P., & Baron, J. B. (1991). *A realization of a national performance-based assessment system.* Prepared for the Assessment Panel of the National Council for Educational Standards and Testing, Washington, DC.

Wolf, D., Bixby, J., Glenn, J., III, & Gardner, H. (1991). To use their minds well: Investigating new forms of student assessment. In G. Grant (Ed.), *Review of Research in Education, 17,* pp. 31–74. Washington, DC: American Educational Research Association.

Cognitive, Metacognitive, and Conative Considerations in Classroom Assessment

Robert J. Marzano

R ecent years have seen a variety of calls for drastic reform in assessment. Some reformers cite a need for more authentic forms of assessment that have a close correspondence to real-world tasks (Baron, 1990; Hart, 1994), whereas others emphasize the importance of demonstrations and products that can be but are not necessarily strongly related to real-world issues (Wiggins, 1989, 1991, 1993). Some researchers emphasize the importance of compilations of student work exhibited in the form of portfolios (LeMahieu, Gitomer, & Eresh, 1995; Wolf, 1989). Still others emphasize the importance of student self-assessment (Hansen, 1994).

One of the fundamental reasons for these calls for reform is the growing influence of cognitive psychology and cognitive science on assessment. As described by Glaser and Bassok (1989), the new understanding about the processes and structures underlying thinking and learning are reshaping people's views of schooling. Snow and Lohman (1989) have described the growing influence on assessment of research and theory on cognitive structures, and Snow (1989) has advanced the discussion to include conative structures. In this chapter, I attempt to expand the discussion to include cognitive, metacognitive, and conative structures and processes. The model used here is an adaptation of that developed by McCombs and Marzano (1990). That model articulates the interaction of three systems: the cognitive system, which encompasses cognitive structures and processes; the metacognitive system, which encompasses metacognitive structures and processes; and the self-system, which encompasses conative structures and processes. The model presented here can also be considered an extension of the metacognitive, cognitive, and affective factors described in the American Psychological Association (APA) learner-centered psychological principles (APA, 1993). That effort is designed to identify those psychological factors internal to the learner that are key variables in the learning process. As discussed in the introduction to this book, 12 principles have been identified and organized into five areas, one of which is the metacognitive and cognitive domain; another is the affective domain.

A Model of the Cognitive, Metacognitive, and Self-Systems During Task Engagement

The self-system, metacognitive system, and cognitive system are engaged anytime an individual is presented with a task. This is depicted in Figure 1. A presenting task is any real or perceived need to change the status quo. For example, an individual might be watching the sunset and be asked by her spouse to complete some household chore. The request to engage in the household chore is a real presenting task. Similarly, the individual observing the sunset might assume that her spouse wishes her to attend to the household chore. This is a perceived presenting task. In both cases, the individual engages her self-, metacognitive, and cognitive systems in response to the presenting task. Although the interaction of the three systems depicted in Figure 1 can be used to explain all types of real and perceived presenting tasks, the discussion in this chapter is limited to academic tasks commonly encountered in kindergarten through 12th-grade (K–12) classrooms.

The self-system contains a hierarchic structure of goals (Glasser, 1981; Powers, 1973), beliefs about self (Markus & Ruvulo, 1990), beliefs about others (Harter, 1980), and beliefs about the nature of the world (Covington, 1983, 1985). The self-system also contains processes that evaluate the importance of the presenting task relative to the hierarchic goal structure and assess the probability of task success relative to the individual's system of beliefs (McCombs & Marzano, 1990).

If the presenting task is judged as important and the probability of success is high, positive affect and high motivation ensue. If the presenting task is evaluated as low relevance and high threat, then negative affect is generated and low task motivation and compensatory activities are selected. Because the mechanisms in the self-systems are the working elements that define motivation and volition in human behavior,

CLASSROOM ASSESSMENT • 243

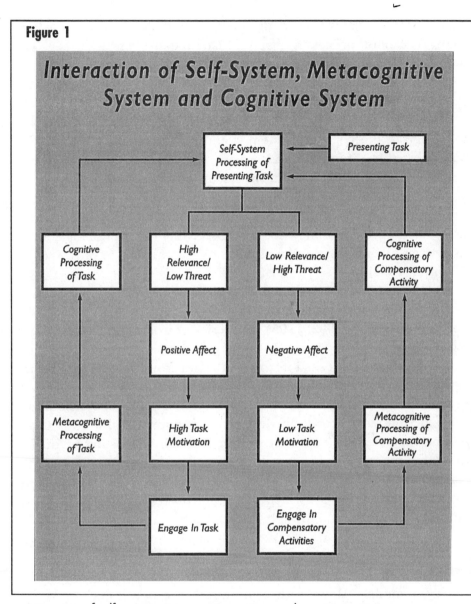

Figure 1

Interaction of Self-System, Metacognitive System and Cognitive System

Interaction of self-system, metacognitive system, and cognitive system.

they have historically been referred to as "conative" structures (Snow & Jackson, 1993).

Regardless of whether the presenting task or compensatory activities are selected, the metacognitive system is engaged. This system contains information about the nature of plans, timelines, resources, and their interactions (Schank & Abelson, 1977). It also contains processes that evaluate progress toward the goals and subgoals within the presenting task and processes that evaluate the use of resources. The metacognitive system is continually interacting with the cognitive system throughout task engagement.

The cognitive system contains information specific to the presenting task. For example, if the presenting task is to read an article about the Civil War, the cognitive system would include general information about the nature of articles and specific facts, concepts, and principles about the Civil War. The cognitive system also contains processes specific to the presenting task. In the reading example, the processes within the cognitive system would be those specific to reading, such as decoding unrecognized or unknown words, discerning the overall logic of the passage, evaluating the validity of the information, and so on (Marzano & Paynter, 1994).

In this model it is assumed that each of the three systems has a similar architecture—specifically, that articulated by Anderson (1982, 1983, 1990a, 1990b, 1993, 1995) in a series of works. Anderson's architecture is depicted in Figure 2. As described by Anderson (1983), the encoding process deposits information taken from the senses (i.e., the outside world) into working memory. Performance processes convert commands in working memory into behavior. The storage process can create permanent records in declarative memory of the contents of working memory and can increase the strength of existing records in declarative memory. In the match process, data in working memory are put in correspondence with the processes housed in procedural memory. The execution process deposits the actions of matched processes into working memory. Through the application cycle, new procedures are learned from the analysis of the history of the applications of existing procedures.

The substructure of procedural memory is a key feature of the Anderson model. Along with a number of other theorists (Bovair, Kieras, & Polson, 1990; Newell, 1991), Anderson postulated that "procedural knowledge takes the form of what are called production rules" (Anderson, 1995, p. 332). Production rules are condition–action structures. In its simplest form, a production rule contains two elements. For example, the following is a production rule for obtaining money from a bank machine:

> If the goal is to get money from the bank machine and I have put
> in my card,

Figure 2

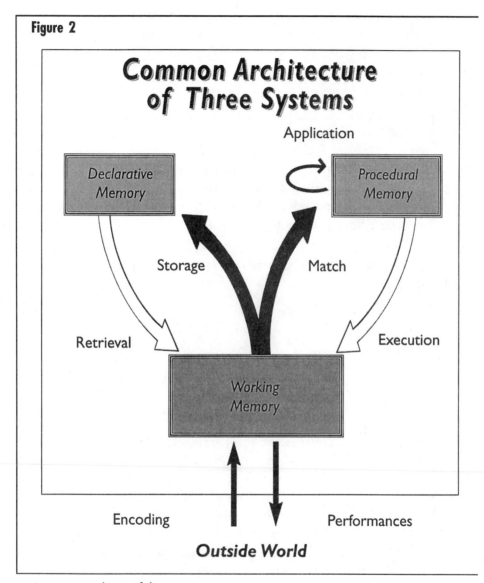

Common Architecture of Three Systems

Application

Declarative Memory

Procedural Memory

Storage

Match

Retrieval

Execution

Working Memory

Encoding

Performances

Outside World

Common attributes of three systems.

THEN type the code, hit Enter and hit withdrawal. (Anderson, 1995, p. 333)

More commonly, procedures comprise long strings of production rules. For example, for the procedure of addition of integers, Anderson described a string of 12 production rules that contain 67 separate elements (Anderson, 1983, pp. 8–9).

The declarative and procedural structures within the three systems have different implications and pose different problems for each of those systems. Given that the vast majority of assessment efforts in K–12 education are focused on it, the cognitive system is considered first, although it is subordinate to the metacognitive and self-systems.

The Cognitive System

The cognitive system is responsible for processing the knowledge specific to the presenting task. The differences in the structures of declarative knowledge and procedural knowledge encountered in academic tasks have strong implications for assessment.

Procedural Knowledge in the Cognitive System

Procedural knowledge as it relates to academic tasks can be organized in a hierarchic fashion relative to level of generality. At the top of the hierarchy are highly robust and comprehensive processes that have a diversity of possible products or outcomes and involve the execution of many interrelated subprocesses. Robust processes that have these characteristics are referred to as *macroprocesses* (Kendall & Marzano, 1994). For example, writing fulfills the defining characteristics of a macroprocess. Writing has a variety of possible products in that it can generate a variety of types of discourses, such as expository discourse, narrative discourse, and so on. In addition, to perform or execute the macroprocess of writing, one must execute at an automatic or at least semiautomatic level a multitude of subprocesses such as correcting faulty diction, correcting mechanical errors, controlling for logic of presentation, controlling for clarity of expression, and so on.

Somewhat in the middle of the hierarchy are procedures that do not generate the variety of products possible from macroprocesses, and do not incorporate within them as wide a variety of subprocesses as do macroprocesses. These procedures are commonly referred to as *strategies*. For example, an individual may have a strategy for reading a histogram. Commonly, strategies are not composed of a set of steps to be performed in a specific order. Rather, they are composed of general rules. For example, a strategy for reading a histogram might include production rules that address (a) identifying the elements depicted in the legend, (b) determining what is reported by each axis on the graph, and (c) determining the relationship between the elements in the two axes. Although there is a general pattern in the sequence in which these steps are executed, there is no rigid set of steps.

Finally, at the bottom of the procedural hierarchy are *algorithms*. These procedures normally do not vary in application, have very specific outcomes, and must frequently be learned to the level of automaticity to be useful. For example, many computing processes in mathematics and decoding processes within reading are algorithmic in nature. Again, algorithms are frequently the subcomponents of macroprocesses and strategies.

Assessing Procedural Knowledge in the Cognitive System

Not coincidentally, there is a strong relationship between the structure of procedural knowledge in the cognitive system and performance assessment. The use of performance tasks as a vehicle for informal and formal assessment is one of the most popular topics in educational assessment (Stiggins, 1994). Resnick and Resnick (1992) asserted that performance tasks greatly expand the scope of what can be assessed. They explained that whereas traditional tests provide assessment data regarding what information students know and what basic skills they can execute, performance tasks indicate how well students apply information:

> Properly developed and implemented, they [performance tasks] allow for reliable measurement of thinking and reasoning in school subject matters. They offer a way to release educators from pressures toward fractionated, low-level forms of learning rewarded by most current tests. (p. 72)

Other reasons commonly given for the use of performance tasks include (a) they provide clear guidelines for students about teacher expectations (Berk, 1986), (b) they reflect real-life challenges and situations (Hart, 1994), (c) they make effective use of teacher judgment (Archbald & Newmann, 1988), and (d) they allow for student differences in style and interest (Mitchell, 1992).

A defining feature of performance assessments is that they involve some type of process that results in a product (Baron, 1990; Wiggins, 1989, 1991, 1993). Consequently, they have been used for years within subject areas that are procedurally based. As Siegel (1986) noted, performance tasks were developed within domains involving technical "jobs" such as carpentry, welding, brick laying, lathe turning, and electronic assembly (p. 127). To demonstrate competence in these areas, students were typically asked to perform the job-related skills—they were asked to use the lathe, lay bricks, weld, and so on. Much of what one does within these domains is procedural in nature. When one lays bricks, he or she is executing a process that involves a complex set of production rules as is the case when one uses a lathe, engages in carpentry, and so on.

Performance tasks, then, are quite compatible with content areas that are heavily laced with procedural knowledge. For example, consider the subject area of mathematics. A recent study by Kendall and Marzano (1995) indicates that the mathematics content covered in K–12 curriculums is about 50% procedural in nature. To illustrate, the procedures of addition, subtraction, multiplication, division, constructing and converting ratios, decimals and percents, solving different types of problems, and the like are inherent in the subject area of mathematics. Creating performance tasks within mathematics can be a simple matter of inserting the procedures inherent in that content area into realistic situations. For example, a performance task in mathematics might be structured around the procedures of addition, subtraction, multiplication, and division by asking students to calculate how many squares of tile of a specific size would be necessary to cover the classroom floor. Although all procedures are amenable to performance tasks, procedures at the highest levels of generality are most effectively used within them. This is because the more general procedures are best suited to the construction of performance standards—a key feature of effective performance assessments.

Most discussions of standards make a distinction between content standards and performance standards. This distinction was formalized and perhaps legitimized in the 1993 report to the National Education Goals Panel by the National Education Standards and Improvement Council (NESIC). Commonly referred to as the "Malcom Report" in deference to Shirley M. Malcom, chair of the Goals 3 and 4 Standards Review Technical Planning Group, the report makes a clear distinction between content standards and performance standards and establishes the validity of both:

> Content standards specify "what students should know and be able to do." They indicate the knowledge and skills—the ways of thinking, working, communicating, reasoning, and investigating, and the most important and enduring ideas, concepts, issues, dilemmas, and knowledge essential to the discipline—that should be taught and learned in school. (NESIC, 1993, p. ii)

> Performance standards specify "how good is good enough." They

relate to issues of assessment that gauge the degree to which content standards have been attained. While others use the term differently, in this report "performance standards" are not the skills, modes of reasoning, and habits mentioned above [in the description of content standards] that assessments attempt to measure. Instead, they are the indices of quality that specify how adept or competent a student demonstration must be. (NESIC, 1993, p. iii)

In general, it is easier to construct performance standards for macroprocesses than for strategies or algorithms. For example, if a macroprocess such as writing has been selected as the focus of a performance task, then the performance standard would specify those subprocesses that are to be executed without significant errors. To illustrate, the performance standard for a writing task might explicitly state that students are expected to perform the writing process without making significant errors in the following writing subprocesses: controlling for the overall logic of the composition, ensuring that effective transitional devices are used, controlling for effective word choice, and controlling for proper use of conventions. Which subprocesses are targeted for mastery at a particular age or grade level is, of course, a key part of setting performance standards. Whereas educators might expect high school students to have mastered the composing subprocesses of controlling for the overall logic of a composition and the effective use of transitional devices, they would not have the same expectations of students in the primary grades.

It is important to note that expectations about the physical product of the writing process would be drawn from the expectations regarding the subcomponents of the writing process. Given the expectations of secondary students regarding their mastery of subcomponents of the writing process, high school students would be expected to produce compositions with a clear, comprehensive, overall logic that hold tightly together and that display effective transitional devices, whereas primary students would not. In short, stating performance standards in terms of expectations about subprocesses within a macroprocess implicitly defines expectations about the final product of the macroprocess.

In summary, when a macroprocess is used as the basis for constructing performance tasks, setting performance standards amounts to specifying expectations about the subprocesses within the macroprocess. Unfortunately, when a strategy or algorithm is used as the basis of a performance task, setting expectations about subcomponents can be problematic. This is because many strategies and algorithms have no clear superordinate–subordinate structure of subcomponents. Rather, the subcomponents are individual steps all of which must usually be performed at the same level of accuracy and efficiency for the procedure to work at all. For example, which component parts of the process of multiplication would one expect students to execute with no errors, and which component parts would one not expect students to execute? Could students multiply integers correctly but make errors in carrying and still be judged as meeting the performance standard for multiplication? Obviously not. Algorithms and strategies are composed of fairly uniform sets of steps or heuristics, all of which must be executed at the same level of accuracy for the strategy or algorithm to be even moderately useful. For this reason, performance tasks are more effectively designed around macroprocesses than they are around strategies or algorithms.

Declarative Knowledge in the Cognitive System

As is the case with procedural knowledge, declarative knowledge can be ordered in somewhat of a hierarchic fashion on the basis of levels of generality. At the bottom end of the hierarchy are facts about specific persons, places, things, and events; at the top are concepts and generalizations. For example, the statement "John Kennedy was assassinated on November 22, 1963" is a fact. The statement "People holding high political office put their lives in jeopardy" is a generalization. The phrase "political assassinations" is a concept.

Although facts are important, they are not transferable, whereas generalizations and concepts are. For instance, both the generalization about people in high political office and the concept of political assassinations can be applied across countries, situations, and ages, whereas the fact of Kennedy's assassination is a specific event that does not directly transfer to other situations. This is not to say that facts are unimportant. On the contrary, to truly understand generalizations and concepts, one must be able to support them with exemplifying facts. For instance, to understand the generalization about people in high political office, one needs a rich set of illustrative facts, one of which is probably that of Kennedy's assassination.

Facts versus concepts or generalizations, then, represent two ends of the spectrum in terms of declarative knowledge. In between are structures that might be thought of as organized sets of facts. Some of these structures are time sequences, causal networks, events, and episodes. (For a detailed discussion of the different types of declarative knowledge see Kendall and Marzano, 1994, and Marzano, 1991.)

Assessing Declarative Knowledge in the Cognitive System

Just as performance tasks designed around procedural knowledge are most effectively organized around high-level macroprocesses, so too are performance tasks designed around declarative knowledge most effectively constructed around high-level declarative structures—in this case, concepts and generalizations. That is to say it is much more effective to construct a performance task around the generalization that people holding high political office put their lives in jeopardy or the concept political assassinations than it is to construct a performance task around the fact of Kennedy's assassination. However, a troublesome issue automatically arises whenever one attempts to construct a performance task for even the most general declarative knowledge—declarative knowledge does not inherently involve performances and products as does procedural knowledge, and, as has been shown, performances and products are central to performance tasks. To illustrate, no matter what type of procedural knowledge one identifies, it will automatically involve a performance and a product. For example, the use of the algorithmic procedure of division always involves the performance or execution of the steps involved in the algorithm and it always involves the production of new information (new, at least, to the learner), namely the answer. Using the macroprocess of writing will always involve the execution of the embedded subprocesses and it will always involve a product, a composition. However, declarative knowledge is not inherently performance and product oriented. Understanding the concept of political assassination is evidenced by recalling, or at least recognizing specific pieces of information and their relationship to one another. Unless one considers the acts of recalling and recognizing performances, declarative knowledge does not inherently involve a performance. In addition, no "new product" is created when the concept of political assassinations is recalled or recognized because the information necessarily resides in long-term memory of the individual being assessed or it could not have been recalled or recognized in the first place. In short, no performance is executed and nothing new is created when one recognizes or recalls declarative knowledge. Constructing performance tasks around declarative knowledge, then, requires the addition of a new component— mental operations that "apply" declarative knowledge and involve performances and products.

Because declarative knowledge does not inherently involve performances and products, one must identify operations that can be performed on that type of knowledge and inherently involve performances

---

Exhibit 1

Cross-Disciplinary Procedures

1. Applying processes that are based on identifying similarities and dissimilarities: comparing, contrasting, classifying
2. Applying basic principles of presenting an argument
3. Applying basic principles of logic and reasoning
4. Applying basic principles of hypothesis testing and scientific inquiry
5. Applying basic trouble-shooting and problem-solving techniques
6. Applying basic decision-making techniques

---

and products. Stated more technically, one must identify productions that can be applied to declarative knowledge. One source for a list of such processes is the national standards that have been established within the various content domains. For example, the National Council of Teachers of Mathematics (NCTM, 1989) has articulated its content standards in the document *Curriculum and Evaluation Standards for School Mathematics*. Science standards have been identified by the American Association for the Advancement of Science (AAAS, 1993) in the document *Benchmarks for Science Literacy*. In effect, these standards documents are listings of the subject-specific, cognitively based declarative and procedural knowledge within academic domains. Those processes that are identified within a majority of the standards documents can be considered cross-disciplinary procedures. In a recent set of studies, six of these cross-disciplinary procedures were identified (Kendall & Marzano, 1994, 1995). They are listed in Exhibit 1.

When these procedures are applied to declarative knowledge, a performance task emerges. To illustrate, assume that a teacher had identified the following generalization as the declarative knowledge around which to construct a performance task: "Historical events commonly happen in patterned ways." The teacher would use the list of cross-disciplinary procedures in Exhibit 1 to identify one that can be easily applied to this generalization. The teacher might determine that a useful application of the declarative knowledge would be to match it without other similar level of generality by constructing categories. The teacher would construct a performance task by presenting students with a number of historical events that they have studied and ask the students to classify those events into two or more categories each of which exemplifies the generalization that "Historical events happen in patterned ways." Students might be asked to report on the categories they identified, the rules for category membership, and the extent to which their categories exemplify the target generalizations. This task would now have (a) a clear performance component—the execution of the cross-disciplinary procedure of classification, (b) a clear product—the students' description of their categories and the rationale behind them, and (c) a specific declarative knowledge component—the students' understanding of the generalization that "Historical events happen in patterned ways."

The Metacognitive System

The distinction between declarative and procedural knowledge within the metacognitive system is a clear one, but it is not as important to assessment as it is to the cognitive system. Declarative memory within the metacognitive system contains information about the nature of goals, plans, timelines, resources, and their interactions. For example, assume a student in a science class accepts the presenting task of researching various opinions about the alleged effects of global warming. The student's metacognitive declarative knowledge would include an understanding of the defining characteristics of an effective goal. In addition, the student's metacognitive declarative knowledge would include an awareness of the component parts of an effective plan, including such elements as timelines and milestones.

Metacognitive declarative knowledge also involves an awareness of what many researchers and theorists refer to as dispositions of intelligent behavior. For example, if one incorporates the work of Amabile (1983), Brown (1978, 1980), Costa (1984, 1991), Ennis (1985, 1987, 1989), Flavell (1976, 1977), Paul (1984, 1986, 1990), and Perkins (1984, 1985, 1986), the following set of dispositions can be identified:

- being accurate and seeking accuracy
- being clear and seeking clarity
- being open-minded
- restraining impulsivity
- taking a position when the situation warrants it
- being sensitive to others' feelings and levels of knowledge
- engaging intensely in tasks even when answers or solutions are not immediately apparent
- generating, trusting, and maintaining your own standards of evaluation

- generating new ways of viewing a situation outside the boundaries of standard conventions

It is important to note that the declarative knowledge in the metacognitive system would not involve the processes for carrying out these dispositions, only the awareness that these dispositions are important and perhaps exemplar episodes depicting their use.

Procedural metacognitive knowledge involves the processes responsible for actually setting a goal, devising a plan, and carrying out the plan. For example, the student in the history class would have to establish the goal of finishing the project by a certain date. Procedural metacognitive knowledge would also include productions that address the establishment of milestones, monitor the extent to which milestones are being met, reset milestones when necessary, and evaluate the effectiveness of the entire process once it is completed. Also within the metacognitive procedural system are productions that monitor the extent to which the dispositions of intelligent behavior are being addressed. For example, one production would monitor the extent to which the student was seeking clarity, another would monitor the extent to which the student was resisting impulsivity, and so on. The combined set of procedures that addresses the goal-setting process and the dispositions of intelligent behavior are the mechanisms that generate what Sternberg (1979, 1983, 1984) referred to as "executive control" of a task.

Assessing the Metacognitive System

At the classroom level there are a number of techniques that can be used to assess the metacognitive system. Many of the formal techniques have been described by Snow and Jackson (1993). Guidelines for assessment of this domain are also described in the learner-centered psychological principles (APA, 1995). Here I focus on techniques that can be used as a regular part of classroom instruction and emphasize student self-assessment. One of the most powerful of these techniques is journal writing. Of course, journals have long been a classroom staple within English and the language arts (Atwell, 1987; Calkins, 1986; Macrorie, 1984). In addition to the central role journals play in the composing process, they can be used as a vehicle for self-analysis and understanding of the metacognitive system.

Hansen (1994) detailed the use of journals in combination with portfolios within the context of the English language arts. In Hansen's study, teachers had students write their reflections regarding the process of constructing portfolios that represented personal goals about which they were highly interested. The teachers reported that students naturally began to analyze the types of goals they set, how effectively they pursued their goals, and the extent to which they used the dispositions of intellectual behavior (although students did not use this terminology). Hansen concluded that understanding the metacognitive system is one of the highest forms of learning and that journals are a powerful tool to this end.

Rubrics are another tool that can be used to stimulate self-assessment of the metacognitive system. For example, Marzano, Pickering, and McTighe (1993) designed the following rubrics to be used by students to assess their understanding and effectiveness at setting goals.

I plan carefully before I begin to work.

4 I set clear goals and describe each step I must take to achieve them. I make a detailed schedule for each step and closely follow the schedule.

3 I set clear goals and describe some steps I must take to achieve them. I make and use a schedule.

2 I begin working with only unclear goals. I describe few of the steps I must take to achieve my goals, and I make an incomplete schedule.

1 I begin working and just let things happen as they happen. I do not describe the steps I must take and I do not make a schedule. (p. 126)

I am aware of available resources that could help me complete a task.

4 I describe in detail all the resources I think I might need before I start working on a task. I search for the resources available to me and, if something I need is not available, I describe other places I might get this help or information. I also predict what parts of the task will require the use of the most resources.

3 I list the most important resources I might need before I start working on a task. I review the resources that are available and describe other resources that I may have to find.

2 I begin working on a task and look for resources when I need them. This slows my work because I have to keep stopping to find the resources. When a resource is not available, I do not find other resources that might help.

1 As I am working on a task, I use resources only if they happen to be readily available. I do not use many resources that are available. (p. 126)

Similarly, Marzano et al. (1993) offered the following rubrics for student self-assessment of two of the dispositions of intellectual behavior.

I push myself to try things that I'm not sure I can do.

4 I look for tasks that I'm not sure I can do and stick with them until I've accomplished them or until I have learned all I can.

3 I try tasks that are given to me even when I'm not sure I can do them, and I stick with them until I've accomplished them or until I have learned all I can.

2 I try tasks that are given to me even when I'm not sure I can do them, but I give up before I accomplish them or before I have learned from them.

1 I avoid tasks that I'm not sure I can do. (p. 133)

I create, trust, and use standards for evaluating my own work.

4 I create and trust standards for evaluating my own work. The standards I set are high enough to make me produce something of high quality. I make sure my final product meets those standards.

3 I create and trust standards for evaluating my own work. I make sure my final product meets those standards.

2 I create and trust standards for evaluating my own work, but I don't make sure my final product meets those standards.

1 I do not create standards for evaluating my own work. (p. 133)

As these examples illustrate, rubrics are descriptions of levels of understanding and performance. They not only serve as a vehicle for self-assessment but they are also instructive in that they provide students with models of varying levels of understanding and performance.

The Self-System

As is the case with the metacognitive system, the distinction between declarative and production knowledge in the self-system is not as important to assessment as is that distinction within the cognitive system. The declarative component of the self-system is composed of the beliefs one has about oneself and about the world in general. A useful construct in understanding the power of beliefs within the self-system is the "contextual frame" (Marzano, 1991).

A contextual frame has at least three general components: (a) an object, (b) a judgment about the object's value, and (c) a judgment as to whether the object can be controlled. Objects of a contextual frame can be events, people, places, things, and even abstractions. For example, a student might have a contextual frame relative to the event "mathematics class." Similarly, a student might have a contextual frame for the person "my science teacher." In fact, proponents of the semiotic extension theory assert that human beings tend to partition the world around them into distinctive persons, places, things, events, and abstractions (McNeil, 1975) even when their environment does not necessarily fit into this partitioning.

Along with an object, a contextual frame contains a judgment about the value of the object. This value parameter has two dimensions: (a) important versus unimportant and (b) positive versus negative. For example, a student's frame about the object "mathematics class" would include a judgment as to whether it is important or unimportant relative to his or her life. If mathematics class is judged as unimportant or of little worth, then the learner will expend little energy relative to the object of the frame, in spite of his or her skills and abilities. However, if the student perceives mathematics class as important, he or she will bring all available skills and abilities to bear on the task. The second aspect of the value parameter is a judgment as to whether the object of the frame is positive or negative. Such a judgment is certainly related to the judgment of importance of the object, but the two are not in a fixed relation. For example, an individual can consider an object to be highly important, yet negative—an object can be considered relevant to one's life because it is very threatening. Conversely, an object can be considered unimportant (not relevant), yet positive in a general sense.

When an object is judged as important and positive, the individual will be strongly motivated to engage in or approach the object. When an object is judged as important and negative, the individual will be strongly motivated to avoid the object or destroy or alter it. When an object is judged as unimportant and either positive or negative, the individual will have little motivation relative to the object. Exhibit 2 depicts the interrelationship between these two dimensions of value and motivation.

The final aspect of a contextual frame is the perception of control over the object of the frame. This parameter affects the learner's decision to expend energy attempting to engage the object or attempting to avoid it. For example, even if mathematics class is perceived as important and negative, the learner must believe that he or she has the necessary resources to effect change in the object (i.e., make it a more positive experience) or he or she will expend energy avoiding it. Re-

---

Exhibit 2

Motivation and the Two Dimensions of Value

Positive

	Little motivation relative to object	Motivation to engage in or approach the object	
Unimportant	Little motivation relative to object	Motivation to avoid or destroy/alter object	Important

Negative

---

sources can include personal skills and psychological power as well as pragmatic necessities such as time, materials, money, and so on.

To summarize, the declarative knowledge in the self-system contains contextual frames for persons, places, things, events, and abstractions. These frames are composed of beliefs and attitudes about the value of the object as well as beliefs and attitudes about the individual's ability to effect change in the object. These frames dictate the extent to which one is motivated and how one makes decisions relative to the persons, places, things, events, and abstractions of the world.

Procedural knowledge in the self-system comprises productions that address the evaluation of the contextual frames involved in a presenting task. For example, if a student is presented with the task of writing a research report, the self-system will activate procedures for evaluating the value parameters and the control parameter. It is the output of these procedures that establishes the affective state of high motivation or low motivation.

Assessing the Self-System

Assessing the self-system is a matter of self-analyzing one's contextual frames and their impact on perception and behavior. The importance of self-analysis is heavily emphasized by the learner-centered psychological principles (APA, 1995). Formal methods of assessing the self-system have been described by Snow and Jackson (1993), but, again, the focus here is on self-assessment techniques that can be used as a part of reg-

---

Exhibit 3

Self-Journal Entries on Components of a Contextual Frame

10/8
The object I'm studying is essay tests. I guess they're a necessary evil—I have to take them in almost every class. I don't think I'll ever be good at them though. They're not good measures of what I know—I'm not good at essay tests because I never really learned how to write. I just don't know how to put the right words on what I want to say.

---

ular classroom instruction. The process of self-assessment is greatly facilitated by the use of self-journals. The term *self-journal* is meant to illustrate the student's exploration of the self-system. Closely related to a dialogue journal (Staton, 1980), a self-journal is a record of a student's thinking recorded for the purpose of discovering the nature and function of specific contextual frames. To illustrate, consider Exhibit 3.

In Exhibit 3, a student has described the components of her contextual frame for the event (object) "essay tests." Relative to this object, the student has identified beliefs about the importance of essay tests and beliefs about her ability to control her performance relative to this event. The student apparently believes that essay tests are important in her life ("I have to take them in almost every class") and negative ("They are not good measures of what I know"). She also believes that she has little control over her performance on essay tests ("I don't think I'll ever be good at them"). In addition to her statement of beliefs relative to the object, the student has attempted to identify reasons or justifications for her belief ("I never really learned how to write"). This can be one of the most enlightening aspects of examining one's self-system. Research and theory support the contention that beliefs can be a product of irrational generalizations made from specific events. For example, Holland, Holyoak, Nisbett, and Thagard (1987) postulated that the human mind has a built-in "generalizer"—a mechanism that automatically associates specific events with other events related by general characteristics. For example, assume the student who wrote the journal entries in Exhibit 3 had a negative experience with an essay exam on a previous occasion. According to Holland et al., the student would initially store this specific experience in long-term memory, but over time the specific experience would be generalized. Instead of remembering that she did poorly on one essay exam, she would translate this stored experience into the belief that she does poorly on *all* essay

Exhibit 4

Free Association Entries in Self-Journal

10/10
Essay tests—English class ninth grade—I didn't really study—tried to bluff my way through—didn't work—elementary school—we started to have to take a lot of them—4th grade is when it really started—May—we have to take our first big essay test—I panicked—didn't even finish. Everyone else did great.

exams. When an experience has been encoded at this general level, it has become an attitude or a belief. Unfortunately, the generalizing process does not always follow a logical course. In fact, such theorists as Ellis (1977) and Meichenbaum (1977) asserted that attitudes and beliefs are all too commonly irrational generalizations from specific events. A child is bitten by a small dog and grows up as an adult who is afraid of dogs of all types. A young girl observes that her mother is not good at writing and generalizes that she cannot be good at writing.

Given the power of attitudes and beliefs and the somewhat irrational nature of the generalizing process, it is useful for students to trace the reasons they give for their beliefs back to some initiating event by using free association. For example, the student who wrote the responses in Exhibit 3 might find that she can trace her attitude about essay tests back to the specific incident. This type of free association writing is depicted in Exhibit 4.

In Exhibit 4, the student has concluded that it was in a fourth-grade class that she began to doubt her ability at essay exams. This tracing of her beliefs back to a single event can be the beginning of the breakup of her ineffective contextual frame relative to essay exams. As the student begins to see the illogical reasoning that led to her present frame, she becomes open to replacing her old beliefs with new beliefs.

In addition to analyzing the reasons behind certain attitudes and beliefs within a contextual frame, students can also analyze the behaviors generated by a given contextual frame. Such observation is most valid if extended over a prolonged interval of time. For example, after selecting a frame for study (e.g., essay tests), the student might observe her behavior relative to that frame for a 2-week period. Exhibit 5 contains an example of the student's entries in the self-journal.

The student has noted that she behaves in certain predictable ways every time she takes an essay examination ("I get very nervous . . . I hand in the test early"). This can be a very powerful realization for

---

Exhibit 5

Behavior Entries in Self-Journal

10/13
One thing I notice about how I act when I take an essay test is that I get very nervous. I start worrying about two days before I take it. As a matter of fact, I start worrying as soon as the teacher assigns it. When I actually sit down to take the test I don't even really concentrate. I usually hand in the test early.

---

students; people seldom recognize that their behavior is related to their beliefs and even less commonly realize that their beliefs can generate their behaviors (Ellis, 1977; Meichenbaum, 1977). Such awarenesses are at the core of "reframing."

Reframing: The Ultimate Form of "Learner-Centeredness"

In a series of articles, McCombs and her colleagues (McCombs, 1984, 1986, 1989; McCombs & Marzano, 1990) described *learner-centeredness*. At the core of this construct is an awareness of oneself as agent:

> The self as agent, as the basis of will and volition, can be thought of, in part, as a generative structure that is goal directed, purposeful, or teleological in nature. Out of this generative and self-determining structure, our experience of being is supported.

> It may not be scientifically observable, measurable or predictable. It does, however, consciously or unconsciously define who we are, what we think, and what we do. (McCombs & Marzano, 1990, p. 66)

The experience of self as agent can be enhanced through reframing, and reframing is intimately tied to contextual frames. Specifically, because contextual frames are the filters through which events, situations, people, places, things, and abstractions are experienced, changing one's contextual frames can actually change one's experiences. Some theorists (Kuhn, 1962; Schwartz & Ogilvy, 1979; Watzlawick, Weakland, & Fisch, 1974) refer to consciously changing one's frame as a paradigm shift.

Reframing is defined here as the process of systematically addressing and, over time, changing the parameters of a specific contextual frame. At the outset, reframing is undertaken at the level of declaration—simply declaring or affirming new beliefs and attitudes. This technique assumes a different role for language than that commonly ascribed to it. The common conception of language is that it is a fairly passive process by which one describes the experiences one has. However, some theorists have viewed language as a vehicle that can shape rather than describe human experience. Benjamin Whorf is perhaps most commonly associated with this position. Whorf (1956) asserted that on a moment-by-moment basis, people use language to organize the somewhat random array of stimuli they are bombarded with. That is, language plays an active role in shaping our perceptions as opposed to a passive role of simply describing them. Similarly, Heidegger (1968), in his landmark work *What Is Called Thinking?*, described how the awareness and subsequent utilization of the power of language to shape experience is the ultimate self-actualization skill.

Operationally, reframing means stating new parameters for a particular contextual frame—actually saying or writing new attitudes and beliefs. For example, the student who wrote the entries in the self-journal in Exhibit 3 might begin to reframe her context for essay examinations by stating new attitudes and beliefs such as, "I can do well on essay tests." Of course, declarations are not actually attitudes and beliefs when initially generated. They are more like symbols of the attitudes and beliefs the student would like to possess. The student would practice or rehearse these newly declared beliefs whenever the object of the frame was encountered. For example, whenever the student took an essay examination, she would mentally restate her newly declared beliefs by making internal statements to herself such as, "I will do well on this test. It will be a true reflection of my knowledge. I will be calm throughout the test." Suinn (1983) noted that mental rehearsal of this type is commonly practiced by peak performers in a variety of situations. While affirming the newly declared beliefs, the student would also try to monitor any negative self-talk. Ellis (1977) and Meichenbaum (1977) noted that negative inner dialogue holds negative contextual frames in place. Over time, the process of affirming new attitudes and beliefs through monitoring and changing negative inner dialogue can totally alter a frame.

Conclusion

In this chapter, I have outlined an explanatory model of human response to presenting tasks. This model involves three interactive systems—the self-system, the metacognitive system, and the cognitive system. Understanding the declarative and procedural structures within these systems can provide guidance for classroom assessment. However, this guidance points to new types of assessment not standard fare in K–12 classrooms. This is particularly the case regarding the self-system and metacognitive system. Ideally, the model presented in this chapter will stimulate interest and discussion in these nontraditional domains of learning and assessment. Finally, the model presented here should be viewed in the context of the current attempts to articulate the defining characteristics of learner-centered schooling. The learner-centered psychological principles (APA, 1995) are certainly a giant step forward in this endeavor. Models like the one presented in this chapter are attempts to fill in the fine detail of the broad brush strokes generated by the principles. Certainly, there are many other interpretations of the learner-centered psychological principles as they relate to classroom assessment. It is hoped that this interpretation is a useful one to practitioners.

References

Amabile, T. M. (1983). *The social psychology of creativity.* New York: Springer-Verlag.

American Association for the Advancement of Science. (1993). *Benchmarks for science literacy.* Oxford, England: Oxford University Press.

American Psychological Association Presidential Task Force on Psychology in Education. (1995, Dec.). *Learner-centered psychological principles: A framework for school redesign and reform* [On-line]. Available: http://www.apa.org/ed/lcp.html.

Anderson, J. R. (1982). Acquisition of cognitive skills. *Psychological Review, 89,* 369–406.

Anderson, J. R. (1983). *The architecture of cognition.* Cambridge, MA: Harvard University Press.

Anderson, J. R. (1990a). *The adaptive character of thought.* Hillsdale, NJ: Erlbaum.

Anderson, J. R. (1990b). *Cognitive psychology and its implications* (3rd ed.). New York: W. H. Freeman.

Anderson, J. R. (1993). *Rules of the mind.* Hillsdale, NJ: Erlbaum.

Anderson, J. R. (1995). *Learning and memory: An integrated approach.* New York: Wiley.

Archbald, D. A., & Newmann, F. M. (1988). *Beyond standardized testing: Assessing authentic achievement in the secondary school.* Reston, VA: National Association of Secondary School Principals.

Atwell, N. C. (1987). *In the middle.* Portsmouth, NH: Heinemann.

Baron, J. B. (1990). Performance assessment: Blurring the edges among assessment, curriculum, and instruction. In A. B. Champagne, B. E. Lovitts, & B. J. Calinger (Eds.), *Assessment in the service of instruction* (pp. 127–147). Washington, DC: American Association for the Advancement of Science.

Berk, R. A. (Ed.). (1986). *Performance assessment: Methods and applications.* Baltimore, MD: Johns Hopkins University Press.

Bovair, S., Kieras, D. E., & Polson, P. G. (1990). The acquisition and performance of text-editing skill: A cognitive complexity analysis. *Human Computer Interaction, 5,* 1–48.

Brown, A. L. (1978). Knowing when, where and how to remember: A problem of metacognition. In R. Glaser (Ed.), *Advances in instructional psychology* (Vol. 1, pp. 77–165). Hillsdale, NJ: Erlbaum.

Brown, A. L. (1980). Metacognitive development and reading. In R. J. Spiro, B. C. Bruce, & W. F. Brewer (Eds.), *Theoretical issues in reading comprehension* (pp. 453–481). Hillsdale, NJ: Erlbaum.

Calkins, L. M. (1986). *The art of teaching writing.* Portsmouth, NH: Heinemann.

Costa, A. (1984). Mediating the metacognitive. *Educational Leadership, 42,* 57–62.

Costa, A. L. (1991). Toward a model of human intellectual functioning. In A. L. Costa (Ed.), *Developing minds: A resource book for teaching thinking* (Vol. 1, pp. 137–140). Alexandria, VA: Association for Supervision and Curriculum Development.

Covington, M. V. (1983). Motivation cognitions. In S. G. Paris, G. M. Olson, & H. W. Stevenson (Eds.), *Learning and motivation in the classroom* (pp. 139–164). Hillsdale, NJ: Erlbaum.

Covington, M. V. (1985). Strategic thinking and the fear of failure. In J. W. Segal, S. F. Chipman, & R. Glaser (Eds.), *Thinking and learning skills: Vol. 1, Relating instruction to research* (pp. 389–416). Hillsdale, NJ: Erlbaum.

Ellis, A. (1977). The basic clinical theory of rational-emotive therapy. In A. Ellis & R. Grieger (Eds.), *Handbook of rationale-emotive therapy.* New York: Springer.

Ennis, R. H. (1985). Goals for a critical thinking curriculum. In A. Costa (Ed.), *Developing minds: A resource book for teaching thinking* (pp. 54–57). Alexandria, VA: Association for Supervision and Curriculum Development.

Ennis, R. H. (1987). A taxonomy of critical thinking dispositions and abilities. In J. Baron & R. Sternberg (Eds.), *Teaching thinking skills: Theory and practice.* New York: Freeman.

Ennis, R. H. (1989). Critical thinking and subject specificity: Clarification and needed research. *Educational Researcher, 18*(3), 4–10.

Flavell, J. H. (1976). Metacognition and cognitive monitoring: A new area of psychological inquiry. *American Psychologist, 34,* 906–911.

Flavell, J. H. (1977). *Cognitive development.* Englewood Cliffs, NJ: Prentice-Hall.

Glaser, R., & Bassok, M. (1989). *Learning theory and the study of instruction* (Technical Report No. 11). Pittsburgh, PA: University of Pittsburgh, Learning Resource and Development Center.

Glasser, W. (1981). *Stations of the mind.* New York: Harper & Row.

Hansen, J. (1994). Literacy portfolios: Windows on potential. In S. W. Valencia, E. H. Hiebert, & P. P. Afflerrbach (Eds.), *Authentic reading assessment: Practices and possibilities* (pp. 26–40). Newark, DE: International Reading Association.

Hart, D. (1994). *Authentic assessment: A handbook for educators.* Menlo Park, CA: Addison Wesley.

Harter, S. (1980). The perceived competence scale for children. *Child Development, 51,* 218–235.

Heidegger, M. C. (1968). *What is called thinking?* New York: Harper & Row.

Holland, J. H., Holyoak, K. J., Nisbett, R. E., & Thagard, P. R. (1987). *Induction: Processes of inference, learning and discovery.* Cambridge, MA: MIT Press.

Kendall, J. S., & Marzano, R. J. (1994). *The systemic identification and articulation of content standards and benchmarks: Update, January 1994.* Aurora, CO: Mid-Continent Regional Educational Laboratory.

Kendall, J. S., & Marzano, R. J. (1995). *The systematic identification and articulation of content standards and benchmarks: Update, March 1995.* Aurora, CO: Mid-Continent Regional Educational Laboratory.

Kuhn, T. (1962). *The structure of scientific revolutions.* Chicago: University of Chicago Press.

LeMahieu, P. G., Gitomer, D. H., & Eresh, J. T. (1995). Portfolios in large scale assessment: Difficult but not impossible. *Educational Measurement: Issues and Practices, 14*(3), 11–28.

Macrorie, K. (1984). *Writing to be read.* Upper Montclair, NJ: Boynton/Cook.

Markus, H., & Ruvulo, A. (1990). Possible selves. Personalized representations of goals. In L. Pervin (Ed.), *Goal concepts in psychology* (pp. 211–241). Hillsdale, NJ: Erlbaum.

Marzano, R. J. (1991). *Cultivating thinking in English and the language arts.* Urbana, IL: National Council of Teachers of English.

Marzano, R. J., & Paynter, D. E. (1994). *New approaches to literacy: Helping students develop reading and writing skills.* Washington, DC: American Psychological Association.

Marzano, R. J., Pickering, D. J., & McTighe, J. (1993). *Assessing student outcomes.* Alexandria, VA: Association for Supervision and Curriculum Development.

McCombs, B. L. (1984). Processes and skills underlying intrinsic motivation to learn: Toward a definition of motivational skills training intervention. *Educational Psychologist, 19,* 197–218.

McCombs, B. L. (1986). The role of the self-system in self-regulated learning. *Contemporary Educational Psychology, 11,* 314–332.

McCombs, B. L. (1989). Self-regulated learning and academic achievement: A phenomenological view. In B. J. Zimmerman & D. H. Schunk (Eds.), *Self-regulated learning and academic achievement: Theory research and practice* (pp. 51–82). New York: Springer-Verlag.

McCombs, B. L., & Marzano, R. J. (1990). Putting the self in self-regulated learning: The self as agent in integrating will and skill. *Educational Psychologist, 25*(1), 51–69.

McNeil, D. (1975). Semiotic extension. In R. L. Solso (Ed.), *Information processing and cognition: The Loyola Symposium* (pp. 22–42). Hillsdale, NJ: Erlbaum.

Meichenbaum, D. (1977). *Cognitive behavior modification.* New York: Plenum Press.

Mitchell, R. (1992). *Testing for learning: How new approaches to evaluation can improve American schools.* New York: The Free Press.

National Council of Teachers of Mathematics. (1989). *Curriculum and evaluation standards for school mathematics.* Reston, VA: Author.

National Education Standards and Improvement Council. (1993). *Promises to keep: Creating high standards for American students. Report on the review of education standards from the goals 3 and 4 technical planning group to the National Education Goals Panel.* Washington, DC: National Goals Panel.

Newell, A. (1991). *Unified theories of cognition.* Cambridge, MA: Harvard University Press.

Paul, R. W. (1984). Critical thinking: Fundamental to education for a free society. *Educational Leadership, 42*(1), 4–14.

Paul, R. W. (1986, December). *Critical thinking, moral integrity, and citizenship: Teaching for the intellectual virtues.* Paper distributed at ASCD Wingspread Conference on Teaching Skills, Racine, WI.

Paul, R. (1990). Socratic questioning. In R. Paul (Ed.), *Critical thinking: What every person needs to survive in a rapidly changing world.* Rohnert Park, CA: Sonoma State University, Center for Critical Thinking and Moral Critique.

Perkins, D. N. (1984). Creativity by design. *Educational Leadership, 42*(1), 18–25.

Perkins, D. N. (1985). *Where is creativity?* Paper presented at University of Iowa Second Annual Humanities Symposium, Iowa City.

Perkins, D. N. (1986). *Knowledge as design.* Hillsdale, NJ: Erlbaum.

Powers, W. T. (1973). *Behavior: The control of perception.* Chicago: Aldine.

Resnick, L. B., & Resnick, D. P. (1992). Assessing the thinking curriculum: New tools for educational reform. In B. R. Gifford & M. C. O'Connor (Eds.), *Changing assessments: Alternative views of aptitude, achievement and instruction* (pp. 37–75). Boston: Kluwer.

Schank, R. C., & Abelson, R. (1977). *Scripts, plans, goals and understanding.* Hillsdale, NJ: Erlbaum.

Schwartz, P., & Ogilvy, J. (1979). *The emergent paradigm: Changing patterns of thought and belief.* Menlo Park, CA: Values and Lifestyles Program.

Siegel, A. I. (1986). Performance tests. In R. A. Berk (Ed.), *Performance assessment: Methods and applications* (pp. 121–142). Baltimore, MD: Johns Hopkins University Press.

Snow, R. E. (1989). Toward assessment of cognitive and conative structures in learning. *Educational Researcher, 18*(9), 8–14.

Snow, R. E., & Jackson, N. D. (1993). *Assessment of conative constructs for educational research and evaluation: A catalogue* (CSE Technical Report No. 354). Los Angeles, CA: University of California, National Center for Research in Evaluation, Standards, and Student Testing.

Snow, R. E., & Lohman, D. F. (1989). Implications of cognitive psychology for educational assessment. In R. L. Linn (Ed.), *Educational measurement* (3rd ed., pp. 263–331). New York: Macmillan.

Staton, J. (1980). Writing and counseling: Using a dialogue journal. *Language Arts, 57,* 514–518.

Sternberg, R. J. (1979). The nature of mental abilities. *American Psychologist, 34,* 214–230.

Sternberg, R. J. (1983). Criteria for intellectual skills training. *Educational Researcher, 12,* 6–12.

Sternberg, R. J. (1984). *Beyond IQ: A triarchic theory of human intelligence.* Cambridge, England: Cambridge University Press.

Stiggins, R. J. (1994). *Student-centered classroom assessment.* New York: Merrill.

Suinn, R. M. (1983). Imagery and sports. In A. A. Sheikh (Ed.), *Imagery: Current theory, research, and application* (pp. 501–534). New York: Wiley.

Watzlawick, P., Weakland, J., & Fisch, R. (1974). *Change: Principles of problem formation and problem resolution.* New York: W. W. Norton.

Whorf, B. L. (1956). *Language, thought and reality.* Cambridge, MA: MIT Press.

Wiggins, G. (1989). Teaching to the (authentic) task. *Educational Leadership, 46*(7), 41–47.

Wiggins, G. (1991, February). Standards, Not Standardization: Evoking Quality Student Work. *Educational Leadership, 48*(5), 18–25.

Wiggins, G. (1993). *Assessing student performance: Exploring the purpose and limits of testing.* San Francisco: Jossey-Bass.

Wolf, D. P. (1989). Portfolio assessment: Sampling student work. *Educational Leadership, 46,* 35–40.

Part III

Dilemmas in Assessment: Policy and Educational Reform

Higher Education Assessment and National Goals for Education: Issues, Assumptions, and Principles

Marcia Mentkowski

My purpose in this chapter is to connect learning and assessment in discussions about undergraduate educational reform among educators, policy makers, assessment practitioners, and psychologists. I hope to encourage postsecondary educators to collaborate with colleagues across the educational spectrum, from preschool through professional school, as they assess student learning in ways that reflect learner-centered principles. I believe that each student can improve his or her learning through effective assessment. Educators can also use assessment information to continuously improve educational programs and to demonstrate accountability to students, policy makers, and the public. Psychologists can use such information to further refine learner-centered psychological principles.

This chapter is an outgrowth of a panel presentation at the Wingspread Conference on Assessment, sponsored by the American Psychological Association's Task Force on Psychology in Education and the Mid-Continent Regional Educational Laboratory, Wingspread, Racine, Wisconsin, November 8–10, 1991. It is based, in part, on an invited address and paper presented at the Fourth National Conference on Assessment in Higher Education sponsored by the American Association for Higher Education, Atlanta, June 1989, Catching Theory Up With Practice: Establishing the Validity and Integrity of Higher Education Assessment; on a symposium presentation at the August 1990 meeting of the American Psychological Association, Boston, Higher Education Assessment: Connecting to Its Conceptual Base (Cassette Recording No. APA-90-164), and on an invited address to Division 2 at the August 1995 meeting of the American Psychological Association, New York, "The Future of Assessment: Taking Responsibility for Student Learning." I acknowledge my Alverno College colleagues in the development of these ideas.

To set context for practice and policy, I review the assessment movement in higher education and examine reasons for higher education's increasing involvement. I discuss efforts to identify broad educational goals proposed at the national and state levels. I review some of the issues that characterize discussions about how assessment can effectively challenge and support educational reform efforts. I frame nine polarities as dimensions of assessment, rather than as dichotomies, so that discussants may better address and resolve controversies.

In my experience, effective conversations about assessment move quickly to probing educational commitments, goals, and values. To this end, I identify some of the educational assumptions that are emerging from higher education philosophy and practice, that are in harmony with advances in psychology, and that have implications for assessment. I discuss four categories of assumptions: defining learning outcomes as abilities integrated with content, understanding learning, defining change as development, and creating coherent curricula.

Further, I cite some principles learned from ability-based, learner-centered assessment. These are drawn from Alverno College theory, research, and practice in designing, implementing, and evaluating assessment at the level of each student (student assessment-as-learning), the curriculum (program assessment), and the college (institutional assessment), and from Alverno educational research on abilities, learning, development, and performance during and after college. My colleague and I (Loacker, 1991; Mentkowski, 1991b) formulated these principles for consideration by the U.S. Department of Education in designing a national assessment system for assessing progress on the National Education Goals as specified in *America 2000: An Education Strategy* (1991). The National Education Goals are part of a long-term strategy adopted by the National Governors' Association and supported by the executive branch of the U.S. government. I use the national goals effort as a policy context because it became an occasion for various groups to converse about assessment. I also include principles formulated by a range of other practitioners and institutions. I expect that the reader will make relationships between these principles and the learner-centered psychological principles (APA, 1993) discussed in Part I of this volume.

This chapter reflects my experiences as a developmental and educational psychologist in program and institutional assessment. I close this chapter with some comments on the potential contributions from psychology and from professors of psychology to the design and implementation of assessment in their classrooms, departments, institutions, and states, as well as nationally.

Contexts for Practice and Policy

The Assessment Movement in Higher Education

The assessment movement, which emerged nationally in 1985 as part of undergraduate reform, has been well documented and discussed (Astin, 1991; Banta & Associates, 1993; Banta, Lund, Black, & Oblander, 1996; Erwin, 1991; Ewell, 1991; Halpern & Associates, 1994; Hutchings & Marchese, 1990; Loacker, Cromwell, & O'Brien, 1986; Mentkowski, 1991a; Mentkowski & Loacker, 1985). Although the movement seemed fueled by state mandates and concerns for public accountability, a few institutions in both the public and private sector had created assessment programs well in advance of external pressures. These institutions (Alverno College, Northeast Missouri State University [now Truman State University], University of Tennessee–Knoxville) are commonly cited as standard bearers (*Time for Results: The Governors' 1991 Report on Education*, 1986; Ewell, 1984). The Fund for the Improvement of Postsecondary Education supported assessment efforts, in particular, an assessment forum conducted by the American Association for Higher Education (AAHE).

What progress has been made? In 1995, the American Council on Education reported that 94% of colleges and universities, up from 55% in 1988, now say they are engaged in activities to assess student learning—that is, they are assessing actual learning outcomes through portfolios and other techniques developed in the 1980s. Most institutions (76%) say that assessment has led to program or curricular changes. However, study director Elaine El-Khawas (1995) concluded that although colleges and universities have become aware of assessment, and have gained some experience with it, they remain skeptical about its uses, particularly if they connect assessment with new reporting requirements and if they worry about how the data are used. In my view, assessing student learning is focused mostly at the program level: *Assessment* is defined as gathering and analyzing information about student learning outcomes and using it to improve programs. Assessment is less well focused at the level of the individual student wherein assessment is directly integral to learning, and wherein each student self-assesses and uses faculty feedback to improve performance. Thus, what assessment is and how it makes a difference is far from resolved in the academic mindset and experience. From the policy maker's perspective, potential benefits are far from realized.

What state and national policy makers continue to want to know is are students achieving complex, multidimensional learning outcomes? Needed now and later? Compared with what standards? To the level students, faculty, and the public expect? As a result of curriculum? These expectations for assessment are complex. Assessment is expected to serve each student's learning, to help faculty ensure *teaching for learning*, to stimulate college-wide discourse about the improvement of education, and to guide public policy on how and where education should be fixed and funded. Each of these levels of practice (individual student, department, institution, discipline, profession, accrediting agency, state, nation) is expected to demonstrate that students are learning and performing in ways that enable them to contribute to work and civic life.

How did psychology, as discipline and profession, respond? A 1991 American Psychological Association (APA) Wingspread conference on assessment issues in kindergarten through 12th grade (K–12) resulted in learner-centered psychological principles that undergird this book. The Presidential Task Force on Psychology in Education noted, for example, "The fundamental purpose of any educational assessment of students should be to promote meaningful learning" (*Learner-Centered Psychological Principles: Guidelines for School Redesign and Reform*, APA, 1993, p. 20). At the postsecondary level, the steering committee for the APA National Conference to Enhance the Quality of Undergraduate Education in Psychology (prepared *Principles for Quality Undergraduate Psychology Programs*. For example, "Quality undergraduate programs set clear and high expectations for their students, promote their active learning, and give students systematic assessment and feedback on their progress" (*Handbook for Enhancing Undergraduate Education in Psychology*, McGovern, 1993, p. 18).

Concurrently, selected members of the American Association for Higher Education—including persons from a number of levels of practice—developed *Principles of Good Practice for Assessing Student Learning*. Principles include, "The assessment of student learning begins with educational values; assessment is most effective when it reflects an understanding of learning as multidimensional, integrated, and revealed in performance over time" (Astin et al., 1992, p. 2). In 1994, AAHE discussions by interdisciplinary assessment practitioners from the classroom to the state level advised the Joint Committee revising the Standards for Educational and Psychological Testing that assessment is justified because it facilitates learning by the student, the department, and by the institution. Assessment should be flexible in mode, avoid harm, and promote learning, assess educational outcomes as advertised and that students have had an opportunity to learn, provide students opportunity to question assessments, and provide prompt and comprehensive feedback on performance useful to the student, faculty, and institution for further learning (AAHE Testimony to the Joint Committee on the Standards for Educational and Psychological Testing, 1994).

At my own institution, faculty have inferred principles from their own research and practice. For example, "assessment is integral to learning" (Alverno College Faculty, 1979, 1985, 1994, p. 4). Alverno also convened consortia of institutions to infer shared educational assumptions from practice, including one consortium composed of 11 institutions across the educational spectrum, from high school through professional school (Consortium for the Improvement of Teaching, Learning and Assessment, 1992). Assumptions include, "Student learning is a primary purpose of an educational institution; assessment is integral to learning" (p. 49).

What is striking is that all six groups—across levels of practice—focus on student learning as central to assessment. Aspects of APA's learner-centered psychological principles (APA, 1993) emerged independently in a range of discussions by higher education practitioners. This suggests that policy and practice in higher education encourages the use of these principles. Nevertheless, a variety of factors account for an emphasis on assessment in higher education. A range of definitions and purposes for assessment blossomed following the 1985 convergence of interest. I now broaden the picture by a look at policy at the national level.

The Assessment Movement and National Goals

The inclusion of higher education in the language and intent of *America 2000: An Education Strategy* (1991; National Education Goals Panel, 1991, 1992), although not as encompassing as some in higher education might have hoped, linked the search for national goals to higher education's assessment movement.

Several assessment issues arose in debates and discussions around national goals: how to achieve them and how best to know whether and how students are meeting skills standards implied by the goals.

Achieving some consensus on skills standards is driven by a growing recognition that education must prepare students to perform in more demanding work and civic arenas. In National Goal 5, the language is more specifically attuned to postsecondary education:

Goal 5: By the year 2000, every adult American will be literate and will possess the knowledge and skills necessary to compete in a global economy and exercise the rights and responsibilities of citizenship.

Objectives:

- Every major American business will be involved in strengthening the connection between education and work.
- All workers will have the opportunity to acquire the knowledge and skills, from basic to highly technical, needed to adapt to emerging new technologies, work methods, and markets through public and private educational, vocational, technical, workplace, or other programs.
- The number of quality programs, including those at libraries, that are designed to serve more effectively the needs of the growing number of part-time and mid-career students will increase substantially.
- The proportion of those qualified students, especially minorities, who enter college; who complete at least two years; and who complete their degree programs will increase substantially.
- The proportion of college graduates who demonstrate an advanced ability to think critically, communicate effectively, and solve problems will increase substantially. (*America 2000*, 1991, p. 39)

Goals defined through criteria or skills standards communicate how students perform when the goals are met (U.S. Department of Labor, The Secretary's Commission on Achieving Necessary Skills, 1991). This implies an assessment system. Thus, there are arguments for continued commitment of higher education to assessment, and for subsequent involvement in goal setting at the state level, as interest in quality issues shifts to the states (e.g., Education Commission of the States, 1995). Edgerton (1991) claimed that higher education's voice was noticeably absent during the creation of the national goals—many of the goals appear framed more for K–12 than for postsecondary education. He argued that higher education educators and policy makers should become more involved for several reasons: As high school graduation requirements change, colleges will need to adjust their requirements and should be concerned about what standards will be set and who will set them. Students should experience their education as continuous. Resolving the old debate about access versus excellence means achieving both access and excellence by raising standards without closing doors. He argued that higher education should pay closer attention to "authentic assessment" (Wiggins, 1993) and "performance assessment" to improve ways to assess student achievement. Finally, Edgerton claimed that national goals are an opportunity for each campus to orient itself to the framework created by the governors and others as representing crucial social needs. Subsequently, a broad range of educators committed themselves to defining the skills to be taught, learned, and assessed at the national (National Center for Education Statistics, 1993, 1994) and state levels.

Educational reform efforts have been focused on the quality of undergraduate education, the quality of teaching, and school and college collaboration. Currently, discussions include concerns about diversity, productivity, school-to-work transition, and involvement in community service. Each of these topics involves the purposes and practices of assessment.

Assessment Issues in Higher Education

Paradoxes and Polarities in Assessment

Higher education is not immune to controversies about the role of assessment in effectively challenging and supporting educational reform efforts. There is a growing consensus that program assessment is here to stay in some form in American colleges and universities. Nevertheless, paradoxes, conundrums, and dynamic tensions characterize discussions in higher education as educators, committed to effective student assessment, explore ways to ensure that assessment meets its intended purposes. These paradoxes can sometimes evolve as dichotomies that separate persons into camps with special interests.

Dimensions of Assessment

My approach is to view these paradoxes as dimensions that can illuminate the problems that educators and policy makers confront. When issue discussions revolve around dimensions of assessment, they can sometimes be resolved. In my experience, a next step is to review the educational assumptions that give rise to a dimension, provided that these assumptions are grounded in practice as well as research. Attempting to resolve dichotomies by discussing dimensions, and then assumptions, does not always work, of course. Some assumptions may be perceived as too idealistic, and their implications too difficult to implement. Current assessment experience or technology may not meet a vision of effective assessment. Some assessment purposes and practices are genuinely contradictory. I now discuss nine assessment dimensions that, in my experience, can be resolved. Then, I review assumptions and implications that, in my experience, can work.

Focusing on the Learner

Should one assess at the level of the individual learner, or some aspect of the system (course, curriculum) or level of practice (department, institution, state, nation)? For example, should one center the role of assessment in individual student development or in a system?

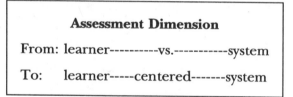

Assessment Dimension

From: learner----------vs.-----------system

To: learner-----centered-------system

The level at which one works (the student, the faculty member in the classroom, the department chair, the curriculum designer, the academic dean, the president and board, the state department of education, the federal department of education) can lead to single-mindedness about the purposes of assessment associated with particular responsibilities (to give feedback to each student in a course and to certify his or her achievement, to improve the curriculum, to report to a state board). Ultimately, however, *each of us is centered on improving learning at the level of the individual student, within an educational system.* When one takes this perspective, faculty build assessment systems that are integral to educational processes that each student experiences directly, and faculty design systems based on the performance of each student. Then, faculty and professional staff design assessment systems for synthesizing information on student performance that can be used by faculty, departments, and institutions to learn about student learning. Professionals who design assessment systems at the state or national level can also take the individual learner perspective, although they report aggregate patterns. However, educators who create learner-centered systems also have responsibilities to communicate to external constituencies and policy makers how students are meeting and exceeding learning goals, and how this information is used to improve systems.

In my experience, there seems to be less attention given to learner-centered assessment. Campuses may differ in this regard because they differ in the priority they place on undergraduate learning. Campuses may, at first, perceive assessment as a response to an external press for accountability. They may fail to clarify who does assessment and who it is for, who is involved, who is primarily responsible, and who primarily benefits. Centering assessment systems on the student and his or her learning as an essential priority may ultimately connect higher education from K–12 to professional schools, and so may enhance the goal of developing continuity across the educational spectrum.

Connecting Assessment and Learning

Should the focus be on improving learning experiences or on assessing outcomes?

Assessment Dimension

From: assessment-----vs.----learning

To: assessment----for----learning

Some argue, "We already know where our problems are. Too much emphasis on assessment can be a barrier to learning. Let's concentrate our resources on the curriculum. Focusing on evaluation rather than intervention will distract us from our major responsibility as educators: to ensure learning." Others argue, "If we don't know how students are performing, and don't feed that information back to them or to us, we could end up neither delivering the curriculum effectively nor maximizing learning for the individual student."

For me, the ultimate test for the practice of assessment is whether assessment leads to learning on the part of each student, each department, each curriculum designer, each institution, or each public policy maker. Does the individual student improve his or her performance as a result of involvement in assessment? Do graduates perform effectively as lifelong learners, and have they internalized a system of self-assessment that continues to serve them in work, personal, and civic roles?

Using assessment for improvement means analyzing teaching and learning on campus. Does the department improve instruction? Thus, the explicit connection between assessment, teaching, and learning is essential. I believe that assessment should be viewed as a continuum, centered on the individual student, whose learning cycle includes performance, self-assessment, and feedback. Faculty and staff experience a similar learning cycle in departments and at the institutional level. For each person involved in assessment, one goal is to link learning to improvement and, thus, to enable accountability to the student, and to various publics. Assessing student performance is for the purpose of learning, which can lead to improvement.

Including Accountability and Improvement

When assessment is connected to learning, can we design assessment for accountability and for the sake of improvement?

> **Assessment Dimension**
>
> From: accountability------------vs.------------improvement
>
> To: accountability----for the sake of----improvement

"The purpose of assessment is to improve things, not to have some external indicator or standard that we meet just to please some outside group," is one argument. "But how will we communicate that we are contributing unless we can show we are meeting our goals?" is one response. "Concern for the individual's personal growth and concern for the individual as a contributing professional and citizen are both essential. An assessment system should meet both accountability and improvement goals within the same system."

This polarity can arise because the educator focuses first on individual achievement, second on demonstrating achievement that defines a particular major or college curriculum, third on strategies that enable an institution to judge its progress over time in relation to standards for excellence, and fourth on overall performance of college students in relation to state and national goals and performance standards. For the policy maker or the public, this progression is usually reversed. Currently, higher education discusses the importance of both improvement and accountability. Systems that bridge the dichotomy can work when policy makers and the public view program accountability as a means to improving graduates' preparation and performance.

Integrating Knowledge and Performance

What should be assessed, knowledge or performance?

Assessment Dimension

From: knowledge------------------vs.---------------performance

To: knowledge----demonstrated through----performance

Traditionally, most instruments that classroom faculty or college boards have used to create either an individual or general picture of student achievement have relied on subject area tests or tests of knowledge. A shared concern is that content will disappear if these kinds of measures are discarded. Admittedly, these tests have come under fire for a number of reasons. First, they are less likely to assess the complex abilities that have long been associated with upper level work in the liberal arts and in the disciplines or professional areas. The student's response may be constrained by the test format, such as multiple choice, rather than enabling the student to demonstrate the full extent of the abilities being assessed. Some advocates press for opportunities for students to demonstrate complex abilities, such as critical thinking, ethical decision making, communication, problem solving, and self-sustained learning. They argue for assessing performance in ways that show what the student is able to do with what he or she knows. Gradually, higher education is beginning to incorporate definitions of assessment that include performance assessment, wherein the educator critically analyzes what students know in relation to what they do and then constructs feedback about the integration of knowledge and performance.

Coming to Consensus

How can we come to consensus around goals and performance standards? Should these be distinct for a department or institution, or common across them?

Assessment Dimension

From: coherence--------vs.------diversity

To: coherence-----within----diversity

"Our strength is in our diversity in higher education," argue some.

"But we have to come to some consensus about how we define the major and general education. How else can students experience a coherent curriculum?" say others. Interdisciplinary educators continue to create diversity in instruction and assessment through the disciplines, and also move to create coherence across the curriculum that enables students to integrate their learning. They ask, "Can we assess learning outcomes across a curriculum within diverse departments?" Some educators have moved from identifying differences among the majors to include building consensus around those abilities, such as "writing across the curriculum." All students demonstrate these abilities within the disciplines and professions to achieve the degree. For those institutions committed to participating in the national effort to improve education, a challenge remains. What picture could each institution create that could show that students meet or exceed state or national goals?

Connecting Inputs, Interventions, and Outcomes

In the past, large-scale assessment concentrated on "inputs" to education, on emphasizing institutional prestige rather than student performance.

Assessment Dimension

From: inputs--------------------------vs.------------------------outcomes

To: inputs---interacting with curriculum generate---outcomes

Inputs include student selectivity data, the number and variety of courses, or the percentage of instructors with a terminal degree in their field. Some educators are distressed by what appears to be a shift in the opposite direction, that is, to a concentration on outcomes defined as indicators of quality alone (Gaither, 1995). The concern is that these performance indicators could easily be divorced from instruction, and –from information about individual differences in student preparation and background that are essential to effective teaching and learning. Several authors in higher education (Astin, 1991, 1993; Mentkowski, 1988; Mentkowski & Doherty, 1983, 1984a, 1984b; Pascarella & Terenzini, 1991) have demonstrated the importance of including inputs, instructional processes, and outcomes in a model of assessment that relates changes in student learning outcomes over time to the curriculum—an important advance in individual student assessment as well as program and institutional assessment.

Integrating Norms and Standards

How will we know if each student has met educational goals? Should the focus be on normative descriptions of current performance, or on aspirational performance standards that describe future expectations? What should be the basis of the comparison?

Assessment Dimension

From: norms------------vs.-----------standards

To: norms-----in relation to-----standards

This dimension reflects one of the most difficult issues in the assessment arena (Howe, 1994). Psychological measurement has introduced strategies for enabling comparisons between student performance and educators' expectations. In recent years, however, many of these strategies have led to invidious comparisons among colleges and universities based on averages, or norms. Often, the source of the norms is obscure rather than public, and the averages cited do not provide the kind of picture of performance educators need to improve curricula. One response to this problem is to move from norm-referenced to criterion-referenced measurement, and to set standards that capture both high aspirations for students and characterize performance needed for future roles. "We should set high standards and hold everyone to them; if we don't, then we are not giving students the benefit of equal expectations," is the argument. Not everyone is satisfied with this solution, however. They respond, "But not all students can meet these standards; we will set students up for failure if we don't consider individual differences on a whole host of dimensions—that is, where students are, what they can reasonably achieve, and the opportunities they have for learning."

Rather than polarizing this dilemma, educators might create developmental performance criteria. When criteria for student abilities illuminate a range of current performances, along with a picture of how we ultimately expect students to perform, criteria can elicit compelling but reasonable aspirations, and suggest future goals. The standards that result are flexible goalposts, and they better reflect concern for individual differences. However, we need thoughtful discussion about this dimension: We have neither a clear picture of how students presently perform on complex abilities and an adequate picture of their potential, nor what will be needed to perform in future roles.

Inherent in this discussion are some of the challenges we have as an assessment community if we act out of this AAHE (1994) principle of good practice for assessing student learning. "Assessment is most effective when it reflects an understanding of learning as multidimensional, integrated, and revealed in performance over time" (p. 2). If we think of learning that way, then standard-setting becomes quite complex. To simplify would be to work against this goal: to judge human abilities such as critical thinking in disciplinary and professional contexts while students are still in school so that they are prepared to perform effectively in work and civic life.

Synthesizing Judgment and Measurement

What seems to make collective standard setting so complex is that "standard-setters" are considering fundamental questions: How "good" is "good enough" and who gets to decide? What is expert judgment? What is good evidence that the judgment process is valid? Effective strategies exist for establishing the validity of measurement, but there are fewer tools for establishing the validity of expert judgment (Mentkowski, 1996; Rogers, 1988).

Assessment Dimension

From: expert judgment------------vs.------------measurement

To: expert judgment-----in relation to-----measurement

For learning to happen, faculty must constantly make expert judgments—in setting standards and in assessing student work. They are making judgments about an aspect or level of a complex, multidimensional ability such as critical thinking—made explicit through criteria that are the basis for judgment. This judgment is expert because faculty bring the rigor of the discipline to these judgments, their experience with students, their education, and their scholarship. However, this is only a starting point for assessing complex performance. Is judgment, they ask, informed, evidence-based, insightful, fair, and wise? Is the evidence that is the basis for judgment not only accurate and credible, but comprehensive and representative? Is it meaningful and conceptually grounded? Is this evidence confirmed through study and experience? Is the evidence drawn from multiple sources, perspectives, and settings? Is it compelling?

Sometimes faculty rightly note that "You can't measure that." Using commonly available tools, one cannot really "measure" all of the complexities of critical thinking. However, experienced faculty can "take a measure of it." In my experience, the phrase, "take a measure," means combining measurement and judgment. Experienced professionals often use a combination of measurement tools and judgment to decide when a learner is ready to move to the next step, particularly when there are human consequences (e.g., a student nurse works with actual clients).

As educators, we often expect to "measure" all aspects of complex abilities, and yet, we do not trust the quality of human judgment generally (Hammond, 1996). We often express this as concern about measurement validity and reliability. However, I think assessment includes a synthesis of judgment and measurement. I am not arguing against measurement or statistics. Rather, I am arguing that when we use judgment, we must develop our understanding of it at the same level we have developed psychometric theory. Educators have a long history of generating evidence that leads to measurement, but little history in public dialogue and conversation about evidence that leads to judgment. In higher education, this kind of "expert" judgment about standards and evidence has too often been cloaked in professional enigma—in part because we have closed, disciplinary languages to discuss criteria; in part because it is difficult to be explicit about insights based on years of practice and experience. Another reason is that when we assess complex abilities in the disciplines, we tend to make broader discriminations, estimates, and interpretations, rather than decisions or conclusions alone. Sometimes, we must do both. Not only do we have to look for cohesion, patterns, and profiles based on our experience, we also need some level of consistency when we certify student performance. When abilities are complex, we must look for patterns and specifics. To give feedback after an assessment, we need specific evidence; but to certify, we need to make a broad, valid judgment, especially when we are judging whether a student teacher will be licensed to work with young children. To turn standard setting into effective assessment of student learning, faculty draw standards from multiple disciplinary perspectives, as well as experience with actual student performance.

In my view, when standard setting works well, faculty also take collective responsibility for culling performance standards from various sources: disciplinary criteria drawn from a particular field based on student performances; a combination of criteria from disciplinary, professional, and postcollege performance examples; and those that seem to capture public expectations. Deriving standards from multiple sources can significantly influence how well prepared the student will be in novel situations that call for more complex forms of an ability such as critical thinking. Then, clearly, faculty will be particularly responsive to what new abilities and standards contemporary life requires.

In a sense, faculty engaged in standard setting try to make explicit what Robert Sternberg (Sternberg & Kolligan, 1990) termed *tacit knowledge*. Tacit knowledge is contextual in nature, procedural in structure, practical in attainment of goals, and based on questions acquired from experience, not just formal studies. Faculty colleagues probe the basis for judgment—the criteria that form the judgment in a particular time and place. These criteria cannot take the place of judgment, but they can make it accessible so that it can be questioned. As long as the processes we have for questioning judgment make sense, then we seem to be more willing to trust human judgment.

One problem is developing new ways to question our own judgments as faculty. At Alverno, we have learned that time spent in interdisciplinary discussion about the basis for our expert judgment is a most intellectually stimulating and engaging activity. In a learner-centered environment, interaction between students and faculty around faculty judgment is one key place for such learning to occur. When faculty make their reasons for judgment explicit through criteria or standards, students learn better. The more active and involved the student is in learning and performing, the more he or she will become a partner with faculty in standard setting. A student performance influences how faculty think about the meaning of an ability in a particular context, what level they can expect, and how the unique, unusual aspects of abilities appear integrated with content in a particular course. An advanced student discovers and sets his or her own criteria for performance, which stretches faculty thinking about an ability.

For standard setting to improve learning on the spot, in the classroom, or in the field, students and faculty need to be able to refine standards. For standard setting to lead to expert judgment, students and faculty need to be able to differentially apply standards as they judge performance in various contexts. How well they do that determines how valid the assessment is—and validity lies in how well each reads the context, considers the consequences, and incorporates what they already know about the meaning of an ability and all its unique, complex aspects (such as dispositions, attitudes, and knowledge).

Assessment as a Means to Transformative Education

Who does assessment? What is its role in educational change?

Assessment Dimension

From: assessment----causes----------educational transformation

To: educational transformation---informed by---assessment

Clearly, assessment is a means to improvement; it cannot, alone, provide the impetus for change in a classroom, institution, or state. That is why it takes students, educators, and policy makers together to identify goals and provide the conditions for learner-centered assessment.

Educational Assumptions Drawn from Practice, Supported by Advances in Psychology, and Implications for Assessment

Now that I have discussed some assessment dimensions, I explore some of the emerging educational assumptions or frameworks that are driving advances in higher education assessment (Mentkowski, Astin, Ewell, & Moran, 1991). These frameworks reflect advances in psychology; have roots in Alverno College theory, research, and practice; and, more broadly, reflect advances across higher education. The assumptions are (a) defining learning outcomes as abilities, (b) understanding learning, (c) defining change as development, and (d) creating coherent curricula. In each, I draw implications for assessment.

Defining Learning Outcomes as Abilities Integrated With Content

One of the objectives of National Goal 5 states that the proportion of college graduates who demonstrate an advanced ability to think critically, communicate effectively, and solve problems will increase substantially. Many institutions are making learning outcomes explicit by defining abilities they expect students to master by the end of general education or the major field (Exhibit 1). These include critical thinking, communicating, problem solving, and ethical decision making (Alverno College Faculty, 1976, 1985, 1992; King's College: Farmer, 1988; Kean College of New Jersey: Presidential Task Force on Student Learning and Development, 1986; University of Tennessee–Knoxville: Office

---

Exhibit 1

Defining Learning Outcomes as Abilities Integrated With Content

Emerging educational assumptions	Implications for assessment
• Student learning outcomes are multidimensional abilities that are complex rather than simple and unitary. Abilities are integrated, developmental, and transferable processes that are qualities of the person. Abilities include multiple components, such as motives or dispositions, self-perceptions and attitudes, skills and behaviors, as well as knowledge, concepts, and constructs. • Student learning outcomes should include not only what students know but what they are able to do.	• Making expected outcomes/abilities explicit and public to all, identifying developmental criteria for performance, and communicating them to students from the beginning contribute to effective performance by making learning more accessible and enabling performance. • When assessing complex abilities, measure constructed performance. Expand the conception of "good" evidence from choosing test item alternatives to include proactive, open, interactive, dynamic, sustained performances, such as the essay, interview, portfolio, project, and so on. • Abilities, performance criteria, and standards will change as we learn to assess effectively and as students begin to improve.

---

of the Executive Vice-Chancellor for Business, Planning and Finance, 1987).

Higher order abilities such as critical thinking or ethical decision making are multidimensional, rather than simple, unitary constructs. These abilities are holistic; that is, they include qualities of the person. Abilities have multiple aspects including knowledge, skills, attitudes, behaviors, and dispositions. Critical thinking and ethical decision making have cognitive, affective, kinesthetic, and social dimensions. They are defined as transferable. They are expected to last a lifetime, and to transfer to multiple aspects of work, personal, and civic life after college.

The definition of these abilities is expanding from faculty teaching experience (Cromwell, 1986; Earley, Mentkowski, & Shafer, 1980; Halonen, 1986, 1995; Loacker, Cromwell, Fey, & Rutherford, 1984), from the psychological literature (Sternberg & Kolligian, 1990), and from studies conducted as a follow-up to the National Goals effort (Jones, 1995; National Center for Education Statistics, 1993, 1994, 1995). For example, while Lawrence Kohlberg (1981) and Carol Gilligan (1982) have expanded definitions of *moral reasoning*, Muriel Bebeau (Bebeau & Brabeck, 1987) has expanded definitions of *moral sensitivity*, confirming that moral development is multidimensional and also developed in the professions (Rest & Narváez, 1994). Similarly, critical thinking definitions are informed by new definitions of intelligence (McClelland, 1973). Howard Gardner's (1983) multiple frames of mind and Robert Sternberg's (1985) triarchic theories of intelligence describe the complexities that counter measurement of critical thinking as a unitary construct. That is important because many of the available psychometric procedures treat constructs as unitary rather than multidimensional (Frederiksen, 1986).

One implication is that the more complex the ability, the more the student will benefit when educators make abilities explicit and public prior to learning experiences, and to assessment. When an ability is described by developmental criteria that are further delineated as applying to beginning, proficient, or advanced performance, the student can more clearly construct a picture of required performance.

Another implication for assessment systems in higher education is that assessment designers consider the complexity of student demonstrations of their abilities. Alverno faculty assessment designers (Alverno College Faculty, 1979, 1985, 1994) began to rethink this question, "What is 'good' evidence?" One strategy is to elicit complex performance, rather than to use a test item as a unit of analysis. The unit of analysis, that is, "good evidence," is expanding from student selection of predetermined test item alternatives—or even short answer—to include proactive, open, interactive, dynamic, sustained student performance. These methods use multiple response modes such as the essay, the interview, the critical incident log, the journal, the oral presentation, the discussion, the performance in a laboratory, the recital, the sculpture, the portfolio, the interaction with a school class, standardized patient, or actual client. Thus, performance assessment is tugging at the edges of traditional measurement (Baron, 1990; Linn, Baker, & Dunbar, 1991; Rogers, 1994).

In institutional assessment, examples include the essay (cf. New Jersey Department of Higher Education, 1988, *Tasks in Critical Thinking*, now available through Higher Education Assessment, Educational Testing Service), the interview (Appalachian Consortium: Carey, 1987), the narrative transcript (The Evergreen State College: *The Evergreen State College Catalog*, 1995), or the critical incident (Flanagan, 1954) or behavioral event interview (McClelland, 1978) wherein students or alumnae describe performance in a dynamic situation (Alverno College: Rogers & Reisetter, 1989; Rhode Island College: "Student Potential Assessed at Rhode Island College," 1989). These methods often use expert judgment to assess such performance.

Still another implication of these assumptions is that faculty will begin assessing these complex abilities even though they are just beginning to define them through performance criteria and standards in the context of the discipline or professional major. Psychologists concerned with defining the meaning of abilities and validating assessment instruments may ask, "How should we define construct validity?" (Cronbach, 1989; Norris, 1983). What is construct validity when multidimensional abilities are not fully defined, when definitions of the abilities emerge in part during the assessment process while the assessor is assessing (e.g., "I haven't seen that response before. It's unique.")? Clearly, expanding assumptions about abilities are likely to challenge traditional assessment approaches and even challenge what is valuable and valid assessment. The inclusion of consequential validity in emerging definitions of validity is a case in point. Our definitions, criteria, and standards will change as students begin to improve. The picture of how students learn these complex abilities draws us deeper into thinking through assessment.

Understanding Learning

Many educators are defining learning as a complex process that happens experientially, where students use different learning styles, where knowledge is linked to action (Exhibit 2). Hutchings and Wutzdorff's (1988) *Knowing and Doing: Learning Through Experience*, Kolb's (1984) experiential learning theory, and Brown's (1994) view of learners as active constructors are examples. Lesley College, The Evergeen State College, and a consortium of Washington state institutions associated with Evergreen's Washington Center are exploring collaborative learning that occurs in interaction with others (MacGregor, 1993). Adult learning is defined by psychologists as socially constructed, as described in *Women's Ways of Knowing* by Mary Belenky, Blythe Clinchy, Nancy Goldberger, and Jill Tarule (1986), and by William Perry (1970) in *Forms of Intellectual and Ethical Development in the College Years*, where shifts occur in how adults think about their learning. Students effectively transfer college-learned abilities when they develop learning-to-learn

---

Exhibit 2

Understanding Learning

Emerging education assumptions	Implications for assessment
• Expand the definitions of learning from understanding information alone to include learning as self-directed, active and interactive, collaborative, experiential, and socially constructed. • Learning to learn, or self-sustained learning, enables the transfer of abilities learned in college to work, personal, and civic roles. • When assessment is connected to learning, assessment leads to learning.	• Assess performance that is the product of interactive, experiential, collaborative, and self-sustained learning. • Assessment strategies that require students to demonstrate performance that is connected to future performance situations in work and civic roles help develop student knowledge and abilities. • Assessment leads to learning when students receive feedback on their performance in relation to criteria and when they have opportunities to self-assess. • Feedback on performance in relation to developmental criteria and the opportunity to interpret that information leads to further learning and improvement of student and program performance.

---

skills, or self-sustained learning. Self-sustained learning that links education to postcollege performance is an important outcome that enables continued learning, adaptation and integration of abilities, and further learning within and across roles and settings.

Defining learning as a complex process where the student learns actively and in interaction with others, and develops self-sustained or lifelong learning, implies measuring and judging complex performance. The implication is that we assess performance that requires the student to link knowledge to action, and to interact with others. Here, more is required than expanding the nature of the task. For example, key ingredients of effective assessment-as-learning are public and explicit abilities and outcomes, developmental performance criteria, multiplicity of performances across varied contexts, expert judgment, feedback, and self-assessment (Loacker & Mentkowski, 1993).

Information from assessments of learning outcomes during college and at graduation may leave unanswered a question that students, educators, employers, and policy makers are often most interested in, "Does college learning transfer to work and civic service, and does college prepare individuals not only for entry-level positions and beginning roles, but also for future positions and roles, that may be as yet undefined or unimagined? How do we know which abilities last a lifetime, which are needed for the 21st century, and which of these should be developed during college?" Thus, an assessment system should assess and research how abilities are actually performed in the workplace so that a college education incorporates societal expectations that higher education be responsible for students' immediate and future application of college-learned abilities. Thus, although the primary investment is in the assessment of the college student, the consequent questions that arise from assessment information immediately redirect public interest in how college-learned abilities connect to work and citizenship following graduation.

How do we best assess when an individual student's performance should reflect how students learn and perform during and after college? Assessment is a new challenge for faculty and administrators who are interested in looking for learning in its most complex forms, and in eliciting performance that is true to what students will be expected to do after college, and across their life span. This challenge is further complicated by defining change as development.

Defining Change as Development

An educational assumption that undergirds assessment is the definition of *change* as development where structural shifts in thinking and learning occur (Exhibit 3). Nor are these changes limited to the cognitive sphere: Socioemotional and affective dimensions also change during college. Therefore, educators are concerned with the students' personal development as well as their performance in general education and the major field.

Concern with student development means measuring change. One might argue that measuring change is not a new topic in higher education and certainly not a new topic in psychology (Collins & Horn, 1991; Harris, 1963). True, prior research on college outcomes (e.g., Astin, 1993; Feldman & Newcomb, 1969) found that college makes a difference, and that traditional-aged students who attend college benefit from it in contrast to those who do not attend or graduate from college.

Exhibit 3

Defining Change as Development

Emerging educational assumptions	Implications for assessment
• The aims of education include developing the whole person as well as learning a discipline or profession. • Individuals recycle through earlier forms of thinking when they meet new situations. • Changes in student learning outcomes, including development over time, are to be demonstrated and linked to courses, curriculum, and college culture. • When an assessment system examines changes in student learning outcomes over time, including who changes and why, and relates those changes to the curriculum, the system yields information necessary for meaningful improvement. • Definitions of learning outcomes and developmental performance criteria change as the result of assessing abilities effectively, and as students master them, because information from assessment improves understanding. Thus, students continue to be challenged by the high aspirations inherent in changing criteria and dynamic standards, and continue to improve.	• Assume change rather than consistency. Expand assumptions expecting consistency over time to include change over time, and from expecting additive/quantitative change to include qualitative/nonlinear change patterns. • Expand the definition of *standards* from static, indirect, endpoint indicators to include dynamic, observed, developmental performance criteria. • Expand the focus on input, resource, or reputational indicators to include changes in student performance over time as a result of curriculum. Assess intra- and inter-individual patterns in individual student learning outcomes as a result of instruction, and in relation to postcollege performance. • Use assessment information to improve individual student learning, faculty learning, programs, and institutional or organizational learning.

Ernest Pascarella and Patrick Terenzini (1991) reviewed studies that link college outcomes to particular aspects of the college environment, but not necessarily to a recognizably coherent curriculum.

Thus, the assessment movement asks a new question: Can we as educators link student learning outcomes to learning in college—to a course, to a general education program, to a major, to a curriculum? What is needed is to show that what faculty systematically do to plan and implement learning and instruction can be linked to student learning outcomes over time.

This fundamental assumption drives the assessment movement: Change is an outcome to be demonstrated. At my college, we hold the traditional belief that development in student abilities and learning is an aim of education. However, we do not assume that students will automatically develop their abilities to the fullest if they are "exposed" to our "best" college environments, nor that students who receive diplomas automatically perform effectively in work, family, and civic roles. We assume that changes in desirable student learning outcomes occur for each student when a curriculum is organized around individual student learning.

Those of us engaged in assessing student learning outcomes in individual courses, general education, the major, or the broad outcomes of a curriculum or college note the difficulties of selecting or designing instruments that might measure change and possible strategies to analyze change, should it occur. But as we create a picture of graduating student or alumni outcomes—a picture of endpoint achievements—we naturally move toward considering change as an outcome. Students are expected to change in some important ways from when they enter a postsecondary curriculum to when they exit. These changes go beyond those that can be attributed to maturation, family and economic history, prior educational opportunity and achievement, cultural background, and individual differences at entrance to college (Astin, 1991; Ewell, 1991; Mentkowski & Strait, 1983; Pascarella, Edison, Amaury, & Hagedorn, 1995; Pike et al., 1991; Winter, McClelland, & Stewart, 1981).

However, the purpose of assessment at the program level goes beyond demonstrating student achievement by showing mean differences between beginning and graduating students, and factoring out the influences of unalterable variables so one can make plausible links to curriculum. A major purpose of assessment is to generate information that can be used to improve individual student learning and programs. Aggregate information that communicates average differences between groups often does not give the kind of information that educators need to improve teaching and curriculum. The question of who changes and why is therefore central. How does change occur and for whom? How does development toward desirable outcomes happen and for whom? What educators need is information on intra- and interindividual patterns.

Faculty are interested in individual scores, but they are as interested in patterns of student change and the kinds of changes that are likely to occur. This information is different from data about individual differences among students on entry to a course or program. Faculty are interested in individual differences—in learning style or course sequences completed—but my experience suggests that faculty are even more interested in the patterns of change that occur while the student is learning. Differences in change patterns are important because faculty intend to intervene to promote learning for each student.

An instructor who teaches large classes is interested in differential patterns for various groups because he or she may not have as many opportunities for one-on-one instruction. A faculty member can develop different learning paths with information on differential patterns of achievement. Measurement strategies that provide averages from aggregate performance at the beginning and end of a course or sequence of courses are not very helpful when faculty seek to improve learning for each student by constructing different learning paths, or for understanding learning blocks when students have consistent difficulties.

Interindividual and intraindividual change patterns can be particularly helpful to those educators who believe that students learn best when they receive individual feedback on their performance on classroom assessments (Schulte & Loacker, 1994). Thus, instruments should yield a performance profile—even when a primary purpose of an out-of-class measure is to demonstrate aggregate student changes toward broad curricular goals, for purposes of broad curriculum improvement. For both purposes, feedback from change patterns is much more meaningful.

To return to earlier themes, what are individual and group patterns in the development of complex, higher order abilities that are multidimensional, developable and expected to transfer? When we are looking for critical thinking in a student performance at the end of a student's work in the major or across a portfolio, will we expect to see more of the same if we look for that ability at the end of a seminar or 5 years after graduation? We will expect to see a qualitatively different ability, particularly when he or she demonstrates that ability in a setting that is quite different from the college. Our developmental models must assume change, not persistence, because abilities may take a quite different form in classroom assessments than they do in cross-college assessments, or in studies of performance in the workplace.

Although these immediate assessment questions drive our interest in measuring change, our institutional mission statements have set other, broad goals for a college education. At the institutional level, we ask basic questions about the ways that college learning makes a difference after college. Thus, assessment of broad, long-term outcomes is essential. Likewise, developmental educators consider complex, cognitive–developmental changes as student learning outcomes and look for these changes beyond college in order to validate educational principles and programs. Outcome measures include ego and moral and intellectual development. Outcomes include evidence of integration of abilities; adaptability and flexibility in the workplace; and the ability to integrate career and family, to demonstrate civic responsibility, and so on (Mentkowski & Rogers, 1993).

Once again, such complex outcomes call for some rethinking around the kinds of assessment models that will work. As psychologists, we are used to measurement models that measure change not by describing qualitative transitions, but rather, by adding up the number of items correct on a test and giving us a quantitative picture of amounts of change from two repeated administrations of the same measure. A more appropriate measurement model, whether qualitative or quantitative, is development and change, not consistency across time, or continuation of a similar ability. Samuel Messick (1988) argued that assuming change rather than consistency should influence our expectations; I think it changes our ideas about what is valid measurement as well. Once again, we might rethink what is "good" assessment and the models we use to analyze change.

Assuming change means that prediction will not necessarily rest on an additive model. That is, we will not necessarily expect to see "more of the same" after instruction or after college, but rather, qualitatively different learning outcomes. What kinds of measures and analytic strategies will validly take this assumption into consideration? What happens when we add the assumption that development is, at times, nonlinear? Alverno longitudinal study results (Mentkowski, 1988) suggest that individuals recycle through earlier forms of thinking when they meet new situations. Positive change is not always consistent, "upward" movement on measures of development. This can shape the assumptions about nonlinear learning underlying models of institutional assessment where one is demonstrating that curriculum makes a difference in student changes in abilities, learning, and personal growth.

We have come full circle to our "new" assessment questions: Can we demonstrate that the complex abilities that are outcomes of active, experiential, collaborative, and socially constructed learning are linked to curriculum? How best do we show change patterns in student learning outcomes as a function of learning? Which assessment strategies will lead to insights about the impact of a course? of a general education curriculum? of a particular major or professional program? of a faculty-designed coherent curriculum? of a particular college? What analytic strategies best describe change patterns after college? Assumptions about how students change and develop have implications for creating performance standards. Rather than defining standards as static, we tend to consider them as changeable, and we create and expand our performance criteria to reflect the full range of individual differences in student learning and the kind of change patterns that characterize it.

Creating Coherent Curricula

Recent developments in higher education suggest a fundamental rethinking rather than just a reflection of disciplinary developments in psychology or any other field. This reconceptualization around the purposes, functions, and student learning outcomes of undergraduate education was initiated inside higher education (Study Group on the Conditions of Excellence in American Higher Education, 1984) and from outside it by society's primary beneficiaries.

The search for coherence emerges from the charge that educational goals are not well articulated, and that educational methods and modes of inquiry are not symbiotic with the goals and purposes of liberal arts education (Select Committee of the Project on Redefining the Meaning and Purpose of Baccalaureate Degrees, 1985). For example, the knowledge explosion has led to separation of content from the processes by which it is best learned; knowledge is separated from its application in particular situations. These and other curricular incoherencies are reflected against a backdrop of specialized, fragmented disciplines.

The search for coherence in curriculum is one response to this fragmentation (Exhibit 4). Assessment in higher education is one means to deal not only with an inherent fragmentation within and among the disciplines, but also with a dysfunctional separation of educational purposes and practices that occur within an overly diversified general education curriculum, set of majors, or institution. Thus, assessment has emerged in part (a) to link measurement of student-learning outcomes to curricular goals, (b) to design assessment as an integral part of teaching and learning, and (c) to connect student outcomes

---
Exhibit 4

Creating Coherent Curricula

Emerging educational assumptions	Implications for assessment
• An understanding of curricular coherence moves beyond describing a broad institutional mission or a series of related courses to articulating learning outcomes that cross the curriculum and that are integrated in student learning. Connect curricular components across the diversity of courses and majors. • Developing coherent curricula means interdisciplinary engagement that builds on the diversity of the disciplines. • A coherent curriculum calls for faculty investment in a community of learning and judgment about how students are achieving college outcomes and how college prepares them for work and civic roles. • Educational frameworks for teaching, learning, and assessment should be constructed collaboratively based on our best understanding of what abilities students need, how they learn, and how development happens, as well as disciplinary and professional frameworks.	• Integrate educators' experience with their disciplinary expertise. • Promote interdisciplinary approaches in assessment design. • Expand faculty judgment of student work in courses to include an assessment system that delivers ongoing, meaningful feedback to individual students and faculty. • Expand the community of judgment about what should be learned in college to include alumni, practicing professionals, employers, and graduate faculty. Assess student performance during college with an eye toward postcollege performance. • Expand occasional, discrete program evaluations by external evaluators, and institutional self studies for accreditation purposes, to include institutionalized, continuous improvement processes that monitor and compare performance to a range of internal and external standards. • Expand the conception of faculty scholarship from expanding the knowledge base of a discipline or profession to include educational research on teaching, abilities, learning, and human development.
---

information from various forms of assessment processes at the student, program, and institutional levels.

One result of these changing assumptions is the recasting of educational research and evaluation from a specialization in educational psychology or a psychologist's method to a key curricular component and an integral part of a higher education institution. Institutions, in turn, have created a new role for educational psychologists (Mentkowski, 1994).

This also means integrating educators' experiences with their disciplinary expertise. In a sense, the assessment movement is a response to the view that teaching, adult learning and development, measurement, research and evaluation—key concepts in educational and developmental psychology—have become separated in discussions at the national level. APA's Task Force on Psychology in Education and the Committee on Undergraduate Education (McGovern, 1993) are working to deal with this fragmentation. If one views the assessment movement only as another hybrid, one will miss the why of its evolution. Assessment is here to curtail the separation between teaching experience and measurement, research and evaluation expertise.

Thus, assessment is an effort to reconnect the educator role with disciplinary expertise. Strategies that support individual faculty to conduct research on teaching and learning connections in the classroom are important new developments (Angelo & Cross, 1993).

Assessment can be a positive thrust if it is successful in integrating the teaching and assessment experience of faculty with the sources of expertise in the disciplines—psychology included—to help guide future directions in assessment. This also means promoting interdisciplinary approaches in assessment design. By drawing from a number of modes of inquiry, faculty colleagues in a number of disciplines help identify alternate approaches to assessment that recognize and capitalize on some of the basic distinctions among the disciplines. This interdisciplinary activity helps to rethink assessment theory, draw many disciplines into the discussion, and to push practice further.

Respected thinkers in educational measurement, research, and evaluation are considering new approaches that draw from several disciplines. They reflect the kind of reexamination occurring in behavioral science methodology that is currently the discipline from which much of testing technology and criteria for establishing the validity of that technology are drawn. In fact, professional groups in educational testing are currently including these new perspectives.

Those who review that literature have noted that there seems to be a general call for considering alternative paradigms for shaping our methodological approaches in educational psychology, thus expanding the boundaries of conventional science. Robert Stake (1967),

Michael Parlett and David Hamilton (1976), Ernest House (1976), Michael Patton (1986), and Egon Guba and Yvonna Lincoln (1981) have done so in evaluation. Jane Loevinger (1957), Samuel Messick (1988), Carol Kehr Tittle (1989), Pamela Moss (1995), Wayne Camara and Diane Brown (1995), and Kate Lenzo (1995) have done so in measurement; Harland Bloland (1989) has done so in higher education.

Others have explored social constructionism as an alternative paradigm. They include Kenneth Gergen (1985), Mary Poplin (1988), Peter Johnston (1989), Yvonna Lincoln (1989), Jennifer Greene (1990), Thomas Schwandt (1989), John Smith (1985), and John Crane (1988). In my experience, these debates in the literature are reflected in the evolving practices of higher education assessment and they are reflected in the assumptions that undergird assessment strategies. These debates are yet another indicator that assessment as an emerging movement is likely to ultimately be based on theoretical frameworks that incorporate recent shifts in how we define scientific methods.

For example, Cleo Cherryholmes (1988) argued that in most approaches to traditional measurement, elements such as consistency, replicability, and stability are valued and pursued, often relentlessly, in the context of change and instability. Some years ago, Elliot Mishler (1979) commented that the importance of context has been largely ignored in methodological approaches. Our field of psychology can help create a role for an educational psychologist in our own immediate, institutional context, where change rather than stability is the rule; where the situation varies and is expected to vary; where purposes, definitions, curricula, and faculty-designed instruments undergo revision over time.

Searching for coherence within the multiple perspectives of the liberal arts and the diversity of courses and majors, and considering curricular connections in an ongoing, changing, context—our own—have the most far-reaching implications for assessment strategies. Here, it becomes essential to reconstruct assessment. Here, assessment becomes an organized process for establishing the validity of learning processes and programs and, most important, the validity of an individual student's performance of essential learning outcomes. Assessment has a critical place in our organized search for coherence within a department and even across an institution.

Principles Learned from Learner-Centered Assessment-as-Learning at Alverno College

Principles learned from Alverno research and practice are described and substantiated in two studies commissioned by the National Center for Education Statistics in response to the National Education Goals Panel: *America 2000: An Education Strategy* (1991; Loacker, 1991; Mentkowski, 1991b) (see Exhibits 5 and 6). These principles reflect the work of Alverno faculty and staff for over 20 years. Alverno College, a liberal arts institution that prepares women for the professions, initiated an ability-based curriculum with performance assessment in 1973 and institutional and program assessment approaches in 1976. Alverno has collaborated with many other institutions in annual workshops and through consortia funded by the U.S. Department of Education and foundations (e.g., Consortium for the Improvement of Teaching, Learning and Assessment, 1992; Schulte & Loacker, 1994). These principles also reflect feedback and insights from these colleagues.

Principles Learned from Other Contributors to Learner-Centered Assessment

This section describes principles agreed on by a consortium of educators, from high school to college to professional school, who are committed to learner-centered assessment, and by another group of assessment practitioners convened by the AAHE Assessment Forum (see Exhibits 7 and 8). This section also briefly describes *Principles of Good Practice for Assessing Student Learning* (Astin et al., 1992) developed under the auspices of the AAHE, which sponsors the Assessment Forum, including an annual conference on assessment for practitioners.

The Role of Psychologists as Experts and as Participants in Assessment

No discussion about the potential contributions of psychologists to assessment is complete without a charge to psychologists themselves to become involved. University faculty—and psychologists are no exception—are experienced in serving as experts to others outside the university. There are other roles for a psychologist than as an expert.

Exhibit 5

Principles learned from Alverno assessment theory, research, and practice (Loacker, 1991):

1. An ability-based performance assessment system, with certain key elements,* can work both to evaluate student performance and to develop student knowledge and ability.
   - Meeting "exit" standards can be effectively combined with individual student development as criteria for excellence.
   - Incentive and feedback elements can be effectively combined to ensure that students are invested in performing their best and can receive feedback that they can use to improve.
   - Both an accountability and an improvement agenda can, therefore, be met with the same system.

     *Public abilities/outcomes and developmental performance criteria, multiplicity of performances across varied contexts, expert judgment, feedback, and self-assessment

2. Making expected outcomes/abilities explicit and public to all, identifying developmental criteria for performance, and communicating them to students ahead of time contributes to effective performance by making learning more accessible and enabling performance.
3. Feedback on performance in relation to developmental criteria and the opportunity to interpret that information leads to further learning and improvement of student and program performance.
4. Students learn complex abilities, including self-sustained learning, in the curriculum through a variety of contexts.
5. Students can transfer abilities when they are assessed in contexts that are valid for what students learned and for how they will perform abilities later.
6. When an assessment system examines changes in student abilities/outcomes over time, including who changes and why, and relates those changes to the curriculum, the system yields information necessary for meaningful improvement.
7. We can validate an ability-based performance assessment process and institute an instrument validation process that gradually improves instrument validity. We can establish the educational value, impact, validity, and effectiveness of the abilities/outcomes.
8. A dynamic assessment system incorporating input from and feedback to faculty, as well as administrators, provides for the effective use of information to keep abilities, performance criteria, and standards responsive to and in advance of the needs of our society.
9. Creating a context for assessment is as important as creating the assessment method.

continued

10. The effectiveness of an assessment system concerned with the improvement of learning depends partially on a coherence that comes from the following articulated components:

  • educational values, assumptions, and principles that are tied to the mission statement of the institution
  • an assessment theory (what are the components of good assessment?) consistent with those values and assumptions
  • a psychometric theory and theory of judgment (how do we best judge, measure, and credential performance, and give feedback to students on their abilities?) consistent with those values and assumptions

Note: Principles from "Designing a National Assessment System: Alverno's Institutional Perspective," by G. Loacker, 1991. Reprinted with permission from Alverno College. Copyright 1991 from Alverno Productions.

Most psychology faculty teach, and there are opportunities for faculty to improve the ways they define student outcomes in the major field and the ways they assist students to demonstrate their abilities. It is here that psychologists can continue to explore their role as educator and find new ways to link instruction and assessment. Further, many psychologists are becoming involved as assessment specialists on faculty assessment committees, or in designing and implementing assessment systems. Research is needed to improve our understanding and practice of effective assessment. Psychologists are in a unique position to integrate their day-to-day experience with their disciplinary expertise. Indeed, each psychologist who teaches is an educational psychologist when he or she integrates such research in the discipline with classroom teaching practice.

Summary and Conclusion

Assessment in higher education should be derived from educational goals in the context of practice and policy. Some of the paradoxes, polarities, and dilemmas in assessment give rise to changing educational assumptions and learning principles in higher education that reflect higher education research and practice; Alverno College theory, research, and practice; and psychological theory and research.

How might learner-centered psychological principles, drawn principally from elementary and secondary education practice and psycho-

---

Exhibit 6

Principles learned from assessing abilities that connect education, work, and citizenship (Mentkowski, 1991b):

1. Abilities integrated with content can be defined in ways that connect education, work, and citizenship. These can be assessed within professional roles in appropriate contexts, as well as in college, in order to achieve both accountability and improvement.
2. Abilities defined as having multiple components, and as integrated, developmental, and transferable, are likely to make sense both to educators and employers.
3. Thinking critically, communicating effectively, and solving problems are abilities common to college education, work, and citizenship. Effective performance at work is integrated; it is made up of both intellectual and interpersonal abilities.
4. To effectively transfer college-learned abilities, students need to develop learning-to-learn skills, or self-sustained learning. Assessment that incorporates feedback and opportunities to self-assess fosters self-sustained learning.
5. Comparing faculty-defined abilities to those demonstrated by outstanding professionals enables faculty to identify abilities students need for particular professions.
6. Complex abilities that connect education and work—including self-sustained learning—can be assessed in graduates' work performance in a variety of professional contexts. Some abilities can be linked to college learning, and some distinguish effective performance at work.
7. Faculty, professionals, and employers will invest in understanding the relationship between education and work if they can create contextually rich descriptions of performance in relation to their judgment of what abilities to develop.

Note: Principles reprinted with permission from Alverno College. Copyright 1991 by Alverno Productions.

logical research, relate to higher education assessment practice? It seems clear that assessment is a means to educational goals; it is not an end in itself. Psychology as a discipline makes learning the purpose of assessment and the student the center of a learning process that respects individual differences and diversity in talent and experience. In my view, higher education practice would do well to emulate this emphasis. Higher education practitioners might also note that psychological principles tend to give as much attention to student motivation, attitudes, and affect as they do to the construction of knowledge in the disciplines and professions. In my view, practitioners in higher educa-

Exhibit 7

Principles of Good Practice for Assessing Student Learning (developed under the auspices of the American Association for Higher Education)

1. The assessment of student learning begins with educational values.
2. Assessment is most effective when it reflects an understanding of learning as multidimensional, integrated, and revealed in performance over time.
3. Assessment works best when the programs it seeks to improve have clear, explicitly stated purposes.
4. Assessment requires attention to outcomes but also and equally to the experiences that lead to those outcomes.
5. Assessment works best when it is ongoing, not episodic.
6. Assessment fosters wider improvement when representatives from across the educational community are involved.
7. Assessment makes a difference when it begins with issues of use and illuminates questions that people really care about.
8. Assessment is most likely to lead to improvement when it is part of a larger set of conditions that promote change.
9. Through assessment, educators meet responsibilities to students and to the public.

tion might benefit from greater attention to these dimensions of student learning. Generally, however, emerging educational assumptions in higher education are in concert with a socially constructionist view of knowledge and a view of learning as interactive, collaborative, and contextual. Those who prepare students for professions would agree, for example, that standards should be high, yet developmental, and they would integrate faculty expectations with those from professional practitioners and policy makers.

The issues, assumptions, and principles drawn from higher education practice, theory, and research do not resolve all the paradoxes educators face in implementing effective assessment—certainly not for everyone in every setting! Nor can this chapter delineate all the research and practice that undergirds these principles. But I hope to move the discussion forward, and to encourage all of us to continue to clarify our issues, assumptions, and principles. Through sharing how we conceptualize the purposes and practices of assessment, and by advancing and discussing them, I trust we will become more effective at designing and implementing assessment that furthers student, state, and national commitments to higher education.

Exhibit 8

Shared Educational Assumptions (developed under the auspices
of the Consortium for the Improvement of Teaching,
Learning, and Assessment)

"The following educational assumptions grew out of a series of discussions we
have had over the past several years as we worked together in different partnerships and, most recently, as a consortium. They are rooted in the experience
of our individual institutions; however, we have come to appreciate how important it is to try to express some understandings that might be common to
education from high school through college/university through professional
school. We offer this current draft of our shared educational assumptions as a
contribution to the ongoing public conversation about the improvement of education."

Student Learning and Assessment

Assumption 1:   Student learning is a primary purpose of an educational institution.
Assumption 2:   Education goes beyond knowing to being able to do what
one knows.
Assumption 3:   Learning must be active and collaborative.
Assumption 4:   Assessment is integral to learning.
Assumption 5:   Abilities must be developed and assessed in multiple modes
and contexts.
Assumption 6:   Performance assessment—with explicit criteria, feedback,
and self assessment—is an effective strategy for ability-
based, student-centered education.

Curricular Coherence and Development

Assumption 7:   A coherent curriculum calls for faculty investment in a community of learning and judgment.
Assumption 8:   The process of implementation and institutionalization of a
curriculum is as important as the curriculum: the process is
dynamic, iterative, and continuous.
Assumption 9:   Educators are responsible for making learning more available by articulating outcomes and making them public.
Assumption 10: Responsibility for education involves assessing student outcomes, documenting inputs, and relating student perfor-
mance over time to the curriculum.

References

Alverno College Faculty. (1976). *Liberal learning at Alverno College*. Milwaukee, WI: Al-
verno Productions.
Alverno College Faculty. (1979). *Assessment at Alverno College*. Milwaukee, WI: Alverno
Productions.

Alverno College Faculty. (1985a). *Liberal learning at Alverno College.* Milwaukee, WI: Alverno Productions.

Alverno College Faculty. (1985b). *Student assessment-as-learning at Alverno College.* Milwaukee, WI: Alverno Productions.

Alverno College Faculty. (1992). *Liberal learning at Alverno College.* Milwaukee, WI: Alverno College Institute.

Alverno College Faculty. (1994). *Student assessment-as-learning at Alverno College.* Milwaukee, WI: Alverno College Institute.

America 2000: An Education Strategy. (1991, rev. ed.). Washington, DC: U.S. Department of Education.

American Association for Higher Education. (1994, October). American Association for Higher Education testimony to the Joint Committee on the Standards for Educational and Psychological Testing: Testimony version (M. Mentkowski, AAHE Advisor). In *Open conference on the revision of the standards: Oral testimony summaries.* Crystal City, VA: Joint Committee on the Standards for Educational and Psychological Testing.

American Psychological Association National Conference to Enhance the Quality of Undergraduate Education in Psychology. (1991). *Principles for quality undergraduate psychology programs.* Washington, DC: American Psychological Association.

American Psychological Association Presidential Task Force on Psychology in Education. (1993, January). *Learner-centered psychological principles: Guidelines for school redesign and reform.* Boulder, CO: American Psychological Association and the Mid-Continent Regional Educational Laboratory.

Angelo, T. A., & Cross, K. P. (1993). *Classroom assessment techniques: A handbook for college teachers* (2nd ed.). San Francisco: Jossey-Bass.

Astin, A. W. (1991). *Assessment for excellence: The philosophy and practice of assessment and evaluation in higher education.* New York: Macmillan.

Astin, A. W. (1993). *What matters in college? Four critical years revisited.* San Francisco: Jossey-Bass.

Astin, A. W., Banta, T. W., Cross, K. P., El-Khawas, E., Ewell, P. T., Hutchings, P., Marchese, T. J., McClenney, K. M., Mentkowski, M., Miller, M. A., Moran, E. T., & Wright, B. D. (1992). Principles of good practice for assessing student learning. *AAHE Bulletin, 45*(4).

Banta, T. W., & Associates. (1993). *Making a difference: Outcomes of a decade of assessment in higher education.* San Francisco: Jossey-Bass.

Banta, T. W., Lund, J. P., Black, K. E., & Oblander, F. W. (1996). *Assessment in practice: Putting principles to work on college campuses.* San Francisco: Jossey-Bass.

Baron, J. B. (1990, May). A new kind of test being tested. *Newsletter for Educational Psychologists,* p. 1.

Bebeau, M. J., & Brabeck, M. (1987). Integrating care and justice issues in professional moral education: A gender perspective. *Journal of Moral Education, 16*(3), 189–203.

Belenky, M. F., Clinchy, B. M., Goldberger, N. R., & Tarule, J. M. (1986). *Women's ways of knowing: The development of self, voice, and mind.* New York: Basic Books.

Bloland, H. G. (1989). Higher education and high anxiety: Objectivism, relativism, and irony. *Journal of Higher Education, 60*(5), 519–543.

Brown, A. L. (1994, November). The advancement of learning. *Educational Researcher, 23*(8), 4–12.

Camara, W. J., & Brown, D. C. (1995, Spring). Educational and employment testing: Changing concepts in measurement and policy. *Educational Measurement: Issues and Practice, 14*(1), 5–11.

Carey, K. (1987). *Appalachian College Assessment Program: Assessing general education interview questions for seniors.* Lexington: University of Kentucky, College of Education, Educational Policy Studies and Evaluation.

Cherryholmes, C. H. (1988). Construct validity and the discourses of research. *American Journal of Education, 93*(3), 420–457.

Collins, L. M., & Horn, J. L. (1991). *Best methods for the analysis of change: Recent advances, unanswered questions, future directions.* Washington, DC: American Psychological Association.

Consortium for the Improvement of Teaching, Learning and Assessment. (1992). *High school to college to professional school: Achieving educational coherence through outcome-oriented, performance-based curricula.* (Final Report to the W. K. Kellogg Foundation). Milwaukee, WI: Alverno Productions.

Crane, J. A. (1988). Evaluation as scientific research. *Evaluation Review, 12*(5), 467–482.

Cromwell, L. (Ed.). (1986). *Teaching critical thinking in the arts and humanities.* Milwaukee, WI: Alverno Productions.

Cronbach, L. (1989). Construct validation after thirty years. In R. Linn (Ed.), *Intelligence: Measurement, theory and public policy: Proceedings of a symposium in honor of Lloyd G. Humphreys* (pp. 147–171). Urbana: University of Illinois Press.

Earley, M., Mentkowski, M., & Shafer, J. (1980). *Valuing at Alverno: The valuing process in liberal education.* Milwaukee, WI: Alverno Productions.

Edgerton, R. (1991, December). National standards are coming! . . . National standards are coming! *AAHE Bulletin, 44*(4), 8–12.

Education Commission of the States. (1995). *Making quality count in undergraduate education.* Denver, CO: Author.

El-Khawas, E. (1995). *Campus trends.* Washington, DC: American Council on Education.

Erwin, D. T. (1991). *Assessing student learning and development.* San Francisco: Jossey-Bass.

The Evergreen State College Catalog. (1995). Olympia, WA: The Evergreen State College.

Ewell, P. T. (1984). *The self-regarding institution: Information for excellence.* Boulder, CO: National Center for Higher Education Management Systems.

Ewell, P. (1991). To capture the ineffable: New forms of assessment in higher education. In G. Grant (Ed.), *Review of research in education* (pp. 75–125). Washington, DC: American Educational Research Association.

Farmer, D. W. (1988). *Enhancing student learning: Emphasizing essential competencies in adademic programs.* Wilkes-Barre, PA: King's College.

Feldman, K. A., & Newcomb, T. M. (1969). *The impact of college on students.* San Francisco: Jossey-Bass.

Flanagan, J. C. (1954). The critical incident technique. *Psychological Bulletin, 51*(4), 327–358.

Frederiksen, N. (1986). Toward a broader conception of human intelligence. *American Psychologist, 41*(4), 445–452.

Gaither, G. H. (Ed.). (1995). Assessing performance in an age of accountability: Case studies: *New Directions for Higher Education,* 91. San Francisco: Jossey-Bass.

Gardner, H. (1983). *Frames of mind: The theory of multiple intelligence.* New York: Basic Books.

Gergen, K. J. (1985). The social constructionist movement in modern psychology. *American Psychologist, 40*(3), 266–275.

Gilligan, C. (1982). *In a different voice: Psychological theory and women's development.* Cambridge, MA: Harvard University Press.

Greene, J. C. (1990). Three views on the nature and role of knowledge in social science. In E. G. Guba (Ed.), *The paradigm dialog* (pp. 227–245). Newbury Park, CA: Sage.

Guba, E., & Lincoln, Y. (1981). *Effective evaluation: Improving the usefulness of evaluation results through responsive and naturalistic approaches.* San Francisco: Jossey-Bass.

Halonen, J. (Ed.). (1986). *Teaching critical thinking in psychology.* Milwaukee, WI: Alverno Productions.

Halonen, J. (1995, February). Demystifying critical thinking. *Teaching of Psychology, 22*(1), 79–81.

Halpern, D. F., & Associates. (1994). *Changing college classrooms: New teaching and learning strategies for an increasingly complex world.* San Francisco: Jossey-Bass.

Hammond, K. (1996). *Human judgment and social policy.* New York: Oxford University Press.

Harris, C. W. (Ed.). (1963). *Problems in measuring change.* Madison: University of Wisconsin Press.

House, E. R. (1976). Justice in evaluation. In G. Glass (Ed.), *Evaluation Studies Review Annual* (Vol. 1, pp 75–100). Beverly Hills, CA: Sage.

Howe, K. R. (1994, November). Standards, assessment, and equality of educational opportunity. *Educational Researcher, 23*(8), 27–33.

Hutchings, P., & Marchese, T. (1990, September–October). Watching assessment: Questions, stories, prospects. *Change,* pp. 12–38.

Hutchings, P., & Wutzdorff, A. (Eds.). (1988). Knowing and doing: Learning through experience. *New Directions for Teaching and Learning, 35.* San Francisco: Jossey-Bass.

Johnston, P. J. (1989). Constructive evaluation and the improvement of teaching and learning. *Teachers College Record, 90*(4), 509–528.

Jones, E. (1995, April). Defining essential critical thinking skills for college graduates. In S. Swayze (Chair), *Student cognition.* Paper presented at the annual meeting of the American Educational Research Association, Boston, MA.

Kolb, D. A. (1984). *Experiential learning: Experience as the source of learning and development.* Englewood Cliffs, NJ: Prentice-Hall.

Kohlberg, L. (1981). *Essays on moral development: The philosophy of moral development* (Vol. I). San Francisco: Harper & Row.

Lenzo, K. (1995, May). Validity and self-reflexivity meet poststructuralism: Scientific ethos and the transgressive self. *Educational Researcher, 24*(4), 17–23, 45.

Lincoln, Y. (1989). Trouble in the land. In J. Smart (Ed.), *Higher education: Handbook of theory and research* (Vol. 5, pp. 57–133) New York: Agathon Press.

Linn, R. L., Baker, E. L., & Dunbar, S. B. (1991, November). Complex, performance-based assessment: Expectations and validation criteria. *Educational Researcher, 20*(8), 15–21.

Loacker, G. (1991). *Designing a national assessment system: Alverno's institutional perspective.* Paper commissioned by the U.S. Department of Education, National Center for Education Statistics, in response to the National Education Goals Panel: America 2000: An Education Strategy, Milwaukee, WI: Alverno Productions.

Loacker, G., Cromwell, L., Fey, J., & Rutherford, D. (1984). *Analysis and communication at Alverno: An approach to critical thinking.* Milwaukee, WI: Alverno Productions.

Loacker, G., Cromwell, L., & O'Brien, K. (1986). Assessment in higher education: To serve the learner. In C. Adelman (Ed.), *Assessment in American higher education* (pp. 47–62). Washington, DC: Office of Educational Research and Improvement, U.S. Department of Education.

Loacker, G., & Mentkowski, M. (1993). Creating a culture where assessment improves learning. In T. W. Banta & Associates (Eds.), *Making a difference: Outcomes of a decade of assessment in higher education* (pp. 5–24). San Francisco: Jossey-Bass.

Loevinger, J. (1957). Objective tests as instruments of psychological theory. *Psychological Reports, 3,* 635–694.

MacGregor, J. (Ed.). (1993, Winter). Student self-evaluation: Fostering reflective learning. New Directions for Teaching and Learning, 56. San Francisco: Jossey-Bass.

McClelland, D. (1973). Testing for competence rather than for "intelligence." *American Psychologist, 28,* 1–14.

McClelland, D. C. (1978). *Guide to behavioral event interviewing.* Boston: McBer & Company.

McGovern, T. V. (1993). *Handbook for enhancing undergraduate education in psychology.* Washington, DC: American Psychological Association.

Mentkowski, M. (1988). Paths to integrity: Educating for personal growth and professional performance. In S. Srivastva & Associates (Eds.), *Executive integrity: The search for high human values in organizational life* (pp. 89–121). San Francisco: Jossey-Bass.

Mentkowski, M. (1991a). Creating a context where institutional assessment yields educational improvement. *Journal of General Education, 40,* 255–283.

Mentkowski, M. (1991b). *Designing a national assessment system: Assessing abilities that connect education and work.* Paper commissioned by the U.S. Department of Education. National Center for Education Statistics, in response to the National Education Goals Panel: America 2000: An Education Strategy. Milwaukee, WI: Alverno Productions.

Mentkowski, M. (1994, January–February). How assessment practitioners who are educational researchers can contribute to assessment in higher education. *Assessment Update, 6*(1), 1–2, 10–11.

Mentkowski, M. (1996). Reflecting on our practice: Research to understand and improve student learning across the curriculum. In G. Gibbs (Ed.), *Improving student learning: Using research to improve student learning* (pp. 12–32). Oxford, England: The Oxford Centre for Staff Development.

Mentkowski, M., Astin, A. W., Ewell, P. T., & Moran, E. T. (1991). *Catching theory up with practice: Conceptual frameworks for assessment.* Washington, DC: The AAHE Assessment Forum, American Association for Higher Education.

Mentkowski, M., & Doherty, A. (1983). *Careering after college: Establishing the validity of abilities learned in college for later careering and professional performance* (Final report to the National Institute of Education: Overview and Summary). Milwaukee, WI: Alverno Productions.

Mentkowski, M., & Doherty, A. (1984a). Abilities that last a lifetime: Outcomes of the Alverno experience. *AAHE Bulletin, 36*(6), 5–6, 11–14.

Mentkowski, M., & Doherty, A. (1984b). *Careering after college: Establishing the validity of abilities learned in college for later careering and professional performance* (Final report to the National Institute of Education: Overview and Summary). Milwaukee, WI: Alverno Productions.

Mentkowski, M., & Loacker, G. (1985). Assessing and validating the outcomes of college. In P. Ewell (Ed.), Assessing educational outcomes. *New Directions for Institutional Research* (Vol. 47, pp. 47–64). San Francisco: Jossey-Bass.

Mentkowski, M., & Rogers, G. (1993, Summer). Connecting education, work, and citizenship: How assessment can help. *Metropolitan Universities: An International Forum, 4*(1), 34–46.

Mentkowski, M., & Strait, M. (1983). *A longitudinal study of student change in cognitive development, learning styles, and generic abilities in an outcome-centered liberal arts curriculum* (Final Report to the National Institute of Education: Research Report No. 6). Milwaukee, WI: Alverno Productions.

Messick, S. (1988). The once and future issues of validity: Assessing the meaning and consequence of measurement. In H. Wainer & H. I. Braun (Eds.), *Test validity*, (pp. 33–40). Hillside, NJ: Erlbaum.

Mishler, E. G. (1979). Meaning in context: Is there any other kind? *Harvard Educational Review, 49*(1), 1–19.

Moss, P. A. (1995, Summer). Themes and variations in validity theory. *Educational Measurement: Issues and Practice, 14*(2), 5–13.

National Center for Education Statistics. (1993). *National assessment of college student learning: Getting started* (NCES 93-116). Washington, DC: U.S. Department of Education, Office of Educational Research and Improvement.

National Center for Education Statistics. (1994). *The national assessment of college student learning: Identification of the skills to be taught, learned, and assessed* (NCES 94-286). Washington, DC: U.S. Department of Education, Office of Educational Research and Improvement.

National Center for Education Statistics. (1995). *National assessment of college student learning: Identifying college graduates' essential skills in writing, speech and listening, and critical thinking* (NCES 95-001). Washington, DC: U.S. Department of Education, Office of Educational Research and Improvement.

National Education Goals Panel. (1991). *The national education goals report: Building a nation of learners.* Washington, DC: Author.

National Education Goals Panel. (1992). *Report of the task force on assessing the national goal relating to postsecondary education* (Report No. 92-07). Washington, DC: Author.

New Jersey Department of Higher Education. (1988). *Tasks in critical thinking.* Princeton, NJ: Educational Testing Service.

Norris, S. P. (1983). The inconsistencies at the foundation of construct validation theory. In E. R. House (Ed.), *Philosophy of evaluation.* New Directions for Program Evaluation, 19, 53–74. San Francisco, CA: Jossey-Bass.

Office of the Executive Vice-Chancellor for Business, Planning and Finance. (1987, October). *University of Tennessee expectations.* Knoxville: University of Tennessee.

Parlett, M., & Hamilton, D. (1976). Evaluation as illumination: A new approach to the study of innovatory programs. In G. Glass (Ed.), *Evaluation Studies Review Annual* (Vol. 1, pp. 140–157). Beverly Hills, CA: Sage.

Pascarella, E. T., Edison, M., Amaury, N., & Hagedorn, L. S. (1995, April). Effect of teacher organization/preparation and teacher skill/clarity on general cognitive skills in college. In S. Swayze (Chair), *Student cognition.* Paper presented at the annual meeting of the American Educational Research Association, Boston, MA.

Pascarella, E. T., & Terenzini, P. T. (1991). *How college affects students: Findings and insights from twenty years of research.* San Francisco: Jossey-Bass.

Patton, M. Q. (1986). *Utilization-focused evaluation* (rev. ed.). Newbury Park, CA: Sage.

Perry, W., Jr. (1970). *Forms of intellectual and ethical development in the college years: A scheme.* New York: Holt, Rinehart & Winston.

Pike, G. R., Phillippi, R. H., Banta, T. W., Bensey, M. W., Melbourne, C. C., & Columbus, P. J. (1991). *Freshman to senior gains at the University of Tennessee, Knoxville.* Knoxville, TN: Center for Assessment, Research and Development.

Poplin, M. S. (1988). Holistic/constructivist principles of the teaching/learning process: Implications for the field of learning disabilities. *Journal of Learning Disabilities, 21*(7), 401–416.

Presidential Task Force on Student Learning and Development. (1986). *Conclusions and recommendations in a proposal for program assessment at Kean College of New Jersey.* Union, NJ: Kean College.

Rest, J. R., & Narváez, D. F. (1994). *Moral development in the professions: Psychology and applied ethics.* Hillsdale, NJ: Erlbaum.

Rogers, G. (1988). *Validating college outcomes with institutionally developed instruments: Issues in maximizing contextual validity.* Paper presented at the annual meeting of the American Educational Research Association, New Orleans. Milwaukee, WI: Alverno Productions.

Rogers, G. (1994, January–February). Measurement and judgment in curriculum assessment systems. In M. Mentkowski (Ed.), How educational research can contribute to assessment in higher education. *Assessment Update, 6*(1), 6–7.

Rogers, G., & Reisetter, J. (1989). *Flexible strategies for behavioral event interviewing: Exploring events and situations.* Milwaukee, WI: Alverno Productions.

Schulte, J., & Loacker, G. (1994). *Assessing general education outcomes for the individual student: Performance assessment-as-learning, Part I: Designing and implementing performance assessment instruments.* Milwaukee, WI: Alverno College Institute.

Schwandt, T. A. (1989, March). *Paths to inquiry in the social disciplines: Scientific, constructivist, and critical science methodologies.* Paper presented at the Alternative Paradigms for Inquiry Conference, Phi Delta Kappa International and Indiana University, San Francisco.

Select Committee of the Project on Redefining the Meaning and Purpose of Baccalaureate Degrees. (1985). *Integrity in the college curriculum.* Washington, DC: Association of American Colleges.

Smith, J. K. (1985). Social reality as mind-dependent versus mind-independent and the interpretation of test validity. *Journal of Research and Development in Education, 19*(1), 1–9.

Stake, R. E. (1967). The countenance of educational evaluation. *Teachers College Record, 68,* 523–540.

Sternberg, R. J. (1985). *Beyond IQ.* Cambridge, England: Cambridge University Press.

Sternberg, R. J., & Kolligian, J., Jr. (Eds.). (1990). *Competence considered.* New Haven, CT: Yale University Press.

Student potential assessed at Rhode Island College. (1989). *Assessment Update, 1*(2), 10.

Study Group on the Conditions of Excellence in American Higher Education. (1984, October). *Involvement in learning: Realizing the potential of American higher education.* Washington, DC: U.S. Department of Education, National Institute of Education.

Time for Results: The Governors' 1991 Report on Education. (1986, August). Washington, DC: National Governors Association Center for Policy Research and Analysis.

Tittle, C. K. (1989). Validity: Whose construction is it in the teaching and learning context? *Educational Measurement: Issues and Practice, 8*(1), 5–13, 34.

U.S. Department of Labor, The Secretary's Commission on Achieving Necessary Skills. (1991, June). *What work requires of schools: A SCANS report for America 2000.* Washington, DC: Author.

Wiggins, G. P. (1993). *Assessing student performance: Exploring the purpose and limits of testing.* San Francisco: Jossey-Bass.

Winter, D. G., McClelland, D. C., & Stewart, A. J. (1981). *A new case for the liberal arts: Assessing institutional goals and student development.* San Francisco: Jossey-Bass.

Educational Assessment and Diversity

Trevor E. Sewell, Joseph P. DuCette, and
Joan Poliner Shapiro

The Metaphor of the Melting Pot in American Schools

America has traditionally viewed itself as a unique combination of unity
and plurality, a perception perfectly captured in the metaphor of the
American melting pot and in the national motto of *e pluribus unum*—
from many, one. In essence, the prevailing ideology has stated for years
that America can be characterized not simply by cohesion and diversity,
but rather by cohesion despite diversity. This ideology has maintained
for over 200 years that the unique American experience is to take a
dizzying array of peoples, cultures, and races and to homogenize them
into a new entity called *American.*

This metaphor of the American melting pot is clearly reflected in
the account of America envisaged by de Crevecoeur in 1782:

> Whence came all these peoples? They are a mixture of English,
> Scotch, Irish, French, Dutch, Germans and Swedes. From this pro-
> miscuous breed, that race now called Americans, have arisen. What
> then is the American, this new man? He is either a European, or
> the descendent of a European, hence that strange mixture of blood,
> which you will find in no other country. Here individuals of all
> nations are melted into a new race of men. (Schwarz, 1995, p. 60)

In this ''new race of men'' was placed the hope for a future devoid
of the problems endemic in the old world: wars based on ethnic and
racial differences, prejudice based on class distinctions, unequal opportunities for advancement based on the vagaries of birth. Moreover, this
melting together was supposed to occur automatically and painlessly
through a natural process based on the inherent desire of men (for the

founding fathers were as little concerned about gender equality as was de Crevecoeur) to find a new and better way that would create the promised opportunities for life, liberty, and the pursuit of happiness for all Americans.

But how was this new and better way to be derived? How were the disparate cultures, races, and ideologies to be forged into this new breed of human being who would constitute the American persona? As Americans have traditionally done throughout our history, the schools were turned to for the answer to this question. The metaphor of the melting pot leads inevitably to the idea that all who come to these shores can be, and should be, assimilated by an open society that transforms disparate peoples into Americans. In an age before radio and television, with their vast potential to homogenize culture and transmit it to all parts of the country, it was the unique role of the schools to accomplish this transformation. Obviously, it was the schools that were supposed to educate students so that they could read and write and calculate. More profoundly, however, the schools were supposed to produce citizens who spoke a common language, understood a common history, and believed in a common set of goals, principles, and values. While this task was never easy, it has become increasingly difficult in recent years due to a daunting array of factors both within education and within society. The purpose of this chapter is to review and summarize the implications of these factors for American education in general, and for education assessment in particular.

Even in this time when a common culture is disseminated through the television set each night of the week, the schools still function as the one essential experience shared by all Americans. It is amazing that, despite vast changes in American society, many schools still portray the "ideal" American in a fashion that has not significantly changed in more than 100 years. This concept was well captured by Cushner, McClelland, and Safford (1989):

> Real Americans are white and they are adult; they are middle-class (or trying very hard to be); they go to church (often Protestant, but sometimes Catholic as well, although that is a bit suspicious); they are married (or aim to be) and they live in single-family houses (which they own, or are trying to); they work hard and stand on "their own two feet"; they wash themselves a good deal, and generally try to "smell good"; they are patriotic and honor the flag; they are heterosexual; they are often charitable, only expecting a certain amount of gratitude and a serious effort to "shape up" from

those who are the objects of their charity; they eat well; they see that their children behave themselves. (p. 216)

Whether this is a valid characterization of the way schools portray the "real American" is less important than the essential fact that American schools have traditionally been expected to present some single and unifying view of the American culture. It is the schools, then, that have borne the burden of producing the social and cultural integration required to generate the new and better race of human beings. And it is the schools in contemporary society that have become the central agencies in which the competing visions of America are debated and attempts to resolve major cultural conflicts are made.

Diversity in American Schools

The reality of the American melting pot, of course, has never totally lived up to its expectations nor matched its ideology. In reality, the conceptual vision of the melting pot was never fully realized and any progress achieved to that end during the last 3 centuries on the American continent is due much less to a natural and painless process and far more to power and hegemony. As Schwarz (1995) commented

> Thus, long before the United States' founding, and until probably the 1960's, the "unity" of the American people derived not from their warm welcoming of and accommodating to nationalist, ethnic, and linguistic differences but from the ability and willingness of an Anglo elite to stamp its image on other peoples coming to this country. That elite's religious and political principles, its customs and social relations, its standards of taste and morality, were for 300 years America's, and in basic ways they still are, despite our celebration of "diversity." Whatever freedom from ethnic and nationalistic conflict this country has enjoyed has existed thanks to a cultural and ethnic predominance that would not tolerate conflict or confusion regarding the national identity. (p. 62)

This reconceptualization of the American experience does not modify the historical role of the schools, but it does place that role in a far less positive light. Rather than being viewed as the vehicle by which "Americanization" occurred, the schools can now be viewed as the instrument through which the powerful and the dominant subjugated and submerged competing philosophies, ideologies, and cultures. Whatever history one wishes to believe, however, it is clear that the schools, and the American culture that these schools reflect, can no longer be characterized in any single or unifying way. Americans have entered an age of diversity and, in such an age, many believe that commonality and agreement about core values and principles are neither achievable nor desirable.

We are faced, then, with a profound change in the way Americans view ourselves. On the one hand, there is the reality of those who have long dominated the culture—witness Schwarz's Anglo elite who are no longer willing or able "to impose their hegemony on society as a whole" (Schwarz, 1995, p. 63). On the other hand, there are those ethnic, linguistic, religious, and various other types of minorities who cannot or do not choose to be assimilated into the dominant culture. America has moved, then, to a situation where the melting pot no longer serves as a viable metaphor. Indeed, some would argue that the appropriate metaphor is the "Chinese hot pot" (Tek Lum, 1987, p. 105), where various foods are cooked together yet maintain their unique flavors and textures. Whatever constitutes the proper metaphor for this age, it is clear that America has moved beyond a point where it is meaningful to speak of the American culture as a unified entity. As always, this profound change has the greatest impact in the schools.

Diversity and Educational Reform

This change in perspective, coupled with the increasing school enrollment of a number of minority children, has had a significant effect on many aspects of American life. One of the most widely discussed effects is the call for a profound change in the curriculum of American schools at all levels—from elementary to college. Stated most simply, this new social reality requires that the curricula of American schools move away from a unified, single concept of the knowledge and skills that American children should possess, toward a pluralistic concept recognizing and incorporating diversity. This movement has produced a fundamental problem in the way the role of the schools is conceptualized.

The central issue underlying the call for a curriculum that is responsive to diversity is that no single description of the real American is possible, and that American schools should stop trying to create one (Gollnick, 1992a, 1992b). But if the goal of the schools is no longer focused on producing the prototypic American, what experience should the schools provide? It can be argued that the answer to this question has been the central focus of American education throughout its history. The critical difference is that today's discussion encounters a politically charged and acrimonious debate in which the possibility of a single answer becomes increasingly problematic.

The call for diversity in the curriculum in which an attempt is made to reflect and incorporate all of the elements of American society presents both a unique challenge and a unique problem for American schools (see Banks, 1991, 1993, and Grant & Secada, 1991, for discussions of this issue). In a previous publication, we have defined diversity as

> encompassing the domain of human characteristics which affect an individual's capacity to learn from, respond to, or interact in a school environment. These characteristics can be overt or covert, recognized by the individual or not recognized, and biologically or environmentally or socially determined. Some of the characteristics are meaningful only as they describe an individual; others are more meaningful as they describe a group. (Shapiro, Sewell, & DuCette, 1995, p. 2)

In essence, we believe that a curriculum that appreciates diversity must include not only racial, ethnic, gender, and social class differences, but also a range of other variables that impact on the ability to learn. We also believe that a curriculum that appreciates diversity will focus attention on learner growth and in so doing increase it. As defined, this curriculum is similar to, yet more inclusive than, what many call a *multicultural curriculum*. According to Banks (1991), in a fully implemented multicultural curriculum all historical and social events are viewed from the perspectives of different cultural and ethnic groups. While Banks' distinction between four models of a multicultural curriculum (from a mainstream-centric model at one end of the spectrum to an ethnonational model at the other) is valuable, we believe his frame of reference needs to be considerably broadened. This thinking is similar in many ways to Tetreault's (1989) discussion of the five phases of curriculum development in women's studies. Again, we agree with these perspectives, although our focus is always broader and more inclusive. We recognize, however, that inclusiveness and breadth have their own drawbacks, and we have previously discussed possible options for the narrowness-versus-breadth dilemma (DuCette, Shapiro, & Sewell, 1992, 1995; Shapiro, Sewell, & DuCette, 1995).

According to some, any curriculum that emphasizes difference rather than similarity has the potential to produce a crisis for American schools. With the decline in the belief in the American melting pot, each of the groups which compose the American people has begun to demand that its unique values, history, and viewpoint be respected, studied, and incorporated into the curriculum (Brown, 1992). Undoubtedly, many positive outcomes can be derived from this movement: ethnic pride, a sense of community within groups sharing a common culture, a richer sense of heritage. The negative side of this movement, however, is that consensus about what America is and, more critically, what it should become may be unattainable.

One of the major historical functions of schools has been to assimilate diverse group into the mainstream culture. This has usually meant that the curriculum, teaching techniques, and methods of testing and assessment were identical (or at least very similar) for all students. If a curriculum in which diversity is a core concept can be created, it follows that teaching techniques and methods of testing and assessment should also be varied. However, if alternative forms of teaching and a variety of pedagogical methods are offered, the demands for standards and accountability that currently permeate American society will present many unusual challenges. A related dilemma also arises from the demand for a curriculum that appreciates diversity: Can schools be reconceptualized to represent and value this diversity while simultaneously maintaining their historical role of transmitting the dominant culture? This latter problem would be acute under any circumstance. It becomes almost insolvable in light of the recent reform movements that stridently demand accountability through the use of standardized tests and the consistent reliance on the human capital model of schooling.

Assessment and Accountability in Educational Reform

Since the publication of *A Nation at Risk: The Imperative for Educational Reform* (National Commission on Excellence in Education, 1983), the seminal critique of American education credited with starting the current reform movement, at least 57 national and organizational reports have followed (Jackson, 1991). Although these reports vary considerably in detail, most seem to agree on a few core issues:

- American education is in a state of crisis.
- This crisis is a major (or, is the major) reason why America's competitive edge in the global marketplace is severely challenged.
- To reestablish America's place in the world, students in American

schools must attain "world-class" standards in core academic subjects.

- To ensure that these standards are attained, American schools, the students in these schools, their teachers, and administrators must be held accountable.
- The major way that this accountability should be achieved is through some form of assessment by which schools, states, and nations can be compared.

While the reports vary in the specificity with which they define or elaborate on the theme of accountability, the majority consider this a central issue. This is clearly articulated in two recent and well-known national reports: *America 2000: An Education Strategy* (1991) and its follow-up report, *Goals 2000: Educate America Act* (1993). These reports provide clear examples of America's unwavering faith in the power of standardized tests to produce accountability to dictate the parameters of educational reform. In addition, they are national reports that have received a great deal of scrutiny from educators, politicians, and many other groups interested in education. As such, they represent more than historical records and warrant attention for what they might predict about the future of the educational reform movement.

There are many contradictions in *America 2000* (1991) and in *Goals 2000* (1993), but their strong belief in the power of accountability, monitored through tests, can be seen throughout the reports. In fact, in *America 2000* it can be argued that accountability is the central concept. (The word *accountability* itself occurs 23 times, which is approximately once per page.) Moreover, the new national achievement tests that represent the major vehicle by which this accountability is to be attained are probably as representative of what politicians consider the promised land of educational reform as one could reasonably hope to find in a political and legislative document. The evidence for this contention can be found throughout the plan's various components:

- *America 2000* calls for parents to have the option of sending their children to the school of their choice, which they will determine by comparing schools' test scores.
- America's students are to become competitive with students from other nations, and we will know that our students have achieved this "world-class status" by comparing the test results from American schools to the results from the schools of other nations.
- Communities throughout the nation are to develop "report

cards'' on their schools, and the basic component of the grades for these report cards are test results.

As many writers have pointed out (see, e.g., Gandal, 1995; Pitsch, 1995), the major difference between *America 2000* and *Goals 2000* is that the latter remands to the states rather than to the nation the responsibility to "establish clear standards for student achievement and to refocus their educational efforts around these standards" (Gandal, 1995, p. 16). In almost every other way, however, the rhetoric and underlying assumptions of the two documents are identical. Our central concern about these reform efforts, and the concern of anyone who takes seriously learner-centered education, is that both *America 2000* and *Goals 2000* place far too much emphasis on accountability monitored by standardized tests rather than on student improvement monitored by educational assessment over time.

To be fair, these reform documents give lip service to assessment through other means (some of which we describe subsequently). In practice, however, we believe that these movements will inevitably lead to a centralized system of standards that will, in turn, inevitably lead back again to the "coin of the realm in public education" (Haladyna, Nolen, & Haas, 1991, p. 2): the standardized achievement test. Whether these tests are national, regional, or state designed, a strong possibility exists that they will be neutralized in such a way that they will be devoid of context and single-minded in purpose.

To cite one immediately evident problem, there is a strong and lengthy tradition in testing to use test scores to compare the performance of students, or, in the aggregate, to compare the performance of schools, school districts, or states. As many have pointed out (see, e.g., Garcia & Pearson, 1994; Sewell, DuCette, & Shapiro, 1991; Shapiro, Sewell, & DuCette, 1992), these comparisons almost always ignore glaring disparities in the opportunity to learn. This practice treats significant differences in sociocultural experiences, inequities in school funding, and disparities in curriculum content and instructional resources as if they were insignificant and meaningless.

However, the rhetoric surrounding the current reform movement seems to negate these troubling realities in the way schools are evaluated. This is perhaps best captured by citing two controversial parts of *Goals 2000.* In HR-1804, the Congress of the United States proposed the following two principles:

> Each State shall establish strategies for improving teaching and learning, including:

> A process for developing and implementing a valid and nondiscrim-
> inatory assessment system or set of locally-based assessment systems
> that is capable of providing coherent information about student at-
> tainments relative to the State content standards. The process shall
> also provide for monitoring the implementation of such system or
> systems and the impact on improved instruction for all students;

> and,

> Each State plan shall establish a strategy and timetable for:

> (1) adopting or establishing opportunity-to-learn standards;
> (2) ensuring that every school in the State achieves the State's
>   opportunity-to-learn standards;
> (3) ensuring that the State's opportunity-to-learn standards address
>   the needs of all students. (*Goals 2000*, 1993, pp. 49–50)

Although the opportunity to learn standards did not pass the
House of Representatives, they still represent a clear call for equity in
the way all students are educated. The dilemma facing those legislators
who proposed these standards, and for those teachers, administrators
and State Department of Education officials who might be faced with
the difficulty of implementing them, is to somehow find a way to provide "valid" and "nondiscriminatory" assessment in the context of environments where the opportunity to learn is unquestionably unequal,
and where the needs of all students have never been fairly or equitably
met. In recent years, the typical response to this dilemma has been to
cite the potential of so-called alternative assessment to address the glaring problems in standardized tests. In fact, the notable shift from measurement and testing to assessment is perhaps coincidentally related to
the current interest in many forms of alternative assessment.

Learner-Centered Psychological Principles

We have presented the background material on a curriculum sensitive
to the issues of diversity and on national standards as an introduction
to the 14 recently approved learner-centered psychological principles
(American Psychological Association [APA], 1995). As stated in the pre-
amble to these principles,

> the learner-centered psychological principles are expected to pro-
> vide an essential framework to be incorporated in new designs for
> curriculum and instruction, assessment systems for evaluating edu-
> cational goal attainments, as well as for the systematic redesign of
> professional development programs and education system struc-
> tures. (APA, 1995, p. 2)

It is our intention in this chapter to look at these principles in the context that the movement that we have indicated seems to lead inevitably toward a curriculum in which diversity is a core concept. How can these learner-centered principles further this movement? What aspects of these principles might need revision, expansion, or elaboration in light of the demands created by diversity in American education? Or, if the underlying assumptions of the principles are valid, how should assessment be conceptualized, developed, and implemented in the context of an appreciation of diversity?

Although all of the 14 principles can and should be investigated, we will focus our discussion in this chapter on Principles 12, 13, and 14. These are

12. Individual differences in learning. Learners have different strategies, approaches, and capabilities for learning that are a function of prior experience and heredity.

13. Learning and diversity. Learning is most effective when differences in learners' linguistic, cultural, and social backgrounds are taken into account.

14. Standards and assessment. Setting appropriately high and challenging standards and assessing the learner as well as learning progress—including diagnostic, process, and outcome assessment—are integral parts of the learning process. (APA, 1995, pp. 8–9)

We believe that these principles provide a solid underpinning for the development of a curriculum that encompasses diversity as well as a set of guidelines for a revised system of educational assessment. As stated in the principles: "The same basic principles of learning, motivation, and effective instruction apply to all learners. However, language, ethnicity, race, beliefs, and socioeconomic status all can influence learning" (APA, 1995, p. 9). This and other comments throughout the document demonstrate that the learner-centered principles have made diversity an integral part of the educational reform effort. Clearly, we applaud this effort. As we have indicated throughout this chapter, however, applying the "basic principles" of learning in a context where diversity is given priority is a formidable challenge. This challenge takes on even greater difficulty when accountability is accepted as a legitimate demand.

Although we do not want to overemphasize the difficulty, we do want to stress the enormity and complexity of the task facing educators who take seriously learner-centered principles. As the APA's principles state, assessment must accommodate individual differences in learning and diversity in cultural and social factors while establishing challenging standards. In addition, the current reform efforts envision standards explicitly tied to accountability, and accountability has almost always meant a consistent and uniform reporting system. Uniformity and consistency have almost always meant the use of standardized tests rather than assessment of what an individual student has learned over time. Moreover, there are an increasing number of calls for an assessment system that can contribute to the instructional needs of students, diagnose learning strengths and weaknesses, and provide valuable and accessible information to teachers, parents, and students to help develop strategies to improve achievement. Can these varied purposes of testing and assessment be incorporated into one acceptable assessment strategy? If such a task is technically possible, can such a system be afforded in this time of shrinking education budgets and rollbacks in many programs? As we argue in the rest of this chapter, this is a daunting challenge, but not an unsolvable one.

Restating the Dilemma

Thus far we have presented a review of two major contemporary themes—namely, a curriculum of diversity on one hand, and educational assessment as seen in expectations regarding accountability on the other—to highlight what we perceive as a dilemma. We should emphasize that the major proponents of both positions have generally taken the public stance that their views are reconcilable. But what is possible in theory may not be as possible in the day-to-day reality of America's classrooms.

As we have previously stated, it is our opinion that both positions, taken to their logical extremes, are essentially contradictory. Moreover, we believe that the forces at work in American society—forces which have generated these positions in the first place—not only can, but will take them to their logical conclusions. At that point, the question becomes whether learner-centered principles will have an opportunity to work, or whether the political climate is so unstable and inflammatory that the competing forces in our society will have a corrosive effect on reform efforts.

If the curriculum of American schools is to move away from a unified view, it is hard to believe that this process can be limited in any legitimate way. American society is diverse in many ways and, as we have indicated in our definition of diversity, all of these ways can have an impact on learning. Consequently, each aspect of diversity could (or should, if the strongest proponents of multiculturalism are taken into account) become elements of the curriculum. Race, gender, social class, ethnicity, sexual orientation, disability, bilingualism, and different learning styles are all legitimate arenas for curricular development. If students learn better when the curriculum reflects their unique backgrounds (as the APA principles rightfully contend), then a curriculum that appreciates differences is a curriculum with almost infinite variation. Moreover, such a curriculum will vary from one region of the country to another, from one school district to another, even from one class within a school to another class within the same school. This variation will occur, in theory, even when high, rigorous content standards are maintained across districts, schools, and classrooms. The enormous impact of such learner variation on achievement is precisely what is stated in APA's Principle 13, which speaks of the power of linguistic, cultural, and social backgrounds to affect learning.

From the perspective of those who believe in a curriculum of diversity, the previous depiction of the implications of difference is neither negative nor frightening. For those who equate testing to accountability, however, the depiction must seem a nightmare. If national or state standards are to be developed, and if the attainment of these standards is to be assessed in a way that is comparable for all students, then inconsistent curricula are inherently indefensible. How can communities produce a report card for the nation (to use a term in common use) if students are learning different material, at different times and under different conditions, although the element of high standards is never negated? How can numbers reflecting the attainment of national goals be produced (for as a nation we have become so used to capturing reality by numbers that anything less would be considered a dereliction of duty) if there is no consistent core of information on which many elements of the curriculum are based? How can we meet the APA's call for diagnostic, process, and outcome assessment (Principle 14) in any meaningful, valid, and useful way if each student—to carry the idea to a logical conclusion—is treated as a completely unique recipient of a completely individualized yet rigorous curriculum?

And so we believe that there is a dilemma. Taken to their extremes, a curriculum of diversity and the accountability movement leave American schools with a difficult choice: curricula that are varied, complex, and highly responsive to learner needs, but that may be fragmented and surely unmanageable from a traditional assessment perspective; or, curricula that are consistent, uniform, and easily assessed through standardized means, but that exclude the ways of knowing of a large and growing number of American students. Stated differently, the dilemma we face is to implement the APA's Principles 1 through 11 in the face of individual differences and diversity principles (i.e., Principles 12 and 13), while developing a meaningful way to adopt Principle 14 on standards and assessment.

Assessment and Accountability in the Context of Learner-Centered Principles

In this section of the chapter, we focus on alternative assessment as one way of confronting the dilemma facing educators who are attempting to develop and apply APA's learner-centered principles in the context of accountability and diversity. If one accepts the premise that some form of accountability is necessary and assumes that standardized tests will inevitably constitute a major element of the assessment package, a broadened assessment process that includes a variety of measurement instruments becomes absolutely crucial. But what criteria will be used to determine the choice of tests or procedures? From a psychometric perspective, whether the purpose of assessment is focused on cognitive, achievement, or personality factors, the emphasis will be on tests and measurement approaches in which psychometric properties such as reliability and validity are well established. This will certainly be true if the discussion focuses on psychological principles, for standard psychometric theory is one of psychology's major achievements. Others will unquestionably raise issues concerning the negative consequences or outcomes inherent in the psychometric tradition of testing. Thus, they are likely to propose alternative assessment approaches to meet a variety of assessment objectives without giving the technical psychometric criteria primary consideration.

Our intention in highlighting differences among an increasingly diverse population with the objective of examining individual learner and group differences in achievement is to suggest that no one model of assessment can fulfill the political, professional, and individual purposes of assessment. Differences in achievement attributable to factors related to learning styles, sociocultural experiences, racial and ethnic distinctiveness, and levels of ability necessarily require an assessment system diverse in conceptualization, ideology, methodology, and purpose. In this context, we refer to several orientations for assessment. These approaches will diversify the assessment process to satisfy a wide range of purposes associated with accountability, learning and instructional processes, and diagnostic objectives.

In the context of national political objectives, the use of standardized tests as measures of cognitive ability, academic achievement, or "competence" is currently viewed by policy makers as a catalyst for school reform. The currency and pervasiveness of this belief was well captured by a recent editorial in *Education Week* (Bleich, 1995):

> [S]tandardized tests are among the most useful tools we have to help students calibrate their work to a higher standard; for teachers to identify problem areas in their students' abilities and in their own teaching; and for the public to gauge school and student performance.... Test results set a common competitive standard colleagues and employers value and students and teachers can use to compare their own results against. If a disadvantaged student wants to attend Harvard, go to medical school, or become a police cadet, he or she will need to know what is required and how to pass the appropriate tests. Tests show students what they are expected to know and be able to do and how well they perform. (p. 33)

This editorial, whose sentiments could be duplicated endlessly, stresses the underlying belief that many of the significant outcomes of education can be objectively measured and that the preferred method of such measurement is norm-referenced standardized tests. Highly touted international achievement standards, the merits of widely differing restructuring efforts, differential effects of various instructional strategies, and individual differences in learning ability and achievement are all expected to be assessed by these tests. And because assessment, implicitly or explicitly, continues to drive the curriculum, the nature of this assessment has become one of the major issues of concern and controversy in contemporary educational practice (Sewell & Hines, in press; Shapiro, Sewell, & DuCette, 1995). We therefore accept the premise that accountability, as publicly defined, is necessary and assume that standardized tests will inevitably constitute one important element of the assessment process. However, despite our acceptance of standardized tests as part of the assessment package, we advocate a broadening of the assessment process to include such alternate forms of assessment as performance assessment, portfolios, and dynamic assessment.

This approach acknowledges that strides are being made in test construction and that those who design standardized tests are beginning to take into account multiple intelligences as well as alternative forms of assessment. For example, Gardner and Hatch (1989) and Sternberg (1990) are developing assessment devices focusing on multiple intelligences as a way of assessing cognitive performance. Additionally, the Educational Testing Service (ETS) and the American College Testing Program (ACT) are designing and pilot testing standardized tests that focus on alternative forms of measurement. Of all the alternative forms, performance assessment appears to hold the promise of standardization more than any of the others. Thus, ETS and ACT seem to have made a commitment to redesigning tests with performance assessment in mind. In this way, standardized test designers have either recognized the merits of alternative assessment or, more cynically, hope to pacify critics who charge that standardized tests do not tap higher order thinking nor do they measure multiple intelligences.

Alternative Assessment

It logically follows from everything that has been said up to this point that the choice of assessment procedures should be dictated by the testing objectives. Darling-Hammond (1994) stated this well in her summary of the lack of educational utility of many standardized tests:

> For most of this century, much of the energy of the U.S. measurement experts has been invested in developing tests aimed at ranking students for sorting and selecting them into and out of particular placements. Standardized test developers have devoted much less energy to worrying about the properties of these instruments as reflections of—or influences on—instruction. As a consequence, the tests generally do not reflect actual tasks educators and citizens expect students to be able to perform, nor do they stimulate forms of instruction that are closely connected to development of performance abilities. (p. 23)

Along with our belief that the testing objectives should determine the choice of assessment procedures, we also agree that "We need some measures that would allow students to pursue their own strengths, interests, and ways of demonstrating knowledge" (Viadero, 1994, pp. 24–25).

Wiggins (1989, 1991) made a point similar to Darling-Hammond's when he argued that educational assessment should use standards, but that standardization, in its common psychometric sense, should be eliminated. Wiggins is not alone in his thinking as there is widespread disdain for standardized tests because of their inherent biases against poor and minority children. The elimination of standardized testing has been frequently discussed, particularly when these tests are used to make high-stake decisions about students (Garcia & Pearson, 1994; Glaser & Silver, 1994).

However, because of our belief that assessment choices should be appropriate to testing objectives, we are aware that as long as educational accountability is a goal, there will continue to be expectations that some kinds of standardized comparisons be made. Turning away from a psychometric approach to assessment, it seems to us that alternative assessment approaches may have the potential to recognize students' instructional needs and their differences in learning styles, as well as the enormous shift in teaching–learning processes based on new standards and new knowledge bases in curriculum content. This premise is stated forcefully by Resnick and Resnick (1992): "Alternative forms of assessment, forms currently within reach, can adequately reflect today's educational goals and, if properly used, serve as positive tools in creating schools truly capable of teaching students to think" (p. 38).

Despite the recent trend toward using these alternative assessment methods to attain the goal of accountability, underlying the alternative or so-called authentic approaches is a continuing emphasis on the instructional process of learning, particularly from a longitudinal perspective. Glaser and Silver (1994) concur: "In this vision of the future, testing is seen as being less about sorting and selecting and more about offering information on which students and teachers can build" (p. 412).

The new forms tend to be more qualitative than quantitative. They also tend to be more process than product oriented, although they do include such approaches as performance assessment, which is really an end product, but preferably not in a standardized test format (Hutchings, 1989). Under the rubric of alternative assessment, there are portfolios (Camp, 1990; Hutchings, 1990; Murphy & Smith, 1990; Walters & Gardner, 1981; Walters & Seidel, 1991), student journals, dialogic journals, teacher logs (Cohen, Landa, & Tarule, 1990; Silberman, 1989), and other innovative assessment approaches designed to determine what students are learning over time. These types of assessments also include one of the oldest forms of alternative assessment (Garcia & Pearson, 1994): dynamic assessment (Feuerstein, 1979; Sewell, 1987).

Above all, these diverse forms of assessment resist labeling a student based on a single test result.

Complex times with complex interdisciplinary knowledge bases require complex ways of assessing what students have learned. However, rather than try to cover all of the forms of alternative assessment that are being discussed and used in this era, we focus briefly on three forms: portfolio assessment, performance assessment, and dynamic assessment. These seem most suited to dealing with the issues of assessment within the parameters established by APA's learner-centered principles and have the ability to assist students with not only improving their learning but with preparing them for taking and doing well on standardized tests.

Portfolio Assessment

Portfolio assessment has been defined by Hutchings (1990) as a collection of student work done over time. It has also been defined by Walters and Seidel (1991) as "a record of learning that focuses on students' work and their reflections on that work" (p. 1). Beyond these broad definitions, the collection or record is often varied: some portfolios include only written work; others contain a broader array of materials that may resemble products (Hutchings, 1990).

Perhaps portfolio assessment has emerged as a major form of alternative assessment because of the variety of instruction-related decisions that the portfolio can be used to make. From an instructional perspective, Murphy and Smith (1990) cited essential features of the teaching–learning process—student motivation, self-assessment, personal growth monitoring, curriculum revisions—in which portfolio assessment can be used.

Unquestionably, the most positive aspect of portfolio assessment is its focus on self-assessment for the student (Walters, Seidel, & Gardner, 1994). Critical appraisal of one's own work should ultimately lead to higher level thinking and to providing rich products for assessment (Travers, 1991). In answering, for example, what is one's best and worse work and why, teachers can learn a great deal about the thinking processes of their students. Above all, students can learn a great deal about themselves and reflect on how and what they learn.

Performance Assessment

When not used in a standardized form, *performance assessment* is another promising alternative approach (Chittenden, 1991). Its focus on the direct measurement of performance has the distinct advantage of assessing complex processes associated with the learning or mastery of specific tasks across the curriculum in a variety of contexts. It is frequently viewed as a culminating project for students to accomplish as one final test of *knowledge in action* (Hutchings, 1989). This concept is derived from the arts where a senior-level recital, exhibit, or performance of some kind occurs. Performance assessment has the potential to affect achievement through the motivation of students, their academic self-evaluation, and the monitoring of their personal growth.

An interesting and informative review of performance assessment in medical fields, where it has been used for many years, has recently been published (Swanson, Norman, & Linn, 1995). The authors present several lessons that they believe have been learned from the use of performance assessment in these specific areas. These lessons concern both the strengths and weaknesses of performance assessment, as well as several practical issues that anyone attempting to use this type of assessment must consider. They conclude their article by saying

> Performance-based tests, used well, can clearly assess skills that cannot be measured with traditional tests. At the same time, performance-based tests have significant disadvantages as well, in large part because of context specificity: Scores do not generalize well across situations and tasks. As a result, in areas where assessment of breadth of knowledge and skills is a major concern, the testing time and resource requirements for performance-based assessment to achieve adequate domain coverage make these methods impractical. (p. 11)

The authors recommend that a blend of both alternative and traditional assessment is desirable. Of special interest is their comment that performance assessment has had its greatest impact on multiple choice tests used for licensing purposes in medical areas. These licensing tests now consist almost exclusively of items based on simulations of decision-making situations in patient care. Although this technique may not be completely generalizable to all achievement domains, many of the lessons learned in the relatively narrow arena of medical examinations are likely to be relevant to other domains.

Overall, then, performance assessment offers a potentially valuable addition to traditional tests. This type of assessment allows students the opportunity to demonstrate competence in ways that can use their strengths, and can be flexible in handling individual differences. The following summary by Swanson, Norman, and Linn (1995), although again focusing on medical examinations, seems a reasonable conclusion for this area in general:

> The use of a battery of methods, combining the efficient sampling of . . . written tests with complementary in-depth performance-based assessment, should be more successful than the use of either family of methods in isolation, both psychometrically and educationally. (p. 11)

Dynamic Assessment

Dynamic assessment (Feuerstein, 1979; Sewell, 1987) is a process-sensitive model of assessment designed to facilitate the instructional needs of students. Assuming that one accepts the proposition that assessment should help fuel the educational reform movement, then priority must be given to the instructional advantage of the assessment procedure. It is in this context that dynamic assessment procedures with a focus on linking assessment to the prescriptive and instructional needs of students claim an impressive advantage. For if cultural experiences have poorly equipped the student to deal with standardized tests, intervention in the assessment process becomes crucial in determining instructional needs, learning potential, and levels of academic attainment.

Educational intervention generated from every conceivable school reform movement is geared to bring about change in students' performance. The nature of cognitive competence and how responsive specific learning problems are to instruction are at the core of the theoretical or pragmatic concerns for low-achieving students. The emphasis on both the processes and products of assessment is the unique feature of a variety of approaches to dynamic assessment that have demonstrated diagnostic and instructional sensitivity to the needs of the learner (Day & Cordón, 1993; Pena, Quinn, & Iglesias, 1992; Spector, 1992). The interactive nature of the testing situation in dynamic assessment provides the opportunity to explore areas of perceived deficits or weaknesses with the ultimate goal of assessing strategies for modifiability.

From a multicultural perspective, dynamic assessment has the potential to be helpful with students who are learning English as a second language. Through a process in which teachers are encouraged to provide increasing amounts of instructional support (what Bruner, 1985, calls *scaffolding*) or social guidance (Gamlin, 1989) to determine which tasks students can complete independently and which they can complete with varying levels of assistance (Garcia & Pearson, 1994), dynamic assessment displays possibilities for increasing a student's ability to comprehend and translate another language. It is even possible that the interactive nature of dynamic assessment in some ways may simulate the interactive process of mother–child relations in a home when a first language is being informally taught (Sewell & Price, 1991). The underlying assumption of dynamic assessment is that any student—irrespective of social class, race, ethnicity, or gender—can complete a task, provided that the appropriate amount of social guidance or scaffolding is offered.

Dynamic assessment has at its heart the broader issues of social justice and equality of educational opportunities. The assessment paradigm of dynamic assessment enables children from diverse backgrounds to have a chance to succeed (Babad & Budoff, 1974). However, Sewell (1987) provided a caveat when they wrote

> It should not be assumed that the high potential of any low-socioeconomic-status child, determined by the degree of modifiability considered feasible, will be necessarily translated into school achievement. If this is not happening, that is, if those children with demonstrated capability of learning are not learning, the focus of assessment should be redirected from the child to the instructional program, the family, the community, and not least of all, to the social system where social and political ideologies often determine educability as well as retardation. (p. 441)

Conclusion: Equity and Assessment

In this chapter, we have discussed various forms of alternative assessment as one of the ways out of the dilemma created by the call for a curriculum responsive to diversity in the face of mounting calls for increased accountability throughout all aspects of American education. We reemphasize our belief that both of these movements are inevitable, and that simply dismissing one or the other is neither wise nor legitimate. This dilemma places the issue of assessment where it belongs: at the heart of the educational process. For despite skepticism and denial, assessment has frequently driven and continues to drive the curriculum. This point is at least tacitly recognized in the 14 APA learner-centered principles, which culminate in the principle presenting APA's views on assessment.

Psychological and educational assessment have substantially influenced the theory, research, and practice in education related to human growth and development, intellectual ability, sound learning, and instructional methods. It is noteworthy that long-standing traditions in education embraced objectives and practices in which the scientific knowledge from psychology, particularly standardized testing, made substantial contributions. If labeling, tracking, sorting, selection, and diagnosis for special class placement were primary needs of the educational process, standardized testing provided the philosophical rationale and the empirical justification for its preeminent status. But the new waves of educational reform, embedded in a changing political and cultural climate, have broadened the dimensions underpinning the purposes of assessment. For as Curtis and Glaser (1981) noted, "In a society struggling to provide equal opportunities for all its members, classification and predicting are no longer the prevalent social needs" (p. 133). Thus, the complex issues that have emerged are broadly debated within the context of the following three objectives: accountability, instructional benefits, and equity and social justice.

Driven by powerful international competitive economic forces, the current school reform movement is marked by transformed cultural expectations that achievement in America's schools will reach world-class standards. Furthermore, if our children are achieving high rigorous standards, it should be documented in a scientific manner that permits valid and reliable data for comparative analysis based on individual, state, and national performance. It should not be surprising, therefore, that accountability is deeply interwoven in the rhetoric of the reform literature. In the political climate in which American education finds itself at the end of the 20th century, this movement toward higher standards represents an imperative that can be neither denied nor ignored. This premise was summarized well by Lewis (1995) when she stated

> For the past half-century, the standards represented in texts and tests have reflected the commercial market for "dumbed-down" resources to a greater degree than they have reflected any public consensus on what teachers should teach and students should learn. Until recently, state policies were also mired in a swamp of low standards, as states put their energies and resources into the pursuit of functional literacy or the design of basic competency tests.
>
> The current debate is about much higher standards. It is driven by what we have learned about children's cognitive growth and by what we know of the curricula in other countries. Moreover, the process of developing standards has been open to professional and public scrutiny, not tightly guarded and exclusive, as in the devel-

opment of a textbook. This very openness has invited controversy.
(p. 746)

In light of this movement toward higher standards, and the controversy that surrounds it (see, e.g., Cohen, 1995), the *Learner-Centered Principles* should be able to play a central role. With their emphasis on learners and their deemphasis on curricular and administrative issues, the principles can fulfill the goal of providing "an essential framework to be incorporated in new designs for curriculum and instruction, assessment systems for evaluating educational goal attainments, as well as for the systemic redesign of professional development programs and educational system structures" (APA, 1995, p. 2). By constantly focusing on the learner, and by emphasizing those psychological and pedagogical principles that can facilitate the attainment of the high standards that are now so much in vogue, the principles represent one of the best hopes to navigate the treacherous political waters that constitute the current national debate on educational reform.

Our intention in this chapter was not to debate whether high standards are necessary, nor even to question whether it is important to assess what students know and are able to do. Clearly, the political climate, if nothing else, makes both of these questions moot. Because educational reform will always be both an educational and a political process, the central issue is to develop the best set of educational standards and the fairest system of educational assessment possible while meeting the political demands for accountability. The fundamental problem is that the history of testing in America does not engender confidence that the standards, and the standardized tests that are so likely to assess them, will address the myriad concerns surrounding diversity and learner differences, opportunity to learn, and the contributions of assessment to instructional practices. The central problem is the expectation that our assessment procedures reflect the fundamental democratic tenets of fairness and equity without sacrificing individual differences in learning as embodied in the learner-centered psychological principles.

It must be recalled that, from its inception in America, standardized testing incorporated a political philosophy that reflected the cultural and racial bias of the nation and established differential academic expectations among various racial, ethnic, and social class groups. Nevertheless, standardized tests, based on the psychometric model—one of psychology's most telling accomplishments—have the capacity to produce understandable achievement data in a relatively efficient manner and thus satisfy the public's demand for accountability. The central problem, however, is that it has considerable limitations in being responsive to the individuality that is called for by a curriculum that incorporates a broad range of diversity. From an historical perspective, standardized testing has not sensitively factored into its assumptions the glaring discrepancies in opportunity to learn, nor has it focused on the instructional needs or pedagogical concerns that must be the cornerstone of reform efforts.

At the heart of the reform movement is the objective of raising the academic performance of students. Assessment as manifested in a traditional standardized testing format is inadequate to contribute to this objective. Alternative assessment, which is conceptually rooted in its responsiveness to individual characteristics and learning needs, is perceived to be the assessment approach most likely to fulfill the higher achievement levels envisioned by the reform agenda. This approach to assessment, however, has not yet established the validity and reliability in technical properties to elicit the confidence of the stakeholders: parents, politicians, educators, and pundits. Assessment procedures must now satisfy at least these two pronounced and distinct objectives and herein lies the dilemma and the challenge.

How, then, can the dilemma be solved? We do not pretend to have a complete answer, but we believe that certain principles can serve as starting points for the discussion:

1. The standardized tests that will inevitably form a part of the assessment process must be constructed, validated, scored, and used in a way that incorporates and values diversity. As we have repeatedly stated throughout this chapter, contemporary standardized achievement tests do not offer the options needed for assessing what children have learned in a complex era in which a diverse curriculum is being developed and used in many schools. No matter how reliable and valid these standardized tests are, they will be too narrow and limited in their scope unless diversity is explicitly recognized and valued. Additionally, these tests demonstrate only one way that children learn. They may not properly demonstrate what other children learn because some have exceptionalities, some come from different cultures, and some simply have different ways of knowing.

   Furthermore, a test score is not always equitable, of course, because all children have not had and still do not have the basic opportunity to learn. Those who come from poverty often arrive in schools battered from an environment that has made it difficult for them to even reach the schoolhouse door, let alone be prepared for taking standardized tests. Unlike their middle-class peers, these students often do not have the help at home they need nor have they learned the skills for being "test-wise." Thus, a one-shot test designed in such a way that certain children are better prepared to take it than others appears to be an inappropriate measure of what all children really know.

Additionally, standardized tests are designed in such a way that students are not treated with respect, but instead are forced to undergo a process characterized by secrecy rather than openness, by anxiety rather than comfort, and by summative rather than by formative evaluation where no feedback for improvement is provided. On this issue, Wiggins (1993) wrote

> To develop an educational system based on the premise that all children will learn, we need assessment systems that treat each student with respect, assume greater promise about gains (and seek to measure them), and offer more worthy tasks and helpful feedback than are provided in our current culture of one short, "secure" testing. (p. 6)

It is obvious that standardized tests of the type Wiggins is criticizing do not have the focus on student learning that APA advocates. It is unarguably the case that the time has long since passed when this form of test, and this type of testing procedure, should have been eliminated as the primary means to make judgments about individuals. Psychologists have spent a considerable portion of the 20th century developing and using sophisticated and complex psychometric principles. As Garcia and Pearson (1994) pointed out, this model suffers from a "mainstream bias," which systematically penalizes anyone who differs from the norm. But what has been historically true about psychology's development and use of standard psychometric theory does not need to be true in the future. In all likelihood, these principles can be modified to reflect diversity. We do not lack the tools to make this change; what we seem to lack is the will. It is time for this change to take place.

2. Alternative assessment must be given equal weight in the assessment process. We believe that it is not enough to simply use various forms of alternative assessments such as portfolios, performance appraisal, or dynamic assessment. These forms must

be allowed equal weight in any assessment system in which decisions are made concerning individual students. As several writers have pointed out (Walters & Gardner, 1981; Wiggins, 1993), standardized tests are useful for aggregate reporting of the type where schools, districts, and states are evaluated, whereas alternative assessment is valuable for investigating individual growth. This is an acceptable use of the current technology in assessment, and these applications present no major problems in themselves. Systems must be developed, however, where standardized tests can also be used to reflect individual growth, and alternative assessment can be used for accountability and aggregate reporting as well. This will require a major shift in emphasis, but, as before, the time has come for this shift to occur.

3. Finally, and most important, it is time for equity to become a major underlying principle in all educational assessment. The evidence is compelling that all children are not beginning at the same starting point in reference to equal opportunity to learn and achieve. In reality, the assumption that individuals at a given chronological age or grade level would have been exposed to the relevant information in order to correctly respond to a test question on a standardized test is decidedly wrong. In light of our discussion, one might ask such questions as the following: Can equity exist when many of the standardized tests continue to have racial, gender, and social class biases? Can equity in assessment ever occur when some children come to testing situations from lives battered by drugs, crime, violence, toxicity, poor nutrition, and ill health, while others come from an environment hardly affected by such factors?

In summary, we believe that APA's learner-centered principles, with their explicit recognition of diversity as a focal point for educational reform, have the potential to place equity for the student at the center of any discussion of assessment. The application of these principles can lead in the direction of an assessment system that displaces standardized tests from their historical place of prominence. As stated previously, we also believe that current national reports have placed too much emphasis on accountability monitored by standardized tests rather than on student improvement by educational assessment over time. Above all, we hope that these learner-centered principles are taken seriously and create an environment in which equitable approaches to assess student learning will be discussed, debated, challenged and ultimately selected with care.

References

America 2000: An education strategy. (1991). Washington, DC: U.S. Government Printing Office.

American Psychological Association Board of Educational Affairs. (1995, Dec.). *Learner-centered principles: A Framework for school redesign and reform* [On-line]. Available: http://www.apa.org/ed/lcp.html.

Babad, E., & Budoff, M. (1974). Sensitivity and validity of learning potential measurement in three levels of ability. *Journal of Educational Psychology, 66,* 439–447.

Banks, J. A. (1991). *Teaching strategies for ethnic studies.* Boston: Allyn and Bacon.

Banks, J. A. (1993). The canon debate, knowledge construction, and multicultural education. *Educational Researcher, 22*(5), 4–14.

Bleich, M. (1995, June 14). All schools can learn. *Education Week, 14*(38), 4–7.

Brown, C. (1992). Restructuring for a new America. In M. Dilworth (Ed.), *Diversity in teacher education: New expectations* (pp. 1–22). San Francisco: Jossey-Bass.

Bruner, J. (1985). Vygotsky: A historical and conceptual perspective. In J. V. Wertsch (Ed.), *Culture, communication and cognition: Vygotskian perspectives.* New York: Cambridge University Press.

Camp, R. (1990). Thinking together about portfolios. *The Quarterly of the National Writing Project and the Center for the Study of Writing, 12*(2), 8–24.

Chittenden, E. (1991). Authentic assessment, evaluation, and documentation of student performance. In V. Perrone (Ed.), *Expanding student assessment* (pp. 22–31). Washington, DC: Association for Supervision and Curriculum Development.

Cohen, D. (1995). What standards for national standards. *Phi Delta Kappan, 76*(10), 751–757.

Cohen, S. B., Landa, A. M., & Tarule, J. M. (1990). *The collaborative learning assessment packet.* Cambridge, MA: Lesley College.

Curtis, M. E., & Glaser, R. (1981). Changing conceptions of intelligence. *Review of Research in Education 9,* 111–148.

Cushner, K., McClelland, A., & Safford, P. (1989). *Human diversity in education.* New York: McGraw-Hill.

Darling-Hammond, L. (1994). Performance-based assessment and educational equity. *Harvard Educational Review, 64*(1), 5–29.

Day, J., & Cordón, L. A. (1993). Static and dynamic measures of ability: An experimental comparison. *Journal of Educational Psychology, 85*(1), 75–82.

DuCette, J. P., Shapiro, J. P., & Sewell, T. E. (1992, April). *Cultural diversity, national testing, and the multicultural curriculum.* Paper presented at the annual meeting of the American Educational Research Association, San Francisco.

DuCette, J. P., Shapiro, J. P., & Sewell, T. E. (1995). Diversity in education: Problems and possibilities. In F. Murray (Ed.), *The teacher educators' handbook* (pp. 323–380). San Francisco: Jossey-Bass.

Feuerstein, R. (1979). *The dynamic assessment of retarded performers: The learning potential assessment device, theory, instruments, and techniques.* Baltimore: University Park Press.

Gamlin, P. J. (1989). Issues in dynamic assessment/instruction. *The International Journal of Dynamic Assessment and Instruction, 1*(1), 13–25.

Gandal, M. (1995). Not all standards are created equal. *Educational Leadership, 52*(6), 16–21.

Garcia, G. E., & Pearson, P. D. (1994). Assessment and diversity. In L. Darling-Hammond (Ed.), *Review of research in education* (Vol. 20, pp. 337–389). Washington, DC: American Educational Research Association.

Gardner, H., & Hatch, T. (1989). The multiple intelligences go to school. *Educational Researcher, 18,* 4–10.

Glaser, R., & Silver, E. (1994). Assessment, testing, and instruction: Retrospect and prospect. In L. Darling-Hammond (Ed.), *Review of research in education* (Vol. 20, pp. 393–419). Washington, DC: American Educational Research Association.

Goals 2000: Educate America Act. (1993). Washington, DC: U.S. Government Printing Office.

Gollnick, D. M. (1992a). Multicultural education: Policies and practices in teacher education. In C. A. Grant (Ed.), *Research and multicultural education* (pp. 218–239). London: Falmer.

Gollnick, D. M. (1992b). Understanding the dynamics of race, class, and gender. In M. E. Dilworth (Ed.), *Diversity in teacher education: New expectations* (pp. 63–78). San Francisco: Jossey-Bass.

Grant, C. A., & Secada, W. G. (1991). Preparing teachers for diversity. In W. R. Huston (Ed.), *Handbook of research on teacher education* (pp. 403–422). New York: MacMillan.

Haladyna, T. M., Nolen, S. B., & Haas, N. C. (1991). Raising standardized achievement test scores and the origins of test score pollution. *Educational Researcher, 20*(5), 2–7.

Hutchings, P. (1989). *Behind outcomes: Contexts and questions for assessment.* Washington, DC: American Association of Higher Education.

Hutchings, P. (1990). Learning over time: Portfolio assessment. *American Association of Higher Education Bulletin, 42*(8), 6–8.

Jackson, B. (1991, November). *The school reform reports and commissions: Where is gender?* Paper presented at the University Council for Educational Administration Convention, Baltimore.

Lewis, A. C. (1995). An overview of the standards movement. *Phi Delta Kappan, 76*(10), 744–750.

Murphy, S., & Smith, M. A. (1990). Talking about portfolios. *The Quarterly of the National Writing Project and the Center for the Study of Writing, 12*(1), 1–3.

National Commission on Excellence in Education. (1983). *A nation at risk: The imperative for educational reform.* Washington, DC: U.S. Government Printing Office.

Pena, E., Quinn, R., & Iglesias, A. (1992). The application of dynamic methods to language assessment: A nonbiased procedure. *Journal of Special Education, 26*(3), 269–280.

Pitsch, M. (1995). Goals 2000 fails to gain firm foothold. *Education Week, 14*(37), 12–14.

Resnick, L. B., & Resnick, D. P. (1992). Assessing the thinking curriculum: New tools for educational reform. In B. R. Gifford & M. C. O'Connor (Eds.), *Changing assessment: Alternative view of aptitude, achievement and instruction* (pp. 37–75). Boston: Kluwer.

Schwarz, B. (1995). The diversity myth: American's leading export. *The Atlantic Monthly, 275,* 57–66.

Sewell, T. E. (1987). Dynamic assessment as a nondiscriminatory procedure. In C. Lidz (Ed.), *Dynamic assessment.* New York: Guilford.

Sewell, T. E., DuCette, J. P., & Shapiro, J. P. (1991). *Cultural diversity and educational assessment.* Paper presented at the 99th Annual Convention of the American Psychological Association, San Francisco.

Sewell, T. E., & Hines, C. (in press). Restructuring American schools: A perspective on testing and assessment. In L. Castenell & J. Tarule (Eds.), *The minority voice in educational reform: An analysis by minority and women college of education deans.* New York: Ablex.

Sewell, T. E., & Price, V. D. (1991). Mediated learning experience: Implications for achievement motivation and cognitive performance in low socio-economic and minority children. In R. Feuerstein, P. Klein, & A. Tannenbaum (Eds.), *Mediated learning experience: Theoretical, psychological and learning implications.* London: Freund Publishing House.

Shapiro, J. P., Sewell, T. E., & DuCette, J. P. (1992). *Towards a resolution of a paradox between diversity and accountability for school administrators: Application of the principles of feminist assessment.* Paper presented at the University Council for Educational Administration Convention, Minneapolis, MN.

Shapiro, J. P., Sewell, T. E., & DuCette, J. P. (1995). *Reframing diversity in education.* Lancaster, PA: Technomic Publishing.

Silberman, A. (1989). *Growing up writing.* New York: Time Books.

Spector, J. (1992). Predicting progress in beginning reading: Dynamic assessment of phonemic awareness. *Journal of Educational Psychology, 84*(3), 353–363.

Sternberg, R. (1990). *Wisdom: Its nature, origins, and development.* New York: Cambridge University Press.

Swanson, D. B., Norman, G. R., & Linn, R. L. (1995). Performance-based assessment: Lessons from the health professions. *Educational Researcher, 24*(5), 5–12.

Tek Lum, W. (1987). *Expounding the doubtful points.* Honolulu, HI: Bamboo Ridge Press.

Tetreault, M. K. T. (1989). Integrating content about women and gender into the curriculum. In J. A. Banks and C. A. McGee Banks (Eds.), *Multicultural education: Issues and perspectives* (pp. 124–144). Boston: Allyn and Bacon.

Travers, J. R. (1991). Testing in educational placement: Issues and evidence. In K. Heller, W. Holtzman, & S. Messick (Eds.), *Placing children in special education: A strategy for equity* (pp. 230–261). Washington, DC: National Academy Press.

Viadero, D. (1994). Teaching to the test. *Education Week, 13*(39), 21–25.

Walters, J., & Gardner, H. (1981). *Portfolios of student projects: Continuing research on a new approach to assessment* (Project Zero Report to the Lilly Endowment). Cambridge, MA: Harvard Graduate School of Education.

Walters, J., & Seidel, S. (1991). *The design of portfolios for authentic student assessment.* Cambridge, MA: Harvard Graduate School of Education.

Walters, J., Seidel, S., & Gardner, H. (1994). Children as reflective practitioners: Bringing metacognition to the classroom. In C. Collins & J. Mangieri (Eds.), *Mindfulness: Creating powerful thinkers* (pp. 145–164). Fort Worth, TX: Harcourt, Brace, and Jovanovich.

Wiggins, G. P. (1989). A true test: Towards a more authentic and equitable assessment. *Phi Delta Kappan, 70,* 703–713.

Wiggins, G. (1991). Standards, not standardization: Evoking quality student work. *Educational Leadership, 48*(5), 18–25.

Wiggins, G. P. (1993). *Assessing student performance.* San Francisco: Jossey-Bass.

Dilemmas in Assessing Academic Achievement

Andrew C. Porter

he United States is in the middle of the most ambitious curriculum reform ever undertaken. The essence of this curriculum reform can be seen in our national educational goal:

> By the year 2000, all students will leave grades 4, 8, and 12 having demonstrated competency over challenging subject matter including English, mathematics, science, ... history, and geography, and every school in America will ensure that all students learn to use their minds well, so that they may be prepared for responsible citizenship, further learning, and productive employment in our nation's modern economy. (*Goals 2000*, 1994)

The phrases in this goal that characterize today's curriculum reform are "challenging subject matter," "learn to use their minds," and "all students." Clearly if all students are to reach this goal, the school curriculum will need to be revised to reflect a much greater emphasis on knowledge use in a variety of applications. The shift in curriculum emphasis will need to occur not only for the academically elite, but for students who struggle as well. The reference to "demonstrated competency" makes clear that assessment is to play a prominent role in pursuing the goal.

Like the American Psychological Association's (APA) *Learner-Centered Psychological Principles: A Framework for School Redesign and Reform* (APA, 1995), the national education goal focuses on student learning. As stated in the *Learner-Centered Psychological Principles*, "Educational

This article draws heavily from a presentation at the Assessing Learning and Educational Achievement Conference sponsored by The American Psychological Association and the Mid-Continent Regional Educational Laboratory, Wingspread, CO, November 8–9, 1991.

practice will be most likely to improve when the educational system is redesigned with a primary focus on the learner'' (p. 3). Goals and assessment are key pieces of the education system.

In pursuing the reforms necessary to reach the national education goal, most of the assessment work has been at the policy level. A great deal of effort is being given to changing assessments at the national (e.g., National Assessment of Educational Progress [NAEP]) and at the state levels. External assessments at the national, state, and even district levels of the education hierarchy, however, often do a poor job of centering attention on the classroom and are rarely designed to assess student progress in learning. Instead, they are used for descriptive and accountability purposes at macro-levels. These external assessments do frequently (but not always) report individual student performance, but they rarely assess student achievement at frequent enough intervals to be good assessments of growth in achievement at the student level. Thus, there are several ways in which the changes in assessment are not as tightly tied to the *Learner-Centered Psychological Principles* as might be desired.

The purpose of the present chapter is to consider the several dilemmas that today's reforms in curriculum and assessment create and to do so from the perspective of the *Learner-Centered Psychological Principles*. The focus is on external assessment used at the national, state, and district levels because that is where changes in assessment practice have received the most attention. Nevertheless, most assessment in education occurs at the classroom level and is instructionally embedded. Some attention is given to this disjuncture.

Historically, the focus in education assessment has been on accuracy and efficiency. This focus has led to the dominance of multiple-choice testing, which produces highly reliable summaries of what students know in a given academic area while requiring minimum amounts of student time. Because the typical multiple-choice item takes less than a minute to complete, multiple-choice tests produce large samples of information in the form of student responses to separate items. Total scores produced by summing across items are based on a large and diverse sample of information that provides a highly stable result (i.e., different sets of items sampled from a common domain tend to lead to the same conclusion about student achievement).

The emerging alternative to multiple-choice testing is performance assessment. As the name implies, performance assessments are designed to measure how students actually perform in using their knowledge.

Performance assessments differ primarily in the degree to which they are standardized so that all students are assessed under the same conditions (e.g., highly structured on-demand performance assessment) or are uniquely tailored to each student (e.g., portfolios produced by the students). Ideally, performance assessments capture how well students "learn to use their minds." Performance assessment can be consistent with the strategic thinking learner-centered psychological principle that states that students "understand and can use a variety of strategies to help them reach learning and performance goals, and to apply their knowledge in novel situations" (APA, 1995, p. 5). To some extent it is also consistent with the intrinsic motivation principle that states that "intrinsic motivation is facilitated on tasks that learners perceive as personally relevant and meaningful" (APA, 1995, p. 7).

Many measurement dilemmas are created by the need to reform assessment to better serve students and teachers (Porter, 1991a). The dilemmas do not, however, appear to hinge primarily on solutions to technical problems, which historically have been the major contributions of psychology. The most important issues concern what to assess, who to assess, and what to do with the results. These are not uniquely measurement issues; they fall at the intersection of the educational, political, and measurement arenas. Five key dilemmas are

- Should assessment be aligned to instruction, or should it be aligned to a vision of what educational reformers would like instruction to become?
- Should assessment serve the purpose of describing progress toward achieving national or state goals, or is assessment needed to serve accountability purposes at local levels?
- Should assessment array student performance against criteria of what students should know and be able to do, or should assessment report student performance in norm-referenced terms?
- Should limited resources available for external assessment be focused exclusively on student performance, or is it necessary to assess school inputs and school processes as well?
- Is external assessment the best focus for assessment reform, or should the focus be on instructionally embedded classroom assessment?

Dilemmas are created when only disagreeable alternatives for action exist. These are difficult and perplexing choices that must be faced, but most appear to allow for the possibility of a promising resolution.

Alignment

The dilemma is whether to align assessment to the vision of curriculum reform or to the curriculum that students are experiencing. Either choice has its problem. If we assess students against the reform, their performance will almost certainly be terrible, at least initially. Not only is it unlikely that students will have learned what they have not been taught, but conceptual understanding and application are simply more difficult to master than are facts and skills. On the other hand, if students are assessed against the curriculum they experience, results will be better, but the information will provide no real knowledge of progress toward the goal. Worse, an assessment aligned to current practice will become an anchor to that practice.

There is a second part to the alignment dilemma. Will assessment be aligned to what we want to assess, or will it instead be aligned to what we know how to test? This second part may appear trivial or foolish, but in practice it is not. Performance assessment as an alternative to multiple-choice testing is in its infancy (Berlak et al., 1992). The attraction of performance assessment is the potential to have better measures of students' ability to use their knowledge to reason and to solve novel problems (Wiggins, 1989). However, thus far performance assessments have suffered from low reliability, calling into question whether they can be used to report on achievement at the level of the individual student (Baxter, Shavelson, Goldman, & Pine, 1992).

Indicators of Accountability

Assessment for descriptive purposes does not require reliable and valid information at the individual student level. Reliability and validity are only required at the lowest level of aggregation for which reporting will be done. Sampling procedures comparable to those used currently (NAEP) would be sufficient (although there would be arguments from subject matter experts about whether or not NAEP assessments are appropriately aligned with the vision of the current curriculum reforms).

Assessment that serves descriptive purposes only reveals whether progress toward achieving the goals is being made. It does not influence that progress. Assessment that serves accountability purposes, however, can be a lead policy instrument in achieving reform goals. The idea is simple enough: If all students are assessed against the national goals, and if performance holds consequences for students, teachers, schools, districts, and states, then preparation for doing well will become important.

Unfortunately, assessments that serve accountability purposes are much more expensive than assessments that serve only descriptive purposes. If students are to be held accountable, then all students must be assessed. This census approach is expensive in its own right. It also eliminates the possibility of different students responding to different assessment exercises, which in turn either narrows the sample of assessment exercises or greatly extends response time for each student. Second, because performance on the assessments would be of great importance, steps would need to be taken to standardize administration and scoring procedures so that each student had an equal opportunity to do his or her best. Rules would need to be enforced concerning students excused from assessment. Cheating would need to be prevented.

New assessment exercises would need to be used at each time of assessment. Not only would it be impossible to guarantee security of a high-stakes assessment over time, but it would be counterproductive. One purpose of accountability based on assessment is to move practice in the desired directions captured in the assessment. After each assessment, the items should be widely circulated so that everyone knows in detail the kinds of knowledge and skills students are to possess. Further, using different samples of assessment tasks at each administration ensures that instruction does not become tied to a particular set of assessment tasks, but rather to the domain from which the samples of tasks are drawn.

Criterion-Referenced or Norm-Referenced Assessment

The controversy between assessment that is *norm referenced* (e.g., percentile-scored standardized testing) and assessment that is *criterion referenced* (i.e., measured against meaningful criteria) is classic. Certainly the bulk of achievement testing in U.S. schools today emphasizes normative reporting of results. Parents and students want feedback in terms of percentile rank. Everybody wants above-average students and schools.

For the past 20 years or so there has been a persistent minority of educators who have emphasized the importance of giving feedback on performance against some meaningful criterion (Fremer, 1994). The notion is to report results in terms of what students know and know how to do. Probably, if there were greater agreement on what constitutes worthwhile knowledge, the criterion-referenced movement would be further along. The content-standard-setting movement in U.S. education, which began in the late 1980s, has found that getting consensus on what students should know and be able to do is extremely challenging. For example, there are three sets of national content standards in science, but scientists still argue about important science that has been left out of all three.

Another stumbling block for criterion-referenced assessment is the difficulty of finding parsimonious ways to provide feedback on performance. A percentile rank is a single number. Until recently, most criterion-referenced feedback has come in the form of a long list of concepts, skills, and applications, with degrees of mastery reported for each. Such detailed feedback makes answers to questions of "How'd you do?" complicated and conditional. Recent emphasis on judgmental performance standards that specify desired levels of student accomplishment may offer greater parsimony in the reports of criterion-referenced results. Thus far, performance standards have found their way into the scoring rubrics of countless performance-assessment tasks, distinguishing levels of performance from "expert" to "novice" to "unacceptable." More difficult has been the setting of criterion-referenced performance standards on total performance (when an overall score results from summing across several tasks). The National Assessment Governing Board is required by law to set performance standards for NAEP. Thus far the standards that they have set have been heavily criticized by the National Academy of Education (Panel, 1993) and the U.S. General Accounting Office (1993) as being misleading and not valid for the interpretations offered. Still, if performance standards can be set that are acceptable, they will offer a parsimonious way of reporting results from criterion-referenced assessments.

At least in theory, a single assessment can serve both norm-referenced and criterion-referenced purposes. A criterion-referenced assessment must be constructed. This task is not easy. It requires careful mapping of knowledge and knowledge-use domains and careful sampling of assessment exercises from those domains in ways that have content validity and that provide stable estimates of performance for each of the various domains deemed important. Once an assessment with these properties is available, norms are easily achieved through administration to appropriate samples.

School Process Indicators

High-quality indicators of student outcomes are essential to monitoring the health of our nation's schooling efforts. There is even considerable agreement that indicators are needed of the inputs to our educational system: the quality of teachers in our schools, the fiscal and other resources that schools are provided to do their work, and the entry characteristics of students who attend schools. What has been less clear is the need for and feasibility of indicators that make it possible to monitor the nature of schooling: the curriculum students study, the instruction teachers provide, and the environment in which teaching and learning take place.

There are at least three motivations for creating a system of indicators about school processes (Porter, 1991b). One is purely descriptive. Schools provide educational opportunity; they do not directly produce student learning. It is important to know, therefore, about the nature of educational opportunity as a direct policy output of schools. A second motivation is to have indicators of school processes that serve as an evaluation instrument in monitoring school reform. For example, the National Council of Teachers of Mathematics, in *Curriculum and Evaluation Standards for School Mathematics* (1989), calls for major changes in mathematics content. How can the degree of success in achieving these changes be measured? A third motivation for indicators of school processes is to provide explanatory information when student output goals are not reached. School process indicators may point to possible causes and, thus, to possible solutions for inadequacies in school outputs.

When interests in student-level accountability based on assessment are considered, issues of fairness become prominent. Is it fair to hold a student accountable on an assessment that covers content for which the student has not been provided an adequate opportunity to learn? The best school-controlled predictors of student achievement are indicators of the enacted curriculum and especially the content of instruction (Porter, 1995).

The Need for Description

As a nation, we invest a great deal in education. As taxpayers, we underwrite the costs of public education. As students and parents, a significant fraction of us purchase private education. As United States citizens, we have the right and the responsibility to know the nature of education being provided. Information should be available to describe the probability that a particular type of student will receive good teaching of worthwhile content. When high-stakes assessments are in place, descriptions of student opportunity to learn may be required by law (Debra P. v. Turlington, 1981).

The descriptive questions of interest concern issues of amount, quality, and distribution of education. Do children from poor families have the same opportunity in school to learn higher order thinking and problem solving as do children from affluent families? What groups of students take coursework in high school that satisfies college entrance requirements? To what extent is there equal access to technology across race, gender, socioeconomic status, and geographic location? To what extent does access to technology vary by subject matter area?

Curiously, the sheer magnitude of descriptive information that is of interest can be used as an argument against building a system of indicators of school processes. An indicator system that did justice to the complexity of our education system would surely cost more than it is worth; such a system might not even be feasible. Hard choices must be made about which information to collect and report.

Monitoring Reform

The ambitious reforms of the 1980s and 1990s call for substantial change from current practice: change in curriculum, change in organizational structure, change in pedagogical practices, change in the distribution of opportunity across types of students. Although the motivation for reform is usually a concern for student outcomes (as reflected in the National Education Goal cited previously), the focus of reform is always on educational practice. Thus, seeing whether the changes envisioned by reform occur requires looking into schools and classrooms. A system of indicators on organizational and instructional processes of schooling would provide the needed information.

Diagnosing the Education System

When student achievement is not improved, corrective actions must be taken. Indicators of school processes can point in promising directions. If student achievement is better than predicted in one district than another or one state than another, then knowledge of differences in curriculum, instruction, and school practices can give clues about why. Does one set of curriculum policies provide better guidance and support for effective schooling than another? Are there differences in the instructional materials available? Are the teachers in one location better trained? Are the connections between school and community stronger in one place than another?

Establishing causal relations between indicators of school processes and student achievement is complicated, and the results always tentative, especially from correlational studies such as those an indicator system would support. Although there are differences of opinion about how useful such analyses can be in diagnosing the relative usefulness of different types of educational practices, most agree that such indicator data is better than no information at all.

Instructionally Embedded Assessment

The motivation to reform assessment of student achievement is to improve student learning. As has been described, the focus has been on external assessment. The belief is that academic achievement assessments can (a) serve to clarify the goals of schooling and, in so doing, make the system more efficient toward reaching those goals; (b) describe progress toward reaching those goals and, in so doing, diagnose successes and failures in teaching and learning; and (c) serve purposes of accountability for students, teachers, schools, and school systems, thus enhancing their motivation for pursuing the goals. These are reasonable assumptions supported by a considerable body of research (Airasian, 1988; Madaus, 1991; Smith, 1991). But clear goals, monitoring progress toward those goals, and accountability by themselves will not be enough to improve teaching and learning. There must also be capacity at the classroom level to provide quality instruction. One important component of classroom instruction is the assessments that teachers and students use during the normal course of instruction for such purposes as placement of students in instructional groups, pacing decisions, and student evaluation (Kuhs et al., 1985). These instructionally embedded assessments, which take place routinely in the classroom, both formally and informally, are typically no better and are often poorer than the instruction within which they occur.

Clearly, issues of alignment discussed previously generalize to instructionally embedded assessment. Unfortunately, reform of assessment at the classroom level will not occur as easily as reform of external assessments. Teachers must be convinced of the need for revising their assessment procedures and provided the professional development that will give them the expertise to make those changes. For example, curriculum materials will need to be revised, so that end-of-chapter tests are consistent with external assessments.

Some may think that instructionally embedded assessments can also serve the purposes of external indicators of student academic achievement and accountability. At least in the near term, this seems unlikely. Reform of instructionally embedded assessment will require massive changes in classroom practices. Such changes will come slowly and will occur unevenly across classrooms. An indicator system or an accountability system must, at a minimum, have the property that every child has an equal chance to demonstrate his or her best. Further, assessments that require scoring by a third party (e.g., experts external to the classroom) typically do not provide information to teachers and students in a timely enough fashion to be useful for instructional purposes.

Reform of instructionally embedded assessments would be a more frontal attack on improving teaching and learning than are efforts to reform external assessment. Both seem useful, but neither seems likely to be sufficient by itself. To date, far too little attention has been given to the reform of classroom assessment; staff development, demonstration projects, and materials development are needed in all subjects and at all grade levels.

Conclusion

A key to successful curriculum reform is timely and valid information on school inputs, practices, and outputs. The place to start is with the desired outputs: What is it that students are to know and be able to do? Our national education goals are unprecedentedly ambitious in calling for all students to demonstrate competence over challenging subject matter and learn to use their minds well. The focus is learner centered just as APA's learner-centered psychological principles are. But setting clear goals is just the first step. An important additional step is to reform assessment of student achievement so that the assessment provides strong support of the goals. The task of assessment reform, however, runs head-on into a number of dilemmas. The purpose here has been to articulate those dilemmas and, for each, point toward promising resolutions.

External assessment procedures should possess the following characteristics: They should be norm referenced in the sense that they report progress over time and within time on contrasts among types of students. The assessments should be comprehensive across subject matter areas, grades, and levels of student accomplishment. Thus, influences on practice will be applied evenly in all areas of need. The assessments must have the weight necessary to influence practice. Among other things, the assessments should serve accountability purposes. Accountability must follow a period of implementation so that schools, teachers, and students all have had an opportunity to achieve the goals before they are held accountable. The assessments should be standardized and unbiased so that they provide valid contrasts over time and across subgroups. The assessments should be repeated frequently enough that data are current and progress toward goals can be steadily monitored. For diagnostic purposes, the assessments should be coupled with indicators of inputs and educational procedures. In addition, instructionally embedded classroom assessment must be reformed to directly support teaching and learning on a daily basis, and to be consistent with valued outputs of schooling and aligned to the system of external assessments.

References

Airasian, P. W. (1988). Symbolic validation: The case of state-mandated, high-stakes testing. *Educational Evaluation and Policy Analysis, 10*, 301–313.

American Psychological Association Board of Educational Affairs. (1995). *Learner-centered psychological principles: A framework for school redesign and reform* [On-line]. Available: http://www.apa.org/ed/lcp.html.

Baxter, G. P., Shavelson, R. J., Goldman, S. R., & Pine, J. (1992). Evaluation of procedure-based scoring for hands-on science assessment. *Journal of Educational Measurement, 29*, 1–17.

Berlak, H., Newmann, F. M., Adams, E., Archbald, D. A., Burgess, T., Raven, J., & Romberg, T. A. (1992). *Toward a new science of educational testing and assessment.* Albany: State University of New York Press.

Fremer, J. J. (1994). Criterion-referenced testing [Entire issue]. *Educational measurement: Issues and practice, 13*(4).

Debra P. v. Turlington. 474 F. Supp 244 (M.D. Fla. 1979); affirmed in part 664 F. 1d 397 (5th Cir., 1981).

Goals 2000: Educate America Act of 1994, 20 U.S.C.S. § 5812 et seq. (Lexis-Nexis 1997).

Kuhs, T., Porter, A., Floden, R., Freeman, D., Schmidt, W., & Schwille, J. (1985). Differences among teachers in their use of curriculum-embedded tests. *The Elementary School Journal, 86*(2), 141–153.

Madaus, G. F. (1991). The effects of important tests on students: Implications for a national examination system. *Phi Delta Kappan, 73*, 226–231.

National Council of Teachers of Mathematics. (1989). *Curriculum and evaluation standards for school mathematics.* Reston, VA: Author.

Panel on the Evaluation of the NAEP Trial State Assessment. (1993). *The trial state assessment: Prospect and realities.* The third report of the Panel. Stanford, CA: National Academy of Education.

Porter, A. C. (1991a). Assessing national goals: Some measurement dilemmas. In *The assessment of National Educational Goals: Proceedings of the 1990 ETS Invitational Conference* (pp. 21–42). Princeton, NJ: Educational Testing Service.

Porter, A. C. (1991b). Creating a system of school process indicators. *Educational Evaluation and Policy Analysis, 13*, 13–29.

Porter, A. C. (1995, May 18). *The uses and misuses of opportunity-to-learn standards.* Paper presented at a Brookings Institution conference, Beyond Goals 2000: The Future of National Standards and Assessment in American Education, Washington, DC.

Smith, M. L. (1991). Put to the test: The effects of external testing on teachers. *Educational Researcher, 20*(5), 8–11.

Wiggins, G. (1989). A true test: Toward more authentic and equitable assessment. *Phi Delta Kappan, 70*, 703–713.

U.S. General Accounting Office. (1993). *Educational achievement standards: NAGB's approach yields misleading interpretations.* Washington, DC: Author.

Part IV

Teacher Education for the Learner-Centered Classrooms of the Future

Cognitive Theory for Education: What Teachers Need to Know

14

Richard E. Mayer

What is the connection between psychological theories of how students learn and educational practices involving how teachers teach? This chapter is concerned with the relation between cognition and instruction, with a special focus on what teachers need to know. Five topics are explored: (a) an historical review of the relation between psychology and education during the past 100 years, (b) a comparison of three views of learning and instruction that have dominated psychology and education during the past 100 years, (c) examples of some of the contributions of cognitive theory for instruction, (d) an analysis of the implications of cognitive theory for learner-centered schools, and (e) recommendations for what teachers need to know about cognitive theory.

Psychology and Education in Historical Perspective

The Potential Relation Between Education and Psychology

I begin with a vision of how the practice of education could be improved by the science of psychology:

> The efficiency of any profession depends in large measure upon the
> degree to which it becomes scientific. The profession of teaching

---

This chapter is an extended version of an article titled, "Cognition and Instruction: Their Historic Meeting Within Educational Psychology," which was published in the *Journal of Educational Psychology, 84*, 1992, pp. 405–412. The reproduced portions of the original article are reprinted with permission of the American Psychological Association.

will improve (1) in proportion as its members direct their work by the scientific spirit and methods, that is by honest, open-minded consideration of facts, by freedom from superstitions, fancies or un-verified guesses, and (2) in proportion as the leaders in education direct their choices of methods by the results of scientific investigation rather than by general opinion. (Thorndike, 1906, p. 257)

This quote, from E. L. Thorndike's *The Principles of Teaching Based on Psychology*, exemplifies that at the opening of this century, confidence that science could improve practice in the field of education was high.

For 100 years, psychologists and educators have recognized the potential relation between their fields. As early as 1892, William James (1899/1958) presented his famous lectures on psychology applied to education and later published them as *Talks to Teachers*. As it is today, the field of education was in ferment, with educators searching for reforms that would bring respect to the teaching profession. Although he recognized the potential value of psychology for education, James (1899/1958) was somewhat hesitant in making specific recommendations:

The desire of the schoolteachers for a completer professional training, and their aspiration toward the professional spirit in their work, have led more and more to turn to us for light on fundamental principles. And in the few hours which we are to spend together you look to me, I am sure, for information concerning the mind's operation, which may enable you to labor more easily and effectively in the several classrooms over which you preside. Far be it from me to disclaim for psychology all title to such hopes. Psychology ought certainly to give the teacher radical help. And yet I confess that, acquainted as I am with the height of your expectations, I feel a little anxious lest, at the end of these simple talks of mine, not a few of you may experience some disappointment at the net results. (p. 22)

James acknowledged two difficulties in applying psychology to education. First, he noted that psychology's description of "the elements of the mental machine . . . and their workings" (James, 1899/1958, p. 26) does not translate directly into specific educational prescriptions— foreshadowing the modern distinction between descriptive learning theory and prescriptive instructional theory (Bruner, 1964). James (1899/1958) warned teachers, "You make a great, a very great mistake, if you think that psychology, being a science of the mind's laws, is something from which you can deduce definite programmes and schemes and methods of instruction for immediate schoolroom use" (p. 23). It is unrealistic for teachers to expect simple, step-by-step procedures guaranteed to work for all children in all situations, and it is unethical for psychologists to profess to be able to supply them.

Second, James (1899/1958) correctly noted that in 1892 psychology lacked the necessary data base:

> We have been experiencing something like a boom in psychology in this country. Laboratories and professorships have been founded, and reviews established. . . . "The new psychology" has thus become a term to conjure up portentous ideas. . . . In my humble opinion there is no "new psychology" worthy of the name. There is nothing but the old psychology which began in Locke's time, plus a little physiology . . . and theory of evolution, and few refinements of introspective detail, for the most part without adaptation to the teacher's use. (pp. 22–23)

As have other educational psychologists throughout this century, I have been haunted by the words of James (1899/1958) and Thorndike (1906) concerning the relation between psychology and education. While sharing their 100-year-old dream that the "proper application of psychological findings might lead the way to better instruction in all schools" (Woodring, 1958, p. 6), I also share their concerns about the appropriate relation between science and practice.

At the opening of this century, educational psychology began as what Cubberly (1920) called a "guiding science of the school" (p. 755), a discipline whose content was defined by the problems of education and whose methods were defined by the science of psychology. In his preface to the first issue of the *Journal of Educational Psychology*, Thorndike (1910) proclaimed that educational psychology would apply the methods of exact science to the problems of education (see also Levin, 1992; Walberg & Haertel, 1992).

The Actual Relation Between Education and Psychology

Despite the high hopes of early educational psychologists, the discipline was in disarray by midcentury. Grinder (1989) summarized three ways in which educational psychology lost its mantle as a guiding science for education: (a) through withdrawal, educational psychologists failed to accept responsibility for contributing to educational policy; (b) through fractionation, educational psychologists failed to achieve a coherent theoretical perspective; and (c) through irrelevance, educational psychologists failed to study practical educational problems in natural settings.

As the end of the 20th century approaches, the problems of education remain, but the science of educational psychology has begun to overcome many of the problems cited by Grinder (1989). Withdrawal is giving way to participation in public policy debates, fractionation is giving way to a unified cognitive approach and irrelevance is giving way to the study of how real students learn real educational subject matter.

First, educational psychologists have become increasingly involved in educational policy issues. For example, the development of the learner-centered psychological principles (APA, 1995) that are the centerpiece of this volume reflects a growing commitment by psychologists to participate in the educational reform movement. The six national educational goals (see U.S. Department of Education, Office of Educational Research and Improvement, 1991) currently under discussion include objectives that are of interest to educational psychologists, such as ensuring that students achieve "competency over challenging subject matter including English, mathematics, science, history, [and] geography" and that students develop "the ability to reason, solve problems, apply knowledge, and write and communicate effectively" (pp. 3–4).

Second, the behaviorist movement, which dominated psychology until the 1950s, stifled much useful research in the discipline. In contrast, educational psychology has experienced what Scandura et al. (1981) called "the paradigm shift from S-R [stimulus-response] to information processing" (p. 367) and what DiVesta (1989) recognized as "the recent era of transition from behavioral to cognitive psychology" (p. 39). Instead of focusing on the role of reinforcers in creating behavior, cognitive psychology has "brought about a renewal of concern about the learner's role in instruction" (DiVesta, 1989, p. 39). In particular, "an important aspect of the cognitive movement in education was the conscious recognition of the learner as an active participant in the learning process" (DiVesta, 1989, p. 54).

Third, educational psychology has moved from the study of behavior on artificial tasks in sterile laboratory environments to the study of the cognitive processes of students as they engage in school tasks in more natural settings. These trends are exemplified in the *Handbook of Educational Psychology* (Berliner & Calfee, 1996). For example, instead of studying rote memorization of lists of nonsense syllables, researchers in educational psychology now investigate how to improve the understandability of school textbooks; instead of measuring the rate at which rats run through mazes, researchers now evaluate the strategies that children use on school tasks; and instead of studying how adults solve puzzles, researchers now investigate why children make errors on mathematics and science problems.

Can educational psychology regain its position as the guiding science of education? Fortified with methods and theories that did not exist in Edward L. Thorndike's time, educational psychology can fulfill Wittrock's (1967) vision as the "scientific study of human behavior in educational settings" (p. 4). For example, Wittrock (1989) predicted that "recent advances in the study of cognition will lead to a useful and prescriptive theory of instruction and teaching" (p. 75).

Three Views of Learning and Teaching

Over the course of this century, the view of learning and instruction has changed in ways that have affected educational practice and research. In short, the following three metaphors of learning are relevant to instruction: learning as response acquisition, learning as knowledge acquisition, and learning as knowledge construction (Mayer, 1992a).

Learning as Response Acquisition

During the first half of this century, the learning as response acquisition metaphor dominated psychological theory and educational practice. Based on research on response learning in animals, learning was viewed as a mechanistic process in which successful responses are automatically strengthened and unsuccessful responses are automatically weakened, or more correctly, associations are strengthened or weakened according to environmental feedback. Within this behaviorist-inspired metaphor, the learner is a passive being whose repertoire of behaviors is determined by rewards and punishments encountered in the environment. Dewey (1902) disparagingly described this view of the passive learner: "The child is simply the immature being who is to be matured; he is the superficial being who is to be deepened. . . . It is his to receive, to accept" (p. 8).

The metaphor of learning as response acquisition has straightforward implications for instruction, namely, creating situations that elicit responses from learners and providing appropriate reinforcement for each response. Drill and practice is the epitome of instruction within this view of learning. For example, the student is given a response-eliciting question such as, "How do you spell *California?*" If the student produces the correct sequence of letters—"C-a-l-i-f-o-r-n-i-a"—the teacher smiles and says, "Right!" But if the student produces an incorrect sequence such as, "C-o-w-i-l-l-f-o-u-r-n-y-a," the teacher says, "You better look at the spelling list." If the learner is a passive recipient, then the teacher can be viewed as the active dispenser of feedback, that is, someone who rewards correct responses and punishes incorrect ones.

According to this view of learning, the goal of instruction is to increase the number (or strength) of correct behaviors in the learner's repertoire. Learning outcomes can be evaluated by measuring the amount of behavior change, such as noting that a learner correctly spelled 5 of 12 words on Monday and correctly spelled 12 of 12 on Friday. By focusing on "how much is learned," the task of the teacher becomes one of shaping changes in specific responses. Although the behaviorist movement from which the metaphor of learning as response acquisition is derived has not fared well in the second half of this century, its remnants can be seen in modern theories of learning and instruction. For example, automatization of basic skills has become a component in modern theories of reading (LaBerge & Samuels, 1974), writing (Scardamalia, Bereiter, & Goelman, 1982), and mathematics (Fuson, 1982), as well as problem solving (Case, 1985; Mayer 1992b; Siegler, 1986) and skill learning (Anderson, 1983; Singley & Anderson, 1989).

Learning as Knowledge Acquisition

The cognitive revolution of the 1950s and 1960s emphasized a new metaphor: learning as knowledge acquisition. As the focus of research shifted from laboratory studies of animal learning to laboratory studies of human learning, psychologists shifted their theoretical focus from the strengthening and weakening of responses to the acquisition of knowledge. Within this new cognitive metaphor, the learner becomes a processor of information and the teacher becomes a dispenser of information. As the acquisition of knowledge becomes the focus of psychologists, the curriculum becomes the focus of instruction. Dewey (1902) described the curriculum-centered approach as follows:

> Subdivide each topic into studies; each study into lessons; each lesson into specific facts and formulae. Let the child proceed step by step to master each one of these separate parts, and at last he will have covered the entire ground. (p. 8)

The learning-as-knowledge acquisition metaphor has straightforward implications for instruction, namely, increasing situations in which students can acquire knowledge. Through this metaphor, teaching basic information from textbooks and lectures becomes a focus of research and practice. According to this view of learning, the goal of instruction is to increase the amount of knowledge in the learner's repertoire so that learning outcomes can be evaluated by measuring the amount of knowledge acquired. For example, a multiple-choice reading comprehension test allows measurement of how much is learned, and the achievement test becomes the most popular evaluation device.

Learning as Knowledge Construction

As cognitive theory matured during the 1970s and 1980s, the dominant metaphor became learning as knowledge construction. Researchers moved from studying the learning of abstract materials in artificial settings to studying subject-based learning in more realistic situations. As a result, the view of the learner changed from that of a recipient of knowledge to that of a constructor of knowledge, an autonomous learner with metacognitive skills for controlling his or her cognitive processes during learning. Learning involves selecting relevant information and interpreting it through one's existing knowledge. As Resnick (1989) aptly noted, "learning occurs not by recording information but by interpreting it" (p. 2). Dewey (1902) described this process of active learning 90 years earlier: "Learning is active. It involves reaching out of one's mind. It involves organic assimilation from within" (p. 9). Accordingly, the teacher becomes a participant with the learner in the process of shared cognition, that is, in the process of constructing meaning in a given situation.

Concerning instruction, the focus changed from the curriculum to the cognition of the child. Dewey (1902) defined this child-centered approach as follows: "The child is the starting point, the center, the end. His development, his growth is the ideal" (p. 9). Thus, instruction is geared toward helping the student to develop learning and thinking strategies that are appropriate for working within various subject domains. Correspondingly, evaluation is qualitative rather than quantitative, determining how the student structures and processes knowledge rather than how much is learned.

Throughout this century, the dominant metaphor has changed from a view of the learner as a response-acquisition machine, to the learner as a recipient of knowledge, to the learner as a constructor of knowledge. Although the third view appears to be new, it has had numerous proponents in the past (Bartlett, 1932; Piaget, 1954; Tolman,

1932). For this chapter, I adopt the learning-as-knowledge-construction metaphor in hopes of shedding light on the relation between cognition and instruction.

A Closer Look at Learning as Knowledge Construction

In contrast to the classic behaviorist view of the learner as a passive recipient whose learning is automatically shaped by practice and reinforcements, the cognitive theory that has come to dominate psychology provides a vision of the learner as an active processor of information. In contrast to the behaviorist view of learning as the automatic strengthening or weakening of associations, cognitive theory offers the view of learning as the construction of knowledge by the learner. In contrast to the classic behaviorist focus on instruction that elicits individual responses that are immediately reinforced, a central instructional issue in cognitive theory concerns how to help students become more effective processors of information.

The main components in a cognitive model of the learning–instruction process (Mayer, 1987) include the following: *instructional manipulations* (the external events concerning what is taught and how it is taught), *learner characteristics* (the internal existing knowledge and information-processing system), *learning processes* (the internal cognitive processes engaged during learning), *learning outcomes* (the internal cognitive structures constructed during learning), and *outcome performance* (the external performance of the learner on tests).

This cognitive model includes internal factors that were ignored in behaviorist theory: learner characteristics (which can lead to individual differences in the process of learning), learning processes (which manipulate information), and learning outcomes (which contain the newly constructed knowledge). Learning processes—information processes that affect the way in which new knowledge is constructed—provide an aspect of cognitive theory that is particularly relevant to education. For example, Figure 1 summarizes three cognitive learning processes involved in meaningful learning, which I have proposed previously (Mayer, 1984, 1987, 1989b). According to the model, meaningful learning occurs when the learner selects relevant information, organizes that information into a coherent whole, and integrates that information with appropriate existing knowledge. In previous work I have called these three learning processes, respectively, *selecting, organizing,* and *integrating* (Mayer, 1984, 1987, 1989b, 1992a). These processes correspond

Figure 1

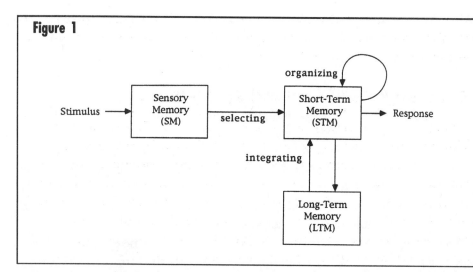

A cognitive model of knowledge construction. Figure from "Guiding Students' Cognitive Processing of Scientific Information," p. 246, by R. E. Mayer, 1992, in *Promoting Academic Competence and Literacy: Cognitive Research and Innovation.* San Diego, CA: Academic Press. Copyright 1992 by Academic Press. Reprinted with permission.

respectively to Sternberg's (1985, 1988) three knowledge-acquisition components: selective encoding, selective combination, and selective comparison. Instructional manipulations are effective to the extent that they elicit cognitive learning processes.

The first process involves focusing attention on relevant pieces of the presented information and is indicated in Figure 1 by the arrow running from sensory memory to short-term memory. *Selecting* involves "selecting information from the text and adding that information to working memory" (Mayer, 1984, p. 32), and selective encoding involves a "sifting out of relevant from irrelevant information" (Sternberg, 1985, p. 107).

The second process requires building internal connections among (or organizing) the selected pieces of information, as indicated in Figure 1 by the arrow running from short-term memory back to short-term memory. *Organizing* involves organizing the selected information in working memory into a coherent whole" (Mayer, 1984, p. 32), and selective combination involves "combining selectively encoded information in such a way as to form an integrated . . . internally connected whole" (Sternberg, 1985, p. 107).

The third process requires building external connections between the organized new knowledge and organized existing knowledge, as indicated in Figure 1 by the arrow directed from long-term memory to short-term memory. *Integrating* is "connecting the organized information to other familiar knowledge structures already in memory" (Mayer, 1984, p. 33), and selective comparison involves "relating newly acquired or retrieved information . . . to old knowledge so as to form an externally connected whole" (Sternberg, 1985, p. 107).

In cognitive theory, the learner is an active processor of information who is trying to make sense of the presented material. The self-regulated learner must appropriately control his or her learning processes by selecting and organizing relevant information and building connections from relevant existing knowledge. Accordingly, a primary goal of education is to help students develop expertise in how to learn and to use that expertise to construct useful knowledge within each subject domain. Although as educators we expect students to become expert learners, we rarely provide students with the opportunities they need to construct useful learning strategies (Mayer, 1987, 1992a; Norman, 1980; Pressley, 1990; Pressley & Levin, 1983a, 1983b; Weinstein & Mayer, 1985).

On the basis of current cognitive theory, Resnick (1989) has identified "three instructional aspects of learning that together call for forms of instructional theory very different from those that grew out of earlier associationist and behaviorist psychologies": (a) "learning is a process of knowledge construction, not knowledge recording or absorption," (b) "learning is knowledge-dependent" in that "people use current knowledge to construct new knowledge," and (c) "learning is highly tuned by the situation in which it takes place" (p. 12). The constructive, knowledge-based, and situational aspects of learning have important implications for instructional research and practice, which are discussed in the next section.

Advances in Cognition and Instruction

With the reemergence of cognitive approaches to instruction now in full swing, it is fruitful to ask whether any new contributions have emerged and whether any are likely to emerge in the future. My reading of the educational psychology literature has convinced me that educational psychology has a unique and important role within the fields of psychology and education. In particular, I am struck by two contributions: a focus on cognition and instruction within subject matter domains (rather than on context-free general laws of learning and cognition) and a focus on detailed descriptions of individual differences in learning strategies and learning outcomes (rather than on average group differences).

First, in being driven by educational problems, educational psychologists are concerned with the ecological validity of their theories for real learning of real material in real situations. The development of psychologies of subject matter represents a unique contribution of educational psychology. For example, to paraphrase Resnick and Ford (1981), instead of asking, "How do people learn?," we ask, "How do people learn to read and write and compute?" Whereas a focus on general psychology failed to produce general laws of learning and cognition, domain-based research offers a potentially productive attempt to understand human learning within specific subject-matter domains.

Second, by focusing on the psychological processes and structures of individual learners, educational psychologists have opened a powerful line of study to further psychology's goal of understanding what James (1899/1958) called the "mental machine . . . and its workings" (p. 26). The focus on learning strategies, including metacognitive strategies, and the focus on techniques for describing and evaluating knowledge structures represent unique contributions of educational psychology. Whereas measuring the average amount learned has not yielded a satisfactory psychology of learning, a more promising approach involves detailed evaluation of the learning processes and knowledge outcomes in individual learners.

In summary, two central aspects of the cognitive theory that have developed within educational psychology are a focus on learning and cognition within subject-matter domains and a focus on the detailed evaluation of individual learning strategies and outcomes. In the remainder of this section, I provide selected examples of the contribution of cognitive theory to the understanding of learning and instruction within the subject domains of reading, writing, and mathematics.

Reading

One of the major goals of reading instruction is *reading comprehension,* that is, helping readers become effective processors of prose information. Cognitive theory emphasizes the constructive nature of reading comprehension and the central role of the reader's existing knowledge. The cognitive strategies used by successful readers include the following: determining importance, summarizing information, drawing inferences, generating questions, and monitoring comprehension (Dole, Duffy, Roehler, & Pearson, 1991). An implication, worthy of intensive study, is that instruction in reading comprehension should focus on helping readers develop these useful cognitive strategies.

The strategy of determining importance involves distinguishing between important and unimportant information, such as distinguishing between the main idea and minor details. The strategy of summarizing involves taking the important information and organizing it, in one's own words, into a coherent structure. The strategy of drawing inferences involves filling in information omitted in a text to construct meaning for that text. For example, in hearing, "Our neighbor unlocked the door," a useful inference is that a key was used (Paris & Lindauer, 1976). The strategy of generating questions occurs when the reader asks specifically relevant questions about the text in advance of reading it and attempts to answer the questions while reading. Given the possibility that students may generate irrelevant questions, students appear to need specific training in how to generate useful questions (Pressley, 1990). The strategy of comprehension monitoring involves detecting that one does not understand a passage and correcting this lack of understanding, such as recognizing when there is a contradiction in a passage. Each of these strategies has been successfully taught to young readers in a way that has yielded improved performance on tests of reading comprehension, so each strategy is "a strong candidate for inclusion in our cognitively based comprehension curriculum" (Dole et al., 1991, p. 244).

In summary, cognitive theory has altered educators' views of how reading comprehension should be taught:

> In rapid retreat is the view that comprehension ability consists of the independent sequential development of a set of hierarchically related skills, each learned to some level of mastery. . . . The development of reading comprehension ability is better viewed as a process of emerging expertise, where readers develop strategies for comprehending increasingly sophisticated texts. (Dole et al., 1991, p. 255)

Additional research is needed to determine how best to help students develop expert reading comprehension strategies.

Writing

In writing instruction, students learn to express their ideas in written form. Cognitive theory emphasizes writing as communication rather than as composition, that is, the goal of writing is to communicate with an audience rather than solely to compose a technically correct product. The cognitive strategies used by successful writers include planning, translating, and reviewing (Flower & Hayes, 1980).

Planning involves generating information to be used in the essay, organizing that information into a writing plan, and establishing goals for writing. For example, to teach effective planning strategies, Fitzgerald and Teasley (1986) asked writers to begin by answering questions on a planning work sheet, such as "Who am I writing for?," "Why am I writing this?," "What do I know?," and "How can I group my ideas?"

Translating involves carrying out a plan by actually generating some written text. A major impediment for young writers is that the motoric (e.g., penmanship) and syntactic (e.g., spelling, punctuation, and grammar) demands of translating require so much mental effort that students do not pay attention to the semantic and pragmatic demands of writing, that is, making sure that the essay has the correct meaning and is appropriate for the intended audience. An instructional technique for improving the semantic and pragmatic aspects of translating is to remove the motoric and syntactic constraints on writing, at least during the first draft—that is, to allow students to orally dictate or to write in rough form without concern for spelling, punctuation, and grammar (Glynn, Britton, Muth, & Dogan, 1982).

The *reviewing* process involves detecting and correcting errors in written text. For example, Fitzgerald and Markman (1987) successfully taught young writers to conduct four types of revisions: additions, deletions, substitutions, and rearrangements. During instruction, teachers described their thought processes as they revised a text, asked students to describe their processes, and provided constructive feedback to students.

In short, Flower and Hayes' (1980) cognitive analysis of writing has led to an explosion of cognitively based writing programs that are beginning to be tested and refined. Cognitive theory has precipitated a fundamental shift from overemphasis on low-level skills (such as penmanship, spelling, and punctuation) to making room in the curriculum for the development of the processes central to writing, namely, planning, translating, and reviewing (Graham & Harris, 1988).

Mathematics

One of the major goals of mathematics instruction is the student's development of expertise in mathematical problem solving, such as the solving of word problems. Cognitive theory emphasizes the role of qualitative reasoning that enables successful mathematical problem solvers to understand the problem, devise and monitor a plan, and carry out the plan (Mayer, 1985, 1992b). An implication, worthy of intensive study, is that instruction in mathematical problem solving should focus on helping readers develop these useful cognitive strategies.

Strategies for problem understanding involve translating each sentence from the problem statement into an internal mental representation and then organizing the relevant information into a coherent mental representation of the situation described in the problem statement (Kintsch & Greeno, 1985). To understand a problem, the problem solver must possess relevant *factual knowledge* (such as knowing that there are 12 inches in a foot), *linguistic knowledge* (such as knowing that "Joe has 5 more marbles than Pete" implies that "Pete has fewer marbles than Joe"), and *schematic knowledge* (such as knowing the difference between a river-crossing problem and a work problem). The literature on the teaching of strategies for problem understanding is growing (Mayer, 1987, 1989a); for example, Lewis (1989) has successfully taught students how to translate sentences from a word problem into a diagrammatic representation.

Planning strategies involve breaking a problem into parts—that is, establishing subgoals—and determining which operations are needed to accomplish each subgoal. Monitoring strategies involve making sure that the plan is working and that the operations carried out are those called for in the plan. Can strategic knowledge, such as how to plan and monitor, be taught? There are encouraging signs that the answer is yes; for example, Schoenfeld (1985) has shown that students can be taught to use planning strategies, such as breaking a problem into smaller parts.

Finally, the research on the automatization of arithmetic procedures shows that students sometimes possess faulty procedures. For example, Brown and Burton (1978) found that the error patterns of individual children in three-column subtraction could be accounted for by assuming that they correctly applied a subtraction procedure that contained one or more bugs, such as always subtracting the smaller number from the larger in a column. Detailed descriptions of students' procedural knowledge (including the bugs in faulty procedures) allow teachers to provide individualized corrective instruction for each student.

Cognitive theory represents a change in focus for mathematics education. Instead of asking which procedures the student should master, cognitive theorists ask what it means to think mathematically (Schoenfeld, 1985). Instead of overemphasizing the product of problem solving (i.e., obtaining the right answer), cognitive theory suggests including an emphasis on the process of problem solving (i.e., what takes place in people's minds as they engage in solving complex mathematics problems).

In contrast to classical experimental psychology, which has sought general laws of learning and cognition, psychologies of subject matter show promise of making substantial contributions to educational practice. For example, by comparing the cognitive processes of successful and less successful students in domains such as reading comprehension, essay writing, or mathematical problem solving, psychologists of subject matter lay the groundwork for cognitively based instructional programs that help students develop domain-specific strategies.

In summary, psychologies of subject matter can provide the basis for educational reform. Recently, I described the role of psychologies of subject matter as follows:

> Why have psychologies of subject matter flourished in the 1980s? Psychologists with an interest in human learning and cognition have become dissatisfied with studying solely contrived learning of artificial materials in laboratory settings and educators with an interest in subject matter have become unwilling to limit their studies to the nontheoretical issues of day-to-day classroom practices. The result is that the best of both worlds is emerging within the discipline of educational psychology: The methods and theories of cognitive psychology are being challenged by the educational problems of how students learn real subject matter. In short, this fruitful area of research called psychologies of subject matter is unique to the discipline of educational psychology. (Mayer, 1989a, p. 452)

The merger of cognitive and educational psychology that reenergized psychologies of subject matter during the 1980s offers a promising path to educational reform in the 1990s.

Implications for Learner-Centered Schools

Throughout the history of psychology and education, psychological principles have been abstracted from the psychological research base and applied to educational practice. During the behaviorist reign, the database consisted mainly of experimental research on animal learning in well-controlled laboratory settings, and the principles focused on the elicitation of responses from students and the administration of rewards and punishments by teachers. During the information-processing period, the database consisted mainly of experimental research on humans in well-controlled laboratory settings, and the principles focused on the efficient design of instructional systems. During the constructivist period, the database consisted of a broader array of experimental and observation studies of people in both laboratory and natural settings, and the principles focused on fostering the active learning of students in realistic contexts.

The learner-centered psychological principles (APA, 1995) builds on the constructivist vision of education that has emerged as educational psychology's dominant view of how people learn. Two themes of the constructivist approach are particularly relevant to school reform: *active learning* and *learning in context.* Active learning refers to the idea that people learn by engaging in a process of sense making. This process requires the learner's orchestration of a collection of cognitive processes, as summarized in Figure 1. The instructional implications of this view include that students need practice in exercising and managing basic cognitive skills. Hands-on activity is not necessarily the same thing as active learning. Instructional methods aimed at active learning seek to engage the learner's cognitive processes, such as helping the learner select relevant information, organize that information into a coherent representation, and integrate that representation with existing knowledge. Instructional methods that emphasize learning by doing can sometimes stimulate active learning, but may sometimes stimulate rote learning. The goal is not to provoke behavioral activity per se, but rather to provoke productive kinds of cognitive activity.

Learning in context refers to the idea that each subject discipline requires its own ways of thinking that are best learned from concrete experience on realistic tasks. An important instructional implication is that students learn from working on authentic problems that interest them. The Cognition and Technology Group at Vanderbilt (1990) has used the term *anchored instruction* to refer to the idea that learning abstract ideas should be tied to concrete situations. For example, in mathematics, students can learn the concept of functional relations by analyzing the expenses and income of several businesses that are competing for the school cafeteria's pizza contract.

The development of the learner-centered psychological principles (APA, 1995) represents a reasonable effort to produce consensus on what is known about how students learn based on the current status of cognitive theory. In particular, the first six principles emphasize cognitive and metacognitive factors, and reflect a fundamental shift in the view of learning and teaching, away from the response-acquisition view and the knowledge-acquisition view, and toward the knowledge construction view. They are based on the idea that students are sense makers who actively construct their knowledge. A theme running through these principles is that learning can be a meaningful activity rather than a rote one. These six principles are reviewed below:

The learning of complex subject matter is most effective when it is an intentional process of constructing meaning from information and experience. This principle emphasizes the constructive nature of learning and the view of the learner as an active sense maker.

The successful learner, over time and with support and instructional guidance, can create meaningful, coherent representations of knowledge. This principle emphasizes the goal of learning as the creation of meaningful knowledge. Consistent with current cognitive theory, the learner's representation of knowledge is at the heart of the learning process.

The successful learner can link new information with existing knowledge in meaningful ways. This principle emphasizes a central cognitive process in meaningful learning, namely the integration of incoming and existing knowledge. The outcome of learning depends both on what is presented and on how the learner connects a representation of that information with existing knowledge.

The successful learner can create and use a repertoire of thinking and reasoning strategies to achieve complex learning goals. This principle emphasizes the variety of cognitive strategies involved in meaningful learning. Interestingly, the repertoire of strategies that are useful in one subject-matter domain may be different from those in another domain.

Higher order strategies for selecting and monitoring mental operations facilitate creative and critical thinking. This principle points to the role of metacognitive strategies in meaningful learning. Students not only need to possess relevant knowledge, they also need to know when and how to use that knowledge in solving novel problems.

Learning is influenced by environmental factors, including culture, technology, and instructional practices. This principle reflects the need to extend the view of meaningful learning beyond the purely cognitive realm, to include cultural and other influences on the construction of knowledge.

Many of the additional principles reflect the need to extend the view of meaningful learning beyond the purely cognitive realm, to include motivational, affective, social, developmental, biological, and cultural influences on the construction of knowledge.

What Teachers Need to Know About Cognition and Instruction

Courses in educational psychology often summarize educational research and derive recommendations for classroom practice. Happily, recent research in educational psychology has become more and more relevant to classroom practice, so the task of deriving recommendations is becoming more straightforward. Clearly, prospective teachers need to know about how students learn, how they develop, and how they think, particularly in the context of specific subject domains. Although a knowledge of the relevant research base and its educational implications is a well-accepted component of teacher education, I address four additional areas in this section—the need for teachers to become informed consumers of educational research, to develop a vision of their instructional goals, to create a personal theory of learning, and to build a personal teaching style.

Becoming a Consumer of Educational Research

Becoming a teacher involves the development of knowledge and strategies for teaching that can be informed by an educational research base. However, given the ever growing number of fads and claims made by promoters of various educational methods, teachers need to become informed consumers of educational research. Rather than relying on what "experts" say or on the notoriously unreliable flood of testimonials for a given method, teachers need to be able to critically assess the available research base. This includes being able to critically review the methodology for possible flaws, and being able to determine whether the conclusions follow from the data.

For example, suppose a blue-panel commission on reading instruction proclaims that the whole-language approach to reading instruction should be replaced with a phonics approach. A teacher needs to be able to critically assess such recommendations based on the available research. Programs such as cognitive-guided instruction represent an important attempt to help teachers integrate research-based knowledge with the development of effective teaching (Carpenter & Fennema, 1992).

Developing a Vision of the Instructional Goals

Becoming a teacher involves the development of a vision of the goals of instruction, that is, a vision of the desired learning outcomes. Learning outcomes can be assessed using two basic kinds of tests—*retention tests*, which seek to evaluate whether the student remembers what was taught, and *transfer tests*, on which the student must apply what has been learned to a novel situation. The outcomes of learning can be divided into three main categories: no learning, rote learning, and meaningful learning. If a student has not learned, then one can expect poor retention and poor transfer performance. If a student has learned in a rote way, then one can expect good retention and poor transfer. If a student has learned in a meaningful way, then one can expect both good retention and good transfer.

Although no one is likely to select "no learning" as the goal of instruction, some prospective teachers bring a "rote learning" goal to the classroom. Those who harbor a rote learning view are likely to agree with assertions such as "The goal of instruction is to help students learn the material as efficiently as possible" or "The teacher is responsible for covering each of the topics in the curriculum." In short, the hallmark of a rote learning goal is a focus solely on retention as the test of learning outcomes.

In contrast, when the goal of instruction is "meaningful learning," the appropriate tests of learning outcomes include both retention and transfer. Those who harbor a meaningful learning view are likely to agree with assertions such as, "Students need to apply what they have learned to solve new problems." Although the goals for rote learning outcomes are consistent with a curriculum-centered approach, goals for meaningful learning outcomes mesh with the learner-centered approach advocated in this book.

Constructing a Personal Theory of Learning

Becoming a teacher includes the development of a personal theory of learning. A teacher's personal theory of learning can influence his or her teaching practices—including decisions about what to teach and how to teach. It may be necessary, in the course of teacher education, to help prospective teachers articulate their personal theories of learning and to help them draw the logical implications.

One popular theory of learning among prospective teachers is what can be called the *response-acquisition view*—the idea that learning involves adding new behaviors to one's repertoire and, consequently, that teaching involves dispensing rewards and punishments. Proponents of this view are likely to agree with assertions such as "Drill and practice on short problems is the best way to teach mathematics" and "When students read aloud to the class, teachers should immediately correct each error and praise each correctly read sentence." Although the response-acquisition view has led to some important innovations in educational practice, it offers a somewhat limited set of teaching methods and goals. Classrooms based on the response-acquisition view can be criticized on the grounds that students are learning specific skills, but are doing so in a rote way that will not lead to transfer.

Another popular theory of learning among prospective teachers is what can be called the *knowledge-acquisition view*—the idea that learning involves adding new information to one's memory and, consequently, that teaching involves dispensing of information. Proponents of this view are likely to agree with assertions such as "Students need to be able to correctly execute solution procedures in mathematics, so it is important to make sure that they know each step in the procedure" or "In reading, students need to acquire comprehension strategies such as being able to figure out the meaning of a word from context." Like the response-acquisition view, the knowledge-acquisition view has led to important improvements in educational practice, but still offers a limited approach to teaching. To view learners as empty vessels that need to be filled creates a curriculum-centered classroom in which the goal is systematically to cram as much information into students as possible. Again, the main problem with a knowledge-acquisition approach is that students may learn by rote and not be able to transfer what they have learned in new situations.

When students find fault with their existing theories of learning, a prime candidate for a new theory is the *knowledge-construction view*—the idea that learning involves an effort to make sense of the presented material and that teaching involves serving as a sort of cognitive guide for students engaged in authentic academic tasks. Proponents of the knowledge-construction theory of learning are likely to agree with assertions such as "Students need to understand arithmetic procedures such as by using concrete manipulatives" or "Students need to be able to plan an essay for a specific audience rather than merely to convey information." Although the knowledge-acquisition theory leads to a curriculum-centered view of education, the knowledge-construction theory is consistent with the learner-centered approach advocated in this volume.

Developing a Personal Teaching Style

Having established one's view of the goals of teaching and the nature of learning, prospective teachers can establish their own style of teaching. A learner-centered approach—based on the goal of meaning-learning outcomes and the view of learning as knowledge construction—can be manifested in many ways. For example, a mathematics teacher who wishes to teach about functions must make decisions about what to teach, how to teach, and where to teach. Concerning what to teach, the teacher can focus on basic skills in equation solving or on how to represent a problem in words, tables, graphs, and equations. Concerning how to teach, the teacher can provide direct instruction in how to solve equations followed by drill and practice on similar problems or can allow for open discussion of alternative methods for representing and solving a challenging realistic problem. Concerning where to teach, the teacher can focus on each new equation-solving technique in isolation or can embed the lesson within a meaningful context such as examining the profitability of a business. In each case, a teacher who has opted for a learner-centered approach is more likely to develop a personal teaching style in which what to teach includes an understanding of key ideas, how to teach involves an emphasis on the process of problem solving, and where to teach involves a realistic context.

Conclusion

Cognitive theory offers a fundamentally new vision of what to teach, how to teach, and where to teach. The issue of what to teach involves focusing on abstract independent skills or concrete domain-based strategies; the issue of how to teach involves focusing on product (e.g., through drill and practice) or process (e.g., through modeling of underlying cognitive processes); and the issue of where to teach involves teaching in isolation or teaching within the context of a real problem or task. Instead of teaching individual behavioral skills in isolation through drill and practice (such as exercises in adding the suffix *s* to change a singular noun into a plural noun or adding a constant to both sides of an algebraic equation), cognitive theory suggests teaching of domain-based strategies within the context of larger problems through modeling of the required thinking processes (such as describing how one plans to write an essay on "How I Spent My Summer Vacation" or describing one's plan for solving a two-step word problem).

The years ahead promise to be exciting for those interested in fulfilling Thorndike's vision of improving educational practice on the basis of scientific research. The cognitive theory that has come to dominate psychology was nurtured by educational demands and has finally begun to exert its influence on education. As the behaviorist grip on educational practices is replaced with cognitively oriented methods, the time is ripe for fundamental changes in the process of instruction.

A discussion of the *Learner-Centered Psychological Principles* belongs at the center of the educational reform process. Current cognitive theory points to the active nature of learning and the situated nature of learning. The increasing relevance of cognitive theory for education places new demands on teachers to become prudent consumers of educational research, to develop a productive vision of instructional goals, to construct a useful theory of how students learn, and to develop appropriate instructional methods.

The educational reform movement, including the six national educational goals, is replete with high-sounding proclamations from political leaders. However, educational psychologists have unique contributions to make to the success of this movement, so the educational decision makers would be missing a necessary component if they failed to base instructional changes on an understanding of how people learn, think, and develop. The *Learner-Centered Psychological Principles* represent an exemplary review of how psychology can contribute to the educational reform movement.

References

American Psychological Association Board of Educational Affairs. (1995). *Learner-centered psychological principles: A framework for school redesign and reform* [On-line]. Available: http://www.apa.org/ed/lcp.html

Anderson, J. (1983). *The architecture of cognition.* Cambridge, MA: Harvard University Press.

Bartlett, F. C. (1932). *Remembering.* Cambridge, England: Cambridge University Press.

Berliner, D., & Calfee, R. (1996). (Eds.). *Handbook of educational psychology.* New York: Macmillan.

Brown, J. S., & Burton, R. R. (1978). Diagnostic models for procedural bugs in basic mathematical skills. *Cognitive Science, 2,* 155–192.

Bruner, J. S. (1964). Some theorems on instruction illustrated with reference to mathematics. In E. Hilgard (Ed.), *The sixty-third yearbook of the National Society for the Study of Education: Part 1. Theories of learning and instruction* (pp. 306–335). Chicago: National Society for the Study of Education.

Carpenter, T. P., & Fennema, E. (1992). Cognitively guided instruction: Building on the knowledge of students and teachers. *International Journal of Educational Research, 17,* 457–470.

Case, R. (1985). *Intellectual development: Birth to adulthood.* San Diego, CA: Academic Press.

Cognition and Technology Group at Vanderbilt. (1990). Anchored instruction and its relation to situated cognition. *Educational Researcher, 19*(6), 2–10.

Cubberly, E. P. (1920). *The history of education.* Boston: Houghton Mifflin.

Dewey, J. (1902). The child and the curriculum. Chicago: University of Chicago Press.

Di Vesta, F. J. (1989). Applications of cognitive psychology to education. In M. C. Wittrock & F. Farley (Eds.), *The future of educational psychology* (pp. 37–73). Hillsdale, NJ: Erlbaum.

Dole, J. A., Duffy, G. C., Roehler, L. R., & Pearson, P. D. (1991). Moving from the old to the new: Research on reading comprehension instruction. *Review of Educational Research, 61,* 239–264.

Fitzgerald, J., & Markman, L. R. (1987). Teaching children about revision in writing. *Cognition and Instruction, 4,* 3–24.

Fitzgerald, J., & Teasley, A. B. (1986). Effects of instruction in narrative structure on children's writing. *Journal of Educational Psychology, 78,* 424–432.

Flower, L. S., & Hayes, J. R. (1980). Identifying the organization of writing processes. In L. W. Gregg & E. R. Steinberg (Eds.), *Cognitive processes in writing* (pp. 3–30). Hillsdale, NJ: Erlbaum.

Fuson, K. C. (1982). An analysis of the counting-on solution procedure in addition. In T. P. Carpenter, J. M. Moser, & T. A. Romberg (Eds.), *Addition and subtraction: A cognitive perspective* (pp. 67–81). Hillsdale, NJ: Erlbaum.

Glynn, S. M., Britton, B. K., Muth, K. D., & Dogan, N. (1982). Writing and revising persuasive documents: Cognitive demands. *Journal of Educational Psychology, 74,* 557–567.

Graham, S., & Harris, K. R. (1988). Instructional recommendations for teaching writing to exceptional students. *Exceptional Children, 54,* 506–512.

Grinder, R. E. (1989). Educational psychology: The master science. In M. C. Wittrock & F. Farley, (Eds.), *The future of educational psychology* (pp. 3–18). Hillsdale, NJ: Erlbaum.

James, W. (1958). *Talks to teachers.* New York: Norton. (Originally published 1899)

Kintsch, W., & Greeno, J. G. (1985). Understanding and solving word arithmetic problems. *Psychological Review, 92,* 109–129.

LaBerge, D., & Samuels, S. J. (1974). Toward a theory of automatic information processing in reading. *Cognitive Psychology, 6,* 293–323.

Levin, J. R. (1992). Editorial. *Journal of Educational Psychology, 84,* 3–5.

Lewis, A. B. (1989). Training students to represent arithmetic word problems. *Journal of Educational Psychology, 81,* 521–531.

Mayer, R. E. (1984). Aids to text comprehension. *Educational Psychologist, 19,* 30–42.

Mayer, R. E. (1985). Mathematical ability. In R. J. Sternberg (Ed.), *Human abilities: An information processing approach* (pp. 127–150). New York: Freeman.

Mayer, R. E. (1987). *Educational psychology: A cognitive approach.* New York: Harper Collins.

Mayer, R. E. (1989a). Introduction to the special section. *Journal of Educational Psychology, 81,* 452–456.

Mayer, R. E. (1989b). Models for understanding. *Review of Educational Research, 59*, 43–64.

Mayer, R. E. (1992a). Guiding students' cognitive processing of scientific information. In M. Pressley, K. Harris, & J. Guthrie (Eds.), *Promoting academic competence and literacy: Cognitive research and instructional innovation* (pp. 243–258). San Diego, CA: Academic Press.

Mayer, R. E. (1992b). *Thinking, problem solving, cognition* (2nd ed.). New York: Freeman.

Norman, D. A. (1980). Cognitive engineering and education. In D. Tuma & F. Reif (Eds.), *Problem solving and education* (pp. 97–107). Hillsdale, NJ: Erlbaum.

Paris, S. G., & Lindauer, B. K. (1976). The role of inference in children's comprehension and memory for sentences. *Cognitive Psychology, 8*, 217–227.

Piaget, J. (1954). *The construction of reality in the child.* New York: Ballantine Books.

Pressley, M. (1990). *Cognitive strategy instruction that really improves children's academic performance.* Cambridge, MA: Brookline Books.

Pressley, M., & Levin, J. R. (Eds.). (1983a). *Cognitive strategy research: Educational applications.* New York: Springer-Verlag.

Pressley, M., & Levin, J. R. (Eds.). (1983b). *Cognitive strategy research: Psychological foundations.* New York: Springer-Verlag.

Resnick, L. B. (1989). Introduction. In L. B. Resnick (Ed.), *Knowing, learning, and instruction: Essays in honor of Robert Glaser* (pp. 1–24). Hillsdale, NJ: Erlbaum.

Resnick, L. B., & Ford, W. W. (1981). *The psychology of mathematics instruction.* Hillsdale, NJ: Erlbaum.

Scandura, J. M., Frase, L. T., Gagne, R. M., Stolurow, K. A., Stolurow, L. M., & Groen, G. (1981). Current status and future directions of educational psychology as a discipline. In F. Farley & N. J. Gordon (Eds.), *Psychology and education* (pp. 367–388). Berkeley, CA: McCutchan.

Scardamalia, M., Bereiter, C., & Goelman, H. (1982). The role of production factors in writing ability. In M. Nystant (Ed.), *What writers know* (pp. 173–210). San Diego, CA: Academic Press.

Schoenfeld, A. H. (1985). *Mathematical problem solving.* San Diego, CA: Academic Press.

Siegler, R. S. (1986). *Children's thinking.* Englewood Cliffs, NJ: Prentice-Hall.

Singley, M. K., & Anderson, J. R. (1989). *The transfer of cognitive skill.* Cambridge, MA: Harvard University Press.

Sternberg, R. J. (1985). *Beyond IQ: A triarchic theory of human intelligence.* Cambridge, England: Cambridge University Press.

Sternberg, R. J. (1988). *The triarchic mind: Conceptions of the nature of intelligence.* Cambridge, England: Cambridge University Press.

Thorndike, E. L. (1906). *The principles of teaching based on psychology.* Syracuse, NY: Mason-Henry Press.

Thorndike, E. L. (1910). The contribution of psychology to education. *Journal of Educational Psychology, 1*, 5–12.

Tolman, E. C. (1932). *Purposive behavior in animals and men.* New York: Appleton-Century-Crofts.

U.S. Department of Education, Office of Educational Research and Improvement. (1991). *Striving for excellence: The national educational goals.* Washington, DC: Author.

Walberg, H. J., & Haertel, G. D. (1992). Educational psychology's first century. *Journal of Educational Psychology, 84*, 6–19.

Weinstein, C. E., & Mayer, R. E. (1985). The teaching of learning strategies. In M. C. Wittrock (Ed.), *Handbook of research on teaching* (3rd ed., pp. 315–327). New York: Macmillan.

Wittrock, M. C. (1967). Focus on educational psychology. *Educational Psychologist, 4,* 1–7.

Wittrock, M. C. (1989). Educational psychology and the future of research in learning, instruction, and teaching. In M. C. Wittrock & F. Farley (Eds.), *The future of educational psychology* (pp. 75–89). Hillsdale, NJ: Erlbaum.

Woodring, P. (1958). Introduction. In W. James, *Talks to teachers* (pp. 6–17). New York: Norton.

Integrating Metacognition, Affect, and Motivation in Improving Teacher Education

Barbara L. McCombs

It is almost an understatement today to say the American educational system is in crisis. Citizens and professionals at all levels of society are calling attention to notable failures of the current system with respect to alarmingly high rates of student dropout, school failure, unsatisfactory levels of achievement, and associated problems such as delinquency, teenage pregnancy, drug and alcohol abuse, and even suicide. Although these problems are not solely attributable to failures of the educational system, relationships between students' achievement in school and these related problems point to the critical role schools, administrators, and teachers can play in reducing the negative trends. At the same time, however, there is rising agreement that schools and educators by themselves cannot solve all of the problems affecting today's youth and that it is the joint responsibility of educators, families, and communities to work together in designing and operating a better system. In response, there are a growing number of schools and school districts that are making significant progress in redesign efforts. Accumulated evidence suggests that learner-centered restructuring efforts can offset or ameliorate underlying problems of alienation, fear of failure, and perceived lack of personal relevance, all of which contribute both to youth's devaluing of education and to their search for other, often negative, alternatives to meet their needs to feel valued, competent, and in control.

This chapter is based in part on a paper presented at the symposium on Using Cognitive, Affective, and Motivation Theory to Improve Education, as part of the Contributions of Psychology to Learning and Education miniconvention at the 99th Annual Convention of the American Psychological Association, San Francisco, August 1991.

To understand why learner-centered models based on well-researched principles of learning, motivation, and individual differences are achieving success, it is helpful to consider the educational reform journey. A case can be made that reform efforts of the past have primarily focused on technical content and its delivery and the organizational structures and processes required to promote learning, achievement, and efficient and effective system management. For many participants in the system—including students, teachers, and parents—feelings of alienation, frustration over lack of control, and inadequacy in performing at acceptable or potentially exceptional levels interfere with successful learning and achievement. Furthermore, expectations about what the system should do, look like, or achieve are often based on outdated notions about learning and individual differences, making change difficult.

Interventions that focus on the people in the system—particularly teachers and their beliefs and practices as they relate to student learning—show particular promise in addressing personal issues and promoting student motivation and achievement. These interventions are geared toward (a) creating a positive context for learning at the classroom and schools levels for all constituents and (b) supporting the change in thinking and perspective required at all system levels and for all constituents for successful and sustainable system change. They stem from the knowledge that personal and interpersonal concerns are at the heart of why some of the best technical (e.g., performance-based assessment and cooperative learning) and organizational (e.g., shared decision making) strategies work well in one context but fail in another.

As a result, current reform movements in education are calling for teachers to attend to the needs of the whole student in achieving high academic standards as well as to provide more integrative and personally relevant curricula and learning assessments. Along with these efforts toward holistic educational methods, psychological theorizing has begun to move in the direction of more integrative, cross-disciplinary accounts of human nature and functioning and how these apply to learning and motivation. To address the complexity of meaningful learning experiences in and outside of the classroom, both new and experienced teachers need to understand theories of learning and psychological functioning that can explain the interrelationships between higher order metacognitive processes, affect, and motivation. Furthermore, teachers need to develop attitudes, skills, and strategies for capitalizing on this understanding in enhancing motivation and learning for all students.

In this chapter, I present a research-based, learner-centered framework for describing these interrelationships. I conclude with implications of this framework for educational practice, new paradigms of learning and motivation, and teacher education that recognizes the teacher as learner. To better set the context for the framework, however, I first describe the need for this model as evidenced by concerns of educators and students.

What Educators and Students Are Saying About Education

A common concern among teachers and other educators across the country is that students appear unmotivated to learn, are bored with school, do not seem to value learning, and have an increasing disregard for what adults can teach them. In addition, many students tell us they do not experience school as relevant to their personal interests or to life, do not believe most teachers care about them or what they think, and are frustrated by a system in which teachers or other adults seem burned out or are "going through the motions." Educators think these students do not care. However, students say they do care about learning, but they are not getting what they need. Furthermore, educators themselves are frustrated because they do not know how to deal with the increasing diversity of students in today's schools, do not understand how to best meet diverse student needs, and do not believe they are being supported by their administration and communities in sharing responsibility for demanding accountability standards.

It is apparent, however, that when students feel alienated and disconnected from the process of learning and from the social context of learning, levels of achievement are lowered. Meeting students' needs for a positive learning climate based on quality student-teacher relationships is a key issue from students' points of view. When students are asked what makes school a place where they want to learn, they report that they want (a) "rigor and joy" in their schoolwork, (b) a balance of complexity and clarity, (c) opportunities to discuss meaning and values, (d) learning activities that are relevant and fun, and (d) learning experiences that offer some choice and require action (Strong, Silver, & Robinson, 1995).

Many researchers have found that what students say they like best about school are teachers and other people who care about them. For example, researchers at the Claremont Graduate School in California spent a year in four schools (two elementary, one middle, and one high school) asking students, teachers, administrators, and parents what they thought was "right" about their schools (Institute for Education in Transformation, 1992; Poplin & Weeres, 1993). The following are common comments from students:

> "What I like about school is one of my teachers. I like the way she talks to me like I am a human. My other teacher, I can't think of a thing I like. She looks over my shoulder when I am working. I can't stand it."
>
> "When I walk into my second period class, my teacher is there to meet you with a handshake and a smile, which makes you know it's going to be a good day. He knows your name, which makes you feel good."

Most frequently mentioned by all groups of students in the Claremont study were "human" issues—relationships, a mix of races and cultures, values, and classroom aesthetics. These mattered most, with quality human relationships characterized by caring, listening, honesty and openness, understanding, and respect at the top of the list. People in the schools studied were clear that educational reform cannot be discussed without these issues—that go beyond the academic—at the center of the discussions.

In commenting about their teachers and classrooms, students clearly focused on the affective factors of learning and teaching. Although such factors may be most salient to students, research indicates that there are other factors that lead to supportive learning environments and, ultimately, to student achievement (e.g., Goldenberg, 1991; Resnick, 1987). For example, effective teachers provide an optimal amount of structure that is neither laissez-faire nor authoritarian, invite students to participate in classroom decision making, maintain high expectations for all students, instruct in developmentally appropriate ways that challenge all students, help instill a sense of purpose in what students are doing, and encourage students to take responsibility for their own learning. In essence, effective practices are those that integrate strategies that focus on the learner *and* learning.

How does one resolve the differing perspectives of educators and students and design educational systems that are responsive to the concerns of both educators and students? I believe that the answers can be found by taking a careful look at schools that are successful for all learners—including teachers, administrators, and parents—and by understanding the knowledge base on both learners and learning. In my examination of both areas, I have found that an understanding of the learner-centered perspective and the research base that supports it is essential to successful schools.

What Defines Successful Educational Interventions?

In examining the characteristics of successful programs, some interesting commonalities can be noted. For example, in a review of successful dropout prevention interventions, Peck, Law, and Mills (1989) discovered that those program elements that clearly contributed to program success were relatively simple and straightforward. The common element across successful programs centered on the quality of the relationship established between adults and youth and a genuine caring for students and an understanding of the optimal climate for learning. Almost irrespective of specific program elements and focus, the single most important factor in the success or failure of a program was this quality relationship, including the quality of people carrying out the program. Thus, it matters less what is done than who does it and how. As Peck and her colleagues state,

> all research concludes that at-risk youth have poorer self-concepts than other students, higher insecurity about their ability to fit in at school, and higher subjective perceptions that school is not for them. Staff must be the kind of people who are not only committed to, but optimistic about, reaching these youth. They must also be the kind of people who are able to bypass this insecure frame of reference and reach students at a deeper level of mental health, motivation, and common sense. (p. 19)

The development of a caring culture in schools requires a change in attitude—not just a restructuring of policies, curricula, and systems. In essence, schools must be learner centered and consider the personal needs and development of all learners—students and teachers included—within the larger context of their families and communities. Caring is what Lipsitz (1995) argued is necessary for establishing an effective culture for learning. It does not replace the need to have high standards and expectations for learning, but it represents a core set of beliefs about how we should treat others.

In addition to the impact of caring and quality relationships on learning, Chaskin and Rauner (1995) argued that there is an important effect of the teacher-student relationship that is often overlooked: the ability of such relationships to offset students' feelings of frustration with or alienation from school. Caring was found to be what differentiated successful from unsuccessful programs in research funded by the Lily Endowment's Research Program on Youth and Caring. A *caring environment* was defined as one in which (a) an atmosphere was created that helped young people feel welcome, respected, and comfortable; (b) experiences were structured to provide opportunities for students to develop caring relationships with both adults and peers; (c) information was provided to students about what it means to care for themselves and others; and (d) opportunities and training were provided to encourage students to engage in projects that contribute to the "greater good," such as service, advocacy, and active problem solving of critical human issues. Research has shown that when youth have opportunities to care for others, they have an increased sense of social responsibility, higher self-esteem, better school attendance, and decreased depression.

Others have argued that to impact student motivation and achievement, change must start with the attitudes and conceptions of educators (e.g., Sarason, 1995). Not only is the attitude dimension often ignored but also power relationships and how they need to be altered to support learning for students and teachers alike. Sarason (1995) argued that the overarching purpose of schooling "is to stimulate, capitalize on, and sustain the kind of motivation, intellectual curiosity, awe, and wonder that a child possesses when he or she begins schooling" (p. 85).

Several important implications emerge with regard to these findings: (a) What works in successful programs is an intervention that addresses the whole person. (b) The whole person intervention is best implemented by caring individuals in quality relationships with youth. (c) The result is that by accessing deeper levels of mental health and motivation, youth are able to make positive changes for themselves.

An essential question, then, is how we—as psychologists and educators—can best contribute to an understanding of those qualities of human relationships that (a) foster an optimal climate for learning and (b) can unlock students' natural health and motivation to learn. We also need to clarify the nature of motivation in complex school settings and how what we know about metacognition, affect, and motivation can be integrated to improve both teacher education and educational practice in general. This chapter focuses on these latter issues in particular, while also addressing how significant developments in psychological research and theory have led to practical implications for education in general and a learner-centered model for professional development in particular.

The Need for an Integrative Framework

In searching for a clearer understanding of the nature of motivation to learn and how it is fostered in classroom settings, it is easy to be overwhelmed by the complex array of psychological, demographic, and contextual variables to be considered. There is no question that significant person–environment interactions exist and account for important differences in student expectations to succeed, motivation, and performance. But are researchers looking in the right direction? A number of psychologists suggest that we may not be. They suggest that there may be some basic, fundamental principles of psychological functioning that can explain complex individual differences and their interactions with the vast array of external variables. They suggest that these fundamental principles move us in the direction of attending to the role of higher order self-processes and metacognitive self-awareness of individuals' personal agency in overriding or bypassing the deterministic role cognitions—including personal interpretations and constructed knowledge and beliefs—and external situational and environmental factors play in motivation and performance. What is exciting about this direction is that it promises to not only clarify our understanding of motivational phenomena, but it also offers a potentially useful framework for designing improved practices in teacher education. By identifying unifying and basic principles of human psychological functioning that explain external behavioral and social phenomena, lawful relationships can be defined between internal individual differences (cognitive capabilities, knowledge and belief structures, and motivational processes) and external factors (background, genetics, and environment). The complexity of individual differences and their interactions with external factors has led psychology on the path of complex and often competing theories of human behavior, cognition, emotion, learning, and motivation. By shifting our search to fundamental, verifiable assumptions about human nature and functioning that can integrate and explain competing theories, we can build a foundation for guiding educational practices for teachers and students.

Exploring the Higher Order Nature of the Self

How do we explain the behavior of individuals such as our colleagues, students, experimental subjects, and even ourselves—that falls outside of what is considered predictable—by past histories, personal characteristics, internal belief systems, or external conditions? How do we account for the self-determining aspects of human nature and our own phenomenological experience of higher order agency in understanding and directing lower order intellectual, emotional, and behavioral processes? It is questions like these that have prompted psychologists from a variety of disciplines to search for more comprehensive models of human psychological functioning.

Noteworthy in this regard is the work of Mills (1990, 1991, 1995) and his colleagues (Mills, Dunham, & Alpert, 1988; Mills, Olson, & Bailey, 1994; R. Suarez, Mills, & Stewart, 1987). The focus of this work has been to specify fundamental principles of psychological functioning and mental health, verify these principles with applied research, and develop interventions to promote the psychological health and well-being of individuals caught in negative cycles of thinking, feeling, and behaving. The "wellness" framework articulated in Mills's work posits the following principles and assumptions:

- Individuals begin life with the inherent capacity for psychological health, including an unconditional sense of self-esteem, capacity for common sense, intrinsic motivation to learn, and capacity for insight and creativity.

  This inner core of health is posited as a tangible part of the self that operates outside the cognitive or intellectual system. It is accessed at higher levels of consciousness in which one sees beyond his or her conditioned belief system or personal frame of reference. This level of awareness is naturally and directly available to all human beings at any time.
- Thought creates each individual's unique experience of reality.
- Knowing how thought operates to create personal "realities" and how one can reconstruct negative perspectives and patterns of thinking is what helps any individual regain his or her innate ability to be motivated from the metacognitive self as agent. Understanding the role of thought allows individuals to function in a state of mind prior to thought in which they are free from, or outside of, their habitual self-conscious ways of thinking and can

see clearly what thoughts are (i.e., self-constructed interpretations of reality).

- Individuals have the capacity to operate at different levels of awareness (consciousness) of their basic nature and the function of thought.

In states of consciousness (pure awareness, the ability to experience life) that are less contaminated by self-conscious thoughts, individuals function directly from their inner core of psychological wellness. When individuals understand differences between the qualities of their feelings in the intrinsic, as opposed to their conditioned, self-conscious states of awareness, they are able to notice those times when they are in lower states of functioning. They can then reduce their self-conscious thinking to a degree that allows consciousness of their higher self to reemerge.

The most dramatic demonstration of the validity of these principles is Mills's (1990, 1991, 1995) study with residents in two housing projects in Miami. Mills contributed the success of his intervention with the residents to their ability to see that they already had the resources to solve the problems in their lives and their environment. Through developing quality relationships with residents, building trust, and teaching principles of psychological functioning, Mills was able to help the residents access their natural self-esteem, common sense, and inner wisdom. Once they "saw" (realized and knew) their own inherent potential and understood that they were responsible for the quality of their lives, they began to see more positive future possibilities for themselves, their families, and their community. A sense of hope replaced previous feelings of despair and negative cycles of thinking, and it was at this point that their goals changed. Thus, the intervention was true empowerment in that it released the natural potential for people to change themselves and transform their ways of looking at themselves and their circumstances.

Related research supporting Mills's work includes that on intrinsic motivation by Deci and Ryan (1991) and Ryan (1995). This research defines *self-determination* as an awareness or realization of one's source of agency and personal control. *Agency* is described as an inherent tendency of the self to originate behavior, to relate to and assimilate events, and to gain a sense of effectance. In this view, awareness of agency is the basis for self-determination; it is a basic motivational process of the self that goes deeper than cognition. The self is said to have at its core an energizing component termed *intrinsic* or *growth* motivation. The "true self" is in operation when one's actions are endorsed by oneself —with integrity and cohesion. *Authenticity* is self-determination, with the person viewing the self as the locus of active development. The self is intrinsically motivated and actively engaged in knowing and directing itself at levels of functioning that lay outside the cognitive system.

Harter (1990) turned her attention to higher order self-processes in her work on "the self beyond the me in the mirror." She emphasizes that researchers need to move away from the descriptive and evaluative aspects of self-concept and self-esteem and focus more on the deep understanding of the self as outside of or beyond these constructions. Her research has demonstrated that individuals with more internalized, unconditional feelings of self-worth experience more positive affect and intrinsic motivation to learn.

Lazarus (1991) contended that the mind cannot be equated with cognition, individuals differ in their awareness or consciousness of the particular thought that produces an emotion, and people personally construct and "carry around with them" personal meanings and interpretations that form the basis for their emotional reactions. Lazarus defined *mental health* as a recognition of the inner agency of mind; an understanding of the rules that apply to one's construction of his or her inner and outer life; a harmonious integration of mind, cognition, motivation, and emotion; and a realization and experience of higher stages of consciousness.

Further delving into a deeper understanding of higher order self-processes, Ridley (1991) provided an interesting conceptualization and empirical corroboration of the impact of differences in reflective self-awareness on individuals' self-regulated behaviors, motivation, and goals. Ridley was able to verify that higher level awareness and understanding of one's personal agency over lower order cognitive processes, thoughts, and beliefs positively impact affect, motivation, and performance in a learning situation. Similarly, research by Borkowski, Day, Saenz, Dietmeyer, and Estrada (1990) has begun to uncover the role of higher order metacognitive self-processes in enhancing motivation, the effectiveness of cognitive interventions, and student performance.

These are but a few examples of many efforts within multiple fields of psychology to enlarge the paradigm of human psychological functioning, focusing on the primary role of the self and its higher level processes in motivation and meaningful learning. Next, I discuss evidence that these efforts are moving in a direction that can be helpful for teacher education.

Supporting Research Evidence for Successful Educational Interventions

Earlier, I introduced evidence that successful interventions were those that addressed the whole person, were implemented by caring adults who established quality relationships with youth, and were those that helped youth access deeper levels of mental health and motivation that made it possible for them to make positive changes for themselves. These key elements are consistent with recent directions in the study of motivation as presented in the preceding section—directions that emphasize the inherent mental health or wellness of even the most troubled and disadvantaged youth. They also point to the importance of empowerment as a strategy for uncovering this health and enabling natural motivation to learn to reemerge, and the focus on meeting higher order needs for self-determination and personal control or agency.

Research that substantiates the importance of these directions for helping teachers and teacher educators understand how best to enhance student motivation and learning can be grouped into several categories. All of this research examines how an understanding of basic psychological principles of learning and overall functioning (including an understanding of the self as agent) can impact on student motivation, access to higher order metacognitive and self-regulatory learning processes, and performance. For teachers and teacher educators, however, categories with particular relevance include research that explores (a) teacher qualities and relationship variables; (b) strategies such as goal setting for promoting the personal relevance and meaningfulness of learning experiences; and (c) empowerment approaches directed at enhancing students' recognition of their personal agency.

Teacher Qualities and Relationships

First, in the area of teacher variables, Bernieri (1991) reported that in an investigation of the amount of complex vocabulary definitions learned by high school students as a function of teachers' interpersonal sensitivity in dyadic teaching interactions, the cluster of teacher qualities that was most strongly related to amount learned included the following: seeing things from the students' perspective, being genuinely interested in and concerned for their students, being person oriented and involving, and displaying responsibility and valuing order. The multiple correlation was .74, indicating an extremely strong impact of the teacher sensitivity cluster on learning.

Further substantiating the universality of this finding is research by Helmke and Schrader (1991) with German fifth graders and their teachers in 39 classes. The goal of this research was to determine whether teachers who are strongly achievement oriented in their instruction sacrifice affective goals, such as positive student attitudes toward themselves and learning. Findings of particular relevance were that those classes in which students both learned the most and had the highest positive attitudes toward themselves (their self-concept of ability) and learning had teachers characterized as (a) sensitive to and tolerant of (patient with) student differences in learning ability ($r = .84$); (b) adaptive to individual differences in their instructional approach ($r = .58$); (c) task-oriented and focused on presenting content in interesting and involving ways ($r = .57$); (d) attentive to affective climate, using praise and humor ($r = .35$); and (e) capable of clearly presenting information and making sure students are comprehending what is presented ($r = .32$). This positive cluster defines teachers who attend to both cognitive and affective instructional goals. What is particularly striking is that far and away the most important teacher characteristic for maximum positive affect and learning was the teachers' sensitivity and respect for individual students and their differences in ability. Helmke and Schrader concluded that this variable plays a key role in the simultaneous attainment of cognitive and noncognitive growth in students. Also of interest in this study is the finding that the teacher—and not the classroom context—is central in the achievement of multiple goals. Teachers exhibiting the qualities that produced the most favorable results were in relatively unfavorable contexts—classes that had students of lower ability, had a higher percentage of foreign students, and were of moderate size.

Research by Ryan and his colleagues (Ryan, 1995; Ryan & Powelson, 1991; Ryan & Stiller, 1991) also clarifies qualities of teacher–student relationships that foster higher order learning, motivation, and autonomy. Results from a series of school and classroom-based studies reveal that both teacher qualities and the social context of schools significantly impact psychological health and positive cognitive outcomes. Key findings include the following:

- Children in the classrooms of teachers who are more autonomy oriented (vs. controlling) report more curiosity, more desire for challenge, more independent mastery attempts, greater perceived competence in school, and higher general self-worth.
- Students who view their interactions with teachers as controlling

act more like "pawns" and may make teachers more controlling as a reciprocal influence, whereas students who are more self-regulating may facilitate responsiveness and support from teachers, which leads to greater self-determination.

- Students experiencing more controlling and externally set performance goals (e.g., grades) engage in less active assimilation and integration of what is learned and demonstrate lower long-term retention than students in less directed and pressured learning environments.
- Students receiving support for autonomy from parents engage in more self-regulated learning activities, are rated more highly by teachers on competence and adjustment, and attain higher grades and achievement levels than students in controlling homes.
- Teachers who believe students are extrinsically motivated are more controlling than teachers who believe students are intrinsically motivated.
- Teachers who work for controlling administrators report less satisfaction with their work, less trust in district and building policies, and more concern with extrinsic outcomes, such as pay and benefits than those whose administrators are more supportive of autonomy.
- Teachers' capacity to promote self-regulation and internalization of value for learning in students is intertwined with teachers' opportunities to regulate their own activities and be creative, innovative, and intrinsically motivated on a day-to-day basis.
- Policies that pressure teachers toward standards or performance requirements for their students result in more controlling versus autonomy-supportive styles in teachers, which, in turn, leads to student performance decrements and lower level cognitive outcomes (e.g., less creative and less capable of critical thinking) as well as deepening feelings of alienation and disengagement from learning.
- Changing teacher and student perceptions of autonomy support as well as the quality of relatedness facilitate positive relationships that, in turn, promote more active student engagement, volition, and confidence in learning.

Ryan and his colleagues (Ryan, 1995; Ryan & Powelson, 1991; Ryan & Stiller, 1991) concluded that an understanding of the psychological needs of individuals clearly points to the fact that autonomy and relatedness are fundamental for learning and motivation. Thus, facilitating environments are those that provide interpersonal involvement and support for autonomy for both students and their teachers.

Weinstein (chap. 4, this volume) argues that concern with motivation to learn is critical because of the central role motivation plays in academic success and in sustained commitment to learning across the life span. She points out that expectations about learning capability play a critical role in motivation. Efforts to promote "positive expectancy climates" are particularly needed in this time of increasing diversity of learners. Weinstein sees the learner-centered psychological principles as helping to define the conditions for creating such climates and presents an integrative model that defines effective expectancy practices in terms of curriculum, grouping, evaluation, motivation, responsibility for learning, class relations, parent–class relations, and school–class relations. These include strategies that reduce ability comparisons among students, foster beliefs that a range of abilities are valued, promote student choice and agency, increase warmth and trust, broaden communication opportunities, and increase leadership and chances for success at both school and classroom levels.

To accomplish these changes, it is necessary to help both teachers and students "change their minds" or modify current thinking. One critical task is to help teachers learn to value student perceptions of practice and increase negotiation strategies in which students and teachers work together collaboratively to define changes in practice and expectations. When beliefs change, practices and climate change, and student outcomes shift to more positive expectations, higher motivation, and higher achievement. Perceived obstacles are translated into opportunities, as teachers collaboratively reframe their work with students, other teachers, and administrators.

My own work supports these findings (McCombs, 1990, 1991a, 1991b, 1991c; McCombs & Marzano, 1990, in press; McCombs & Whisler, 1989, 1997). My colleagues and I have focused on promoting the mental health and potential of high-risk youth through addressing will, skill, and social support components. Within this model, *will* is defined as an innate or "self-actualized" state of motivation, an internal state of well-being, in which individuals are in touch with their natural self-esteem, common sense, and intrinsic motivation to learn. *Skill* is defined as an acquired cognitive or metacognitive competency that develops with training and practice. *Social support* is the enabling interpersonal context for the empowerment of will and the development of skill components, specifically through quality relationships and interactions with others.

Empowerment in this model is reciprocal and is embodied in training for parents, teachers, administrators, and students. As parents, teachers, and administrators develop positive belief systems in themselves and their students, and as they acquire a higher level understanding of students' inherent mental health and how to uncover it through enhanced communication and interactions (will component), they are empowered to create a positive emotional climate and to develop enhanced interpersonal relationships with their students that embody qualities of mutual trust, respect, caring, and concern (social support component). This positive emotional climate—in combination with teaching students mental health principles from the will component—helps uncover students' natural motivation to acquire and develop the knowledge and skills imparted through the schooling process (skill component). As students display enhanced will and skill, teachers, parents, and administrators are empowered by seeing and realizing how they can nurture children's inner potential to learn and develop in positive ways. In addition, administrators are empowered by seeing and realizing how they can nurture teachers' inner potential for creative and wise educational practices that lead to enhanced student outcomes. Thus, common principles of empowerment work reciprocally for all individuals in the system.

Whisler (1991) described evidence that supports this model. Following a year of involvement with students, teachers, parents, and administrators in a middle school located in the heart of Denver's most severe gang and drug problems, Whisler noted dramatic changes in the emotional climate, mental health, and academic performance of area students. Teachers and parents gained a new and more positive view of their students' potential and responded with more understanding in the classroom and at home. Administrators were more supportive of teacher needs and requests for autonomy and innovation in the classroom and began to find more ways to involve parents in school activities and students in their own education. A group of the most high-risk sixth and seventh grade students who had special support in learning about their own psychological functioning and in developing enhanced self-monitoring and self-regulation skills calmed down, had fewer discipline referrals, had begun attending school more regularly, showed improved grades, and reported more positive attitudes toward school.

Strategies for Promoting Personal Relevance

Most people can remember those learning experiences that particularly aroused their interest and involvement. They were activities that no doubt were in some way related to our personal interests, needs, or goals. Research verifies that these types of learning experiences are indeed the ones most conducive to student motivation and learning. Covington (1991, 1992), for example, conducted research showing that the motives or reasons for learning that students bring to a situation are powerful organizers of the perceived need and motivation to learn. Aligning student and instructional "motives" or goals is thus one critical way to enhance students' perceptions that learning is meaningful. Furthermore, seeing one's higher self as "valued agency" in the sense that "at the center of our being resides a decent, resourceful, basically playful source of energy" is what Covington (1991, p. 87) suggests can further enhance students' abilities to see themselves as capable of learning and thereby enhance motivation to learn.

Newby (1991) explored motivational strategies used by 30 elementary school classroom teachers and the impact of these strategies on students' on-task behaviors and interest. Strategies used by teachers were grouped into the following categories: focusing attention, providing relevance, building confidence, and administering rewards and punishments. Although the most frequently used strategies were administering rewards and punishments (58.31%), correlations between on-task behaviors indicated that providing relevance was the most significantly and positively related to on-task behaviors ($r = .61$), whereas building confidence ($r = .25$) and focusing attention ($r = .22$) were only moderately related to on-task behaviors, and administering rewards ($r = -.28$) or punishments ($r = -.23$) was negatively related to on-task behaviors. The important implication here is that motivating more active student involvement in learning activities can be accomplished by the addition of relevance—an intrinsically oriented strategy that engages students' natural motivation to learn those activities that are perceived to be related to personal interests, goals, or needs. Similarly, research by Bergin (1991) with preservice teacher education students revealed that promoting learning goals that focus students on developing a preference for challenge and learning new skills rather than outperforming their peers increased both achievement and enjoyment of learning. Again, natural motivation to learn was enhanced by focusing on self-relevant learning goals.

Schunk and Swartz (1991) also found positive effects of process goals and progress feedback on fifth-grade children's self-efficacy and writing skills. Because goals help students focus on goal-relevant activities, students are motivated to expend effort and persist on learning tasks, particularly when they value the goal and believe they are capable of achieving it. Helping students learn a strategy they believed was useful for accomplishing their performance goals further enhanced writing performance through its positive effects on students' judgments of self-efficacy. Research by Pintrich and his colleagues (Garcia & Pintrich, 1991; Pintrich & DeGroot, 1990) supports similar relationships—specifically, that motivation is a function of students' beliefs about (a) their ability to perform a task and their responsibility for their own performance, (b) their goals and beliefs about the importance and interest of the task, and (c) their feelings about these appraisals and the task. In addition, when students believed they were capable and adopted a learning and mastery orientation, they exhibited deeper levels of cognitive engagement in self-regulated learning.

Empowerment Approaches for Enhancing Agency

Dweck (1991; Dweck & Leggett, 1988), in his studies of the impact of adaptive versus maladaptive belief systems in children's motivation, found that adopting learning goals leads to positive beliefs about efficacy and agency. Research on the relationships between cognitions and affect, however, also shows that if students think that their competence or worth is somehow threatened in particular learning situations, their self-ruminations and goals will be more ego-focused and attention will be distracted from concerns with learning. If students can be helped to become task involved, however, less self-conscious task involvement is promoted. This is what Graham and Golan (1991) found in two studies with fifth- and sixth-grade students. When students' thoughts and feelings of agency and worth are enhanced and learned self-conscious cognitions are absent, students' natural tendencies to enjoy learning and experience feelings of well-being are elicited.

Whisler (1991) found even more positive motivational effects for student learning. According to Whisler, approaches that assume that motivational problems are indicators of a deficit to be fixed or a skill that is missing in students are basically disempowering and lead to short-term results, at best. Empowerment approaches need to help students access higher levels of consciousness regarding their agency so that students can begin to naturally function with more maturity and common sense, better behavior, more positive attitudes, better problem-solving ability, and increased motivation to learn. Results with this approach by Stewart (1984) and Timm and Stewart (1990) have shown that it (a) elevates student moods and produces substantial reading achievement gains, and (b) helps at-risk high school students increase their grades and reduce their suspensions from school.

Finally, in summarizing research and theory on motivation, Bob Marzano and I (McCombs & Marzano, 1990, in press) described the trend to focus on an understanding of the self as agent. Within this framework, constructed self-knowledge and beliefs play a primary role in motivation and behavior only to the extent that individuals are not aware of their role in choosing how to view the influence of these thoughts and beliefs. Supporting research by E. Suarez (1988) shows that if individuals do not recognize the choice to selectively use their thought system, they operate unconsciously within the limits of that thought system. Suarez argues that it is the function of thought that provides a more primary level of agency than the content of thought. Thought is both the immediate cause of all beliefs and can be controlled consciously and voluntarily. Mills's (1990, 1995) work with residents of a housing project shows that if individuals understand the function of thought, they are empowered by experiencing voluntary control of their thinking and, in turn, their emotions, motivation, and behavior.

Recent theories and research in motivation and self-processes indicate that the content of thought (e.g., beliefs, goals, expectancies, and values) causes motivation only to the degree that individuals are unaware of their role as thinker or agent in constructing and directing thoughts—in choosing the level of influence specific beliefs will have in a given situation. At higher levels of understanding about how beliefs function, individuals can "override" their influence through the choice of thoughts. Conditions that facilitate individuals' higher level understanding and access to their natural motivation to learn include supportive instructional environments of socioemotional support from teachers, classmates, and other participants in the system and instructional practices that provide opportunities for the development of self-awareness and high-level understandings of the self as agent. When students can be helped to understand, with the aid of this support—their own psychological functioning and their agency in that functioning, their inherent capacities for higher level thinking, metacognition, and motivation to learn—are elicited and developed. Self-regulation becomes a self-confirming cycle, and a positive spiral of higher level understanding and functioning results. These basic principles, which expand on many of those cited in the learner-centered psychological principles, need to be part of teacher education.

The Emerging Model of Motivation

The paradigm that Mills (1995) suggests (and that other emerging models and related research corroborates) is one that separates psychological and intellectual (cognitive) functioning. It helps us see that what human beings possess in common is the capacity for mental health (higher levels of awareness and consciousness, unconditional self-esteem, common sense, and inner wisdom). The principles of self, thought, and consciousness as general principles of psychological functioning can describe human motivation and behavior independently of the unique intellectual or physical capabilities of individuals. In addition, the positing of these general principles helps clarify why it is possible for very gifted people to feel insecure or very mentally impaired people to feel efficacious. That is, because people can operate outside the boundaries of their thoughts and conditioned belief systems, and see these cognitions as personal constructions of reality that have nothing to do with inner worth, mental health is possible for all individuals regardless of their particular intellectual or physical talents. It is when individuals get trapped into a conditional self-concept or conditional feelings of self-worth that mental health and motivation suffer. Promoting higher levels of metacognitive self-awareness of personal agency, the function of thought, and access of higher levels of consciousness promises to be an important breakthrough in how motivation operates in complex school settings and how schools can be redesigned to promote healthy functioning.

In terms of a framework that can have practical implications for education and, specifically, the learner-centered redesign of schools, as well as suggest how what research shows about metacognition, affect, and motivation can be integrated to improve practice—the reciprocal empowerment model delineated by McCombs (1990) and reported by Whisler (1991) is helpful. This model illustrates how will, skill, and social support components—combined with an understanding of individuals' basic psychological functioning and core of mental health—can operate to produce a positive climate for learning. Within this climate, the foundation is provided for introducing more socially and personally relevant curricula; innovative instructional methods that encourage student choice, involvement, and responsibility; and administrative and physical structures that support a learner-centered learning environment.

For teachers to understand and apply this model, however, it needs to be introduced in teacher education or professional development programs such that basic principles of learning, motivation, and psychological functioning are personally validated and experienced. Educational programs for teachers need to be designed to engage participants in learning activities that are themselves in keeping with these principles. Further implications for teacher education are discussed in the following sections.

Implications for Practice

A self-as-agent understanding reflects a metacognitive level of self-awareness analogous to higher level consciousness of one's role in directing, selecting, and regulating the intellectual system. In this context, metacognition becomes a tool of agency (McCombs, 1991a). Metacognitive processes such as self-reflection, self-monitoring, and self-awareness lead to higher level executive strategies such as planning, goal setting, and self-regulation in general. Agency and efficacy beliefs are a natural outgrowth of students' recognition of self-agency. Even if students perceive that certain background or ability factors can interfere with their success—being able to recognize that their thoughts about these factors will interfere with their positive affect and motivation to learn—allows them to choose to redirect their thoughts, gain a different perspective, and work to overcome these barriers with effort and training in skill-enhancing strategies that can offset these negative influences.

In terms of practical implications for all learners, three general principles emerge:

1. Learners are motivated by learning situations and activities that (a) challenge them to become personally and actively involved in their own learning and (b) allow them personal choice and control matched to their abilities and learning task requirements.

2. Learners' motivation is enhanced if they perceive that learning tasks (a) directly or indirectly relate to personal needs, interests,

and goals and (b) are of appropriate difficulty levels such that they can accomplish them successfully.

3. Learners' natural motivation to learn can be elicited in safe, trusting, and supportive environments characterized by (a) quality relationships with caring adults that see their unique potential, (b) instructional supports that are tailored to students' unique learning needs, and (c) opportunities for students to take risks without fear of failure.

These principles apply both to the design of teacher education programs and how teachers design learning environments for their own students. In addition, what these basic principles imply for the teacher's role is that it involve

- diagnosing and understanding students' unique needs, interests, and goals;
- helping students define personal goals and their relationships to general learning goals;
- relating learning content and activities to students' personal needs, interests, and goals, and helping students define these relative to learning goals;
- structuring learning goals and activities such that each student can accomplish his or her own goals and experience success;
- challenging students to invest effort and energy in taking personal responsibility and being actively involved in learning activities;
- providing students with opportunities to exercise personal control and choice over carefully selected task variables, such as type of learning activity, level of mastery, amount of effort, or type of reward;
- creating a safe, trusting, and supportive climate by demonstrating real interest, caring, and concern for each student;
- attending to classroom goal structures and goal orientations such that noncompetitive structures and learning goals are emphasized over competitive structures and performance goals;
- highlighting the value of student accomplishment, the value of students' unique skills and abilities, and the value of the learning process and learning task; and
- acknowledging students' accomplishments and encouraging them to reward themselves and develop pride in their accomplishments.

These practices are themselves in keeping with basic principles of learning, motivation, and psychological functioning and are best learned when experienced as part of teacher preparation and professional development. In addition, new understandings of changes in teacher and student roles in the learning process emerge.

Shifts in Teacher and Student Roles

Shared responsibility for learning that occurs between teachers and students is a cornerstone of learner-centered practices. A critical defining characteristic of this shared responsibility is a shift in teacher and student roles and relationships. According to Vatterott (1995), the teacher no longer delivers the curriculum but mediates it in three ways: (a) by designing active learning tasks in which students learn through their actions on concepts, with opportunities for choice, autonomy, integration of content in more than one subject, application of skills and content knowledge, demonstrations of creativity and personal expression in projects or products they present or display; (b) by designing assessments, ideally in partnership with students and with their input, as exhibitions or performances that encourage students to produce knowledge, create products, or engage in personal reflections; and (c) by redirecting time and energy away from content presentation or paper grading to the development of activities that focus students on products they create, focusing on creating options for structuring and individualizing learning that are based on learning styles or multiple intelligences. Students' roles become more active. They construct their own knowledge, make their own meaning, and evaluate their own learning. Perhaps of most importance, however, is a change in the traditional or conventional teacher–student relationship. This relationship becomes more collaborative, students have more voice, and there in an underlying trust and respect often absent in traditional teacher-centered models of learning. Students are encouraged to take responsibility for asking questions and guiding their own learning. The result is higher student motivation and achievement.

The knowledge and skills needed to support this shift in roles is also being explored. For example, Sternberg and Horvath (1995) listed features of the expert teacher that reflect knowledge and thinking skills necessary for effective teaching. These include content, pedagogical (both specific and general) and practical (explicit and tacit) content, efficiency (automatization, executive control—that is, planning, monitoring, and evaluating—and reinvestment of cognitive resources), and insight (selective encoding, selective combination, and selective comparison). Explicitly addressing these knowledges and skills is helpful in professional development experiences.

In determining the qualities of expert teachers—teachers who consistently help students achieve high academic standards—Henry (1994) compared experienced teachers with expert teachers. He found that expert teachers were more concerned with student enjoyment while learning and with the compatibility of the instruction to their own philosophy and experiences of success. Expert teachers' decision-making process is centered in the self (i.e., is compatible with values and beliefs about teaching, learning, and individual differences), is directed by personal feelings of competence, and is primarily student centered (concerned with how instructional practice motivates students and enhances student understanding and enjoyment). Expert teachers were defined by criteria similar to those that define the "learner-centered teacher." These include the following: knowledgeable about content, able to work with all students, nurturing, inclined to take risks, respectful, interested in each student's needs, engaged in ongoing professional development, self-confident and reflective, able to adjust the context to learners, slow to end the learning process, able to acknowledge own lack of knowledge, enthusiastic, and inclined to use a variety of learning strategies.

In too many instances, however, professional development experiences leave teachers inadequately prepared. Linda Darling-Hammond (1994) argued that this is often the case for those who will teach in urban schools, where there is even greater student diversity and a critical need for teachers to value, respect, and encourage the development of students' unique talents and natural motivation to learn. As a result, a number of psychologists and educators are examining the usefulness of the psychological perspective for teachers and teacher educators, particularly educational psychologists. For example, Anderson et al. (1995) suggested that there are four elements of teacher expertise that need to be developed: analyzing situations, drawing on principled knowledge, drawing on technical knowledge, and choosing among goals for a given situation and acting on the choices made. The authors emphasize that teachers, as are all learners, are influenced in the learning process by their prior knowledge and beliefs about teaching and learning. To encourage the kinds of learning necessary for expert teaching, Anderson et al. (1995) recommend that educational psychology classes include strategies consistent with new views of learning. That is, they should include tasks that provide multiple representations of key ideas across situations, that help make explicit prospective teachers' beliefs and conceptions and engage them in examining their own beliefs and considering alternative points of views, and tasks that create opportunities for public interaction among the students and between the instructor and students, and grading and assessment practices that are consistent with new views on learning.

Another area of beliefs that needs to be addressed in teacher education is that of beliefs about personal efficacy. Soodak and Podell (1995) found that teacher efficacy is made up of three uncorrelated factors: personal efficacy, outcome efficacy, and teaching efficacy. This implies that teachers can hold two independent beliefs—beliefs that they can teach and beliefs that student outcomes are dependent on their teaching. Because these beliefs are independent, they can differentially influence instructional decisions, and they point to different kinds of change strategies depending on which beliefs are interfering with student achievement and motivation. Soodak and Podell (1995) stated that

> efficacy beliefs among teachers may be best conceptualized as following a developmental sequence in which confidence in one's future field may be important until an individual has an opportunity to develop a sense of efficacy as a professional within the field. (p. 18)

This implies that professional development needs to concern itself with providing meaningful field experiences that promote a positive sense of personal efficacy among prospective teachers.

The kinds of beliefs that can shape teaching practices also include preconceptions about (a) the nature of what is being taught, (b) learning and how it takes place, (c) students' capabilities, (d) priorities and constraints that are part of the professional and institutional context, and (e) their own efficacy in influencing student learning that can limit what is thought to be useful or possible. Hasseler (1995) recommends that teachers make these preconceptions, perceptions, and beliefs explicit and question their views in light of contradictory evidence, thereby challenging these beliefs. Teachers need to be supported in assessing their changes and helped to see how their own changes are influenced by school policies and how they can take an increased leadership role in aligning practices and policies to be more consistent with current views of learning.

Role of Beliefs and Assumptions About Learners, Learning, and Teaching

Any major change or paradigm shift requires a transformation in thinking, seeing, or interpreting reality. In this era of educational reform, many shifts in thinking are being proposed. Teachers and educators are being asked to adopt thinking that holds that "all students can learn" and to see education as a "shared responsibility" among all constituencies—students, teachers, administrators, parents, and community members. They are also being asked to confront old models and beliefs about how people learn and how best to promote the learning process. In any time of significant change, people are forced to confront old beliefs and assumptions and to challenge themselves to revise these views on the basis of evidence that a change is needed. For this process to be successful, however, people need to know why such a shift is needed, what the shift entails, and how to make the shift.

Teachers, themselves, are also often resistant to change. First, there always seems to be a new "bandwagon"—one that often comes in with a bang and goes out with a whimper. Policies, programs, and practices often change with changes in school administrations or legislative mandates. Rather than evaluating each bandwagon in terms of its impact on learners and learning, many teachers, somewhat understandably, hope it goes away, as have so many other reform fads. Second, teachers often feel saddled with all of the responsibility for student success or failure in school and in life. They know that what they do in school, no matter how positive, can get "undone" outside of school. What they sometimes forget is that, although their concern is valid and they are often undermined, one teacher frequently does make the crucial difference for at-risk students.

Even for those who are open to change, there is uncertainty as to what kind of changes will be most effective and how best to go about making the changes. There is also the question of whether the changes can be successful given what appears to be a complex and overwhelming set of problems and issues underlying educational systems change. Feelings of fear, frustration, hopelessness, and despair abound, as well as a sense that "we're already doing so much—how can we possibly do more?" In such an atmosphere, it is easy to hold on to old beliefs and assumptions, to stay within the comfort zone of old ways of thinking about education, and to avoid the problem as long as possible. What is the way out of this dilemma? What can increase willingness to and hope-fulness about change?

Self-Assessing Personal Beliefs

My colleagues and I have examined our own beliefs and thinking about learning, learners, and teaching. We have looked to the research liter-ature to inform us about what needs to change and why. We have learned to question even the most pervasive assumptions and ideas be-ing proposed. For example, we have learned from the research on learning that not only *can* all students learn, but also that all students *do* learn. Research from cognitive and developmental psychology is clear that learning is a natural and ongoing process, that it occurs continu-ously for all learners from cradle to grave. We have examined the dif-ferences in educational systems on the basis of the "can learn" versus "do learn" philosophy and have seen clear evidence of the superiority of those systems that assume all students do learn. The do-learn envi-ronments respect and accommodate student diversity by variable learn-ing methods, content, and performance demonstrations. They are in-clusive and accepting of multiple abilities, and they value the cultivation and demonstration of diverse talents—both academic and nonaca-demic.

This examination has led to a recognition that educational systems designed from a research-based set of principles—that focus on learn-ers and learning as well as on basic principles of psychological func-tioning that are translated into a core philosophy and culture—are more successful. We have also realized that change is more likely to occur when educators and others are assisted in self-assessing and re-flecting on their basic beliefs and assumptions, and in engaging in crit-ical inquiry on issues identified in the research on learners and learn-ing. We believe these are essential steps in the change process.

Conclusion

A number of knowledge gaps still exist in making the aforementioned changes in teacher education practices (cf. McCombs & Whisler, 1997). Research is needed on how best to provide opportunities for prospective teachers to consider and appreciate different perspectives and how to accommodate these perspectives in their instructional practices. The promise of self-assessment and reflection tools as a strategy to stimulate change needs to be explored (McCombs, 1997). Although current staff development models emphasize teachers' taking increased responsibility for their own professional development and advocate self-assessment and reflection strategies as well as learning through inquiry, tools do not currently exist for teachers to engage in a continual, ongoing, respectful, nonthreatening, supportive, and self-directed process of assessing and changing their practices to increase their instructional effectiveness with individual students. There is also a need for tools that address personal discomforts associated with change by all constituencies (or stakeholders) and how to encourage teachers to view the discomfort associated with change from a more positive perspective (e.g., as an idea trying to break through).

Interventions for enhancing motivation, learning, and human development are concerned with the "psychology of learning and change" as well as the personal needs and individual perceptions that support motivation, learning, and change. Of the variables that are related to (a) creating a positive learning context, (b) supporting personal change in thinking, and (c) enhancing students' motivation, learning, and academic achievement, the following are identified in the literature as among the most critical:

- Need for and individual perceptions of interpersonal caring, acceptance, and support;
- Need for and individual perceptions of personal voice, control, and autonomy;
- Need for and individual perceptions of meaningfulness and relevancy of learning activities;
- Need for and individual perceptions of personal competence and capacity to succeed; and
- Need for and individual perceptions of being understood and respected as an individual.

These needs and perceptions are necessary for all constituents and at all levels of the system. Current research, however, indicates that teacher changes in thinking and practice have a high payoff in terms of student motivation and achievement. In addition to attention to teacher role implications, the emerging model of motivation has implications for the design of curricula and instructional practices, the design of administrative supports, and the design of the interface of schools and the larger community. People are at the heart of any living system; attention to learner-centered goals for educational redesign puts the focus where there is the maximum probability of enhancing positive outcomes. I believe that focusing on the nature of human psychological functioning, its implications for learning and motivation, and the design of schooling is a start in the right direction.

References

Anderson, L. M., Blumenfeld, P., Pintrich, P. R., Clark, C. M., Marx, R. W., & Peterson, P. (1995). Educational psychology for teachers: Reforming our courses, rethinking our roles. *Educational Psychologist, 30,* 143–157.

Bergin, D. A. (1991, April). *Mastery versus competitive learning situations: Two experimental studies.* Paper presented at the annual meeting of the American Educational Research Association, Chicago.

Bernieri, F. J. (1991). Interpersonal sensitivity in teaching interactions. *Personality and Social Psychology Bulletin, 17,* 98–103.

Borkowski, J. G., Day, J. D., Saenz, D., Dietmeyer, S., & Estrada, T. M. (1990). Expanding the boundaries of cognitive interventions. In T. E. Scruggs & B. Wong (Eds.), *Intervention research in learning disabilities* (pp. 46–61). New York: Springer-Verlag.

Chaskin, R. J., & Rauner, D. M. (1995). Youth and caring: An introduction. *Phi Delta Kappan, 76,* 667–674.

Covington, M. V. (1991). Putting the self back in the process: A discussant's perspective [Special issue]. *Journal of Experimental Education, 60*(1), 82–88.

Covington, M. V. (1992). *Making the grade: A self-worth perspective on motivation and school reform.* Cambridge, England: Cambridge University Press.

Darling-Hammond, L. (1994). Who will speak for the children? How "Teach for America" hurts urban schools and students. *Phi Delta Kappan, 76,* 21–34.

Deci, E. L., & Ryan, R. M. (1991). A motivational approach to self: Integration in personality. In R. Dienstbier (Ed.), *Nebraska Symposium on Motivation: Vol. 38. Perspectives on Motivation* (pp. 237–288). Lincoln: University of Nebraska Press.

Dweck, C. S. (1991). Self-theories and goals: Their role in motivation, personality and development. In R. Dienstbier (Ed.), *Nebraska Symposium on Motivation: Vol. 38. Perspectives on Motivation* (pp. 199–235). Lincoln: University of Nebraska Press.

Dweck, C. S., & Leggett, E. L. (1988). A social–cognitive approach to motivation and personality. *Psychological Review, 95,* 256–273.

Garcia, T., & Pintrich, P. R. (1991, April). *Student motivation and self-regulated learning: A LISREL model.* Paper presented at the annual meeting of the American Educational Research Association, Chicago.

Goldenberg, C. (1991, June). *Two views of learning and their implications for literacy education.* Paper presented at the Language Minority Literacy Roundtable, Santa Barbara, University of California.

Graham, S., & Golan, S. (1991). Motivational influences on cognition: Task involvement, ego involvement, and depth of information processing. *Journal of Educational Psychology, 83,* 187–194.

Harter, S. (1990). *Visions of self: Beyond the me in the mirror.* Unpublished manuscript, University of Denver, CO.

Hasseler, S. S. (1995, April). *Missing links: The complexities of supporting teacher learning in school contexts.* Paper presented at the annual meeting of the American Educational Research Association, San Francisco.

Helmke, A., & Schrader, F. W. (1991, April). *Cognitive, affective and motivational goals of classroom instruction: Are they incompatible?* Paper presented at the annual meeting of the American Educational Research Association, Chicago.

Henry, M. A. (1994, February). *Differentiating the expert and experienced teacher: Quantitative differences in instructional decision making.* Paper presented at the annual meeting of the American Association of Colleges for Teacher Education, Chicago.

Institute for Education in Transformation. (1992, November). Voices from the inside: A report on schooling from inside the classroom. Claremont, CA: The Claremont Graduate School.

Lazarus, R. S. (1991). Cognition and motivation in emotion. *American Psychologist, 46,* 352–367.

Lipsitz, J. (1995). Prologue: Why we should care about caring. *Phi Delta Kappan, 76,* 665–666.

McCombs, B. L. (1990). *The reciprocal empowerment model: A key to positive motivation and development.* Unpublished manuscript, University of Denver, CO.

McCombs, B. L. (1991a, April). *Metacognition and motivation for higher level thinking.* Paper presented at the annual meeting of the American Educational Research Association, Chicago.

McCombs, B. L. (1991b). Motivation and lifelong learning. *Educational Psychologist, 26,* 117–127.

McCombs, B. L. (1991c). Overview: Where have we been and where are we going in understanding human motivation? [Special issue]. *Journal of Experimental Education, 60,* 5–15.

McCombs, B. L. (1997). Self-assessment and reflection: Tools for promoting teacher changes toward learner-centered practices. *NASSP Bulletin, 81,* 1–14.

McCombs, B. L., & Marzano, R. J. (1990). Putting the self in self-regulated learning: The self as agent in integrating will and skill. *Educational Psychologist, 25,* 51–69.

McCombs, B. L., & Marzano, R. J. (in press). What is the role of the will component in strategic learning? In C. E. Weinstein & B. L. McCombs (Eds.), *Strategic learning: Skill, will, and self-regulation.* Hillsdale, NJ: Erlbaum.

McCombs, B. L., & Whisler, J. S. (1989). The role of affective variables in autonomous learning. *Educational Psychologist, 24,* 277–306.

McCombs, B. L., & Whisler, J. S. (1997). *The learner centered classroom and school: Strategies for enhancing student motivation and achievement.* San Francisco: Jossey-Bass.

Mills, R. C. (1990, June). *Substance abuse, dropout and delinquency prevention: An innovative approach.* Paper presented at the Eighth Annual Conference of the Psychology of Mind, St. Petersburg, FL.

Mills, R. C. (1991). A new understanding of self: The role of affect, state of mind, self understanding, and intrinsic motivation [Special issue]. *Journal of Experimental Education, 60,* 67–81.

Mills, R. C. (1995). *Realizing mental health.* New York: Sulbuger & Graham.

Mills, R. C., Dunham, R. G., & Alpert, G. P. (1988). Working with high-risk youth in prevention and early intervention programs: Toward a comprehensive model. *Adolescence, 23,* 643–660.

Mills, R. C., Olson, P., & Bailey, J. (1994). *Treatment effects of short-term therapy based on psychology of mind.* Unpublished manuscript, University of Minnesota, School of Professional Psychology.

Newby, T. J. (1991). Classroom motivation: Strategies of first-year teachers. *Journal of Educational Psychology, 83,* 195–200.

Peck, N., Law, A., & Mills, R. C. (1989). *Dropout prevention: What we have learned.* Ann Arbor, MI: ERIC Counseling and Personnel Services Clearinghouse.

Pintrich, P. R., & DeGroot, E. V. (1990). Motivational and self-regulated learning components of classroom academic performance. *Journal of Educational Psychology, 82,* 33–40.

Poplin, M., & Weeres, J. (1993). Listening at the learner's level. *The Executive Educator, 15*(4), 14–19.

Resnick, L. B. (1987). Learning in school and out. *Educational Researcher, 16*(9), 13–20.

Ridley, D. S. (1991). Reflective self-awareness: A basic motivational process [Special issue]. *Journal of Experimental Education, 60,* 31–48.

Ryan, R. M. (1995). Psychological needs and the facilitation of integrative processes. *Journal of Personality, 63,* 397–427.

Ryan, R. M., & Powelson, C. L. (1991). Autonomy and relatedness as fundamental to motivation and education [Special issue]. *Journal of Experimental Education, 60,* 49–66.

Ryan, R. M., & Stiller, J. (1991). The social contexts of internalization: Parent and teacher influences on autonomy, motivation, and learning. In M. L. Maehr & P. R. Pintrich (Eds.), *Advances in motivation and achievement* (Vol. 7, pp. 115–149). Greenwich, CT: JAI Press.

Sarason, S. B. (1995). Some reactions to what we have learned. *Phi Delta Kappan, 77,* 84–85.

Schunk, D. H., & Swartz, C. W. (1991, April). *Process goals and progress feedback: Effects on children's self-efficacy and skills.* Paper presented at the annual meeting of the American Educational Research Association, Chicago.

Soodak, L. C., & Podell, D. M. (1995, April). *Teacher efficacy: Toward the understanding of a multifaceted construct.* Paper presented at the annual meeting of the American Educational Research Association, San Francisco.

Sternberg, R. J., & Horvath, J. A. (1995). A prototype view of expert teaching. *Educational Researcher, 24,* 9–17.

Stewart, D. (1984). *The effect of teacher/student states of mind in raising reading achievement in high risk, cross cultural youth.* Paper presented at the Fourth Annual Conference of the Psychology of Mind, Honolulu, Hawaii.

Strong, R., Silver, H. F., & Robinson, A. (1995). What do students want? (and what really motivates them)? *Educational Leadership, 53,* 8–12.

Suarez, E. M. (1988). A neo-cognitive dimension. *The Counseling Psychologist, 16,* 239–244.

Suarez, R., Mills, R. C., & Stewart, D. (1987). *Sanity, insanity, and common sense.* New York: Fawcett Columbine.

Timm, J., & Stewart, D. (1990). *The thinking teacher's guide to self-esteem.* Tampa, FL: Florida Center for Human Development.

Vatterott, C. (1995). Student-focused instruction: Balancing limits with freedom. *Middle School Journal, 27*(11), 28–38.

Whisler, J. S. (1991). The impact of teacher relationships and interactions of self-development and motivation [Special issue]. *Journal of Experimental Education, 60,* 15–30.

Developmental Psychology as a Guide for Teaching and Teacher Preparation

Paul Ammon and Allen Black

There are, of course, many psychologies and many ways in which they might be brought to bear on educational practice. We are concerned here with developmental psychology—particularly psychology in the tradition of Piaget—and with its use as a basis for teaching and teacher preparation. This focus reflects, in part, our own academic backgrounds and our professional activities over the past several years. Our purpose in this chapter is to argue that Piagetian developmental psychology provides an especially firm foundation for teaching, and that the education of teachers is an especially important area of activity for building effectively on Piagetian theory in educational practice. We believe our argument is well grounded in Piaget's work (and more recent extensions of his work), and in the experience that we and our colleagues have had as teacher educators attempting to address the requirements of effective teaching. Additional contexts for this discussion will include earlier attempts to "apply Piaget" in education, recent innovations in teaching, and current ideas in the general discourse about educational reform in general, and the learner-centered psychological principles articulated by the American Psychological Association's (APA) Presidential Task Force on Psychology in Education (1993). We begin with a brief analysis of what is required for schools to improve and a discussion of why Piagetian theory seems particularly germane to that analysis.

Requirements for Improvement in Education and the Relevance of Piagetian Theory

Some Propositions About Educational Improvement

The issue of educational improvement has numerous facets, but three propositions about what is required should suffice to build a rationale for the rest of our discussion. These propositions indicate the importance of learner-centered psychological principles that include a *learning*-centered perspective as well.

1. *To improve the quality of education in our schools, the area that needs most attention is the interface between the curriculum and the individual learner, that is, the teacher–learning process.* Although the alarm over an educational crisis in the 1980s (National Commission on Excellence in Education, 1983) may well have been overblown (Berliner & Biddle, 1995), there can be little doubt that many students continue to learn with inadequate understanding of concepts and without mastery of important skills. Since conceptual development and learning are well established domains of inquiry in psychology, it seems that psychology should contribute more to educational reform than just devising objective tests to assess new grade-level standards. Most teachers we know make little use of standardized test results because these tests do not inform teachers about what to do, nor do they capture their students' understandings and interests. Moreover, there are psychological grounds for questioning the current enthusiasm for grade-level standards, even where such standards seem somewhat informed by studies of learner development.

2. *To meet the challenge of teaching in classrooms that include students with diverse backgrounds and diverse levels of achievement, teachers must be better able to monitor the course of learning for each student.* In today's classrooms, the teacher needs to be someone who marshalls individuals' resources for learning, rather than someone who delivers a curriculum prescribed by experts far removed from the specific individuals in the classroom. Attempts to produce "teacher proof" curricula are not only demeaning to teachers, but also counterproductive to learning.

3. *To teach effectively, teachers must be able to link knowledge of children with knowledge of subject matter.* During the current period of reform in education, ambiguity about what constitutes expertise

in teaching was apparent in the first wave of proposals for changes in teacher preparation. For example, the original report of the Holmes Group (1986) emphasized increased knowledge of subject matter for prospective teachers, whereas the Carnegie Forum (1986) leaned more toward increasing the kind of knowledge that can be derived directly from teaching practice. Only in the second wave of proposals has attention been given to pedagogy, most notably in the work of Shulman (1987) and his colleagues on *pedagogical content knowledge*, that is, knowledge of the subject matter that is needed for teaching, but is not part of the subject itself. Shulman's work was directed mainly at secondary teaching and came from a different theoretical perspective than the one we are taking here, but the fundamental issue raised is key. What teachers need to know that others do not is determined in part by the nature of the subject and in part by other factors—most importantly, characteristics of the learner.

If these three propositions are accepted, then it seems clear that progress toward the goal of educational improvement can be advanced if teaching is well informed by psychological studies of the processes that children go through in coming to know what they are expected to learn in school. Developmental studies by Piaget and his followers offer a great deal in this regard, and the conclusions drawn from them seem consistent with APA's learner-centered psychological principles.

Why Piaget?

The body of theory and research associated with Piaget can be recommended as a foundation for educational improvement by virtue of its sheer extent along several relevant dimensions. First, it addresses issues of knowledge and development from earliest childhood into adulthood, thereby providing a basis not only for the teaching of children and adolescents, but also for the professional education of their teachers. Second, it encompasses social and affective development as well as intellectual development in a variety of content domains (number, space, time, physical objects, written language, the social world, morality) and therefore it speaks to issues of learning and motivation as they relate to the school curriculum and the school setting. Finally, there is an extensive research base supporting Piagetian developmental theory, including not only Piaget's monumental oeuvre but a host of related studies as well.

The work of Piaget and other Piagetians has never been without its critics, but there seemed to be an especially notable crescendo of criticism around the time of Piaget's death in 1980 (e.g., Cohen, 1983; Modgil & Modgil, 1982). Today, even among those psychologists who seek to build on Piaget's foundation, controversies abound over fundamental issues such as the nature (or existence) of stages (e.g., Levin, 1986) and the relationship between development and learning (e.g., Kuhn, 1995). Our purpose here is neither to defend the Piagetian perspective in general nor to engage in debate over the particulars of Piagetian or neo-Piagetian theory. Rather it is to demonstrate that Piagetian developmental psychology (as we understand it) constitutes, quite plausibly, a suitable vehicle for educational improvement through its use as core knowledge in the preparation of teachers. Just how suitable it will prove to be is, in the long run, an empirical question to be addressed by examining educational outcomes—but only in the long run, after considerable efforts have gone into the matter of establishing conditions that will make it possible for the ultimate question to be addressed. Having been engaged for several years in just such an effort, in the form of a teacher education program, we draw on that experience in the remainder of this chapter. First, however, we briefly discuss previous efforts to use Piagetian theory as a basis for educational improvement.

Previous Applications of Piaget in Education

Back in the sixties and on into the seventies, there was a great deal of excitement over Piaget among educators, and among psychologists interested in education (see Resnick & Ford, 1981, chapters 5 and 7). That excitement came in the wake of an earlier educational "crisis"—the one precipitated by Sputnik and the "race for space" between the United States and the Soviet Union. It seems fair to say, though, that previous attempts to apply Piaget in mainstream education have met, at best, with only modest success—else there would not have been the more recent sense of crisis. One can cite a number of reasons for this disappointing result, not the least of which is massive inertia in the existing educational system due to a variety of political, economic, and social constraints. But we also think there have been some problems with the ways in which Piagetian applications in education have been approached in the past.

On the one hand, there has been a tendency for experts to prescribe educational practices from afar, by designing "developmentally appropriate" curricula to be used by teachers in their classrooms. Such an approach seems to underestimate the diversity that real teachers find in children and in the settings in which they work—diversity that includes individual differences not only in rate of development (both within and between domains of knowledge) but also in motivational and contextual factors that determine the types of learning activities children find most engaging. Thus a better alternative, in our view, is to help teachers attain the kinds of understandings they need in order to construct developmentally appropriate curricula according to the needs of the particular students they teach.

On the other hand—and in contrast to the curriculum-centered approach—there is an approach that seems overly centered on the child. The basic premise is that children learn in their own time and through their own actions, so that teachers can do little more than provide environments rich in opportunities for children to "invent" what they are ready to understand at a particular stage of development. Our concern is not with the concept of invention per se, but with the way this approach seems to reflect poor understandings about the role of maturation in development, and about the idea that knowledge is "self-constructed" by the individual. It seems more aligned with the romanticism of Rousseau than with the learner-centered approach advocated here.

In Piagetian theory, constructivism is a basic principle—one that holds that individuals of whatever age acquire understandings of the world about them primarily through an analysis of their own actions upon the world, not by passive "growth," or by imitation or memorization, although these factors make contributions (Piaget, 1970b). Moreover, the knowledge-construction process does involve self-regulation. Learning, in the sense of making associations, is subordinated to a process of active assimilation, whereby new information is interpreted in terms of current understandings, which in turn are transformed by an internal process (equilibration) that seeks to resolve contradictions and incompatibilities in the knowledge system, insofar as they are perceived (Piaget, 1964, 1985). But the process is not all assimilatory; there is an accommodatory pole as well, in that the information obtained is heavily dependent on the opportunities and challenges available in the environment.

Acknowledging development and the process of knowledge construction does imply that learning cannot be forced, but it does not mean that it cannot be facilitated. Schools exist so that individual children are not faced with reinventing all knowledge on their own. Thus a better alternative to the overly child-centered approach is one that helps teachers acquire the knowledge they need in order to facilitate learning of the curriculum as they orchestrate activities in the classroom.

Previous attempts to apply Piaget in education have served useful purposes. The curriculum-centered approach has challenged the wisdom of designing curricula based entirely on adults' logical analyses of the disciplines to be taught, whereas the child-centered approach has challenged the adequacy of the traditional show-and-tell type of instruction. In order to capitalize on the important insights behind these challenges, however, it is necessary to take a more balanced approach— one that treats school learning as the result of facilitated *interactions* between students and appropriate curricula. As the chief facilitator of such interactions, it is also necessary for the teacher to understand both the student and the curriculum in developmental terms. That is the goal of the teacher education program in which we have worked, and that we now describe briefly as a context for further discussion.

The Developmental Teacher Education Program at Berkeley

The Developmental Teacher Education Program (DTE) was founded in 1980 by a group of psychologists in the Graduate School of Education at the University of California at Berkeley, in collaboration with teachers and other educators in the surrounding area.[1] Its goal was to treat developmental psychology as core knowledge in the preparation of teachers for elementary schools, and that remains its goal today. The typical teacher credentialling program in California comprises one postbaccalaureate year. In contrast, DTE is a 2-year graduate program that combines the master of arts (MA) degree with the teaching credential. The MA degree acknowledges the academic work in developmental psychology as well as the completion of a master's research project on some aspect of the relationship between development and education. The program is also relatively small and intimate: At present about 20 students are admitted each year, and they progress through the program

---

[1]Colleagues who collaborated closely with us in planning and initiating the Developmental Teacher Education Program were Nadine Lambert, Elliot Turiel, and Margaret Wilcox.

as a cohort, which provides a source of mutual support and collegial interactions.

In its evolution over the past 15 years, DTE has undergone a number of changes. We describe the program here with an emphasis on basic structural features that have remained more or less the same and that seem most pertinent to the goal of using developmental psychology as core knowledge (see also Ammon & Levin, 1993; Black & Ammon, 1992). Coursework and student teaching go on simultaneously in DTE throughout the 2 years students are enrolled. In the first year, there are somewhat separate sequences of coursework on developmental theory and on methods of teaching basic school subjects. In second-year courses, both of these areas are revisited with the goal of integrating theory and practice more systematically than before. In one second-year class, for example, student teachers use developmental principles to design teaching strategies for enhancing children's understandings of the mathematics they are being taught. In another, the students are given a group assignment to produce a document that explains and illustrates developmental approaches to the teaching of literacy and the language arts.

Students in DTE experience two short "participant observer" placements in elementary school classrooms during their first semester, and then one longer student teaching placement in each of the three remaining semesters. Only gradually during the first year do they assume responsibility for leading instruction in the classroom, so that they have the time and energy to engage in formal and informal field studies of children, including assignments from courses in developmental theory and in methods of instruction. The field placements are coordinated to some extent with the coursework. For example, students are placed in primary-grade classrooms at the beginning of the first semester while studying the development of cognition and language in young children, and then in upper elementary grades while studying development in older children.

The multiplicity of field placements allows student teachers to experience not only a variety of age groups, but also a variety of cultures and socioeconomic backgrounds (which ties in with coursework on social development, the sociology of urban education, and the teaching of linguistic and cultural minority students, and is consistent with the learner-centered principles regarding social and contextual factors in learning). In addition, it allows student teachers to experience a variety of teaching styles as they work with a number of different cooperating teachers, some of whom are DTE graduates, but many of whom are not. It is hoped that all this diversity—in children, in settings, and in co-operating teachers—will leave student teachers with no illusions about there being one "developmentally correct" way of teaching that they can learn by imitation. Rather we want them to see the necessity of constructing multiple ways of teaching that are consistent with the needs of particular children and with principles of development as understood by the teacher. Support for learning to teach in this way comes from a group of campus-based supervisors of student teaching who have had extensive teaching experience themselves, and graduate work in education that generally includes some study of development.

Developmental Pedagogy

In order for the DTE program to pursue its main agenda, it has been necessary for those of us who participate, both faculty and students, to meet the challenge of formulating a developmental pedagogy based on theory and research not undertaken originally for that purpose. As illustrated in Figure 1, such a pedagogy derives from two sources—knowledge of children and knowledge of subject matter. Also shown in Figure 1 are the two components that a developmental pedagogy must include to be usable in a classroom setting. The first of these (on the left) concerns the scope and sequence of the curriculum, within and across subject areas. The second (on the right) is concerned with classroom organization and management. The first component is more closely related to the teacher's role as facilitator of individual learning, the second to the teacher's role as orchestrator of the group.

In their basic studies of developing intelligence, researchers working in the tradition of Piaget have addressed numerous topics entailed in the first component of developmental pedagogy, that is, curriculum scope and sequence, although many education-related details have remained to be worked out. Until recently, however, developmentalists have had relatively little to say about the second, classroom organization component. Therefore the formulation of a developmental pedagogy —particularly with regard to the second component—involves drawing on the work of others, such as teaching methods devised by educators who may or may not have been influenced by developmental theory.

Fortunately, there are ample resources in key areas. In mathematics instruction, for example, there is the rich legacy of manipulative-based

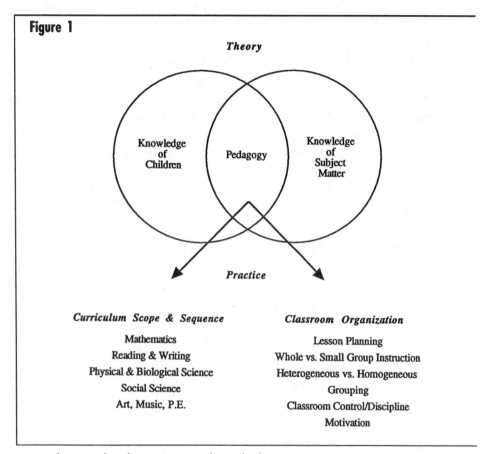

Figure 1

Developmental pedagogy. P.E. = physical education.

methods that emphasize the active construction of mathematical concepts (Baratta-Lorton, 1976; Burns, 1975, 1982; Kamii, 1985; Kamii & Joseph, 1989). Similarly, the "hands-on" approach to science instruction emphasizes the acquisition of scientific knowledge through the doing of science, not just through reading or hearing about scientific facts and principles (e.g., Lowery, 1985; Science Curriculum Framework and Criteria Committee, 1984). Furthermore, although the teaching of literacy has not had as strong a connection with Piagetian theory as mathematics and science instruction, there are nonetheless methods available that seem quite consistent with constructivism. Approaches to literacy education such as *language experience* (Stauffer, 1970) or *whole language* (Goodman, 1986; Goodman, Hood, & Goodman, 1991) emphasize the active and authentic use of written language to construct and communicate meaning, rather than the accumulation of reading and writing skills out of context.

All of these teaching methods lend themselves to a view of the student as an active learner and the teacher as a facilitator. As it happens, they also help teachers meet the challenge of orchestrating activities in a classroom containing two or even three dozen children. That is, they involve activities that children can engage in to some extent on their own, either individually or in small groups. Where interaction between children is entailed, it relates directly to the interest educators have had in cooperative learning or group work, with both social and academic objectives in mind (Cohen, 1986; Johnson, Johnson, Holubec, & Roy, 1984).

Recent theoretical and empirical research by developmentalists promises to support the interest in social-interactive aspects of learning among educators. This research concerns an additional principle of development that we refer to as the *social construction of knowledge*. Although Piaget often mentioned the importance of social interaction for intellectual development and also described parallels between levels of cognitive development and levels of social interaction (Piaget, 1971a), he only began to investigate this process himself in the area of moral development (Piaget, 1932). More recently, however, there has been research on the ways in which social interactions promote intellectual development in general (Damon, 1984; Doise & Mugny, 1984; Murray, 1972), leading to the current enthusiasm for what is called *co-construction of knowledge*. Similar work on the social construction of knowledge has been undertaken by educational researchers in school settings, particularly in the area of literacy development (Daiute, 1993; Dyson, 1987).

Filling out both components of our model of developmental pedagogy presents a considerable challenge, but working it out on the level of educational practice with bright, reflective teachers as collaborators, consumers, and critics, has proven to be stimulating and rewarding for us. There is a sense, though, in which this work must go on indefinitely because we do not believe it possible simply to hand down "best practice" to new teachers. Rather, good developmental practice must continually be reinvented to suit new situations. As teacher educators, then, the key for us is to help teachers acquire the conceptual tools of invention—a developmental process to be taken up in the latter part of this chapter. First, however, we turn to some additional topics that relate to each component of developmental pedagogy.

Curriculum Scope and Sequence, and Individualized Instruction

Much of the potential of Piagetian research for the scope and sequence component of developmental pedagogy is suggested by the matrix of subject areas by stages in Figure 2. In his own research, Piaget worked his way through about half of the subject areas starting on the left of the matrix (Piaget, 1960, 1970a, 1971b; Piaget & Inhelder, 1967, 1975; Piaget, Inhelder, & Szeminska, 1964; Piaget & Szeminska, 1965), and did a seminal study of moral development (Piaget, 1932), which is listed on the right. His usual mode of analysis was to describe the development of knowledge within each area as a sequence of steps, which were further explicated in terms of characteristics of the four general stages listed on the vertical axis.

Here we consider briefly three ways in which these analyses are

Figure 2

Subject Areas

Grade Levels and Student Achievement		Mathematics			Probability	Physical/ Biological Science	Literacy		Social Science	Social/Moral Development
		Number	Measurement				Reading	Writing		
			Space	Time						
Stage	Grade									
Preparations	K									
	1									
Early Concrete Operations	2									
	3									
Late Concrete Operations	4									
	5									
Early Formal	6									

Curriculum scope and sequence. K = kindergarten.

helpful to teachers, and one way in which they are not. The first thing that is helpful is the hierarchical analysis within each subject area—that is, the ordering of knowledge development. These orderings are described in terms of conceptual difficulties encountered by children as they progress in their understandings of each area. For the most part, these are the same sorts of difficulties children encounter in school. Therefore, the information in the matrix makes it possible to devise curriculum sequences and instructional strategies to address such difficulties.

The second way in which Piagetian analyses are helpful is by providing a general theory of knowledge, an epistemology, that identifies common points of reference across domains of knowledge. These commonalities can be used to compare children's levels of understanding in different areas of the curriculum. To illustrate, in Piaget's theory the ability to establish one-to-one correspondences and then to classify and order objects is related to knowledge development in all areas of the curriculum. So in kindergarten, for example, a teacher has a way to relate a child's performance in gathering objects together by color to the same child's understanding of correspondences between letters and sounds, and to the strategies the child uses when counting. This is not to say that one should expect to find complete synchrony in the development of theoretically related cognitive operations across subject areas, as the existence of asynchronies has certainly been confirmed by Piaget (his *horizontal décalages*) and many others. However, the matrix does serve as a source of pedagogically relevant questions. For instance, does a lag in operative development in one area relative to others indicate a kind of readiness that has yet to be tapped in the child's experience with that area?

A third way in which the matrix can be helpful—seemingly opposite to the second—is that the epistemological analyses also identify unique qualities which distinguish areas of knowledge from one another—including areas that are often confused by children and by teachers, such as numerical versus spatial knowledge (Piaget, Inhelder, & Szeminska, 1964) or moral issues versus matters of social convention (Turiel, 1983). The fact that we cannot delve into domain-specific aspects of development here should not be interpreted to mean that we attach little importance to them.

There is a possible interpretation of the matrix in Figure 2 that seems not only unwarranted by the data on development, but also unhelpful to teachers. It is that one can use the classic Piagetian tasks that look like direct measures of operational development, such as classification or seriation, to assess a child's general stage of development, as in the tradition of measuring general intelligence. The concept of general intelligence (or general operational level) is one that has understandably been of interest to psychologists, but it tends to be useless for teachers because its relationship to what they teach is fairly obscure.

Early in the DTE program we do ask student teachers to conduct clinical interviews based on Piagetian tasks like classification and seriation with children, but our goal is not to train teachers in the use of such tasks to assess general levels of development in children. Rather, it is to help student teachers learn the clinical method and understand Piagetian explanations of children's thinking well enough to see how operational development might play itself out within the various domains of content taught in school. Indeed, the next step for our student teachers is to use the clinical method for curriculum-based assessment of children's understandings of subject matter, with less attention to general stages than to domain-specific aspects of development.

In general, it helps to think of Figure 2 as both similar to and different from the kinds of curriculum guidelines published by school districts. These are frequently summarized in grids where the boxes contain grade-level expectations (or "standards") for subject areas, such as the mastery of double-digit addition and subtraction in third grade arithmetic. But, of course, some children can understand this aspect of arithmetic before third grade and others not until later, and the same children may be at different developmental levels with respect to other content. Our point, then, is that the two grids—the curriculum grid and the developmental grid—must be in correspondence for the individual child if that child is going to thrive in school. The need for individualized adjustment of the curriculum to the learner takes us back to the importance of curriculum-based assessment for the teacher, and forward to the topic of errors as a key basis for such assessments.

Errors

Piaget's work demonstrates the value of regarding children's errors not just as incorrect responses, but as manifestations of their own ways of understanding. With respect to children's understandings of the content taught in school, there have been many analyses of the errors they make in solving arithmetic problems (such as double-digit addition and subtraction; e.g., Brown & Burton, 1978) and much interest in their misconceptions or *alternative frameworks* in science (Carmichael et al., 1990). But errors have proven to be a rich source of data on children's acquisition of literacy as well. Analyses of children's miscues when reading aloud have shed light on the knowledge that children apply to the task of making meaning from print (Goodman, 1973; Simons & Ammon, 1989). Ferreiro and her coworkers (Ferreiro & Teberosky, 1982; Goodman, 1990) have shown that young children's initial attempts to use writing as a mode of representation, while far from correct, reveal interesting hypotheses that children entertain in the process of constructing the principle of alphabetic writing. Others (Henderson & Beers, 1980) have pursued the qualitative changes that occur in children's invented spellings even after the basic alphabetic principle is understood.

Kamii and Randazzo (1985) replicated some of Ferreiro's work on early writing development with similar results. However, they also found what they called *unnatural* forms of invented spelling at each level of development. They hypothesized that these learning anomalies resulted from efforts to teach the correct alphabetic system by means of direct instruction without helping children construct the more naturally occurring sequence of levels themselves, and thus bypassing the process of self-regulation.

The literature on mathematics learning includes numerous case studies that are instructive about the dangers of teaching only the memorization of procedures rather than teaching for understanding (e.g., Black, 1985; Davis & Greenstein, 1969; Erlwanger, 1973). Frequently it is found that errors like those in Figure 3 do not reflect carelessness or total misunderstandings, but show creative attempts at putting together partially understood "facts" or algorithms. In making sense of such errors, it helps to look for what could be considered correct rather than incorrect. It then becomes easy to see, for example, how 4,808 divided by 8 might equal 61, when one has learned that 0 means nothing; or that $14 - 8$ equals 14, when one has learned to subtract the smaller number from the larger one. In a way $12 + 6$ does equal 9, because $1 + 2 + 6$ equals 9. Studies of errors like these also suggest ways in which an understanding of development can be used to avoid the dangers of just memorizing facts and procedures or used to remediate the result. Because constructivist developmental teaching is sometimes seen as unable to address the needs of children who lag behind others in learning, we focus particularly on "remediation" in the discussion of individualized instruction that follows.

Figure 3

12 +6 9	6 x ? = 9 ? = 15
14 -8 14	14 +8 112
13 x12 26 13 39	6 1 8⟌4808
3/6 > 3/4 (because 6 > 4)	3 + 2 = 5 5 6 11

Some common types of arithmetic errors.

Developmental Principles for Individualizing Instruction

With the goal of using developmental theory to guide a teacher's response to children's errors, we offer the following principles:

1. *Errors generally reflect knowledge, and they frequently represent an over-generalization of a partial understanding or a lack of integration with other knowledge.* The errors in Figure 3 involve partial knowledge and result from struggles to put together what is understood.

2. *The child's misunderstanding is likely to extend further back in the hierarchy of subject knowledge than it first appears. Instead of immediately confronting the child with the error and teaching the correct algorithm, probe to reveal the basis for the misapplied knowledge and to find a bedrock of conceptual understanding.* Just teaching how to get a correct answer will not do; that is often what has led to the errors. It is necessary to find a level of understanding in the hierarchy where the child is a virtuoso, and then work back up from there. Go (at least) two steps backward for one step forward.

3. *Discover and maintain a balance between computational procedures and conceptual knowledge.* Computational skills should not be allowed to get too far ahead of understanding. Algorithms are helpful tools that can be used automatically after understanding is achieved, but they are no substitute for understanding.

4. *Disequilibrium that leads to progressive understanding results from conflicting understandings already held by the learner, not from getting a wrong answer.* Here *disequilibrium* refers to that aspect of self-regulation that motivates children's efforts to self-correct because something does not make sense to them—a kind of intrinsic motivation. The teacher's job is to present problems where the self-regulating process will be engaged, for example, by situating a problem in a realistic context where the student has a clear expectation as to what a correct answer might look like, but also has an approach that produces a different answer. In the early grades, simply using money or ages as content for math can be helpful in that regard. In general, this fourth principle seems especially important not only for learning with understanding, but for learning to learn with understanding, which is a key metacognitive objective.

5. *Facility or virtuosity at one level of understanding is necessary for achieving a higher level of understanding.* If a learner is going to move forward, prerequisite knowledge must be well learned. Readiness to learn multiplication, for example, is indicated by facility with addition and subtraction. Without that facility, the new operations will be confused with the old ones.

In some respects, these principles for individualizing instruction hardly seem unique to the Piagetian developmental perspective. Principle 5, for example has much in common with the behaviorist approach called *mastery learning* (Block & Anderson, 1975; Bloom, 1976). Principle 4, on the other hand, does seem more uniquely Piagetian. In general, constructivist developmental psychology, as applied, does not so much reject other perspectives on learning and development as it subsumes and extends them. Taken together, these five principles recognize the interactionist nature of development in that the teacher structures the learning environment to match the demands of the task with the individual child's current level of understanding, and with the self-regulatory process by which children achieve better understandings.

Assessment and Remediation in Mathematics: An Example

To further illustrate a developmental approach to curriculum-based assessment and individualized instruction, we present an example based on remedial work that Allen Black carried out in a classroom where a DTE student had been placed for student teaching early in the program. It has to do with some third graders who were experiencing particular difficulty with double-digit addition and subtraction using the standard "carrying" and "borrowing" algorithms. Prolonged drill and practice with the algorithms had failed, and the teacher was quite concerned about what to do. She wanted the student teacher to conduct a general cognitive assessment of some kind. Instead, a more developmental, curriculum-based assessment was done using the principles just presented. This investigation has since served as one model for the projects DTE students carry out in the second-year course on development and mathematics education.

Underlying the carrying and borrowing algorithms is the concept of place value in base 10, which proves difficult for many children. And underlying place value is the simpler matter of just composing and decomposing small numbers in various ways, for example, in number families such as $12 = 8 + 4 = 6 + 6 = 3 + 9$, and so on. A related problem—notoriously difficult for young children—is the "missing addend" problem: Children who can solve a problem such as $6 + 3 = ?$, for example, may still be unable to solve $6 + ? = 9$, and often give 15 as an answer. Gaining facility in composing and decomposing small numbers and in dealing with missing addends constitutes an important step toward understanding the composition and decomposition of larger numbers in base 10 (e.g., $18 = 10 + 8$), and hence toward understanding place value and the borrowing and carrying algorithms.

With this analysis of the knowledge hierarchy that underlies the carrying and borrowing algorithms as background, a set of tasks was assembled to serve as clinical assessment and teaching tools for work with the third graders who were having problems. Instead of immediately attempting remedial instruction on the borrowing and carrying algorithms, the goal was to determine the levels at which the children understood the composing and decomposing of numbers, because that is where the conceptual difficulties were suspected to lie.

With the tasks ordered from most to least difficult, the children were first clinically interviewed using some double-digit addition and subtraction problems of the sort that had been giving them difficulty. In general it was found that they made many errors (including some that we have already seen), but occasionally got correct answers by simply adding on or subtracting off by ones (a strategy that breaks down with double-digit numbers). One boy, however, appeared to be decomposing numbers with an unconventional left-to-right procedure, which is conceptually valid, but is in conflict with the algorithms being taught (e.g., $17 + 25 = 15 + 20 + 2 + 5$).

Next the children were asked a question that Kamii and Joseph (1989) used to assess place value understanding. Given the written numeral *16* and sixteen counters, they were asked to show with the counters what the 1 in the numeral stands for and what the 6 stands for. Younger children tend to select one counter for the 1 and six counters for the 6, leaving nine counters unused.

Then came an adaptation of Piaget and Henriques-Christophides' (1980) "transfer of *n*-elements" task. After seeing two equal rows of counters in one-to-one correspondence, the children were shown two or more counters in one row being transferred to the other while one of the rows was screened from view. The question was how many more counters there were in one row than in the other as a result of the transfer. Understanding that, say, there are 4 more in one row after the transfer of just 2, is somewhat like understanding that there are 10 more units in the ones column after borrowing just 1 from the tens column.

Another kind of task entailed solving simple addition and subtraction problems, as well as missing addend problems with small numbers (e.g., $5 + 4 = ?, 7 - 3 = ?, 5 + ? = 7$). These were presented both in paper and pencil form and by means of a two-armed balance where equilibrium could be established by hanging unit weights from both arms of the balance at distances corresponding to the numbers involved on both sides of a given equation problem (e.g., $5 + 2$ on one side balanced with 7 on the other). Working with a balance is a particularly effective way for children to gain facility in composing and decomposing numbers.

The children also were asked simply to construct various number families, in as many different ways as they could, using unifix cubes (e.g., $9 = 5 + 4 = 6 + 3 = 7 + 2 = 8 + 1$). In addition, when it seemed appropriate they were given Piaget's classic conservation of number task, in which children are asked whether two parallel rows of objects, shown to be equal in number by one-to-one correspondence, are still equal when one row is spread out to be larger than the other (Piaget & Szeminska, 1965), because it would be a potentially serious problem if a third grader were still uncertain about number invariance.

Almost all of these tasks lend themselves to teaching as well as assessment, and that is how they were used here, in accord with the developmental principles of instruction discussed previously. Each of the three third graders responded somewhat differently. The boy who was trying to decompose numbers from left to right to add and subtract instead of using the standard algorithms initially failed Piaget's transfer of *n*-elements task, but then mastered it and Kamii's place value task easily. He needed help in connecting the knowledge of composing and decomposing numbers that he already possessed to an appreciation of borrowing and carrying with the base-10 algorithms, so that he could work from right to left and achieve greater accuracy. It was important for the teacher to learn that this student's errors revealed more knowledge than she thought. She also was encouraged to pay closer attention to individually constructed solutions to mathematics problems in the future—perhaps even to structure her mathematics program around them, along the lines that Kamii (1985; Kamii & Joseph, 1989) has proposed and demonstrated.

The second child was not good at composing and decomposing large numbers, but was facile with small ones. She needed help to take a step up to where the first child was already comfortable, by composing and decomposing larger and larger numbers in more and more flexible ways before the algorithms were reintroduced. The third child was not good at composing and decomposing small numbers, but he did show some signs of conserving numbers, so that even in his case there was a bedrock of understanding for further work on small number families. However, the standard third grade curriculum had left him behind, and further drill and practice would only increase his frustration and the teacher's.

These particular procedures are of interest here only to help us make some general points about the approach taken. First, because a hierarchical theory of knowledge acquisition within the subject area was available, it was possible to place children along a developmental continuum that suggested what a teacher could do next in each case. Second, reliable assessment was achieved by means of the clinical method combined with teaching and not by means of an object test. And third, although some Piagetian tasks were included, they were used not to make general stage assessments, but because they fell within the mathematical domain and were related to the difficulties the children were having in that domain.

This type of clinical assessment and individualized instruction represents the most analytic aspect of developmental teaching. It contrasts sharply with a traditional approach limited to memorizing number facts and practicing algorithms. But because it is so analytic, the developmental approach also raises questions about its practicality, due to the time it requires of teachers. Yet there are ways to create opportunities for it in the classroom by, for example, engaging the whole class in independent activities as individuals or in small groups so that there is time for the teacher to spend with particular individuals or with her own small group. Thus we turn now to the organizational, orchestrating side of developmental pedagogy.

The Developmental Teacher as Orchestrator

To provide a picture of what a "developmental classroom" might look like, we relate some results from a study that Kroll and Black (1993) conducted to assess the classroom practices of graduates from the DTE program. In order to design an instrument that would identify developmentally compatible teaching methods in mathematics and literacy, Kroll and Black took some principles of development that we have already discussed and matched them with instructional practices that seemed consistent with the principles. We illustrate these matches here with reference to literacy instruction.

Constructivism was matched with such practices as integrating reading and writing, invented spelling, and the use of children's literature (not "Dick and Jane" readers) with an emphasis on children making meaning from text. *Self-regulation* was matched with children making choices (e.g., what to write about), engaging in self-evaluation, and responding as they saw fit to timely feedback from others. *Social construction of knowledge* was matched with small group interactions such as teacher–student or peer conferences about pieces of writing (in contrast to direct instruction by the teacher, followed by individual seat work). The *interactional nature of learning* was matched with a teacher's efforts to integrate the district-mandated curriculum with her understanding of students' learning needs in order to find opportunities for ongoing assessments of student learning.

With an observational instrument based on these matches between developmental principles and teaching practices, a study was carried out to compare the practices of three DTE graduates with those of three traditional teachers who were recognized as good teachers by their colleagues and principals. Although the groups were small, the results seem promising, in that they include striking differences in the use of teaching methods. Because this is not a complete research report, we have summarized only the striking differences in Table 1.

In general, DTE graduates seemed to function more as orchestrators of activities than as direct transmitters of knowledge. They showed more flexible use of grouping for instruction, and they made group-work assignments that would promote social development as well as the learning of subject matter. The group work provided a wider variety of activities and choices for students, and it also allowed more time for individual evaluation by the teacher. In traditional classrooms, most of

Table 1

Summary of Teachers' Organization for Instruction and Implementation of Developmentally Consistent Curricula

Characteristics		Traditional Teachers	DTE Graduates
Type of Instruction	Kind: Mix:	Mostly whole class Mostly homogeneous by ability	Mostly small group Mostly either heterogeneous or student choice
Development of Lesson Products		Mostly by individuals	Many more by pairs or groups
Evaluation of Lessons	Who:	Mostly by the teacher alone	Mostly either by the student with teacher or students with each other
	When:	Less frequently during the lesson	More frequently during the lesson
Source of Materials for Reading		Basal text the basis of curriculum	Basal texts used for supplementary reading
		Literature-based trade books used for supplementary reading	Literature-based trade books are the basic reading materials
Integration of Skills		Some	Lots
Purpose of Lesson Communicated		Infrequently	Frequently

the evaluation was done without the students' direct involvement, whereas in DTE classrooms most evaluation was done either by the teacher with the student, or by the students with each other.

With regard specifically to literacy, the traditional teachers depended primarily on basal series for reading instruction, whereas the DTE teachers made extensive use of other materials, including children's literature. They also integrated reading and writing more as, for example, books written by students were part of the classroom library. In writing, DTE teachers encouraged the use of invented spelling to

Table 2

Several Teaching Methods Likely to be Found in a Developmental Classroom

Domain	Method
General	More small-group than whole-class instruction.
	More heterogeneous grouping than homogeneous grouping.
	Interaction between children seen as an important source of new knowledge.
	Children offered choices in grouping and in the content of lessons.
	A functional basis for learning is emphasized.
	Children given reasons for learning particular lessons.
Literacy	Writing to read and reading to write emphasized.
	Whole-language approach to reading is integrated into program.
	Literature-based versus basal reader-based reading program.
	Communication of meaning emphasized as source of specific skill acquisition, not the converse.
	Peer and teacher conferencing as well as editing of written products.
Mathematics and Science	Hands-on science and manipulative-based mathematics instruction emphasized.
	Mathematics and science texts supplement teacher-organized curriculum.
	Science as a reading actively deemphasized and science as observation, experimentation, and communication emphasized.
	Mental mathematics, problem-solving, and estimation emphasized over memorization of facts and algorithms.

compose stories and other meaningful texts, whereas traditional teachers tended to focus on learning correct spellings out of functional context. The results for mathematics instruction were quite similar.

Table 2 presents a more general list of teaching methods, which, if used with understanding, are consistent with a developmental approach. It should be noted that, unlike some child-centered approaches, our vision of developmental teaching does not overlook skills. However, the learning of skills is pursued in a context that encourages students to understand why the skills are useful.

Although the methods listed in Table 2 stand in contrast to those that comprise traditional practice, it is not all that unusual these days to find them being used in classrooms. However, it is still quite unusual, we believe, to find them being used by teachers who understand why such methods succeed when they do, how to choose and integrate them wisely, and how to develop variations and extensions of them to make them work better in a given situation. Since it is just this sort of understanding on the part of the teacher that the DTE program aims to promote, we must concern ourselves with the question of how teachers can be helped to attain understandings that are consistent with what has been learned from the scientific study of development. This is a problem of applied psychology, and—not surprisingly—we think of it, more specifically, as a problem of applied developmental psychology.

Teacher Development: From Behaviorism to Constructivism

What makes the Piagetian constructivist tradition challenging as a basis for both teaching and teacher education is that it differs in fundamental ways from a kind of conventional wisdom about teaching that seems much more in keeping with the empiricist–behaviorist tradition in psychology. This conventional wisdom comes in both formal-theoretical and everyday, "common sense" versions. The same also can be said about developmental constructivism, except that the common sense versions of constructivism are not nearly so common. Essentially what we are concerned with here is the transformation of everyday behaviorism into everyday constructivism because everyday behaviorism (rather than scientific or theoretical behaviorism) is what most teachers seem to start with and everyday constructivism (rather than formal constructivist theory) is what informs a constructivist teacher's day-to-day decision making and problem solving in the classroom. But we also are concerned with the study of formal developmental psychology as a means of helping new teachers move from behaviorism to constructivism in their everyday thinking.

In teaching constructivist developmental psychology for teachers, we are faced with a problem analogous to the one that has received much attention in the teaching of science—namely that naive theories or misconceptions based on a great deal of ordinary experience become so firmly entrenched that they tend to resist the impact of formal, academic instruction on thinking about practical problems (or even about theoretical problems, for that matter). When there is evidence that formal instruction has failed to overcome this resistance (as indicated by lack of transfer, etc.), it is often inferred that the students did not entirely give up their naive understandings in favor of the correct ones that were taught.

From a developmental perspective, it is important to bear in mind, however, that all understandings are at least partially correct, and that good understandings are gained neither in one fell swoop nor through simple accretion, but rather through a series of qualitative transformations, or stages, whereby more adequate understandings evolve from less adequate ones. Thus the developmental perspective leads to an understanding of everyday conventional wisdom about learning and teaching not just as a set of misconceptions, nor as an adversary to be overcome, but rather as an earlier stage of development from which more advanced pedagogical understandings can evolve through some regular progression. Moreover, the constructivist perspective leads us to expect that this evolution will be driven, at least in part, by the student teacher's own self-regulated activity.

It follows from this line of thought that two interrelated questions must be addressed: First, what might the progression in the development of a teacher's pedagogical conceptions look like (i.e., what are the qualitative transformations, or stages, the teacher would go through)? And second, what sorts of activities might lead to these transformations, and how might teacher educators guide such activities in order to facilitate the process of development? It is possible to begin answering the second question in some very general ways, for example, by talking about action and reflection on the part of the teacher. But more specific answers to the second question require at least some tentative answers to the first question. Thus a systematic description of stages in the development of pedagogical thinking might go a long way toward providing a scientific basis for the education of teachers, just as we have argued that careful descriptions of developmental stages in the basic school subjects can provide a scientific basis for the education of children.

Proposed Levels of Development in Teachers' Pedagogical Thinking

Other educational researchers have written about teacher development, and some have even identified stages thereof (e.g., Fuller, 1969), but our own studies differ from most by focusing specifically on the development of teachers' pedagogical conceptions. We began by examining some transcripts from interviews that had been conducted with student teachers in the DTE program, interviews that were designed to get at thinking about a variety of issues related to teaching. We searched the interview transcripts for evidence of differences in pedagogical thinking that might reflect different levels of understanding as student teachers move from empiricist–behaviorist conceptions to constructivist conceptions. These initial data were cross-sectional in that some interviews were with students who were just entering our 2-year program, whereas others were with different students at the time of their graduation. We found quite a range of pedagogical conceptions that looked like they might be ordered developmentally, and on that basis we proposed five tentative levels of understanding.

A highly abbreviated representation of the five levels is displayed in Table 3, which includes a name for each level—designated in terms

Table 3

Levels of Pedagogical Conception

Qualitative Level	What learning comes from	What teaching essentially is
1. Naive empiricism	Experiencing	Showing and telling
2. Everyday behaviorism	Doing (i.e., practicing)	Modeling and reinforcing
3. Global constructivism	Exploring	Providing hands-on experience
4. Differentiated constructivism	Sense making	Guiding thinking within domains
5. Integrated constructivism	Problem solving	Guiding thinking across domains

of familiar philosophical or psychological positions—together with core ideas in two developmental strands that have to do with learning and teaching. There is, of course, much more to be said about the learning and teaching strands within each level, and two other strands having to do with child behavior and development are not included in the table at all. However, the present table should suffice as a basis for the discussion that follows. (A more elaborated, but still condensed representation of the levels is contained in Ammon and Hutcheson [1989].)

Now, what reason do we have for believing that these different levels actually constitute a developmental progression, that is, are ordered as we say they are? In particular, why do we say that the various forms of constructivist thinking are more advanced than empiricist or behaviorist conceptions, aside from our own belief that constructivism represents a more adequate perspective? After all, other researchers have identified alternative orientations or philosophies among teachers and have sometimes described them in terms that are similar to some of our levels, but without making claims that they are ordered developmentally. Metz (1978), for example, described two major groups of teachers in the junior high schools she studied, whom she called *incorporative* and *developmental* teachers. From our vantage point, these two groups correspond approximately to Level 2 (everyday behaviorism) and Level 4 (differentiated constructivism). Another, less frequent philosophy that Metz called *nondirective guidance* may correspond to our Level 3 (global constructivism) and also to the overly child-centered approach we cited previously.

Metz (1978) did not explicitly judge any of these philosophies to be better or more advanced than others. Nevertheless, she did make a couple of observations about differences between the incorporative and developmental groups that suggest that their philosophies can, in fact, be ordered. First, she noted that, whereas developmental teachers could characterize incorporative teachers in terms of a particular way of thinking that was different from their own, that such was not the case with the incorporative teachers, who only saw that the developmental teachers did not use all the "direct" instructional strategies they would use themselves. Second, developmental teachers sometimes reported that they had once been in the incorporative camp, but apparently there were no reports of movement in the reverse direction by teachers in the incorporative group.

Findings like Metz's (1978) are suggestive, but not persuasive. A case for the proposed ordering from behaviorism to constructivism might also be based on the history of ideas in philosophy and psychology, but we will not try to make that case here. In any case, there is no adequate substitute for more direct, longitudinal data on changes in teacher thinking over time. Fortunately, we have been accumulating such longitudinal data in the DTE program. Unfortunately, the analyses we have carried out so far are small in scale and must be regarded essentially as pilot studies. However, the results seem promising, and are worth reviewing for the present discussion.

Our first longitudinal analysis was a comparison of interviews from the same sample of five students upon entry into and graduation from the DTE program (Ammon, Hutcheson, & Black, 1985). Some results are displayed in Table 4. In four of the five cases, we found evidence of a shift from a preponderance of Level-2 thinking at entry to a preponderance of Level-3 or -4 thinking at graduation. We say "preponderance" because an individual's thinking never seems to be entirely at one level at any one time, but is distributed across two or more adjacent levels. This sort of heterogeneity is entirely consistent with, and is ar-

Table 4

Modal and Mean Levels of Student Teachers' Responses Regarding Behavior, Development, Learning, and Teaching When Entering and Graduating

Student	Entering				Graduating			
	Behav	Devel	Learn	Teach	Behav	Devel	Learn	Teach
mode	2	2	2	2(4)[a]	4	3	4(3)	4
1 mean	1.6	2.1	2.5	2.6	3.8	3.0	3.2	3.6
mode	2	2	2	2	2	2	2	2
2 mean	1.9	2.0	1.9	2.0	2.4	2.1	2.3	2.3
mode	2	2	2,3[b]	2	4	3	4	4
3 mean	2.2	2.1	2.7	2.5	3.3	2.6	3.4	3.5
node	2	2	2	2	3,4,5	2(3)	4	4
4 mean	1.9	1.9	1.9	2.2	3.7	2.6	3.6	3.8
mode	2(3)	2	2	2	3	3	3	4
5 mean	2.5	2.3	2.1	2.7	2.7	3.0	2.9	3.3

[a]Parentheses indicate secondary mode. [b]Multiple entries indicate equally high frequencies.

guably inherent in, the notion of developmental stages (Turiel & Davidson, 1986). The important question is whether an individual's distribution moves up through the proposed levels over time.

Although the initial analysis of entry and graduation interviews showed movement in some instances from Level 2 to Level 4, it was not clear whether there had been a preponderance of Level-3 thinking at some point in the interim. To explore that question, Hutcheson and Ammon (1986) analyzed weekly journal entries that two of the students (Students 3 and 4) had written about their classroom experiences as student teachers. As shown in Figure 4, we graphed the percentages of ideas at different levels across the five student teaching placements that each student had had—three in the first year and two in the second. Figure 4 also shows similar percentages for the entry and graduation interviews. (Levels 1 and 5 are not represented in the graphs because of their low frequencies, and the percentages for the remaining levels were obtained by combining data from the four strands of development—behavior, development, learning, and teaching.) It can be seen that in both cases there was, in fact, an intermediate point at which Level-3 ideas were most frequent as the students were progressing through the program.

In another longitudinal analysis, follow-up interviews were conducted with four DTE graduates during their third year of teaching—graduates who had not been involved in the preceding studies. By coding all three of the interview transcripts available for each teacher—entry to DTE, graduation, and follow-up—we were able to graph changes in the predominant level of thinking within each strand of development over a period of nearly 5 years, as shown in Figure 5. Three findings from this study are of particular interest here. First, there is new evidence of conceptual development during the preservice years, between entry and graduation. Second, there is also evidence of further growth between graduation and third-year teaching. This is a gratifying result, given that one of our goals in DTE is to provide a foundation for continued professional development during the inservice years. And third, although there is variability in exactly when particular levels are reached, all four teachers showed general progress through the levels, and there were no regressions.

The findings reviewed thus far from all of these studies seem quite consistent with the hypothesis that our proposed levels represent stages in the development of increasingly more adequate pedagogical understandings. However, they also raise questions regarding the extent to

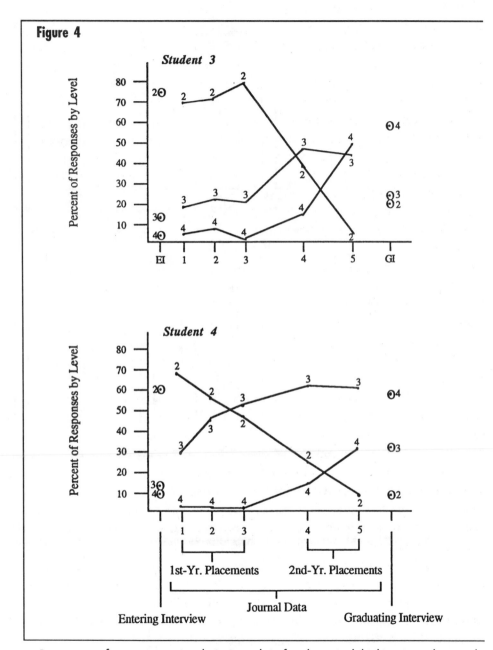

Percentage of responses at Levels 2, 3, and 4 of pedagogical thinking in student teachers' interviews and journals over 2 years.

Figure 5

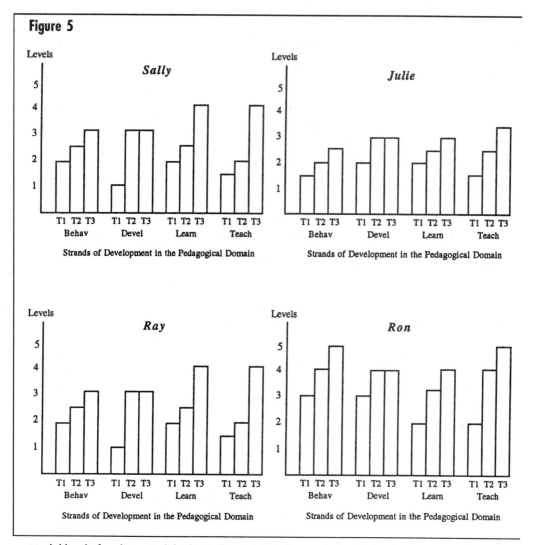

Modal level of pedagogical thinking about child behavior (Behav), development (Devel), learning (Learn), and teaching (Teach) in interviews at entry to program (T1), graduation (T2), and third year of teaching (T3).

which these findings might be specific to the DTE program, and the extent to which assessments of pedagogical understandings are related to the pedagogical practices teachers actually use in the classroom. Rather than address these questions immediately, we will return to them later, after discussing the issue of how to facilitate the sort of conceptual change our data appear to show.

Facilitating the Process of Teacher Development

Assume for the moment that the levels discussed do capture something of the steps that teachers go through in constructing pedagogical understandings—understandings that presumably have a significant influence on the ways in which teachers actually teach. The question then becomes one of how we, as teacher educators, can promote their progress. It seems clear, from what we said previously about the dominance of the empiricist–behaviorist conventional wisdom, that teachers generally do need help in arriving at constructivist understandings. We suspect that "self-made" constructivist teachers have travelled a long, hard road in getting there, and probably could have gone somewhat faster and farther with more support.

Ammon and Hutcheson (1989) suggested that one form of support would be simply to provide student teachers with many opportunities to work through their own current ways of thinking. That suggestion was made with the expectation that our DTE students would thereby gain facility with some bedrock ideas (in accord with the principles of remediation we outlined) and also would eventually discover the contradictions and limitations inherent in lower-level understandings, which in turn would motivate the construction of better understandings in order to resolve and transcend them. If we knew what level teachers' dominant levels of thinking were, then we could try to encourage a lot of thinking at that level, that is, we could try to promote horizontal development. Although that strategy seems consistent with explanations of *spontaneous development* in children (e.g., the attainment of Piagetian conservations), fostering development in adolescents and adults (and sometimes in children also) may require a lot more direct attention to vertical development. Teachers will use their own current ways of thinking in any case, to the extent that they have time to think about their work, but the things they have to think about are so complex in nature that conceptual progress to a higher level is likely to be difficult without some guidance.

We will suggest here, then, that such guidance can be particularly effective if it is directed toward both the "leading edge" and the "trailing edge" of development. Given that an individual's pedagogical thinking is typically distributed over two or more levels at the same time, one might think of the upper end of this distribution as the leading edge of development, and the lower end as the trailing edge. We want to consider briefly here how we might, in fact, be directing student teachers' attention to the leading and trailing edges of their own thinking by means of some current practices in the DTE program. We offer these ideas simply as plausible hypotheses worthy of further investigation.

With regard to promoting development at the leading edge, we think the sequence of academic coursework in our program may be well suited to doing just that. Students typically seem to enter our program with little in the way of thinking beyond Level 2. However, even Level-2 thinking includes the idea that there are some sorts of developmental constraints on what can be learned through practice and reinforcement, although the nature of these constraints is not yet well specified. When Level-2 thinking reaches its most advanced form, these constraints may be regarded as the absence of some general (but still unspecified) cognitive skills that emerge in the process of maturation. It probably is fortunate, then, that the first course in our development and education sequence suggests a way of specifying what those cognitive skills might be when we focus initially on Piaget's general stages of development. The idea that there is domain-specific development and the idea that development does not reduce to maturation are also discussed at that time, but usually they are not yet well understood because they are more in keeping with Level 4. What we see instead, then, in response to formal instruction is the emergence of constructivist ideas that are still global (Level 3) through a process that reminds one of Vygotsky's (1962) thinking about the interaction of spontaneous and scientific concepts.

Our reference to advanced Level-2 thinking grows out of an early suspicion of Ammon and Hutcheson (1989) that it would be possible to distinguish further levels of behavioristic thinking within Level 2, analogous to the global, differentiated, and integrated forms of constructivist thinking beyond Level 2. Perhaps Ammon and Hutcheson did not further differentiate behaviorist thinking within their model because they were concerned primarily with the development of constructivist thinking. However, from an instructional standpoint, it might be important to make this differentiation more clearly, at least for those students whose thinking about pedagogy is limited to more global behaviorist ideas, in order that we might address their leading edges. Their thinking might actually be advanced in the first-year courses that all students take on methods of teaching the basic school subjects to the extent that examination of skills-oriented curriculum guides might suggest ways of differentiating and integrating specific skills within and between learning tasks, which represents a step toward Level 3.

With regard to development beyond Level 3, our curriculum addresses such Level-4 ideas as domain-specific development by means of second-year courses that are devoted to a closer look at development within school subject areas. We suspect that most instruction in developmental psychology for teachers does not go very far into domain-specific development (because of the time it requires) and therefore is not very helpful from a practical standpoint. It should be noted, also, that both development and the learning of school subjects are treated recursively in DTE, as they are studied in both the first and the second year of the program. This sort of spiral curriculum seems quite consistent with the idea that more advanced understandings are constructed gradually.

Finally, with regard to those students who have already reached Level-3 thinking near the beginning of the program, we note again that Level-4 concepts are already represented to some extent in the curriculum during the first year, for those students who are ready to appropriate them. In general, it seems important that multiple levels of thinking be represented in our curriculum at any one time because the students will be at somewhat different levels and will have different leading edges.

The issue of development at the trailing edge can be addressed with reference to course work too. But, because course work is only one part of our program, let us turn to the more individualized kind of teaching and learning that occurs particularly in the context of student teaching. Students in DTE are encouraged to engage in a great deal of self-evaluation of their own teaching through such activities as journal writing and conferencing with supervisors and master teachers. When they focus critically on what they perceive as their shortcomings in teaching, student teachers are sometimes criticizing practices that would be more consistent with the kinds of lower-level thinking they still sometimes engage in themselves, at their trailing edges. Of course in doing so, they are also making use of ideas from higher levels, but one effect of that is probably for them to become clearer about the limitations of ideas at lower levels, which would tend to advance their trailing edges. In their conferences with student teachers, supervisors and master teachers can seek to enhance this sort of effect.

Student teachers are also inclined to direct their criticism toward the teaching of others—particularly their master teachers. This sort of criticism is not discouraged in DTE, but of course for interpersonal reasons it must be handled diplomatically. From an intellectual standpoint, the criticism sometimes reflects a poor understanding on the part of the student teacher as to what the master teacher is doing. In other cases, however, the student's own understandings are relatively advanced, and they lead the student to criticize observed practices that would, in fact, be more consistent, say, with everyday behaviorism or with global constructivism. (No one can be a perfect constructivist teacher, and some of our master teachers could be characterized most accurately as good behaviorist teachers, as in the study by Kroll and Black [1993].) When engaging in the latter sort of criticism with respect to other teachers, student teachers are probably criticizing themselves in some sense as well, that is, they are again criticizing the kinds of thinking that linger at the trailing edges of their own understandings.

Issues Regarding the Proposed Developmental Levels

Returning now to our pilot data on the proposed levels of teacher development, it should be clear that a number of questions remain to be answered. Exactly what do the levels represent? Might they simply show that DTE students become increasingly adept at saying what we want to hear as they go through the program, or that the apparent changes in their thinking only mirror the curriculum sequence we described earlier? Would similar levels be found in settings other than the DTE program? Do our levels relate at all to what teachers actually do in their classrooms? We can at least begin to address these questions on the basis of data that already exist, and we can also consider some of the issues involved in hopes of suggesting directions for future research.

It seems noteworthy that all of our analyses of preservice students in DTE have shown individual differences in the rate of progress through the proposed levels, even within a single cohort of students who have experienced essentially the same curriculum from one semester to another. This suggests that their interview responses and journal writings reflected changes from one time to another in their assimilations of the DTE curriculum, rather than just a parroting of what they had heard most recently.

Levin and Ammon's (1992) finding of continued development beyond graduation from DTE provides another piece of evidence that the changes represented in our model are not completely dependent on the DTE curriculum. We do not mean to suggest that this postgraduate development was completely independent of DTE either. As noted previously, we try to provide a foundation for later development while students are still in the program. In addition, the graduates in Levin and

Ammon's study had stayed in touch with DTE through their contacts with other graduates, and through their service as master teachers for later preservice students. But once they had graduated, they were not involved in any systematic effort on the part of DTE staff to promote their further development.

Kroll (1991) reported similar developmental progressions among student teachers at Mills College, in terms of our proposed levels. It is true that Kroll was a teacher and supervisor in the DTE program at Berkeley for several years, and that she is now involved at Mills with another constructivist developmental program. However, despite their philosophical similarities, the Mills and Berkeley programs are also different in some important respects, and that makes the observed similarities in teacher development seem all the more significant. Programs with philosophies that differ greatly from ours probably are not appropriate settings for research on the kind of development we are concerned with here because it generally makes little sense to study development in an unsupportive environment (unless one already knows what development looks like and wishes to determine whether or not a given environment supports it).

The issue of thoughts in relation to actions is another one that we can pursue through existing data. We discussed how Kroll and Black (1993) found that a small sample of DTE graduates were much more likely to use constructivist teaching practices in their classrooms than a comparison sample of experienced traditional teachers. One of those DTE graduates was Student 4 in the initial analyses of preservice interviews and journals (Ammon et al., 1985; Hutcheson & Ammon, 1986), so we know that she was capable of thinking about her work as an inservice teacher from at least a Level-4 perspective. In the Levin and Ammon (1992) study of other DTE graduates, third-year teachers were not only interviewed, but also observed while teaching. In general, good correspondences were found between their thoughts in the interview and their actions in the classroom, together with a few interesting inconsistencies.

It is important to note that we should not expect to find exact correspondences between thought and action in all cases. Some discrepancies are inherent in development, because—as we have seen—there are heterogeneities and inconsistencies in pedagogical thinking itself at any one time. In addition, to borrow from Piaget (1978), thought and action are separate (but not unrelated) planes of development; sometimes success precedes understanding, and sometimes understanding comes first. It might be useful, however, to consider some factors that can cause discrepancies between thought and action, in that it may clarify what our levels of pedagogical thinking include by highlighting what they do not include.

Our pedagogical levels do not include understandings in a number of other knowledge domains that bear on teachers' actions. The decisions a teacher makes are based on a number of important considerations in addition to those that are purely pedagogical. These other considerations involve the teacher's understandings of moral and societal issues, interpersonal relations, and subject matter, together with practical constraints and self-interest. When these sorts of considerations are at odds with and outweigh those that are purely pedagogical, there will be discrepancies between the teacher's pedagogical understandings and the teacher's actions. Thus, for example, many teachers end up teaching to standardized tests, for a variety of reasons, even though it does not seem very sensible to them from a purely pedagogical standpoint. How teachers coordinate the various issues involved in teaching and how their coordinations change over time are certainly interesting topics for further research.

Also not included in our pedagogical levels is the kind of intuitive, situation-specific, automatic, and skill-type knowledge that is undoubtedly important for making things go well in the classroom. Without that kind of knowledge, constructivist approaches to teaching may be implemented quite poorly. And with it, behaviorist approaches may be implemented rather effectively. Thus the absence of intuitive and situation-specific knowledge from our levels may strike some people as a glaring omission, especially in view of the fact that it has been given a central role in some accounts of teacher expertise (Berliner, 1986). We wonder, though, whether teachers who have gone far on the basis of such knowledge could not have gone even farther had they received adequate support for the development of the more explicit and generalizable understandings that are represented in the higher levels of our model.

If today's good teachers are found to have a kind of expertise that consists primarily of intuitive, situation-specific knowledge, is that something we should try to replicate in the teachers of tomorrow, or is it something we should try to transcend? Would it not be desirable if teachers were more able to share important elements of their expertise with others, and to generalize it to new situations they face themselves? Karmiloff-Smith and Inhelder (1975) said, "If you want to get ahead, get a theory." Theories help individuals make increasingly good sense of their experience, and that is a vital function when experience is so complex and fraught with uncertainty that the "law of effect" becomes a questionable shaper of behavior. Theories are also generalizable and sharable. Consequently, when held by teachers, they lend themselves to such laudable enterprises as teacher research and productive collegiality. In other words, they can help make teaching a true profession, and not just an art or a skilled trade.

Of course the ultimate question is whether the advantages of constructivist understandings for teachers pay off in advantages for their students as well. Do their students end up with better understandings of curriculum content? We have not yet formally investigated that question as a program in DTE. But our students, in carrying out research projects for their courses or their masters degrees, have sought to evaluate or inform constructivist methods of instruction by assessing children's understandings through clinical interviews and other means, and by carrying out developmental analyses of longitudinal and cross-sectional data. And, of course, they are encouraged to do the same sorts of things in less formal ways as a means of monitoring their own teaching. Anyone else who wanted to assess the effectiveness of DTE graduates as teachers would presumably need to use the same sorts of methods, but perhaps more formally.

Conclusion

With this last thought, we have come full circle. Because Piagetian developmental psychology has provided important insights into child development, along with fruitful methods of assessing children's understandings, it can serve as a useful guide for teaching. Therefore, it can also serve as a core subject of study for teachers. In addition, principles of developmental psychology can guide us in teaching teachers, and in assessing and understanding their development. Finally, developmental psychology has provided ways in which developmentally oriented teachers, and their observers, can assess the effects of their approach to teaching on children. Moreover, because teachers and classroom life generally have not figured importantly in past developmental research, systematic use of developmental principles and methods in teaching and teacher education may further enrich developmental psychology itself. In that regard, the learner-centered psychological principles discussed in the present volume, as sound as they seem to us now, can only be expected to evolve further, in response to future advances in psychology and education.

References

Ammon, P., & Hutcheson, B. P. (1989). Promoting the development of teachers' pedagogical conceptions. *Genetic Epistemologist, 17*(4), 23–29.

Ammon, P., Hutcheson, B. P., & Black, A. (1985, April). *Teachers' developing conceptions about children, learning, and teaching: Observations from a clinical interview.* Paper presented at the meeting of the American Educational Research Association, Chicago.

Ammon, P., & Levin, B. B. (1993). Expertise in teaching from a developmental perspective: The Developmental Teacher Education Program at Berkeley. *Learning and Individual Differences, 5*(4), 319–326.

Baratta-Lorton, M. (1976). *Mathematics their way.* Menlo Park, CA: Addison-Wesley.

Berliner, D. C. (1986). In pursuit of the expert pedagogue. *Educational Researcher, 15*(7), 5–13.

Berliner, D. C., & Biddle, B. J. (1995). *The manufactured crisis: Myths, fraud, and the attack on America's public schools.* Reading, MA: Addison-Wesley.

Black, A. (1985, April). Structural-developmental theory and elementary school teaching. In L. Nucci (Chair), *New developments in Piagetian theory and their implications for education.* Symposium conducted at the meeting of the American Educational Research Association, Chicago.

Black, A., & Ammon, P. (1992). A developmental-constructivist approach to teacher education. *Journal of Teacher Education, 43*(5), 323–335.

Block, J. H., & Anderson, L. W. (1975). *Mastery learning in classroom instruction.* New York: Macmillan.

Bloom, B. S. (1976). *Human characteristics and school learning.* New York: McGraw-Hill.

Brown, J. S., & Burton, R. R. (1978). Diagnostic models for procedural bugs in basic mathematical skills. *Cognitive Science, 2,* 153–192.

Burns, M. (1975). *The "I hate mathematics!" book.* Boston: Little, Brown.

Burns, M. (1982). *Math for smarty pants.* Boston: Little, Brown.

Carmichael, P., Driver, R., Holding, B., Phillips, I., Twigger, D., & Watts, M. (1990). *Research on students' conceptions in science: A bibliography.* Leeds, England: Centre for Studies in Science and Mathematics Education, University of Leeds.

Carnegie Forum on Education and the Economy. (1986). *A nation prepared: Teachers for the 21st Century.* Washington, DC: Author.

Cohen, D. (1983). *Piaget: Critique and assessment.* London: Croom Helm.

Cohen, E. G. (1986). *Designing groupwork: Strategies for the heterogeneous classroom.* New York: Teachers College Press.

Daiute, C. (Ed.). (1993). The development of literacy through social interaction. *New Directions for Child Development.* San Francisco: Jossey-Bass.

Damon, W. (1984). Peer education: The untapped potential. *Journal of Applied Developmental Psychology, 5,* 331–343.

Davis, R. B., & Greenstein, R. (1969). Jennifer. *New York State Mathematics Teachers Journal, 19*(3), 94–103.

Doise, W., & Mugny, G. (1984). *The social development of the intellect.* New York: Pergamon.

Dyson, A. H. (1987). The value of "time off task": Young children's spontaneous talk and deliberate text. *Harvard Educational Review, 57*(4), 396–420.

Erlwanger, S. H. (1973). Benny's conception of rules and answers in IPI mathematics. *Journal of Children's Mathematical Behavior, 1*(2), 7–26.

Ferreiro, E., & Teberosky, A. (1982). *Literacy before schooling* (K. G. Castro, Trans.). Exeter, NH: Heinemann. (Original work published 1979)

Fuller, F. F. (1969). Concerns of teachers: A developmental conceptualization. *American Educational Research Journal, 6*, 207–226.

Goodman, K. (Ed.). (1973). *Miscue analysis: Applications to reading instruction.* Urbana, IL: National Council of Teachers of English.

Goodman, K. (1986). *What's whole in whole language?* Postsmouth, NH: Heinemann.

Goodman, Y. M. (Ed.). (1990). *How children construct literacy: Piagetian perspectives.* Newark, DE: International Reading Association.

Goodman, Y. M., Hood, W. J., and Goodman, K. S. (Eds.). (1991). *Organizing for whole language.* Portsmouth, NH: Heinemann.

Henderson, E. H., & Beers, J. W. (Eds.). (1980). *Developmental and cognitive aspects of learning to spell: A reflection of word knowledge.* Newark, DE: International Reading Association.

Holmes Group Executive Board. (1986). *Tomorrow's teachers: A report of the Holmes Group.* East Lansing, MI: Holmes Group.

Hutcheson, B. P., & Ammon, P. (1986, April). *The development of teachers' conceptions as reflected in their journals.* Paper presented at the meeting of the American Educational Research Association, San Francisco.

Johnson, D. W., Johnson, R. T., Holubec, E. C., & Roy, P. (1984). *Circles of learning.* Alexandria, VA: Association for Supervision and Curriculum Development.

Kamii, C. (1985). *Young children reinvent arithmetics.* New York: Teachers College Press.

Kamii, C., & Joseph, L. L. (1989). *Young children continue to reinvent arithmetic: Second grade.* New York: Teachers College Press.

Kamii, C., & Randazzo, M. (1985). Social interaction and invented spelling. *Language Arts, 62*(2), 124–133.

Karmiloff-Smith, A., & Inhelder, B. (1975). If you want to get ahead get a theory. *Cognition, 3*, 195–212.

Kroll, L. (1991, April). Linking teacher development and teacher reflection: A case study of two beginning teachers. In A. Richert (Chair), *Cases of teacher education: Ways of doing, ways of seeing.* Symposium conducted at the meeting of the American Educational Research Association, Chicago.

Kroll, L., & Black, A. (1993). Developmental theory and teaching methods: A pilot study of a teacher education program. *The Elementary School Journal, 93*(4), 417–441.

Kuhn, D. (Ed.). (1995). Development and learning: Reconceptualizing the intersection. *Human Development, 38*(6).

Levin, B. B., & Ammon, P. (1992). The development of beginning teachers' pedagogical thinking: A longitudinal analysis of four case studies. *Teacher Education Quarterly, 19*(4), 19–37.

Levin, I. (Ed.). (1986). *Stage and structure: Reopening the debate.* Norwood, NJ: Ablex.

Lowery, L. (1985). *The everyday science sourcebook: Ideas for teaching in the elementary and middle school.* Palo Alto, CA: Seymour Publications.

Metz, M. H. (1978). *Classrooms and corridors: The crisis of authority in desegregated secondary schools.* Berkeley, CA: University of California Press.

Modgil, S., & Modgil, C. (1982). *Jean Piaget: Consensus and controversy.* London: Holt, Rinehart & Winston.

Murray, F. B. (1972). Acquisition of conservation through social interaction. *Developmental Psychology, 6*, 1–6.

National Commission on Excellence in Education. (1983). *A nation at risk: The imperative for educational reform.* Washington, DC: Author.

Piaget, J. (1932). *The moral judgment of the child* (M. Gabain, Trans.). London: Routledge and Kegan Paul.

Piaget, J. (1960). *The child's conception of physical causality* (M. Gabain, Trans.). Totowa, NJ: Littlefield. (Original work published 1927)

Piaget, J. (1964). Development and learning. In R. E. Ripple & V. N. Rockcastle (Eds.), *Piaget rediscovered.* Ithaca, NY: Cornell University School of Education.

Piaget, J. (1970a). *The child's conception of time* (A. J. Pomerans, Trans.). New York: Basic Books. (Original work published 1946)

Piaget, J. (1970b). Piaget's theory. In P. Mussen (Ed.), *Carmichael's manual of child psychology* (3rd ed., pp. 703–732). New York: Wiley.

Piaget, J. (1971a). *Biology and knowledge* (B. Walsh, Trans.). Chicago: University of Chicago Press. (Original work published 1967)

Piaget, J. (1971b). *The child's conception of movement and speed* (G. E. T. Holloway & M. J. MacKensie, Trans.). New York: Ballantine. (Original work published 1946)

Piaget, J. (1978). *Success and understanding* (A. J. Pomerans, Trans.). Cambridge, MA: Harvard University Press. (Original work published 1974)

Piaget, J. (1985). *The equilibration of cognitive structures: The central problem of intellectual development* (T. Brown & K. J. Thampy, Trans.). Chicago: University of Chicago Press. (Original work published 1975)

Piaget, J., & Henriques-Christophides, A. (1980). Simple or reciprocal transfers from one collection to another. In J. Piaget, *Experiments in contradiction.* (D. Coltman, Trans.). Chicago: University of Chicago Press. (Original work published 1974)

Piaget, J., & Inhelder, B. (1967). *The child's conception of space* (F. J. Langdon & J. L. Lunzer, Trans.). New York: Norton. (Original work published 1948)

Piaget, J., & Inhelder, B. (1975). *The origins of the idea of chance in the child* (L. Leake, P. Burrell, & H. D. Fishbein, Trans.). New York: Norton. (Original work published 1951)

Piaget, J., Inhelder, B., & Szeminska, A. (1964). *The child's conception of geometry.* New York: Harper & Row. (Original work published 1960)

Piaget, J., & Szeminska, A. (1965). *The child's conception of number* (C. Gattegno & F. M. Hodgson, Trans.). New York: Norton. (Original work published 1941)

Resnick, L. B., & Ford, W. W. (1981). *The psychology of mathematics instruction.* Hillsdale, NJ: Erlbaum.

Science Curriculum Framework and Criteria Committee. (1984). *Science framework addendum for California public schools.* Sacramento, CA: California State Board of Education.

Shulman, L. S. (1987). Knowledge and teaching: Foundations of the new reform. *Harvard Educational Review, 57*(1), 1–22.

Simons, H. D., & Ammon, P. (1989). Child knowledge and primerese text: Mismatches and miscues. *Research in the Teaching of English, 23*(4), 380–398.

Stauffer, R. G. (1970). *The language-experience approach to the teaching of reading.* New York: Harper & Row.

Turiel, E. (1983). *The development of social knowledge: Morality and convention.* Cambridge, England: Cambridge University Press.

Turiel, E., & Davidson, P. (1986). Heterogeneity, inconsistency, and asynchrony in the development of cognitive structures. In I. Levin (Ed.), *Stage and structure: Reopening the debate* (pp. 106–143). Norwood, NJ: Ablex.

Vygotsky, L. S. (1962). *Thought and language* (E. Hanfmann & G. Vakar, Trans.). Cambridge, MA: M.I.T. Press.

Teaching Educational Psychology: Learner-Centered and Constructivist Perspectives

Hermine H. Marshall

The preceding chapters in this section together with several chapters from earlier sections provide some background for what appears in this chapter. Mayer has described the movement in educational psychology beyond behaviorism to information processing and cognitive psychology. Wittrock (chapter 6) has pointed out the importance of "generative teaching theory" and principles of cognitive learning and teaching for preservice teachers' learning with understanding. Generative teaching theory overlaps in a number of ways with the constructivist perspectives and learner-centered principles that are described in this chapter. McCombs has presented evidence supporting learner-centered and constructivist principles. (Other research evidence supporting these principles has been reviewed by Alexander and Murphy. See chapter 2, this volume.) Ammon and Black have described a teacher education program based on developmental and constructivist principles.

The focus of this chapter is on the implications of learner-centered principles and constructivist approaches for teaching educational psychology in teacher education programs. As a guide for those who teach educational psychology in teacher education programs, *Learner-Centered Psychological Principles: Guidelines for the Teaching of Educational Psychology in Teacher Education Programs* (American Psychological Association [APA], 1995) was adapted from the *Learner-Centered Psychological Principles: Guidelines for School Redesign and Reform* (APA Presidential Task Force on Psychology in Education, 1993). As a reference, the 12 learner-centered principles and the section Implications for Teacher Education as revised for the teaching of educational psychology are presented in the appendix to this chapter. Although the School Redesign and Reform version includes a number of principles derived from a constructivist perspective (e.g., Cobb, 1994; Marshall, 1992a, 1992b, 1996a; Newman, Griffin, & Cole, 1989; Steffe & Gale, 1995), more of a constructivist approach is included in the Teaching of Educational Psychology version.

Constructivist approaches to learning have added new ways of looking at learning and teaching that need to be considered as the field moves beyond earlier behaviorist, information processing, and cognitive psychological approaches. In order to adequately understand learner-centered principles, those who are concerned with teaching educational psychology must also have an adequate understanding of constructivist perspectives[1] and how these differ from earlier views.

After briefly outlining some differences between constructivist perspectives and earlier views of learning, I describe a number of obstacles that sometimes impede adequate understanding and implementation of constructivist and learner-centered principles by those in teacher-education programs. I then suggest some implications of the learner-centered principles for teaching educational psychology in teacher education programs with the goal of promoting change.

Constructivist Approaches to Learning

Constructivist views differ from earlier information-processing views in a number of ways. Both views contend that the learner is active. However, two major differences between these perspectives center on questions of (a) whether knowledge can accurately reflect external reality and (b) how knowledge is acquired (from an information-processing view) or constructed (from a constructivist view). From an *information-processing* perspective, knowledge is acquired, stored, and retrieved, built on the basis of previously acquired facts, skills, and knowledge (Mayer, 1992). Acquisition of knowledge implies that something is taken in that accurately reflects what exists in the external world. This view also implies that what is taken in, stored, and retrieved from memory serves in a relatively unchanged form as blocks for building new knowledge.

[1]Those involved in teaching educational psychology also need to be informed about sociocultural perspectives on learning. However, these views are beyond the scope of this chapter. See for example, John-Steiner & Mahn, 1996; Lave & Wenger, 1991; Moll, 1990; Rogoff, 1990; and Wertsch, 1985.

In contrast, *constructivist* views hold that knowledge is not a replica of something that exists in the external world, but that it is constructed based on previously constructed and interpreted knowledge. Knowledge is thus not a direct copy of something external (cf. Ernest, 1995). From this constructivist perspective, new experiences and materials are interpreted through previously constructed cognitive structures and in interaction with the experiential world and thus may lead to somewhat unique representations of the world. This is not to deny the existence of external reality, but rather to point out that there is no way of knowing whether what people perceive and believe they understand exactly matches that reality. However, people can test their representations of the world through continuing interactions with the world and with others. For example, my understanding of constructivism or information processing is somewhat different from yours. In interaction, we may come to closer agreement or negotiated understanding about the meaning of concepts, such as constructivism and information processing. Similarly, children's understanding of sources of heat may have more to do with their own experiences with "warm sweaters" than the sun, but through guided experimentation, reflection, and discussion, they can come to construct understandings closer to those currently accepted by scientists (Watson & Konicek, 1990). In a similar way, preservice teachers who have come to understand developmental constructivist principles can then help children overcome computational errors based on "partially understood 'facts' or algorithms" that were probably acquired through inadequate memorization and interpretation of procedures (Ammon & Black, this volume).

It should be noted, however, that from a constructivist perspective, all knowledge is constructed—even when information is presented in a teacher-directed, lecture format (cf. Wittrock, this volume). Individuals take that information and try to make sense of it from their own framework based on past experiences. Learner-Centered Principle 2 reflects this process, stating that "the learner seeks to create meaningful, coherent representations of knowledge regardless of the quantity and quality of data available" (p. 2). In doing so, learners interpret and reconstruct in their own terms the information presented. However, where learning situations are set up specifically so that learners have opportunities to interact actively with problems relevant to their own goals and discuss these with others, learning is more likely to be deeper and more meaningful.

Although there is some commonality among the variety of constructivist perspectives (see, for example, Cobb, 1994; Steffe & Gale, 1995), cognitive and social constructivists (and sociocultural researchers)[2] vary regarding the nature and influence of the social world in the process of knowledge construction (Cobb & Yackel, 1996; Marshall, 1996b; Nuthall, in press). Cognitive constructivist views of learning suggest that the learner constructs knowledge—often with the guidance of an expert—as exemplified by the previous example of computation. In contrast, social constructivists place greater emphasis on the role of the social interaction through which contexts, knowledge, and meanings in everyday life are constructed and reconstructed.[3] According to a social constructivist framework, learning and thinking are situated in social contexts rather than occurring mainly in an individual's mind (e.g., Newman, Griffin, & Cole, 1989; Wertsch, 1985; Vygotsky, 1978). Through discussion with others—where ideas are shared, challenged, negotiated, and justified—new levels of conceptual understanding can be reached (Edwards & Mercer, 1987; Vygotsky, 1978). From this perspective, learning occurs on an interpersonal plane as individuals participate in activities (Rogoff, 1990). This process of social negotiation is illustrated by a sixth grade student's essay describing her learning with her "table group" in a bilingual class:

> [W]hen we were studying on the "Tropical Rain Forest" . . . [e]ach table had to work together on a layer of the rain forest; some would study on the animals of the layer and others would study trees and plants. We took notes from rain forest books. We also had to do a painting about the layer. Then we presented it and talked about it in both languages. Again, we understood what was going on. . . . I guess the way we really function together as learners is that when someone says something, depending on what we are talking about and what the classmate says, we will either agree or say what our point of view is. (Yaeger, Floriani, & Green, 1996)

Knowledge of the world is thus based on negotiated understandings (Ernest, 1995). Nevertheless, although individuals participate in the negotiation of shared understandings, their use of this shared understanding reflects their own involvement in that activity (Rogoff, 1990).

Moreover, social constructivists contribute to the understanding that it is not only substantive knowledge in the formal sense that is

---

[2]Although there are distinctions between social constructivism and sociocultural approaches, these distinctions are not relevant to the argument presented here. Interested readers are referred to Cobb (1994), Ernest (1995), and the special issue of the *Educational Psychologist* edited by Marshall (1996b) for enlightening comparisons.

[3]However, it appears that a number of cognitive (radical) constructivists appear to be coming closer to incorporating more of the social constructivist views (Ernest, 1995).

constructed (the sources of heat or definition of constructivism, for example), but how and what it means to be a student (for example, listening and taking notes or actively participating in the construction of understandings) and what is of value and worth knowing (for example, "right answers" or justification and reasoning) that are continually constructed in dynamic and ongoing interactions among the participants. This, in turn, influences learners' processing of substantive content and their level of understanding. Within the social context, students essentially learn how to "do school," how to "be a student" in the particular setting. (See Marshall [1992a] for further elaboration of these notions.) And this has implications not only for preschool, elementary, and secondary teaching, but for how teachers are prepared as well. For example, most students entering a teacher-education program expect to absorb and reproduce the material in the text and instructors' lectures to do well, based on their construction of what it means to be a student in a college class. For change to occur, the meaning of being a student must be reconstructed in conjunction with instructors and peers to a more active and reflective form.

The notion of the construction of knowledge through the negotiation of understandings in interaction with others at different levels is incorporated to some extent in the *Learner-Centered Psychological Principles: Guidelines for the Teaching of Educational Psychology in Teacher Education Programs* (APA, 1995). Following are some barriers to understanding and implementing learner-centered and constructivist principles in teacher education programs.

Impediments to Implementing Constructivist and Learner-Centered Principles

Although many of the learner-centered principles, such as "Individuals progress through stages of physical, intellectual, emotional, and social development that are a function of unique genetic and environmental factors" (Principle 8, p. 8), may seem self-evident, a number of obstacles may hinder understanding and implementation of these and the constructivist principles. These hindrances include (a) educators' education and beliefs, (b) available textbooks and resources for teaching, and (c) preservice teachers' education and beliefs.

Educators' Training and Beliefs

Traditional education for educational practitioners has included a heavy dose of behaviorism. Although educators have been exposed to the benefits of intrinsic motivation, educators have also learned to believe in the effectiveness of external reinforcements in our professional education as well as through our own experiences in schools. This has resulted, for example, in the use of rewards and punishments as the motivational strategy most commonly used by beginning teachers, despite that fact that making learning relevant was found to be most effective (Newby, 1991). Educators are also products of the efficiency movement in education (Johnson & Brooks, 1979; Marshall, 1988). Efficient methods of producing batches of "educated citizens" were believed to include competition and grouping them according to ability. However, many of these methods run counter to the learner-centered principles and are in fact only mentioned in the learner-centered document as strategies to avoid. The deeply rooted beliefs of some teacher educators are difficult to dislodge, and often hamper both the acceptance of new knowledge as well as the ability to convey newer views to their students.

Moreover, teaching loads and time constraints can overwhelm opportunities to keep up with the latest research that supports newer views of learning. As a consequence, many instructors rely on textbooks to keep them and their students abreast of current thinking.

Available Textbooks

Until recently, a second roadblock to implementing these learner-centered and constructivist principles was set up by the available educational psychology textbooks. For decades, these texts have been based on the traditional, transmissive, behaviorist-, associationist-, and efficiency-derived views. Not only is at least one chapter in most textbooks devoted entirely to behaviorist views of learning, but chapters on other topics like motivation, classroom management, evaluation, and even development are often interwoven with traditional transmissive notions. Textbook readers are told, for example, that young children like praise and rewards. In contrast, if learners are naturally curious, as is stated in Learner-Centered Principle 6, it follows that they do not need praise and rewards to learn what they are naturally curious about, even though educators have been socialized to believe that they do. Children may need praise and rewards only for decontextualized, overly easy, or overly difficult tasks. But these qualifications and their implications are omitted from most textbooks. In contrast, the learner-centered principles suggest that natural curiosity needs to be supported through interpersonal interactions, strategies for self-control, and authentic learning tasks of optimal difficulty and novelty for each learner (Principles 6 and 7).

Fortunately, some modifications in textbooks have been made over the past several years in recognition of the importance of constructivist principles, although chapters on behaviorism seem not to have been reduced proportionately. Sections or chapters on constructivist learning have been added. Many textbooks now incorporate the broader implications of constructivist principles for motivation and classroom management as well. As more textbooks present better explanations and examples of constructivist principles, this barrier will be further reduced.

Preservice Students' Education and Beliefs

A third set of obstacles to implementing learner-centered principles and constructivist views and to students' understanding of these views comes from our preservice students. For 12 to 16 years, most of them have swallowed a pretty solid diet of direct instruction, memorization, and regurgitation. Many have come to believe that teachers and texts are the sole sources of knowledge and fail to trust their own critical thinking abilities—at least in academic settings. These students also survived the competition that left many others behind. Those others may not have learned the strategies to cope, to pass the tests, and to jump through the hoops or may not have wanted to subject themselves to a system that was incompatible with their styles of learning and experiences and consequently dropped out. The survivors in our teacher-education programs are likely to believe in the efficacy of the ways in which they were taught: teacher presentation of information; praise, rewards, and punishments; and batch-processing via ability grouping and tracking. They are unaware that these methods are ineffective for many, particularly those whose backgrounds differ from their own. Their experiences and the "folk wisdom" perpetuated in the traditional schools that most of them attended have entrenched these beliefs. Ammon and Black (chapter 16, this volume) present evidence that many students enter teacher education with levels of thinking that can be described as *naive empiricism* and *everyday behaviorism*. In the Developmental Teacher Education program that Ammon and Black describe, students are helped to progress through a developmental sequence in levels of thinking toward increasingly integrated constructivist views. Unfortunately, the obstacle of preservice students' beliefs is compounded where students believe that knowledge is stored in teachers and texts, but instructors are not adequately informed about new conceptions of learning and the texts do not present an adequate picture of these principles.

To overcome these problems, attention needs to be paid to the background and training of instructors. Rather than just drawing from a pool of graduate students, care must be taken that instructors for educational psychology courses are thoroughly grounded, not just in learner-centered and constructivist principles, but in classroom learning and teaching as well as the backgrounds and learning styles of those from different cultural groups. Where instructors have not had first-hand experience as classroom teachers, they need to have experience observing in a variety of types of classrooms and talking to learners and teachers regarding the process of learning and the problems encountered. Extensive and intensive experience observing in classrooms that exemplify the type of learning and teaching that reflects learner-centered principles and constructivist approaches will be a better foundation for creating the conditions for preservice teachers to construct their own knowledge of these views of learning (see Marshall, 1996a).

Other Barriers

Other barriers to implementing these newer views derive from the traditional academic settings in which teacher educators teach. These constraints apply to teacher education programs in general, rather than just the teaching of educational psychology and include factors such as time slots for courses, grading policies, and testing for competencies.

Learner-Centered Principles as a Guide for Overcoming Obstacles and Promoting Change

The *Learner-Centered Psychological Principles: Guidelines for the Teaching of Educational Psychology in Teacher Education Programs* (APA, 1995) can provide clues as to how to overcome these obstacles along two dimensions. One dimension is helping teachers understand the substantive content reflected in the learner-centered principles and constructivist views, for example, understanding that learning is an active process, both internally and socially mediated (Principle 1). Teachers need to be provided with classroom examples of this and other principles to facilitate this understanding. One illustration of this principle is provided by Brilliant-Mills (1993) and Floriani (1993). Both articles highlight the social mediation of learning in their descriptions of how one sixth grade teacher sets up her classroom so that students come to see themselves as learners who collaborate in small groups as they develop their understanding of how mathematicians, historians, and anthropologists analyze data. These authors provide a sense of how learners, in this case sixth graders, gradually construct knowledge from evidence in social interaction with teacher and peers. From the first day when students were asked to work in groups to come up with the best estimate for the weight and price per pound of a watermelon, gather more data, and record their data in a notebook, this teacher conveyed the notion that learning is an active process requiring both individual contributions and social negotiation. Multiple examples of each principle are needed to provide opportunities for discussing and constructing understandings of each of the principles.

The second dimension refers to the actual learning processes that preservice teachers go through. If those preparing to teach are expected to follow these learner-centered and constructivist principles, they must experience these principles as learners themselves. The question becomes one of how students can be encouraged to move beyond believing that "the answers are in the back of the book" toward understanding that knowledge is not fixed and does not exist somewhere in the external world to be incorporated into students' minds unchanged. Students must understand that learning is a continuing process of interpreting and revising understandings. What, then, are some methods and strategies that may prove useful in moving beyond the traditional, teacher front-and-center, student-as-passive-receptor approaches?

For learners who have been socialized to absorb information passively, a first step is to help them acquire new strategies to critically evaluate what they are reading and hearing and to trust their own reflective powers, critical thinking, and integrating abilities (cf. Belenky, Clinchy, Goldberger, & Tarule, 1986). A major dilemma, then, is how to change these preservice students' beliefs and strategies and how to open their senses to other ways of learning, of constructing their own knowledge so that ultimately they may be able to change the ways that their pupils learn. Principle 4 suggests that one place to begin the process of encouraging "critical thinking and the development of exper- tise" is with helping students develop "higher-order strategies for 'thinking about thinking and learning' " (APA, 1995, p. 3). Supporting this principle, McCombs (chapter 15, this volume) has described the importance of higher order metacognitive self-processes in promoting learning and developing agency. Wittrock (chapter 6, this volume) also points out the place of metacognitive processes in relating prior knowl- edge to the learning of subject matter. Teacher education programs like those described by Ammon and Black (chapter 16, this volume) and Fosnot (1989, 1996) deliberately plan activities where students are en- couraged to reflect on their own and others' learning and thinking.

In addition to higher order and critical thinking, Principle 7 sug- gests that "curiosity, creativity, and higher-order thinking are stimulated by relevant, authentic learning tasks" (p. 4). *Authentic learning tasks* can be those based on (a) authentic situations and problems from real class- rooms or (b) tasks or problems that are as difficult for preservice can- didates to solve as problems found in elementary or secondary school are for those pupils. Both types of authentic tasks can be presented and discussed to illustrate research-based principles. However, for tasks to be derived from real classrooms, it seems important for preservice can- didates to have concurrent field placements, particularly in classrooms that implement learner-centered principles, both to draw on and to test out what they are learning (see Marshall, 1996a). Ammon and Black (chapter 16, this volume) suggest how preservice candidates can learn, for example, about the place of "errors" in the construction of knowl- edge by assessing individual children's understanding of subject matter using Piaget's clinical method and then providing experiences at the child's level of understanding (see also Fosnot, 1989, 1996).

In addition, both students and instructors can bring in situations or "cases" from their own experience in their classrooms or from books or videos or from descriptions of particular teachers teaching—such as "Keisha Coleman" (Peterson, 1992), "Janet Ferero" (Putnam & Burke, 1992), Beth Yaeger (Yaeger, Floriani, & Green, 1996; Brilliant-Mills, 1993; Floriani, 1993) or Teachers A and B described by Blumenfeld, Puro, and Mergandoller (1992)—to stimulate discussion and new learn- ing. The case of Keisha Coleman demonstrates one teacher's move from a traditional didactic teacher who believed in "teaching-as-telling" to one who began to understand that learners must have a hand in actively constructing their own learning. Janet Ferero and Beth Yaeger illustrate the establishment of a community of learners. Contrasting Teacher A with Teacher B can demonstrate how teachers can implement some of the learner-centered constructivist principles to different degrees and with differing effects. Bringing in such cases allows students to test out their own beliefs based on a mutually shared experience and in interaction with their peers and instructors' probing questions so as to negotiate, share, and construct more sophisticated meanings and understandings (Principle 1).

An equally compelling way to develop preservice candidates' sensitivity to the learning process that younger or less proficient learners go through is to present students with problems that are difficult at their own level (see Fosnot, 1989, 1996; Marshall, 1996a). As the students discuss their reasoning and solutions first in small groups and then as a whole class, such challenges can help them make the link between their own learning and that of those they will be teaching.

However, this implies that a safe and respectful environment in which students feel free to express their ideas and feelings and to challenge other ideas must be established. As Principle 10 emphasizes, "learning and self-esteem are heightened when individuals are in respectful and caring relationships with others who see their potential, genuinely appreciate their unique talents, and accept them as individuals" (APA, 1995, p. 4). McCombs' chapter (chapter 15, this volume) presents the research support for the benefits for learning where instructors are sensitive and caring.

In a safe environment where discussion is facilitated and individuals' critical thinking is validated, students are more likely to move beyond accepting the authority of text or teacher and reflect on their own and others' views. Instructional strategies must include opportunities for small group discussion and dialogue. Students are then more likely to learn through the "process of discovering and constructing meaning from information and experience, filtered through each individual's unique perceptions, thoughts, and feelings—as shared understandings are negotiated with [others]" (Principle 1, APA, 1995, p. 2).

In addition, if "personal beliefs, thoughts, and understandings resulting from prior learning and interpretations become the individual's basis for constructing reality and interpreting life experiences" (APA, 1995, p. 5)—as is stated in Principle 12—continued opportunities to revisit and confront learners' current understandings need to be provided, thereby stimulating the emergence of more complex understandings, as does Ammon and Black's teacher education program (chapter 16, this volume). By assuring that courses and programs are themselves consistent with the *Learner-Centered Psychological Principles*, preservice teachers will have opportunities to learn the substantive content of the principles through the processes described in the principles.

The *Guidelines for the Teaching of Educational Psychology* (APA, 1995) itself describes further the implications for teacher education. Like the original *Guidelines for School Redesign and Reform* (APA, 1993) on which it is based, it is being revised periodically based on the suggestions of those in the field. *The Guidelines for the Teaching of Educational Psychology* represents a distillation of knowledge based on research to date and will continue to be modified as educational researchers' understanding changes. Readers are referred to the latest version for further implications.

References

American Psychological Association Division 15 Committee on Learner-Centered Teacher Education for the 21st Century (1995). *Learner-centered psychological principles: Guidelines for the teaching of educational psychology in teacher education programs.* Washington, DC: American Psychological Association.

American Psychological Association Presidential Task Force on Psychology in Education. (1993). *Learner-centered psychological principles: Guidelines for school redesign and reform.* Washington, DC: American Psychological Association and the Mid-Continent Regional Educational Laboratory.

Belenky, M. F., Clinchy, B. M., Goldberger, N. R., & Tarule, J. M. (1986). *Women's ways of knowing: The development of self, voice, and mind.* New York: Basic Books.

Blumenfeld, P., Puro, P., & Mergandoller, J. (1992). Translating motivation into thoughtfulness. In H. H. Marshall (Ed.), *Redefining student learning: Roots of educational change.* Norwood, NJ: Ablex.

Brilliant-Mills, H. (1993). Becoming a mathematician: Building a situated definition of mathematics. *Linguistics and Education, 5*, 301–334.

Cobb, P. (1994). Where is the mind? Constructivist and sociocultural perspectives on mathematical development. *Educational Researcher, 23*(7), 13–20.

Cobb, P., & Yackel, E. (1996). Constructivist, emergent, and sociocultural perspectives in the context of developmental research. *Educational Psychologist, 31*, 175–190.

Edwards, D., & Mercer, N. (1987). *Common knowledge: The development of understanding in the classroom.* New York: Methuen.

Ernest, P. (1995). The one and the many. In L. Steffe & J. Gale (Eds.), *Constructivism in education* (pp. 459–486). Hillsdale, NJ: Erlbaum.

Floriani, A. (1993). Negotiating what counts: Roles and relationships, texts and contexts, content and meaning. *Linguistics and Education, 5*, 241–276.

Fosnot, C. T. (1989). *Enquiring teachers, enquiring learners: A constructivist approach for teaching.* New York: Teachers College Press.

Fosnot, C. T. (1996). Teachers construct constructivism: The Center for Constructivist Teaching/Teacher Preparation Project. In C. T. Fosnot (Ed.), *Constructivism: Theory, perspectives and practice.* New York: Teachers College Press.

John-Steiner, V., & Mahn, H. (1996). Sociocultural approaches to learning and development: A Vygotskyian framework. *Educational Psychologist.*

Johnson, M., & Brooks, H. (1979). Conceptualizing classroom management. In D.

Duke (Ed.), *Classroom management: 78th Yearbook of the National Society for the Study of Education* (Part 2, pp. 1–43). Chicago: University of Chicago Press.

Lave, J., & Wenger, E. (1991). *Situated learning: Legitimate peripheral participation.* Cambridge, England: Cambridge University Press.

Marshall, H. H. (1988). Work or learning: Implications of classroom metaphors. *Educational Researcher, 17,* 9–16.

Marshall, H. H. (1992a). *Redefining student learning: Roots of educational change.* Norwood, NJ: Ablex.

Marshall, H. H. (1992b). Seeing, redefining, and supporting student learning. In H. H. Marshall (Ed.), *Redefining student learning: Roots of educational change* (pp. 1–32). Norwood, NJ: Ablex.

Marshall, H. H. (1996a). Clarifying and implementing contemporary psychological perspectives. *Educational Psychologist, 31,* 29–35.

Marshall, H. H. (Ed.). (1996b). Recent and emerging theoretical frameworks for research on classroom learning: Contributions and limitations. *Educational Psychologist, 31*(3/4).

Mayer, R. E. (1992). Cognition and instruction. *Journal of Educational Psychology, 84,* 405–412.

Moll, L. (Ed.). (1990). *Vygotsky and education: Instructional implications and applications of sociohistorical psychology.* New York: Cambridge University Press.

Newby, T. J. (1991). Classroom motivation: Strategies of first-year teachers. *Journal of Educational Psychology, 83,* 195–200.

Newman, D., Griffin, P., & Cole, M. (1989). *The construction zone: Working for cognitive change in school.* New York: Cambridge University Press.

Nuthall, G. (in press). Understanding student thinking and learning in the classroom. In B. J. Biddle, T. L. Good, & I. F. Goodson (Eds.), *International handbook of teachers and teaching.* Kulwer Academic Publishers.

Peterson, P. L. (1992). Revising their thinking: Keisha Coleman and her third-grade mathematics class. In H. H. Marshall (Ed.), *Redefining student learning: Roots of educational change* (pp. 151–176). Norwood, NJ: Ablex.

Putnum, J., & Burke, J. B. (1992). *Organizing and managing classroom learning communities.* New York: McGraw-Hill.

Rogoff, B. (1990). *Apprenticeship in thinking: Cognitive development in social context.* Oxford, England: Oxford University Press.

Steffe, L. P., & Gale, J. (1995). *Constructivism in education.* Hillsdale, NJ: Lawrence Erlbaum.

Vygotsky, L. (1978). *Mind in society: The development of higher psychological processes.* Cambridge, MA: Harvard University Press.

Watson, B., & Konicek, R. (1990). Teaching for conceptual change: Confronting children's experience. *Phi Delta Kappan, 71,* 680–685.

Wertsch, J. (1985). *Vygotsky and the Social Formation of Mind.* Cambridge, MA: Harvard University Press.

Yaeger, B., Floriani, A., & Green, J. (1996). Learning to see learning in the classroom: Developing an ethnographic perspective. In A. Egan-Robertson & D. Bloome (Eds.), *Students as researchers of culture and language in their communities.* New York: Hampton Press.

Appendix
Learner-Centered Psychological Principles: Guidelines for the Teaching of Educational Psychology in Teacher Education Programs

Metacognitive and Cognitive Factors

Principle 1: The Nature of the Learning Process. Learning is a natural process of pursuing personally meaningful goals and it is active, volitional, and *both* internally and *socially* mediated; it is a process of discovering and constructing personal and shared meaning from information and experience, filtered through each individual's unique perceptions, thoughts, and feelings—as well as *through negotiations with others.*

Learners have a natural inclination to learn and pursue personally relevant learning goals. They are capable of assuming personal responsibility for learning—monitoring, checking for understanding, and becoming active, self-directed learners—in an environment that takes past learning into account, ties new learning to personal goals, and actively engages *individuals* in their own learning process. In meaningful life

---

The twelve learner-centered principles as modified for the *Teaching of Educational Psychology* are presented here as is the section on Implications for Teacher Education. Changes from the original version for school redesign and reform are indicated with italics. From *Learner-Centered Psychological Principles: Guidelines for School Redesign and Reform,* by the American Psychological Association (APA) Presidential Task Force on Psychology in Education and the Mid-Continent Regional Educational Laboratory (McREL), 1993. Copyright 1993 by McREL.

situations, even very young children naturally engage in self-directed learning activities to pursue personal goals. During the learning process, individuals create and construct their own meanings and interpretations, *often in interaction with others,* on the basis of previously existing understandings and beliefs.

Principle 2: Goals of the Learning Process. The learner seeks to create meaningful, coherent representations of knowledge regardless of the quantity and quality of data available.

Learners generate integrated, commonsense representations and explanations for even poorly understood or communicated facts, concepts, principles, or theories. Learning processes operate holistically in the sense that internally consistent understandings emerge that may or may not be valid from an objective, externally-oriented perspective. As *learners negotiate understandings with others and* internalize values and meanings within a discipline, however, they can refine their conceptions by filling gaps, resolving inconsistencies, and revising prior conceptions.

Principle 3: The Construction of Knowledge. The learner links new information with existing and future-oriented knowledge in uniquely meaningful ways.

Given that backgrounds and experiences of individual learners can differ dramatically, and given that the mind works to link information meaningfully and holistically, learners interpret and organize information in ways that are uniquely meaningful to them. A goal in formal education is to have all learners create shared understandings and conceptions regarding fundamental knowledge and skills that define and lead to valued learning outcomes. In these situations, teachers can assist learners in acquiring and integrating knowledge (e.g., *by creating opportunities for discussion and dialogue and interaction among learners and between learners and adults;* by teaching them strategies for constructing meaning, organizing content, accessing prior knowledge, relating new knowledge to general themes or principles, storing or practicing what they have learned, and visualizing future uses for the knowledge).

Principle 4: Higher-Order Thinking. Higher-order strategies for "thinking about thinking *and learning"* —for overseeing and monitoring mental operations—facilitate creative and critical thinking and the development of expertise.

During early to middle childhood, learners become capable of a metacognitive or executive level of thinking about their own thinking that includes self-awareness, self-inquiry or dialogue, self-monitoring, and self-regulation of the processes and contents of thoughts, knowledge structures, and memories. Learners' awareness of their personal agency or control over thinking and learning processes promotes higher levels of commitment, persistence, and involvement in learning. To foster this self-awareness of *personal control,* learners need settings where their personal interests, values, and goals are respected and accommodated.

Affective Factors

Principle 5: Motivational Influences on Learning. The depth and breadth of *understandings constructed,* and what and how much is learned and remembered, are influenced by (a) self-awareness and beliefs about personal control, competence, and ability; (b) clarity and saliency of personal and social values, interests, and goals; (c) personal expectations for success or failure; (d) affect, emotion, and general states of mind; and (e) the resulting motivation to learn.

The rich internal world of beliefs, goals, expectations, and feelings can enhance or interfere with learners' quality of thinking and *understandings created.* The relationship among thoughts, mood, and behavior underlies individuals' psychological health and ability to learn. Learners' interpretations or constructions of reality can *facilitate* or impede positive motivation, learning, and performance. Positive learning experiences can help reverse negative thoughts and feelings and enhance student motivation to learn.

Principle 6: Intrinsic Motivation to Learn. Individuals are naturally curious and enjoy learning, but intense negative cognitions and emotions (e.g., insecurity, worrying about failure, being self-conscious or shy, fearing punishment or verbal ridiculing or stigmatizing labels) thwart this enthusiasm.

Educators must support and develop learners' natural curiosity or intrinsic motivation to learn.[1] Also, both positive interpersonal support and instruction in self-control strategies can offset factors that interfere with optimal learning—factors such as low self-awareness; negative beliefs; lack of learning goals; negative expectations for success; and anxiety, insecurity, or pressure.

Principle 7: Characteristics of Motivation—Enhancing Learning Tasks. Curiosity, creativity, and higher-order thinking are stimulated by rele-

---

[1]Negatively phrased aspects were omitted here.

vant, authentic learning tasks of optimal difficulty, challenge, and novelty for each *learner*.

Positive affect, creativity, and flexible and insightful thinking are promoted in contexts that *learners* perceive as personally relevant and meaningful. For example, learners need opportunities to make choices in line with their interests and to have the freedom to change the course of learning in light of self-awareness, discovery, or insights. Projects that are comparable to real-world situations in complexity and duration elicit learners' higher-order thinking skills and creativity. In addition, curiosity is enhanced when *learners* can work on personally relevant learning tasks of optimal difficulty and novelty *as well as in interaction with others*.

Developmental Factors

Principle 8: Developmental Constraints and Opportunities. Individuals progress through stages of physical, intellectual, emotional, and social development that are a function of unique genetic and environmental factors.

Individuals learn best when material is appropriate to their developmental level and is presented in an interesting way, while challenging their intellectual, emotional, physical, and social development. *Beginning at birth*, unique environmental factors (e.g., the quality of language interactions between adult and child, parental involvement in the child's schooling, *and cultural background*) can influence development in each area. The cognitive, emotional, and social development of individual learners and how they interpret life experiences are affected by prior schooling, home, culture, and community factors. An overemphasis on developmental readiness, however, may preclude learners from demonstrating that they are more capable intellectually than schools, teachers, or parents allow them to show. *Young children, in particular, need appropriate stimulation to encourage their development. Moreover, individuals can also learn in interaction with others who are at different developmental levels.* Awareness and understanding of developmental differences of learners with special abilities and disabilities can greatly facilitate efforts to create optimal contexts for learning.

Personal and Social Factors

Principle 9: Social and Cultural Diversity. Learning is facilitated by social interactions and communication with others in flexible, diverse (*in age, culture, family background, etc.*), and adaptive instructional settings.

Learning is facilitated when the learner has an opportunity to interact and *collaborate* with a variety of students representing different cultural and family backgrounds, interests, and values. Learning settings that allow for *social interactions* and *that* respect diversity encourage flexible thinking as well as social competence and moral development. In such settings, individuals have an opportunity for perspective taking and reflective thinking, thereby leading to insights and breakthroughs to new knowledge.

Principle 10: Social Acceptance, Self-Esteem, and Learning. Learning and self-esteem are heightened when individuals are in respectful and caring relationships with others who see their potential, genuinely appreciate their unique talents, and accept them as individuals.

Quality personal relationships give the individual access to higher-order, healthier levels of thinking, feeling, and behaving. Teachers' (or other significant adults') states of mind, stability, trust, and caring are preconditions for establishing a sense of belonging, self-respect, self-acceptance, and positive climate for learning. Healthier levels of thinking are those that are less self-conscious, insecure, irrational, and/or self-deprecating. Self-esteem and learning are mutually reinforcing.

Individual Differences

Principle 11: Individual and Cultural Differences in Learning. Although basic principles of learning, motivation, and effective instruction may apply to all learners (regardless of ethnicity, race, language, gender, physical ability, religion, or socioeconomic status), learners have different capabilities and preferences for learning mode and strategies. These differences are a function of environment (what is learned and communicated in different cultures or other social groups) and heredity (what occurs naturally as a function of genes). *Learning is most effective when differences in learners' linguistic, cultural, and social backgrounds are taken into account.*

The same basic principles of learning, motivation, and effective instruction may apply to all learners. However, individuals are born with and develop unique capabilities and talents and have acquired through learning and social acculturation different preferences for how they like to learn and the pace at which they learn. Also, learner differences and curricular and environmental conditions are key factors that greatly affect learning outcomes. Understanding and valuing cultural differences and the cultural contexts in which learners develop—*including language, ethnicity, race, beliefs and socioeconomic status*—enhances the possibilities for designing and implementing learning environments that are optimal for all *learners*.

Principle 12: Cognitive and Social Filters. Personal thoughts, beliefs, and understandings resulting from prior learning and interpretations become the individual's basis for constructing reality and interpreting life experiences.

Unique cognitive *and social* constructions form a basis for beliefs about and attitudes toward others. Individuals then operate out of these "separate realities" as if they were true for everyone, often leading to misunderstandings and conflict. *Through interactions with others, learners increase their* awareness and understanding of these phenomena *and the value of multiple perspectives*. Increased understandings allow greater choice in what one believes and more control over the degree to which one's beliefs influence one's actions and enable one to see and take into account others' points of view. The cognitive, emotional, and social development of a child and the way that child interprets life experiences is a product of prior schooling, home, culture, and community factors.

Implications for Teacher Education

Instruction

Effective Instruction

- Involves students in their own learning, with opportunities for teacher and peer interactions that engage students' natural curiosity and opportunities for personal reflection and self-study;
- Encourages students to link prior knowledge with new information by providing multiple ways of presenting information (e.g., auditory, visual, kinesthetic);
- Attends to the *content* of curriculum domains and to generalized and domain-specific *processes* that facilitate the acquisition and integration of knowledge in these domains;

- *Provides stimulating, guiding questions to help students and groups of students rethink their understandings, come closer to more powerful concepts and ways of thinking;*
- Includes constructive and informative feedback regarding the learner's instructional approach and products, as well as sufficient opportunities to practice and apply new knowledge and skills to developmentally appropriate levels of mastery;
- Offers opportunities for acquiring and practicing various learning strategies in different content domains to help students develop and effectively use their minds while learning;
- Encourages problem solving, planning, complex decision-making, debates, group discussions, and other strategies that enhance the development of higher-order thinking and use of metacognitive strategies;
- Helps students understand and respect individual differences by learning principles of thinking and psychological functioning and how these operate in building attitudes and belief systems about others;
- Enables learners to plan future directions and apply what they learn;
- Maintains fair, consistent, and caring policies that respect the individual student by focusing on individual mastery and cooperative teamwork rather than competitive performance goals;
- Provides opportunities for learners to construct their own knowledge and shared understandings through groupwork and dialogue with others; and
- Ensures that all students have experience with (a) teachers interested in their area of instruction, (b) teachers who respect and value them as individuals, (c) positive role modeling and mentoring, (d) constructive and regular student evaluations, (e) optimistic teacher expectations, and (f) use of questioning skills to actively involve them in the learning process.

Curriculum

Effective Curricula

- Attend to affect and mood as well as cognition and thinking in all learning activities and experiences, thereby engaging the learner;
- Include assessments from students, peers, and teachers to check

for student understanding of the subject matter, including implications and applications of knowledge;

- Have an affective and cognitive richness that helps students generate positive thoughts and feelings of excitement, interest, and stimulation;
- Help students engage in higher-order thinking and practice metacognitive strategies, including reflective self-awareness and goal setting;
- Help students to be more aware of their own psychological functioning and how it relates to their own learning;
- Include authentic tasks (relevant to the real world) and assessments that help students integrate information and performance across subject matter disciplines, while allowing students to choose levels of difficulty for challenge or novelty;
- Are developmentally appropriate to the unique intellectual, emotional, physical, and social characteristics of the individual;
- *Incorporate meaningful materials and activities relevant to different cultural groups;*
- Help students increase awareness and understanding of how thought processes operate to produce separate, self-confirming realities so that they can better understand different individuals, as well as different social, cultural, and religious groups;
- Encourage students to see positive qualities in all groups of learners, regardless of race, sex, culture, language, physical ability, or other individual differences; and
- Include activities that promote empathy and understanding, respect for individual differences, and valuing of different perspectives, including materials from a multi-cultural perspective.

Assessment

Effective Assessment

- Is integrated with instruction to continue learning progress and is authentic in content and performance requirements;
- Measures personal progress and achievement, rather than comparing an individual's performance with the performance of others, and fosters personal learning goals;
- Redefines *success*; standards should be based not on competition,

but on self-selected or collaborative learning goals that promote self-generated solutions;

- Enables students to make various choices, including the types of products for demonstrating achievement of educational standards;
- Measures student growth and allows for the highest levels of performance on developmentally appropriate standards; standards are formulated in such a way that every student has an opportunity to excel at something;
- Promotes students' self-reflection on their growth by providing opportunities for self-assessment and thoughtful feedback on learning progress; and
- Considers alternative scoring and reporting strategies that focus on individual achievement of valued standards rather than normative grading practices.

Instructional Management

Effective Schools and Classrooms

- Accommodate mentoring and make time and physical space and facilities for students to pursue individual learning goals and activities;
- Are flexible in matching individual student needs with variations in instructional format and processes, including content, organization, strategies, and social settings;
- Encourage cooperation and respect for diversity and individual differences and discourage practices that are not inclusive of all learners;
- Accommodate differences in intelligence and other special talents in the artistic, musical, spatial, physical, and social domains;
- Provide alternative technologies or paths to learning for students with special needs (e.g., total communication systems for hearing impairments, Braille systems for visual impairments, argumentative communication for multiple impairments), and teachers qualified to use them;
- Provide supports for both students and teachers to deal constructively with expectations to master challenging curricula and exhibit quality performance (e.g., through individual attention and support groups); and
- Meet the needs of the whole child (emotional, intellectual, so-

cial, physical) by providing integrated health, mental health, and social services in addition to academic services.

Effective Learning Environments

- Encourage student choice in areas such as topics of learning, types of projects on which to work and whether to learn independently or in groups;
- Are flexible in matching individual student needs with variations in instructional format and processes, including content, organization, strategies, and social settings;
- Emphasize respect and acceptance of differences, and avoid stigmatizing practices such as labeling, tracking, or grade level retention;
- Include the flexible and creative use of cross-age and peer tutoring models; *flexible grouping is based on students' needs for new understandings and additional help from teachers and peers for particular skills and concepts rather than long-term ability grouping;*
- *Provide for an appropriate diversity of language, abilities, ages, cultures, and other individual differences in grouping students;*
- *Include materials that provide opportunities for students to participate at different levels and* avoid grade level materials that are too easy for fast-learning students and too difficult for slow-learning students;
- Foster quality adult–student relationships based on understanding and mutual respect; such relationships reciprocally reduce levels of stress and insecurity in teachers and students;
- Are conducive to quiet, reflective thought and cooperative social interaction;
- Support students in developing ideas through student-centered projects and activities that promote student choice and responsibility;
- Attend to meaningful performance contexts (e.g., apprenticeship settings) wherein knowledge can be anchored to meaningful prior knowledge and experience;
- Are warm, comfortable, and supportive; they provide a climate that minimizes students' insecurities and promotes a sense of belonging; and
- Provide high standards and optimistic expectations for all students, while respecting cultural and linguistic diversity, developmental variations, and other individual differences.

Effective Teacher Education Programs

- Include standards for teacher and staff selection that attend to attitudes and beliefs that reflect the teacher's orientation to different student groups;
- Are based on the preceding principles of learner-centered instruction in both pre- and in-service teacher education programs;
- *Provide opportunities for pre- and in-service teachers to acquire new strategies to critically evaluate their beliefs and experiences;*
- *Build on experiences and assignments that are related to the real world of complex classrooms and authentic problems;*
- *Provide opportunities for pre- and in-service teachers to interact with their peers and more experienced teachers, to reflect on their experiences; and in interaction with others, to negotiate, share, and construct meanings and understandings;*
- Offer strategies for establishing positive climates for learning and methods teachers can use to promote positive and reverse negative thoughts and moods in teachers and students that interfere with teaching and learning;
- Help teachers see how their own attitudes and motivation for teaching and learning affect student motivation and learning in the classroom;
- Provide the knowledge base about the cognitive, emotional, and motivational processes that affect learning so that teachers can promote higher-order thinking and learning processes;
- Include information about general and domain-specific metacognitive strategies and how they can most effectively be taught to students of differing abilities and backgrounds;
- Encourage teachers to "think out loud" during explanations as a strategy for making learning and problem solving explicit and transparent, thus modeling metacognitive thinking and teaching strategies for their students;
- Provide information about intellectual, emotional, physical, social, linguistic, and cultural characteristics of students at various development levels, as well as methods for assessing and accommodating developmental and intellectual differences in learning ability;
- Help teachers become more aware of (a) the need to relate instructional content and processes to the cultural contexts of their students and (b) the differences that cultures impose on public displays of volunteering information, asking questions, asking for help,

discussing personal concerns in public, and a host of other cultural values and constraints that can enrich the classroom when recognized, or lead to chaos and misattributions when ignored;

- *Emphasize ways to actively involve students in the learning process and to elicit the material or solutions from the students themselves in a way that is supportive and that will trigger students' creative thinking;*
- Focus on strategies for diagnosing and encouraging students' use of self-directed motivational and learning processes;
- Help teachers understand how each student learns best and to relate subject matter being taught to each student's interests in a manner that triggers the student's curiosity and innate interest in learning;
- Include information on how to engage students' excitement and intrinsic interest in learning in a way that bypasses students' self-consciousness, concern about self-image, or need to prove themselves and without relying on external rewards that undermine natural learning interest;
- Help teachers understand how to continually demonstrate respect and caring for students in the classroom, while maintaining an organized classroom in an authoritative (as opposed to authoritarian) manner;
- Include strategies for selecting curricula that provide appropriate levels of cognitive complexity and authenticity for students at different developmental and ability levels *and from different cultural groups;*
- *Include strategies for working closely with families and subcultures in aiding student learning;*
- *Include stress management training that emphasizes principles of mind—emotion—behavior relationships and how to provide climates of socioemotional support;*
- *Include attention to personal "self-care and renewal" as ways for teachers to avoid burn-out as well as model these strategies to their students;*
- *Focus on helping teachers learn ways to take increasing responsibility for their own professional and personal needs as a strategy for enhancing the professionalism of teaching; and*
- *Help teachers see relationships between the psychology of learning and the psychology of change as well as their leadership roles in creating educational systems as learning communities dedicated to continuous learning, ongoing assessment and evaluation of practices, and continuous improvement.*

Part V

Summary and Conclusion

What Have We Learned and Where Are We Going in School Reform?

Barbara L. McCombs and Nadine M. Lambert

If education is not transformative, it is nothing.
—Global Association for Transformative Education

Gradually we began trying some new approaches. One change led to another and another and another, like dominos. I started to see what people meant by systemic change. A new energy and excitement surged among us as hope grew and the cloudy vision of what we wanted became clearer and clearer.

—High school principal

As we saw at the beginning of this book, American education is in an era of radical educational reform—our very notions about teaching, learning, and the whole enterprise of schooling are being challenged and transformed. Many educators and psychologists are no longer aiming to improve the existing system. Many believe that the existing system is not working and that basic assumptions underlying this system are fundamentally flawed (e.g., Berliner & Biddle, 1995; Covington, 1991; Eisner, 1991; Hargreaves, 1995; Levin, 1991; Sizer, 1995; Skrtic, 1991). These educators at least implicitly acknowledge that comprehensive, learner-centered, and systemic redesign strategies are required. The strategies must holistically address the unique needs of individuals, the family and social systems of which they are a part, and the educational and administrative systems that interface with the learner and his or her supporting social systems. Strategies for improv-

Portions of this chapter are based on ideas developed in B. L. McCombs and J. S. Whisler (1997), *The learner-centered classroom and school: Strategies for enhancing student motivation and achievement.* San Francisco: Jossey-Bass.

ing student achievement are being considered in the larger context of transformed views of teaching and learning. We believe that the views represented by the authors of the chapters in this volume have converged on creating a transformed, learner-centered view of what is necessary for our educational reform agenda to have the necessary impact on learning, motivation, and achievement for all learners. Our purpose in this final chapter is to summarize conclusions reached in the preceding chapters and provide a selective review of the broad-based research support for applications of the current knowledge base on learning and learners in educational reform. We discuss what we see as conclusions and implications of the learner-centered psychological principles (APA, 1993; APA, 1995) and the resulting learner-centered model from a policy and school change perspective. We end with a challenge for a learner-centered reform agenda for maximizing the achievement of all learners.

Summary of Promising Learner-Centered Educational Practices

Beginning the chapters detailing theory and research relevant to learner-centered schools, teaching, assessment, teacher education, and policy development is the section on learner-centered perspectives for classroom teaching. We summarize these chapters first, and follow with summaries of learner-centered perspectives on assessment and the current dilemmas in assessment policy and educational reform, and then summarize the learner-centered perspectives on teacher education.

Learner-Centered Applications in the Classroom

Alexander and Murphy's chapter (chap. 2) summarizes the research base for the learner-centered psychological principles (APA, 1993; APA, 1995). The authors note correctly that the principles were written to stress the within-individual processes and conditions that are central to learning. The principles are concerned more with the internal state of human learning than with social or contextual considerations. In this sense the principles are "learner-centered"; they describe what is going on with learners in school contexts. However, as Alexander and Murphy point out, the learner never works in isolation of contextual factors, but always in a social context. They offer their views on the research base for school redesign and educational practice as a contribution to reasoned and informed practice, rather than as offering support for particular policy or political actions regarding educational change. To fulfill the promise of utilization of scientific knowledge in educational reform, the psychologist as educational researcher has to become a partner in change with the teachers, educators, parents, and members of the community. In other words, utilization of research findings is always contextual, and the scientist accepting this premise will engage in efforts to examine the ways that his or her research findings influence practice; in turn, the scientist's research and theory development will be influenced by practice.

Frisby (chap. 2) provides details on the kinds of home, neighborhood, and demographic contextual factors that influence learners independently from those factors that influence learners in school contexts. Teachers understand the products of community, social class, family configuration, and home environment contexts as those conditions that students bring to the classroom. But it is the classroom context over which the teacher can have control. And teachers' effectiveness will be directly related to the extent that they share perspectives on effective strategies for taking into account learner background contextual factors. These factors include the learner's prior experiences and ways of knowing and understanding that provide a rich foundation for school learning experiences.

Two examples of classroom practices that reflect learner-centered principles follow. The first is Kroll's (chap. 5) exploration of ways that cognitive principles can be applied to literacy development in young children just beginning school. After showing how Piaget's perspective on the development of logical thinking contributes to an understanding of writing development, Kroll explores ways that children's early attempts at writing reflect their development of logical reasoning within the context of early literacy. Although Kroll's own research has centered on four strands of development—physical, symbolic, semantic, and social—her chapter focuses on how children's use of physical and symbolic representational systems represents the development of meaning. Then using data from 1 year's critical exploration of children's writing samples, she develops a sequence of development in the semantic strand and describes the essence of learner-centered teaching.

Moving to the affective and motivational domains, Weinstein (chap. 4) provides a second classroom teaching application by showing how a learner-centered perspective can be informed by studying teacher expectations of students and teachers' differential interactions with stu-

dents of differing characteristics. Students are aware of these teacher
expectations and report that low achievers receive more negative feedback and teacher direction than high achievers. In turn, higher achievers were judged by their classmates to benefit from higher teacher expectations and more opportunity and choice. Not only do students
report differences among their classmates in teachers' expectations of
them, but also student awareness of these expectations can have profound effects on their own academic expectations and ultimately their
achievement. Although there is only sparse evidence in the literature
for classroom interventions that alter these expectancy effects, Weinstein offers an array of possibilities for teachers to consider and a promising intervention at the high school level.

Wittrock (chap. 6) outlines a psychological research perspective
that provides details on research on strategies for instruction in different subject matter areas. The explicit acknowledgment of what is known
about different psychological processes associated with subject matter
learning leads the way to considering ranges of individual differences
in learning processes within subject matter. Acknowledgment of these
differences can consequently assist in the identification of learner differences that are relevant to more learner-centered teaching.

Brown and Campione's (chap. 7) proposal for a community of
learners shows how classrooms can be constructed so that a social context for learning and sharing one's learning can be created—classrooms in which every child is a participant at a level of accomplishment
consistent with his or her own development. They view their contribution as the formation of a new theory of learning in which learners are
active constructors of knowledge, rather than passive recipients of static
knowledge. In this new theory, the learner is encouraged to actively
speculate, to develop metacognitive awareness of what is being learned
and how the learner feels about that new learning. And although every
learner is actively involved in the classroom learning community, Brown
and Campione remind us of the importance of individual differences,
and that some learners are predisposed to learn some things more readily than others. As they outline this approach within the guidelines of
the proposed new theory of learning, they caution the reader, quite
appropriately we believe, that the results of the research in their "real
world" laboratories cannot be expected to be "taught" to other teachers, but teachers using these methods have to design their own application of them. In other words, successful utilization of psychological
research in other classrooms will have to become "teacher-centered"

wherein teachers are the learners and designers of the applications. Just as we have learned that top-down teacher instruction does not succeed for all learners, top-down teacher training in how to use research findings will not work either. The same learner-centered psychological principles apply to all learners in the system.

Learner-Centered Perspectives in the Design of Assessment Systems and Classroom Assessments

Throughout the period in which the learner-centered psychological principles were under development, the debate was well underway on the importance to educational reform of high stakes testing, setting and measuring national standards for achievement, and abandoning these more traditional types of assessment for classroom-based, or "authentic," assessment. The group of chapters in the Learner-Centered Perspectives in the Design of Assessment Systems section offers motivational and emotional counterparts of assessment, shows how knowledge of metacognitive and cognitive processes can be derived from authentic assessment, and charts ways that large-scale assessments can be compatible with learner-centered schools.

The question, What if they gave a test and nobody came? follows from Paris's chapter (chap. 8) on how affective and developmental factors affect the accuracy of learner assessments. Paris shows how the relationship between difficulty levels or inappropriateness of assessment tasks can alter motivation and learning from the student's perspective. And in this context he warns us that high stakes assessment, inappropriately selected difficulty levels in test items, and comparisons with normative standards can impact negatively on student performance in the classroom, as well as on student test performance. In contrast, his recommendations for alternative assessment practices that enhance student involvement and learning show that testing experiences can be positive and viewed favorably.

Boykoff Baron (chap. 9) challenges us to consider the potential of learner-centered assessment in the context of large-scale state and national testing programs. She outlines three elements of learner-centered assessment. The first involves test situations in which the content, skills, and dispositions that society values and that the learner can perform are presented. The second element is that a learner-centered assessment task is a learning event that involves application of knowledge and transfer of the products of the task to a new situation. The third feature is that the learner is involved in continuously assessing his or her own progress in these assessment processes. By becoming more invested in representing what they know and what they can do, learners become involved in their own standard setting, thereby accepting a performance standard as something they want to accomplish.

Marzano (chap. 10) introduces his chapter with a conceptual framework for cognitive processes that includes the metacognitive system, how individuals think and plan about carrying out a task; the self system, the individual's awareness of his or her individual differences, interests, and goals; and the cognitive system, the knowledge a student brings to the learning task. Marzano proposes that understanding the declarative and procedural structures within these three systems can guide classroom assessment. Because most classroom assessment methods include little, if any, information about the metacognitive processes involved in classroom tasks, and rarely consider the self system as an assessment challenge, the chapter serves to stimulate interest in methods for using these aspects of cognitive processing as they influence ways that learners become and remain involved in classroom learning activities and programs.

Because learner-centered assessments, as described by Boykoff Baron, ultimately involve the aspects of cognitive processes outlined by Marzano, and take into account the emotional and motivational factors set forth by Paris, these chapters lay out an important agenda for school restructuring by redesigning ways that learners become knowledgeable about what they know and what they can do. Boykoff Baron also describes how this information can be transferred into evidence for local, state, and national standards.

Dilemmas in Assessment: Policy and Educational Reform

The policy section begins with Mentkowski's chapter wherein she argues for a perspective in which national goals for kindergarten through 12th grade (K–12) education are framed in the larger context of lower and higher education. Current priorities are that students leaving K–12 schools will be prepared to work or prepared for higher education. This requires that linkages between the goals for the different segments of our educational systems become an imperative. As Mentkowski develops a set of objectives designed by those involved in setting standards and assessment methods for higher education, the commonality between the activities of higher educators and K–12 becomes immediately apparent.

Ultimately, questions about whether educators should assess individuals, or the products of courses, or the success of the system, are policy questions. In K-12 programs, authentic assessment focuses on the individual, grade level performance assesses the "courses," and comparisons from district-wide tests assess school district effectiveness against a state, national, or international standard. Mentkowski's examples from deliberations about these issues from a higher education perspective help to cast the importance of learner-centered perspectives in a new light. When we expect a graduate to be prepared for work, or a student to be prepared for freshman college classes, we are focusing on the learner, not the course, nor the system. By shifting the focus to college undergraduate programs Mentkowski provides a way of thinking about the belief systems that are brought to the table when policies are set forth for designing assessment programs at any level of the educational system.

Sewell, DuCette, and Shapiro (chap. 12) provide a cultural or diversity perspective in the policy discussion on the utility of a learner-centered perspective. If schools are to become more involved with student diversity—and at least in some ways recognize diversity in the curriculum—major considerations that must be resolved are issues of what standards should be set, what should be assessed, and how results should be evaluated? Persuasive arguments for using performance, portfolio, and dynamic assessments are presented in a context that compares these assessments against standards. Sewell et al. contend that standardizing assessments should be avoided because standardized scores invite comparisons that would be difficult to make fairly in a diverse learner context.

Given that the current sense of a crisis in education centers on outcomes of schooling, it is perhaps fitting that Porter (chap. 13) concludes our group of invited chapters with a perspective on dilemmas in achievement assessment. Mentkowski has shown that assessments of education outcomes are derived from policy, and thus are policy statements or policy imperatives. Sewell and his colleagues remind us that assessment ultimately does make comparisons among individuals, and if we believe in a pluralistic society, then assessment must represent fairly appropriate outcomes for every student from every background. If assessment policy describes what learners are expected to know, it might be considered to be learner centered. But as Porter makes clear, the key to successful reform relies on inputs, practices, and outputs. Policy makers focus on outputs, and in turn must decide what students are to know and what they are able to do. The task for learner-centered schools is to design methods of assessing the outputs that consider ways of measuring individual student progress over time. These methods must also be helpful in making informed normative comparisons of assessments with standards, and must consider the practice implications of assessments as well as the ways that the assessments influence future behavior. Porter concludes by stating an obvious fact—we are engaged in a very difficult and challenging policy debate about restructuring schools that has enormous implications for teaching and learning, and for the well-being of our society. We hope that the learner-centered psychological principles for school redesign will inform that debate because we believe that reform centered on learners and learner outcomes has the best chance of making lasting changes in our educational system over time.

Teacher Education Challenges for Learner-Centered Schooling

The most prominent involvement of psychology in education over the past decades has been the teaching of psychology thought to be essential for teaching to those enrolled in teacher-education programs. But even those psychologists, the ones who have been gratified by their success in preparing the future teacher to meet the challenges of diverse learners, would be among the first to acknowledge the difficulty of framing psychology subject matter in such a way that teachers accept it as a necessary and crucial preparatory experience for teaching. The chapters in the Teacher Education for the Learner-Centered Classrooms of the Future section acknowledge this challenge and propose some new directions worthy of serious consideration as teacher-education programs become part of the school redesign discussion.

Mayer (chap. 14) approaches the topic from a more "traditional" perspective. Mayer's historical overview of research on cognition and its applications forms the basis of recommendations for ways to reconstruct teacher-education programs not only by acquiring knowledge of cognition and relevant implications for instruction and learning but also by assisting teachers to develop their own personal theories of teaching. In this latter regard, Mayer's view would suggest that teachers should not model their teaching after the "master" teacher. Rather, they should develop their own styles, be their own consumers of educational research, and develop a vision of instructional goals for learners that is consistent with district standards but appropriate to the learners in the classroom. In this regard, Mayer outlines a learner-centered approach in teacher education—focusing on the teacher as learner—that the following three chapters in this section develop further.

McCombs (chap. 15) maps out the territory for reforms in teaching that involve more than just knowing about subject matter and relevant cognitive processes, but that also focus on the development of teacher and student roles wherein there is shared responsibility for learning between teachers and students. This involves the teacher in designing classroom tasks that invite active learning by providing opportunities for choice, autonomy, and demonstrations of personal creativity. Teachers develop assessment methods that encourage students to show what they know, lead them to new applications of knowledge, and engage them in reflecting on their own development. Teachers also involve students directly in setting classroom standards and learning goals. In such classrooms, teachers create an atmosphere of trust in which learners experience a sense of personal efficacy, and learners become aware of the teacher as guiding competence and identity development. To create such conditions, teacher-education programs must focus on helping teachers acquire a deep understanding of the knowledge base on learners and learning, develop learner-centered attitudes and practices, and accept increasing responsibility for their own professional development and learning.

Teacher development in the context of learner development follows from Ammon and Black's (chap. 16) proposals for developmental teacher education. The Developmental Teacher Education Program focuses on helping teachers become knowledgeable agents in using developmental theory to design their own classroom programs. The results are learner-centered classrooms. But perhaps more important, each teacher creates her or his own strategies for utilizing a developmental perspective. The studies of teaching and teachers that have been undertaken by Ammon and Black have shown that by providing ways for teachers to become their own instruments of theory application—rather than to rely on a "teacher-proof" curriculum—teachers develop over time as well. From the beginning in a program where they acquire knowledge about theory, to their first applications of theory to a teaching unit, to considering ways that theory informs them about why there is success in one learning task but failure in another, to the development of ongoing personal teaching theories, the Developmental Teacher Education Program shows its essential qualities in being both a learner-centered and a teacher-centered teacher-education program.

Marshall (chap. 17) provides a useful perspective on ways that the teaching of psychology in teacher-education programs should change. Using a learner-centered perspective, she presents issues from a review of the content of available textbooks, educator beliefs about teaching and learners, and the prior experience of direct instruction from undergraduate programs experienced by those entering the teaching profession. If teachers teach the way they have been taught, then Marshall proposes that more learner-centered teacher-education programs, based on learner-centered models for students in the schools, will have a much greater payoff for altering the shape of instruction in the schools of tomorrow. Given these perspectives, we turn our attention next to the broad-based support for learner-centered practices in education.

Support for Application of the Principles in Educational Interventions

Research has demonstrated that teaching in ways derived from a learner-centered model and perspective can enhance students' motivation to learn as well as their actual learning and performance (cf. APA, 1993; McCombs & Whisler, 1997). When students can be involved in directing their own learning and making important decisions about classroom procedures, instruction, and curriculum; when students believe that teachers listen to them and try to get to know them; when students think that what they are learning is somehow connected to the real world and their personal interests—with teacher guidance and support—students' natural curiosity will guide their learning. Students become more effective, more interested, and more independent learners. They develop skills, such as learning to question, analyze, think about their thinking, and make decisions. They also develop social skills; a deeper respect for their classmates, teachers, and other individuals; and realize how much they can learn from each other.

In general, a learner-centered model or perspective leads to interventions that focus on will to learn, intrinsic motivation, and self-regulated learning. Interventions focus on an understanding of basic learner needs, interests, and learning capacities as well as on an understanding of the personally and socially constructive nature of the learning process (Brooks & Brooks, 1993). Psychological research from such areas as human development, learning, cognition, and motivation are being integrated in ways that can contribute directly to practices that are responsive to the individual learner. Ornstein (1993) argued that key in those practices that foster motivation and engagement in learning is good teaching and teachers that emphasize the personal and social development of learners. He cited a variety of research indicating that people perform best when they feel respected and valued, when they can develop their own unique strengths, and when they are helped to take control of their learning and their lives. Furthermore, Oldfather (1991, 1993) contended that students' continuing impulse to learn is propelled and focused by conditions that are learner-centered as defined from the perspectives of students. Her research indicates that higher levels of intrinsic motivation are evoked in contexts that honor students' self-expression—when their voices are heard, taken seriously, and acted on.

In addition to the benefits of enhanced motivation to learn, the research shows a number of other benefits of interventions that are learner centered and focus on providing more learner choice and control. Benefits for students include a greater display of active planning and monitoring of learning, higher levels of student awareness of their own learning progress and outcomes, more resourcefulness and efficiency in using learning resources, and higher levels of sensitivity to the social learning context (Zimmerman, 1996). Benefits also include broader educational outcomes such as staying in school, higher academic performance, self-regulation of learning such as doing school work, feelings of competence and self-esteem, enjoyment of academic work, and satisfaction with school (Deci & Ryan, 1991; McCombs & Marzano, in press).

The learner-centered psychological principles on which the learner-centered model is based provide a foundation and rationale for designing and implementing effective classroom practices and supportive school climates. The principles focus attention on the importance of meeting learners' basic needs, treating learners individually and respectfully, acknowledging learner frames of reference, and challenging students to achieve their best and develop their unique potentials. This focus on the individual learner leads to instructional implications that share basic concepts and attributes but that, in practice, may look different with different students and different school and classroom contexts. In fact, a test of "learner-centeredness" is that learner-centered schools and classrooms will not have a single blueprint, a single design. They will be as diverse as the students and communities they serve.

How "Learner-Centeredness" Addresses the Personal Needs of Individual Learners

Examples abound of schools that are implementing practices consistent with the latest research on learning. In some cases, these schools have been highly successful in enhancing student motivation, learning, and achievement. In others, they have not. What accounts for this difference? From our analysis, the critical difference is how these practices are implemented and whether there is explicit and shared attention given to each learner and that learner's unique needs.

Let's consider two hypothetical schools. Both schools are focused on student learning, but one is learner centered, whereas the other is not. In the first case, teachers and other adults in the school are explicitly supported and given time to explore, inquire, and understand the knowledge base that addresses individual differences in cognitive and metacognitive abilities important to learning; the role of affective and motivational variables in influencing these cognitive and metacognitive differences; how different personal and social needs can impact learning; how individuals differ in their development across physical and emotional as well as intellectual domains; and how various cultural and family backgrounds and experiences can enhance or impede school learning. On the basis of this understanding, there is a shared commitment to know and respect each learner and to provide the personal context that best meets each learner's needs. In the second case, the knowledge about and commitment to individual learners is only implicitly recognized, is often given lip service, and is attended to by only some of the staff. The focus is on learning outcomes and accountability, and there is an atmosphere of stress and pressure that further alienates students and staff.

The result in the first school is that all students know they have the respect and support they need; in the second school, some of the students believe they have the respect and support they need, whereas others do not. Attendance, dropout rate, and achievement levels are more positive in the first school than in the second in spite of the fact that they share many of the same practices—practices that have been shown to increase learning. Furthermore, measures of learning and achievement are higher in the first school because motivation to learn is higher. Perhaps the greatest benefit of all is that more students in the first school choose to stay in school—thereby increasing their potential for productive lives.

As borne out in work by Damico and Roth (1994), students who want to learn and stay in school, compared with students who drop out, characterize their schools as having a facilitative orientation toward students, with adults who treat them in positive ways, communicate high expectations, and also advocate joint responsibility for learning by staff and students. Students in schools with high graduation rates as contrasted with students in schools with low graduation rates also report that these schools have strong support systems, fair and consistent discipline policies, and give students a strong and active role and voice in school practices. On the other hand, schools with low graduation rates are described by students as punitive and authoritarian, unfair and inconsistent, and having teachers who are demoralized, paying little attention to individual student learning needs, or are unsure what type of learning environment they should be creating. Students are very clear and articulate about what needs to change. Damico and Roth concluded that for schools to change in positive ways—ways that will make a difference in whether students want to be in school and graduate—students need to be included in regular assessments of specific school policies and practices that create a positive learning environment. Beyond this, students need to be involved on the front end in defining these policies and practices. The more voice and control learners have in their own learning process, the more commitment and ownership is established.

Successful Schools Reflect Applications of Learner-Centered Principles

One of the initially unexpected outcomes we discovered in our analysis of successful schools—as judged by high levels of student engagement, motivation, learning, and achievement for all students—was the high energy, positive attitudes, feelings of hopefulness, and commitment to making a difference for all students among school staff. Many teachers expressed that teaching in these schools had rejuvenated them and helped them reconnect with their initial teaching goals. Because students were learning and were motivated to learn, teachers and administrators felt reinforced, and parents were enthusiastic and willing to be involved in their children's education. The students themselves were turned on to school and to learning. A positive reciprocal cycle was in place for all learners in the system.

In contrast, in less successful schools—even those with a learning focus—many of these benefits were noticeably absent, except in isolated classrooms in which teachers intuitively implemented learner-centered approaches with their students or in schools in which administrators intuitively implemented learner-centered approaches with their staff. We thus learned that an understanding of basic psychological principles of learning, human development, motivation, and individual differences was common to those successful schools. Learner-centered approaches were critical to the creation of optimal learning climates at all levels of the system and for all participants. Successful schools operated as learning communities, and learning was explicitly valued. The systemic implementation of learner-centered principles had the effect of enhancing the well-being and learning of all. Our own observations have been confirmed in research on new models of schooling that are consistent with the learner-centered psychological principles, such as Comer's (1993) Learning Communities (Ramirez-Smith, 1995), Central Park East's alternative high school for students at risk of dropout and school failure (Meier, 1995), Levin's Accelerated Schools (Keller, 1995), and Sizer's Coalition of Essential Schools (O'Neil, 1995).

From our work with learner-centered models of education (McCombs, 1995; McCombs & Whisler, 1997) that builds on the *Learner-Centered Psychological Principles: A Framework for School Redesign and Reform* (APA, 1995), it is clear that redesigning school and classroom practices and structures in keeping with what educational and psychological research shows about learners and learning can also lead to outcomes that extend to enhanced student valuing of schooling and learning, as well as a reduction in students' feelings of alienation, boredom, and frustration. In turn, by functioning from a learner-centered model and perspective—including strategies that provide for critical dimensions of choice, relevancy, control, responsibility, and connection with others— other outcomes are possible—outcomes such as reduced dropout and associated problems (e.g., drug use, gang involvement, and other negative outcomes).

Studies of successful schools show that the articulation and alignment of the learner-centered psychological principles (that define the knowledge base on learning and learners) with educational practices at all levels of the educational system enables educators to determine what needs to be designed and why. We further realize that these same learner-centered principles can define a change process that is in keeping with this knowledge base and that addresses the personal as well as technical and organizational dimensions of systemic educational change. Learning is change and change involves learning. Both processes are continual and ongoing; they are complementary and reciprocal.

The answer to the question we ask in the title of chapter 1, Why Learner-Centered Schools and Classrooms as a Direction for School Reform?, can be summarized as follows:

- The research evidence is clear that the most successful schools are those that focus on both learners and learning.
- The benefits of learner-centered practice extend to students, teachers, administrators, parents, and others involved in the educational system.
- The changes in our society have necessitated a change in the role and function of schools to better meet the needs of the whole person as a learner, whether that person is a student, teacher, administrator, or parent.
- The change process itself is a transformation in thinking and thus a process of learning that can be facilitated by an understanding of basic principles about learning and learners.

The principles provide a systemic framework that can guide decisions about the content, environment, and opportunities for learning beyond the student in the classroom and help define a dynamic learning context that is continuously improving. Of perhaps even greater importance, the principles confirm the knowledge and experience of our best teachers and other educators while at the same time providing research justification for the practices of these teachers and their administrators.

Learner-Centered Principles in a Policy and School Change Perspective

Educators and researchers recognize that prior reform strategies have made assumptions that are no longer tenable regarding what needs to change and how to address the underlying factors impacting student achievement. In general, new designs for education have come in response to an observed need for a change in the outcomes of education—first to an industrial society, then to a competitive world, and then to changing cultural values. Even in today's debates, we face a dilemma in terms of contradictory goals for education. For example, some would argue that there are dual, conflicting goals for education (Cuban, 1986, 1990): Socialize all children, yet nourish each child's individuality; teach history, but ensure that the child possesses the practical skills marketable in the community; demand obedience to authority, but teach children to think and question; teach children the value of cooperation, but also teach them to compete.

Critics and advocates of public education mainly agree on one thing: The educational system must change to meet the needs of an increasingly diverse and seemingly less well-educated or prepared young population of students for the complex needs of the 21st century. To meet these needs, visionaries are going a step further and arguing that the current system cannot be restructured; it must be transformed. What does that mean? In a literal sense, transformation is a shift in thinking, perception, or behavior. It results in a fundamentally different way of being. A transformation of our educational system means a rethinking of the basic purposes of schooling, the creation of a new vision, and the development of a new culture. In the context of all "living systems"—those systems such as education that support a human purpose—the transformation must consider the people it serves and how best to serve them in accomplishing the desired mission of learning and academic achievement for every learner.

For some, transformation of the educational system is necessary due to the revolution in our thinking about the "nature of things" that occurred in the early part of this century with the revolution in the field of physics (Garmston & Wellman, 1995). New fields of quantum mechanics, chaos theory, complexity theory, fractal geometry, and the new biology are all reshaping human thought. According to Garmston and Wellman schools must be adaptive as well as create adaptivity in order to be successful. They believe adaptivity can be created by

- basing decisions on the questions of "who are we" and "what is our purpose?"—filtered through agreed-on core values, such as a respect for human differences and respect and caring for others;
- shifting decision-making authority to the people most influenced by the decision;
- restructuring the day and year to increase the time teachers have to act collegially with one another;
- setting outcomes and standards that signal a passion for excellence and attention to qualities that are based on real-world needs; and
- supporting faculty members in collaboratively setting and working toward self-defined goals. (see Garmston & Wellman, 1995, p. 8)

Garmston and Wellman (1995) further argued that five human "energy fields" must be used to help schools and the people in them to be continuously adaptive: efficacy (believing one can achieve and being willing to exert effort necessary to achieve), flexibility (ability to appreciate multiple perspectives), craftsmanship (standards of excellence in thinking and actions), consciousness (awareness of thoughts, feelings, intentions, and behaviors and one's personal agency or control as well as awareness of other's styles, values, and behaviors), and interdependence (seeing benefits of connections and collaboration as opportunities to learn). These states of mind can be used to develop personal and organizational capacities in a shared leadership model that can capitalize on and value the diversity of those in the system.

In keeping with this vision, a current goal of educational reform is to create and sustain self-governing learning communities (Meier, 1995). Such communities require, at their heart, a new school culture dedicated to continuous learning and improvement for the purpose of better preparing students with the mental, moral, and social standards required for their maximum productivity and personal development in meeting the challenges of our complex and changing world. In a word, the culture must be one that strives to develop the potential of every learner, with a respect for the diversity of talents, interests, and capabilities each student has to offer. It is a culture dedicated to helping all students achieve the highest standards on the basic knowledge and skills required while at the same time nurturing those unique skills and abilities that are a source of needed diversity in life.

How do cultures dedicated to these goals develop? We know from the research on successful schools—schools that are reaching the goal of high achievement for all students—that they have created a new culture that sees continuous improvement and learning as an ongoing goal for all, including not only the students but the teachers, parents, administrators, and community members as well (e.g., Anderson, 1993; Baum, Renzulli, & Hebert, 1994; Bennett & O'Brien, 1994; Boyd & Hord, 1994; Hargreaves, 1995; Kruse, Seashore-Louis, & Bryk, 1994; Meier, 1995). The culture developed in a process that included sharing a common purpose or goal, being dedicated to continuous improvement and lifelong learning rather than to maintaining the status quo, and having a sense of shared responsibility for reaching this goal among all participants of the system. There are shared norms and values at the core, with a collective focus on learners and learning, but the development of the culture emerges in a process involving reflective dialogue and collaboration (Kruse et al., 1994; McCombs & Whisler, 1997).

Equally critical, however, in building and sustaining a culture committed to continuous learning and change is continual and simultaneous attention to the organizational, personal, and technical supports needed. That is, from the *organizational* perspective there must be time to meet and talk, physical proximity for team planning and collaboration, communication structures such as regular meetings or electronic mail systems, and shared decision-making strategies (Kruse et al., 1994; Sagor, 1995). From a *personal* perspective, there needs to be a sense of community, quality personal relationships and constructive dialogue, an openness to improvement, trust and respect, supportive leadership, and processes for socializing new members into the culture (Kruse et al., 1994; McCombs, 1995). In the *technical* area, providing all members of the community with the knowledge and skills they need to take risks, learn new knowledge and skills when needed, and take responsibility for their own professional development, continuous improvement, and lifelong learning are also key (Kruse et al., 1994; McCombs, 1991). In research by the Center for School Restructuring collected in 15 schools, however, Kruse et al. (1994) found that attention to the personal domain—to the human resources in the system—was more critical to the development of a sense of professional community or culture than structural conditions. They concluded,

> This finding adds weight to the argument that the structural elements of restructuring have received too much emphasis in many reform proposals, while the need to improve the culture, climate and interpersonal relationships in schools has received too little attention. (p. 6)

To develop new cultures that are collaborative and centered on a shared vision for seeing to it that all students learn according to valued standards and to their potentials, Hargreaves (1995) pointed out that a key component is the "willful" involvement of all influenced by the changes. It is, therefore, essential that strategies consistent with the transformed vision and respectful of the diversity of expertise that is available—in even the most critical and skeptical examples—be used. This places a focus on the central importance of building personal relationships as an initial support system for sustaining the changes. These personal needs must be supported organizationally and "collaborative cultures" established that value both individual and shared learning (Hargreaves, 1995). Change becomes learning, learning becomes intrinsically motivating and valued, and the negative associations of change as aversive can be transformed into the view that change is learning, and learning is fun.

For students, the culture is defined by student experiences at both the school and classroom levels. In discussing the kind of culture that can meet the goal of high achievement for all students, Baum et al. (1994) said the first step is understanding underachievement from the perspective of the learners themselves. When students are asked why they fail to achieve, the reasons they give are not that they didn't study, didn't do their homework, didn't get good grades, or didn't try to please their teachers. All of these reasons may have been true from the perspective of an outside observer, but from the students' perspectives, the reasons were associated with emotional issues such as trying to gain positive attention from a caring adult, peer group pressure to under-achieve as a way to gain popularity, or lack of a curriculum that they perceived as interesting and in keeping with how they liked to learn.

Reversing the underachievement pattern required that teachers (a) took the time to know each student; (b) used their time with students to facilitate learning rather than counsel students about their underachievement; (c) understood students' needs to make choices and share their expertise and competence; (d) recognized the need for observation, reflection, and ongoing experimentation with strategies for helping students overcome their learning and motivational problems; and (e) consistently demonstrated patience and their belief in each student's ability to succeed (Baum et al., 1994). The transformation occurred in thinking and practice, in moving from a deficit to an enrichment model that encouraged students to pursue an area of interest in their preferred learning style. The model provided students with general exploratory experiences to stimulate new areas of interest, training in research and learning-to-learn skills necessary for pursuing an interest in greater depth, and guidance in pursuing both individual and small group investigations of meaningful, real problems that are designed to have an impact on a real audience. With this model, the underachievement cycle was reversed for nearly 90% of students classified as underachievers and the improvements were sustained following the intervention for over the 2 years following the study.

For teachers, the culture that supports student learning and achievement needs to be based on principles that also support teachers' needs as learners. In addressing the nature of the culture that is formed among teachers committed to high achievement for all learners, Fullan (1993) suggested the following guiding principles: (a) being committed to being agents of educational and social improvement; (b) being committed to continuous improvement through program innovation and evaluation; (c) valuing and practicing exemplary teaching; (d) engaging in constant inquiry; (e) modeling and developing lifelong learning among staff and students; (f) modeling and developing collaboration among staff and students; (g) being respected and engaged as a vital part of the whole system; (h) forming partnerships with relevant groups and agencies; (i) being visible and valued in the local and global community; and (j) working collaboratively to build regional, national, and international networks.

To support teachers in developing a culture of learning and change, teachers need the organizational and personal support to be knowledgeable about, committed to, and skilled in areas identified by Fullan (1993), including (a) working with all students in a caring, equitable, and effective manner by respecting diversity and individual student needs; (b) being active learners and reflective practitioners throughout their careers; (c) developing and applying the research knowledge needed to implement and monitor effective and evolving programs and practices for all learners; (d) initiating, valuing, and practicing collaboration and partnerships; (e) appreciating and practicing the principles, ethics, and legal responsibilities of teaching as a profession; and (f) developing a personal philosophy of teaching.

In a similar vein, Boyd and Hord (1994) discussed the role of school principals in creating schools as learning communities. Building on Senge's (1990) definition, learning communities are seen as organizations (or cultures) wherein people are continually expanding their capacity to create what they desire, new and expansive patterns of thinking are nurtured, and there is the freedom to be creative and continually learn how to learn together. Consistent with this definition, a learning organization has at its heart a shift of mind to seeing ourselves as connected to each other and the world. People begin to see that they create their reality and they can change it. A particularly important shift is required in the leadership role of school principals. They need to see that learning and change are two sides of the same coin. From Boyd and Hord's (1994) research, the primary leadership functions conducive to change are (a) reducing isolation, (b) increasing staff capacity, (c) providing a caring and productive environment, and (d) promoting increased quality. These functions are fulfilled by modeling, coaching, attending to detail, observing ceremonies, rituals, and traditions, and telling stories that identify heroes and heroines who support the school's mission. When these functions are being fulfilled, norms change and a new culture develops. Furthermore, Reitzug and Burrello (1995) reported that one of the most critical roles for principals is to facilitate teachers' reflective practice by asking challenging questions, providing constructive feedback from their own observations, challenging program regularities, and enhancing resource supports.

Three further points are critical in the development of a culture that sees change as learning. First, the culture must build on the concept of inclusion that is based on true valuing and respect for multiple perspectives—including the perspectives of those who might be seen as "resistors." When there is room for everyone and no one has to be wrong, agreement on a common vision is more likely and negative conflict can often be avoided. Thus, although creating a culture of learning and change can benefit from leadership that uses conflicts as opportunities to promote interaction and discussion about the vision—and staff can benefit from training in conflict resolution and other team building skills, as advocated by Boyd and Hord (1994)—a new vision that is more inclusive may avoid the kind of negative conflict and need for resistance that has occurred in past reform efforts. When diversity is celebrated by all who serve and are served by the system, a new culture can be created with minimum conflict, as reported by Roesener (1995) after a 2-year study of urban school reform.

Second, the change literature—particularly with respect to personal change—supports the role of "hope" and creative tension in facilitating willingness to change as well as inspiration or excitement in considering new options and ways of thinking and acting (e.g., APA, 1993; McCombs & Whisler, 1997). One of the by-products that can be expected from a shift in understanding change as learning and the development of a new culture devoted to learning and continuous improvement is the generation of excitement, experimentation, and hope. Facilitating an attitude of hopefulness is a deliberate part of the culture-building activities. This may mean developing what Bennett and O'Brien (1994) termed a *creative tension* between current reality and the desired future. Strategies such as encouraging a look at discrepancies between ideal and actual practices from varying perspectives, sharing success stories generated by real schools and the people in them, having the opportunity to observe a diverse set of successful models and options for reaching the shared vision, and creating positive support teams and networks that go beyond the school walls are all ways that have been successful in generating and sustaining hope (McCombs, 1995;

McCombs & Whisler, 1997). Models such as *accelerated schools* that are based on a philosophy of providing the best possible education for each child (Keller, 1995), Sizer's Coalition of Essential Schools that demonstrates a principle-driven approach to empowering local schools and communities to prepare all students for a 21st century world (O'Neil, 1995), or Comer's model that emphasizes students' social, emotional, and academic development (Ramirez-Smith, 1995) all provide success stories and optional approaches for collaboratively working toward the vision of high levels of achievement and learning for all students.

Finally, it is critical that change and transformation as well as the building of a culture of learning and change must be accomplished from within the organization. The process must be one that supports continuous examination and improvement of education at every level (Joyce & Calhoun, 1995). Critical inquiry into ways of helping students learn better must become a normal activity that involves the whole faculty and is used to build community. An important outcome of facilitating this kind of change from within, as reported in research by Joyce and Calhoun (1995), is that faculty begin to realize that teaching and learning is a never-ending process of trying to reach all students in the best ways currently envisioned. The vision must be subject to change, and the whole system must maintain flexibility and openness to new learning, transformation, and change. The challenge is in part what Anderson (1993) expressed as nurturing change in all aspects of the educational system while helping stakeholders rise above their singular viewpoints.

From Content to Learning and Learners

In the past, educators have most often approached the business of schooling with a concentration on content—that is, on what and how much must be taught in various academic content areas—with learning and learners of secondary concern. This is particularly true at the high school level and beyond, and is supported by the kind of teacher preparation given: a focus on discipline knowledge rather than pedagogical knowledge and skills. With the popularity of the standards movement, which identifies what is important for learners to know and be able to do, there has been a shift from what to teach to a focus on learning— that is, can the learner perform or demonstrate the knowledge or skills identified as important.

This shift in focus from teaching required content to learning valued knowledge and skills goes only half the distance necessary, however, if our goal is that all students learn these valued knowledge and skills. Why? Because without a corresponding focus on individual learners, we will continue to ignore students' calls for help when they say they think school is irrelevant, they report feeling disconnected from their teachers and peers, or they drop out both mentally and physically because they just don't want to be there. The best and most challenging standards in the world won't address these concerns. Focusing on standards and learning is thus a necessary but insufficient direction. The learner-centered model focuses equally on the learner and learning. The ultimate goal of schooling is to foster the learning of learners; and learners learn best when they are an integral part of the learning equation— when the relevance and meaningfulness of what they are being asked to learn, their distinctive perspectives and unique differences, the support they receive from the environment and relationships within which their learning occurs, and the view that learning is natural and learners fundamentally want to learn and succeed are recognized and taken into account in their school experiences.

A Learner-Centered Reform Agenda

This sampler of teaching, assessment, policy initiatives, and teacher development is directed at strategies and practices that are based on the research on learners and learning. The emphasis is on high standards, thematic and integrated curricula, and instructional practices that help students take a more active and responsible role in directing their own learning. Assessment methods focus not only on what students know but also on what they can do to demonstrate and apply that knowledge in real-life or life-like settings. Teacher education models become more learner-centered in that teachers are encouraged to construct their own applications of theory to classroom practices that they judge to be appropriate to the development of their students. Changes in school organization, management structures, and policies acknowledge the important social and organizational factors that contribute to effective schooling, such as physical space and facilities for organizing teachers and students in teams. Schools are being reorganized to increase the time spent on learning activities, taking into account the diversity in students' cultural and personal histories, and changing policies that govern grading practices and graduation requirements such that students are held accountable for reaching high academic standards.

Although these technical and organizational changes have occurred in response to what is now known about how learning occurs best and are known to be necessary for achieving higher levels of learning, researchers and educators have given little attention to their potential impact on outcomes such as student attendance, discipline, or dropout rates. We believe, and the research demonstrates, that these changes are not sufficient for addressing such outcomes because they do not include an emphasis on the learner and learning environment, nor do they focus on or provide effective strategies for offsetting the problems of student alienation, fear of failure, or disinterest in being in or learning in schools. To address learning and achievement as well as outcomes related to motivation to learn and stay in school, we believe that in addition to a focus on learning and learning standards, it is critical that there be an equal focus on the learner. We believe that the knowledge base on both learners and learning must be considered if new designs for schools are going to have their maximum impact on increasing learning and achievement for all learners. That means an increased attention to the personal as well as the technical and organizational components of school design.

More and more educators, researchers, and parents believe that schools, to be most effective, should build on students' cognitive and social competencies; pay attention not only to academic but also personal, social, emotional, and physical needs; and give all students the same chance to blossom in all areas or aspects of life and learning. Educators also are concerned with making schools more equitable, making schools more just, and respecting of the integrity of every child (Raywid, 1992).

We believe that the learner-centered model—with its combined focus on learning and learners—is so critical that, if ignored, efforts to raise the educational achievement levels of all students will be undermined, the sustainability of needed changes in the educational system will be impeded, and increased frustration and burn-out of both educators and students alike will increase. Basing school reform efforts on an understanding of the learner-centered psychological principles leads to a different concept of schooling than reform efforts based primarily on, for example, content standards or performance-based assessment models. The learner-centered model leads to a concept of schooling that has at the center a concern with each student and that student's maximum achievement and development. This model guides decisions about learning standards, curriculum, assessment, and instructional approaches by taking into account learner needs, capacities, and frames of reference. A focus is on creating quality learning environments and the personal relationships that make that possible on the basis of an understanding of learners and learning. There is a balance of individual learner considerations and what is known to be best for all learners. There is also a balance of concerns with learner needs and concerns with learning those standards and content that define an educated and productive citizen.

Putting the learner at the center of current reform efforts is a view supported by Elliott Eisner (1994). Decrying reform efforts solely centered on defining curriculum standards, Eisner stated,

> Rather than trying to ensure that every student gets to the same place at the same time, schools should strive to raise the mean in performance and increase the variance of students' interests and strengths. Educators ought to be cultivating productive idiosyncrasy, playing to the youngsters' talents . . . in the long haul it's the cultivation of these positive aptitudes that will feed back into the culture. (pp. 6–7)

It needs to be emphasized that a learner-centered perspective is not just one more recipe for better learning to add to the pile of educational trends that are popular today. Focusing on the learner provides a research-based foundation for school design decisions. It provides coherence to site-based decision making, cooperative learning, and higher order thinking, and gives educators a way to develop, organize, and plan significant educational innovations. By focusing on students and bringing their frames of reference to the implementation of educational innovations, we believe—and the research supports—that more students will be successful and satisfied in school, and current innovations will be more effective in improving achievement, learning, and motivation for all students. We also believe that we will begin to help reinstill the love of learning in those growing numbers of students most alienated and turned off to school. We must be willing to value all learners, respect their differences, and challenge them. This includes addressing the needs of teachers as learners—teachers who have all too frequently become demoralized, frustrated, and burned out by the increasing demands placed on them by the reform agenda. The time for research-based, learner-centered practice in our schools is now.

References

American Psychological Association Board of Educational Affairs. (1995, Dec.). *Learner-centered psychological principles: A framework for school redesign and reform* [On-line]. Available: http://www.apa.org/ed/lcp.html.

American Psychological Association Presidential Task Force on Psychology in Education. (1993, January). *Learner-centered psychological principles: Guidelines for school redesign and reform.* Washington, DC: American Psychological Association and the Mid-Continent Regional Educational Laboratory.

Anderson, B. L. (1993). The stages of systemic change. *Educational Leadership, 51*(1), 14–17.

Baum, S. M., Renzulli, J. S., & Hebert, T. P. (1994). Reversing underachievement: Stories of success. *Educational Leadership, 52*(3), 48–52.

Bennett, J. K., & O'Brien, M. J. (1994, June). The building blocks of the learning organization. *Training, 3,* 41–49.

Berliner, D. C., & Biddle, B. J. (1995). *The manufactured crisis: Myths, fraud, and the attack on America's public schools.* Reading, MA: Addison-Wesley.

Boyd, V., & Hord, S. M. (1994, April). *Principals and the new paradigm: Schools as learning communities.* Paper presented at the annual meeting of the American Educational Research Association, New Orleans.

Brooks, J. G., & Brooks, M. G. (1993). *The case for constructivist classrooms.* Alexandria, VA: Association for Supervision and Curriculum Development.

Comer, J. (1993, March). *Creating learning communities: The Comer process. Experimental session.* Annual Conference of the Association for Supervision and Curriculum Development, Washington, DC.

Covington, M. V. (1991, August). *Motivation, self-worth, and the myth of intensification.* Paper presented at the Contributions of Psychology to Learning and Education Miniconvention at the 99th Annual Convention of the American Psychological Association, San Francisco.

Cuban, L. (1986). *Teachers and machines: Classroom use of technology since 1920.* New York: Teachers College Press.

Cuban, L. (1990). Reforming again, again, and again. *Educational Researcher, 19*(1), 3–13.

Damico, S. B., & Roth, J. (1994, April). *Differences between the learning environments of high and low graduation schools: Listening to general track students.* Paper presented at the annual meeting of the American Educational Research Association, New Orleans.

Deci, E. L., & Ryan, R. M. (1991). A motivational approach to self: Integration in personality. In R. Dienstbier (Ed.), *Nebraska Symposium on Motivation. Vol. 38: Perspectives on motivation* (pp. 237–288). Lincoln: University of Nebraska Press.

Eisner, E. W. (1991). What really counts in schools. *Educational Leadership, 48*(3), 10–17.

Eisner, E. W. (1994). Opinions clash on curriculum standards. *ASCD Update, 36*(1), 6–7.

Fullan, M. G. (1993). Why teachers must become change agents. *Educational Leadership, 51*(7), 12–17.

Garmston, R., & Wellman, B. (1995). Adaptive schools in a quantum universe. *Educational Leadership, 52*(7), 6–12.

Hargreaves, A. (1995). Renewal in the age of paradox. *Educational Leadership, 52*(7), 14–19.

Joyce, B., & Calhoun, E. (1995). School renewal: An inquiry, not a formula. *Educational Leadership, 52*(7), 51–55.

Keller, B. M. (1995). Accelerated schools: Hands-on learning in a unified community. *Educational Leadership, 52*(5), 10–13.

Kruse, S., Seashore-Louis, K., & Bryk, A. (1994). *Building professional community in schools.* Madison: University of Wisconsin, Center for School Restructuring.

Levin, H. (1991, April). *Building school capacity for effective teacher empowerment: Applications to elementary schools with at-risk students.* Paper presented at the annual meeting of the American Educational Research Association, Chicago.

McCombs, B. L. (1991). Motivation and lifelong learning. *Educational Psychologist, 26*(2), 117–127.

McCombs, B. L. (1995, May). *Facilitating change at the personal level.* Invited presentation at the Facilitating Systemic Change Conference, University of Nebraska, Lincoln.

McCombs, B. L., & Marzano, R. J. (in press). What is the role of the will component in strategic learning. In C. E. Weinstein & B. L. McCombs (Eds.), *Strategic learning: Skill, will, and self-regulation.* Hillsdale, NJ: Erlbaum.

McCombs, B. L., & Whisler, J. S. (1997). *The learner-centered classroom and school: Strategies for enhancing student motivation and achievement.* San Francisco: Jossey-Bass.

Meier, D. (1995). How our schools could be. *Phi Delta Kappan, 40*(4), 373.

Oldfather, P. (1991, April). *When the bird and the book disagree, always believe the bird: Children's perceptions of their impulse to learn.* Paper presented at the annual meeting of the American Educational Research Association, Chicago.

Oldfather, P. (1993, Summer). *Students' perspectives on motivating experiences in literacy learning.* Athens, GA: National Reading Research Center.

O'Neil, J. (1995). On lasting school reform: A conversation with Ted Sizer. *Educational Leadership, 52*(5), 4–9.

Ornstein, A. C. (1993). How to recognize good teaching. *American School Board Journal, 80*(1), 24–27.

Ramirez-Smith, C. (1995). Stopping the cycle of failure: The Comer model. *Educational Leadership, 52*(5), 14–19.

Raywid, M. A. (1992). Why do these kids love school? *Phi Delta Kappan, 73*(9), 631–633.

Reitzug, U. C., & Burrello, L. C. (1995). How principals can build self-renewing schools. *Educational Leadership, 52*(7), 48–50.

Roesener, L. (1995). Changing the culture at Beacon Hill. *Educational Leadership, 52*(7), 28–32.

Sagor, R. (1995). Overcoming the one-solution syndrome. *Educational Leadership, 52*(7), 24–27.

Senge, P. (1990). *The fifth discipline.* New York: Doubleday.

Sizer, T. (in O'Neil, J., 1995). On lasting school reform: A conversation with Ted Sizer. *Educational Leadership, 52*(5), 4–9.

Skrtic, T. M. (1991). The special education paradox: Equity as the way to excellence. *Harvard Educational Review, 61*(2), 148–206.

Zimmerman, B. J. (1996). Dimensions of academic self-regulation: A conceptual framework for education. In D. H. Schunk & B. J. Zimmerman (Eds.), *Self-regulation of learning and performance: Issues and educational applications* (pp. 3–21). Hillsdale, NJ: Erlbaum.

Appendix: Original Version of the Learner-Centered Psychological Principles: Guidelines for School Redesign and Reform (Mid-Continent Regional Educational Laboratory, 1993)

The following 12 psychological principles pertain to the *learner* and the *learning process*. They focus on psychological factors that are primarily internal to the learner while recognizing external environment or contextual factors that interact with these internal factors. These principles also attempt to deal holistically with learners in the context of real-world learning situations. Thus, they must be understood as an organized set of principles and not be treated in isolation. The first 10 principles subdivide into those referring to *metacognitive and cognitive, affective, developmental*, and *social* factors and issues. Two final principles cut across the prior principles and focus on what psychologists know about *individual differences*. Finally, the principles are intended to apply to *all learners*, beginning with preschoolers.

Metacognitive and Cognitive Factors

Principle 1
The nature of the learning process. **Learning is a natural process of pursuing personally meaningful goals, and it is active, volitional, and**

Copies of the complete version of this document are available from the Mid-Continent Regional Educational Laboratory (McREL), 2550 South Parker Road, Suite 500, Aurora, CO 80014-1678. Reprinted with permission of APA and McREL.

internally mediated; it is a process of discovering and constructing meaning from information and experience, filtered through the learner's unique perceptions, thoughts, and feelings.

Students have a natural inclination to learn and pursue personally relevant learning goals. They are capable of assuming personal responsibility for learning—monitoring, checking for understanding, and becoming active, self-directed learners—in an environment that takes past learning into account, ties new learning to personal goals, and actively engages students in their own learning process. In meaningful life situations, even very young children naturally engage in self-directed learning activities to pursue personal goals. During the learning process, individuals create their own meanings and interpretations on the basis of previously existing understandings and beliefs.

Principle 2

Goals of the learning process. **The learner seeks to create meaningful, coherent representations of knowledge regardless of the quantity and quality of data available.**

Learners generate integrated, commonsense representations and explanations for even poorly understood or communicated facts, concepts, principles, or theories. Learning processes operate holistically in the sense that internally consistent understandings emerge that may or may not be valid from an objective, externally oriented perspective. As learners internalize values and meanings within a discipline, however, they can refine their conceptions by filling in gaps, resolving inconsistencies, and revising prior conceptions.

Principle 3

The construction of knowledge. **The learner links new information with existing and future-oriented knowledge in uniquely meaningful ways.**

Given that backgrounds and experiences of individuals can differ dramatically, and given that the mind works to link information meaningfully and holistically, learners organize information in ways that are uniquely meaningful to them. A goal in formal education is to have all learners create shared understandings and conceptions regarding fundamental knowledge and skills that define and lead to valued learning outcomes. In these situations, teachers can assist learners in acquiring and integrating knowledge (e.g., by teaching them strategies for constructing meaning, organizing content, accessing prior knowledge, relating new knowledge to general themes or principles, storing or practicing what they have learned, and visualizing future uses for the knowledge).

Principle 4

Higher-order thinking. **Higher-order strategies for "thinking about thinking"—for overseeing and monitoring mental operations—facilitate creative and critical thinking and the development of expertise.**

During early to middle childhood, learners become capable of a metacognitive or executive level of thinking about their own thinking that includes self-awareness, self-inquiry or dialogue, self-monitoring, and self-regulation of the processes and contents of thoughts, knowledge structures, and memories. Learners' awareness of their personal agency or control over thinking and learning processes promotes higher levels of commitment, persistence, and involvement in learning. To foster this self-awareness of agency, learners need settings where their personal interests, values, and goals are respected and accommodated.

Affective Factors

Principle 5

Motivational influences on learning. **The depth and breadth of information processed, and what and how much is learned and remembered, are influenced by (a) self-awareness and beliefs about personal control, competence, and ability; (b) clarity and saliency of personal values, interests, and goals; (c) personal expectations for success or failure; (d) affect emotion, and general states of mind; and (e) the resulting motivation to learn.**

The rich internal world of beliefs, goals, expectations, and feelings can enhance or interfere with learners' quality of thinking and information processing. The relationship among thoughts, mood, and behavior underlies individuals' psychological health and ability to learn. Learners' interpretations or cognitive constructions of reality can impede positive motivation, learning, and performance, as can negative thoughts and feelings. Conversely, positive learning experiences can help reverse negative thoughts and feelings and enhance student motivation to learn.

Principle 6

Intrinsic motivation to learn. **Individuals are naturally curious and enjoy learning, but intense negative cognitions and emotions (e.g., feeling insecure, worrying about failure, being self-conscious or shy, and fearing corporal punishment, ridicule, or stigmatizing labels) thwart this enthusiasm.**

Educators must support and develop students' natural curiosity or intrinsic motivation to learn, rather than "fixing them" or driving them by fear of corporal punishment or excessive punishments or any kind. Also, both positive interpersonal support and instruction in self-control strategies can offset factors that interfere with optimal learning—factors such as low self-awareness; negative beliefs; lack of learning goals; negative expectations for success; and anxiety, insecurity, or pressure.

Principle 7

Characteristics of motivation-enhancing learning tasks. **Curiosity, creativity, and higher-order thinking are stimulated by relevant, authentic learning tasks of optimal difficulty and novelty for each student.**

Positive affect, creativity, and flexible and insightful thinking are promoted in contexts that learners perceive as personally relevant and meaningful. For example, students need opportunities to make choices in line with their interests and to have the freedom to change the course of learning in light of self-awareness, discovery, or insights. Projects that are comparable to real-world situations in complexity and duration elicit students' higher-order thinking skills and creativity. In addition, curiosity is enhanced when students can work on personally relevant learning tasks of optimal difficulty and novelty.

Developmental Factors

Principle 8

Developmental constraints and opportunities. **Individuals progress through stages of physical, intellectual, emotional, and social development that are a function of unique genetic and environmental factors.**

Children learn best when material is appropriate to their developmental level and is presented in an enjoyable and interesting way, while challenging their intellectual, emotional, physical, and social development. Unique environmental factors (e.g., the quality of language interactions between adult and child and parental involvement in the child's schooling) can influence development in each area. An overemphasis on developmental readiness, however, may preclude learners from demonstrating that they are more capable intellectually than schools, teachers, or parents allow them to show. Awarencess and understanding of developmental differences of children with special emotional, physical or intellectual disabilities as well as special abilities can greatly facilitate efforts to create optimal contexts for learning.

Personal and Social Factors

Principle 9

Social and cultural diversity. **Learning is facilitated by social interactions and communication with others in flexible, diverse (in age, culture, family background, etc.), and adaptive instructional settings.**

Learning is facilitated when the learner has an opportunity to interact with various students representing different cultural and family backgrounds, interests, and values. Learning settings that allow for and respect diversity encourage flexible thinking as well as social competence and moral development. In such settings, individuals have an opportunity for perspective taking and reflective thinking, thereby leading to insights and breakthroughs to new knowledge.

Principle 10

Social acceptance, self-esteem, and learning. **Learning and self-esteem are heightened when individuals are in respectful and caring relationships with others who see their potential, genuinely appreciate their unique talents, and accept them as individuals.**

Quality personal relationships give the individual access to higher-order, healthier levels of thinking, feeling, and behaving. Teachers' (or other significant adults') states of mind, stability, trust, and caring are preconditions for establishing a sense of belonging, self-respect, self-acceptance, and positive climate for learning. Healthier levels of thinking are those that are less self-conscious, insecure, irrational, and self-deprecating. Self-esteem and learning are mutually reinforcing.

Individual Differences

Principle 11

Individual differences in learning. **Although basic principles of learning, motivation, and effective instruction apply to all learners (regardless of ethnicity, race, gender, physical ability, religion, or socioeconomic status), learners have different capabilities and preferences for learning mode and strategies. These differences are a function of environment (what is learned and communicated in different cultures or other social groups) and heredity (what occurs naturally as a function of genes).**

The same basic principles of learning, motivation, and effective instruction apply to all learners. However, individuals are born with and develop unique capabilities and talents and have acquired through learning and social acculturation different preferences for how they like to learn and the pace at which they learn. Also, student differences and curricular and environmental conditions are key factors that greatly affect learning outcomes. Understanding and valuing cultural differences and the cultural contexts in which learners develop enhances the possibilities for designing and implementing learning environments that are optimal for all students.

Principle 12

Cognitive filters. **Personal beliefs, thoughts, and understandings resulting from prior learning and interpretations become the individual's basis for constructing reality and interpreting life experiences.**

Unique cognitive constructions form a basis for beliefs and attitudes about others. Individuals then operate out of these "separate realities" as if they were true for everyone, often leading to misunderstandings and conflict. Awareness and understanding of these phenomena allow greater choice in what one believes and more control over the degree to which one's beliefs influence one's actions and enable one to see and take into account others' points of view. The cognitive, emotional, and social development of a child and the way that child interprets life experiences are a product of prior schooling, home, culture, and community factors.

Author Index

Numbers in italics refer to listings in the reference sections.

Subject Index

A

Accountability, 4
  assessment for, 278, 342–343
  curriculum of diversity and, 321–323
  education reform goals, 317–318,
    331–332
  principles of learner-centered educa-
    tion, 323–325
Active learning, 10, 178, 368
Administration and management
  for changing expectancies, 95–96,
    100–101
  decentralized decision-making, 4
  flexibility in, for revitalizing schools,
    76
  ideological thinking in, 76–77
  for large-scale learner-centered as-
    sessment, 235
  learner-centered culture, 494–495,
    496–497
  qualities of principals, 69–70, 496–
    497
  school environment shaped by, 68–
    70
  student outcomes in different school
    settings, 73
  student participation in decision-
    making, 11
  teacher autonomy, 391
Affective processes
  benefits of caring environment, 383–
    384, 389

  principles of learner-centered educa-
    tion, 8, 18–19, 464–465, 507–508
  psychological models, 386–388
  research base, 34–36
  teacher qualities in student out-
    comes, 390–391
Alienation, 380, 381, 384
Alternative schools, 70–71
America 2000: An Education Strategy, 5,
  270, 273–274, 299
  accountability goals, 317–318
  assessment in, 317–318
  significance of, 317
Anchored instruction, 40, 41, 368
Anxiety, effects on learning, 18
Argumentation skills, 167
Assessment, 13, 43, 276–277
  abilities as learning outcomes, 285–
    288
  for accountability, 278, 342–343
  alternative designs, 324–330, 333,
    334–335
  characteristics of learner-centered,
    212–213
  classroom implementation, 233–234
  cognitive model of task engagement,
    241–242, 262–263
  in community of learners, 153–154
  of community of learners, 162–167
  concept of learning in, 288–290
  conceptual trends, 297–298
  consensus-building, 279–280
  construct validity, 288

in motivation, 36
principles of community of learners concept, 179–180
principles of learner-centered approach, 8, 466–467, 510
principles of learner-centered education, 12, 21–22
research base, 36–38
Individualized instruction, 423–424
Information processing
goals of learner-centered education, 16–17
vs. constructivist learning theory, 450
See also Construction of knowledge
Integration and synthesis of knowledge
integrating information and memory, 361–362
learner-centered assessment, 212
Interest, 35–36
Interpersonal interaction
environment for learner-centered education, 10
principles of learner-centered education, 20
qualities of successful programs, 383–384, 389–393
student motivation outcomes, 385
student preferences for learning environment, 382
See also Social context; Teacher-student relationship
Intrinsic motivation, 11
facilitation of, 19
indicators of, 19
principles of learner-centered approach, 19, 82, 464, 508
psychological process, 387–388
strategy for positive enhancement, 93–94
IQ, 85

J

James, William, 354–355
Jigsaw, 41, 157, 158, 174
Journals, self-assessment, 254–255, 259

K

Knowledge in action, 328

L

Law, 149
Learner-centered education
accountability in, 323–325
assessment design for, 323–330, 341
assessment goals, 220–221, 299, 301–303
assessment rationale, 214, 233, 276–277
as basis for educational reform, 12–13, 106, 332, 335–336, 380–381, 491, 499–501
characteristics of successful implementation, 488–491
contributions of psychology profession, 3, 13, 368–370
cultural change for, 493–495
definition, 9–10
design of interventions, 486–487
developmental model of writing development, 115–116, 139
distinguishing characteristics, 81–82
educational psychology textbooks, 454–455
general premises, 10–11, 25–26
implications for teacher education, 14, 467–473
interactive dimensions, 43–44
issues for psychological research, 6–7
large-scale assessment, 211, 233–235
learning theory in, 11–12, 16, 144–145
obstacles to implementation, 453, 456
perspectives needed for implementation of, 2, 76–77, 498–499
psychological principles, 7–9, 15–16, 27, 28, 81–82, 319–321, 505–510. *See also specific principle*
rationale, 6
research base in support of, 26, 28, 478–479
for teacher development, 449–450
teacher education for implementation of, 456–460
teacher expectancies, 105–107
teaching style, 372
Learner-Centered Psychological Principles: Guidelines for School Design and Reform, 7–8, 62, 339–340, 449, 505–510

About the Editors

Nadine M. Lambert, PhD, received her doctoral degree in psychology from the University of Southern California and her master's degree in education from Los Angeles State University. Dr. Lambert is currently professor in the Graduate School of Education, University of California at Berkeley, where she has been since 1964. During her more than 30-year career in psychology and education, Dr. Lambert has made major contributions in both areas. She was director of the School Psychology Training Program for the Berkeley campus and also served as Associate Dean for Student Affairs in the School of Education. She continues to be a leader within the American Psychological Association (APA), serving as one of the co-chairs for the Presidential Task Force on Psychology in Education that resulted in the creation of the learner-centered psychological principles. She has also headed a number of other special APA committees and played a major role in establishing the APA Education Directorate. Dr. Lambert's School Psychology Program at Berkeley was supported by the National Institute of Mental Health as a model of education and training programs from 1966 to 1987. During this time and to the present, this work and her program evaluation studies demonstrate that teachers, principles, and other school administrators perceived the positive impact of the school psychologists on the academic, personal, and social well-being of students in the system. The scientist-professional model of the program has set a standard for a comprehensive service-delivery role of school psychologists in California as well as those trained by graduates of Berkeley's program nationally. Dr. Lambert has authored major books in the fields of education and psychology and has served in an editorial capacity on several significant professional journals in both fields.

Barbara L. McCombs, PhD, received her doctoral degree in educational psychology from Florida State University. Dr. McCombs is presently senior director for the Human Development and Motivation Group at the Mid-Continent Regional Educational Laboratory in Colorado. She has more than 20 years of experience directing research and development efforts in a wide range of basic and applied areas. These include large-scale projects for the U.S. Department of Education on learning and motivational strategies for students and teachers, and social skills training curricula for enhancing job success. Dr. McCombs's expertise is in motivational and self-development training programs for empowering youth and adults. She is co-author of the *McREL Middle School Advisement Program* for enhancing student self-development in critical nonacademic areas. She is also the primary author of the *Learner-Centered Psychological Principles: Guidelines for School Redesign and Reform* (1993), written by APA's Presidential Task Force on Psychology in Education, which she co-chaired. Under Dr. McCombs's direction, her Human Development and Motivation Group at McREL has recently completed a professional development program for teachers that is based on the learner-centered principles, titled For Our Students, For Ourselves: Putting Learner-Centered Principles to Practice. In addition, she is directing a project to inspire a new vision of American education and to bring information and useful strategies related to effective practice to school administrators, teachers, parents, and school boards through the use of telecommunications technologies. Included in these strategies is the use of the Internet for the professional development of teachers of students at risk of educational failure, the All Children's Education Network (ACEnet). Dr. McCombs's work extends to systemic reform strategies, including community involvement and empowerment programs for schools with a high percentage of students at risk of academic failure.